THE WORLD ALMANAC®
OF THE U.S.A.

Allan Carpenter and Carl Provorse

WORLD ALMANAC BOOKS
An Imprint of K-III Reference Corporation
A K-III Communications Company

World Almanac Books

Vice President and Publisher: Richard W. Eiger

Editor:
Robert Famighetti

Sales Manager:
James R. Keenley

Director of Marketing:
Joyce H. Stein

Editorial Staff: William A. McGeveran, Jr., Deputy Editor; Christina Cheddar, Matthew Friedlander, Judith Leale, Associate Editors; Melissa Janssens, Desktop Publishing Associate

K-III Reference

Vice President and Editorial Director: Leon L. Bram
Vice President of Manufacturing: Sally McCravey
Director of Editorial Production: Andrea J. Pitluk

Contributors

Cover Design: Todd Cooper, Bill Smith Studio
Copyediting: Jacqueline Laks Gorman
Index: AEIOU Inc.

Flags produced by Lovell Johns, U.K. and authenticated by the Flag Research Center, Winchester, MA 01890, U.S.A.

Library of Congress Cataloging-in-Publication Data

Carpenter, Allan, 1917-
      The world almanac of the U.S.A. / Allan Carpenter and Carl Provorse and editors of
The world almanac.
          p. cm.
      Includes index.
      ISBN 0-88687-792-X(hard cover). — ISBN 0-88687-791-1 (pbk.)
      1. United States—Miscellanea. 2. Almanacs, American.
  I. Provorse, Carl. II. Title.
  E156.C3644   1996
  973--dc20

                                                                                    96-975
                                                                                    CIP

Printed in the United States of America

World Almanac® Books
An Imprint of K-III Reference Corporation
One International Boulevard
Mahwah, NJ 07495-0017

10   9   8   7   6   5   4

CONTENTS

AUTHORS' NOTE

The World Almanac of the U.S.A. is the most exhaustive single-volume reference work of its kind. It provides in one source the widest variety of information and statistical data on the United States as a whole and on the fifty states, the District of Columbia, Puerto Rico, and U.S. associated regions.

This completely revised and expanded edition opens with an all-new, fact-packed section entitled Portrait of the U.S.A. It provides a well-rounded miniature portrait of this great nation, past and present, adding a new dimension to the book. Included are rankings that enable the reader to compare the United States today with other major nations of the world in key categories.

Part II, Portraits of the States, offers an in-depth profile of each state. Significant physical characteristics, historical milestones, and contemporary facts are interwoven in the early part of each chapter. Notable personalities, illuminating quotations, and colorful historical details highlight the text.

Each state chapter includes general information such as state capital, official nickname, motto, slogan, song, and symbols. The chapters also provide a wealth of statistical data for each state, under such categories as land, climate and environment, major cities, people, vital statistics, health, housing, crime, teaching and learning, law enforcement, religion, personal income, economy and business, travel and transportation, government, law, attractions, and sports.

How do the states compare with one another? In Part III, The States Compared, readers will be able to find in one place figures and rankings for all the states in many of the most useful categories presented in Part II. Some valuable additional information has also been included. Almost every table catches the eye with striking comparisons in such areas as climate, growth of the elderly population, highest and lowest housing values, teachers' salaries, SAT scores, average income per person, numbers of prisoners on death row, travel time to work, and size of the state debt. Each table has its own story to tell.

The authors believe that users will find the information in this volume indispensable and highly enlightening.

The statistical data are the most recent available at press time. Dates for statistical information are generally noted; when no date is specified, the information is based on 1990 data. Indexes of people, places, and topics are provided.

Allan Carpenter
Carl Provorse

Allan Carpenter is the author of 119 volumes on the U.S.A., a substantial portion of the 228 books that bear his name. His recent works include a new edition of his first book, *Between Two Rivers: Iowa Year by Year.* Carl Provorse joined with Allan Carpenter as coauthor in four of his recent works. Provorse is known for his knowledge of the widest variety of sources of information and for his copyrighted system used in organizing the masses of data required for his work on this volume and others.

ACKNOWLEDGMENTS

The authors acknowledge with pleasure the valuable assistance provided by Yoland Weschind and the library and staff of Loyola University, Chicago, and by Edward Kobak, Jr., editor of *The Sports Address Bible.* We also wish to thank the U.S. Census Bureau, especially Glenn King and Marie Pees, as well as the other agencies of the U.S. government and the many state and private agencies that have furnished data and other assistance.

PART I:
PORTRAIT OF
THE U.S.A.

O beautiful for spacious skies,
For amber waves of grain,
For purple mountain majesties
Above the fruited plain.
America! America!
God shed His grace on thee,
And crown thy good with brotherhood
From sea to shining sea.

Katharine Lee Bates

On a visit to Colorado in 1893, Wellesley College professor Katharine Lee Bates stood on the summit of Pikes Peak and gazed at an expanse of purple mountains and waves of grain. The dramatic view inspired perhaps the most descriptive brief word "portrait" of the United States ever made—"America the Beautiful."

So They Say

"It was then and there, as I was looking out over the sea-like expanse of fertile country spreading away so far under those ample skies, that the opening lines of the hymn floated into my mind."

Katharine Lee Bates

FROM SEA TO SHINING SEA—A NATION OF VAST EXTENT

The United States is indeed, as Katharine Lee Bates proclaimed, a land of spacious skies, majestic mountains, and rich plains. The country's 50 states encompass a total area of 3,717,522 square miles (including inland, coastal, and Great Lakes waters). The conterminous (48 contiguous) states are made up of a vast central plain, mountains in the west, and hills and low mountains in the east, along with numerous rivers and lakes, deep gorges, and even active volcanoes. Of the two non-contiguous states, Alaska is characterized by

tall mountains and broad river valleys, Hawaii by rugged volcanic peaks. Structural additions made to the landscape of the United States include some of the world's tallest buildings, longest bridges, and grandest dams. Alaska is the largest of the 50 states, with Rhode Island being the smallest.

The conterminous United States is bounded by Canada to the north, Mexico and the Gulf of Mexico to the south, the Atlantic Ocean to the east, and the Pacific Ocean to the west.

If all 50 states could be fitted into a gigantic rectangle, the tip of Point Barrow, Alaska, would stand at the northernmost edge of that figure, with the southern beaches of Hawaii at the southern perimeter. Quoddy Head, Maine, on the eastern limit and Cape Prince of Wales in Alaska on the west would complete the great quadrangle.

However, the nation's reach extends much farther—all the way to Guam in the west, to American Samoa in the far south, and to the Virgin Islands in the east. Largest and most populous of U.S. "territories" is Puerto Rico, now under much discussion as to its future relationship with the United States. Less well-known to most Americans are other dots of U.S. land scattered about the Pacific, such as Wake Island and its sister islands of Wilkes and Peale, or the tiny Johnston Atoll, administered by the U.S. federal government.

SUPERLATIVES

- The world's only remaining superpower.
- Initiated the atomic age.
- Landed the first and only men on the moon.
- *Mariner 9*—first spacecraft to orbit Mars, 1971.
- Largest portrait art—Mount Rushmore.
- World's first air mail.
- One of the world's greatest engineering feats—the reversal of the Chicago River, creating a water route from the Great Lakes to the Gulf of Mexico.
- World's first oil well.
- World's first powered air flight.
- World's largest cavern—Carlsbad, in New Mexico.
- The Declaration of Independence, whose statement of the right of self-determination was a landmark in the history of freedom.
- World's largest economy, or biggest gross national product.

THE EARLIEST TIMES

From Time Immemorial. When did humans first reach what is present-day America? The estimates cover an almost ridiculous range, from 12,000 to 40,000 years ago. These ancient peoples may first have trudged over a "land bridge" that is now covered by the Bering Strait. Such a land route was formed when the seas were lower at the point of Alaska where the United States "touches fingers with Siberia." (Today this icy strait separates the mainland of Asia and the Americas by only about 50 miles.)

Actually, Russia and the United States lie even closer together, with only three miles of ocean separating Russia's Big Diomede Island from America's Little Diomede Island. Experts point out that human wanderers could have crossed the narrow waters without a land bridge. Following the crossing—whenever it took place—men and women made their way across and down the Western Hemisphere, until they finally reached the easternmost and southernmost extent of the current United States.

Known Only to Archaeology. The prehistoric Americans produced many well-developed civilizations about which modern archaeologists continue to make exciting discoveries. Remains that permit continuing study were left by the native peoples of the far north, who were skilled hunters and craftsmen, and by the ancestral Hawaiians, the Pueblo peoples of the Southwest, the Mound Builders of the Midwest, and others.

The Fringes of History. History is vague about the earliest Europeans who touched what is now U.S. soil. Phoenician sailors may possibly have reached U.S. soil in ancient times, and finds continue to be made that shed light on pre-Columbian discoveries. The famed Kensington Runestone, dug up on a Minnesota farm in 1898, may have been one of these discoveries, or it may be a fraud. In any case, it appears that Norse adventurers visited North America around the 11th century. The voyages of Christopher Columbus to the Caribbean region in the late 15th century finally brought Europe and the Americas together.

So They Say

"Eight Goths [Swedes] and twenty-two Norwegians, on a journey of discovery from Vinland westward. We had a camp by two skarries [islands] one day's journey north of this stone. We were out fishing one day. When we returned home, we found ten men red of blood and dead. Ave Virgo Maria. Save us from evil...[We] have ten men by the sea to look after our ships fourteen days' journeys from this island [in the year of our Lord] 1362."

Transcription of a portion
of the Kensington Runestone

The Indian Nations. Early explorers and settlers were introduced to the diverse Indian tribes, many of whom had created highly civilized nations which even today have not been adequately recognized. Among the most important of these were the powerful confederacies of the Six Nations and of Chief Powhatan. Other indigenous groups include the Pueblo, Caddo, Algonquin, and Iroquois nations and the many remarkable aboriginal peoples of the Pacific areas associated with the United States.

MOMENTS IN RECORDED HISTORY

Early Recorded History (1497-1619)

1497—John Cabot reaches present-day Massachusetts

1519—Alvarez de Pineda may have discovered the Mississippi River

1524—Giovanni de Verrazano enters New York harbor

1539—Father Marcos de Niza explores Southwest, brags of cities of gold

1540—Francisco Vásquez de Coronado's great party begins exploration of Southwest

1541—Hernando de Soto reaches the Mississippi River

1542—Juan Rodriguez Cabrillo discovers San Diego Bay

1565—St. Augustine, Florida, founded

1570—(approx.) Iroquois Federation founded

1579—Sir Francis Drake explores Pacific coast

1586—Drake plunders St. Augustine

1587—First English colony in North America is established in North Carolina, at Roanoke

1598—Don Juan de Onate explores Southwest

1607—Jamestown, Virginia, founded; first permanent English settlement in North America

—First ship constructed in the Americas, Popham, Maine

1609—Santa Fe, New Mexico, founded

—Henry Hudson explores the Hudson River

—Samuel de Champlain explores the Northeast

1614—Captain John Smith explores New Hampshire region

1619—House of Burgesses formed in Jamestown

Growth Continues (1620-1735)

1620—Plymouth, Massachusetts, founded by Pilgrims

1624—New Amsterdam (New York City) founded

1630—Puritans settle Boston area

1632—King grants Lord Baltimore a charter for Maryland

1634—Benjamin Syms endows first U.S. free school, in Hampton, Virginia

—Jean Nicolet passes through straits of Mackinac

1636—Harvard University founded, first university in United States

—Rhode Island is acquired by Roger Williams, who founds Providence.

1638—Swedes begin settlement at what is now Wilmington, Delaware

1643—Tinicum Island is site of first European settlement in Pennsylvania

1664—British conquer New Netherland (New York)

1670—Charleston, South Carolina, founded, soon becomes early cultural center

1673—Jacques Marquette and Louis Jolliet discover upper Mississippi, explore vast area

1675—King Philip's War with the Wampanoag Indians begins

1676—Nathaniel Bacon leads Virginia planters in the first conflict over British rule

1682—Robert Cavelier, Sieur de La Salle, claims vast Louisiana region for France

—Ysleta founded, first permanent European settlement in Texas

1692—Witchcraft trials and executions take place in Salem, Massachusetts

1701—Detroit founded by Antoine de la Mothe, Sieur de Cadillac

1704—First regular United States newspaper published, in Boston

1718—Sieur de Bienville founds New Orleans, Louisiana

1729—Baltimore, Maryland, founded

1733—James Oglethorpe begins establishment of Georgia

1735—Trial of John Peter Zenger recognizes freedom of the press

The Early Frontier (1736-1764)

1741—Vitus Bering becomes first explorer known to reach Alaska

1748—Ohio Company of Virginia organized to begin Ohio settlement

1754—French and Indian War begins

1760—French rule in Detroit ends

1761—First regular U.S. stagecoach run is begun, from Boston to Portsmouth, New Hampshire

1763—French control in North America ends with British victory in French and Indian War

—Chief Pontiac's siege of Detroit begins

1764—St. Louis, Missouri, established

Seeds of Rebellion (1765-1774)

1765—Stamp Act incites the colonists against taxation without representation
—Patrick Henry fans the flames of the colonists' discontent
1769—First visit made by Daniel Boone to Kentucky
1770—Boston Massacre occurs
1772—Rhode Island residents burn British ship *Gaspee* to protest tax laws
1773—Boston Tea Party takes place
1774—Rhode Island abolishes slavery
—First Continental Congress meets in Philadelphia

The Revolution (1775-1783)

1775—Coxsackie declaration of independence signed
—Bruno Heceta discovers the Columbia River
—Midnight ride of Paul Revere alerts patriots to approach of British troops; battles of Lexington and Concord fought
—Battle of Bunker Hill, first major battle of Revolution, takes place
—Second Continental Congress names George Washington commander-in-chief of Continental Army
1776—Enemy troops enter, then are forced to withdraw from Boston
—Declaration of Independence is approved by the Continental Congress on July 4
—Colonists driven back and defeated in Battle of Long Island
—General Washington crosses Delaware River, wins Battle of Trenton
1777—Washington loses Battle of Brandywine
—British troops led by Lord William Howe enter Philadelphia
—Continental Congress flees to York
—Desperate winter spent by Continental Army at Valley Forge
—Decisive Battle of Saratoga won by Americans
—Articles of Confederation adopted by Continental Congress
1778—Battle of Rhode Island fought
—Captain James Cook arrives in Hawaii
—Savannah, Georgia, is captured by the British
—Benjamin Franklin brings about alliance with France

1779—George Rogers Clark's capture of Vincennes, Indiana, confirms U.S. control in Midwest
1780—French army of over 5,000 lands at Newport, Rhode Island
—British fleet arrives at Newport and blocks Washington's attempt to retake New York
1781—Lord Cornwallis arrives in Virginia, is overtaken by Washington and allies; surrenders at Yorktown
—Los Angeles founded
1782—Americans recapture Georgia
1783—Treaty of Paris officially ends Revolutionary War

Becoming a Nation (1784-1815)

1784—"State of Franklin" proclaimed in Tennessee
—Russia establishes settlement in Kodiak, Alaska
1786—Last of the eastern states cede western land claims
1787—Constitutional convention adopts Constitution of the United States
—Delaware is first state to ratify new Constitution
—Northwest Ordinance establishes Northwest Territory
1788—Cincinnati founded, becomes "Queen City of the West"
1789—Washington is inaugurated as first U.S. president
1790—Rhode Island is last of the 13 original colonies to ratify Constitution
1791—Vermont becomes a state
1792—Kentucky becomes a state
—American explorer Captain Robert Gray passes the treacherous Columbia River mouth
1793—Eli Whitney invents the cotton gin
1795—King Kamehameha I conquers most of Hawaii
1796—Tennessee becomes a state
1800—U.S. government moves to District of Columbia
1803—Ohio becomes a state
—Vast Louisiana Territory purchased from France
1804—Great expedition of Meriwether Lewis and William Clark leaves St. Louis
—Duel between Alexander Hamilton and Aaron Burr; Hamilton is killed, Burr becomes a fugitive

1805—Lewis and Clark expedition reaches the Pacific
—Zebulon Pike begins two years of exploration of the Southwest
1806—Lewis and Clark bring back much knowledge of the Northwest
1807—Robert Fulton's steamboat *Clermont* sails up the Hudson River
1811—First steamship sails on Ohio River
—Indians under the Prophet defeated by William Henry Harrison at Battle of Tippecanoe
—Strong U.S. earthquake devastates central Mississippi River region, forms Reelfoot Lake in what is now Tennessee
1812—Fort Ross is built by the Russians in what is now California
—War of 1812 begins
—Louisiana becomes a state
—Fort Dearborn (Chicago) massacre by Potawatomi Indians
1813—Detroit recaptured by United States
—Oliver Hazard Perry's victory over the British at Put-in-Bay ensures U.S. control of Great Lakes
1814—British attack, are defeated at Fort McHenry; "Star-Spangled Banner" is composed
—British burn Washington, DC
—Battle of Plattsburgh brings U.S. control of Lake Champlain
1815—Treaty of Ghent ends War of 1812
—Andrew Jackson wins Battle of New Orleans after War of 1812 ends
—Power loom introduced to the United States

Expansion and Controversy (1816-1860)

1816—Indiana enters the Union
1817—Mississippi enters the Union
—Indian resettlement begins in Oklahoma
1818—Illinois enters the Union
—First steamboat sails on the Great Lakes
1819—Alabama enters the Union
1820—Maine becomes a state
1821—Andrew Jackson's successes in Indian wars bring Florida to the United States
—First U.S. cathedral is consecrated in Baltimore
—Missouri becomes a state (after Missouri Compromise on slavery is reached)
1822—Santa Fe Trail blazed

1824—First great annual fur "rendezvous" held in West
—Dr. John McLoughlin establishes Fort Vancouver, Washington
1825—Mexico takes control in California
—Erie Canal opens
1827—First American, Jedediah Smith, struggles overland to California
—Mechanics Union of Trade Associations formed, in Philadelphia
1828—America's first passenger railroad, which is horse-drawn, begins operation
—Gold discovered in northern Georgia
1830—Country's first railroad built for a steam engine begins operation in South Carolina
1832—Black Hawk War pushes Indians west
—Henry R. Schoolcraft discovers source of Mississippi River: Lake Itasca, in Minnesota
1834—Indian Territory established in present-day Oklahoma
—Cyrus McCormick invents reaper, revolutionizing agriculture
1835—Fire destroys 600 New York City buildings
1836—Texans besieged by Mexican troops at the Alamo
—Seminole War begins in Florida, as Indians protest forced removal
—Sam Houston's Texans defeat Mexican leader Santa Anna in Battle of San Jacinto
—Texas becomes an independent republic
—Arkansas becomes a state
1837—Electric motor invented by Thomas Davenport, in Vermont
—John Deere invents steel plow
—Michigan becomes a state
1838—Last of Cherokee forced over infamous "Trail of Tears" to Oklahoma, where Indian nations begin their great advances
—First Mardi Gras parade held in New Orleans
1841—William Henry Harrison becomes the first president to die in office
—First commercial use of natural gas, in Malden, West Virginia
1842—Dr. Crawford W. Long is first to use ether as an anesthetic
—Webster-Ashburton Treaty establishes northeast border with Canada
1843—First major westward immigration begins, from Missouri
—Hawaii recognized as an independent nation

1844—Mormon leader Joseph Smith murdered; Mormons leave Iowa

1845—Texas and Florida become states
—Naval Academy founded at Annapolis
—California Republic is formed

1846—Oregon and Washington come under U.S. control after agreement with Britain; expansionists had called for "54° 40′ or fight" boundary
—War with Mexico over disputed southwest lands
—Iowa becomes a state
—Elias Howe invents sewing machine

1847—Mormon pioneer refugees found Salt Lake City

1848—Treaty of Guadalupe Hidalgo with Mexico adds Southwest region to United States
—Wisconsin becomes a state

1849—Unparalleled gold rush begins, with arrival of California 49ers

1850—California becomes a state

1853—Gadsden Purchase completes U.S. lands in the Southwest
—New York holds nation's first world's fair

1854—Republican Party formed

1855—Sault Ste. Marie canal opens, eventually becomes world's busiest

1856—Slave disagreement grows, flares into Kansas/Missouri guerrilla war

1858—Minnesota becomes a state
—Debates between Stephen Douglas and Abraham Lincoln focus national attention on Lincoln

1859—Comstock silver boom begins in Nevada
—Five Civilized Tribes hold council, consolidate their gains, in present-day Oklahoma
—John Brown seizes federal arsenal at Harpers Ferry, West Virginia; is tried and executed
—Oregon becomes a state
—World's first petroleum well pumps in Titusville, Pennsylvania

1860—Pony Express begins its brief life
—Regular steamboat runs begin in upper Missouri River
—Lincoln elected president

Times of Great Travail (1861-1865)

1861—Kansas enters the Union as a free state
—Southern states, eventually numbering 11, form Confederacy
—Civil War begins with Confederate attack at Fort Sumter, South Carolina
—North American continent is spanned by telegraph
—Northern forces routed at first Battle of Bull Run
—Confederates seize Fort Pulaski, Georgia, many other strongholds

1862—Northern drive on Richmond, Virginia, fails
—Battle of the *Monitor* and *Merrimac*
—Battle of Antietam, Maryland, halts Confederates' northern advance
—Union drive defeated by Robert E. Lee at Fredericksburg, Virginia
—Battles of Pea Ridge and Prairie Grove, Arkansas
—Battles of Shiloh, Iuka, Booneville, Mississippi
—Decoration Day first celebrated, Mississippi
—Union forces capture New Orleans

1863—Lincoln issues Emancipation Proclamation, freeing slaves
—Ulysses S. Grant lays siege to Southern stronghold of Vicksburg, Mississippi
—Battle of Gettysburg halts Lee's drive north, is decisive turning point of Civil War
—Federal forces defeated at Chickamauga
—William Clarke Quantrill burns Lawrence, Kansas
—Vicksburg, Jackson, and Natchez fall to North; Union forces completely control Mississippi River
—West Virginia becomes state, maintains Union sympathies
—Battle of Missionary Ridge provides an important Union victory

1864—Grant placed at head of all Union armies
—Captain David Farragut captures Mobile Bay (Alabama)
—Sand Creek massacre of Indians in Colorado
—General William Tecumseh Sherman captures and burns Atlanta, captures Savannah
—Nevada becomes a state

1865—Petersburg and Richmond fall to Union forces
—Lee surrenders at Appomattox Court House, Virginia
—Lincoln is assassinated

—Jefferson Davis captured in Irwinville, Georgia

—Jesse Chisholm blazes Chisholm Trail

Reconstruction, Recovery, Road to Greatness (1866-1899)

1866—First bridge built across Ohio River

1867—Alaska purchased from Russia by the United States

—Nebraska enters the Union

—C. Latham Sholes invents the typewriter

1868—President Andrew Johnson is impeached, cleared by Senate

1869—First transcontinental railroad connects east and west coasts

1871—Great Chicago fire

1872—Yellowstone becomes first national park

1874—George Armstrong Custer expedition finds Black Hills gold in South Dakota

1875—First Kentucky Derby in Louisville

1876—Custer defeated, his troops wiped out, at Battle of Little Bighorn, Montana

—Centennial Exposition held in Philadelphia

—Colorado becomes a state

1877—Chief Joseph defeated in Nez Percé War

—Thomas Edison invents the phonograph

1878—Devastating yellow fever epidemic strikes the South

1880—Gold rush in Juneau, Alaska

1881—President James Garfield is assassinated in Washington, DC

1884—Cigarette-making machinery fuels growth of smoking

—First U.S. golf course opens in White Sulphur Springs, West Virginia

—Minnesota iron ore dominance begins

1885—Washington Monument dedicated

—World's first steel frame skyscraper rises in Chicago

1886—Coca-Cola is formulated and introduced in Atlanta

—Statue of Liberty dedicated

—American Federation of Labor formed, in Pittsburgh

1887—Bauxite (aluminum) discovered in Arkansas

1888—Great Blizzard causes 400 deaths in eastern United States

1889—First "run" for land titles begins Oklahoma land boom

—Johnstown, Pennsylvania, flood kills 2,200 people

—North and South Dakota, Montana, and Washington enter the Union

1890—Sioux leader Sitting Bull is killed by U.S. forces

—South Dakota is site of last Indian battle in United States, at Wounded Knee

—Wyoming and Idaho enter the Union

> ## So They Say
>
> President and Mrs. Benjamin Harrison were so afraid of the electric lights that had been newly installed in the White House that they always called for the servants to operate the switches.

1893—Hawaiian monarchy is overthrown

—World's Columbian Exposition in Chicago, most splendid ever

1894—First "modern" automobile perfected by Elwood Haynes

1896—Utah enters the Union

1898—U.S. battleship *Maine* blown up in Havana Harbor, Cuba, igniting Spanish-American War

—U.S. Marines invade Cuba, capture Philippines and Puerto Rico

—War success asserts U.S. presence in Caribbean and Pacific

—Hawaii is annexed by the United States

—City of New York created by combining five boroughs

—Kensington Runestone discovered in Minnesota

—Mississippi International Exposition held in Omaha, Nebraska

1899—Nome, Alaska, gold rush occurs

World Conflict/World Power (1900-1920)

1900—Chicago River is reversed, creating water route from the Great Lakes to the Gulf of Mexico

—International Ladies' Garment Workers Union founded in New York City

1901—Carlsbad Caverns discovered in New Mexico

—President William McKinley assassinated at Buffalo world's fair; Theodore Roosevelt becomes president

> ### So They Say
>
> In reporting Theodore Roosevelt's 1901 swearing-in ceremony, a New York newspaper reported, "...surrounded by the cabinet and a few distinguished citizens, Mr. Roosevelt took his simple bath, as President of the United States." A typo had changed the "o" in oath to "b." British newspapers carried the story without change.

—Spindletop oil flows in Texas, heralds age of petroleum

1902—Nation's first national forest established, in Wyoming
—Social reforms of Governor Robert M. La Follette in Wisconsin set national pattern

1903—Gold discovered in Fairbanks, Alaska
—Panama Canal Zone comes under U.S. jurisdiction
—Wright Brothers make world's first powered airplane flight
—Louisiana Purchase Exposition held in St. Louis, Missouri

1906—Diamonds discovered in Arkansas
—San Francisco devastated by earthquake and fire

1907—Oklahoma enters the Union

1908—First Model T Ford introduced

1911—First Indianapolis 500 automobile race held
—President Theodore Roosevelt dedicates Roosevelt Dam in Arizona
—Rebecca Felton, of Georgia, is appointed as first woman U.S. senator
—World's first overland airmail, from Des Moines, Iowa, to Chicago

1912—Georgia is birthplace of Girl Scouts of America
—Women gain right to vote in Oregon and Kansas
—Railroad is built across sea over the Florida Keys, from Miami to Key West
—Arizona and New Mexico become last of the conterminous states

1913—Grand Canyon becomes national park

1914—Panama Canal opens, just as Germany declares war on France

1916—Jeannette Rankin of Montana is first woman elected to Congress

—Virgin Islands purchased from Denmark by the U.S.

1917—The United States joins Allied forces opposing the German alliance in World War I

1918—World War I ends with Allied victory
—Large-scale influenza epidemic ravages the nation

1919—Boston police strike broken by National Guard

1920—World's first commercial broadcasting station established in Pittsburgh
—19th Amendment ratified, giving women right to vote

Peace and Depression (1921-1940)

1921—Great destruction of cotton crops by boll weevil

1922—Lincoln Memorial dedicated

1923—President Warren G. Harding dies; Calvin Coolidge becomes president

> ### So They Say
>
> When the laconic President Calvin Coolidge died, columnist Dorothy Parker wrote: "How could they tell?"

1924—George Gershwin's *Rhapsody in Blue* introduces symphonic jazz
—All Native American Indians are made U.S. citizens
—Nellie Tayloe Ross of Wyoming is elected as the first woman governor in the United States

1927—First airplane flight from mainland to Hawaii
—Charles Lindbergh makes first solo flight across the Atlantic

1929—Stock market collapse ignites the Great Depression

1930—First America's Cup race in the United States, at Newport, Rhode Island

1931—George Washington Bridge, Empire State Building opened

1932—Winter Olympics are held in the United States for the first time, at Lake Placid
—First woman elected to U.S. Senate, Hattie Caraway of Arkansas

1933—Franklin D. Roosevelt becomes president, begins "100 Days" and New Deal to combat Depression

1934—Nebraska becomes only state with a unicameral legislature

1935—Will Rogers and Wiley Post killed in Alaska plane crash

—Controversial Louisiana politician Huey Long assassinated

1936—Hoover Dam begins operation

1937—Golden Gate Bridge opens in San Francisco

—Dirigible *Hindenburg* explodes at Lakehurst, New Jersey

—Worst Ohio River floods yet

1938—Oregon's Bonneville Dam begins operation

1939—President Roosevelt opens New York World's Fair

1940—Roosevelt elected to unprecedented third term

—Nation's first peacetime draft anticipates war needs

The Nation at War Once More (1941-1945)

1941—Grand Coulee Dam completed in Washington

—U.S. Lend-Lease aid extended to Britain and Soviet Union

—U.S. ships attacked at sea by German submarines

—United States attacked by Japan at Pearl Harbor; declares war

1942—Corregidor falls; Japanese take control of the Philippines

—Americans of Japanese ancestry (Nisei) moved to isolated camps

—American and Philippine prisoners forced on "death march" by Japanese

—Japanese suffer severe naval defeat at Battle of Midway

—Americans land on Guadalcanal Island, take control after bitter battle

—General Dwight Eisenhower lands U.S. forces in North Africa

—First controlled nuclear chain reaction produced at University of Chicago

1943—Allied leaders hold series of meetings at Casablanca, Cairo, and Teheran

—Japanese defeated in Battle of Bismarck Sea with great losses

—U.S. forces free Aleutian Islands

—Allied forces capture Sicily, reach Italian mainland

—U.S. Marines capture "impregnable" Tarawa

—First subway operates in Chicago

1944—50,000 U.S. troops withstand long siege in Casino, Italy

—Eisenhower prepares to attack main German defenses in northern Europe

—American forces capture the Marshall Islands

—American Fifth Army enters Rome

—Vast Allied forces land in Normandy, France (D-Day)

—American forces   Saipan and Marianas

—With slight losses, American forces win Battle of Philippine Sea

—U.S. forces capture Guam in march across the Pacific

—Allied forces enter Paris

—General Douglas MacArthur returns to Philippines, as he promised

—Allies experience severe losses in the Battle of the Bulge

—Allied bombers carry out 40,000 sorties against Germany

1945—Roosevelt, Winston Churchill, and Joseph Stalin meet at Yalta

—Buchenwald extermination camp liberated by U.S. forces

—President Roosevelt dies; Harry S Truman becomes president

So They Say

Harry S Truman had only the initial S as his middle name, without a period. It was the result of a family disagreement on whether his middle name should be Shippe or Solomon, last names from two sides of the family.

—United Nations founded at San Francisco

—Germany surrenders unconditionally

—World's first atomic bomb explosion, at Alamogordo, New Mexico

—Dropping of atomic bombs on Hiroshima and Nagasaki brings Japanese surrender

A Cold War World (1946-1959)

1946—In speech at Fulton, Missouri, Churchill coins the phrase "Iron Curtain"

—United States gives the Philippines complete independence

—Mother Frances Xavier Cabrini becomes nation's first Catholic saint

1947—The nation undertakes its responsibilities as a superpower
—United States begins oversight of Trust Territory of the Pacific Islands
—Marshall Plan leads way toward European recovery from war
—Voice of America begins broadcasts to Soviets
—Sound barrier is broken by Charles Yeager
—Jackie Robinson becomes first black in modern major league baseball
1948—United States is the first nation to recognize Israel
—Soviets blockade Berlin; U.S./British airlift overcomes the move
1949—Rocket projects begin at Huntsville, Alabama
—United States joins North Atlantic Treaty Organization (NATO)
—Truman announces that Soviets have the atomic bomb
—South Dakota becomes nation's leading gold producer
1950—Truman sends combat troops to Korea
—Wisconsin Senator Joseph McCarthy begins anti-Communism campaign
—Lava flow from Hawaii's Mauna Loa is largest in modern times
—Ute Indians receive $31,700,000 for lands taken from them
1951—With U.S. help, UN forces capture Seoul, Korea
—Korean War becomes a stalemate
—Atomic-powered electricity operates for first time, in Arco, Idaho
—Ratification of 22nd Amendment limits presidents to two terms of office
1952—First experimental H-bomb exploded at Pacific proving grounds
—Eisenhower elected president
—Puerto Rico becomes a U.S. commonwealth
—Iowa is first state to produce a billion-dollar corn crop
—United Nations moves to New York City headquarters
1953—Eisenhower reaches difficult armistice in Korea
1954—Supreme Court decision *Brown* v. *Board of Education* declares school segregation unconstitutional
—First atomic-powered submarine launched at Groton, Connecticut

—McCarthy censured by Senate; McCarthyism fades
—First Newport jazz festival held in Rhode Island
1955—Polio conquered by new vaccine discovered by Dr. Jonas Salk
—Rosa Parks contests "Jim Crow" segregation in Montgomery, Alabama
—Supreme Court expands desegregation rulings
—Major unions form AFL-CIO
—Air Force Academy opens in Colorado Springs
1957—Eisenhower sends federal troops to enforce historic court order mandating school desegregation in Little Rock, Arkansas
—First nuclear electric power plant opens in Shippingport, Pennsylvania
—First Soviet satellite brings space race
—Mackinac Bridge is built
1958—*Explorer 1*, first U.S. satellite, launched
—First scheduled jet plane crosses the Atlantic
—American Van Cliburn wins Soviet's Tchaikovsky contest
1959—Alaska and Hawaii become the 49th and 50th states
—St. Lawrence Seaway brings ocean shipping to Great Lakes
—First schools integrated in Virginia
—Widespread earthquake damages Yellowstone National Park
—Soviet Premier Nikita Khrushchev visits United States; first hints of better U.S./Soviet relations

A New World in the Making (1960-1990)

1960—American U-2 reconnaissance plane is shot down over Soviet Union
1961—First American troops arrive in Vietnam
—Freedom Riders challenge Southern segregation practices
—President John F. Kennedy establishes the Peace Corps
1962—Astronaut John Glenn makes first U.S. orbital flight
1963—President Kennedy assassinated in Dallas; Lyndon B. Johnson becomes president
—California becomes largest state in population

1964—Reported attack on U.S. destroyers in Gulf of Tonkin; Johnson orders major U.S. involvement in Vietnam
—Landmark Civil Rights Act passed
—Beatles perform first U.S. concert, in New York's Carnegie Hall
—Disastrous Alaska earthquake strikes
—FTC requires health warnings on all cigarette packages

1965—Hurricane Betsy ravages much of the Gulf Coast
—North American Air Defense Command begins operations in Colorado

1966—Gateway Arch dedicated in St. Louis

1967—Thurgood Marshall sworn in as first African-American on Supreme Court

1968—Dr. Martin Luther King, Jr., is shot and killed in Memphis, Tennessee
—Large oil deposits discovered at Prudhoe Bay, Alaska
—Senator Robert F. Kennedy is shot and killed in Los Angeles

1969—Neil Armstrong becomes the first person to walk on the moon
—Harvard scientists discover a single gene, basic unit of heredity

1970—McClellan-Kerr Arkansas River Navigation System begins operations

1971—Spacecraft *Mariner 9* orbits Mars

1972—President Richard Nixon makes historic trip to China
—First major league baseball strike, lasts for 13 days

1973—U.S. involvement in Vietnam War ends ingloriously, with 50,000 U.S. servicepersons dead
—In *Roe* v. *Wade* decision, Supreme Court rules that abortion is legal
—Senate hearings begin into break-in at Democratic National Committee offices at the Watergate
—Wounded Knee, South Dakota, occupied during Indian protest

1974—Nixon becomes first U.S. president to resign
—Chicago's Sears Tower becomes world's tallest building

1975—Columbia/Snake River navigation system completed
—Elizabeth Ann Seton named first American-born saint
—Ella T. Grasso of Connecticut becomes first woman elected governor without family ties

1976—Bicentennial recognized with extensive national celebrations
—Agreement makes the Mariana Islands a U.S. commonwealth
—Legionnaire's disease identified

1977—First landing of Concorde SST in United States
—Singer Elvis Presley dies
—Trans-Alaska pipeline opens

1978—Hannah Gray becomes president of University of Chicago, first woman to head a major U.S university

1979—Three Mile Island nuclear power plant malfunctions in Pennsylvania

1980—Ronald Reagan is elected president
—First woman graduates from U.S. Military Academy at West Point
—Mt. St. Helens erupts in Washington; ash covers 120 square miles
—Former Beatle John Lennon is shot and killed

1981—Iran releases 52 Americans held hostage for 444 days
—Reagan is shot and wounded
—First space shuttle is launched
—Sandra Day O'Connor is sworn in as first woman on the Supreme Court

1983—Bomb destroys U.S. Marine headquarters in Beirut, Lebanon, killing 241 servicepersons
—Sally Ride is first U.S. woman in space

1986—Space shuttle *Challenger* explodes; six astronauts and teacher Christa McAuliffe killed
—Congressional hearings begin into Iran/Contra affair

1989—U.S. forces invade Panama, overthrow General Manuel Noriega
—Largest oil spill in U.S. history at Prince William Sound, Arkansas
—L. Douglas Wilder of Virginia is first African-American elected governor of a U.S. state since Reconstruction

1990—U.S. forces reach Persian Gulf to defend area against Iraq

Alone at the Top (1991-)

1991—Soviet Union in disarray, separates into individual nations; United States is only remaining "superpower"
—United States and allies defeat Iraq, liberate Kuwait in Gulf War
—California wildfires bring destruction and 24 deaths

1992—Riots in Los Angeles follow the acquittal of four policemen on trial for beating a black man

—Hurricane Andrew hits Florida and Gulf states, causing massive destruction

—Carol Moseley-Braun of Illinois is first African-American woman elected to Senate

1993—Midwest suffers one of the most disastrous floods in its history

—Terrorist bomb explodes in New York City's World Trade Center; six people are killed

—Branch Davidian cult headquarters burns at Waco, Texas, during FBI raid; more than 70 cult members die

1994—Earthquake strikes Los Angeles, claiming 61 lives

—Jacqueline Kennedy Onassis dies

—Republicans gain control of both houses of Congress

—Major league baseball players go on strike; World Series canceled

1995—California suffers disastrous floods following torrential rains

—Federal building in Oklahoma City bombed in terrorist attack, killing 169

—Massive heat wave kills over 800 in Midwest and Northeast

—Football great O. J. Simpson is acquitted of murder

—An African-American "Million Man March" is held in Washington, DC

1996—Blizzard strikes Northeast

—President Bill Clinton and Congress grapple over the federal budget

GENERAL

Independence declared: July 4, 1776
Capital: Washington, DC
Motto: In God We Trust
Bird: Bald eagle
Song: "The Star-Spangled Banner"

THE LAND

Area: 3,717,522 sq. mi.
  Land: 3,536,338 sq. mi.
  Water: 181,184 sq. mi.
    Inland water: 78,641 sq. mi.
    Coastal water: 42,491 sq. mi.
    Great Lakes: 60,052 sq. mi.
Topography: Vast central plain, mountains in west, hills and low mountains in east; rugged mountains and broad river valleys in Alaska; rugged, volcanic topography in Hawaii

Number of counties: 3,096
Geographic center: Butte County, South Dakota, W of Castle Rock, approx. 44°58'N 103°46'W
Highest point: 20,320 ft. (Mount McKinley, Alaska)
Lowest point: −282 ft. (Death Valley, California)
Coastline: 12,373 mi.

ENVIRONMENT

Hazardous waste sites (1995): 1,227
  Federal sites: 153
  Nonfederal sites: 1,074

LARGEST CITIES, POPULATION, 1990 PERCENTAGE INCREASE, 1980-90

Chicago, 2,783,726— −7.37%
Houston, 1,630,553—2.22%
Los Angeles, 3,485,398—17.41%
New York City, 7,322,564—3.55%
Philadelphia, 1,585,577—6.08%

THE PEOPLE

Population (1995): 262,755,270
  Percent change (1990-95): 5.64%
Population (2000 proj.): 276,242,000
  Percent change (1990-2000): 11.07%
Per sq. mi. (1995): 70.68
Percent in metro. area (1992): 79.7%
Foreign born: 19,767,000
  Percent: 7.9%
Top three ancestries reported:
  German, 23.30%
  Irish, 15.57%
  English, 13.13%
White (1994): 216,470,000, 83.0%
Black (1994): 32,672,000, 12.5%
Native American (1994): 2,210,000, 0.8%
Asian, Pacific Islander (1994): 8,989,000, 3.4%
Hispanic origin (1994): 26,077,000, 10.0%
Percent over 5 yrs. old speaking language other than English at home: 13.8%
Percent never married: males, 23.27%; females, 18.37%
Percent males: 48.72%
Percent females: 51.28%
Marriages per 1,000 (1993): 9.0

Divorces per 1,000 (1993): 4.6
Median age (1994): 34.0
Under 5 years old (1994): 7.58%
Under 18 years (1994): 26.13%
65 years & older (1994): 12.7%
Percent increase among the elderly (1990-94):
6.62%

OF VITAL IMPORTANCE

Live births per 1,000 pop. (est. 1995): 15.25
Infant mortality rate per 1,000 births (est.
1995): 7.9
   Rate for blacks (1992): 16.8
   Rate for whites (1992): 6.9
Births to unmarried women, % of total
(1992): 30.1%
Births to teenage mothers, % of total (1992):
12.7%
Abortions (1992): 1,528,930
   Ratio per 1,000 live births: 379
   Rate per 1,000 women 14-44 years old:
   25.9
   Percent change (1988-92): -5%
Life expectancy at birth (1995): males, 73;
females, 80
Deaths per 1,000 pop. (1994-95): 8.7
Causes of death per 100,000 pop. (1994):
   Accidents & adverse effects: 34.6
   Atherosclerosis (1991): 6.9
   Cancer: 206.0
   Cerebrovascular diseases: 59.2
   Chronic liver diseases & cirrhosis: 9.9
   Chronic obstructive pulmonary diseases: 39.1
   Diabetes mellitus: 21.2
   Diseases of heart: 281.6
   Pneumonia, flu: 31.5
   Suicide: 12.4

KEEPING WELL

Active nonfederal physicians per 100,000 pop.
(1993): 225
Dentists per 100,000 (1991): 59
Nurses per 100,000 (1992): 731
Hospitals per 100,000 (1993): 2.04
   Admissions per 1,000 (1993): 119.28
   Beds per 1,000 (1993): 3.55
   Average cost per patient per day (1993):
   $881
   Average cost per stay (1993): $6,132
   Average stay (1992): 8 days
AIDS, new cases (1994): 61,301
HIV infection, not yet AIDS (1993): 51,439
Population without health insurance (1991-
93): 14.9%

HOUSEHOLDS

Total households (1994): 95,946,000
   Percent change (1990-94): 4.4%
   Per 1,000 pop.: 368.54
   Percent of households 65 yrs. and over:
   21.76
   Persons per household (1994): 2.64

LIVING QUARTERS

Total year-round housing units (1993):
103,253,000
   Occupied units: 94,724,000
      Percent of total: 91.7%
   Owner-occupied units: 61,252,000
      Percent of total: 59.3%
   Renter-occupied units: 33,472,000
      Percent of total: 32.4%
Persons in emergency shelters for homeless
persons: 178,638, 0.072%
Persons visible in street locations: 49,734,
0.0200%
Persons in shelters for abused women: 11,768,
0.0047%
Nursing home population: 1,772,032, 0.71%

CRIME INDEX PER 100,000 (1992-93)

Total reported: 5,482.9
   Violent: 746.1
      Murder, nonnegligent manslaughter: 9.5
      Aggravated assault: 440.1
      Robbery: 255.8
      Forcible rape: 40.6
   Property: 4,736.9
      Burglary: 1,099.2
      Larceny, theft: 3,032.4
      Motor vehicle theft: 605.3
Drug abuse violations (1990): 391.1
Child-abuse rate per 1,000 children (1993):
15.01

TEACHING AND LEARNING

Literacy rate (persons age 15 or older; 1991):
96%
Pop. age 3 and over enrolled in school:
64,519,000
   Percent of pop.: 24.78%
Public elementary & secondary schools (1992-
93): 84,501
   Per 100,000 pop.: 33.13
   Total enrollment (1993): 43,476,267
   Teachers (1993): 2,505,075
   Pupil/teacher ratio (fall 1993): 17.4

Teachers' avg. salary (1993-94): $35,819
Expenditure per capita (1990-91): $3,587.33
Expenditure per pupil (1993): $5,594
Percent of graduates taking SAT (1995): 41%
  Mean SAT verbal scores: 428
  Mean SAT mathematical scores: 482
Percent of graduates taking ACT (1995): 39%
  Mean ACT scores: 20.9
Percent of pop. over 25 completing:
  Less than 9th grade: 10.4%
  High school: 75.2%
  College degree(s): 20.3%
Higher education, institutions (1993-94): 3,632
  Enrollment (1992): 14,491,226
    Percent of pop.: 5.68%
  White non-Hispanic (1992): 10,870,037
    Percent of enroll.: 75.01%
  Black non-Hispanic (1992): 1,393,483
    Percent of enroll.: 9.62%
  Hispanic (1992): 954,422
    Percent of enroll.: 6.59%
  Asian/Pacific Islander (1992): 696,812
    Percent of enroll.: 4.81%
  American Indian/Alaska native (1992): 118,845
    Percent of enroll.: 0.82%
  Nonresident alien (1992): 457,627
    Percent of enroll.: 3.16%
  Female (1992): 7,965,137
    Percent of enroll.: 54.97%
  Public institutions (1993-94): 1,625
    Enrollment (1992): 11,387,725
    Percent of enroll.: 78.58%
  Private institutions (1993-94): 2,007
    Enrollment (1992): 3,103,501
    Percent of enroll.: 21.42%
  Tuition, pub. inst. (avg., 1993-94): $6,374
  Tuition, private inst. (avg., 1993-94): $15,009
Public libraries (1993): 8,929

LAW ENFORCEMENT, COURTS, AND PRISONS

Police protection, corrections, judicial and legal functions expenditures (1992): $79,502,000,000
  Per capita: $312
Police per 10,000 pop. (1993): 35.34
Prisoners (state & fed.) per 100,000 pop. (1993): 3,673.42
  Percent change (1992-93): 7.3%
Under sentence of death (Oct. 1995): 3,046
Executed (1995): 56

MAKING A LIVING

Personal income per capita (1994): $21,809
  Percent increase (1993-94): 4.8%
Disposable personal income per capita (1994): $18,963
Median income of households (1993): $31,241
Percent of pop. below poverty level (1993): 15.1%
Expenditure for energy per person (1992): $1,853

ECONOMY

Civilian labor force (1995): 132,304,000
  Percent of total pop.: 50.35%
  Percent female: 46.06%
Unemployment rate (1995): 5.59%
  Male: 5.58%
  Female: 5.61%
Major occupations, in thousands (1994):
  Managerial & professional: 33,847, 27.5%
  Technical, sales, & admin. support: 37,306, 30.3%
  Services: 16,912, 13.7%
  Manufacturing, mining, transportation, & crafts: 31,365, 25.5%
  Farming, forestry, & fishing: 3,629, 2.9%
Business failure rate per 10,000 concerns (1993): 96
Agriculture farm income:
  Marketing (1993): $175,052,000,000
    Average per farm: $84,647.97
    Average per acre: $178.96
  Leading agricultural products: Cattle, dairy products, corn, soybeans
  Average value land & buildings per acre (1994): $744
    Percent increase (1990-94): 11.38%
  Govt. payments (1993): $13,402,000,000
    Average per farm: $6,480.66
    Average per acre: $13.70
Leading mineral products: Coal, copper, lead, molybdenum, phosphates, uranium, bauxite, gold, iron, mercury, nickel, potash, silver, tungstun, zinc
Leading industries: Petroleum, steel, motor vehicles, aerospace, telecommunications, chemicals, electronics, food processing, consumer goods, lumber, mining
Retail sales (1993): $2,079,201,000,000
  Per household: $21,683
    Percent increase (1992-93): 4.7%

Foreign exports, total value (1994):
$429,808,000,000
Per capita: $1,650.94
Gross domestic product per person (1993):
$25,900
Percent change (1990-94): 1.6%
Patents per 100,000 pop. (1993): 23.69
Public aid recipients (percent of resident pop. 1993): 7.7%
Medicaid recipients per 1,000 pop. (1993): 126.71
Medicare recipients per 1,000 pop. (1993): 137.70

TRAVEL AND TRANSPORTATION

Motor vehicle registrations (1993):
194,063,000
Per 1,000 pop.: 752.82
Motorcycle registrations (1993): 3,978,000
Per 1,000 pop.: 15.43
Licensed drivers (1993):173,149,313
Per 1,000 pop.: 671.69
Deaths from motor vehicle accidents per 100,000 pop. (1993): 16.29
Public roads & streets (1993):
Total mileage: 3,904,721
Per 1,000 pop.: 15.15
Rural mileage: 3,101,643
Per 1,000 pop.: 12.03
Urban mileage: 803,078
Per 1,000 pop.: 3.12
Interstate mileage: 45,530
Per 1,000 pop.: 0.18
Annual vehicle-mi. of travel per person (1993): 8,911
Mean travel time for workers age 16+ who work away from home: 22.4 min.

GOVERNMENT

Percent of voting age pop. registered (1994): 62.0%
Percent of voting age pop. voting (1994): 44.6%
Percent of voting age pop. voting for U.S. representatives (1994): 36.0%
U.S. Congress: Senate, 100; House of Representatives, 435
U.S. federal budget (fiscal 1995):
Total receipts: $1,350.6 bil.
Per capita: $5,120
Total outlays: $1,514.4 bil.
Per capita: $5,740
Public debt outstanding (end of fiscal 1995):
$5,000.9 bil.
Per capita: $18,956

THE U.S.A. IN THE WORLD

The United States is one of the world's largest countries in area. It is close in size to Canada and China, but much smaller than Russia. It ranks a distant third in population, well behind China and India.

With a life expectancy of 75.99 years at birth, Americans can expect shorter lives than people in many other developed countries. Among the "Big Ten" nations listed below, the United States ranked only seventh in life expectancy, and the same in literacy rate. Crude births per 1,000 population were estimated at 15.25 in 1995; two other selected major nations exceeded the U.S. crude birth rate.

In at least one major respect, the United States ranks first among all nations. It has the world's largest economy by far, as measured in gross domestic product.

The following tables compare the United States with the other Group of Seven (G-7) economic giants—Canada, France, Germany, Italy, Japan, and the United Kingdom—plus China, India, and Russia.

AREA
(in square miles)

1.	Russia	6,591,027
2.	Canada	3,850,790
3.	**United States**	3,717,522*
4.	China	3,704,427
5.	India	1,269,010
6.	France	211,154
7.	Japan	145,844
8.	Germany	137,767
9.	Italy	116,275
10.	United Kingdom	94,501

* China is often ranked ahead of the U.S.; this U.S. figure includes inland, Great Lakes, and coastal water.

POPULATION
(1995 estimates)

1.	China	1,203,097,268
2.	India	936,545,814
3.	**United States**	262,755,270
4.	Russia	149,909,089
5.	Japan	125,506,492
6.	Germany	81,337,541
7.	United Kingdom	58,295,119
8.	Italy	58,261,971
9.	France	58,109,160
10.	Canada	28,434,545

LIFE EXPECTANCY
(in years at birth; 1995 estimates)
1. Japan   79.44 yrs.
2. France   78.37 yrs.
3. Canada   78.29 yrs.
4. Italy   77.85 yrs.
5. United Kingdom   77.00 yrs.
6. Germany   76.72 yrs.
7. United States   75.99 yrs.
8. Russia   69.10 yrs.
9. China   68.80 yrs.
10. India   59.04 yrs.

LITERACY RATE
(age 15 and over; estimated)
1. Germany   100%   (1993)
1. Japan   100%   (1992)
1. United Kingdom   100%   (1992)
4. France   99%   (1992)
5. Russia   98%   (1993)
6. Italy   97%   (1993)
7. Canada   96%   (1994)
7. United States   96%   (1991)
9. China   78%   (1992)
10. India   48%   (1993)

BIRTH RATE
(per 1,000 population; 1995 estimates)
1. India   27.78
2. China   17.78
3. United States   15.25
4. Canada   13.74
5. United Kingdom   13.18
6. France   13.13*
7. Russia   12.64
8. Germany   10.98
9. Italy   10.89
10. Japan   10.66
* 1994

ECONOMY
(gross domestic product; 1994)
1. United States $6,738.4 billion
2. China $2,978.8 billion[1]
3. Japan $2,527.4 billion[2]
4. Germany $1,344.6 billion[2]
5. India $1,235.9 billion[2]
6. France $1,081.0 billion[2]
7. United Kingdom $1,045.2 billion[2]
8. Italy $998.9 billion[2]
9. Russia $721.2 billion[2]
10. Canada $639.8 billion[2]

[1] Based on official estimate; could be high.
[2] Estimated

PART II:
PORTRAITS OF
THE STATES

ALABAMA

"I had no idea Alabama had so much to offer. We have wafted over blue Gulf waters, rustled through venerable historic rooms, lilted across pine-ringed lakes, heard our voices echoed from picturesque mountain tops and resounded through mammoth caverns. We have been transported from the historical lands of the Indians, the Spanish, the French, the English, to the roar of the Space Age, and we had them all and much more in star-studded Alabama."

Anonymous travel writer

True to its nickname, Alabama is the "Heart of Dixie," where the Confederate constitution was formulated, but it is also a state that looks to the future. As a pioneer in the iron and steel industry, Alabama took an early lead in manufacturing in the South. It became a leader in the Space Age— Huntsville, "Rocket City, U.S.A.," is the center for research on rockets and space vehicles. Alabama is also filled with beauty, from forests rising from the red clay soil in the north, through pine forests and rolling grasslands of the south, to the swamps and bayous in the Mobile Delta on the Gulf of Mexico. This football-mad state (the University of Alabama has won many national championships) is no longer the rural region it once was, and has become increasingly cosmopolitan.

SUPERLATIVES

• Introduced Mardi Gras to the Western Hemisphere.
• Tuscumbia Railroad, the first west of the Alleghenies.
• The first rocket to put humans on the moon, built in Huntsville.
• First in cast-iron and steel pipe products.

• The only state to possess all the major raw materials needed to make iron and steel.
• World's first electric trolley system— Montgomery, 1886.

MOMENTS IN HISTORY

• In 1540 the Spanish explorer Hernando de Soto and his large party entered Alabama, killing and enslaving the native peoples as they went.
• The Parish of Mobile was organized in 1704.
• The American Revolution had little effect on what is present-day Alabama, but in 1780 the Spanish captured Mobile Bay from the British and held it for Spain during the war.
• Parts of Alabama came to the United States after the Revolution and also following battles with the British during the War of 1812.
• On March 27, 1814, Andrew Jackson's victory at the Battle of Horseshoe Bend brought to an end the power of the formidable Creek Confederacy.
• The pioneer smelters built near Russellville in 1818 were forerunners of the state's later leadership in iron and steel.

• The 1830s witnessed the beginning of one of history's saddest episodes as the Five Civilized Tribes were forced to leave their comfortable homes and move west over the "Trail of Tears." Their valuable property was taken without compensation.

• On January 11, 1861, Alabama seceded from the Union, and on February 4, delegates from six states met at Montgomery and formed the Confederate States of America, with Montgomery as the capital.

• The Confederate flag was designed and first flown in Alabama in 1861.

• Selma, Mobile, Tuscaloosa, and Montgomery fell to Union forces during the Civil War.

So They Say

"Damn the torpedoes—full speed ahead!"

Union Admiral David Farragut, as he moved to capture Mobile Bay—one of the world's most famous battle cries

• After the Civil War, Alabama refused to approve the 14th Amendment, and the state suffered many hardships during the Reconstruction period. Federal troops were not withdrawn from Alabama until 1876, and the state then began a slow recovery.

• After the Civil War the condition of the freed slaves did not improve greatly. Then in 1881, Booker T. Washington took over the Tuskegee Institute and was a pioneer in the education of African-Americans.

So They Say

"...progress in the enjoyment of all the privileges that will come to us must be the result of severe and constant struggle rather than of artificial forcing....It is important and right that all privileges of the law be ours, but it is vastly more important that we be prepared for the exercise of those privileges."

George Washington Carver,
Director of Agricultural Research Dept.
Tuskegee Institute

• Alabama's first steel was produced in 1888.

• In 1898 an entire battalion of black volunteers joined the state's recruits in the Spanish-American War.

• Alabama was figuratively shaken by a worm in 1910, as the boll weevil threatened the state's mammoth cotton crop, the key factor in its economy. Although the insect was controlled, peanut growing became important as a substitute.

• During World War I, Alabama Seaman Osmond Kelly (O. K.) Ingram, one of the 86,916 Alabamans who saw military service in that conflict, was the first U.S. Navy man to be killed.

• In 1932 the judgment of the Alabama Supreme Court was reversed by the U.S. Supreme Court in the famous Scottsboro case, and nine black men were returned for a new trial because their original trial was deemed prejudiced and unfair. Four were later released, and five were convicted.

• In 1933 the Tennessee Valley Authority was established. With its strategic location and pioneer Muscle Shoals dam, Alabama was in an excellent position to benefit from the TVA. Its dams and navigation projects helped to alleviate the severe effects of the Great Depression.

• During World War II, a total of 288,003 Alabamans saw service in the U.S. armed forces.

• In 1950, Dr. Werner von Braun brought 120 German rocket scientists to the small town of Huntsville. This started it on its way to becoming the "Rocket Capital of the World."

• In 1955, Rosa Parks contested "Jim Crow" segregation by refusing to move to the back of the bus.

• On January 31, 1958, *Explorer 1* became the West's first satellite; both the rocket and satellite had been developed at the Army Ballistic Missile Agency at Huntsville, under Werner von Braun.

• On May 15, 1972, while campaigning for the Democratic presidential nomination, Governor George Wallace was shot and partially paralyzed; he lost the nomination but was reelected governor in 1974. (He ran again, and won a fourth term, in 1982.)

• A federal district judge in 1991 ordered Alabama's state universities to hire more minority faculty and staff and alter financial and admission policies.

THAT'S INTERESTING

• An important relic discovered in Russell Cave was the skeleton of a prehistoric man. The tip of the spear that killed him was found lying among his bones.

So They Say

In 1811, Chief Tecumseh met with Creek Indian leaders in Tuckabatchee, Alabama, and tried to persuade them to join him in his fight against the Americans. Unsuccessful, he shouted, "When I get back to Detroit I will stamp my foot upon the ground and shake down every house in Tuckabatchee." A month later the great earthquakes of 1811 shook an enormous region. The Indians at Tuckabatchee hurried to their lodges, exclaiming, "Tecumseh has reached Detroit. Feel the earth move with his foot!"

• During the Civil War, John H. Wisdom became known as the Paul Revere of the South, after he galloped the 67 miles between Gadsden, Alabama, and Rome, Georgia, to warn of a Union attack.
• During his 46 years at Tuskegee Institute, black scientist George Washington Carver discovered 300 new uses for the peanut and 175 for the sweet potato, and made many other important contributions toward feeding the modern world.
• At one time, Alabama claimed to have the "largest representation in Congress." Senator Dixon H. Lewis of Montgomery weighed 500 pounds, and his Senate seat had to be specially made.
• One of the world's most unusual monuments stands at the town of Enterprise—a giant tribute to the boll weevil.

NOTABLE NATIVES

Henry Louis (Hank) Aaron (Mobile, 1934-), baseball player. Tallulah Brockman Bankhead (Huntsville, 1903-1968), actress. Hugo La-Fayette Black (Harlan, 1886-1971), Supreme Court justice. William Crawford Gorgas (Mobile, 1854-1920), army officer/physician. William Christopher Handy (Florence, 1873-1958), musician/composer. Percy Lavon Julian (Montgomery, 1899-1975), chemist.

Helen Adams Keller (Tuscumbia, 1880-1968), author/lecturer. Joe Louis (Lexington, 1914-1981), boxer. Willie Howard Mays, Jr. (Westfield, 1931-), baseball player. Alexander McGillivray (Alabama, 1759?-1793), Indian leader. John Hunt Morgan (Huntsville, 1825-1864), soldier. Jesse Owens (Danville, 1913-1980), athlete.

GENERAL

Admitted to statehood: December 14, 1819
Origin of name: Indian for tribal town, later a tribe (Alabamas or Alibamons) of the Creek confederacy
Capital: Montgomery
Nickname: Cotton State, Heart of Dixie
Motto: *Audemus jura nostra defendere*—We dare defend our rights
Bird: Yellowhammer
Fish: Tarpon (saltwater); largemouth bass (freshwater)
Flower: Camellia
Mineral: Red iron ore (hematite)
Stone: Marble
Song: "Alabama"
Tree: Southern pine

THE LAND

Area: 52,237 sq. mi., 30th
  Land: 50,750 sq. mi., 28th
  Water: 1,487 sq. mi., 20th
    Inland water: 968 sq. mi., 23rd
    Coastal water: 519 sq. mi., 12th
Topography: Coastal plains including Prairie Black Belt give way to hills, broken terrain
Number of counties: 67
Geographic center: Chilton, 12 mi. SW of Clanton
Length: 330 mi.; width: 190 mi.
Highest point: 2,405 ft. (Cheaha Mountain), 35th
Lowest point: sea level (Gulf of Mexico), 3rd
Mean elevation: 500 ft., 40th
Coastline: 53 mi., 17th
Shoreline: 607 mi., 19th

CLIMATE AND ENVIRONMENT

Temp., highest: 112 deg. on Sept. 5, 1925, at Centerville; lowest: –27 deg. on Jan. 30, 1966, at New Market
Monthly average: highest: 91.5 deg., 16th; lowest: 31.0 deg., 42nd; spread (high to low): 60.5 deg., 44th
Hazardous waste sites (1993): 14, 26th

Endangered species: Mammals: 4— Gray bat, Indiana bat, Alabama beach mouse, Perdido Key beach mouse; birds: 3— American peregrine falcon, Wood stock, Red-cockaded woodpecker; reptiles: 4; amphibians: none; fishes: 4; invertebrates: 21; plants: 6

MAJOR CITIES
POPULATION, 1990
PERCENTAGE INCREASE, 1980-90

Birmingham, 265,968— –6.49%
Huntsville, 159,789—12.12%
Mobile, 196,278— –2.08%
Montgomery, 187,106—5.20%
Tuscaloosa, 77,759—3.39%

THE PEOPLE

Population (1995): 4,252,982, 22nd
  Percent change (1990-95): 5.3%, 25th
Population (2000 proj.): 4,485,000, 21st
  Percent change (1990-2000): 11.00%, 23rd
Per sq. mi. (1994): 83.1, 26th
Percent in metro. area (1992): 67.4%, 32nd
Foreign born: 44,000, 35th
  Percent: 1.1%, 46th
Top three ancestries reported:
  African, 20.77%
  American, 17.00%
  Irish, 15.27%
White: 2,975,797, 73.65%, 43rd
Black: 1,020,705, 25.26%, 6th
Native American: 16,506, 0.41%, 26th
Asian, Pacific Isle: 21,979, 0.54%, 44th
Other races: 5,782, 0.14%, 48th
Hispanic origin: 24,629, 0.61%, 48th
Percent over 5 yrs. speaking language other than English at home: 2.9%, 46th
Percent males: 47.92%, 49th; percent females: 52.08%, 3rd
Percent never married: 23.9%, 37th
Marriages per 1,000 (1993): 9.4, 17th
Divorces per 1,000 (1993): 6.5, 3rd
Median age: 33
Under 5 years (1994): 7.16%, 27th
Under 18 years (1994): 25.60%, 32nd
65 years & older (1994): 13.1%, 24th
Percent increase among the elderly (1990-94): 5.55%, 26th

OF VITAL IMPORTANCE

Live births per 1,000 pop. (1993): 15.1, 19th
Infant mortality rate per 1,000 births (1992): 10.5, 3rd

Rate for blacks (1990): 15.9, 28th
Rate for whites (1990): 8.3, 14th
Births to unmarried women, % of total (1992): 32.6%, 14th
Births to teenage mothers, % of total (1992): 18.2%, 3rd
Abortions (1992): 17,450, 21st
  Rate per 1,000 women 14-44 years old: 18.2, 27th
  Percent change (1988-92): –3%, 18th
Average lifetime (1979-81): 72.53, 45th
Deaths per 1,000 pop. (1993): 9.9, 8th
Causes of death per 100,000 pop.:
  Accidents & adverse effects (1992): 49.9, 5th
  Atherosclerosis (1991): 6.4, 32nd
  Cancer (1991): 218.6, 16th
  Cerebrovascular diseases (1992): 66.6, 10th
  Chronic liver diseases & cirrhosis (1991): 9.1, 25th
  Chronic obstructive pulmonary diseases (1992): 35.2, 31st
  Diabetes mellitus (1992): 20.6, 26th
  Diseases of heart (1992): 311.7, 15th
  Pneumonia, flu (1991): 32.8, 18th
  Suicide (1992): 12.6, 24th

KEEPING WELL

Active nonfederal physicians per 100,000 pop. (1993): 170, 40th
Dentists per 100,000 (1991): 42, 46th
Nurses per 100,000 (1992): 673, 35th
Hospitals per 100,000 (1993): 2.77, 17th
  Admissions per 1,000 (1993): 144.68, 5th
  Occupancy rate per 100 beds (1993): 60.7, 29th
  Average cost per patient per day (1993): $775, 33rd
  Average cost per stay (1993): $5,229, 40th
  Average stay (1992): 7.1 days, 27th
AIDS cases (adult, 1993): 733; per 100,000: 17.5, 30th
HIV infection, not yet AIDS (1993): 3,281
Other notifiable diseases:
  Gonorrhea: 533.7, 4th
  Measles: 0.6, 43rd
  Syphilis: 77.6, 7th
  Tuberculosis: 12.0, 14th
Pop. without health insur. (1991-93): 17.4%, 12th

HOUSEHOLDS BY TYPE

Total households (1994): 1,583,000
  Percent change (1990-94): 5.1%, 21st

Per 1,000 pop.: 375.21, 24th
Percent of households 65 yrs. and over: 22.93%, 17th
Persons per household (1994): 2.61, 21st
Family households: 1,103,835
  Percent of total: 73.26%, 6th
Nonfamily households: 402,955
  Percent of total: 26.74%, 46th
Pop. living in group quarters: 92,402
  Percent of pop.: 2.29%, 42nd

LIVING QUARTERS

Total housing units: 1,670,379
Persons per unit: 2.42, 22nd
Occupied housing units: 1,506,790
  Percent of total units: 90.21%, 20th
  Persons per unit: 2.57, 16th
  Percent of units with over 1 person per room: 3.51%, 22nd
Owner-occupied units: 1,061,867
  Percent of total units: 63.57%, 8th
  Percent of occupied units: 70.47%, 6th
  Persons per unit: 2.70, 33rd
  Median value: $53,700, 41st
Renter-occupied units: 444,893
  Percent of total units: 26.63%, 42nd
  Percent of occupied units: 29.53%, 45th
  Persons per unit: 2.44, 14th
  Median contract rent: $229, 48th
  Rental vacancy rate: 9.3%, 19th
Mobile home, trailer & other as a percent of occupied housing units: 15.90%, 12th
Persons in emergency shelters for homeless persons: 1,530, 0.038%, 39th
Persons visible in street locations: 364, 0.0090%, 21st
Persons in shelters for abused women: 127, 0.0031%, 43rd
Nursing home population: 24,031, 0.59%, 38th

CRIME INDEX PER 100,000 (1992-93)

Total reported: 4,878.8, 27th
  Violent: 780.4, 13th
    Murder and nonnegligent manslaughter: 11.6, 8th
    Aggravated assault: 574.3, 8th
    Robbery: 159.5, 23rd
    Forcible rape: 35.1, 32nd
  Property: 4,098.4, 31st
    Burglary: 1,088.6, 19th
    Larceny, theft: 2,672.0, 36th
    Motor vehicle theft: 337.8, 32nd

Drug abuse violations (1990): 188.0, 36th
Child-abuse rate per 1,000 children (1993): 17.76, 17th

TEACHING AND LEARNING

Pop. 3 and over enrolled in school: 1,056,402
  Percent of pop.: 27.3%, 25th
Public elementary & secondary schools (1992-93): 1,294
  Total enrollment (1992): 723,410
    Percent of total pop.: 17.48%, 24th
  Teachers (1992): 41,567
    Percent of pop.: 1.00%, 33rd
  Pupil/teacher ratio (fall 1992): 17.4, 18th
  Teachers' avg. salary (1992-93): $28,913, 45th
Expenditure per capita (1990-91): $2,942.29, 43rd
Expenditure per pupil (1991-92): $3,616, 48th
Percent of graduates taking SAT (1993): 9%, 42nd
  Mean SAT verbal scores: 480, 13th
  Mean SAT mathematical scores: 526, 15th
Percent of graduates taking ACT (1995): 60%, 20th
  Mean ACT scores: 20.0, 45th
Percent of pop. over 25 completing:
  Less than 9th grade: 13.7%, 8th
  High school: 66.9%, 47th
  College degree(s): 15.7%, 45th
Higher education, institutions (1993-94): 80
  Enrollment (1992): 230,537
    White non-Hispanic (1992): 172,209
      Percent of enroll.: 74.70%, 38th
    Black non-Hispanic (1992): 49,466
      Percent of enroll.: 21.46%, 5th
    Hispanic (1992): 1,428
      Percent of enroll.: 0.62%, 44th
    Asian/Pacific Islander (1992): 1,901
      Percent of enroll.: 0.82%, 47th
    American Indian/AK native (1992): 839
      Percent of enroll.: 0.36%, 31st
    Nonresident alien (1992): 4,694
      Percent of enroll.: 2.04%, 39th
    Female (1992): 126,813
      Percent of enroll.: 55.01%, 31st
  Pub. institutions (1993-94): 52
    Enrollment (1992): 206,287
      Percent of enroll.: 89.48%, 8th
      Percent of pop.: 4.99%, 13th
  Private institutions (1993-94): 28
    Enrollment (1992): 24,250
      Percent of enroll.: 10.52%, 44th

Tuition, public institution (avg., 1993-94): $5,287, 33rd

Tuition, private institution (avg., 1993-94): $10,092, 40th

Public library systems: 206

Books & serial vol. per capita: 1.81, 44th

Govt. expenditure per capita: $8.24, 46th

LAW ENFORCEMENT, COURTS, AND PRISONS

Police protection, corrections, judicial and legal functions expenditures (1992): $825,000,000

Per capita: $199, 40th

Police per 10,000 pop. (1993): 20.53, 26th

Prisoners (state & fed.) per 100,000 pop. (1993): 4,454.44, 8th

Percent change (1992-93): 6.7%, 22nd

Death penalty: yes, by electrocution

Under sentence of death (1993): 120, 8th

Executed (1993): 0

RELIGION, NUMBER AND PERCENT OF POPULATION

Agnostic: 5,964—0.20%, 42nd

Buddhist: NA

Christian: 2,782,019—93.30%, 5th

Hindu: 2,982—0.10%, 10th

Jewish: 2,982—0.10%, 43rd

Muslim: 5,964—0.20%, 13th

Unitarian: 2,982—0.10%, 31st

Other: 23,854—0.80%, 37th

None: 116,290—3.90%, 44th

Refused to answer: 38,763—1.30%, 45th

MAKING A LIVING

Personal income per capita (1994): $18,010, 41st

Percent increase (1993-94): 5.1%, 22nd

Disposable personal income per capita (1994): $16,022, 41st

Median income of households (1993): $25,082, 47th

Percent of pop. below poverty level (1993): 17.4%, 12th

Percent 65 and over (1990): 24.0%, 3rd

Expenditure for energy per person (1992): $2,019, 12th

ECONOMY

Civilian labor force (1994): 2,031,000

Percent of total pop.: 48.14%, 44th

Percent 65 and over (1990): NA

Percent female: 46.18%, 28th

Percent job growth (1980-90): 18.99%, 26th

Major employer industries (1994):

Agriculture: NA—2.3%, 29th

Construction: 94,000—5.1%, 9th

Finance, insurance, & real estate: 83,000—4.5%, 37th

Government: 275,000—14.9%, 29th

Manufacturing: 397,000—21.6%, 10th

Service: 339,000—18.4%, 43rd

Trade: 331,000—18.0%, 40th

Transportation, communications, public utilities: 106,000—5.8%, 15th

Unemployment rate (1994): 6.01%, 9th

Male: 4.7%, 37th

Female: 7.5%, 4th

Total businesses (1991): 114,123

New business incorps. (1991): 6,116

Percent of total businesses: 5.36%, 34th

Business failures (1991): 678

Percent of total businesses: 0.59%

Agriculture farm income:

Marketing (1993): $2,910,000,000, 24th

Average per farm: $61,914.89, 37th

Leading products (1993): Broilers, cattle, eggs, greenhouse

Average value land & build. per acre (1994): $964, 26th

Percent increase (1990-94): 14.90%, 25th

Govt. payments (1993): $137,000,000, 25th

Average per farm: $2,914.89, 29th

Construction, value of all: $1,648,000,000

Per capita: $407.86, 40th

Manufactures:

Value added: $21,362,000,000

Per capita: $5,286.86, 22nd

Leading products: Electronics, cast iron and plastic pipe, fabricated steel products, ships, paper products, chemicals, steel, mobile homes, fabrics, and poultry processing

Value of nonfuel mineral production (1994): $576,000,000, 19th

Leading mineral products: Coal, petroleum, natural gas

Retail sales (1993): $29,779,000,000, 24th

Per household: $18,911, 46th

Percent increase (1992-93): 6.2%, 33rd

Tourism revenues: $3.4 bil. (1991)

Foreign exports, in total value (1994): $3,895,000,000, 26th

Per capita: $923.20, 37th

Gross state product per person (1993): $18,106.19, 47th

Percent change (1990-93): 4.23%, 17th

Patents per 100,000 pop. (1993): 7.75, 48th

Public aid recipients (percent of resident pop. 1993): 7.0%, 20th

Medicaid recipients per 1,000 pop. (1993): 124.85, 21st

Medicare recipients per 1,000 pop. (1993): 147.81, 18th

TRAVEL AND TRANSPORTATION

Motor vehicle registrations (1993): 3,390,000
Per 1,000 pop.: 810.81, 23rd

Motorcycle registrations (1993): 40,000
Per 1,000 pop.: 9.57, 42nd

Licensed drivers per 1,000 pop. (1993): 719.68, 12th

Deaths from motor vehicle accidents per 100,000 pop. (1993): 24.30, 4th

Public roads & streets (1993):
Total mileage: 92,209
Per 1,000 pop.: 22.05, 20th
Rural mileage: 72,828
Per 1,000 pop.: 17.42, 23rd
Urban mileage: 19,381
Per 1,000 pop.: 4.64, 3rd
Interstate mileage: 899
Per 1,000 pop.: 0.22, 24th

Annual vehicle-mi. of travel per person (1993): 11,313, 4th

Mean travel time for workers age 16+ who work away from home: 21.2 min., 20th

GOVERNMENT

Percent of voting age pop. registered (1994): 70.6%, 15th

Percent of voting age pop. voting (1994): 45.8%, 28th

Percent of voting age pop. voting for U.S. representatives (1994): 35.5%, 37th

State legislators, total (1995): 140, 28th
Women members (1992): 8
Percent of legislature: 5.7%, 50th

U.S. Congress, House members (1995): 7
Change (1985-95): 0

Revenues (1993):
State govt.: $11,389,000,000
Per capita: $2,723.99, 36th
Parimutuel & amusement taxes & lotteries, revenue per capita: $1.44, 42nd

Expenditures (1993):
State govt.: $10,242,000,000
Per capita: $2,449.65, 36th

Debt outstanding (1993): $4,163,000,000
Per capita: $995.69, 34th

LAWS AND REGULATIONS

Legal driving age: 16

Marriage age without parental consent: 18

Divorce residence requirement: 6 mo., for qualifications check local statutes

ATTRACTIONS (1995)

Major opera companies: 1

Major dance companies: 1

Major professional theater companies (non-profit): 1

State appropriations for arts agencies per capita: $0.48, 38th

State Fair in early October at Birmingham

SPORTS AND COMPETITION

NCAA teams (Division I): Alabama State Univ. Hornets, Auburn Univ. Tigers, Jacksonville State Univ. Gamecocks, Samford Univ. Bulldogs, Troy State Univ. Trojans, Univ. of Alabama Crimson Tide, Univ. of Alabama-Birmingham Blazers, Univ. of South Alabama Jaguars

ALASKA

"The future is bound to be a bright and useful one. You are no longer an Arctic frontier. You constitute a bridge to the continent of Asia and all of its people."

President Dwight D. Eisenhower

Vast Alaska could swallow up Texas, California, and Montana, yet it is the third least populous state. It reaches so far to the west that the international date line had to be bent around it to keep all the state in the same day. Although it is generally thought of as a "frozen" land, vegetables and fruit here can grow two or three times their normal size. Alaska is so large and roads are so few that the airplane becomes the "family car." Alaska is a land where railroads sink into the ground, where the ice barks and huge moose sometimes interfere with golf games. Celebrated for its wild grandeur and vast oil resources, Alaska has been called "America's Last Frontier."

SUPERLATIVES

• Largest of all the states, one-fifth as large as all the other states together.

> ## So They Say
>
> "Claustrophobia is how an Alaskan feels in the heart of Texas. Take all the tall tales you've heard about Texas, multiply by ten, and you have a fairly good starting point in a yarn that nobody will believe because it's too close to the truth."
>
> The Enchantment of Alaska

• Only U.S. state extending into the Eastern Hemisphere.
• Mt. McKinley—the highest mountain in North America.
• Nation's largest forest acreage.

MOMENTS IN HISTORY

• Sent by the Russian Czar, Vitus Bering reached Alaska in 1741. Native groups included the Indian, Eskimo, and Aleut, who were decimated by the Russians.
• Russia's trading headquarters were set up at Kodiak in 1784, the first permanent European settlement in present-day Alaska.

• In 1804, Alexander Baranov routed the Sitka Indians and established Sitka, which soon became the highly civilized capital of Alaska.

> ## So They Say
>
> "Their [Aleuts'] instruments and utensils are all made with amazing beauty and the exactest symmetry....Their boats are infinitely superior to those of any other."
>
> Anonymous early visitor

• As his hold on Alaska weakened, the Russian Czar decided to sell the territory to the United States. Although most Americans thought of Alaska as a barren, frigid waste, on March 30, 1867, the United States bought all of Russian America for $7.2 million.

> ## So They Say
>
> "The mystery is not why Russia wished to sell Alaska but why the United States wanted to buy."
>
> Unnamed journalist

• On October 18, 1867, the Americans present cheered as their flag was raised at Sitka, closing one of the best real estate bargains ever.
• In 1880 prospectors discovered a large gold lode near the headwaters of Gold Creek; in less than a year prospectors and settlers rushed in, and the community was named for prospector Joe Juneau.
• In 1896, thousands of American prospectors crossed Alaska over the treacherous passes to reach the gold discoveries of the Canadian Klondike.
• The gold found exposed on the beaches of Nome in 1899 brought prospectors in near-record numbers. As many as 40,000 scratched for the riches.

• On June 6, 1912, the top of Mt. Katmai exploded with a roar heard 750 miles away. The shock has been considered to be the second worst ever recorded.

So They Say

"A mountain has burst near here, so that we are covered with ashes, in some places ten feet deep....Night and day we light lamps...we are expecting death any moment, and we have no water....Here are darkness and hell, thunder and noise. The earth is trembling."

Unnamed observer,
on the explosion of Mt. Katmai

• On July 15, 1923, at the Tanana River bridge, Alaska's first railroad was dedicated by President Warren G. Harding.
• On August 15, 1935, a pontoon plane crashed, and the "world lost two of its most beloved figures" at a place a few miles from Barrow. Dead were the world famed humorist/philosopher Will Rogers and noted aviator Wiley Post.

So They Say

"One man big, have tall boots. Other man short, have sore eye, rag over eye."

Barrow native Okpeasha, on the crash of Will Rogers and Wiley Post, who wore a patch over one eye

• During World War II, Japanese invaders seized Attu, Kiska, and Agattu islands in 1942, but U.S. forces soon recaptured the Aleutians.
• Alaska became the 49th state on January 3, 1959; it was the first new state in the Union since 1912.
• One of the most disastrous earthquakes ever to hit North America devastated the Anchorage area on March 27, 1964.
• In 1977 the controversial Trans-Alaska pipeline was completed after three years of work, allowing oil to flow from the vast Prudhoe Bay oil field on the Arctic coast.
• By 1985 every Alaskan who applied had received a check of about $400 as a share in the state's revenues from oil.

• The grounding of the *Exxon Valdez* oil tanker in Prince William Sound on March 24, 1989, was one of the nation's worst ecological disasters. A vast oil spill killed unknown numbers of marine and shore animals and birds and affected much of the economy of a vast area. Cleanup costs and damages were staggering. In September 1994, Exxon was ordered to pay $5 billion in damages.
• In the mid-1990s declining oil prices and reserves began to threaten the state's subsidized lifestyle.
• A 1994 order by President Bill Clinton required that the state's aboriginal tribes receive the same deference from the administration as given to state governments.
• In 1994, Mount Cleveland erupted near Anchorage.

So They Say

"As soon as she heard the first sounds, she grabbed the kids and ran out of the house. A minute later the yard and the house—everything—fell into that hole."

Dr. Richard Sutherland,
on his wife's experience in
the 1964 Alaska earthquake

THAT'S INTERESTING

• The state of Rhode Island could fit into Alaska 425 times.
• Self-emptying Lake George is the best known curiosity of its kind. A dam of ice forms each winter and the lake backs up behind it. The pressure of the water causes the dam to burst. The lake empties itself, and the process begins all over.
• The last shot of the Civil War was fired in the remote region of the Bering Sea. The Confederate cruiser *Shenandoah* fired on a Union whaler on June 22, 1865, not knowing the war was over.
• Juneau's gold made prospector Joe Juneau wealthy, but he felt that he had to spend all his money before he died. He squandered his fortune and soon got his wish, dying penniless in Dawson.
• During Alaska's statehood celebration, Fairbanks attempted to turn the Chena River into gold, as a symbol of this source of wealth. However, through some chemical mistake, the river turned a lovely green.

• A map maker, unfamiliar with the name of an Alaskan community, wrote "name?" on the map. His draftsman misread the notation and entered the word "Nome" at that location, literally putting Nome on the map.

ALASKA NOTABLES

Alexander Baranov (Russia, 1747-1819), trader/public official. Rex Ellingwood Beach (Atwood, MI, 1877-1949), author. Vitus Jonassen Bering (Denmark, 1681-1741), explorer. Sheldon Jackson (Minaville, NY, 1834-1909), missionary. John Griffith (Jack) London (San Francisco, CA, 1876-1916), author. John Muir (Scotland, 1838-1914), naturalist/explorer/conservationist.

GENERAL

Admitted to statehood: January 3, 1959
Origin of name: Russian version of an Aleutian (Eskimo) word *alakshak,* for "peninsula," "great lands," or "land that is not an island"
Capital: Juneau
Nickname: Last Frontier, Land of Midnight Sun
Motto: North to the future
Bird: Willow ptarmigan
Fish: King salmon
Flower: Forget-me-not
Gem: Jade
Song: "Alaska's Flag"
Tree: Sitka spruce

THE LAND

Area: 615,230 sq. mi., 1st
   Land: 570,374 sq. mi., 1st
   Water: 44,856 sq. mi., 1st
   Inland water: 17,501 sq. mi., 1st
   Coastal water: 27,355 sq. mi., 1st
Topography: Includes Pacific and Arctic mountain systems, central plateau, and Arctic slope. Mt. McKinley, 20,320 ft., is the highest point in North America.
Number of counties: 25
Geographic center: lat. 63°50'N, long. 152°W, approx. 60 mi. NW of Mt. McKinley
Length: 1,480 mi.; width: 810 mi.
Highest point: 20,320 ft. (Mount McKinley), 1st
Lowest point: sea level (Pacific Ocean), 3rd
Mean elevation: 1,900 ft., 15th
Coastline: 6,640 mi., 1st
Shoreline: 33,904 mi., 1st

CLIMATE AND ENVIRONMENT

Temp., highest: 100 deg. on June 27, 1915, at Fort Yukon; lowest: –80 deg. on Jan. 23, 1971, at Prospect Creek Camp
Monthly average: highest: 71.8 deg., 51st; lowest: –21.6 deg., 1st; spread (high to low): 93.4 deg., 1st
Hazardous waste sites (1993): 8, 41st
Endangered species: Mammals: none; birds: 3—Eskimo curlew, American peregrine falcon, Aleutian Canada goose; reptiles: none; amphibians: none; fishes: none; invertebrates: none; plants: 1

MAJOR CITIES
POPULATION, 1990
PERCENTAGE INCREASE, 1980-90

Anchorage, 226,338—29.76%
College, 11,249—178.23%
Fairbanks, 30,843—36.20%
Juneau, 26,751—36.99%
Sitka, 8,588—10.06%

THE PEOPLE

Population (1995): 603,617, 48th
   Percent change (1990-95): 9.7%, 11th
Population (2000 proj.): 699,000, 47th
   Percent change (1990-2000): 27.08%, 3rd
Per sq. mi. (1994): 1.1, 51st
Percent in metro. area (1992): 41.8%, 42nd
Foreign born: 25,000, 42nd
   Percent: 4.5%, 19th
Top three ancestries reported:
   German, 23.09%
   English, 14.00%
   Irish, 13.45%
White: 415,492, 75.54%, 40th
Black: 22,451, 4.08%, 31st
Native American: 85,698, 15.58%, 1st
Asian, Pacific Isle: 19,728, 3.59%, 5th
Other races: 6,674, 1.21%, 23rd
Hispanic origin: 17,803, 3.24%, 22nd
Percent over 5 yrs. speaking language other than English at home: 12.1%, 15th
Percent males: 52.70%, 1st; percent females: 47.30%, 51st
Percent never married: 27.2%, 17th
Marriages per 1,000 (1993): 9.2, 19th
Divorces per 1,000 (1993): 5.3, 14th
Median age: 29.4
Under 5 years (1994): 9.24%, 2nd
Under 18 years (1994): 31.68%, 2nd
65 years & older (1994): 4.6%, 51st

Percent increase among the elderly (1990-94): 25.17%, 2nd

OF VITAL IMPORTANCE

Live births per 1,000 pop. (1993): 17.6, 5th
Infant mortality rate per 1,000 births (1992): 8.6, 25th
  Rate for blacks (1990): 11.2, 42nd
  Rate for whites (1990): 8.5, 11th
Births to unmarried women, % of total (1992): 27.4%, 28th
Births to teenage mothers, % of total (1992): 10.9%, 33rd
Abortions (1992): 2,370, 47th
  Rate per 1,000 women 14-44 years old: 16.5, 30th
  Percent change (1988-92): –10%, 29th
Average lifetime (1979-81): 72.24, 46th
Deaths per 1,000 pop. (1993): 3.8, 50th
Causes of death per 100,000 pop.:
  Accidents & adverse effects (1992): 60.9, 1st
  Atherosclerosis (1991): NA
  Cancer (1991): 88.1, 51st
  Cerebrovascular diseases (1992): 18.4, 51st
  Chronic liver diseases & cirrhosis (1991): 8.8, 30th
  Chronic obstructive pulmonary diseases (1992): 15.1, 51st
  Diabetes mellitus (1992): 8.0, 51st
  Diseases of heart (1992): 88.1, 51st
  Pneumonia, flu (1991): 9.1, 51st
  Suicide (1992): 15.3, 9th

KEEPING WELL

Active nonfederal physicians per 100,000 pop. (1993): 142, 48th
Dentists per 100,000 (1991): 56, 20th
Nurses per 100,000 (1992): 637, 40th
Hospitals per 100,000 (1993): 2.68, 18th
  Admissions per 1,000 (1993): 62.37, 51st
  Occupancy rate per 100 beds (1993): 52.9, 50th
  Average cost per patient per day (1993): $1,136, 4th
  Average cost per stay (1993): $7,594, 4th
  Average stay (1992): 5.9 days, 47th
AIDS cases (adult, 1993): 70; per 100,000: 1.7, 50th
HIV infection, not yet AIDS (1993): NA
  Other notifiable diseases:
  Gonorrhea: 193.8, 27th
  Measles: 14.5, 5th

Syphilis: 4.7, 40th
Tuberculosis: 12.4, 11th
Pop. without health insur. (1991-93): 14.6%, 18th

HOUSEHOLDS BY TYPE

Total households (1994): 208,000
  Percent change (1990-94): 10.3%, 5th
  Per 1,000 pop.: 343.23, 49th
  Percent of households 65 yrs. and over: 8.17%, 51st
Persons per household (1994): 2.81, 4th
Family households: 132,837
  Percent of total: 70.32%, 27th
Nonfamily households: 56,078
  Percent of total: 29.68%, 25th
Pop. living in group quarters: 20,701
  Percent of pop.: 3.76%, 5th

LIVING QUARTERS

Total housing units: 232,608
  Persons per unit: 2.36, 34th
Occupied housing units: 188,915
  Percent of total units: 81.22%, 49th
  Persons per unit: 2.78, 4th
  Percent of units with over 1 person per room: 8.58%, 3rd
Owner-occupied units: 105,989
  Percent of total units: 45.57%, 50th
  Percent of occupied units: 56.10%, 46th
  Persons per unit: 2.97, 3rd
  Median value: $94,400, 14th
Renter-occupied units: 82,926
  Percent of total units: 35.65%, 8th
  Percent of occupied units: 43.90%, 7th
  Persons per unit: 2.58, 5th
  Median contract rent: $503, 6th
  Rental vacancy rate: 8.5%, 24th
Mobile home, trailer & other as a percent of occupied housing units: 13.08%, 22nd
Persons in emergency shelters for homeless persons: 447, 0.081%, 10th
Persons visible in street locations: 79, 0.0144%, 13th
Persons in shelters for abused women: 157, 0.0285%, 1st
Nursing home population: 1,202, 0.22%, 51st

CRIME INDEX PER 100,000 (1992-93)

Total reported: 5,567.9, 17th
  Violent: 760.8, 16th

Murder and nonnegligent manslaughter:
9.0, 18th
Aggravated assault: 545.6, 9th
Robbery: 122.4, 31st
Forcible rape: 83.8, 1st
Property: 4,807.2, 18th
Burglary: 816.9, 36th
Larceny, theft: 3,539.4, 12th
Motor vehicle theft: 450.9, 22nd
Drug abuse violations (1990): 101.1, 46th
Child-abuse rate per 1,000 children (1993):
36.60, 1st

TEACHING AND LEARNING

Pop. 3 and over enrolled in school: 156,357
Percent of pop.: 30.2%, 4th
Public elementary & secondary schools (1992-93): 494
Total enrollment (1992): 122,487
Percent of total pop.: 20.83%, 4th
Teachers (1992): 7,282
Percent of pop.: 1.24%, 5th
Pupil/teacher ratio (fall 1992): 16.8, 26th
Teachers' avg. salary (1992-93): $46,984, 3rd
Expenditure per capita (1990-91): $9,776.41, 1st
Expenditure per pupil (1991-92): $8,450, 4th
Percent of graduates taking SAT (1993): 42%, 24th
Mean SAT verbal scores: 438, 29th
Mean SAT mathematical scores: 477, 34th
Percent of graduates taking ACT (1995): 40%, 27th
Mean ACT scores: 21.0, 28th
Percent of pop. over 25 completing:
Less than 9th grade: 5.1%, 50th
High school: 86.6%, 1st
College degree(s): 23.0%, 12th
Higher education, institutions (1993-94): 8
Enrollment (1992): 30,902
White non-Hispanic (1992): 24,682
Percent of enroll.: 79.87%, 31st
Black non-Hispanic (1992): 1,143
Percent of enroll.: 3.70%, 33rd
Hispanic (1992): 730
Percent of enroll.: 2.36%, 19th
Asian/Pacific Islander (1992): 799
Percent of enroll.: 2.59%, 18th
American Indian/AK native (1992): 2,852
Percent of enroll.: 9.23%, 2nd
Nonresident alien (1992): 696
Percent of enroll.: 2.25%, 32nd

Female (1992): 18,260
Percent of enroll.: 59.09%, 1st
Pub. institutions (1993-94): 4
Enrollment (1992): 29,037
Percent of enroll.: 93.96%, 4th
Private institutions (1993-94): 4
Enrollment (1992): 1,865
Percent of enroll.: 6.04%, 48th
Tuition, public institution (avg., 1993-94): $5,985, 23rd
Tuition, private institution (avg., 1993-94): $11,057, 35th
Public library systems: 81
Books & serial vol. per capita: 3.13, 17th
Govt. expenditure per capita: $36.18, 1st

LAW ENFORCEMENT, COURTS, AND PRISONS

Police protection, corrections, judicial and legal functions expenditures (1992): $366,000,000
Per capita: $623, 2nd
Police per 10,000 pop. (1993): 17.41, 39th
Prisoners (state & fed.) per 100,000 pop. (1993): 4,520.07, 6th
Percent change (1992-93): −5.7%, 51st
Death penalty: no

RELIGION, NUMBER AND PERCENT OF POPULATION

Agnostic: NA
Buddhist: NA
Christian: NA
Hindu: NA
Jewish: NA
Muslim: NA
Unitarian: NA
Other: NA
None: NA
Refused to answer: NA

MAKING A LIVING

Personal income per capita (1994): $23,788, 9th
Percent increase (1993-94): 3.1%, 48th
Disposable personal income per capita (1994): $21,175, 7th
Median income of households (1993): $42,931, 1st
Percent of pop. below poverty level (1993): 9.1%, 49th
Percent 65 and over (1990): 7.6%, 49th
Expenditure for energy per person (1992): $3,175, 2nd

ECONOMY

Civilian labor force (1994): 305,000
  Percent of total pop.: 50.33%, 33rd
  Percent 65 and over (1990): NA
  Percent female: 45.90%, 32nd
Percent job growth (1980-90): 40.53%, 4th
Major employer industries (1994):
  Agriculture: NA—0.5%, 50th
  Construction: 13,000—4.8%, 15th
  Finance, insurance, & real estate: 12,000—
    4.2%, 42nd
  Government: 76,000—27.7%, 2nd
  Manufacturing: 10,000—3.7%, 50th
  Service: 53,000—4.2%, 38th
  Trade: 47,000—17.2%, 46th
  Transportation, communications, public
    utilities: 22,000—8.1%, 1st
Unemployment rate (1994): 7.87%, 5th
  Male: 9.1%, 2nd
  Female: 6.2%, 16th
Total businesses (1991): 19,262
  New business incorps. (1991): 1,250
    Percent of total businesses: 6.49%, 19th
  Business failures (1991): 124
    Percent of total businesses: 0.64
Agriculture farm income:
  Marketing (1993): $27,000,000, 50th
    Average per farm: $27,000, 48th
  Leading products (1993): Greenhouse, dairy
    products, potatoes, hay
  Average value land & build. per acre
    (1994): NA
  Govt. payments (1993): $2,000,000,
    48th
    Average per farm: $2,000.00, 36th
Construction, value of all: $295,000,000
  Per capita: $536.32, 26th
Manufactures:
  Value added: $1,390,000,000
    Per capita: $2,527.08, 43rd
  Leading products: Fish products, lumber
    and pulp, furs
Value of nonfuel mineral production (1994):
  $429,000,000, 27th
Leading mineral products: Petroleum, natural
  gas, sand/gravel
Retail sales (1993): $5,471,000,000, 48th
  Per household: $26,088, 4th
  Percent increase (1992-93): 5.1%, 35th
Tourism revenues (1994): $863 mil.
Foreign exports, in total value (1994):
  $2,456,000,000, 31st
  Per capita: $4,052.81, 2nd

Gross state product per person (1993):
  $45,694.20, 2nd
  Percent change (1990-93): –3.70%, 51st
Patents per 100,000 pop. (1993): 10.70,
  41st
Public aid recipients (percent of resident pop.
  1993): 7.2%, 18th
Medicaid recipients per 1,000 pop. (1993):
  108.70, 27th
Medicare recipients per 1,000 pop. (1993):
  50.17, 51st

TRAVEL AND TRANSPORTATION

Motor vehicle registrations (1993): 489,000
  Per 1,000 pop.: 817.73, 21st
Motorcycle registrations (1993): 12,000
  Per 1,000 pop.: 20.07, 18th
Licensed drivers per 1,000 pop. (1993):
  732.44, 6th
Deaths from motor vehicle accidents per
  100,000 pop. (1993): 19.57, 18th
Public roads & streets (1993):
  Total mileage: 13,849
    Per 1,000 pop.: 23.16, 18th
  Rural mileage: 12,107
    Per 1,000 pop.: 20.25, 17th
  Urban mileage: 1,742
    Per 1,000 pop.: 2.91, 33rd
  Interstate mileage: 1,087
    Per 1,000 pop.: 1.82, 2nd
Annual vehicle-mi. of travel per person
  (1993): 6,522, 49th
Mean travel time for workers age 16+ who
  work away from home: 16.7 min.,
  45th

GOVERNMENT

Percent of voting age pop. registered (1994):
  71.7%, 13th
  Percent of voting age pop. voting (1994):
    59.1%, 6th
  Percent of voting age pop. voting for U.S.
    representatives (1994): 48.5%, 10th
State legislators, total (1995): 60, 49th
  Women members (1992): 14
    Percent of legislature: 23.3%, 15th
U.S. Congress, House members (1995): 1
  Change (1985-95): 0
Revenues (1993):
  State govt.: $7,358,000,000
    Per capita: $12,304.35, 1st
  Parimutuel & amusement taxes & lotteries,
    revenue per capita: $1.67, 41st

Expenditures (1993):
  State govt.: $5,423,000,000
    Per capita: $9,068.56, 1st
  Debt outstanding (1993): $4,427,000,000
    Per capita: $7,403.01, 1st

LAWS AND REGULATIONS

Legal driving age: 16
Marriage age without parental consent: 18
Divorce residence requirement: For qualifications check local statutes

ATTRACTIONS (1995)

Major opera companies: 1
State appropriations for arts agencies per capita: $1.37, 12th
State Fair in late August at Palmer

SPORTS AND COMPETITION

NCAA teams (Division II): Univ. of Alaska-Anchorage Seawolves, Univ. of Alaska-Fairbanks Nanooks

ARIZONA

"Land of extremes. Land of contrasts. Land of surprises. Land of contradictions. A land that is never to be fully understood but always to be loved....That is Arizona."

Federal Writers' Project, Arizona

The last of the conterminous states to be admitted to the union, Arizona is renowned for its natural wonders, with its magnificent deserts, mountains, and plateaus. The most startling area of the state is, of course, the Grand Canyon, which is one of the Seven Natural Wonders of the World. Long ago, ancient Indian peoples built on Arizona lands great communal cliff dwellings, whose crumbling adobe walls remain as testimony to their culture. The state capital, Phoenix, was founded on Indian ruins and—like its namesake, the mythical bird—grew swiftly out of the remains. In recent years, Arizona has continued to grow spectacularly in population, as its healthful climate and industrious workers have lured both retired persons and industry.

SUPERLATIVES

• The Grand Canyon, one of the world's greatest natural wonders.
• The Arizona trout, found only here.
• Has led the nation in copper production since 1907.
• Leads all states in value of nonfuel mineral production.
• Hoover Dam (partly in Arizona), which impounds the nation's largest artificial body of water.

So They Say

"The Casa Grande—a four story building as large as a castle and equal to the finest church in these lands of Sonora."

Father Eusebio Francisco Kino,
describing that monument
to Pueblo culture

• The largest tribe on the largest U.S. reservation—Arizona's Navajo Indians.
• World's largest solar telescope, at Kitts Peak National Observatory in Sells.

MOMENTS IN HISTORY

• The Pueblo (Spanish for village) peoples flourished from about 700 A.D through the late 1200s—a striking civilization.

So They Say

During the great Pueblo period, grand apartment houses were built with as many as four stories and dozens of rooms. These fantastic structures are found in all parts of Arizona.

The Enchantment of Arizona

• In 1539, Franciscan friar Marcos de Niza failed to find the fabled wealth of the Seven Cities of Cibola.
• The enormous expedition of Francisco Vásquez de Coronado entered present-day Arizona in 1540, made many discoveries, but found no riches.
• Garcia Lopez de Cardenas reached the brink of a great gorge one day in 1540, but failed to appreciate the wonders of what is now called the Grand Canyon.

So They Say

"...Ours has been the first and will doubtless be the last party of whites to visit this profitless locality."

Joseph Ives, describing
the Grand Canyon

• Little attention was paid to the area until the arrival of the Jesuits in 1692, led by Father Eusebio Francisco Kino. He baptized thousands, taught them how to raise crops and livestock, and explored much of the area.
• In 1752, Tubac, in the Santa Cruz Valley, became the first permanent white settlement in what is now Arizona.

• Arizona continued under Spanish and later Mexican rule until the Mexican War, beginning in 1846. In that war a notable military group, the renowned Mormon volunteer battalion, made the longest infantry march on record.

So They Say

Lieutenant Colonel Philip St. George Cooke, leader of the Mormon Battalion, "...in the evening [Dec. 18, 1846], camped without water after traveling 30 miles.... [Dec. 19] Started again...traveled till a little after dark and still no prospects of water....I was almost choked with thirst and hardly able to stand...passed by many lying on the roadside begging for water. Some of the men finally reached the river..." and brought back water.

Henry Standage,
in an unpublished journal

• During the gold rush to California, beginning in 1849, 60,000 persons passed across Arizona, suffering many Indian attacks.
• Gold was discovered north of Fort Yuma in 1858. Soon, Gila City had a population of 1,000, but the boom quickly died.
• In February 1862 Confederate cavalry took over Tucson. Federal troops then occupied Yuma.
• The Battle of Apache Pass, in July 1862, was a major struggle in the Indian wars that took place from the 1860s to the early 1870s. Indians retreated when government troops fired their howitzers.

So They Say

"We would have done well if you hadn't fired wagon wheels at us."

Chief Cochise, commenting on the howitzer fire at the Battle of Apache Pass

---

• During the years 1861 to 1880, travelers and peaceful Indians feared the periodic raids of Chief Geronimo.
• Phoenix originated in 1866 as a hay camp to supply Camp McDowell's fodder. The town grew as soon as Jack Swilling began to restore the prehistoric irrigation canals.

• After several moves the capital was located at Phoenix in 1889.
• Arizona became the 48th state on February 14, 1912.
• In 1916 the already poor relations with Mexico worsened when Mexican revolutionary Pancho Villa was thwarted as he attempted to enter Nogales from Sonora.
• In 1934, Arizona lost the "water war" when the courts awarded a large share of the Colorado River's water to California.
• In the decades from 1960 to 1990, the population grew amazingly, by more than 250%.
• Governor Evan Mecham was convicted in 1988 by the Arizona Senate on charges of misconduct and removed from office (but was then acquitted of a key criminal charge).
• In 1991 the biosphere, designed as supposedly a complete ecosystem, was sealed for two years in Oracle, beginning a controversial experiment.

THAT'S INTERESTING

• The bed of the Colorado River at the Grand Canyon lies at about the same level as it did millions of years ago. The canyon was formed as the ground continued to rise, and the river continued to carve through it as the force of the water and the sand and boulders cut away at the rising land.
• The great dome of the White Dove of the Desert mission was formed over a lofty mound of earth, piled up by the Indian converts. Learning that many coins had been buried in the earth beneath the dome, the eager Indians cleared away the entire earthen form to dig up those "riches."
• Arizona humorist Dick Wick Hall was noted for his tall tales about the state. According to one of his stories, potatoes were really planted so that when onions were scratched the potatoes' eyes would water and irrigate the whole garden.
• Because Arizona's conditions seemed ideal for it, Edward F. Beale brought in camels, which were actually used for a time, but camel transport proved impractical. After the animals were abandoned, "wild" camels remained for years, frightening travelers and their horses.
• Famed Mission San Xavier at Tucson features a carving of a cat. On the opposite side of the mission is the carving of a mouse.

According to Indian legend, the world will
end when that cat catches the mouse.

• Based on the legend of the phoenix bird,
which is burned by fire every 500 years and
then rises from its ashes, the new town that
rose on the "ashes" of the prehistoric Hoho-
kam settlement was named Phoenix.

NOTABLE NATIVES

Cesar Estrada Chavez (Yuma, 1927-1993),
labor leader. Cochise (probably in Arizona,
1812?-1874), Indian leader. Geronimo (in
Arizona, 1829-1909), Indian leader. Barry
Morris Goldwater (Phoenix, 1909-), public
official. Morris (Mo) King Udall (St. Johns,
1922-), public official. Stewart Lee Udall (St.
Johns, 1920-), public official.

GENERAL

Admitted to statehood: February 14, 1912
Origin of name: Spanish version of the Pima
    Indian word for "little spring place," or
    the Aztec word *arizuma*, meaning
    "silver bearing"
Capital: Phoenix
Nickname: Grand Canyon State
Motto: *Ditat Deus*—God enriches
Bird: Cactus wren
Flower: Blossom of the Saguaro Cactus
Song: "Arizona"
Tree: Paloverde

THE LAND

Area: 114,006 sq. mi., 6th
    Land: 113,642 sq. mi., 6th
    Water: 364 sq. mi., 45th
    Inland water: 364 sq. mi., 41st
Topography: Colorado plateau in the N,
    containing the Grand Canyon; Mexi-
    can Highlands running diagonally NW
    to SE; Sonoran Desert in the SW
Number of counties: 15
Geographic center: Yavapai, 55 mi. ESE of
    Prescott
Length: 400 mi.; width: 310 mi.
Highest point: 12,633 ft. (Humphreys Peak),
    12th
Lowest point: 70 ft., (Colorado River), 27th
Mean elevation: 4,100 ft., 7th

CLIMATE AND ENVIRONMENT

Temp., highest: 127 deg. on July 7, 1905, at
    Parker; lowest: –40 deg. on Jan. 7,
    1971, at Hawley Lake

Monthly average: highest: 105.0 deg., 1st;
    lowest: 38.1 deg., 49th; spread (high to
    low): 66.9 deg., 30th
Hazardous waste sites (1993): 10, 36th
Endangered species: Mammals: 6—Sanborn's
    long-nosed bat, Jaguarundi, Ocelot,
    Sonoran pronghorn, Mount Graham
    red squirrel, Hualapai Mexican vole;
    birds: 3—Masked bobwhite, American
    peregrine falcon, Yuma clapper rail;
    reptiles: none; amphibians: none; fishes:
    9; invertebrates: none; plants: 9

MAJOR CITIES
POPULATION, 1990
PERCENTAGE INCREASE, 1980-90

Glendale, 148,134—52.73%
Mesa, 288,091—89.03%
Phoenix, 983,403—24.53%
Tempe, 141,865—32.68%
Tucson, 405,390—22.65%

THE PEOPLE

Population (1995): 4,217,940, 23rd
    Percent change (1990-95): 15.1%, 3rd
Population (2000 proj.): 4,437,000, 23rd
    Percent change (1990-2000): 21.06%, 9th
Per sq. mi. (1994): 35.9, 38th
Percent in metro. area (1992): 84.7%, 12th
Foreign born: 278,000, 14th
    Percent: 7.6%, 13th
Top three ancestries reported:
    German, 23.96%
    English, 15.99%
    Irish, 14.46%
White: 2,963,186, 80.85%, 33rd
Black: 110,524, 3.02%, 37th
Native American: 203,527, 5.55%, 6th
Asian, Pacific Isle: 55,206, 1.51%, 20th
Other races: 332,785, 9.08%, 4th
Hispanic origin: 688,338, 18.78%, 4th
Percent over 5 yrs. speaking language other
    than English at home: 20.8%, 6th
Percent males: 49.40%, 12th; percent females:
    50.60%, 40th
Percent never married: 25.5%, 26th
Marriages per 1,000 (1993): 9.9, 14th
Divorces per 1,000 (1993): 6.2, 7th
Median age: 32.2
Under 5 years (1994): 8.44%, 6th
Under 18 years (1994): 27.95%, 10th
65 years & older (1994): 13.4%, 19th
Percent increase among the elderly (1990-94):
    14.04%, 3rd

OF VITAL IMPORTANCE

Live births per 1,000 pop. (1993): 18.0, 4th
Infant mortality rate per 1,000 births (1992): 8.4, 28th
  Rate for blacks (1990): 16.7, 18th
  Rate for whites (1990): 8.2, 18th
Births to unmarried women, % of total (1992): 36.2%, 5th
Births to teenage mothers, % of total (1992): 15.0%, 15th
Abortions (1992): 20,600, 17th
  Rate per 1,000 women 14-44 years old: 24.1, 16th
  Percent change (1988-92): –16%, 41st
Average lifetime (1979-81): 74.30, 20th
Deaths per 1,000 pop. (1993): 8.2, 35th
Causes of death per 100,000 pop.:
  Accidents & adverse effects (1992): 42.3, 14th
  Atherosclerosis (1991): 6.6, 26th
  Cancer (1991): 194.2, 37th
  Cerebrovascular diseases (1992): 47.6, 43rd
  Chronic liver diseases & cirrhosis (1991): 12.7, 5th
  Chronic obstructive pulmonary diseases (1992): 44.3, 8th
  Diabetes mellitus (1992): 17.2, 39th
  Diseases of heart (1992): 243.1, 35th
  Pneumonia, flu (1991): 31.0, 23rd
  Suicide (1992): 17.0, 6th

KEEPING WELL

Active nonfederal physicians per 100,000 pop. (1993): 194, 28th
Dentists per 100,000 (1991): 50, 33rd
Nurses per 100,000 (1992): 711, 27th
Hospitals per 100,000 (1993): 1.52, 42nd
  Admissions per 1,000 (1993): 102.31, 38th
  Occupancy rate per 100 beds (1993): 57.1, 40th
  Average cost per patient per day (1993): $1,091, 5th
  Average cost per stay (1993): $5,528, 33rd
  Average stay (1992): 5.8 days, 49th
AIDS cases (adult, 1993): 1,200; per 100,000: 31.5, 18th
HIV infection, not yet AIDS (1993): 2,619
Other notifiable diseases:
  Gonorrhea: 145.1, 30th
  Measles: 8.5, 10th
  Syphilis: 35.2, 20th
  Tuberculosis: 7.5, 21st
Pop. without health insur. (1991-93): 17.8%, 11th

HOUSEHOLDS BY TYPE

Total households (1994): 1,503,000
  Percent change (1990-94): 9.8%, 6th
  Per 1,000 pop.: 368.83, 34th
  Percent of households 65 yrs. and over: 22.62%, 20th
  Persons per household (1994): 2.66, 14th
Family households: 940,106
  Percent of total: 68.68%, 41st
Nonfamily households: 428,737
  Percent of total: 31.32%, 11th
Pop. living in group quarters: 80,683
  Percent of pop.: 2.20%, 46th

LIVING QUARTERS

Total housing units: 1,659,430
  Persons per unit: 2.21, 46th
Occupied housing units: 1,368,843
  Percent of total units: 82.49%, 46th
  Persons per unit: 2.59, 15th
  Percent of units with over 1 person per room: 7.42%, 7th
Owner-occupied units: 878,561
  Percent of total units: 52.94%, 44th
  Percent of occupied units: 64.18%, 40th
  Persons per unit: 2.71, 29th
  Median value: $80,100, 20th
Renter-occupied units: 490,282
  Percent of total units: 29.55%, 24th
  Percent of occupied units: 35.82%, 14th
  Persons per unit: 2.46, 12th
  Median contract rent: $370, 18th
  Rental vacancy rate: 15.3%, 1st
Mobile home, trailer & other as a percent of occupied housing units: 20.08%, 4th
Persons in emergency shelters for homeless persons: 2,735, 0.075%, 13th
Persons visible in street locations: 1,897, 0.0518%, 4th
Persons in shelters for abused women: 279, 0.0076%, 6th
Nursing home population: 14,472, 0.39%, 47th

CRIME INDEX PER 100,000 (1992-93)

Total reported: 7,431.7, 3rd
  Violent: 715.0, 19th
    Murder and nonnegligent manslaughter: 8.6, 20th
    Aggravated assault: 505.7, 12th
    Robbery: 162.9, 22nd
    Forcible rape: 37.8, 26th

Property: 6,716.7, 3rd
  Burglary: 1,465.5, 4th
  Larceny, theft: 4,387.4, 4th
  Motor vehicle theft: 863.8, 4th
Drug abuse violations (1990): 382.5, 11th
Child-abuse rate per 1,000 children (1993): 28.72, 6th

TEACHING AND LEARNING

Pop. 3 and over enrolled in school: 991,122
  Percent of pop.: 28.4%, 14th
Public elementary & secondary schools (1992-93): 1,118
  Total enrollment (1992): 673,477
    Percent of total pop.: 17.58%, 21st
  Teachers (1992): 36,076
    Percent of pop.: 0.94%, 40th
  Pupil/teacher ratio (fall 1992): 18.7, 8th
  Teachers' avg. salary (1992-93): $39,211, 13th
  Expenditure per capita (1990-91): $3,421.61, 23rd
  Expenditure per pupil (1991-92): $4,381, 40th
Percent of graduates taking SAT (1993): 28%, 25th
  Mean SAT verbal scores: 444, 25th
  Mean SAT mathematical scores: 497, 25th
Percent of graduates taking ACT (1995): 29%, 30th
  Mean ACT scores: 21.0, 28th
Percent of pop. over 25 completing:
  Less than 9th grade: 9.0%, 29th
  High school: 78.7%, 20th
  College degree(s): 20.3%, 23rd
Higher education, institutions (1993-94): 42
  Enrollment (1992): 275,599
  White non-Hispanic (1992): 208,688
    Percent of enroll.: 75.72%, 36th
  Black non-Hispanic (1992): 8,616
    Percent of enroll.: 3.13%, 36th
  Hispanic (1992): 34,443
    Percent of enroll.: 12.50%, 4th
  Asian/Pacific Islander (1992): 7,065
    Percent of enroll.: 2.56%, 20th
  American Indian/AK native (1992): 9,244
    Percent of enroll.: 3.35%, 7th
  Nonresident alien (1992): 7,543
    Percent of enroll.: 2.74%, 22nd
  Female (1992): 149,054
    Percent of enroll.: 54.08%, 41st
  Pub. institutions (1993-94): 22
    Enrollment (1992): 255,907
    Percent of enroll.: 92.85%, 5th
  Private institutions (1993-94): 20

Enrollment (1992): 19,692
  Percent of enroll.: 7.15%, 47th
Tuition, public institution (avg., 1993-94): $5,462, 29th
Tuition, private institution (avg., 1993-94): $9,201, 44th
Public library systems: 91
  Books & serial vol. per capita: 1.86, 43rd
  Govt. expenditure per capita: $21.20, 13th

LAW ENFORCEMENT, COURTS, AND PRISONS

Police protection, corrections, judicial and legal functions expenditures (1992): $1,404,000,000
  Per capita: $366, 9th
Police per 10,000 pop. (1993): 20.06, 29th
Prisoners (state & fed.) per 100,000 pop. (1993): 4,514.83, 7th
  Percent change (1992-93): 8.1%, 13th
Death penalty: yes, by lethal gas
  Under sentence of death (1993): 112, 9th
  Executed (1993): 2

RELIGION, NUMBER AND PERCENT OF POPULATION

Agnostic: 29,525—1.10%, 6th
Buddhist: 2,684—0.10%, 17th
Christian: 2,133,867—79.50%, 45th
Hindu: NA
Jewish: 42,946—1.60%, 11th
Muslim: 5,369—0.20%, 13th
Unitarian: 5,368—0.20%, 23rd
Other: 61,735—2.30%, 6th
None: 327,461—12.20%, 6th
Refused to answer: 75,155—2.80%, 12th

MAKING A LIVING

Personal income per capita (1994): $19,001, 38th
  Percent increase (1993-94): 5.1%, 22nd
Disposable personal income per capita (1994): $16,748, 38th
Median income of households (1993): $30,510, 28th
Percent of pop. below poverty level (1993): 15.4%, 17th
  Percent 65 and over (1990): 10.8%, 30th
Expenditure for energy per person (1992): $1,797, 36th

ECONOMY

Civilian labor force (1994): 1,988,000
  Percent of total pop.: 48.79%, 42nd

Percent 65 and over (1990): NA
Percent female: 45.27%, 40th
Percent job growth (1980-90): 48.44%, 3rd
Major employer industries (1994):
Agriculture: 42,000—2.4%, 25th
Construction: 98,000—5.7%, 5th
Finance, insurance, & real estate: 111,000—6.4%, 10th
Government: 288,000—16.7%, 20th
Manufacturing: 184,000—10.7%, 40th
Service: 390,000—22.6%, 19th
Trade: 325,000—18.9%, 29th
Transportation, communications, public utilities: 99,000—5.8%, 15th
Unemployment rate (1994): 6.34%, 14th
Male: 5.7%, 24th
Female: 7.1%, 6th
Total businesses (1991): 146,672
New business incorps. (1991): 9,832
Percent of total businesses: 6.70%, 16th
Business failures (1991): 1,090
Percent of total businesses: 0.74%
Agriculture farm income:
Marketing (1993): $1,922,000,000, 31st
Average per farm: $240,250, 2nd
Leading products (1993): Cattle, cotton, dairy products, hay
Average value land & build. per acre (1994): $314, 44th
Percent increase (1990-94): 19.39%, 11th
Govt. payments (1993): $114,000,000, 27th
Average per farm: $14,250.00, 4th
Construction, value of all: $3,207,000,000
Per capita: $874.98, 5th
Manufactures:
Value added: $11,916,000,000
Per capita: $3,251.09, 41st
Leading products: Electronics, printing and publishing, foods, primary and fabricated metals, aircraft and missiles, apparel
Value of nonfuel mineral production (1994): $3,323,000,000, 1st
Leading mineral products: Natural gas, petroleum, coal
Retail sales (1993): $33,825,000,000, 21st
Per household: $22,441, 19th
Percent increase (1992-93): 8.6%, 15th
Tourism revenues (1994): $10.5 bil.
Foreign exports, in total value (1994): $6,467,000,000, 20th
Per capita: $1,586.99, 15th

Gross state product per person (1993): $18,681.61, 41st
Percent change (1990-93): 2.94%, 29th
Patents per 100,000 pop. (1993): 23.52, 20th
Public aid recipients (percent of resident pop. 1993): 6.5%, 28th
Medicaid recipients per 1,000 pop. (1993): 102.41, 31st
Medicare recipients per 1,000 pop. (1993): 140.43, 27th

TRAVEL AND TRANSPORTATION

Motor vehicle registrations (1993): 2,892,000
Per 1,000 pop.: 733.08, 36th
Motorcycle registrations (1993): 73,000
Per 1,000 pop.: 18.50, 22nd
Licensed drivers per 1,000 pop. (1993): 665.15, 35th
Deaths from motor vehicle accidents per 100,000 pop. (1993): 20.35, 15th
Public roads & streets (1993):
Total mileage: 55,763
Per 1,000 pop.: 14.14, 32nd
Rural mileage: 39,423
Per 1,000 pop.: 9.99, 35th
Urban mileage: 16,340
Per 1,000 pop.: 4.14, 5th
Interstate mileage: 1,189
Per 1,000 pop.: 0.30, 12th
Annual vehicle-mi. of travel per person (1993): 9,937, 17th
Mean travel time for workers age 16+ who work away from home: 21.6 min., 16th

GOVERNMENT

Percent of voting age pop. registered (1994): 56.0%, 45th
Percent of voting age pop. voting (1994): 41.6%, 39th
Percent of voting age pop. voting for U.S. representatives (1994): 37.6%, 29th
State legislators, total (1995): 90, 43rd
Women members (1992): 31
Percent of legislature: 34.4%, 1st
U.S. Congress, House members (1995): 6
Change (1985-95): +1
Revenues (1993):
State govt.: $10,843,000,000
Per capita: $2,748.54, 34th
Parimutuel & amusement taxes & lotteries, revenue per capita: $63.88, 29th
Expenditures (1993):
State govt.: $9,783,000,000
Per capita: $2,479.85, 34th

Debt outstanding (1993): $3,053,000,000
Per capita: $773.89, 43rd

LAWS AND REGULATIONS

Legal driving age: 16
Marriage age without parental consent: 18
Divorce residence requirement: 90 days

ATTRACTIONS (1995)

Major opera companies: 2
Major symphony orchestras: 2
Major dance companies: 1
Major professional theater companies (nonprofit): 1

State appropriations for arts agencies per capita:
$0.63, 31st
State Fair in late October-early November at
Phoenix

SPORTS AND COMPETITION

NCAA teams (Division I): Arizona State Univ.
Sun Devils, Northern Arizona Univ.
Lumberjacks, Univ. of Arizona Wildcats
Major league baseball teams: Arizona Diamondbacks to begin play in 1998
NBA basketball teams: Phoenix Suns, America
West Arena
NFL football teams: Arizona Cardinals
(NFC), Sun Devil Stadium

ARKANSAS

"If I could rest anywhere it would be in Arkansaw, where the men are of the real half-horse, half-alligator breed such as grows no-where else on the face of the universal earth."

Attributed to frontiersman Davy Crockett

Long known as "a state which should be better known," Arkansas was thrust into national prominence and scrutiny in 1992 as its native son Bill Clinton campaigned for and won the presidency of the United States. It is a beautiful state of mountains, valleys, thick forests, and fertile plains, and tourism is one of its most important industries. Millions of travelers come to the state every year—many of them to visit the hot springs in Eureka Springs and Hot Springs. Nearly 99% of the people in this westernmost of the Southern states are native-born Americans.

SUPERLATIVES

- The continent's only diamond mine, located near Murfreesboro.
- Magnet Cove region, claiming to possess the world's greatest mineral variety.
- One of the country's leading cotton states.
- Pine Bluff—known as the world center of archery bow production.
- The first woman U.S. senator—Hattie Caraway.

MOMENTS IN HISTORY

- In 1541 the large party of Spanish explorer Hernando de Soto moved across the Mississippi into what is now Arkansas and spent the winter at the Indian village of Utiangue on a bluff over the Ouachita River.
- Early explorers found the Quapaw, Osage, and Caddo Indian confederacies.
- The remarkable party of Father Jacques Marquette and Louis Jolliet reached the mouth of the Arkansas River in 1673.
- The French explorer Robert Cavalier, Sieur de La Salle entered present-day Arkansas in 1682.
- Under Henri de Tonty, stragglers from La Salle's party founded Arkansas Post, the first permanent European settlement in the lower Mississippi Valley, and for 80 years the only outpost in a vast region.

So They Say

"We saw several cottages at certain Distances, straggling up and down as the Ground happens to be fit for Tillage. The Field lies about the Cottage, and at other Distances there are large Huts, not inhabited, but only serving for publick Assemblies, either upon Occasion of Rejoycing, or to consult about Peace and War. The [smaller] cottages that are inhabited, are not each of them for a private Family for in some of them are fifteen or twenty, each of which has its Nook or Corner, Bed and other Utensils to its self...they have nothing in Common besides the Fire, which is in the Midst of the Hut, and never goes out....The Cottages are round at the Top, after the manner of the Bee-Hive."

N. Joutel, an early visitor,
describing the Caddo

- After the United States bought the huge Louisiana Territory from France, U.S. troops took over Arkansas Post in 1804.
- The earthquake that shook the Mississippi Valley in 1811 has been called the strongest ever to strike the continent.

So They Say

"The agitation which convulsed the earth and the waters of the mighty Mississippi filled every living creature with horror. The earth on the shores opened up in wide fissures...threw water, sand and mud in huge jets higher than the tops of trees."

Anonymous account of
the 1811 earthquake

- Despite the opposition to a new slave state, Arkansas became a state on June 15, 1836.
- Fort Smith became a principal outfitting post for travelers to the West, and with the rush of the 1849 gold seekers, it became a rip-roaring frontier settlement.
- Arkansas Governor Henry M. Rector seized Fort Smith and Arkansas joined the Confederacy in 1861.
- When the Civil War ended in 1865, returning Confederate troops found their farms in ruin, their credit gone, and no mules or plows to put in new crops.
- Arkansas was put under U.S. military rule in 1867.
- After Arkansas adopted a new constitution in 1874, the state returned to civilian rule.
- Until federal Judge Isaac C. Parker took over at Fort Smith in 1875, the region to the west was lawless. For the next 21 years, Parker dispensed stern justice on the frontier.
- Large reserves of bauxite were found in 1887.
- In 1906 diamonds were found near Murfreesboro. This proved to be the only "diamond mine" on the continent, but only modest numbers of the stones have been taken out over the years.
- With the beginning of World War I in 1917, Arkansas became one of the major centers for war training camps, such as Camp Pike.
- In 1919 the state's first oil well was brought in near Stephens; the state has continued to be a major oil and gas producer.
- By the end of World War II, more than 200,000 Arkansas men and women had gone into the armed services.
- In the 1957 struggle over school integration, President Dwight Eisenhower sent federal troops to Little Rock to enforce a court integration order.
- Republican Winthrop Rockefeller became governor in 1967, gaining attention as the second Rockefeller brother to govern a state.
- In 1986, Arkansas mounted a yearlong celebration of its 150 years of statehood.
- The 1990 census found Arkansas's population had reached 2,351,000, an increase of 2.8% over 1980.
- In November 1992, Governor Bill Clinton was elected as first U.S. president from Arkansas.

THAT'S INTERESTING

- During a battle of Chickasaw versus Quapaw Indians, the Chickasaw ran out of ammunition. The Quawpaw obligingly gave half of their gunpowder to the enemy, and the battle continued.
- The Brooks-Baxter War, a dispute between two candidates for governor, actually became so fierce that ten persons were killed in the squabble.
- A newly rich oil family at El Dorado bought a home at a high price. When the owners started to take down the family portraits, the buyer shouted: "Oh no you don't. Pitchers is furniture!"
- The farm of John M. Huddleston was so poor that he was about to give up on it when he discovered the continent's only diamond mine on his property.
- Some Arkansas rivers were so shallow that steamboats were designed to operate in as little as a foot of water.
- Sam Walton founded his Wal-Mart Stores merchandising empire in Bentonville and became one of the nation's richest men.

NOTABLE NATIVES

Johnny Cash (Kingsland, 1932-), singer. William Jefferson (Bill) Clinton (Hope, 1946-), U.S. president. Jay Hanna (Dizzy) Dean (Lucas, 1911-1974), baseball player. Orval Faubus (Combs, 1910-), public official. John Johnson (Arkansas City, 1918-), publisher. Scott Joplin (Texarkana, 1868-1917), musician/composer. Douglas MacArthur (Little Rock, 1880-1964), soldier/statesman. Edward Durell Stone (Fayetteville, 1902-1978), architect.

GENERAL

Admitted to statehood: June 15, 1836
Origin of name: French variant of *Quapaw*, a Siouan term meaning "downstream people"
Capital: Little Rock
Nickname: Land of Opportunity, Razorback State
Motto: *Regnat Populus*—The people rule
Bird: Mockingbird
Insect: Honeybee
Flower: Apple blossom
Gem: Diamond
Song: "Arkansas"
Tree: Pine

THE LAND

Area: 53,182 sq. mi., 28th
  Land: 52,075 sq. mi., 27th
  Water: 1,107 sq. mi., 25th
    Inland water: 1,107 sq. mi., 18th
Topography: Eastern delta and prairie, southern lowland forests, and the northwestern highland, which includes the Ozark plateaus
Number of counties: 75
Geographic center: Pulaski, 12 mi. NW of Little Rock
Length: 260 mi.; width: 240 mi.
Highest point: 2,753 ft. (Magazine Mountain), 34th
Lowest point: 55 ft. (Ouachita River), 26th
Mean elevation: 650 ft., 36th

CLIMATE AND ENVIRONMENT

Temp., highest: 120 deg. on Aug. 10, 1936, at Ozark; lowest: –29 deg. on Feb. 13, 1905, at Pond
Monthly average: highest: 93.6 deg., 6th; lowest: 26.6 deg., 38th; spread (high to low): 67.0 deg., 28th
Hazardous waste sites (1993): 12, 29th
Endangered species: Mammals: 3—Gray bat, Indiana bat, Ozark big-eared bat; birds: 3—American peregrine falcon, Least tern, Red-cockaded woodpecker; reptiles: none; amphibians: none; fishes: 1; invertebrates: 4; plants: 1

MAJOR CITIES POPULATION, 1990 PERCENTAGE INCREASE, 1980-90

Fort Smith, 72,798—1.64%
Jonesboro, 46,535—47.59%
Little Rock, 175,795—10.45%
North Little Rock, 61,741— –4.11%
Pine Bluff, 57,140—0.89%

THE PEOPLE

Population (1995): 2,483,769, 33rd
  Percent change (1990-95): 5.7%, 21st
Population (2000 proj.): 2,578,000, 33rd
  Percent change (1990-2000): 9.67%, 28th
Per sq. mi. (1994): 47.1, 36th
Percent in metro. area (1992): 44.7%, 40th
Foreign born: 25,000, 42nd
  Percent: 1.1%, 46th

Top three ancestries reported:
  Irish, 19.74%
  German, 17.01%
  African, 13.06%
White: 1,944,744, 82.73%, 31st
Black: 373,912, 15.91%, 12th
Native American: 12,773, 0.54%, 22nd
Asian, Pacific Isle: 12,530, 0.53%, 47th
Other races: 6,766, 0.29%, 40th
Hispanic origin: 19,876, 0.85%, 42nd
Percent over 5 yrs. speaking language other than English at home: 2.8%, 48th
Percent males: 48.20%, 39th; percent females: 51.80%, 13th
Percent never married: 20.7%, 51st
Marriages per 1,000 (1993): 15.0, 2nd
Divorces per 1,000 (1993): 6.9, 2nd
Median age: 33.8
Under 5 years (1994): 7.01%, 38th
Under 18 years (1994): 26.09%, 24th
65 years & older (1994): 14.8%, 6th
Percent increase among the elderly (1990-94): 3.70%, 39th

OF VITAL IMPORTANCE

Live births per 1,000 pop. (1993): 14.1, 35th
Infant mortality rate per 1,000 births (1992): 10.3, 5th
  Rate for blacks (1990): 13.6, 34th
  Rate for whites (1990): 8.0, 22nd
Births to unmarried women, % of total (1992): 31.0%, 20th
Births to teenage mothers, % of total (1992): 19.4%, 2nd
Abortions (1992): 7,130, 35th
  Rate per 1,000 women 14-44 years old: 13.5, 38th
  Percent change (1988-92): 16%, 3rd
Average lifetime (1979-81): 73.72, 28th
Deaths per 1,000 pop. (1993): 10.9, 2nd
Causes of death per 100,000 pop.:
  Accidents & adverse effects (1992): 47.7, 7th
  Atherosclerosis (1991): 7.0, 24th
  Cancer (1991): 244.2, 6th
  Cerebrovascular diseases (1992): 84.5, 1st
  Chronic liver diseases & cirrhosis (1991): 8.6, 33rd
  Chronic obstructive pulmonary diseases (1992): 39.3, 22nd
  Diabetes mellitus (1992): 21.5, 20th
  Diseases of heart (1992): 344.0, 6th
  Pneumonia, flu (1991): 38.2, 6th
  Suicide (1992): 12.2, 30th

KEEPING WELL

Active nonfederal physicians per 100,000 pop. (1993): 162, 43rd
Dentists per 100,000 (1991): 41, 49th
Nurses per 100,000 (1992): 587, 42nd
Hospitals per 100,000 (1993): 3.59, 10th
  Admissions per 1,000 (1993): 141.01, 7th
  Occupancy rate per 100 beds (1993): 58.3, 37th
  Average cost per patient per day (1993): $678, 40th
  Average cost per stay (1993): $4,585, 50th
  Average stay (1992): 6.7 days, 36th
AIDS cases (adult, 1993): 404; per 100,000: 16.7, 32nd
HIV infection, not yet AIDS (1993): 1,004
Other notifiable diseases:
  Gonorrhea: 362.1, 12th
  Measles: 2.3, 34th
  Syphilis: 55.3, 15th
  Tuberculosis: 13.7, 7th
Pop. without health insur. (1991-93): 18.5%, 10th

HOUSEHOLDS BY TYPE

Total households (1994): 927,000
  Percent change (1990-94): 4.0%, 28th
  Per 1,000 pop.: 377.90, 18th
  Percent of households 65 yrs. and over: 25.35%, 7th
Persons per household (1994): 2.58, 30th
Family households: 651,555
  Percent of total: 73.11%, 7th
Nonfamily households: 239,624
  Percent of total: 26.89%, 45th
Pop. living in group quarters: 58,332
  Percent of pop.: 2.48%, 34th

LIVING QUARTERS

Total housing units: 1,000,667
  Persons per unit: 2.35, 36th
Occupied housing units: 891,179
  Percent of total units: 89.06%, 29th
  Persons per unit: 2.55, 20th
  Percent of units with over 1 person per room: 3.73%, 20th
Owner-occupied units: 619,938
  Percent of total units: 61.95%, 12th
  Percent of occupied units: 69.56%, 14th
  Persons per unit: 2.61, 48th
  Median value: $46,300, 48th
Renter-occupied units: 271,241
  Percent of total units: 27.11%, 38th
  Percent of occupied units: 30.44%, 38th
  Persons per unit: 2.48, 11th
  Median contract rent: $230, 47th
  Rental vacancy rate: 10.4%, 14th
Mobile home, trailer & other as a percent of occupied housing units: 15.87%, 13th
Persons in emergency shelters for homeless persons: 489, 0.021%, 50th
Persons visible in street locations: 62, 0.0026%, 43rd
Persons in shelters for abused women: 105, 0.0045%, 33rd
Nursing home population: 21,809, 0.93%, 14th

CRIME INDEX PER 100,000 (1992-93)

Total reported: 4,810.7, 29th
  Violent: 593.3, 24th
    Murder and nonnegligent manslaughter: 10.2, 15th
    Aggravated assault: 415.8, 23rd
    Robbery: 127.9, 29th
    Forcible rape: 42.4, 21st
  Property: 4,217.5, 27th
    Burglary: 1,099.3, 18th
    Larceny, theft: 2,795.7, 29th
    Motor vehicle theft: 322.5, 35th
Drug abuse violations (1990): 256.0, 24th
Child-abuse rate per 1,000 children (1993): 16.28, 21st

TEACHING AND LEARNING

Pop. 3 and over enrolled in school: 582,405
  Percent of pop.: 25.8%, 43rd
Public elementary & secondary schools (1992-93): 1,090
  Total enrollment (1992): 441,490
  Percent of total pop.: 18.44%, 13th
  Teachers (1992): 25,978
  Percent of total pop.: 1.09%, 18th
  Pupil/teacher ratio (fall 1992): 17.0, 21st
  Teachers' avg. salary (1992-93): $29,232, 43rd
  Expenditure per capita (1990-91): $2,439.92, 51st
  Expenditure per pupil (1991-92): $4,031, 45th
Percent of graduates taking SAT (1993): 6%, 46th
  Mean SAT verbal scores: 478, 15th
  Mean SAT mathematical scores: 519, 19th
Percent of graduates taking ACT (1995): 63%, 16th

Mean ACT scores: 20.2, 40th
Percent of pop. over 25 completing:
  Less than 9th grade: 15.2%, 5th
  High school: 66.3%, 48th
  College degree(s): 13.3%, 50th
Higher education, institutions (1993-94): 35
  Enrollment (1992): 97,435
  White non-Hispanic (1992): 79,602
    Percent of enroll.: 81.70%, 28th
  Black non-Hispanic (1992): 14,014
    Percent of enroll.: 14.38%, 11th
  Hispanic (1992): 511
    Percent of enroll.: 0.52%, 47th
  Asian/Pacific Islander (1992): 1,024
    Percent of enroll.: 1.05%, 43rd
  American Indian/AK native (1992): 578
    Percent of enroll.: 0.59%, 23rd
  Nonresident alien (1992): 1,706
    Percent of enroll.: 1.75%, 46th
  Female (1992): 55,665
    Percent of enroll.: 57.13%, 4th
  Pub. institutions (1993-94): 21
    Enrollment (1992): 85,686
    Percent of enroll.: 87.94%, 13th
  Private institutions (1993-94): 14
    Enrollment (1992): 11,749
    Percent of enroll.: 12.06%, 39th
  Tuition, public institution (avg., 1993-94): $5,334, 31st
  Tuition, private institution (avg., 1993-94): $8,398, 47th
Public library systems: 37
  Books & serial vol. per capita: 1.97, 39th
  Govt. expenditure per capita: $7.25, 50th

LAW ENFORCEMENT, COURTS, AND PRISONS

Police protection, corrections, judicial and legal functions expenditures (1992): $366,000,000
  Per capita: $153, 49th
Police per 10,000 pop. (1993): 13.94, 50th
Prisoners (state & fed.) per 100,000 pop. (1993): 3,555.23, 20th
  Percent change (1992-93): 4.1%, 32nd
Death penalty: yes, by lethal injection, or in some circumstances electrocution
  Under sentence of death (1993): 33, 20th
  Executed (1993): 0

RELIGION, NUMBER AND PERCENT OF POPULATION

Agnostic: 3,459—0.20%, 42nd
Buddhist: 3,459—0.20%, 11th
Christian: 1,549,716—89.60%, 14th
Hindu: NA
Jewish: 1,730—0.10%, 43rd
Muslim: NA
Unitarian: 3,459—0.20%, 23rd
Other: 12,107—0.70%, 43rd
None: 100,317—5.80%, 35th
Refused to answer: 55,347—3.20%, 6th

MAKING A LIVING

Personal income per capita (1994): $16,898, 50th
  Percent increase (1993-94): 5.6%, 14th
Disposable personal income per capita (1994): $14,995, 49th
Median income of households (1993): $23,039, 49th
Percent of pop. below poverty level (1993): 20.0%, 6th
Percent 65 and over (1990): 22.9%, 4th
Expenditure for energy per person (1992): $1,959, 16th

ECONOMY

Civilian labor force (1994): 1,207,000
  Percent of total pop.: 49.21%, 40th
  Percent 65 and over (1990): 2.47%, 34th
  Percent female: 45.90%, 32nd
Percent job growth (1980-90): 18.13%, 30th
Major employer industries (1994):
  Agriculture: 46,000—4.3%, 12th
  Construction: 47,000—4.3%, 23rd
  Finance, insurance, & real estate: 47,000—4.3%, 41st
  Government: 158,000—14.5%, 35th
  Manufacturing: 244,000—22.4%, 7th
  Service: 179,000—16.4%, 50th
  Trade: 202,000—18.5%, 35th
  Transportation, communications, public utilities: 63,000—5.8%, 15th
Unemployment rate (1994): 5.39%, 29th
  Male: 4.7%, 37th
  Female: 6.1%, 18th
Total businesses (1991): 79,276
  New business incorps. (1991): 5,326
    Percent of total businesses: 6.72%, 15th
  Business failures (1991): 266
    Percent of total businesses: 0.34%
Agriculture farm income:
  Marketing (1993): $4,382,000,000, 14th
  Average per farm: $95,260.87, 16th

Leading products (1993): Broilers, soybeans, cotton, cattle
Average value land & build. per acre (1994): $800, 31st
Percent increase (1990-94): 6.67%, 32nd
Govt. payments (1993): $705,000,000, 7th
Average per farm: $15,326.09, 2nd
Construction, value of all: $804,000,000
Per capita: $342.02, 43rd
Manufactures:
Value added: $12,468,000,000
Per capita: $5,303.90, 21st
Leading products: Food products, chemicals, lumber, paper, electric motors, furniture, home appliances, auto components, airplane parts, apparel, machinery, petroleum products
Value of nonfuel mineral production (1994): $392,000,000, 30th
Leading mineral products: Petroleum, natural gas, bromine
Retail sales (1993): $16,998,000,000, 32nd
Per household: $18,295, 47th
Percent increase (1992-93): 6.4%, 31st
Tourism revenues (1994): $2.9 bil.
Foreign exports, in total value (1994): $1,672,000,000, 35th
Per capita: $681.61, 44th
Gross state product per person (1993): $17,292.28, 49th
Percent change (1990-93): 7.89%, 2nd
Patents per 100,000 pop. (1993): 6.35, 49th
Public aid recipients (percent of resident pop. 1993): 6.6%, 27th
Medicaid recipients per 1,000 pop. (1993): 139.74, 12th
Medicare recipients per 1,000 pop. (1993): 169.00, 4th

TRAVEL AND TRANSPORTATION

Motor vehicle registrations (1993): 1,528,000
Per 1,000 pop.: 629.84, 49th
Motorcycle registrations (1993): 14,000
Per 1,000 pop.: 5.77, 50th
Licensed drivers per 1,000 pop. (1993): 721.76, 11th
Deaths from motor vehicle accidents per 100,000 pop. (1993): 24.03, 5th
Public roads & streets (1993):
Total mileage: 77,192
Per 1,000 pop.: 31.82, 12th

Rural mileage: 69,597
Per 1,000 pop.: 28.69, 12th
Urban mileage: 7,595
Per 1,000 pop.: 3.13, 23rd
Interstate mileage: 543
Per 1,000 pop.: 0.22, 23rd
Annual vehicle-mi. of travel per person (1993): 9,893, 19th
Mean travel time for workers age 16+ who work away from home: 19.0 min., 38th

GOVERNMENT

Percent of voting age pop. registered (1994): 60.0%, 37th
Percent of voting age pop. voting (1994): 41.6%, 39th
Percent of voting age pop. voting for U.S. representatives (1994): 39.0%, 25th
State legislators, total (1995): 135, 31st
Women members (1992): 10
Percent of legislature: 7.4%, 46th
U.S. Congress, House members (1995): 4
Change (1985-95): 0
Revenues (1993):
State govt.: $6,446,000,000
Per capita: $2,657.05, 40th
Parimutuel & amusement taxes & lotteries, revenue per capita: $7.01, 37th
Expenditures (1993):
State govt.: $5,915,000,000
Per capita: $2,438.17, 37th
Debt outstanding (1993): $1,884,000,000
Per capita: $776.59, 42nd

LAWS AND REGULATIONS

Legal driving age: 16
Marriage age without parental consent: 18
Divorce residence requirement: 60 days, for qualifications check local statutes

ATTRACTIONS (1995)

State appropriations for arts agencies per capita: $0.42, 45th
State Fair in late September–early October at Little Rock

SPORTS AND COMPETITION

NCAA (Division I) teams: Arkansas State Univ. Indians, Univ. of Arkansas-Fayetteville Razorbacks, Univ. of Arkansas-Little Rock Trojans

CALIFORNIA

"This is one of the most favored spots of the earth."

John Muir, naturalist

"Why! It is even worth the expense of a trip across the continent."

John D. Rockefeller, Sr., industrialist and philanthropist

The most populous state, California is a land of contrasts, with its high mountains, rocky cliffs, sandy beaches, redwood forests, and barren deserts. This state, with its vast vineyards in the north, its glitter in Hollywood and Beverly Hills in the south, and its tremendous farms and ranches almost everywhere, combines the Old World charm of San Francisco with the unusual lifestyles of Los Angeles to maintain its image as a truly unique part of the country. First in manufacturing, first in agriculture, it also contains some of the largest cities in the nation. If famed naturalist John Muir were alive today, he would be even more convinced that he had been very right when he called California "one of the most favored spots on earth!" Millions of visitors have agreed. Despite earthquakes and other traumas, little has occurred to diminish that luster.

SUPERLATIVES

• First state in population.
• World's largest landlocked harbor—San Francisco Bay.
• Lowest point in the Western Hemisphere—Death Valley, 282 feet below sea level.
• Hottest recorded temperature in the United States—Death Valley, 134° F.
• Most life zones in the nation—six.
• World's most fertile valley.
• Most national sites of any state.
• Largest living tree—General Sherman tree, trunk 101.6 feet in circumference, Sequoia National Park.
• The oldest living thing—a bristlecone pine, approximately 4,600 years old, Inyo National Forest.

MOMENTS IN HISTORY

• Nine major tribes were found by the earliest European explorers, beginning circa 1540.

• In 1540, Hernando de Alarcón may have touched California at the Colorado River.
• Sir Francis Drake explored the coast in 1579 and claimed the area for England's Queen Elizabeth.
• In 1769, Gaspar de Portola and Father Junipero Serra founded the mission of San Diego.
• San Francisco was founded in 1776.
• Sleepy El Pueblo de Nuestra Senora la Reina de Los Angeles de Porciuncula (Los Angeles) was founded in 1781.
• At the missions, Indians became Christianized and, some say, were harshly treated.
• In 1812, Russia established Fort Ross, adding to its Alaskan fur trade.
• In 1825, Mexico took over California, with the capital at Monterey.

So They Say

In 1818, Monterey was occupied for a week by the French pirate Hippolyte de Bouchard, who had served with the patriot navy of the Republic of Buenos Aires. So in a sense it might be said that California once was occupied by Argentina.

• The first overland wagon train to California left Missouri and arrived in the San Joaquin Valley on November 4, 1841.

So They Say

"To this gate I gave the name of Chrysolpylae, or Golden Gate....The form... and its advantages for commerce, Asiatic inclusive, suggested to me the name...".

Explorer John Charles Frémont in 1841

• With the 1848 Treaty of Guadalupe Hidalgo, Mexico gave up California.

• A pea-sized metal pellet from Sutter's Millrace changed the course of history in 1848 when it proved to be gold.

> ## So They Say
>
> "Sir: I have to report to the state department one of the most astonishing excitements...now existing in this country...a placer, a vast tract of land containing gold...."
>
> Thomas O. Larkin,
> to President James Buchanan

• News of the gold discovery sparked a record rush to the gold fields. In 1849, thousands of 49ers braved danger and death for riches.

• Congress hesitated to welcome a new free state, but California was at last admitted on September 9, 1850.

• During the Civil War, loyal California's gold helped to support the Union.

• In a last heroic but unsuccessful fight for their rights, the Modoc Indians went to war (1872-1873).

• Land booms, growth of agriculture, and the discovery of oil at Bakersfield in 1899 brought people and prosperity.

> ## So They Say
>
> "Of a sudden we had found ourselves staggering and reeling...a sickening swaying of the earth....a great cornice crushed a man as if he were a maggot...".
>
> P. Barrett, San Francisco Examiner,
> April 19, 1906

• Before the ruins of the earthquake and fire of 1906 had cooled, devastated San Francisco had begun to rebuild.

• In 1916, a Republican dispute gave Woodrow Wilson California's electoral votes, just enough to put him over the top for the White House.

• World War I found California far removed from the conflict, but great numbers of Californians crossed the continent and the sea to serve.

• California was particularly hard hit by the Great Depression. However, despite the Depression, San Francisco's great bridges were opened in 1936-1937, and in 1939 the city celebrated with the Golden Gate International Exposition.

• Thought to be a security threat in World War II, Japanese-Americans were sent to relocation camps where they endured many hardships.

• In 1945 the United Nations was founded at San Francisco.

• Big league baseball came to California in 1958 with the Dodgers at Los Angeles and the Giants at San Francisco.

• By 1963, California could claim to be the nation's most populous state.

• In 1969, Richard Nixon became California's only native U.S. president.

• Los Angeles hosted the financially successful Olympic Summer Games of 1984.

• California's 1980s drought was one of its worst in history; some relief started in 1992.

• Striking just minutes before the start of the third game of the World Series, the 1989 San Francisco earthquake was a major disaster, causing at least 59 deaths and massive property damage.

• 1992 riots in Los Angeles followed the acquittal of four policemen in the beating of a black man, Rodney King.

• A powerful earthquake shook Los Angeles in January 1994.

• In 1995 world attention was riveted on the notorious murder trial of ex-football star O. J. Simpson, who was found not guilty.

THAT'S INTERESTING

• In the Mexican War, the "Paul Revere of the West," John Brown (Lean John), rode horseback from Los Angeles to San Francisco to warn of approaching Mexican troops, making the 500 miles in only five days.

• An 1849 gold rush miner asked Levi Strauss to make a pair of pants. Lacking suitable thread, Strauss stapled the pants at stress points, and Levis have been popular ever since.

• Beginning at San Diego in 1769, Father Junipero Serra established nine thriving missions, centers of civilization in the wild; he became known as the "Father of California."

• In the 1849 gold rush, bar owners hired bartenders with large hands. Drinks sold for a pinch of gold dust—the larger the hands, the bigger the pinch.

• The 1916 drought at San Diego was so severe that the city hired the famous rainmaker Charles Hatfield. Shortly after he set up his rainmaking towers, so much rain fell that disastrous floods were caused, and the city refused to pay Hatfield his $10,000 fee.

• Told by a medium that she would never die as long as she kept building her house in San Jose, wealthy widow Sara Winchester kept carpenters busy creating 1,660 rooms, secret passageways, 40 stairways, blind chimneys, and other novel arrangements. Despite spending $5.5 million, she could not forestall her death in 1922.

NOTABLE NATIVES

Joseph Paul (Joe) DiMaggio, Jr. (Martinez, 1914-   ), baseball player. Robert Lee Frost (San Francisco, 1874-1963), poet. Lillian Moller Gilbreth (Oakland, 1878-1972), consulting engineer. William Randolph Hearst (San Francisco, 1863-1951), publisher. Richard Milhous Nixon (Yorba Linda, 1913-1994), U.S. president. William Saroyan (Fresno, 1908-1981), author. John Ernst Steinbeck (Salinas, 1902-1968), author. Adlai Ewing Stevenson (Los Angeles, 1900-65), public official. Earl Warren (Los Angeles, 1891-1974), public official; chief justice of the United States.

GENERAL

Admitted to statehood: September 9, 1850
Origin of name: Bestowed by the Spanish conquistadors (possibly by Cortez). It was the name of an imaginary island, an earthly paradise, in "Las Serges de Esplandian," a Spanish romance written by Garcí Ordóñez de Montalvo in 1510. Baha California (Lower California, in Mexico) was first visited by the Spanish in 1533. The present U.S. state was called Alta (Upper) California.
Capital: Sacramento
Nickname: Golden State
Motto: *Eureka*—I have found it
Animal: California grizzly bear
Bird: California valley quail
Fish: California golden trout
Flower: Golden poppy
Stone: Serpentine
Song: "I Love You, California"
Tree: California redwood

THE LAND

Area: 158,869 sq. mi., 3rd
  Land: 155,973 sq. mi., 3rd
  Water: 2,896 sq. mi., 12th
  Inland water: 2,674 sq. mi., 8th
  Coastal water: 222 sq. mi., 16th
Topography: Long mountainous coastline; central valley; Sierra Nevada on the E; desert basins of the Southern interior; rugged mountains of the N
Number of counties: 58
Geographic center: 38 mi. E of Madera
Length: 770 mi.; width: 250 mi.
Highest point: 14,494 ft. (Mount Whitney), 2nd
Lowest point: –282 ft. (Death Valley), 1st
Mean elevation: 2,900 ft.; 11th
Coastline: 840 mi., 3rd
Shoreline: 3,427 mi., 5th

CLIMATE AND ENVIRONMENT

Temp., highest: 134 deg. on July 10, 1913, at Greenland Ranch; lowest: –45 deg. on Jan. 20, 1937, at Boca
Monthly average: highest: 92.2 deg., 12th; lowest: 14.3 deg., 16th; spread (high to low): 77.9 deg., 9th
Hazardous waste sites (1993): 95, 3rd
Endangered species: Mammals: 8—San Joaquin kit fox, Salt marsh harvest mouse, Fresno kangaroo rat, Giant kangaroo rat, Morro Bay kangaroo bat, Stephen's kangaroo rat, Tipton kangaroo rat, Amargosa vole; birds: 10—California condor, American peregrine falcon, Aleutian Canada goose, Brown pelican, California clapper rail, Light-footed clapper rail, Yuma clapper rail, San Clemente loggerhead shrike, California least tern, Least bell's vireo; reptiles: 3; amphibians: 2; fishes: 10; invertebrates: 10; plants: 29

MAJOR CITIES
POPULATION, 1990
PERCENTAGE INCREASE, 1980-90

Long Beach, 429,433—18.79%
Los Angeles, 3,485,398—17.41%
San Diego, 1,110,549—26.84%
San Francisco, 723,959—6.63%
San Jose, 782,248—24.28%

THE PEOPLE

Population (1995): 31,589,153, 1st
  Percent change (1990-95): 6.2%, 19th
Population (2000 proj.): 34,888,000, 1st
  Percent change (1990-2000): 17.23%, 14th
Per sq. mi. (1994): 201.5, 13th
Percent in metro. area (1992): 96.7%, 3rd
Foreign born: 6,459,000, 1st
  Percent: 21.7%, 1st
Top three ancestries reported:
  Mexican, 17.88%
  German, 16.58%
  English, 12.25%
White: 20,524,327, 68.97%, 47th
Black: 2,208,801, 7.42%, 25th
Native American: 242,164, 0.81%, 18th
Asian, Pacific Isle: 2,845,659, 9.56%, 2nd
Other races: 3,939,070, 13.24%, 1st
Hispanic origin: 7,687,938, 25.83%, 2nd
Percent over 5 yrs. speaking language other
  than English at home: 31.5%, 2nd
Percent males: 50.06%, 4th; percent females:
  49.94%, 48th
Percent never married: 30.1%, 4th
Marriages per 1,000 (1993): 6.5, 48th
Median age: 31.5
Under 5 years (1994): 9.01%, 3rd
Under 18 years (1994): 27.61%, 12th
65 years & older (1994): 10.6%, 46th
Percent increase among the elderly (1990-94):
  6.74%, 22nd

OF VITAL IMPORTANCE

Live births per 1,000 pop. (1993): 18.9, 2nd
Infant mortality rate per 1,000 births (1992):
  7.0, 44th
  Rate for blacks (1990): 14.2, 32nd
  Rate for whites (1990): 7.6, 33rd
Births to unmarried women, % of total
  (1992): 34.3%, 9th
Births to teenage mothers, % of total (1992):
  11.8%, 30th
Abortions (1992): 304,230, 1st
  Rate per 1,000 women 14-44 years old:
  42.1, 5th
  Percent change (1988-92): –8%, 26th
Average lifetime (1979-81): 74.57, 19th
Deaths per 1,000 pop. (1993): 7.0, 46th
Causes of death per 100,000 pop.:
  Accidents & adverse effects (1992): 30.7,
  37th
  Atherosclerosis (1991): 6.6, 26th
  Cancer (1991): 162.1, 45th
  Cerebrovascular diseases (1992): 49.1, 41st

Chronic liver diseases & cirrhosis (1991):
  12.3, 6th
Chronic obstructive pulmonary diseases
  (1992): 32.6, 40th
Diabetes mellitus (1992): 11.6, 50th
Diseases of heart (1992): 217.2, 45th
Pneumonia, flu (1991): 32.0, 20th
Suicide (1992): 12.1, 31st

KEEPING WELL

Active nonfederal physicians per 100,000 pop.
  (1993): 240, 11th
Dentists per 100,000 (1991): 65, 13th
Nurses per 100,000 (1992): 568, 45th
Hospitals per 100,000 (1993): 1.37, 45th
  Admissions per 1,000 (1993): 97.77, 40th
  Occupancy rate per 100 beds (1993): 61.2,
  27th
  Average cost per patient per day (1993):
  $1,221, 1st
  Average cost per stay (1993): $6,918, 8th
Average stay (1992): 6.1 days, 46th
AIDS cases (adult, 1993): 18,689; per
  100,000: 59.9, 5th
HIV infection, not yet AIDS (1993): NA
Other notifiable diseases:
  Gonorrhea: 185.2, 28th
  Measles: 41.9, 1st
  Syphilis: 54.9, 16th
  Tuberculosis: 16.4, 4th
Pop. without health insur. (1991-93): 19.7%,
  7th

HOUSEHOLDS BY TYPE

Total households (1994): 10,850,000
  Percent change (1990-94): 4.5%, 25th
  Per 1,000 pop.: 345.20, 48th
  Percent of households 65 yrs. and over:
  18.82%, 43rd
  Persons per household (1994): 2.83, 3rd
Family households: 7,139,394
  Percent of total: 68.77%, 40th
Nonfamily households: 3,241,812
  Percent of total: 31.23%, 12th
Pop. living in group quarters: 751,860
  Percent of pop.: 2.53%, 32nd

LIVING QUARTERS

Total housing units: 11,182,882
  Persons per unit: 2.66, 3rd
Occupied housing units: 10,381,206
  Percent of total units: 92.83%, 5th
  Persons per unit: 2.79, 3rd

Percent of units with over 1 person per room: 12.29%, 2nd
Owner-occupied units: 5,773,943
  Percent of total units: 51.63%, 46th
  Percent of occupied units: 55.62%, 47th
  Persons per unit: 2.84, 8th
  Median value: $195,500, 2nd
Renter-occupied units: 4,607,263
  Percent of total units: 41.20%, 4th
  Percent of occupied units: 44.38%, 6th
  Persons per unit: 2.74, 2nd
  Median contract rent: $561, 2nd
  Rental vacancy rate: 5.9%, 46th
Mobile home, trailer & other as a percent of occupied housing units: 6.55%, 40th
Persons in emergency shelters for homeless persons: 30,806, 0.104%, 5th
Persons visible in street locations: 18,081, 0.0608%, 2nd
Persons in shelters for abused women: 1,257, 0.0042%, 35th
Nursing home population: 148,362, 0.50%, 45th

CRIME INDEX PER 100,000 (1992-93)

Total reported: 6,456.9, 5th
  Violent: 1,077.8, 3rd
    Murder and nonnegligent manslaughter: 13.1, 5th
    Aggravated assault: 621.8, 6th
    Robbery: 405.1, 4th
    Forcible rape: 37.7, 27th
  Property: 5,379.1, 9th
    Burglary: 1,327.0, 7th
    Larceny, theft: 3,029.1, 22nd
    Motor vehicle theft: 1,023.0, 2nd
Drug abuse violations (1990): 838.9, 2nd
Child-abuse rate per 1,000 children (1993): 18.81, 14th

TEACHING AND LEARNING

Pop. 3 and over enrolled in school: 8,300,046
  Percent of pop.: 29.3%, 9th
Public elementary & secondary schools (1992-93): 7,665
  Total enrollment (1992): 5,195,370
    Percent of total pop.: 16.82%, 33rd
  Teachers (1992): 215,738
    Percent of pop.: 0.70%, 51st
  Pupil/teacher ratio (fall 1992): 24.1, 2nd
  Teachers' avg. salary (1992-93): $42,975, 8th

Expenditure per capita (1990-91): $3,978.45, 11th
Expenditure per pupil (1991-92): $4,746, 34th
Percent of graduates taking SAT (1993): 47%, 22nd
  Mean SAT verbal scores: 415, 44th
  Mean SAT mathematical scores: 484, 31st
Percent of graduates taking ACT (1995): 12%, 38th
  Mean ACT scores: 20.9, 30th
Percent of pop. over 25 completing:
  Less than 9th grade: 11.2%, 16th
  High school: 76.2%, 28th
  College degree(s): 23.4%, 10th
Higher education, institutions (1993-94): 328
  Enrollment (1992): 1,977,249
  White non-Hispanic (1992): 1,115,374
    Percent of enroll.: 56.41%, 49th
  Black non-Hispanic (1992): 139,665
    Percent of enroll.: 7.06%, 22nd
  Hispanic (1992): 315,261
    Percent of enroll.: 15.94%, 3rd
  Asian/Pacific Islander (1992): 287,194
    Percent of enroll.: 14.52%, 2nd
  American Indian/AK native (1992): 21,919
    Percent of enroll.: 1.11%, 14th
  Nonresident alien (1992): 97,836
    Percent of enroll.: 4.95%, 5th
  Female (1992): 1,075,739
  Pub. institutions (1993-94): 139
    Per 100,000 pop.: 0.45, 46th
    Enrollment (1992): 1,747,895
    Percent of enroll.: 88.40%, 11th
    Percent of pop.: 5.65%, 8th
  Private institutions (1993-94): 189
    Enrollment (1992): 229,354
    Percent of enroll.: 11.60%, 41st
  Tuition, public institution (avg., 1993-94): $7,511, 14th
  Tuition, private institution (avg., 1993-94): $17,432, 11th
Public library systems: 168
  Books & serial vol. per capita: 1.95, 40th
  Govt. expenditure per capita: $18.75, 18th

LAW ENFORCEMENT, COURTS, AND PRISONS

Police protection, corrections, judicial and legal functions expenditures (1992): $14,032,000,000
  Per capita: $454, 5th
Police per 10,000 pop. (1993): 21.02, 23rd

Prisoners (state & fed.) per 100,000 pop. (1993): 3,842.49, 16th
Percent change (1992-93): 9.5%, 9th
Death penalty: yes, by lethal gas
Under sentence of death (1993): 363, 1st
Executed (1993): 1

RELIGION, NUMBER AND PERCENT OF POPULATION

Agnostic: 264,112—1.20%, 2nd
Buddhist: 154,065—0.70%, 1st
Christian: 16,947,158—77.00%, 48th
Hindu: 22,009—0.10%, 10th
Jewish: 506,214—2.30%, 7th
Muslim: 132,056—0.60%, 2nd
Unitarian: 88,037—0.40%, 8th
Other: 418,177—1.90%, 12th
None: 2,861,209—13.00%, 5th
Refused to answer: 616,260—2.80%, 12th

MAKING A LIVING

Personal income per capita (1994): $22,493, 15th
Percent increase (1993-94): 2.7%, 50th
Disposable personal income per capita (1994): $19,593, 13th
Median income of households (1993): $34,073, 14th
Percent of pop. below poverty level (1993): 18.2%, 10th
Percent 65 and over (1990): 7.6%, 49th
Expenditure for energy per person (1992): $1,600, 47th

ECONOMY

Civilian labor force (1994): 15,471,000
Percent of total pop.: 49.22%, 39th
Percent 65 and over (1990): 2.41%, 36th
Percent female: 44.08%, 51st
Percent job growth (1980-90): 32.26%, 10th
Major employer industries (1994):
Agriculture: 436,000—3.1%, 18th
Construction: 548,000—4.0%, 29th
Finance, insurance, & real estate: 856,000—6.2%, 11th
Government: 2,054,000—14.8%, 30th
Manufacturing: 2,004,000—14.5%, 29th
Service: 2,933,000—21.2%, 24th
Trade: 2,550,000—18.4%, 36th
Transportation, communications, public utilities: 711,000—5.1%, 30th
Unemployment rate (1994): 8.60%, 2nd
Male: 8.7%, 3rd
Female: 8.4%, 2nd

Total businesses (1991): 1,097,465
New business incorps. (1991): 36,561
Percent of total businesses: 3.33%, 48th
Business failures (1991): 8,968
Percent of total businesses: 0.82%
Agriculture farm income:
Marketing (1993): $19,850,000,000, 1st
Average per farm: $261,184.21, 1st
Leading products (1993): Dairy products, greenhouse, grapes, cattle
Average value land & build. per acre (1994): $1,722, 10th
Percent increase (1990-94): 1.06%, 45th
Govt. payments (1993): $522,000,000, 9th
Average per farm: $6,868.42, 16th
Construction, value of all: $24,480,000,000
Per capita: $822.58, 9th
Manufactures:
Value added: $149,578,000,000
Per capita: $5,026.14, 27th
Leading products: Foods, printed material, primary and fabricated metals, machinery, electric and electronic equipment, transportation equipment instruments
Value of nonfuel mineral production (1994): $2,497,000,000, 3rd
Leading mineral products: Petroleum, natural gas, cement
Retail sales (1993): $233,725,000,000, 1st
Per household: $21,515, 29th
Percent increase (1992-93): 0.2%, 48th
Tourism revenues (1992): $52.8 bil.
Foreign exports, in total value (1994): $66,292,000,000, 1st
Per capita: $2,109.13, 8th
Gross state product per person (1993): $25,118.36, 11th
Percent change (1990-93): 1.46%, 42nd
Patents per 100,000 pop. (1993): 30.65, 9th
Public aid recipients (percent of resident pop. 1993): 11.2%, 3rd
Medicaid recipients per 1,000 pop. (1993): 154.85, 8th
Medicare recipients per 1,000 pop. (1993): 112.25, 47th

TRAVEL AND TRANSPORTATION

Motor vehicle registrations (1993): 22,824,000
Per 1,000 pop.: 731.14, 37th
Motorcycle registrations (1993): 587,000
Per 1,000 pop.: 18.80, 21st

Licensed drivers per 1,000 pop. (1993): 644.62, 42nd
Deaths from motor vehicle accidents per 100,000 pop. (1993): 12.5, 41st
Public roads & streets (1993):
Total mileage: 169,201
Per 1,000 pop.: 5.42, 47th
Rural mileage: 88,140
Per 1,000 pop.: 2.82, 45th
Urban mileage: 81,061
Per 1,000 pop.: 2.60, 42nd
Interstate mileage: 2,423
Per 1,000 pop.: 0.08, 45th
Annual vehicle-mi. of travel per person (1993): 8,534, 39th
Mean travel time for workers age 16+ who work away from home: 24.6 min., 6th

GOVERNMENT

Percent of voting age pop. registered (1994): 54.2%, 49th
Percent of voting age pop. voting (1994): 45.0%, 31st
Percent of voting age pop. voting for U.S. representatives (1994): 35.9%, 35th
State legislators, total (1995): 120, 36th
Women members (1992): 22
Percent of legislature: 18.3%, 25th
U.S. Congress, House members (1995): 52
Change (1985-95): +7
Revenues (1993):
State govt.: $108,222,000,000
Per capita: $3,466.76, 17th
Parimutuel & amusement taxes & lotteries, revenue per capita: $56.41, 31st
Expenditures (1993):
State govt.: $104,567,000,000
Per capita: $3,349.68, 12th
Debt outstanding (1993): $41,295,000,000
Per capita: $1,322.84, 25th

LAWS AND REGULATIONS

Legal driving age: 18, 16 after driver education course
Marriage age without parental consent: 18
Divorce residence requirement: 6 mo., with qualifications—check local statutes

ATTRACTIONS (1995)

Major opera companies: 12
Major symphony orchestras: 10
Major dance companies: 14
Major professional theater companies (non-profit): 4

State appropriations for arts agencies per capita: $0.40, 46th
State Fair in late August–early September at Sacramento

SPORTS AND COMPETITION

NCAA (Division I) teams: California Polytechnic State Univ. Broncos, California State Univ.-Fullerton Titans, California State Univ.-Northridge Matadors, California State Univ.-Sacramento Hornets, California State Univ.-Fresno Bulldogs, Long Beach State Univ. Forty Niners, Loyola Marymount Univ. Lions, Pepperdine Univ. Waves, Saint Mary's College Gaels, San Diego State Univ. Aztecs, San Jose State Univ. Spartans, Santa Clara Univ. Broncos, Stanford Univ. Cardinals, Univ. of California-Berkeley Golden Bears, Univ. of California-Irvine Anteaters, Univ. of California-Los Angeles Bruins, Univ. of California-Santa Barbara Gauchos, Univ. of the Pacific Tigers, Univ. of San Diego Toreros, Univ. of San Francisco Dons, Univ. of Southern California Trojans
Major league baseball teams: San Diego Padres (NL West), San Diego Jack Murphy Stadium; California Angels (AL West), Anaheim Stadium; San Francisco Giants (NL West), Candlestick Park; Los Angeles Dodgers (NL West), Dodger Stadium; Oakland Athletics (AL West), Oakland-Alameda County Coliseum
NBA basketball teams: Sacramento Kings, ARCO Arena; Los Angeles Clippers, L.A. Memorial Sports Arena and Arrowhead Pond of Anaheim; Los Angeles Lakers, The Great Western Forum; Golden State Warriors, Oakland Coliseum Arena
NFL football teams: San Francisco 49ers (NFC), Candlestick Park; Oakland Raiders (AFC), Oakland-Alameda County Coliseum; San Diego Chargers (AFC), San Diego Jack Murphy Stadium
NHL hockey teams: Anaheim Mighty Ducks, Arrowhead Pond of Anaheim; San Jose Sharks, San Jose Arena; Los Angeles Kings, The Great Western Forum

COLORADO

"Passing through your wonderful mountains and canyons I realize that this state is going to be more and more the playground for the whole republic....You will see this the real Switzerland of America."

President Theodore Roosevelt

A skier's paradise, Colorado is the nation's loftiest state. Its mountain reaches provide some of the nation's most dramatic and beautiful scenery—Colorado vistas inspired "America the Beautiful." From those same mountains flow much of the nation's river waters. It is a center for vacationers, with its cool, pleasant summer climate and its winter supply of powdered snow. But it is also the leading manufacturing area in the Rocky Mountain states and a major agricultural and mining state. Indeed, the story of its gold- and silver-mining boom days has become the theme of two popular musicals—*The Unsinkable Molly Brown* and *The Ballad of Baby Doe*.

SUPERLATIVES

• Highest mean altitude of the states.
• More mountains reaching 14,000 or more feet than any other state.
• Grand Mesa, the world's largest flat-top mountain.
• State where three of the nation's greatest river systems rise.
• Colorado oil shales, thought to contain five times more oil than all the present reserves of the world combined.
• Highest suspension bridge in the world—1,053 feet over the Arkansas River.

MOMENTS IN HISTORY

• The Colorado region was visited by Spanish explorers during the 16th century.
• The first known written record of the Colorado area was left by Diego de Vargas in 1694, as he pursued Indians who had escaped from Taos Pueblo in New Mexico.
• Spain won recognized ownership of the region in 1763.
• In 1803, three years after France acquired eastern Colorado, the United States obtained it as part of the Louisiana Purchase.
• The party of U.S. Lieutenant Zebulon Pike explored present-day Colorado in 1806,

discovering the mountain that now bears Pike's name.

So They Say

When Zebulon Pike discovered Pike's Peak, later named for him, that explorer exclaimed that it was so high and massive that it would never be climbed. Not long afterward, the first climbers reached the peak, and it is perhaps the most "climbed" mountain anywhere today.

The Enchantment of Colorado

• In 1832, William Bent completed the construction of massive Fort Bent, with walls as thick as four feet; this stronghold became the center of trade of a vast region.
• Western Colorado, which Mexico won control of in 1821, became U.S. territory in 1848 after the Mexican War.
• Settlers from Mexican lands in 1851 founded San Luis, the oldest continuously occupied community in Colorado.
• In 1858, thousands rushed to the gold at Cherry Creek, spurred by the slogan "Pike's Peak or bust!"
• By June 1858, the "bust" had come. Little easy-to-reach gold had been found and thousands of disappointed fortune hunters turned back in despair.
• In November 1858, promoter William Larimer and his son William H. H. Larimer came to Cherry Creek and founded Denver, named for the governor of the territory.
• In May 1859, John Gregory made a real gold find; Gregory Gulch was soon to become bustling Central City.
• In 1860, Abe Lee discovered gold in the canyon where the community of Leadville soon developed.
• Retaliating for a ranch massacre, a group of irregulars surprised and massacred a contin-

gent of Indians in 1864 in a slaughter known as the Battle of Sand Creek.

• Enraged over the Sand Creek massacre and other complaints, the Indians attacked, spreading terror. Much of the Indian power was broken in the Battle of Beecher Island, and the last battle with the Indians in Colorado was the Battle of Summit Springs on July 11, 1869. Pawnee Chief Traveling Bear was awarded the Medal of Honor for his support of federal forces in that battle.

• After three tries Colorado was made a state on August 1, 1876.

• Just as Colorado's gold appeared to be running out, new wealth came from the silver found at Leadville in 1877.

• In 1891 gold brought Cripple Creek to world attention. The overall value of gold taken from the Cripple Creek region has been called second only to that from the Witwatersrand mines in South Africa.

• Women of Colorado won the right to vote in 1893.

• World War I called 43,000 to service from Colorado.

• Royal Gorge was spanned in 1929, by what was, at the time, the world's highest suspension bridge.

• The Great Depression was made even more tragic in the 1930s by the worst drought and dust storms in history.

So They Say

"Part of my farm blew off into Kansas yesterday, so I guess I'll have to pay taxes there, too."

An unnamed farmer, responding to the drought and dust storms

• Beginning in 1942, nearly 10,000 persons of Japanese-American descent were brought to resettlement camps at Arkansas Valley near Grenada, because of misplaced fears that they might aid Japan during World War II.

• The U.S. Air Force Academy opened in 1955 and moved to its permanent location near Colorado Springs in 1958.

• Deep within Cheyenne Mountain, the North American Air Defense Command headquarters commenced operations in 1965.

• In 1988 the Rocky Flats nuclear weapons plant was closed after three workers were exposed to radiation.

• Demonstrators attacked a bus carrying Ku Klux Klan members from a Klan rally in Denver on Martin Luther King's birthday in 1992.

THAT'S INTERESTING

• Many explanations have been given for the decline of the Pueblo culture. According to one of the most interesting, the people ground their grain in stone grinders; fine stone mixed with the meal, and their teeth were ground down until they no longer could eat.

• In 1936 in a unique ceremony, Middle Park officially became a part of the United States. The area supposedly had never been included in any of the cessions of territory to the federal government.

• Mining tycoon Auguste Rische was asked to donate a large chandelier to a church he financed. He refused, saying that he could not play a chandelier, and he thought no one else in the congregation could do so.

• Mrs. James J. (Molly) Brown, socialite wife of a Colorado mining tycoon, survived the sinking of the liner *Titanic*. She became famous as "the Unsinkable Molly Brown" in the Broadway hit of that name. Her home is now a Denver museum.

NOTABLE NATIVES

William Harrison (Jack) Dempsey (Manassa, 1895-1983), boxer. **Douglas Fairbanks** (Denver, 1883-1939), actor. **Byron Raymond White** (Fort Collins, 1917-), Supreme Court justice. **Paul Whiteman** (Denver, 1890-1967), musician/conductor.

GENERAL

Admitted to statehood: August 1, 1876
Origin of name: Spanish, red, first applied to
     Colorado River
Capital: Denver
Nickname: Centennial State
Motto: *Nil Sine Numine*—Nothing without
     providence
Animal: Rocky Mountain bighorn sheep
Bird: Lark bunting
Flower: Rocky Mountain columbine
Stone: Aquamarine
Song: "Where the Columbines Grow"
Tree: Colorado blue spruce

THE LAND

Area: 104,100 sq. mi., 8th
     Land: 103,729 sq. mi., 8th

Water: 371 sq. mi., 43rd
Inland water: 371 sq. mi., 38th
Topography: Eastern dry high plains; hilly to mountainous central plateau; western Rocky Mountains of high ranges alternating with broad valleys and deep, narrow canyons.
Number of counties: 63
Geographic center: Park, 30 mi. NW of Pike's Peak
Length: 380 mi.; width: 280 mi.
Highest point: 14,433 ft. (Mt. Elbert), 3rd
Lowest point: 3,350 ft. (Arkansas River), 51st
Mean elevation: 6,800 ft., 1st

CLIMATE AND ENVIRONMENT

Temp., highest: 118 deg. on July 11, 1888, at Bennett; lowest: –61 deg. on Feb. 1, 1985, at Maybell
Monthly average: highest: 98.8 deg., 3rd; lowest: 36.8 deg., 48th; spread (high to low): 62.0 deg., 38th
Hazardous waste sites (1993): 18, 22nd
Endangered species: Mammals: 1—Black-footed ferret; birds: 3—Whooping crane, American peregrine falcon, Least tern; reptiles: none; amphibians: none; fishes: 3; invertebrates: none; plants: 7

MAJOR CITIES
POPULATION, 1990
PERCENTAGE INCREASE, 1980-90

Aurora, 222,103—40.05%
Colorado Springs, 281,140—30.70%
Denver, 467,610— –5.09%
Lakewood, 126,481—11.14%
Pueblo, 98,640— –3.00%

THE PEOPLE

Population (1995): 3,746,585, 25th
Percent change (1990-95): 13.7%, 4th
Population (2000 proj.): 4,059,000, 24th
Percent change (1990-2000): 23.21%, 6th
Per sq. mi. (1994): 35.2, 39th
Percent in metro. area (1992): 81.8%, 18th
Foreign born: 142,000, 18th
Percent: 4.3%, 20th
Top three ancestries reported:
German, 32.30%
English, 17.67%
Irish, 16.33%
White: 2,905,474, 88.19%, 23rd
Black: 133,146, 4.04%, 32nd
Native American: 27,776, 0.84%, 17th

Asian, Pacific Isle: 59,862, 1.82%, 17th
Other races: 168,136, 5.10%, 6th
Hispanic origin: 424,302,12.88%, 5th
Percent over 5 yrs. speaking language other than English at home: 10.5%, 16th
Percent males: 49.52%, 11th; percent females: 50.48%, 41st
Percent never married: 25.8%, 24th
Marriages per 1,000 (1993): 9.5, 16th
Divorces per 1,000 (1993): 5.4, 13th
Median age: 32.5
Under 5 years (1994): 7.39%, 19th
Under 18 years (1994): 26.53%, 19th
65 years & older (1994): 10.1%, 48th
Percent increase among the elderly (1990-94): 11.70%, 6th

OF VITAL IMPORTANCE

Live births per 1,000 pop. (1993): 15.4, 15th
Infant mortality rate per 1,000 births (1992): 7.6, 34th
Rate for blacks (1990): 16.5, 20th
Rate for whites (1990): 8.4, 13th
Births to unmarried women, % of total (1992): 23.8%, 42nd
Births to teenage mothers, % of total (1992): 12.0%, 28th
Abortions (1992): 19,880, 18th
Rate per 1,000 women 14-44 years old: 23.6, 19th
Percent change (1988-92): 6%, 9th
Average lifetime (1979-81): 73.30, 38th
Deaths per 1,000 pop. (1993): 6.7, 47th
Causes of death per 100,000 pop.:
Accidents & adverse effects (1992): 33.1, 32nd
Atherosclerosis (1991): 9.3, 9th
Cancer (1991): 143.0, 49th
Cerebrovascular diseases (1992): 41.3, 47th
Chronic liver diseases & cirrhosis (1991): 9.5, 21st
Chronic obstructive pulmonary diseases (1992): 40.8, 16th
Diabetes mellitus (1992): 12.6, 49th
Diseases of heart (1992): 178.1, 49th
Pneumonia, flu (1991): 28.0, 34th
Suicide (1992): 17.3, 5th

KEEPING WELL

Active nonfederal physicians per 100,000 pop. (1993): 222, 14th
Dentists per 100,000 (1991): 71, 7th
Nurses per 100,000 (1992): 780, 24th
Hospitals per 100,000 (1993): 2.02, 29th

Admissions per 1,000 (1993): 95.40, 43rd
Occupancy rate per 100 beds (1993): 58.6,
  36th
Average cost per patient per day (1993):
  $961, 14th
Average cost per stay (1993): $6,212, 14th
Average stay (1992): 7.2 days, 25th
AIDS cases (adult, 1993): 1,324; per 100,000:
  37.1, 14th
HIV infection, not yet AIDS (1993): 4,942
Other notifiable diseases:
  Gonorrhea: 105.2, 34th
  Measles: 4.2, 26th
  Syphilis: 6.1, 37th
  Tuberculosis: 2.2, 45th
Pop. without health insur. (1991-93): 11.9%,
  34th

HOUSEHOLDS BY TYPE

Total households (1994): 1,417,000
  Percent change (1990-94): 10.5%, 4th
  Per 1,000 pop.: 387.58, 3rd
  Percent of households 65 yrs. and over:
    16.51%, 50th
  Persons per household (1994): 2.52, 48th
Family households: 854,214
  Percent of total: 66.61%, 49th
Nonfamily households: 428,275
  Percent of total: 33.39%, 3rd
Pop. living in group quarters: 79,472
  Percent of pop.: 2.41%, 37th

LIVING QUARTERS

Total housing units: 1,477,349
  Persons per unit: 2.23, 43rd
Occupied housing units: 1,282,489
  Percent of total units: 86.81%, 38th
  Persons per unit: 2.46, 44th
  Percent of units with over 1 person per
    room: 2.97%, 25th
Owner-occupied units: 798,277
  Percent of total units: 54.03%, 41st
  Percent of occupied units: 62.24%, 43rd
  Persons per unit: 2.66, 40th
  Median value: $82,700, 18th
Renter-occupied units: 484,212
  Percent of total units: 32.78%, 14th
  Percent of occupied units: 37.76%, 11th
  Persons per unit: 2.25, 39th
  Median contract rent: $362, 20th
  Rental vacancy rate: 11.4%, 10th
Mobile home, trailer & other as a percent
  of occupied housing units: 7.97%,
  32nd

Persons in emergency shelters for homeless
  persons: 2,554, 0.078%, 11th
Persons visible in street locations: 393,
  0.0119%, 14th
Persons in shelters for abused women: 167,
  0.0051%, 23rd
Nursing home population: 18,506, 0.56%, 41st

CRIME INDEX PER 100,000 (1992-93)

Total reported: 5,526.8, 19th
  Violent: 567.3, 25th
    Murder and nonnegligent manslaughter:
      5.8, 31st
    Aggravated assault: 399.0, 24th
    Robbery: 116.7, 34th
    Forcible rape: 45.8, 15th
  Property: 4,959.5, 15th
    Burglary: 1,009.8, 25th
    Larceny, theft: 3,499.4, 14th
    Motor vehicle theft: 450.3, 24th
Drug abuse violations (1990): 228.3, 30th
Child-abuse rate per 1,000 children (1993):
  8.41, 43rd

TEACHING AND LEARNING

Pop. 3 and over enrolled in school: 896,144
  Percent of pop.: 28.5%, 13th
Public elementary & secondary schools (1992-
  93): 1,399
  Total enrollment (1992): 612,635
    Percent of total pop.: 17.68%, 17th
  Teachers (1992): 33,419
    Percent of pop.: 0.96%, 35th
  Pupil/teacher ratio (fall 1992): 18.3, 11th
  Teachers' avg. salary (1992-93): $35,514,
    24th
  Expenditure per capita (1990-91): $3,418.99,
    24th
  Expenditure per pupil (1991-92): $5,172,
    26th
Percent of graduates taking SAT (1993): 28%,
  25th
  Mean SAT verbal scores: 454, 23rd
  Mean SAT mathematical scores: 509, 21st
Percent of graduates taking ACT (1995):
  63%, 16th
  Mean ACT scores: 21.4, 13th
Percent of pop. over 25 completing:
  Less than 9th grade: 5.6%, 48th
  High school: 84.4%, 3rd
  College degree(s): 27.0%, 4th
Higher education, institutions (1993-94): 59
  Enrollment (1992): 240,163

White non-Hispanic (1992): 197,648
  Percent of enroll.: 82.30%, 27th
Black non-Hispanic (1992): 7,755
  Percent of enroll.: 3.23%, 35th
Hispanic (1992): 20,063
  Percent of enroll.: 8.35%, 6th
Asian/Pacific Islander (1992): 6,616
  Percent of enroll.: 2.75%, 17th
American Indian/AK native (1992): 2,641
  Percent of enroll.: 1.10%, 15th
Nonresident alien (1992): 5,440
  Percent of enroll.: 2.27%, 30th
Female (1992): 128,281
  Percent of enroll.: 53.41%, 46th
Pub. institutions (1993-94): 28
  Enrollment (1992): 211,238
  Percent of enroll.: 87.96%, 12th
Private institutions (1993-94): 31
  Enrollment (1992): 28,592
  Percent of enroll.: 11.91%, 40th
Tuition, public institution (avg., 1993-94):
  $6,183, 22nd
Tuition, private institution (avg., 1993-94):
  $15,235, 16th
Public library systems: 124
  Books & serial vol. per capita: 2.62, 24th
  Govt. expenditure per capita: $18.87, 17th

LAW ENFORCEMENT, COURTS, AND PRISONS

Police protection, corrections, judicial and
  legal functions expenditures (1992):
  $1,051,000,000
Per capita: $303, 16th
Police per 10,000 pop. (1993): 23.29, 16th
Prisoners (state & fed.) per 100,000 pop.
  (1993): 2,654.88, 29th
Percent change (1992-93): 5.2%, 25th
Death penalty: yes, by lethal injection
  Under sentence of death (1993): 3, 31st
  Executed (1993): 0

RELIGION, NUMBER AND PERCENT OF POPULATION

Agnostic: 26,764—1.10%, 6th
Buddhist: 2,433—0.10%, 17th
Christian: 1,944,069—79.90%, 43rd
Hindu: 4,866—0.20%, 3rd
Jewish: 43,796—1.80%, 9th
Muslim: NA
Unitarian: 17,032—0.70%, 4th
Other: 48,663—2.00%, 10th
None: 277,377—11.40%, 8th
Refused to answer: 68,128—2.80%, 12th

MAKING A LIVING

Personal income per capita (1994): $22,333,
  17th
  Percent increase (1993-94): 3.9%, 44th
Disposable personal income per capita (1994):
  $19,022, 20th
Median income of households (1993):
  $34,488, 13th
Percent of pop. below poverty level (1993):
  9.9%, 44th
Percent 65 and over (1990): 11.0%, 29th
Expenditure for energy per person (1992):
  $1,571, 50th

ECONOMY

Civilian labor force (1994): 1,996,000
  Percent of total pop.: 54.60%, 7th
  Percent 65 and over (1990): 2.05%, 43rd
  Percent female: 45.84%, 35th
Percent job growth (1980-90): 24.50%,
  19th
Major employer industries (1994):
  Agriculture: NA—2.1%, 34th
  Construction: 87,000—4.8%, 15th
  Finance, insurance, & real estate:
    107,000—5.9%, 15th
  Government: 272,000—15.1%, 28th
  Manufacturing: 225,000—12.5%, 37th
  Service: 435,000—24.1%, 12th
  Trade: 340,000—18.8%, 31st
  Transportation, communications, public
    utilities: 117,000—6.5%, 7th
Unemployment rate (1994): 4.21%, 45th
  Male: 4.4%, 43rd
  Female: 4.0%, 46th
Total businesses (1991): 156,891
  New business incorps. (1991): 13,583
    Percent of total businesses: 8.66%, 10th
  Business failures (1991): 2,091
    Percent of total businesses: 1.33%
Agriculture farm income:
  Marketing (1993): $4,083,000,000, 16th
    Average per farm: $157,038.46, 5th
  Leading products (1993): Cattle, wheat,
    corn, dairy products
  Average value land & build. per acre
    (1994): $430, 41st
    Percent increase (1990-94): 20.11%,
    9th
  Govt. payments (1993): $250,000,000,
    19th
    Average per farm: $9,615.38, 12th
Construction, value of all: $2,536,000,000
  Per capita: $769.79, 13th

Manufactures:
Value added: $13,819,000,000
Per capita: $4,194.70, 35th
Leading products: Computer equipment, instruments, foods, machinery, aerospace products
Value of nonfuel mineral production (1994): $440,000,000, 25th
Leading mineral products: Petroleum, natural gas, coal
Retail sales (1993): $33,261,000,000, 22nd
Per household: $23,437, 11th
Percent increase (1992-93): 9.9%, 8th
Tourism revenues (1992): $6.4 bil.
Foreign exports, in total value (1994): $3,802,000,000, 27th
Per capita: $1,039.93, 31st
Gross state product per person (1993): $22,848.66, 17th
Percent change (1990-93): 5.48%, 10th
Patents per 100,000 pop. (1993): 29.57, 10th
Public aid recipients (percent of resident pop. 1993): 4.8%, 43rd
Medicaid recipients per 1,000 pop. (1993): 78.84, 49th
Medicare recipients per 1,000 pop. (1993): 111.11, 48th

TRAVEL AND TRANSPORTATION

Motor vehicle registrations (1993): 3,032,000
Per 1,000 pop.: 850.73, 13th
Motorcycle registrations (1993): 88,000
Per 1,000 pop.: 24.69, 12th
Licensed drivers per 1,000 pop. (1993): 726.99, 8th
Deaths from motor vehicle accidents per 100,000 pop. (1993): 15.74, 29th
Public roads & streets (1993):
Total mileage: 78,721
Per 1,000 pop.: 22.09, 19th
Rural mileage: 65,818
Per 1,000 pop.: 18.47, 21st
Urban mileage: 12,903
Per 1,000 pop.: 3.62, 9th
Interstate mileage: 954
Per 1,000 pop.: 0.27, 18th
Annual vehicle-mi. of travel per person (1993): 9,175, 30th
Mean travel time for workers age 16+ who work away from home: 20.7 min., 24th

GOVERNMENT

Percent of voting age pop. registered (1994): 64.3%, 26th
Percent of voting age pop. voting (1994): 46.4%, 24th
Percent of voting age pop. voting for U.S. representatives (1994): 38.9%, 26th
State legislators, total (1995): 100, 42nd
Women members (1992): 31
Percent of legislature: 31.0%, 5th
U.S. Congress, House members (1995): 6
Change (1985-95): 0
Revenues (1993):
State govt.: $10,028,000,000
Per capita: $2,813.69, 32nd
Parimutuel & amusement taxes & lotteries, revenue per capita: $72.11, 26th
Expenditures (1993):
State govt.: $8,673,000,000
Per capita: $2,433.50, 38th
Debt outstanding (1993): $3,117,000,000
Per capita: $874.58, 41st

LAWS AND REGULATIONS

Legal driving age: 18
Marriage age without parental consent: 18
Divorce residence requirement: 90 days

ATTRACTIONS (1995)

Major opera companies: 3
Major symphony orchestras: 2
Major dance companies: 1
Major professional theater companies (nonprofit): 1
State appropriations for arts agencies per capita: $0.44, 42nd
State Fair in August at Pueblo

SPORTS AND COMPETITION

NCAA teams (Division I): Colorado State Univ. Rams, U.S. Air Force Academy Falcons, Univ. of Colorado Buffaloes
Major league baseball teams: Colorado Rockies (NL West), Coors Field
NBA basketball teams: Denver Nuggets, McNichols Sports Arena
NFL football teams: Denver Broncos (AFC), Mile High Stadium
NHL hockey teams: Colorado Avalanche, McNichols Sports Arena

CONNECTICUT

"The warm, very warm heart of 'New England at its best,' such a vast abounding arcadia of mountains, broad vales and great rivers and large lakes and white villages embowered in prodigious elms and maples. It is extraordinarily graceful and idyllic."

Henry James, Sr., writer, philosopher

Although Connecticut is the third smallest of the states geographically, it must rank among the greatest in its contributions to the nation and the world. The state gave the world its "first workable written constitution" and introduced mass production, which paved the way for modern manufacturing. Its inventors and manufacturers introduced a wide variety of inexpensive products. "Yankee pedlars" and the masters of the Yankee clippers carried these products around the nation and the world. Connecticut has long led in the insurance field and in the production of helicopters, jet aircraft engines, submarines, pins and needles, silverware, small firearms, and thread.

SUPERLATIVES

• The first tax-supported library in the United States, at Salisbury.
• Modern manufacturing methods—first developed by Eli Terry and Eli Whitney.
• The first woman to receive a U.S. patent—Mary Kies of South Killingly, for a machine to weave silk and straw.
• America's first cigars, machine-made combs, factory hats, plows, friction matches, and tacks among many other new products.
• The nation's first commercial telephone exchange, in New Haven.
• America's first trade association, founded by Naugatuck Valley manufacturers.
• First in the value of insurance written.

MOMENTS IN HISTORY

• Adriaen Block, a Dutch explorer, discovered and entered the Connecticut River in 1614.
• In 1633 the Dutch built a fort at present-day Hartford. The British countered with a fortified trading post where Windsor now stands.
• Wethersfield was founded in 1634, be-

coming the oldest permanent European settlement in Connecticut.
• To counter the threat of Indian attack, a force under Captain John Mason attacked and destroyed the Indian encampment of Pequot in 1637.

So They Say

"The greatness and the violence of the fire... the shrieks and yells of men and women and children....It was a fearful sight to see them frying in the fire and the streams of blood quenching the same."

Clergyman Cotton Mather, describing the destruction of Pequot

---

• The three towns of Connecticut in 1639 grouped themselves into a commonwealth; they were governed by a covenant known as the Fundamental Orders, sometimes called the first constitution. This document was the first to declare that "the foundation of authority is in the free consent of the people," anticipating the U.S. Constitution.
• The charter granted Connecticut by the English King in 1662 was amazingly liberal. It legalized almost every act previously taken in the Connecticut colony, including the Fundamental Orders.
• In 1687, King James II revoked the Connecticut charter. Royal Governor Sir Edmund Andros attempted to seize the charter, but Joseph Wadsworth stole away with it. Tradition says it was hidden in the hollow of an oak on Samuel Wyllys's property. This "Charter Oak" became a famous landmark.
• In 1770, six years before the Declaration of Independence, Lebanon freemen drafted a declaration of rights, and Old Lyme launched its own "Tea Party" by burning the tea sacks of a traveling peddler.

• During the American Revolution, Connecticut is said to have "furnished more men and money than any other colony except Massachusetts."

• Revolutionary Stonington was attacked in 1775, Danbury was burned and looted in 1777, New Haven in 1779, and Bridgeport and New London in 1781.

• On January 9, 1788, Connecticut became the fifth state, after dropping its claim to extend to the west coast, except for what became the "Western Reserve," now the area of Cleveland, Ohio.

• Connecticut adopted "universal manhood suffrage in 1845," extending the vote to all men, but not to women.

• Beginning in 1861, the state's quota of Civil War volunteers was met five times over. Of the 57,379 Connecticut men and women serving in the war, more than a third (20,573) were killed or missing in action.

• The nation's first code of law for registering airplanes and licensing pilots was inaugurated in Connecticut in 1911.

• During World War I, Connecticut led all the states in production per person.

• In 1954 the Groton shipyards produced the world's first atomic-powered submarine, the *Nautilus*.

• County government was abolished in Connecticut in 1960, the first such step taken by any state. Local government was transferred to an extension of the existing township system.

• Ella T. Grasso was elected governor in 1975, becoming the first woman in any state to be elected governor without having been preceded by her husband.

• Three years of recession in the state by 1992 had resulted in high unemployment and declining budgets. Defense contractors were hardest hit. However, the subsequent recovery was remarkable.

THAT'S INTERESTING

• Early Hartford, described as a Puritan theocracy, was known for its strict religious law. Its "blue laws" called for the death penalty for any son who cursed or struck his parents. Elder Malbone once flogged his daughter Martha on the green for going on a date with a young gentleman.

• The great charter of 1662 extended Connecticut west even to the Pacific Ocean.

• During the American Revolution, Lime Rock metal workers forged a huge chain that was stretched across the Hudson River to keep British ships from sailing up that strategic waterway. Each link was three feet long.

• During the American Revolution, at the age of 15, Samuel Smedley of Fairfield became a captain of a privateer ship. By war's end he had captured more enemy prize ships than any other captain, surpassing even the small U.S. Navy.

So They Say

"There is little hope of conquering an enemy whose very schoolboys are capable of valor equaling that of trained veterans of naval warfare."

Comment of a captured
British sea captain

• Connecticut's Charter Oak gained such fame that it became fashionable to own a product supposedly made from its trunk. It was said that Charter Oak products included walking sticks, dog collars, needle cases, three-legged stools, dinner tables, tenpin alleys, toothpicks, and enough alleged Charter Oak to build a plank road from Hartford to Salt Lake City.

NOTABLE NATIVES

Ethan Allen (Litchfield, 1738-1789), Revolutionary soldier. **Phineas Taylor Barnum** (Bethel, 1810-1891), showman. **John Brown** (Torrington, 1800-1859), abolitionist. **Samuel Colt** (Hartford, 1814-1862), inventor. **John Fitch** (Hartford County, 1743-1798), inventor. **Charles Goodyear** (New Haven, 1800-1860), inventor/manufacturer. **Nathan Hale** (Coventry, 1755-1776), soldier. **Katharine Hepburn** (Hartford, 1907-), actress. **Elias Howe** (Spencer, 1819-1867), inventor. **Collis Potter Huntington** (Harwinton, 1821-1900), railroad builder. **John Pierpont Morgan** (Hartford, 1837-1913), financier. **Harriet Beecher Stowe** (Litchfield, 1811-1896), author. **Eli Terry** (East Windsor, 1772-1852), clock manufacturer. **John Trumbull** (Lebanon, 1756-1843), painter. **Jonathan Trumbull,** (Lebanon, 1710-1785), public official. **Noah Webster** (West Hartford, 1758-1843), lexicographer. **Emma Hart Willard** (Berlin, 1787-1870), educator.

GENERAL

Admitted to statehood: January 9, 1788
Origin of name: From Mohican and other
   Algonquin words meaning "long river
   place"
Capital: Hartford
Nickname: Constitution State, Nutmeg
   State
Motto: *Qui Transtulit Sustinet*—He who
   transplanted still sustains
Animal: Sperm whale
Bird: American robin
Insect: Praying mantis
Flower: Mountain laurel
Mineral: Garnet
Song: "Yankee Doodle"
Tree: White oak

THE LAND

Area: 5,544 sq. mi., 48th
   Land: 4,845 sq. mi., 48th
   Water: 699 sq. mi., 36th
   Inland water: 161 sq. mi., 47th
   Coastal water: 538 sq. mi., 11th
Topography: Western upland, the Berkshires,
   in the NW, highest elevations; narrow
   central lowland; hilly eastern upland
   drained by rivers
Number of counties: 8
Geographic center: Hartford, at East Berlin
Length: 110 mi.; width: 70 mi.
Highest point: 2,380 ft. (Mount Frissell),
   36th
Lowest point: sea level (Long Island Sound),
   3rd
Mean elevation: 500 ft., 41st
Coastline: 0 mi., 24th
Shoreline: 618 mi., 18th

CLIMATE AND ENVIRONMENT

Temp., highest: 105 deg. on July 22, 1926, at
   Waterbury; lowest: −32 deg. on Feb.
   16, 1943, at Falls Village
Monthly average: highest: 84.8 deg., 39th;
   lowest: 16.7 deg., 22nd; spread (high to
   low): 68.1 deg., 27th
Hazardous waste sites (1993): 15, 24th
Endangered species: Mammals: none; birds:
   2—American peregrine falcon, Roseate
   tern; reptiles: 2; amphibians: none;
   fishes: none; invertebrates: none; plants:
   2

MAJOR CITIES
POPULATION, 1990
PERCENTAGE INCREASE, 1980-90

Bridgeport, 141,686— −0.60%
Hartford, 139,739—2.45%
New Haven, 130,474—3.48%
Stamford, 108,056—5.46%
Waterbury, 108,961—5.51%

THE PEOPLE

Population (1995): 3,274,662, 28th
   Percent change (1990-95): −0.4%, 49th
Population (2000 proj.): 3,271,000, 29th
   Percent change (1990-2000): −0.45%, 48th
Per sq. mi. (1994): 676.0, 5th
Percent in metro. area (1992): 95.7%, 5th
Foreign born: 279,000, 13th
   Percent: 8.5%, 11th
Top three ancestries reported:
   Italian, 19.11%
   Irish, 18.68%
   English, 14.09%
White: 2,859,353, 86.99%, 26th
Black: 274,269, 8.34%, 22nd
Native American: 6,654, 0.20%, 44th
Asian, Pacific Isle: 50,698, 1.54%, 19th
Other races: 69,142, 2.10%, 17th
Hispanic origin: 213,116, 6.48%, 12th
Percent over 5 yrs. speaking language other
   than English at home: 15.2%, 10th
Percent males: 48.46%, 33rd; percent females:
   51.54%, 19th
Percent never married: 29.0%, 9th
Marriages per 1,000 (1993): 7.0, 44th
Divorces per 1,000 (1993): 3.1, 44th
Median age: 34.4
Under 5 years (1994): 7.05%, 36th
Under 18 years (1994): 24.06%, 45th
65 years & older (1994): 14.2%, 9th
Percent increase among the elderly (1990-94):
   4.28%, 36th

OF VITAL IMPORTANCE

Live births per 1,000 pop. (1993): 14.0, 39th
Infant mortality rate per 1,000 births (1992):
   7.6, 34th
   Rate for blacks (1990): 16.0, 25th
   Rate for whites (1990): 6.6, 47th
Births to unmarried women, % of total
   (1992): 28.7%, 24th
Births to teenage mothers, % of total (1992):
   8.0%, 48th

Abortions (1992): 19,720, 19th
  Rate per 1,000 women 14-44 years old:
    26.2, 13th
  Percent change (1988-92): –16%, 41st
Average lifetime (1979-81): 75.12, 11th
Deaths per 1,000 pop. (1993): 8.9, 27th
Causes of death per 100,000 pop.:
  Accidents & adverse effects (1992): 27.3,
    44th
  Atherosclerosis (1991): 6.4, 32nd
  Cancer (1991): 217.5, 17th
  Cerebrovascular diseases (1992): 53.5, 34th
  Chronic liver diseases & cirrhosis (1991):
    9.8, 18th
  Chronic obstructive pulmonary diseases
    (1992): 35.4, 30th
  Diabetes mellitus (1992): 16.4, 41st
  Diseases of heart (1992): 294.6, 23rd
  Pneumonia, flu (1991): 32 9, 21st
  Suicide (1992): 9.1, 46th

KEEPING WELL

Active nonfederal physicians per 100,000 pop.
  (1993): 321, 5th
Dentists per 100,000 (1991): 80, 2nd
Nurses per 100,000 (1992): 946, 7th
Hospitals per 100,000 (1993): 1.07, 50th
  Admissions per 1,000 (1993): 105.64, 36th
  Occupancy rate per 100 beds (1993): 74.4,
    5th
  Average cost per patient per day (1993):
    $1,058, 7th
  Average cost per stay (1993): $7,478, 5th
  Average stay (1992): 8.6 days, 11th
AIDS cases (adult, 1993): 1,758; per 100,000:
  53.6, 6th
HIV infection, not yet AIDS (1993): 49
Other notifiable diseases:
  Gonorrhea: 251.3, 21st
  Measles: 6.0, 17th
  Syphilis: 56.6, 14th
  Tuberculosis: 5.0, 33rd
Pop. without health insur. (1991-93): 8.6%, 49th

HOUSEHOLDS BY TYPE

Total households (1994): 1,222,000
  Percent change (1990-94): –0.7%, 49th
  Per 1,000 pop.: 373.13, 30th
  Percent of households 65 yrs. and over:
    23.16%, 15th
  Persons per household (1994): 2.60, 23rd
Family households: 864,493
  Percent of total: 70.26%, 28th
Nonfamily households: 365,986
  Percent of total: 29.74%, 24th

Pop. living in group quarters: 101,167
  Percent of pop.: 3.08%, 14th

LIVING QUARTERS

Total housing units: 1,320,850
  Persons per unit: 2.49, 9th
Occupied housing units: 1,230,479
  Percent of total units: 93.16%, 3rd
  Persons per unit: 2.52, 26th
  Percent of units with over 1 person per
    room: 2.29%, 38th
Owner-occupied units: 807,481
  Percent of total units: 61.13%, 18th
  Percent of occupied units: 65.62%, 34th
  Persons per unit: 2.74, 22nd
  Median value: $177,800, 3rd
Renter-occupied units: 422,998
  Percent of total units: 32.02%, 15th
  Percent of occupied units: 34.38%, 19th
  Persons per unit: 2.30, 32nd
  Median contract rent: $510, 4th
  Rental vacancy rate: 6.9%, 42nd
Mobile home, trailer & other as a percent
    of occupied housing units: 2.52%,
    48th
Persons in emergency shelters for homeless
    persons: 4,194, 0.128%, 3rd
Persons visible in street locations: 221,
    0.0067%, 25th
Persons in shelters for abused women: 155,
    0.0047%, 28th
Nursing home population: 30,962, 0.94%,
    12th

CRIME INDEX PER 100,000 (1992-93)

Total reported: 4,650.4, 32nd
  Violent: 456.2, 32nd
    Murder and nonnegligent manslaughter:
      6.3, 29th
    Aggravated assault: 228.7, 37th
    Robbery: 196.7, 15th
    Forcible rape: 24.4, 48th
  Property: 4,194.2, 28th
    Burglary: 978.1, 29th
    Larceny, theft: 2,620.6, 39th
    Motor vehicle theft: 595.5, 14th
Drug abuse violations (1990): 571.4, 6th
Child-abuse rate per 1,000 children (1993):
    29.77, 4th

TEACHING AND LEARNING

Pop. 3 and over enrolled in school: 805,486
  Percent of pop.: 25.6%, 44th

Public elementary & secondary schools (1992-93): 993
Total enrollment (1992): 488,476
  Percent of total pop.: 14.90%, 44th
Teachers (1992): 34,193
  Percent of pop.: 1.04%, 24th
Pupil/teacher ratio (fall 1992): 14.3, 46th
Teachers' avg. salary (1992-93): $51,233, 1st
Expenditure per capita (1990-91): $4,443.02, 6th
Expenditure per pupil (1991-92): $8,017, 5th
Percent of graduates taking SAT (1993): 88%, 1st
Mean SAT verbal scores: 430, 33rd
Mean SAT mathematical scores: 474, 36th
Percent of graduates taking ACT (1995): 3%, 47th
Mean ACT scores: 21.4, 13th
Percent of pop. over 25 completing:
  Less than 9th grade: 8.4%, 34th
  High school: 79.2%, 17th
  College degree(s): 27.2%, 3rd
Higher education, institutions (1993-94): 42
Enrollment (1992): 165,874
  White non-Hispanic (1992): 138,151
    Percent of enroll.: 183.29%, 23rd
  Black non-Hispanic (1992): 11,036
    Percent of enroll.: 6.65%, 24th
  Hispanic (1992): 6,448
    Percent of enroll.: 3.89%, 11th
  Asian/Pacific Islander (1992): 4,943
    Percent of enroll.: 2.98%, 14th
  American Indian/AK native (1992): 406
    Percent of enroll.: 0.24%, 47th
  Nonresident alien (1992): 4,890
    Percent of enroll.: 2.95%, 18th
  Female (1992): 92,613
    Percent of enroll.: 55.83%, 16th
Pub. institutions (1993-94): 19
  Enrollment (1992): 107,786
    Percent of enroll.: 64.98%, 44th
Private institutions (1993-94): 23
  Enrollment (1992): 58,088
    Percent of enroll.: 35.02%, 8th
Tuition, public institution (avg., 1993-94): $7,926, 7th
Tuition, private institution (avg., 1993-94): $19,708, 2nd
Public library systems: 194
  Books & serial vol. per capita: 3.42, 12th
  Govt. expenditure per capita: $28.10, 3rd

LAW ENFORCEMENT, COURTS, AND PRISONS

Police protection, corrections, judicial and legal functions expenditures (1992): $1,091,000,000
  Per capita: $333, 12th
Police per 10,000 pop. (1993): 25.72, 8th
Prisoners (state & fed.) per 100,000 pop. (1993): 4,176.63, 10th
  Percent change (1992-93): 20.1%, 1st
Death penalty: yes, by electrocution
  Under sentence of death (1993): 5, 31st
  Executed (1993): 0

RELIGION, NUMBER AND PERCENT OF POPULATION

Agnostic: 12,688—0.50%, 27th
Buddhist: 5,075—0.20%, 11th
Christian: 2,167,055—85.40%, 29th
Hindu: 2,538—0.10%, 10th
Jewish: 60,901—2.40%, 6th
Muslim: 2,538—0.10%, 22nd
Unitarian: 7,613—0.30%, 15th
Other: 32,988—1.30%, 24th
None: 147,177—5.80%, 35th
Refused to answer: 98,964—3.90%, 3rd

MAKING A LIVING

Personal income per capita (1994): $29,402, 2nd
  Percent increase (1993-94): 4.4%, 36th
Disposable personal income per capita (1994): $24,732, 2nd
Median income of households (1993): $39,516, 5th
Percent of pop. below poverty level (1993): 8.5%, 50th
Percent 65 and over (1990): 7.2%, 51st
Expenditure for energy per person (1992): $1,980, 14th

ECONOMY

Civilian labor force (1994): 1,726,000
  Percent of total pop.: 52.70%, 15th
  Percent 65 and over (1990): 3.75%, 6th
  Percent female: 47.39%, 12th
Percent job growth (1980-90): 18.58%, 28th
Major employer industries (1994):
  Agriculture: NA—0.9%, 47th
  Construction: 57,000—3.4%, 46th
  Finance, insurance, & real estate: 167,000—9.9%, 1st
  Government: 196,000—11.7%, 50th

Manufacturing: 341,000—20.3%, 13th
Service: 392,000—23.4%, 14th
Trade: 302,000—18.0%, 40th
Transportation, communications, public
utilities: 74,000—4.4%, 38th
Unemployment rate (1994): 5.56%, 26th
Male: 5.3%, 31st
Female: 5.9%, 19th
Total businesses (1991): 139,462
New business incorps. (1991): 8,501
Percent of total businesses: 6.10%, 23rd
Business failures (1991): 435
Percent of total businesses: 0.31%
Agriculture farm income:
Marketing (1993): $521,000,000, 41st
Average per farm: $130,250.00, 9th
Leading products (1993): Greenhouse, eggs,
dairy products, aquaculture
Average value land & build. per acre
(1994): $4,686, 3rd
Percent increase (1990-94): 6.09%, 35th
Govt. payments (1993): $3,000,000, 45th
Average per farm: $750.00, 44th
Construction, value of all: $1,602,000,000
Per capita: $487.36, 30th
Manufactures:
Value added: $23,826,000,000
Per capita: $7,248.30, 5th
Leading products: Aircraft engines and
parts, submarines, helicopters, instru-
ments, machinery & computer equip-
ment, electronics & electrical equip-
ment
Value of nonfuel mineral production (1994):
$97,000,000, 44th
Leading mineral products: Sand and gravel,
stone, limestone, fieldspar
Retail sales (1993): $28,980,000,000, 25th
Per household: $23,621, 10th
Percent increase (1992-93): −1.4%,
50th
Tourism revenues (1993): $3.9 bil.
Foreign exports, in total value (1994):
$5,664,000,000, 22nd
Per capita: $1,729.47, 11th
Gross state product per person (1993):
$29,170.46, 4th
Percent change (1990-93): 2.13%, 37th
Patents per 100,000 pop. (1993): 53.26,
2nd
Public aid recipients (percent of resident pop.
1993): 6.2%, 31st
Medicaid recipients per 1,000 pop. (1993):
101.89, 33rd

Medicare recipients per 1,000 pop. (1993):
149.79, 13th

TRAVEL AND TRANSPORTATION

Motor vehicle registrations (1993): 2,594,000
Per 1,000 pop.: 791.34, 25th
Motorcycle registrations (1993): 37,000
Per 1,000 pop.: 11.29, 36th
Licensed drivers per 1,000 pop. (1993):
665.04, 36th
Deaths from motor vehicle accidents per
100,000 pop. (1993): 10.43, 46th
Public roads & streets (1993):
Total mileage: 20,357
Per 1,000 pop.: 6.21, 43rd
Rural mileage: 8,814
Per 1,000 pop.: 2.69, 46th
Urban mileage: 11,543
Per 1,000 pop.: 3.52, 12th
Interstate mileage: 343
Per 1,000 pop.: 0.10, 43rd
Annual vehicle-mi. of travel per person
(1993): 8,237, 42nd
Mean travel time for workers age 16+ who
work away from home: 21.1 min.,
22nd

GOVERNMENT

Percent of voting age pop. registered (1994):
68.4%, 19th
Percent of voting age pop. voting (1994):
51.3%, 15th
Percent of voting age pop. voting for U.S.
representatives (1994): 43.0%, 17th
State legislators, total (1995): 187, 9th
Women members (1992): 43
Percent of legislature: 23.0%, 16th
U.S. Congress, House members (1995): 6
Change (1985-95): 0
Revenues (1993):
State govt.: $12,744,000,000
Per capita: $3,887.74, 7th
Parimutuel & amusement taxes & lotteries,
revenue per capita: $187.31, 4th
Expenditures (1993):
State govt.: $12,507,000,000
Per capita: $3,815.44, 6th
Debt outstanding (1993): $12,848,000,000
Per capita: $3,919.46, 8th

LAWS AND REGULATIONS

Legal driving age: 18, 16 if completed driver
education course
Marriage age without parental consent: 18

Divorce residence requirement: 1 yr., for qualifications—check local statutes

ATTRACTIONS (1995)

Major opera companies: 3
Major symphony orchestras: 2
Major dance companies: 2
Major professional theater companies (nonprofit): 2

State appropriations for arts agencies per capita: $0.66, 29th

SPORTS AND COMPETITION

NCAA teams (Division I): Central Connecticut State Blue Devils, Fairfield Univ. Stags, Univ. of Connecticut Huskies, Univ. of Hartford Hawks, Yale Univ. Bulldogs
NHL hockey teams: Hartford Whalers, Hartford Civic Center

DELAWARE

"Delaware is like a diamond, diminutive, but having within it inherent value."

John Lofland, poet and author

The distinguished history of the second smallest state geographically extends over more than 300 years. Delaware is proud to be known as the "First State," the first to accept the new U.S. Constitution. It was the only colony to have been claimed by Sweden, Holland, and England. The lotus plants found here have led some specialists to believe that the region may have been visited by early Egyptian explorers. Swedish settlers here introduced the log cabin to American shores, and the nation's first regularly operated steam railroad was started here. Today, Delaware is both a farming and an industrial region and leads the nation in the production of chemicals. More corporations are headquartered in Delaware than in any other state as a result of its corporate laws.

SUPERLATIVES

• The European-style log cabin, introduced to the United States in Delaware.
• The nation's first regularly operated steam railroad, beginning operations out of New Castle in 1831.
• At one time the nation's flour industry center, with the price of wheat set in Wilmington.

MOMENTS IN HISTORY

• Henry Hudson sailed his storied ship, the *Half Moon*, up Delaware Bay in 1609, becoming the first European known to have visited the area.
• In 1613 another explorer, Cornelius Jacobsen Mey, explored and traded in the area.
• Dutch leader Peter Minuit, employed by Sweden, brought settlers in two ships to what is now Wilmington in 1638. They landed on "The Rocks," known as the "Plymouth Rock" of Delaware.
• In 1655, New Amsterdam Governor Peter Stuyvesant brought a large fleet to the area, captured all of New Sweden for the Dutch, and ended Swedish rule in America.

So They Say

He "...did there trade with the inhabitants; said trade consisting of sables, Furs, Robes and other skins.... He hath found the said Country full of trees, to wit: Oaks, hickory and pines; which trees were, in some places covered with vines...in the said country, Bucks and does, turkeys and partridges...."

Cornelius Hendrickson, on the exploration of Cornelius Jacobsen Mey

• In 1682, William Penn, new proprietor of Delaware and Pennsylvania, sailed up the Delaware River past flourishing Christina (Wilmington) on his way to his new capital, Philadelphia. Delaware would be governed from there until it became a British crown colony in 1704.
• In 1776, although he was seriously ill, Caesar Rodney, a member of the Continental Congress, made a famous ride from Wilmington to Philadelphia in order to cast the deciding vote for the Declaration of Independence.
• On August 27, 1776, Delaware's First Regiment played a key role in the important Battle of Long Island.
• Delaware gained distinction as the "First State" when it ratified the U.S. Constitution on December 7, 1787.
• During the War of 1812, Delaware's Captain Thomas Macdonough's victory in the Battle of Lake Champlain became a turning point of that conflict.
• In the Civil War's Battle of Antietam on September 17, 1862, almost half of the Delaware men who took part were killed.
• During the great storm of 1889, 40 ships were destroyed off Lewes and 70 lives were lost.
• The U.S. battleship *Delaware* was commissioned in 1910.

So They Say

"Sir: The Almighty has been pleased to grant us a signal victory on Lake Champlain in the capture of one frigate, one brig, and two sloops of war of the enemy."

Captain Thomas Macdonough reporting to his commander, modestly neglecting to mention that he had brought the entire British fleet into his hands

• The disastrous Pocomoke Swamp fire of 1930 burned the underlying peat for eight months.
• The Delaware Memorial Bridge went into service in 1951, paying tribute to the 800 Delaware men and women who lost their lives during World War II.
• A 1978 order of the U.S. Supreme Court permitted the busing of children from Wilmington to the suburbs to promote racial integration. The decision was a landmark for the establishment of this practice.
• In 1992, Delaware carried out its first execution since 1946, as convicted murderer Steve Brian Pennell was put to death.

THAT'S INTERESTING

• Johan Prinz, capable governor of New Sweden from 1643 to 1653, was the "greatest" of all colonial governors. He weighed 400 pounds and was called the "Big Tub."
• When a ship carrying peas wrecked on a sandbar, the peas grew and collected so much sand that a new island formed, now Pea Patch Island.
• When one of the Du Pont men saw sparks flying from a machine in their blasting powder plant, he dipped his tall silk hat in water and put out the fire before a tremendous explosion could occur.
• One of the most curious exhibits to be found at the Delaware Historical Society is a cigar store white man, a carving of George Washington.
• When Shadrach Cannon of Seaford was bitten by a rabid dog, some of the town's best citizens were selected to smother him to death between two feather beds, in an early mercy killing.

NOTABLE NATIVES

James Asheton Bayard (Wilmington, 1799-1880), politician. Henry Seidel Canby (Wilmington, 1878-1961), author/publisher. Annie Jump Cannon (Dover, 1863-1941), astronomer. John Middleton Clayton (Dagsborough, 1796-1856), jurist/statesman. Alfred Irenee Du Pont (near Wilmington, 1864-1965), industrialist/philanthropist. Henry Du Pont (Wilmington, 1812-1889), industrialist/philanthropist. Henry Algernon Du Pont (near Wilmington, 1838-1926), politician/industrialist. Pierre Samuel Du Pont (Wilmington, 1870-1954), industrialist. Jacob Jones (near Smyrna, 1768-1850), naval officer. Thomas Macdonough (Macdonough, 1783-1825), naval officer. John Phillips Marquand (Wilmington, 1893-1960), author. Howard Pyle (Wilmington, 1853-1911), author/artist. Caesar Rodney (near Dover, 1728-1784), patriot/statesman.

GENERAL

Admitted to statehood: December 7, 1787
Origin of name: Named for Lord De La Warr, early governor of Virginia; the name was first applied to the river, then to the Indian tribe (Lenni-Lenape) and to the state
Capital: Dover
Nickname: Diamond State, First State, Blue Hen State
Motto: Liberty and independence
Bird: Blue hen chicken
Insect: Lady Bug
Fish: Weakfish
Flower: Peach blossom
Mineral: Sillimanite
Song: "Our Delaware"
Tree: American holly

THE LAND

Area: 2,397 sq. mi., 49th
    Land: 1,955 sq. mi., 49th
    Water: 442 sq. mi., 41st
        Inland water: 71 sq. mi., 49th
        Coastal water: 371 sq. mi., 15th
Topography: Piedmont plateau in the northern tip, sloping to a near sea-level coastal plain
Number of counties: 3
Geographic center: Kent, 11 mi. S of Dover

Length: 100 mi.; width: 30 mi.
Highest point: 442 ft. (Ebright Road), 49th
Lowest point: sea level (Atlantic Ocean), 3rd
Mean elevation: 60 ft., 51st
Coastline: 28 mi., 21st
Shoreline: 381 mi., 21st

CLIMATE AND ENVIRONMENT

Temp., highest: 110 deg. on July 21, 1930, at
  Millsboro; lowest: −17 deg. on Jan. 17,
  1893, at Millsboro
Monthly average: highest: 85.6 deg., 35th;
  lowest: 23.2 deg., 32nd; spread (high to
  low): 62.4 deg., 36th
Hazardous waste sites (1993): 19, 21st
Endangered species: Mammals: 1—Delmarva
  Peninsula fox squirrel; birds: 1—
  American peregrine falcon; reptiles: 2;
  amphibians: none; fishes: none; inver-
  tebrates: none; plants: 1

MAJOR CITIES
POPULATION, 1990
PERCENTAGE INCREASE, 1980-90

Brookside, 15,307—0.34%
Dover, 27,630—17.54%
Newark, 25,098— −0.59%
Wilmington, 71,529—1.90%

THE PEOPLE

Population (1995): 717,197, 46th
  Percent change (1990-95): 7.7%, 16th
Population (2000 proj.): 759,000, 46th
  Percent change (1990-2000): 13.94%,
  18th
Per sq. mi. (1994): 361.3, 8th
Percent in metro. area (1992): 82.7%, 16th
Foreign born: 22,000, 44th
  Percent: 3.3%, 24th
Top three ancestries reported:
  Irish, 20.87%
  German, 20.72%
  English, 18.47%
White: 535,094, 80.32%, 34th
Black: 112,460, 16.88%, 10th
Native American: 2,019, 0.30%, 32nd
Asian, Pacific Isle: 9,057, 1.36%, 21st
Other races: 7,538, 1.13%, 24th
Hispanic origin: 15,820, 2.37%, 26th
Percent over 5 yrs. speaking language other
  than English at home: 6.9%, 27th
Percent males: 48.48%, 32nd; percent fe-
  males: 51.52%, 20th
Percent never married: 27.6%, 12th

Marriages per 1,000 (1993): 7.2, 40th
Divorces per 1,000 (1993): 4.5, 26th
Median age: 32.9
Under 5 years (1994): 7.22%, 24th
Under 18 years (1994): 24.79%, 40th
65 years & older (1994): 12.7%, 27th
Percent increase among the elderly (1990-94):
  10.24%, 8th

OF VITAL IMPORTANCE

Live births per 1,000 pop. (1993): 15.1,
  19th
Infant mortality rate per 1,000 births (1992):
  8.6, 25th
  Rate for blacks (1990): 19.4, 5th
  Rate for whites (1990): 7.3, 38th
Births to unmarried women, % of total
  (1992): 32.6%, 14th
Births to teenage mothers, % of total (1992):
  12.4%, 24th
Abortions (1992): 5,730, 39th
  Rate per 1,000 women 14-44 years old:
  35.2, 6th
  Percent change (1988-92): −1%, 15th
Average lifetime (1979-81): 73.21, 40th
Deaths per 1,000 pop. (1993): 8.7, 29th
Causes of death per 100,000 pop.:
  Accidents & adverse effects (1992): 35.8,
  24th
  Atherosclerosis (1991): 3.8, 48th
  Cancer (1991): 223.5, 13th
  Cerebrovascular diseases (1992): 46.9, 44th
  Chronic liver diseases & cirrhosis (1991):
  9.9, 17th
  Chronic obstructive pulmonary diseases
  (1992): 35.9, 28th
  Diabetes mellitus (1992): 30.0, 2nd
  Diseases of heart (1992): 266.9, 32nd
  Pneumonia, flu (1991): 26.6, 39th
  Suicide (1992): 12.7, 20th

KEEPING WELL

Active nonfederal physicians per 100,000 pop.
  (1993): 209, 21st
Dentists per 100,000 (1991): 45, 42nd
Nurses per 100,000 (1992): 894, 11th
Hospitals per 100,000 (1993): 1.15, 48th
  Admissions per 1,000 (1993): 113.61, 27th
  Occupancy rate per 100 beds (1993): 70.9,
  10th
  Average cost per patient per day (1993):
  $1,028, 11th
  Average cost per stay (1993): $7,307, 6th
  Average stay (1992): 6.7 days, 38th

AIDS cases (adult, 1993): 375; per 100,000:
53.6, 7th
HIV infection, not yet AIDS (1993): NA
Other notifiable diseases:
Gonorrhea: 506.3, 5th
Measles: 1.4, 37th
Syphilis: 59.3, 12th
Tuberculosis: 5.7, 30th
Pop. without health insur. (1991-93): 12.7%,
25th

HOUSEHOLDS BY TYPE

Total households (1994): 264,000
Percent change (1990-94): 6.8%, 13th
Per 1,000 pop.: 373.94, 29th
Percent of households 65 yrs. and over:
21.21%, 32nd
Persons per household (1994): 2.59, 26th
Family households: 175,867
Percent of total: 71.06%, 22nd
Nonfamily households: 71,630
Percent of total: 28.94%, 30th
Pop. living in group quarters: 20,071
Percent of pop.: 3.01%, 17th

LIVING QUARTERS

Total housing units: 289,919
Persons per unit: 2.30, 40th
Occupied housing units: 247,497
Percent of total units: 85.37%, 42nd
Persons per unit: 2.55, 20th
Percent of units with over 1 person per
room: 2.27%, 39th
Owner-occupied units: 173,813
Percent of total units: 59.95%, 23rd
Percent of occupied units: 70.23%, 9th
Persons per unit: 2.71, 29th
Median value: $100,100, 11th
Renter-occupied units: 73,684
Percent of total units: 25.42%, 47th
Percent of occupied units: 29.77%, 43rd
Persons per unit: 2.38, 22nd
Median contract rent: $425, 12th
Rental vacancy rate: 7.8%, 33rd
Mobile home, trailer & other as a percent of
occupied housing units: 14.98%, 14th
Persons in emergency shelters for homeless
persons: 313, 0.047%, 25th
Persons visible in street locations: 19,
0.0029%, 38th
Persons in shelters for abused women: 36,
0.0054%, 17th
Nursing home population: 4,596, 0.69%,
29th

CRIME INDEX PER 100,000 (1992-93)

Total reported: 4,872.1, 28th
Violent: 685.9, 20th
Murder and nonnegligent manslaughter:
5.0, 34th
Aggravated assault: 417.1, 22nd
Robbery: 186.7, 19th
Forcible rape: 77.0, 2nd
Property: 4,186.3, 29th
Burglary: 892.0, 31st
Larceny, theft: 2,979.0, 24th
Motor vehicle theft: 315.3, 36th
Drug abuse violations (1990): 333.5, 14th
Child-abuse rate per 1,000 children (1993):
12.98, 30th

TEACHING AND LEARNING

Pop. 3 and over enrolled in school: 171,219
Percent of pop.: 26.9%, 30th
Public elementary & secondary schools (1992-
93): 176
Total enrollment (1992): 104,321
Percent of total pop.: 15.10%, 43rd
Teachers (1992): 6,252
Percent of pop.: 0.90%, 41st
Pupil/teacher ratio (fall 1992): 16.7, 28th
Teachers' avg. salary (1992-93): $38,667,
14th
Expenditure per capita (1990-91):
$4,092.90, 10th
Expenditure per pupil (1991-92): $6,093,
13th
Percent of graduates taking SAT (1993): 68%,
10th
Mean SAT verbal scores: 429, 34th
Mean SAT mathematical scores: 465,
43rd
Percent of graduates taking ACT (1995): 4%,
44th
Mean ACT scores: 21.6, 11th
Percent of pop. over 25 completing:
Less than 9th grade: 7.2%, 43rd
High school: 77.5%, 23rd
College degree(s): 21.4%, 17th
Higher education, institutions (1993-94): 9
Enrollment (1992): 42,763
Percent of pop.: 6.20%, 16th
White non-Hispanic (1992): 35,230
Percent of enroll.: 82.38%, 25th
Black non-Hispanic (1992): 5,156
Percent of enroll.: 12.06%, 14th
Hispanic (1992): 569
Percent of enroll.: 1.33%, 35th

Asian/Pacific Islander (1992): 881
  Percent of enroll.: 2.06%, 24th
American Indian/AK native (1992): 113
  Percent of enroll.: 0.26%, 42nd
Nonresident alien (1992): 814
  Percent of enroll.: 1.90%, 42nd
Female (1992): 24,357
  Percent of enroll.: 56.96%, 9th
Pub. institutions (1993-94): 5
  Enrollment (1992): 35,313
  Percent of enroll.: 82.58%, 28th
Private institutions (1993-94): 4
  Enrollment (1992): 7,450
  Percent of enroll.: 17.42%, 24th
Tuition, public institution (avg., 1993-94):
  $7,811, 8th
Tuition, private institution (avg., 1993-94):
  $10,132, 38th
Public library systems: 29
  Books & serial vol. per capita: 1.68, 47th
  Govt. expenditure per capita: $10.02, 40th

LAW ENFORCEMENT, COURTS, AND PRISONS

Police protection, corrections, judicial and
  legal functions expenditures (1992):
  $259,000,000
Per capita: $375, 7th
Police per 10,000 pop. (1993): 29.65, 5th
Prisoners (state & fed.) per 100,000 pop.
  (1993): 6,031.52, 2nd
  Percent change (1992-93): 3.6%, 34th
Death penalty: yes, by lethal injection
  Under sentence of death (1993): 15, 23rd
  Executed (1993): 2

RELIGION, NUMBER AND PERCENT OF POPULATION

Agnostic: NA
Buddhist: NA
Christian: 429,414—85.40%, 29th
Hindu: NA
Jewish: 7,040—1.40%, 14th
Muslim: NA
Unitarian: NA
Other: 1,509—0.30%, 48th
None: 36,204—7.20%, 20th
Refused to answer: 28,661—5.70%, 1st

MAKING A LIVING

Personal income per capita (1994): $22,828,
  12th
Percent increase (1993-94): 4.5%, 35th

Disposable personal income per capita (1994):
  $19,381, 18th
Median income of households (1993):
  $36,064, 9th
Percent of pop. below poverty level (1993):
  10.2%, 42nd
Percent 65 and over (1990): 10.1%, 40th
Expenditure for energy per person (1992):
  $1,970, 15th

ECONOMY

Civilian labor force (1994): 384,000
  Percent of total pop.: 54.39%, 8th
  Percent 65 and over (1990): 2.49%,
    33rd
  Percent female: 45.05%, 42nd
Percent job growth (1980-90): 35.15%, 7th
Major employer industries (1994):
  Agriculture: 8,000—2.4%, 25th
  Construction: 21,000—5.9%, 3rd
  Finance, insurance, & real estate: 34,000—
    9.5%, 2nd
  Government: 44,000—12.5%, 48th
  Manufacturing: 68,000—19.1%, 14th
  Service: 82,000—23.1%, 16th
  Trade: 63,000—17.8%, 43rd
  Transportation, communications, public
    utilities: 15,000—4.4%, 38th
Unemployment rate (1994): 4.95%, 36th
  Male: 4.5%, 41st
  Female: 5.3%, 29th
Total businesses (1991): 21,542
  New business incorps. (1991): 29,887
    Percent of total businesses: 138.74%,
      1st
  Business failures (1991): 80
    Percent of total businesses: 0.37%
Agriculture farm income:
  Marketing (1993): $622,000,000, 40th
    Average per farm: $207,333.33, 3rd
  Leading products (1993): Broilers, soy-
    beans, corn, greenhouse
  Average value land & build. per acre
    (1994): $2,641, 6th
    Percent increase (1990-94): 16.91%,
      18th
  Govt. payments (1993): $6,000,000,
    42nd
    Average per farm: $2,000.00, 35th
Construction, value of all: $572,000,000
  Per capita: $858.64, 6th
Manufactures:
  Value added: $4,512,000,000
    Per capita: $6,773.07, 8th

of modern history like Franklin Delano Roosevelt and Winston Churchill. You will also be interested to learn about the connections to Freemasonry of many well-known figures from the European Enlightenment that are likely to figure in *The Solomon Key*—people ranging from Mozart to Lafayette and Voltaire.

If you're like me, then despite having a good liberal arts education, you will be surprised to discover that at least eight signers of the Declaration of Independence were Freemasons; that George Washington took his role as a leader of a Masonic lodge very seriously; that Benjamin Franklin and the leading Enlightenment philosopher Voltaire visited the Masonic halls of Paris together; and that a British captain, also a Freemason, released Paul Revere from British custody on the night of his famous ride, after he determined that Revere *himself* was a Mason. You will suddenly wonder why you never realized that the Washington Monument (and a similar monument on Bunker Hill in Boston, and many others elsewhere) was not just coincidentally shaped like an Egyptian obelisk, but was intentionally designed that way to honor Masonic allusions to ancient Egyptian mystical wisdom. You may have heard Mozart's *Magic Flute* many times, but you may never have known that it was written as a Masonic allegory and is filled with Masonic symbolism. You may have read Rudyard Kipling or seen the film version of *The Man Who Would Be King,* but may not have realized that Kipling, too, was a leading Mason and that *The Man Who Would Be King* is also a Masonic allegory.

You may also have seen the 2004 film *National Treasure.* This entertaining and utterly fictional heist film may have stolen a tiny bit of thunder from *The Solomon Key.* It brought into the popular culture a modern-day story that reached back into the time of Benjamin Franklin and depicted some fanciful legends of the Masons and the Knights Templar and their relevance to the Founding Fathers, themes that Dan Brown is likely to explore in *The Solomon Key.* Brown's prior books have been criticized by many for being too unclear in their mix of fact and fiction. *The Solomon Key* will undoubtedly continue Brown's novelistic style of asserting that certain myths, legends, and speculations are "factual." But whatever liberties with history Dan Brown takes in his next book—and he certainly will take many—I expect that once *The Solomon Key* is published, we will find that he has explored these issues in considerably greater depth than the filmmakers of *National Treasure* did.

If at least a significant portion of what you will read in *The Solomon Key* is news to you, you will also want to know why you were never taught these things in school! Or why Brown's version of history isn't recounted in the recent bestselling biographies of the Founding Fathers by leading scholars. Reading *Secrets of the Widow's Son* will fill in many of those blanks and help you develop your own ideas about the wide range of issues Dan Brown's next novel is likely to touch on.

How does David Shugarts know what Dan Brown is going to write about in *The Solomon Key* long before the book is even published?

First, a quick bit of personal history about my involvement with this book. I am the editor of a book called *Secrets of the Code: The Unauthorized Guide to the Mysteries Behind The Da Vinci Code*, which was published in early 2004. That book grew out of my own interest in *The Da Vinci Code*, and my own personal quest to sort out fact from fiction in Dan Brown's work after my fascinating experience reading the novel. A good indicator of the power of *The Da Vinci Code* phenomenon is that *Secrets of the Code* went on to become a blockbusting *New York Times* bestseller in its own right, spending more than twenty weeks on the *Times* bestseller list in 2004, appearing in roughly two dozen international editions and on at least seven global bestseller lists. We have subsequently created a whole series of "Secrets" books, designed to bring the expertise of leading scholars and thinkers to the subjects touched on by the Dan Brown novels, in a way that allows readers to develop their own informed perspective on fact, fiction, speculation, and meaning in these novels.

When my co-editor, Arne de Keijzer, and I were neck deep in producing *Secrets of the Code,* we asked our good friend Dave Shugarts to look into a rumor we'd heard that there was a code buried in the dust jacket flaps of *The Da Vinci Code*. As you will soon discover, Dave is pretty good when it comes to cracking codes. Indeed, he has found

Leading products: Nylon, apparel, luggage, automobiles, processed meats and vegetables, other food products, railroad and aircraft equipment

Value of nonfuel mineral production (1994): $9,000,000, 50th

Leading mineral products: Magnesium compounds, sand/gravel

Retail sales (1993): $6,860,000,000, 45th
  Per household: $26,263, 3rd
  Percent increase (1992-93): 7.3%, 26th

Tourism revenues (1993): $806 mil.

Foreign exports, in total value (1994): $1,498,000,000, 38th
  Per capita: $2,121.81, 7th

Gross state product per person (1993): $30,882.35, 3rd
  Percent change (1990-93): 5.00%, 14th

Patents per 100,000 pop. (1993): 74.64, 1st

Public aid recipients (percent of resident pop. 1993): 5.3%, 37th

Medicaid recipients per 1,000 pop. (1993): 98.85, 37th

Medicare recipients per 1,000 pop. (1993): 137.54, 30th

TRAVEL AND TRANSPORTATION

Motor vehicle registrations (1993): 555,000
  Per 1,000 pop.: 795.13, 24th

Motorcycle registrations (1993): 10,000
  Per 1,000 pop.: 14.33, 29th

Licensed drivers per 1,000 pop. (1993): 724.93, 9th

Deaths from motor vehicle accidents per 100,000 pop. (1993): 16.19, 27th

Public roads & streets (1993):
  Total mileage: 5,544
    Per 1,000 pop.: 7.94, 42nd
  Rural mileage: 3,675
    Per 1,000 pop.: 5.27, 41st
  Urban mileage: 1,869
    Per 1,000 pop.: 2.68, 40th
  Interstate mileage: 41
    Per 1,000 pop.: 0.06, 48th

Annual vehicle-mi. of travel per person (1993): 9,885, 20th

Mean travel time for workers age 16+ who work away from home: 20.0 min., 30th

GOVERNMENT

Percent of voting age pop. registered (1994): 58.7%, 42nd

Percent of voting age pop. voting (1994): 41.2%, 41st

Percent of voting age pop. voting for U.S. representatives (1994): 36.5%, 32nd

State legislators, total (1995): 62, 48th
  Women members (1992): 8
  Percent of legislature: 12.9%, 36th

U.S. Congress, House members (1995): 1
  Change (1985-95): 0

Revenues (1993):
  State govt.: $2,876,000,000
    Per capita: $4,120.34, 5th
  Parimutuel & amusement taxes & lotteries, revenue per capita: $121.78, 14th

Expenditures (1993):
  State govt.: $2,557,000,000
    Per capita: $3,663.32, 8th

Debt outstanding (1993): $3,490,000,000
  Per capita: $5,000.00, 3rd

LAWS AND REGULATIONS

Legal driving age: 18, 16 if complete driver education course

Marriage age without parental consent: 18

Divorce residence requirement: 6 mo.

ATTRACTIONS (1995)

Major opera companies: 1

Major symphony orchestras: 1

State appropriations for arts agencies per capita: $1.84, 7th

State Fair in end of July at Harrington

SPORTS AND COMPETITION

NCAA teams (Division I): Delaware State Univ. Hornets, Univ. of Delaware Fightin' Blue Hens

DISTRICT OF COLUMBIA

"I went to Washington the other day...and I felt that the sun in all its course could not look down upon a better sight than that majestic home of the Republic that had taught the world its best lessons in liberty."

Henry W. Grady, journalist and author

The city of Washington and the District of Columbia—"the District," as residents call it—are one and the same. The site was selected by Congress as the nation's capital, and over the years the District has brought together the nation's most famous statesmen and politicians. The city of Washington was burned by the British in the War of 1812, and its capture was threatened in the Civil War. Events that affect the nation and the world have occurred with regularity in its legislative, executive, and judicial halls. Washington has been the center of national mourning, where martyred presidents were honored. The grandeur of its buildings and monuments and the glamour of its world figures attract tourists from home and abroad. Washington has become an international metropolis in every sense of the word. With its increasing world importance has come an increasing awareness, closer to home, of the District's citizens and their welfare.

MOMENTS IN HISTORY

• In 1790 a bill was passed to locate a new capital on the Potomac River along the Virginia-Maryland border.

So They Say

"No nation ever before had the opportunity offered them of deliberately deciding upon the spot where their capital city should be fixed."

Pierre Charles L'Enfant, planner of the new capital

• The cornerstone of the Capitol was laid in 1793 by George Washington, who was a skilled mason.

• In 1800 the federal government moved to Washington, with 300 clerks, 138 members of Congress, and justices of the Supreme Court and the Circuit Court all crowded into a part of the unfinished Capitol. The East Room of the uncompleted president's house was used by Mrs. John Adams for drying the family laundry.

• The British burned Washington during the War of 1812, and first lady Dolley Madison escaped carrying only a portrait of George Washington, some official papers, and a few valuables.

So They Say

"Mrs. Madison's drawing room was often filled with gallants immaculate in sheer ruffles and small [tight] clothes...dainty belles in frills, flounces and furbellows."

Contemporary account of Dolley Madison's social accomplishments

• The Marquis de Lafayette visited Washington in 1824 and received a gift of the "incredible sum" of $200,000. He was the first foreign dignitary ever to address the full Congress.

• In the 1840s about one-third of the District's territory was returned to Virginia.

So They Say

Washington is "...the central star of the constellation which enlightens the whole world!"

Marquis de Lafayette

In addition, codes are part of the games hosted on *The Da Vinci Code* Web site. For instance, faintly showing and mirror-imaged, in the red portion of the back of the jacket at the edge is a pair of latitude-longitude coordinates:

37 degrees 57 minutes 6.5 seconds North

77 degrees 8 minutes 44 seconds West

Add one degree to the latitude. This will lead to the sculpture of Kryptos at the CIA headquarters. The phrase "only WW knows" is found in a brown area of the *DVC* dust jacket. This refers to William Webster, a former CIA director.

Another code is in a darkly printed circular pattern on the back of the *DVC* dust jacket. It has numbers and little icons of the all-seeing eye within a triangle. If you use the same old Dan Brown technique, the numbers will refer to first letters in the chapters, or

* 20 11 11 68 * 1 10 11 61 15 * 5 8 73 11

becomes * E U U N * R S U P I * M L B U

If you just take this string of characters as something meaningful (which is a leap of faith, of course), you can fool around until you solve it. Or you can just put it into an anagram site on the Web. I went to http://www.crosswordtools.com/anagram-solver/ and it took about five seconds to come up with the famous U.S. motto: "E Pluribus Unum" or "Of many, one."

However, if you discover that the total number of characters, including the little icons, adds up to 16, you again should think of a Caesar's Box code, 4 x 4, which will allow you to fiddle with it awhile and get:

E	U	U	N
*	R	S	U
P	I	*	M
L	B	U	*

To me, it seems possible that Dan Brown conceived the general nature of the Robert Langdon series in the late 1990s, and has been writing it ever since. Therefore, he might have felt as though his Freemasonry research were completed. However, since there are an estimated fifty thousand books on Freemasonry, not to mention all the peripheral theories of conspiracies and other secret societies, it is hard for anyone to know that they have come to the last Freemasonry book on the library shelf. As far as I can tell, there are about ten authors writing new exposés of Freemasonry at any given moment.

So, the way I see it, there's a lot more that Dan Brown has yet to write about the Freemasons, and he's probably going to unload both barrels on us in his next book.

Dan Brown puts together intricate mystery plots, but, to date, they have all showed a simple principle: Conspirators are lurking everywhere, but they are just dupes for other conspirators, the ones *really* pulling the strings. According to Brown, one of the techniques of a secret society such as the Illuminati is to spread plenty of half-truths or downright disinformation. Brown calls this "data sowing," and he asserts that the major intelligence agencies do it, such as the CIA and NSA. The net result is essentially a variation on "hiding things in plain sight."

I believe in listening super-carefully to Dan Brown here. I think deception should never be discounted as a Dan Brown technique for talking about his own book plans.

At any given time, he could be telling a partial truth or just hurling chunks of disinformation. In one of Dan Brown's speeches, for instance, he claimed he had left the "most controversial" assertion out of *DVC*. Even though he had credible evidence that Jesus may have survived the Crucifixion, he said, he left it out of the book. Although this is certainly titillating, I don't think it is likely to come up in the next novel. I view it as a sop we have been thrown, to keep us guessing.

However, in late October of 2004, the press was fed one more vital clue. According to Stephen Rubin, president and publisher of

Doubleday, the new book will be titled *The Solomon Key*. Rubin met with reporters, divulged this one tidbit, and reiterated the earlier statements by Brown that it would focus on Freemasonry and take place in Washington, with its rich symbolic architecture. The various Dan Brown Web sites, which had been predicting the next book's arrival in "summer 2005," were now amended to say, "No release date is scheduled." In New York publishing circles, there is a belief that this now means the book will be published sometime in 2006.

You won't get many clues that come directly from Dan Brown, but I did get one that was nearly as good. As I scampered down the twisted trails of history, I encountered a larger-than-life American of the nineteenth century named Albert Pike. One day, I got an out-of-the-blue call from an author, Warren Getler, mentioning a book that he had written, *Shadow of the Sentinel*. It's about Civil War-era treasure that may have been buried in Arkansas and farther west, perhaps in Arizona. But it also brings up historical figures such as Jesse James and the very same Albert Pike.

Getler recounted a little vignette. It seems that he and Dan Brown attended a publishing luncheon together in the spring of 2003, since both were in the final stages of releasing their books. The two chatted, and when Dan Brown inquired about Getler's book and heard a little about it, up came the name Albert Pike.

According to Getler, Brown "blanched" and said, "I don't think I should talk about this further with you, because my next book is going to be about Albert Pike!"

Of course, this inspired me to roar through Getler's book and then order more tomes related to Pike—who is not an easy figure to figure out. But knowing about Pike is important in the study of Freemasonry, and gives meaning to some of the side issues as well. Pike's life, as we shall see, could give us meaningful clues as to a possible theme in Dan Brown's next book—or maybe just some red herrings.

My Roots

I had better come clean about a couple of personal things here. They have to do with my family roots.

My Dad died recently, and he was, among other things, a very advanced amateur genealogist. He spent some forty years working on our family history, and had amassed some ten thousand pages of genealogical notes by the time of his death. I inherited all these records and began to try to understand them. Believe it or not, the pursuit of Dan Brown's next novel played right into my getting to know my roots.

We think of our family as average Americans, which is to say that our ancestors came from many lands and intermingled, so that we have Welsh, Scottish, English, Irish, Dutch, and German blood, to name just the highlights. But the predominant line of our family descends from the Germans, and not just any Germans, but the waves who immigrated to Pennsylvania in the early eighteenth century and became the Pennsylvania Deutsch, misnamed "Dutch."

They largely came from a region known as the Palatinate, which has historical connections to the origins of the Rosicrucians and also to the Illuminati of Bavaria. (I know of no actual connections between my family and those groups, however.) Rosicrucians and Illuminati are both thoroughly implicated in Dan Brown's Langdon novels.

While my ancestors belonged to many religions, I would say that the most common one among our early American ancestors was the Society of Friends, or Quakers.

I am going to talk a lot about Freemasonry, since Dan Brown's next book will focus on it. I should make it clear that I am not a Freemason. I know that our family includes some Freemasons, including my favorite uncle, but I had never discussed Freemasonry within the family before I began studying Dan Brown's books. (I think a lot of American families might be like that, in that the older generation was involved in fraternal pursuits, but not the younger.)

- Washington might have been captured by the Confederates if they had followed up on their victory after the first Battle of Bull Run on July 21, 1861.
- Abraham Lincoln was shot at Ford's Theater on the evening of April 14, 1865, and died the next day. Washington mourned its leader, martyred on the threshold of Civil War victory.
- President James Garfield died on September 19, 1881, after having been shot in a Washington rail station.
- Protesting unemployment, Jacob Coxey in 1894 "invaded" Washington with 300 followers. Accused of walking on the grass, Coxey was arrested, and his followers were dispersed.
- In March 1952, a total restoration of the White House was finished.
- Residents of Washington were given the right to vote for president and vice president with the ratification of the 23rd Amendment in 1961.
- Under a new home rule charter, Washington's mayor and city council took office in 1975.
- In 1990, Mayor Marion S. Barry was sentenced to jail for six months for cocaine possession. Four years later he was returned to office.
- The White House came under attack in 1994 when a gunman sprayed the north side with rifle bullets and a pilot crashed a small plane on the South Lawn.

THAT'S INTERESTING

- Roosevelt Island in the Potomac River at Theodore Roosevelt Memorial Bridge "grows" about 20 acres every hundred years, as new land forms around the brush and branches that have floated down the river.

So They Say

Washington has a reputation for unpleasant climate that it may not deserve. "With blue skies, soft winds, and rich landscapes, only an ingrate would complain of the few admittedly difficult months."

Federal Writers' Project,
District of Columbia

- In the competition for the design of the Capitol, one plan called for the structure to be topped by the statue of an enormous rooster.
- The name of the play being performed when Abraham Lincoln was shot was *Our American Cousin*.
- House Speaker Joe Cannon gave Congress one of its cherished traditions when he commanded that his famous bean soup be served every day in the Capitol. It has been on the menu since 1907.
- Sudden rises of temperature in the Washington Monument cause the moisture to condense, so that "rain" falls inside.

GENERAL

Origin of District name: For Christopher Columbus
Origin of city name: For George Washington; originally called Federal City
Nickname: Nation's Capital, America's First City
Motto: *Justitia Omnibus*—Justice for all
Bird: Wood thrush
Flower: American beauty rose
Tree: Scarlet oak

THE LAND

Area: 68 sq. mi., 51st
    Land: 61 sq. mi., 51st
    Water: 7 sq. mi., 51st
    Inland water: 7 sq. mi., 51st
Topography: Low hills rise toward N away from the Potomac River and slope to the S.
Geographic center: Near 4th and L Streets NW
Highest point: 410 ft. (Tenleytown at Reno Reservoir), 50th
Lowest point: 1 ft. (Potomac River), 25th
Mean elevation: 150 ft., 48th
Hazardous waste sites (1993): 0, 51st

CLIMATE AND ENVIRONMENT

Temp., highest: 106 deg. on July 20, 1930, at Washington; lowest: −15 deg. on Feb. 11, 1988, at Washington
Monthly average: highest: 87.9 deg., 24th; lowest: 27.5 deg., 40th; spread (high to low): 60.4 deg., 45th
Endangered species: Mammals: none; birds: 1—American peregrine falcon; reptiles: none; amphibians: none; fishes: none; invertebrates: 1; plants: none

MAJOR CITIES
POPULATION, 1990
PERCENTAGE INCREASE, 1980-90

Washington, 606,900— -4.94%

THE PEOPLE

Population (1995): 554,256, 50th
  Percent change (1990-95): -8.7%, 51st
Population (2000 proj.): 537,000, 51st
  Percent change (1990-2000): -11.52%, 50th
Per sq. mi. (1994): 9,347.1, 1st
Percent in metro. area (1992): 100.0%, 1st
Foreign born: 59,000, 31st
  Percent: 9.7%, 6th
Top three ancestries reported:
  African, 51.89%
  German, 6.43%
  Irish, 5.60%
White: 179,667, 29.60%, 51st
Black: 399,604, 65.84%, 1st
Native American: 1,466, 0.24%, 38th
Asian, Pacific Isle: 11,214, 1.85%, 15th
Other races: 14,949, 2.46%, 13th
Hispanic origin: 32,710, 5.39%, 14th
Percent over 5 yrs. speaking language other than English at home: 12.5%, 14th
Percent males: 46.63%, 51st; percent females: 53.37%, 1st
Percent never married: 47.6%, 1st
Marriages per 1,000 (1993): 5.2, 51st
Divorces per 1,000 (1993): 3.4, 40th
Median age: 33.5
Under 5 years (1994): 7.54%, 16th
Under 18 years (1994): 20.88%, 50th
65 years & older (1994): 13.5%, 18th
Percent increase among the elderly (1990-94): -1.09%, 51st

OF VITAL IMPORTANCE

Live births per 1,000 pop. (1993): 16.9, 7th
Infant mortality rate per 1,000 births (1992): 19.6, 1st
  Rate for blacks (1990): 24.4, 1st
  Rate for whites (1990): 12.1, 1st
Births to unmarried women, % of total (1992): 66.9%, 1st
Births to teenage mothers, % of total (1992): 16.3%, 11th
Abortions (1992): 21,320, 16th
  Rate per 1,000 women 14-44 years old: 138.4, 1st
  Percent change (1988-92): -15%, 38th

Average lifetime (1979-81): 69.20, 51st
Deaths per 1,000 pop. (1993): 1.6, 51st
Causes of death per 100,000 pop.:
  Accidents & adverse effects (1992): 31.6, 35th
  Atherosclerosis (1991): 6.9, 25th
  Cancer (1991): 260.9, 2nd
  Cerebrovascular diseases (1992): 57.4, 27th
  Chronic liver diseases & cirrhosis (1991): 25.8, 1st
  Chronic obstructive pulmonary diseases (1992): 28.2, 48th
  Diabetes mellitus (1992): 29.6, 3rd
  Diseases of heart (1992): 314.1, 13th
  Pneumonia, flu (1991): 31.3, 22nd
  Suicide (1992): 5.8, 51st

KEEPING WELL

Active nonfederal physicians per 100,000 pop. (1993): 667, 1st
Dentists per 100,000 (1991): 122, 1st
Nurses per 100,000 (1992): 1,966, 1st
Hospitals per 100,000 (1993): 1.90, 32nd
  Admissions per 1,000 (1993): 270.12, 1st
  Occupancy rate per 100 beds (1993): 73.2, 7th
  Average cost per patient per day (1993): $1,201, 2nd
  Average cost per stay (1993): $8,594, 1st
  Average stay (1992): 8.3 days, 13th
AIDS cases (adult, 1993): 1,585; per 100,000: 274.0, 1st
HIV infection, not yet AIDS (1993): NA
Other notifiable diseases:
  Gonorrhea: 2,419.7, 1st
  Measles: 4.0, 27th
  Syphilis: 488.5, 1st
  Tuberculosis: 26.9, 1st
Pop. without health insur. (1991-93): 22.9%, 1st

HOUSEHOLDS BY TYPE

Total households (1994): 237,000
  Percent change (1990-94): -5.2%, 51st
  Per 1,000 pop.: 415.79, 1st
  Percent of households 65 yrs. and over: 21.52%, 30th
  Persons per household (1994): 2.24, 51st
Family households: 122,087
  Percent of total: 48.91%, 51st
Nonfamily households: 127,547
  Percent of total: 51.09%, 1st
Pop. living in group quarters: 41,717
  Percent of pop.: 6.87%, 1st

LIVING QUARTERS

Total housing units: 278,489
  Persons per unit: 2.18, 48th
Occupied housing units: 249,634
  Percent of total units: 89.64%, 25th
  Persons per unit: 2.31, 51st
  Percent of units with over 1 person per room: 8.25%, 4th
Owner-occupied units: 97,108
  Percent of total units: 34.87%, 51st
  Percent of occupied units: 38.90%, 51st
  Persons per unit: 2.50, 50th
  Median value: $123,900, 9th
Renter-occupied units: 152,526
  Percent of total units: 54.77%, 1st
  Percent of occupied units: 61.10%, 1st
  Persons per unit: 2.12, 50th
  Median contract rent: $441, 10th
  Rental vacancy rate: 7.9%, 30th
Mobile home, trailer & other as a percent of occupied housing units: 1.14%, 51st
Persons in emergency shelters for homeless persons: 4,682, 0.771%, 1st
Persons visible in street locations: 131, 0.0216%, 7th
Persons in shelters for abused women: 49, 0.0081%, 4th
Nursing home population: 7,008, 1.15%, 5th

CRIME INDEX PER 100,000 (1992-93)

Total reported: 11,761.1, 1st
  Violent: 2,921.8, 1st
    Murder and nonnegligent manslaughter: 78.5, 1st
    Aggravated assault: 1,557.6, 1st
    Robbery: 1,229.6, 1st
    Forcible rape: 56.1, 6th
  Property: 8,839.3, 1st
    Burglary: 1,995.5, 1st
    Larceny, theft: 5,449.0, 1st
    Motor vehicle theft: 1,394.8, 1st
Drug abuse violations (1990): 1,647.4, 1st
Child-abuse rate per 1,000 children (1993): 28.93, 5th

TEACHING AND LEARNING

Pop. 3 and over enrolled in school: 151,248
  Percent of pop.: 25.9%, 41st
Public elementary & secondary schools (1992-93): 181
  Total enrollment (1992): 80,937
    Percent of total pop.: 13.84%, 51st

Teachers (1992): 6,064
  Percent of pop.: 1.04%, 24th
Pupil/teacher ratio (fall 1992): 13.3, 51st
Teachers' avg. salary (1992-93): $40,967, 10th
Expenditure per capita (1990-91): $6,935.39, 2nd
Expenditure per pupil (1991-92): $9,549, 1st
Percent of graduates taking SAT (1993): 76%, 4th
  Mean SAT verbal scores: 405, 48th
  Mean SAT mathematical scores: 441, 51st
Percent of graduates taking ACT (1995): 5%, 43rd
  Mean ACT scores: 18.9, 50th
Percent of pop. over 25 completing:
  Less than 9th grade: 9.6%, 23rd
  High school: 73.1%, 39th
  College degree(s): 33.3%, 1st
Higher education, institutions (1993-94): 18
  Enrollment (1992): 81,909
  White non-Hispanic: 40,934
    Percent of enroll.: 49.97%, 50th
  Black non-Hispanic (1992): 25,156
    Percent of enroll.: 30.71%, 1st
  Hispanic (1992): 2,648
    Percent of enroll.: 3.23%, 14th
  Asian/Pacific Islander (1992): 3,742
    Percent of enroll.: 4.57%, 11th
  American Indian/AK native (1992): 202
    Percent of enroll.: 0.25%, 45th
  Nonresident alien (1992): 9,227
    Percent of enroll.: 11.26%, 1st
  Female (1992): 43,573
    Percent of enroll.: 53.20%, 48th
  Pub. institutions (1993-94): 2
    Enrollment (1992): 12,285
    Percent of pop.: 2.10%, 51st
  Private institutions (1993-94): 16
    Enrollment (1992): 69,624
    Percent of enroll.: 85.00%, 1st
  Tuition, public institution (avg., 1993-94): $0, 50th
  Tuition, private institution (avg., 1993-94): $18,004, 7th
Public library systems: 1
  Books & serial vol. per capita: 2.77, 21st
  Govt. expenditure per capita: $32.16, 2nd

LAW ENFORCEMENT, COURTS, AND PRISONS

Police protection, corrections, judicial and legal functions expenditures (1992): $719,000,000
  Per capita: $1,229, 1st

Police per 10,000 pop. (1993): 75.95, 1st
Prisoners (state & fed.) per 100,000 pop.
   (1993): 18,730.57, 1st
   Percent change (1992-93): –0.3%, 45th
Death penalty: no

RELIGION, NUMBER AND PERCENT OF POPULATION

Agnostic: 2,449—0.50%, 27th
Buddhist: 1,469—0.30%, 8th
Christian: 417,806—85.30%, 31st
Hindu: NA
Jewish: 11,266—2.30%, 7th
Muslim: 2,939—0.60%, 2nd
Unitarian: NA
Other: 12,245—2.50%, 4th
None: 30,858—6.30%, 30th
Refused to answer: 10,776—2.20%, 23rd

MAKING A LIVING

Personal income per capita (1994): $31,136, 1st
   Percent increase (1993-94): 5.5%, 16th
Disposable personal income per capita (1994): $25,832, 1st
Median income of households (1993): $27,304, 40th
Percent of pop. below poverty level (1993): 26.4%, 1st
   Percent 65 and over (1990): 17.2%, 12th
Expenditure for energy per person (1992): $1,954, 17th

ECONOMY

Civilian labor force (1994): 314,000
   Percent of total pop.: 55.09%, 5th
   Percent 65 and over (1990): 2.68%, 28th
   Percent female: 48.73%, 1st
Percent job growth (1980-90): 11.01%, 43rd
Major employer industries (1994):
   Agriculture: NA—0.4%, 51st
   Construction: NA—2.1%, 51st
   Finance, insurance, & real estate: 15,000—5.5%, 20th
   Government: 87,000—31.2%, 1st
   Manufacturing: 11,000—3.8%, 49th
   Service: 96,000—34.4%, 1st
   Trade: 29,000—10.5%, 51st
   Transportation, communications, public utilities: 11,000—3.8%, 49th
Unemployment rate (1994): 8.28%, 3rd
   Male: 8.3%, 4th
   Female: 8.0%, 3rd

Total businesses (1991): 28,638
   New business incorps. (est.): 2,256
      Percent of total businesses: 7.88%, 12th
   Business failures (1991): 100
      Percent of total businesses: 0.37%
Agriculture farm income:
   Marketing (1993): $0, 51st
Construction, value of all: $170,000,000
   Per capita: $280.11, 48th
Manufactures:
   Value added: $1,573,000,000
      Per capita: $2,591.86, 42nd
Value of nonfuel mineral production: NA
Retail sales (1993): $3,740,000,000, 50th
   Per household: $15,839, 51st
   Percent increase (1992-93): 7.3%, 27th
Tourism revenues (1994): $3.48 bil.
Foreign exports, in total value (1994): $546,000,000, 45th
   Per capita: $957.89, 35th
Gross state product per person (1993): $63,973.06, 1st
   Percent change (1990-93): 2.70%, 34th
Patents per 100,000 pop. (1993): 10.36, 42nd
Public aid recipients (percent of resident pop. 1993): 15.0%, 1st
Medicaid recipients per 1,000 pop. (1993): 207.25, 1st
Medicare recipients per 1,000 pop. (1993): 134.72, 34th

TRAVEL AND TRANSPORTATION

Motor vehicle registrations (1993): 264,000
   Per 1,000 pop.: 455.96, 51st
Motorcycle registrations (1993): 2,000
   Per 1,000 pop.: 3.45, 51st
Licensed drivers per 1,000 pop. (1993): 623.49, 47th
Deaths from motor vehicle accidents per 100,000 pop. (1993): NA
Public roads & streets (1993):
   Total mileage: 1,107
      Per 1,000 pop.: 1.91, 51st
   Rural mileage: 0
      Per 1,000 pop.: 0, 51st
   Urban mileage: 1,107
      Per 1,000 pop.: 1.91, 49th
   Interstate mileage: 14
      Per 1,000 pop.: 0.02, 51st
Annual vehicle-mi. of travel per person (1993): 6,045, 51st
Mean travel time for workers age 16+ who work away from home: 27.1 min., 2nd

GOVERNMENT

Percent of voting age pop. registered (1994): 66.9%, 20th
Percent of voting age pop. voting (1994): 55.6%, 9th
U.S. Congress, House members (1995): 1 delegate, voting only in committee

LAWS AND REGULATIONS

Legal driving age: 18
Marriage age without parental consent: 18
Divorce residence requirement: 6 mo.

ATTRACTIONS (1995)

Major opera companies: 1
Major symphony orchestras: 1
Major dance companies: 2

Major professional theater companies (non-profit): 2
State appropriations for arts agencies per capita: $3.01, 3rd

SPORTS AND COMPETITION

NCAA teams (Division I): American Univ. Eagles, George Washington Univ. Colonials, Georgetown Univ. Hoyas, Howard Univ. Bison
NBA basketball teams: Washington Bullets (nickname will change to Wizards in 1997), USAir Arena (MD)
NFL football teams: Washington Redskins (NFC), Robert F. Kennedy Memorial Stadium
NHL hockey teams: Washington Capitals, USAir Arena (MD)

FLORIDA

"Florida is today to the United States what the United States was to Europe 100 years ago—a melting pot, a frontier, a place to improve your health or your luck."

Budd Schulberg, author

Florida boasts the nation's oldest European settlement in continuous occupation. A land of sunshine and flowers, Florida has become one of the world's tourist magnets, with Walt Disney World leading the way. The state's gleaming beaches, crystal springs, sophisticated cities, and other recreational opportunities have made it a leading center for retired persons as well as tourists. The quality of its labor and its moderate climate have brought rapidly increasing numbers of industries and businesses. To winter-weary northerners, Florida is an Eden where they might still find Ponce de León's legendary Fountain of Youth. The state has come to increasing recognition of its responsibilities in public safety and in its relationship with a host of newcomers, including many refugees from Cuba, Haiti, and other countries.

SUPERLATIVES

• St. Augustine—the oldest continuously occupied European settlement in North America.
• The nation's fastest growing population in 1980-1990.
• Pan American started flights from Key West to Cuba, bringing commercial aviation to the United States.
• The nation's principal launching pad for space flights—on Cape Canaveral.
• First in the United States in citrus production.
• Walt Disney World in Orlando, luring more visitors than any other single attraction anywhere.
• More than a fourth of all the country's major springs.

MOMENTS IN HISTORY

• Juan Ponce de León sighted present-day Florida on March 27, 1513. Although others knew of the area before, he is generally recognized its "discoverer."

• A 1502 map by Alberto Cantino clearly shows the distinctive Florida outline, but it apparently was not known to Ponce de León.
• Panfilo de Narvaez and his large force entered Tampa Bay in 1528. Only four of his 400 men survived the ensuing hurricanes and other disasters.
• The huge expedition of Hernando de Soto landed at present-day Tampa on May 30, 1539. His letter to the King of Spain is thought to be the first letter mailed from what is today the United States.

> ## So They Say
>
> *"...a country of rivers, havens and islands of such surpassing fruitfulness as cannot by the tongue be expressed."*
>
> Jean Ribaut describing the
> St. Johns River area, 1562

• Pedro Menéndez de Aviles entered a harbor on the Florida peninsula on St. Augustine's feast day. The place he founded there in 1565 took the saint's name, and St. Augustine remains the oldest continuing settlement in the country.
• Englishman Sir Francis Drake captured St. Augustine in 1586 and burned it to the ground, but the Spanish rebuilt the town.
• In 1763 the English returned and captured Cuba from Spain. The British then traded Cuba back to Spain for Florida.
• Florida remained faithful to Britain during the American Revolution, but Spain gave the British the Bahamas and Gibraltar in return for Florida.
• Spain ceded Florida to the United States in 1819, with final ratification two years later. On July 17, 1821, Andrew Jackson received the transfer of Florida from Spain to the United States. The Stars and Stripes then flew over Castillo de San Marcos at St. Augustine, which had never been captured in battle.

• A costly war with the Seminole Indians broke out in the mid-1830s, as the United States sought to "remove" the Seminoles from Florida. It is said that this was the only Indian war never won by the United States, and the $20 million cost was enormous for the time.

• Florida became a state on March 3, 1845, a move delayed by the reluctance of Congress to admit another slave state.

• When the issue of slavery finally led to the Civil War, Florida joined the Confederacy on January 10, 1861.

• Union forces lost the Battle of Olustee on February 20, 1864, the largest battle of the war on Florida soil.

• Florida forces repelled a Union attack on Tallahassee in the Battle of Natural Bridge on March 6, 1865.

So They Say

"From boys of fourteen to men of seventy, from the humble woodsmen to the highest civil dignitaries, all came to the defense of their country."

General William Miller,
on the Battle of Natural Bridge

• Much of Florida's wealth was destroyed by the Civil War, but new development began in earnest in 1881 when Hamilton Disston paid the state $1 million for 4 million acres of state land.

So They Say

"...It is the dream of my life to see this wilderness [Miami] turned into prosperous country and where this tangled mass of vines, brush, trees and rocks now are, to see homes, surrounded by beautiful grassy lawns."

Julia D. Tuttle, an associate of
Henry Flagler, 1890

• Florida became the main point of embarkation for troops and supplies in the Spanish-American War in 1898, expanding business there.

• Florida promoter Henry Flagler built a railroad from Miami to Key West, going "out to sea" on a series of bridges built from island to island in the Florida Keys. The first train reached Key West in 1912.

• The great Florida land boom that began in 1919 was the largest in the country to that time. Carl Fisher founded Miami Beach in that year, and other promoters brought hosts of investors to the state.

So They Say

The college was founded "...with five girls, a small cabin, $1.50 and a million dollars' worth of faith. We used charred splinters as pencils. For ink we mashed up elderberries."

Mary McLeod Bethune, on the founding of Bethune-Cookman College in 1904

• The hurricane of 1926 brought 16 hours of destruction to the Miami area.

• In February 1933 at Miami, President-elect Franklin D. Roosevelt escaped an assassination attempt, but Mayor Anton Cermak of Chicago was fatally shot in the attack.

• During World War II, Florida became one of the greatest wartime military and transportation centers ever known.

• In 1962, John Glenn soared into space from Cape Canaveral, becoming the first American in orbit.

• The early 1980s posed great problems for the state in accommodating the Cuban boat people, refugees from the troubles of their homeland.

• On January 28, 1986, the space shuttle *Challenger* exploded after liftoff from Cape Canaveral, killing the seven persons aboard, including Christa McAuliffe, the first teacher in space.

• In August 1992, Hurricane Andrew devastated southern Florida, claiming more than 60 lives and causing damage estimated as high as $30 billion.

THAT'S INTERESTING

• During the hurricane of 1926, the barometer at Miami reached the country's record low, causing hundreds to faint from lack of oxygen.

• When a British captain's ear was cut off in a war between Spain and England, the conflict, which was waged in Florida, became known as the War of Jenkins's Ear.

• The demand was so great for Florida property during the great land boom that investors paid up to $25,000 for lots that had not yet been dredged up from the ocean.

• Once endangered, alligators increased to become something of a nuisance, sometimes even swallowing small pets. The stomach of one was found to contain a pickle jar, dog collar, and several golf balls.

• After fishing, Florida's anhinga, or water turkey, must dry its feathers in the sun. These birds lie in groups with wings outspread, looking much like a wash left out to dry.

FLORIDA NOTABLES

John James Audubon (Haiti, 1785-1851), ornithologist/artist. **Jacqueline Cochran** (Pensacola, 1910?-1980), aviator/business leader. **Henry Morrison Flagler** (Hopewell, NY, 1830-1913), capitalist/promoter. **John Gorrie** (Charleston, SC, 1803-1855), physician/inventor. **Edmund Kirby-Smith** (St. Augustine, 1824-1893), army officer. **Osceola** (in Georgia, 1804?-1838), Indian leader. **Marjorie Kinnan Rawlings** (Washington, D.C., 1896-1953), writer.

GENERAL

Admitted to statehood: March 3, 1845
Origin of name: Named by Ponce de Leon on *Pascua Florida*, "Flowery Easter," on Easter Sunday, 1513
Capital: Tallahassee
Nickname: Sunshine State
Motto: In God we trust
Bird: Mockingbird
Flower: Orange blossom
Gem: Moonstone
Song: "Swanee River" (*Old Folks at Home*)
Tree: Sabal palmetto palm

THE LAND

Area: 59,988 sq. mi., 23rd
  Land: 53,997 sq. mi., 26th
  Water: 5,991 sq. mi., 7th
    Inland water: 4,683 sq. mi., 4th
    Coastal water: 1,308 sq. mi., 6th
Topography: Land is flat or rolling to highest point, in the NW
Number of counties: 67
Geographic center: Hernando, 12 mi. NNW of Brooksville
Length: 500 mi.; width: 160 mi.
Highest point: 345 ft. (in Walton County), 51st
Lowest point: sea level (Atlantic Ocean), 3rd
Mean elevation: 100 ft., 49th
Coastline: 1,350 mi., 2nd
Shoreline: 8,426 mi., 2nd

CLIMATE AND ENVIRONMENT

Temp., highest: 109 deg. on June 29, 1931, at Monticello; lowest: −2 deg. on Feb. 13, 1899, at Tallahassee
Monthly average: highest: 91.7 deg., 15th; lowest: 39.9 deg., 50th; spread (high to low): 51.8 deg., 49th
Hazardous waste sites (1993): 55, 6th
Endangered species: Mammals: 11—Gray bat, Indiana bat, Key deer, West Indian manatee, Anastasia Island beach mouse, Choctawhatchee beach mouse, Key Largo cotton mouse, Perdido Key beach mouse, Florida panther, Lower Keys rabbit, Key Largo woodrat; birds: 7—American peregrine falcon, Everglade snail kite, Piping plover, Cape Sable seaside sparrow, Florida grasshopper sparrow, Wood stock, Redcockaded woodpecker; reptiles: 5; amphibians: none; fishes: 1; invertebrates: 1; plants: 31

MAJOR CITIES
POPULATION, 1990
PERCENTAGE INCREASE, 1980-90

Hialeah, 188,004—29.43%
Jacksonville, 635,230—17.44%
Miami, 358,548—3.42%
Saint Petersburg, 238,629— −0.01%
Tampa, 280,015—3.11%

THE PEOPLE

Population (1995): 14,165,570, 4th
  Percent change (1990-95): 9.5%, 12th
Population (2000 proj.): 15,313,000, 4th
  Percent change (1990-2000): 18.36%, 11th
Per sq. mi. (1994): 258.4, 11th
Percent in metro. area (1992): 93.0%, 7th
Foreign born: 1,663,000, 3rd
  Percent: 12.9%, 4th
Top three ancestries reported:
  German, 18.63%
  Irish, 14.68%
  English, 14.27%
White: 10,749,285, 83.08%, 29th
Black: 1,759,534, 13.60%, 16th
Native American: 36,335, 0.28%, 34th
Asian, Pacific Isle: 154,302, 1.19%, 23rd
Other races: 238,407, 1.84%, 20th

Hispanic origin: 1,574,143, 12.17%, 7th

Percent over 5 yrs. speaking language other than English at home: 17.3%, 8th

Percent males: 48.40%, 37th; percent females: 51.60%, 15th

Percent never married: 22.6%, 44th

Marriages per 1,000 (1993): 10.4, 11th

Divorces per 1,000 (1993): 6.1, 9th

Median age: 36.4

Under 5 years (1994): 6.89%, 41st

Under 18 years (1994): 23.38%, 49th

65 years & older (1994): 18.4%, 1st

Percent increase among the elderly (1990-94): 8.51%, 17th

OF VITAL IMPORTANCE

Live births per 1,000 pop. (1993): 14.1, 35th

Infant mortality rate per 1,000 births (1992): 8.8, 20th

Rate for blacks (1990): 16.2, 23rd

Rate for whites (1990): 7.6, 33rd

Births to unmarried women, % of total (1992): 34.2%, 10th

Births to teenage mothers, % of total (1992): 13.5%, 19th

Abortions (1992): 84,680, 4th

Rate per 1,000 women 14-44 years old: 30.0, 8th

Percent change (1988-92): –5%, 20th

Average lifetime (1979-81): 74.00, 22nd

Deaths per 1,000 pop. (1993): 10.7, 4th

Causes of death per 100,000 pop.:

Accidents & adverse effects (1992): 36.1, 23rd

Atherosclerosis (1991): 7.8, 17th

Cancer (1991): 260.9, 1st

Cerebrovascular diseases (1992): 64.9, 14th

Chronic liver diseases & cirrhosis (1991): 13.4, 3rd

Chronic obstructive pulmonary diseases (1992): 48.6, 5th

Diabetes mellitus (1992): 22.8, 11th

Diseases of heart (1992): 351 0, 4th

Pneumonia, flu (1991): 25.2, 41st

Suicide (1992): 15.0, 10th

KEEPING WELL

Active nonfederal physicians per 100,000 pop. (1993): 215, 16th

Dentists per 100,000 (1991): 51, 31st

Nurses per 100,000 (1992): 707, 29th

Hospitals per 100,000 (1993): 1.62, 41st

Admissions per 1,000 (1993): 124.26, 20th

Occupancy rate per 100 beds (1993): 60.4, 32nd

Average cost per patient per day (1993): $940, 15th

Average cost per stay (1993): $6,169, 15th

Average stay (1992): 7.0 days, 29th

AIDS cases (adult, 1993): 10,931; per 100,000: 79.9, 3rd

HIV infection, not yet AIDS (1993): NA

Other notifiable diseases:

Gonorrhea: 328.1, 15th

Measles: 4.7, 23rd

Syphilis: 115.9, 4th

Tuberculosis: 14.2, 5th

Pop. without health insur. (1991-93): 19.4%, 8th

HOUSEHOLDS BY TYPE

Total households (1994): 5,456,000

Percent change (1990-94): 6.3%, 16th

Per 1,000 pop.: 391.03, 2nd

Percent of households 65 yrs. and over: 28.98%, 1st

Persons per household (1994): 2.50, 50th

Family households: 3,511,825

Percent of total: 68.39%, 44th

Nonfamily households: 1,623,044

Percent of total: 31.61%, 8th

Pop. living in group quarters: 307,461

Percent of pop.: 2.38%, 39th

LIVING QUARTERS

Total housing units: 6,100,262

Persons per unit: 2.12, 49th

Occupied housing units: 5,134,869

Percent of total units: 84.17%, 44th

Persons per unit: 2.44, 48th

Percent of units with over 1 person per room: 5.79%, 12th

Owner-occupied units: 3,452,160

Percent of total units: 56.59%, 36th

Percent of occupied units: 67.23%, 27th

Persons per unit: 2.49, 51st

Median value: $77,100, 21st

Renter-occupied units: 1,682,709

Percent of total units: 27.58%, 35th

Percent of occupied units: 32.77%, 25th

Persons per unit: 2.39, 18th

Median contract rent: $402, 15th

Rental vacancy rate: 12.4%, 6th

Mobile home, trailer & other as a percent of occupied housing units: 15.99%, 11th

Persons in emergency shelters for homeless persons: 7,110, 0.055%, 20th

Persons visible in street locations: 3,189, 0.0246%, 6th

Persons in shelters for abused women: 601, 0.0046%, 31st

Nursing home population: 80,298, 0.62%, 33rd

CRIME INDEX PER 100,000 (1992-93)

Total reported: 8,351.0, 2nd
Violent: 1,206.0, 2nd
  Murder and nonnegligent manslaughter: 8.9, 19th
  Aggravated assault: 785.7, 2nd
  Robbery: 357.6, 6th
  Forcible rape: 53.8, 8th
Property: 7,145.0, 2nd
  Burglary: 1,835.4, 2nd
  Larceny, theft: 4,413.9, 3rd
  Motor vehicle theft: 895.7, 3rd
Drug abuse violations (1990): 506.1, 8th
Child-abuse rate per 1,000 children (1993): 25.87, 8th

TEACHING AND LEARNING

Pop. 3 and over enrolled in school: 2,926,662
  Percent of pop.: 23.5%, 51st
Public elementary & secondary schools (1992-93): 2,594
  Total enrollment (1992): 1,981,407
    Percent of total pop.: 14.70%, 46th
  Teachers (1992): 107,590
    Percent of pop.: 0.80%, 50th
  Pupil/teacher ratio (fall 1992): 18.4, 10th
  Teachers' avg. salary (1992-93): $33,315, 28th
  Expenditure per capita (1990-91): $3,412.17, 26th
  Expenditure per pupil (1991-92): $5,243, 25th
Percent of graduates taking SAT (1993): 52%, 20th
  Mean SAT verbal scores: 416, 42nd
  Mean SAT mathematical scores: 466, 42nd
Percent of graduates taking ACT (1995): 34%, 28th
  Mean ACT scores: 20.7, 32nd
Percent of pop. over 25 completing:
  Less than 9th grade: 9.5%, 24th
  High school: 74.4%, 37th
  College degree(s): 18.3%, 30th
Higher education, institutions (1993-94): 108
  Enrollment (1992): 618,285
    Percent of pop.: 4.58%, 48th

White non-Hispanic (1992): 435,987
  Percent of enroll.: 70.52%, 42nd
Black non-Hispanic (1992): 72,750
  Percent of enroll.: 11.77%, 15th
Hispanic (1992): 75,270
  Percent of enroll.: 12.17%, 5th
Asian/Pacific Islander (1992): 15,205
  Percent of enroll.: 2.46%, 21st
American Indian/AK native (1992): 2,287
  Percent of enroll.: 0.37%, 28th
Nonresident alien (1992): 16,786
  Percent of enroll.: 2.71%, 23rd
Female (1992): 343,224
  Percent of enroll.: 55.51%, 21st
Pub. institutions (1993-94): 39
  Enrollment (1992): 511,226
  Percent of enroll.: 82.68%, 27th
Private institutions (1993-94): 69
  Enrollment (1992): 107,059
  Percent of enroll.: 17.32%, 25th
Tuition, public institution (avg., 1993-94): $5,855, 25th
Tuition, private institution (avg., 1993-94): $13,722, 20th
Public library systems: 119
  Books & serial vol. per capita: 1.54, 49th
  Govt. expenditure per capita: $13.88, 29th

LAW ENFORCEMENT, COURTS, AND PRISONS

Police protection, corrections, judicial and legal functions expenditures (1992): $5,153,000,000
  Per capita: $382, 6th
Police per 10,000 pop. (1993): 24.32, 11th
Prisoners (state & fed.) per 100,000 pop. (1993): 3,864.78, 15th
  Percent change (1992-93): 9.8%, 8th
Death penalty: yes, by electrocution
  Under sentence of death (1993): 324, 3rd
  Executed (1993): 3

RELIGION, NUMBER AND PERCENT OF POPULATION

Agnostic: 100,717—1.00%, 10th
Buddhist: 10,072—0.10%, 17th
Christian: 8,480,362—84.20%, 38th
Hindu: 10,072—0.10%, 10th
Jewish: 362,581—3.60%, 3rd
Muslim: 10,072—0.10%, 22nd
Unitarian: 30,215—0.30%, 15th
Other: 130,932—1.30%, 24th
None: 725,162—7.20%, 20th
Refused to answer: 211,506—2.10%, 28th

MAKING A LIVING

Personal income per capita (1994): $21,677, 21st

Percent increase (1993-94): 5.0%, 25th

Disposable personal income per capita (1994): $19,076, 19th

Median income of households (1993): $28,550, 36th

Percent of pop. below poverty level (1993): 17.8%, 11th

Percent 65 and over (1990): 10.8%, 30th

Expenditure for energy per person (1992): $1,510, 51st

ECONOMY

Civilian labor force (1994): 6,824,000
Percent of total pop.: 48.91%, 41st
Percent 65 and over (1990): 3.25%, 13th
Percent female: 46.37%, 23rd
Percent job growth (1980-90): 50.14%, 2nd
Major employer industries (1994):
Agriculture: 166,000—2.7%, 20th
Construction: 325,000—5.3%, 8th
Finance, insurance, & real estate: 429,000—7.0%, 8th
Government: 913,000—14.8%, 30th
Manufacturing: 552,000—9.0%, 42nd
Service: 1,578,000—25.6%, 5th
Trade: 1,335,000—21.6%, 2nd
Transportation, communications, public utilities: 361,000—5.9%, 13th
Unemployment rate (1994): 6.57%, 11th
Male: 6.3%, 15th
Female: 6.9%, 8th
Total businesses (1991): 415,975
New business incorps. (1991): 81,083
Percent of total businesses: 19.49%, 3rd
Business failures (1991): 3,665
Percent of total businesses: 0.88%
Agriculture farm income:
Marketing (1993): $5,750,000,000, 8th
Average per farm: $147,435.90, 6th
Leading products (1993): Greenhouse, oranges, tomatoes, cane/sugar
Average value land & build. per acre (1994): $2,205, 8th
Percent increase (1990-94): 5.76%, 41st
Govt. payments (1993): $111,000,000, 28th
Average per farm: $2,846.15, 31st

Construction, value of all: $12,007,000,000
Per capita: $928.05, 4th
Manufactures:
Value added: $29,793,000,000
Per capita: $2,302.76, 45th
Leading products: Electric and electronic equipment, transportation equipment, foods, printing & publishing, machinery
Value of nonfuel mineral production (1994): $1,468,000,000, 6th
Leading mineral products: Phosphate, petroleum, stone
Retail sales (1993): $129,996,000,000, 3rd
Per household: $23,648, 8th
Percent increase (1992-93): 7.9%, 17th
Tourism revenues (1994): $33.0 bil.
Foreign exports, in total value (1994): $16,287,000,000, 8th
Per capita: $1,167.28, 29th
Gross state product per person (1993): $19,190.25, 38th
Percent change (1990-93): 4.08%, 18th
Patents per 100,000 pop. (1993): 15.40, 27th
Public aid recipients (percent of resident pop. 1993): 7.0%, 20th
Medicaid recipients per 1,000 pop. (1993): 127.13, 19th
Medicare recipients per 1,000 pop. (1993): 181.70, 1st

TRAVEL AND TRANSPORTATION

Motor vehicle registrations (1993): 10,170,000
Per 1,000 pop.: 740.93, 32nd
Motorcycle registrations (1993): 189,000
Per 1,000 pop.: 13.77, 31st
Licensed drivers per 1,000 pop. (1993): 784.06, 1st
Deaths from motor vehicle accidents per 100,000 pop. (1993): 19.62, 17th
Public roads & streets (1993):
Total mileage: 112,808
Per 1,000 pop.: 8.22, 41st
Rural mileage: 63,630
Per 1,000 pop.: 4.64, 42nd
Urban mileage: 49,178
Per 1,000 pop.: 3.58, 11th
Interstate mileage: 1,443
Per 1,000 pop.: 0.11, 41st
Annual vehicle-mi. of travel per person (1993): 8,779, 35th
Mean travel time for workers age 16+ who work away from home: 21.8 min., 15th

GOVERNMENT

Percent of voting age pop. registered (1994): 55.5%, 47th

Percent of voting age pop. voting (1994): 42.3%, 38th

Percent of voting age pop. voting for U.S. representatives (1994): 26.3%, 49th

State legislators, total (1995): 160, 18th

Women members (1992): 30

Percent of legislature: 18.8%, 21st

U.S. Congress, House members (1995): 23

Change (1985-95): +4

Revenues (1993):

State govt.: $33,216,000,000

Per capita: $2,419.93, 45th

Parimutuel & amusement taxes & lotteries, revenue per capita: $154.74, 8th

Expenditures (1993):

State govt.: $30,103,000,000

Per capita: $2,193.14, 47th

Debt outstanding (1993): $13,635,000,000

Per capita: $993.37, 35th

LAWS AND REGULATIONS

Legal driving age: 16

Marriage age without parental consent: 18

Divorce residence requirement: 6 mo.

ATTRACTIONS (1995)

Major opera companies: 5

Major symphony orchestras: 7

Major dance companies: 2

Major professional theater companies (non-profit): 1

State appropriations for arts agencies per capita: $1.80, 8th

State Fair in early to mid-February at Tampa

SPORTS AND COMPETITION

NCAA teams (Division I): Bethune-Cookman College Wildcats, Florida A&M Univ. Rattlers, Florida Atlantic Univ. Owls, Florida International Univ. Golden Panthers, Jacksonville Univ. Dolphins, Stetson Univ. Hatters, Univ. of Central Florida Knights, Univ. of Florida Gators, Univ. of Miami Hurricanes, Univ. of South Florida Bulls

Major league baseball teams: Florida Marlins (NL East), Joe Robbie Stadium; Tampa Bay Rays to begin play in 1998

NBA basketball teams: Orlando Magic, Orlando Arena; Miami Heat, Miami Arena

NFL football teams: Jacksonville Jaguars (AFC), Jacksonville Municipal Stadium; Miami Dolphins (AFC), Joe Robbie Stadium; Tampa Bay Buccaneers (NFC), Tampa Stadium

NHL hockey teams: Florida Panthers, Miami Arena; Tampa Bay Lightning, ThunderDome (scheduled to begin play at Ice Palace, October 1996)

GEORGIA

"...the transportation, manufacturing, and marketing hub of the Deep South...the charm of the South as symbolized by Greek porticos, Doric columns, and romantic traditions. Here is a land where modern fortresses [Air Force bases] are not far from communities where sacred harp singing is still carried on...a land of forested mountains, deep lakes, and clear mountain streams, contrasted with miles of sunny beaches and sun-drenched isles, with still further contrast in the misty swamps where alligators splash and exotic tropical birds preen their elaborate plumage."

President Jimmy Carter

Today the commercial leader of its region, Georgia was the only colony to be founded as a refuge for poor and deserving people. Invented in Georgia, the cotton gin revolutionized the South. The state ranks first in the production of peanuts and pecans, lima beans, and pimiento peppers. It leads the nation in production of fine china clays. Savannah is the nation's foremost cotton port, and is often called "the nation's most beautiful city." Atlanta has become the leading transportation center of the Southeast. Georgia gave Coca-Cola to the world, and Atlanta native Margaret Mitchell was the author of one of the world's best-known novels, *Gone With the Wind.* During the mid-1990s, much attention was focused on the 1996 Summer Olympics, hosted by Atlanta.

SUPERLATIVES

• First steamship to cross the Atlantic—the *City of Savannah* sailing from Georgia.
• Site of the first U.S. gold rush, at Dahlonga.
• Home of the cotton gin.
• First U.S. source of aluminum.

MOMENTS IN HISTORY

• In 1540 the great expedition of Hernando de Soto entered what is now Georgia and may have spent a month at the site of Rome. The visit left a never-forgiven legacy of cruelty to the Indians.
• Beginning in 1565, Spaniard Pedro Menéndez de Aviles established forts and missions in the area.
• English and French pirates plagued the Spanish settlements beginning in 1670.

• The pirate Blackbeard made his headquarters on Blackbeard Island in 1716, becoming a de facto lord of the area.
• On February 12, 1733, James Oglethorpe first arrived at present-day Savannah to claim and settle the land he called Georgia in honor of the King of England. He and 125 colonists pitched their tents and founded the last of the original 13 British colonies.

> ### So They Say
> The Georgia charter provided a grant for "...the land lying between the Savannah and Altamaha rivers and westward from the sources to the South Sea" for the purpose of "settling poor persons of London."

• In 1736, Oglethorpe arrived again with a large group of colonists, in "the Great Embarkation." They laid out the city, including the neat pattern of square parks that still distinguish Savannah.
• When the Spanish attempted to take the colony, Oglethorpe's forces won the Battle of Bloody Marsh on July 7, 1742. This small struggle has been called "one of the decisive battles of world history" because it kept the Spanish from pressing their claims northward on the coast.
• In 1752, Georgia became a crown colony.
• During the Revolution, the British captured Savannah in a surprise attack on December 29, 1778.
• On July 11, 1782, Savannah was recaptured by American General Anthony Wayne, and the Revolution was over in Georgia.

• Georgia unanimously ratified the U.S. Constitution and became the fourth state on January 2, 1788.

• After the War of 1812, Georgia entered its "Golden Age of Prosperity."

• In 1838 the Indians remaining in Georgia were forced from their lands and sent west over the "Trail of Tears."

• On January 19, 1861, Georgia joined the Confederacy.

• During the Civil War one of the most important Union aims was to take the state. After many unsuccessful efforts, Union General William Tecumseh Sherman, "marching through Georgia," captured and burned Atlanta and left almost complete destruction in his subsequent path to the sea, capturing Savannah on December 22, 1864.

• After a long, harsh Reconstruction period, Georgia was readmitted to the Union on July 15, 1870.

• More than 3,000 Georgia men volunteered to serve in the Spanish-American War in 1898.

• Although Atlanta suffered a disastrous fire in 1917, the area remained a major military training center during World War I.

• Georgia continued as a center of World War II activity, and the state drew world attention with the death of President Franklin D. Roosevelt at Warm Springs on April 12, 1945.

• Jimmy Carter was inaugurated in 1977, the first U.S. president from the state.

THAT'S INTERESTING

• Rivalry between Indian tribes did not always lead to war. Some disputes between Cherokee and Creek groups were settled by a ball game.

• In the 1740s, Mary Jones was the skillful and successful captain of Fort Wimberley during a Spanish attack.

• Polio victim Franklin D. Roosevelt often visited and enjoyed the waters of Warm Springs. That small community gained world fame when he became president.

• The sculpture created by Gutzon Borglum on the side of Stone Mountain was so grand that Borglum once hosted 20 guests at breakfast on the shoulder of the Robert E. Lee carving. The work was later destroyed to make way for a smaller monument.

• One of the famed incidents of the Civil War was later known as "the Great Locomotive Chase," when Confederate forces pursued and retook a captured locomotive.

NOTABLE NATIVES

James Nathaniel (Jim) Brown (Saint Simons Island, 1936-), football player. **Asa Griggs Candler** (near Villa Rica, 1851-1929), businessman/philanthropist. **James Earl (Jimmy) Carter** (Plains, 1924-), U.S. president. **Tyrus Raymond (Ty) Cobb** (Narrows, 1886-1961), baseball player. **John Charles Frémont** (Savannah, 1813-1890), soldier. **Joel Chandler Harris** (Eatonton, 1848-1908), journalist/author. **Robert Tyre (Bobby) Jones** (Atlanta, 1902-1971), golfer. **Martin Luther King, Jr.** (Atlanta, 1929-1968), religious leader/social reformer. **Sidney Lanier** (Macon, 1842-1881), poet/critic. **Crawford Williamson Long** (Danielsville, 1815-1878), surgeon. **Carson Smith McCullers** (Columbus, 1917-1967), author. **Margaret Mitchell** (Atlanta, 1900-1949), author. **Jack Roosevelt (Jackie) Robinson** (Cairo, 1919-1972), baseball player. **Alexander Hamilton Stephens** (Wilkes County, later Taliaferro County, 1812-1883), statesman.

GENERAL

Admitted to statehood: January 2, 1788
Origin of name: For King George II of England by James Oglethorpe, colonial administrator, 1732
Capital: Atlanta
Nickname: Empire State of the South, Peach State
Motto: Wisdom, justice, and moderation
Bird: Brown thrasher
Fish: Largemouth bass
Flower: Cherokee rose
Song: "Georgia on My Mind"
Tree: Live oak

THE LAND

Area: 58,977 sq. mi., 24th
    Land: 57,919 sq. mi., 21st
    Water: 1,058 sq. mi., 28th
        Inland water: 1,011 sq. mi., 20th
        Coastal water: 47 sq. mi., 18th
Topography: Most southerly of the Blue Ridge Mtns. cover NE and N central; central piedmont extends to the fall line of rivers; coastal plain levels to the coast flatlands.

Number of counties: 159
Geographic center: Twiggs, 18 mi. SE of Macon
Length: 300 mi.; width: 230 mi.
Highest point: 4,784 ft. (Brasstown Bald), 25th
Lowest point: sea level (Atlantic Ocean), 3rd
Mean elevation: 600 ft., 37th
Coastline: 100 mi., 16th
Shoreline: 2,344 mi., 12th

CLIMATE AND ENVIRONMENT

Temp., highest: 112 deg. on July 24. 1953, at Louisville; lowest: −17 deg. on Jan. 27, 1940, at CCC Camp F-16
Monthly average: highest: 92.2 deg., 12th; lowest: 32.6 deg., 44th; spread (high to low): 59.6 deg., 46th
Hazardous waste sites (1993): 13, 27th
Endangered species: Mammals: 3—Gray bat, Indiana bat, West Indian manatee; birds: 3—American peregrine falcon, Wood stock, Red-cockaded woodpecker; reptiles: 3; amphibians: none; fishes: 2; invertebrates: none; plants: 12

MAJOR CITIES, POPULATION PERCENTAGE INCREASE (1980-90)

Albany, 78,122—4.97%
Atlanta, 394,017— −7.29%
Columbus, 178,681—5.45%
Macon, 106,612— -8.78%
Savannah, 137,560— −2.89%

THE PEOPLE

Population (1995): 7,200,882, 10th
 Percent change (1990-95): 11.2%, 7th
Population (2000 proj.): 7,637,000, 10th
 Percent change (1990-2000): 17.89%, 13th
Per sq. mi. (1994): 121.8, 21st
Percent in metro. area (1992): 67.7%, 30th
Foreign born: 173,000, 16th
 Percent: 2.7%, 29th
Top three ancestries reported:
 African, 21.94%
 Irish, 14.99%
 English, 13.74%
White: 4,600,148, 71.01%, 44th
Black: 1,746,565, 26.96%, 5th
Native American: 13,348, 0.21%, 41st
Asian, Pacific Isle: 75,781, 1.17%, 24th
Other races: 42,374, 0.65%, 32nd
Hispanic origin: 108,922, 1.68%, 33rd

Percent over 5 yrs. speaking language other than English at home: 4.8%, 39th
Percent males: 48.54%, 28th; percent females: 51.46%, 24th
Percent never married: 26.2%, 22nd
Marriages per 1,000 (1993): 8.9, 20th
Divorces per 1,000 (1993): 5.5, 11th
Median age: 31.6
Under 5 years (1994): 7.78%, 11th
Under 18 years (1994): 26.83%, 18th
65 years & older (1994): 10.1%, 48th
Percent increase among the elderly (1990-94): 8.52%, 16th

OF VITAL IMPORTANCE

Live births per 1,000 pop. (1993): 16.2, 11th
Infant mortality rate per 1,000 births (1992): 10.3, 5th
 Rate for blacks (1990): 18.0, 10th
 Rate for whites (1990): 9.1, 5th
Births to unmarried women, % of total (1992): 35.0%, 7th
Births to teenage mothers, % of total (1992): 16.2%, 12th
Abortions (1992): 39,680, 11th
 Rate per 1,000 women 14-44 years old: 24.0, 17th
 Percent change (1988-92): 2%, 10th
Average lifetime (1979-81): 72.22, 47th
Deaths per 1,000 pop. (1993): 8.1, 36th
Causes of death per 100,000 pop.:
 Accidents & adverse effects (1992): 38.9, 19th
 Atherosclerosis (1991): 6.0, 36th
 Cancer (1991): 174.2, 42nd
 Cerebrovascular diseases (1992): 54.4, 32nd
 Chronic liver diseases & cirrhosis (1991): 8.7, 32nd
 Chronic obstructive pulmonary diseases (1992): 31.2, 43rd
 Diabetes mellitus (1992): 14.5, 47th
 Diseases of heart (1992): 243.4, 34th
 Pneumonia, flu (1991): 28.6, 31st
 Suicide (1992): 12.0, 33rd

KEEPING WELL

Active nonfederal physicians per 100,000 pop. (1993): 182, 35th
Dentists per 100,000 (1991): 46, 41st
Nurses per 100,000 (1992): 647, 39th
Hospitals per 100,000 (1993): 2.30, 24th
 Admissions per 1,000 (1993): 123.60, 21st
 Occupancy rate per 100 beds (1993): 63.4, 23rd

Average cost per patient per day (1993): $775, 33rd

Average cost per stay (1993): $5,554, 31st

Average stay (1992): 6.7 days, 37th

AIDS cases (adult, 1993): 2,789; per 100,000: 40.3, 13th

HIV infection, not yet AIDS (1993): NA

Other notifiable diseases:
Gonorrhea: 756.7, 2nd
Measles: 5.6, 19th
Syphilis: 142.2, 2nd
Tuberculosis: 12.3, 12th

Pop. without health insur. (1991-93): 17.2%, 13th

HOUSEHOLDS BY TYPE

Total households (1994): 2,581,000
Percent change (1990-94): 9.1%, 7th
Per 1,000 pop.: 365.84, 39th
Percent of households 65 yrs. and over: 17.47%, 49th
Persons per household (1994): 2.67, 12th
Family households: 1,713,072
Percent of total: 72.38%, 12th
Nonfamily households: 653,543
Percent of total: 27.62%, 40th
Pop. living in group quarters: 173,633
Percent of pop.: 2.68%, 29th

LIVING QUARTERS

Total housing units: 2,638,418
Persons per unit: 2.46, 14th
Occupied housing units: 2,366,615
Percent of total units: 89.70%, 24th
Persons per unit: 2.63, 11th
Percent of units with over 1 person per room: 4.05%, 16th
Owner-occupied units: 1,536,759
Percent of total units: 58.25%, 30th
Percent of occupied units: 64.93%, 37th
Persons per unit: 2.76, 20th
Median value: $71,300, 23rd
Renter-occupied units: 829,856
Percent of total units: 31.45%, 17th
Percent of occupied units: 35.07%, 17th
Persons per unit: 2.49, 10th
Median contract rent: $344, 23rd
Rental vacancy rate: 12.2%, 7th
Mobile home, trailer & other as a percent of occupied housing units: 13.85%, 18th
Persons in emergency shelters for homeless persons: 3,930, 0.061%, 17th
Persons visible in street locations: 450, 0.0069%, 24th

Persons in shelters for abused women: 192, 0.0030%, 44th

Nursing home population: 36,549, 0.56%, 41st

CRIME INDEX PER 100,000 (1992-93)

Total reported: 6,193.0, 9th
Violent: 723.1, 18th
Murder and nonnegligent manslaughter: 11.4, 9th
Aggravated assault: 428.3, 21st
Robbery: 248.0, 10th
Forcible rape: 35.4, 29th
Property: 5,469.8, 7th
Burglary: 1,307.3, 9th
Larceny, theft: 3,568.7, 11th
Motor vehicle theft: 593.8, 15th
Drug abuse violations (1990): 271.9, 22nd
Child-abuse rate per 1,000 children (1993): 30.16, 2nd

TEACHING AND LEARNING

Pop. 3 and over enrolled in school: 1,643,859
Percent of pop.: 26.6%, 32nd
Public elementary & secondary schools (1992-93): 1,724
Total enrollment (1992): 1,207,186
Percent of total pop.: 17.82%, 15th
Teachers (1992): 68,942
Percent of pop.: 1.02%, 27th
Pupil/teacher ratio (fall 1992): 18.0, 13th
Teachers' avg. salary (1992-93): $32,535, 31st
Expenditure per capita (1990-91): $3,213.36, 32nd
Expenditure per pupil (1991-92): $4,375, 41st
Percent of graduates taking SAT (1993): 65%, 13th
Mean SAT verbal scores: 399, 50th
Mean SAT mathematical scores: 445, 49th
Percent of graduates taking ACT (1995): 18%, 32nd
Mean ACT scores: 20.2, 40th
Percent of pop. over 25 completing:
Less than 9th grade: 12.0%, 13th
High school: 70.9%, 42nd
College degree(s): 19.3%, 26th
Higher education, institutions (1993-94): 116
Enrollment (1992): 293,162
Percent of pop.: 4.33%, 50th
White non-Hispanic (1992): 211,081
Percent of enroll.: 72.00%, 41st

Black non-Hispanic (1992): 65,261
  Percent of enroll.: 22.26%, 4th
Hispanic (1992): 3,838
  Percent of enroll.: 1.31%, 36th
Asian/Pacific Islander (1992): 5,785
  Percent of enroll.: 1.97%, 25th
American Indian/AK native (1992): 762
  Percent of enroll.: 0.26%, 42nd
Nonresident alien (1992): 6,435
  Percent of enroll.: 2.20%, 35th
Female (1992): 162,785
  Percent of enroll.: 55.53%, 20th
Pub. institutions (1993-94): 72
  Enrollment (1992): 232,634
  Percent of enroll.: 79.35%, 34th
Private institutions (1993-94): 44
  Enrollment (1992): 60,528
  Percent of enroll.: 20.65%, 18th
Tuition, public institution (avg., 1993-94):
  $5,075, 40th
Tuition, private institution (avg., 1993-94):
  $13,066, 24th
Public library systems: 53
  Books & serial vol. per capita: 1.70, 46th
  Govt. expenditure per capita: $8.13, 47th

LAW ENFORCEMENT, COURTS, AND PRISONS

Police protection, corrections, judicial and
  legal functions expenditures (1992):
  $1,806,000,000
  Per capita: $267, 23rd
Police per 10,000 pop. (1993): 28.12, 6th
Prisoners (state & fed.) per 100,000 pop.
  (1993): 4,025.35, 13th
  Percent change (1992-93): 9.9%, 6th
Death penalty: yes, by electrocution
  Under sentence of death (1993): 96, 12th
  Executed (1993): 2

RELIGION, NUMBER AND PERCENT OF POPULATION

Agnostic: 14,253—0.30%, 37th
Buddhist: 4,751—0.10%, 17th
Christian: 4,328,082—91.10%, 7th
Hindu: 9,502—0.20%, 3rd
Jewish: 23,755—0.50%, 27th
Muslim: 14,253—0.30%, 9th
Unitarian: 4,751—0.10%, 31st
Other: 66,513—1.40%, 20th
None: 218,542—4.60%, 43rd
Refused to answer: 66,513—1.40%, 44th

MAKING A LIVING

Personal income per capita (1994): $20,251,
  31st
  Percent increase (1993-94): 5.2%, 21st
Disposable personal income per capita (1994):
  $17,677, 31st
Median income of households (1993):
  $31,663, 22nd
Percent of pop. below poverty level (1993):
  13.5%, 24th
  Percent 65 and over (1990): 20.4%, 8th
Expenditure for energy per person (1992):
  $1,861, 31st

ECONOMY

Civilian labor force (1994): 3,566,000
  Percent of total pop.: 50.55%, 31st
  Percent 65 and over (1990): 2.08%,
  42nd
  Percent female: 47.00%, 15th
Percent job growth (1980-90): 36.84%, 5th
Major employer industries (1994):
  Agriculture: 90,000—2.7%, 20th
  Construction: 149,000—4.6%, 18th
  Finance, insurance, & real estate:
  178,000—5.4%, 23rd
  Government: 544,000—16.6%, 21st
  Manufacturing: 530,000—16.2%, 21st
  Service: 695,000—21.3%, 23rd
  Trade: 597,000—16.3%, 50th
  Transportation, communications, public
  utilities: 203,000—6.2%, 9th
Unemployment rate (1994): 5.19%, 33rd
  Male: 5.0%, 34th
  Female: 5.4%, 24th
Total businesses (1991): 191,583
  New business incorps. (1991): 18,098
  Percent of total businesses: 9.45%, 8th
  Business failures (1991): 1,944
  Percent of total businesses: 1.01%
Agriculture farm income:
  Marketing (1993): $4,211,000,000, 15th
  Average per farm: $93,577.78, 18th
  Leading products (1993): Broilers, peanuts,
  cattle, eggs
  Average value land & build. per acre
  (1994): $983, 23rd
  Percent increase (1990-94): –2.87%,
  47th
  Govt. payments (1993): $226,000,000,
  21st
  Average per farm: $5,022.22, 20th

Construction, value of all: $4,730,000,000
  Per capita: $730.14, 16th
Manufactures:
  Value added: $36,423,000,000
    Per capita: $5,622.38, 18th
  Leading products: Textiles, apparel, foods, transportation equipment, printing and publishing
Value of nonfuel mineral production (1994): $1,535,000,000, 5th
Leading mineral products: Clays, stone, cement
Retail sales (1993): $54,313,000,000, 12th
  Per household: $21,250, 35th
  Percent increase (1992-93): 6.6%, 30th
Tourism revenues (1993): $11.2 bil.
Foreign exports, in total value (1994): $8,237,000,000, 16th
  Per capita: $1,167.54, 28th
Gross state product per person (1993): $21,739.13, 22nd
  Percent change (1990-93): 5.11%, 13th
Patents per 100,000 pop. (1993): 12.47, 36th
Public aid recipients (percent of resident pop. 1993): 8.4%, 10th
Medicaid recipients per 1,000 pop. (1993): 138.37, 13th
Medicare recipients per 1,000 pop. (1993): 114.60, 46th

TRAVEL AND TRANSPORTATION

Motor vehicle registrations (1993): 5,632,000
  Per 1,000 pop.: 816.00, 22nd
Motorcycle registrations (1993): 55,000
  Per 1,000 pop.: 7.97, 49th
Licensed drivers per 1,000 pop. (1993): 668.36, 34th
Deaths from motor vehicle accidents per 100,000 pop. (1993): 20.37, 14th
Public roads & streets (1993):
  Total mileage: 110,879
    Per 1,000 pop.: 16.06, 30th
  Rural mileage: 84,605
    Per 1,000 pop.: 12.26, 29th
  Urban mileage: 26,274
    Per 1,000 pop.: 3.81, 7th
  Interstate mileage: 1,243
    Per 1,000 pop.: 0.18, 33rd
Annual vehicle-mi. of travel per person (1993): 11,359, 3rd

Mean travel time for workers age 16+ who work away from home: 22.7 min., 9th

GOVERNMENT

Percent of voting age pop. registered (1994): 54.9%, 48th
  Percent of voting age pop. voting (1994): 35.4%, 48th
  Percent of voting age pop. voting for U.S. representatives (1994): 29.0%, 47th
State legislators, total (1995): 236, 3rd
  Women members (1992): 34
    Percent of legislature: 14.4%, 34th
U.S. Congress, House members (1995): 11
  Change (1985-95): +1
Revenues (1993):
  State govt.: $16,565,000,000
    Per capita: $2,400.03, 47th
Expenditures (1993):
  State govt.: $15,308,000,000
    Per capita: $2,217.91, 46th
Debt outstanding (1993): $4,519,000,000
  Per capita: $654.74, 44th

LAWS AND REGULATIONS

Legal driving age: 16
Marriage age without parental consent: 16
Divorce residence requirement: 6 mo.

ATTRACTIONS (1995)

Major opera companies: 2
Major symphony orchestras: 2
Major dance companies: 1
Major professional theater companies (nonprofit): 1
State appropriations for arts agencies per capita: $0.49, 37th

SPORTS AND COMPETITION

NCAA teams (Division I): Georgia Southern Univ. Eagles, Georgia State Univ. Crimson Panthers, Georgia Tech Yellow Jackets, Mercer Univ. Bears, Univ. of Georgia Bulldogs
Major league baseball teams: Atlanta Braves (NL East), Atlanta-Fulton County Stadium
NBA basketball teams: Atlanta Hawks, The Omni
NFL football teams: Atlanta Falcons (NFC), Georgia Dome

HAWAII

"The loveliest fleet of islands that lies anchored in any ocean....No other land could so longingly and bewitchingly haunt me, sleeping and waking, through half a lifetime, as that one has done."

Mark Twain, writer

In some ways Hawaii is the nation's most unusual state. "Hawaii rests like a water lily on the swelling bosom of the Pacific," as the first King described his realm. It is the only state ever to have been governed directly by monarchs recognized by international law. The nation's only island state, it forms the world's longest island chain. The only tropical state, it has a climate that "sweetens one's bones," as Robert Louis Stevenson described it. Consequently, the language of Hawaii has no word for weather. Among Hawaii's natural wonders is stupendous Waimea Canyon, which rivals that of the Colorado River. The island chain was the home of unique prehistoric peoples who left mysterious evidence of their culture. They were followed by native peoples noted for their wisdom, strength, bravery, and loyalty. In its "most fortunate location," Hawaii is master of the Pacific. With the greatest ethnic and racial diversity of any state, Hawaii maintains constant vigil over the rights of its many peoples, giving particular attention to the native and mixed native peoples.

SUPERLATIVES

• World's most active volcano—the crater of Kilauea on Mauna Loa.
• World's bulkiest mountain—Mauna Loa.
• "The wettest place on earth" —Mt. Waialeale.
• Only state that has an official native language.
• King Kalakaua, the first reigning monarch ever to visit the United States (1874).
• World's most diverse population mix.
• Leader in pineapple production.

MOMENTS IN HISTORY

• As early as 500 B.C. expert navigators arrived at Hawaii in their double-hulled canoes, bringing evidence of their Indo-Malay culture.
• In 1778 native Hawaiians were astonished to see two "floating islands" carrying strange white-skinned men. Captain James Cook had arrived at Kauai, and he named the archipelago the Sandwich Islands.
• On the Big Island (Hawaii), Cook was killed in 1789 in revenge for the many injustices he and his men had committed against the islanders.
• In 1795, King Kamehameha I conquered Oahu; he soon extended his rule across the islands, acquiring the title of "the Great."
• The first American missionaries arrived in 1820 aboard the *Thaddeus*, in a move that was to transform the islands.

So They Say

"It is no small thing to say of the missionaries...that in less than 40 years they have taught this whole people to read and to write, to cipher, and to sew. They have given them an alphabet, grammar, and dictionary, preserved their language...given [them] a literature, and translated into it the Bible and works of devotion, science, and entertainment...."

Richard Henry Dana, lawyer and author

• During the reign of Kamehameha III, in 1840, the feudal system was changed into a constitutional monarchy.
• The new constitution of 1852 created a two-house legislature and courts of law. Religious freedom was guaranteed.
• Queen Liliuokalani, the last Hawaiian monarch, was overthrown and a temporary republic set up in 1893.
• In 1898 the Hawaiian republic transferred sovereignty to the United States by a treaty accepted on both sides.
• In 1900, Hawaii became a U.S. territory, with all residents becoming U.S. citizens.

• In 1903 the first Hawaiian pineapple was packed, and the islands' commerce increased so rapidly that many Asian immigrants were brought in as workers.

> ### So They Say
>
> "This is a blessed country....There is not a locked door in Hilo, and nobody makes anybody else afraid....I never saw such healthy bright complexions...or such sparkling smiles....The population at Cook's time may have been 300,000 in 1779. In 1872 it was only 49,000. It is a pity the race is dying out. It has shown a singular aptitude for politics and civilization."
>
> British travel writer Isabella Bird, describing the Hawaii of the 1870s

• Beginning in 1917, World War I brought many Hawaiians into service.

• Hawaiian isolation became a thing of the past after the first flight arrived from the mainland in 1927, and radio-telephone communication came in 1931.

• During the 1930s, Hawaii felt little effect of the Great Depression, partly because of the enormous military buildup.

• The Japanese bombing of Pearl Harbor on December 7, 1941, was a "day of infamy" never to be forgotten. Hawaii then became the principal Pacific fortress of the war, the greatest arsenal the world had ever known.

• The 1950 lava flow from the Mauna Loa eruption was considered to have been the largest in historic times.

• The first proposal for Hawaiian statehood was made during the time of Kamehameha II. Statehood finally occurred on August 21, 1959, and the United States had its 50th state.

• The 1990 census revealed that Hawaii's population had increased almost 15% in the past decade. The population is composed of perhaps the world's greatest racial and ethnic mixture, with more than 60 different racial combinations, all living together in harmony.

• In the 1990s a growing movement sought to gain some form of sovereignty for part-native Hawaiians.

• The U.S. government in 1994 returned the island of Kahroolawe to the state; it had been used as a target practice and bombing range.

THAT'S INTERESTING

• As many as 100 people often crowded into a single Polynesian double-hulled canoe as the seaworthy ships sailed the thousands of stormy ocean miles from the South Pacific to populate Hawaii.

• When the Hawaiians killed Captain Cook in 1789, they prepared his body as they would have their own great chief, removing the flesh from the bones before burial.

• In 1825, Hawaiian chieftess Kapiolani defied the volcano goddess Pele and ate the sacred ohelo berries to prove that the old religion was no longer effective.

• Hawaiian kings were noted for their great size and strength. Kamehameha I once moved a 4,500-pound stone. His Queen, Kaahumanu, weighed 300 pounds.

• The Robinson family, owners of the island of Niihau, have for years done everything in their power to preserve the ways of early Hawaii, making the island an off-limits place of mystery.

NOTABLE NATIVES

Samuel Chapman Armstrong (Maui, 1839-1893), educator. **Sanford Ballard Dole** (Honolulu, 1844-1926), public official. **Luther Halsey Gulick** (Honolulu, 1865-1918), educator. **Don Ho** (Kakaaho, Oahu, 1930-), singer. **Daniel K. Inouye** (Honolulu, 1924-), public official. **Kamehameha I** (Hawaii Island, 1758?-1819), king of Hawaii. **Kamehameha II** (Hawaii Island, 1796?-1824), king of Hawaii. **Kamehameha III** (Oahu, 1813-1854), king of Hawaii. **Kamehameha IV** (Oahu, 1834-1863), king of Hawaii. **Kamehameha V** (Oahu, 1830-1872), king of Hawaii. **Liliuokalani** (Oahu, 1838-1917), queen of Hawaii.

GENERAL

Admitted to statehood: August 21, 1959
Origin of name: Possibly derived from native word for homeland, *Hawaiki* or *Owyhyhee*
Capital: Honolulu
Nickname: Aloha State
Motto: *Ua Mau Ke Ea O Ka Aina I Ka Pono*—The life of the land is perpetuated in righteousness
Bird: Nene (Hawaiian goose)
Flower: Red hibiscus
Song: "Hawaii Ponoi"
Tree: Kukui (candlenut)

THE LAND

Area: 6,459 sq. mi., 47th
Land: 6,423 sq. mi., 47th
Water: 36 sq. mi., 50th
Inland water: 36 sq. mi., 50th
Topography: Eight main islands, which are the tops of a chain of submerged volcanic mountains; active volcanoes: Mauna Loa, Kilauea
Number of counties: 5
Geographic center: Hawaii, 20°15'N, 156°20'W, off Maui Island
Length: 1600 mi.
Highest point: 13,796 ft. (Mauna Kea), 6th
Lowest point: sea level (Pacific Ocean), 3rd
Mean elevation: 3,030 ft., 10th
Coastline: 750 mi., 4th
Shoreline: 1,052 mi., 17th

CLIMATE AND ENVIRONMENT

Temp., highest: 100 deg. on April 27, 1931, at Pahala; lowest: 12 deg. on May 17, 1979, at Mauna Kea
Monthly average: highest: 87.1 deg., 26th; lowest: 65.3 deg., 51st; spread (high to low): 21.8 deg., 51st
Hazardous waste sites (1993): 3, 47th
Endangered species: Mammals: 1—Hawaiian hoary bat; birds: 29—Hawaii 'akepa, Maui 'akepa, Kauai 'akialoa, 'Akiapolaau, Hawaiian coot, Hawaiian creeper, Molokai creeper, Oahu creeper, Hawaiian crow, Hawaiian duck, Laysan duck, Laysan finch, Nihoa finch, Hawaiian goose, Hawaiian hawk, Crested honeycreeper, Nihoa millerbird, Hawaiian common moorhen, Nukupu'u, Kauai 'o'o, Hawaiian 'o'u, Palila, Maui parrotbill, Hawaiian dark-rumped petrel, Po'ouli, Hawaiian stilt, Large Kauai thrush, Molokai thrush, Small Kauai thrush; reptiles: 2; amphibians: none; fishes: none; invertebrates: 1; plants: 19

MAJOR CITIES POPULATION, 1990 PERCENTAGE INCREASE, 1980-90

Hilo, 37,800—7.18%
Honolulu, 365,272—0.06%
Kailua, 36,818—2.81%
Kaneohe, 35,448—18.48%
Pearl City, 30,993— –27.20%

THE PEOPLE

Population (1995): 1,186,815, 40th
Percent change (1990-95): 7.1%, 17th
Population (2000 proj.): 1,327,000, 39th
Percent change (1990-2000): 19.74%, 10th
Per sq. mi. (1994): 183.5, 14th
Percent in metro. area (1992): 74.7%, 23rd
Foreign born: 163,000, 17th
Percent: 14.7%, 3rd
Top three ancestries reported:
Japanese, 23.65%
Filipino, 15.88%
Hawaiian, 14.17%
White: 369,616, 33.35%, 50th
Black: 27,195, 2.45%, 38th
Native American: 5,099, 0.46%, 24th
Asian, Pacific Isle: 685,236, 61.83%, 1st
Other races: 21,083, 1.90%, 19th
Hispanic origin: 81,390, 7.34%, 11th
Percent over 5 yrs. speaking language other than English at home: 24.8%, 4th
Percent males: 50.88%, 3rd; percent females: 49.12%, 49th
Percent never married: 29.8%, 5th
Marriages per 1,000 (1993): 14.9, 3rd
Divorces per 1,000 (1993): 4.2, 30th
Median age: 32.6
Under 5 years (1994): 8.06%, 7th
Under 18 years (1994): 25.78%, 27th
65 years & older (1994): 12.1%, 34th
Percent increase among the elderly (1990-94): 12.80%, 4th

OF VITAL IMPORTANCE

Live births per 1,000 pop. (1993): 16.7, 8th
Infant mortality rate per 1,000 births (1992): 6.3, 48th
Rate for blacks (1990): 11.5, 41st
Rate for whites (1990): 5.1, 51st
Births to unmarried women, % of total (1992): 26.2%, 35th
Births to teenage mothers, % of total (1992): 10.0%, 40th
Abortions (1992): 12,190, 30th
Rate per 1,000 women 14-44 years old: 46.0, 3rd
Percent change (1988-92): 7%, 7th
Average lifetime (1979-81): 77.02, 1st
Deaths per 1,000 pop. (1993): 6.2, 48th
Causes of death per 100,000 pop.:
Accidents & adverse effects (1992): 25.4, 48th
Atherosclerosis (1991): 2.6, 50th

Cancer (1991): 151.9, 48th
Cerebrovascular diseases (1992): 48.2, 42nd
Chronic liver diseases & cirrhosis (1991): 6.0, 50th
Chronic obstructive pulmonary diseases (1992): 16.4, 50th
Diabetes mellitus (1992): 14.8, 45th
Diseases of heart (1992): 184.8, 48th
Pneumonia, flu (1991): 26.4, 40th
Suicide (1992): 11.2, 39th

KEEPING WELL

Active nonfederal physicians per 100,000 pop. (1993): 244, 10th
Dentists per 100,000 (1991): 78, 4th
Nurses per 100,000 (1992): 697, 32nd
Hospitals per 100,000 (1993): 1.72, 37th
Admissions per 1,000 (1993): 83.10, 50th
Occupancy rate per 100 beds (1993): 83.1, 1st
Average cost per patient per day (1993): $823, 30th
Average cost per stay (1993): $7,633, 3rd
Average stay (1992): 8.5 days, 12th
AIDS cases (adult, 1993): 359; per 100,000: 30.6, 19th
HIV infection, not yet AIDS (1993): NA
Other notifiable diseases:
Gonorrhea: 54.5, 41st
Measles: 3.7, 28th
Syphilis: 3.0, 42nd
Tuberculosis: 17.7, 3rd
Pop. without health insur. (1991-93): 8.1%, 51st

HOUSEHOLDS BY TYPE

Total households (1994): 381,000
Percent change (1990-94): 7.1%, 12th
Per 1,000 pop.: 323.16, 50th
Percent of households 65 yrs. and over: 21.26%, 31st
Persons per household (1994): 2.99, 2nd
Family households: 263,456
Percent of total: 73.95%, 3rd
Nonfamily households: 92,811
Percent of total: 26.05%, 49th
Pop. living in group quarters: 37,632
Percent of pop.: 3.40%, 9th

LIVING QUARTERS

Total housing units: 389,810
Persons per unit: 2.84, 2nd
Occupied housing units: 356,267
Percent of total units: 91.40%, 14th

Persons per unit: 2.99, 2nd
Percent of units with over 1 person per room: 15.92%, 1st
Owner-occupied units: 191,911
Percent of total units: 49.23%, 47th
Percent of occupied units: 53.87%, 49th
Persons per unit: 3.19, 2nd
Median value: $245,300, 1st
Renter-occupied units: 164,356
Percent of total units: 42.16%, 3rd
Percent of occupied units: 46.13%, 3rd
Persons per unit: 2.78, 1st
Median contract rent: $599, 1st
Rental vacancy rate: 5.4%, 48th
Mobile home, trailer & other as a percent of occupied housing units: 1.71%, 50th
Persons in emergency shelters for homeless persons: 854, 0.077%, 12th
Persons visible in street locations: 1,071, 0.0966%, 1st
Persons in shelters for abused women: 73, 0.0066%, 9th
Nursing home population: 3,225, 0.29%, 50th

CRIME INDEX PER 100,000 (1992-93)

Total reported: 6,277.0, 7th
Violent: 261.2, 44th
Murder and nonnegligent manslaughter: 3.8, 40th
Aggravated assault: 120.1, 46th
Robbery: 103.6, 37th
Forcible rape: 33.6, 37th
Property: 6,015.8, 4th
Burglary: 1,135.7, 15th
Larceny, theft: 4,429.4, 2nd
Motor vehicle theft: 450.8, 23rd
Drug abuse violations (1990): 324.6, 15th
Child-abuse rate per 1,000 children (1993): 7.68, 45th

TEACHING AND LEARNING

Pop. 3 and over enrolled in school: 290,578
Percent of pop.: 27.4%, 23rd
Public elementary & secondary schools (1992-93): 238
Total enrollment (1992): 177,449
Percent of total pop.: 15.35%, 41st
Teachers (1992): 10,083
Percent of pop.: 0.87%, 45th
Pupil/teacher ratio (fall 1992): 17.6, 14th
Teachers' avg. salary (1992-93): $38,560, 15th

Expenditure per capita (1990-91): $4,597.48, 5th

Expenditure per pupil (1991-92): $5,420, 21st

Percent of graduates taking SAT (1993): 56%, 18th

Mean SAT verbal scores: 401, 49th

Mean SAT mathematical scores: 478, 32nd

Percent of graduates taking ACT (1995): 14%, 35th

Mean ACT scores: 21.8, 6th

Percent of pop. over 25 completing:

Less than 9th grade: 10.1%, 21st

High school: 80.1%, 13th

College degree(s): 22.9%, 14th

Higher education, institutions (1993-94): 16

Enrollment (1992): 61,162

Percent of pop.: 5.30%, 32nd

White non-Hispanic (1992): 17,075

Percent of enroll.: 27.92%, 51st

Black non-Hispanic (1992): 1,446

Percent of enroll.: 2.36%, 40th

Hispanic (1992): 1,229

Percent of enroll.: 2.01%, 23rd

Asian/Pacific Islander (1992): 36,112

Percent of enroll.: 59.04%, 1st

American Indian/AK native (1992): 225

Percent of enroll.: 0.37%, 28th

Nonresident alien (1992): 5,075

Percent of enroll.: 8.30%, 2nd

Female (1992): 33,383

Percent of enroll.: 54.58%, 35th

Pub. institutions (1993-94): 10

Enrollment (1992): 49,605

Percent of enroll.: 81.10%, 30th

Private institutions (1993-94): 6

Enrollment (1992): 11,557

Percent of enroll.: 18.90%, 22nd

Tuition, public institution (avg., 1993-94): $0, 50th

Tuition, private institution (avg., 1993-94): $9,514, 43rd

Public library systems: 1

Books & serial vol. per capita: 2.15, 34th

Govt. expenditure per capita: $19.81, 16th

LAW ENFORCEMENT, COURTS, AND PRISONS

Police protection, corrections, judicial and legal functions expenditures (1992): $407,000,000

Per capita: $352, 10th

Police per 10,000 pop. (1993): 23.06, 17th

Prisoners (state & fed.) per 100,000 pop. (1993): 2,683.53, 28th

Percent change (1992-93): 6.9%, 20th

Death penalty: no

RELIGION, NUMBER AND PERCENT OF POPULATION

Agnostic: NA

Buddhist: NA

Christian: NA

Hindu: NA

Jewish: NA

Muslim: NA

Unitarian: NA

Other: NA

None: NA

Refused to answer: NA

MAKING A LIVING

Personal income per capita (1994): $24,057, 7th

Percent increase (1993-94): 2.4%, 51st

Disposable personal income per capita (1994): $20,587, 10th

Median income of households (1993): $42,662, 2nd

Percent of pop. below poverty level (1993): 8.0%, 51st

Percent 65 and over (1990): 8.0%, 48th

Expenditure for energy per person (1992): $1,702, 44th

ECONOMY

Civilian labor force (1994): 583,000

Percent of total pop.: 49.45%, 37th

Percent 65 and over (1990): 3.53%, 8th

Percent female: 48.71%, 2nd

Percent job growth (1980-90): 25.55%, 18th

Major employer industries (1994):

Agriculture: 14,000—2.6%, 22nd

Construction: 42,000—7.5%, 1st

Finance, insurance, & real estate: 41,000—7.4%, 5th

Government: 114,000—20.4%, 7th

Manufacturing: 20,000—3.5%, 51st

Service: 142,000—25.4%, 6th

Trade: 108,000—19.4%, 14th

Transportation, communications, public utilities: 37,000—6.6%, 6th

Unemployment rate (1994): 6.00%, 21st

Male: 7.1%, 9th

Female: 5.0%, 34th

Total businesses (1991): 31,188

New business incorps. (1991): 3,792
Percent of total businesses: 12.16%, 4th
Business failures (1991): 149
Percent of total businesses: 0.48%
Agriculture farm income:
Marketing (1993): $492,000,000, 43rd
Average per farm: $123,000.00, 11th
Leading products (1993): Sugar, pineapples, greenhouse, nuts
Average value land & build. per acre: NA
Govt. payments (1993): $3,000,000, 46th
Average per farm: $750.00, 45th
Construction, value of all: $2,116,000,000
Per capita: $1,909.35, 1st
Manufactures:
Value added: $1,558,000,000
Per capita: $1,405.85, 50th
Leading products: Sugar, canned pineapple, apparel, foods, printing and publishing
Value of nonfuel mineral production (1994): $137,000,000, 41st
Leading mineral products: Stone, cement, sand/gravel
Retail sales (1993): $13,244,000,000, 36th
Per household: $34,454, 1st
Percent increase (1992-93): 7.6%, 20th
Tourism revenues (1993): $8.7 bil.
Foreign exports, in total value (1994): $297,000,000, 50th
Per capita: $251.91, 51st
Gross state product per person (1993): $27,336.86, 7th
Percent change (1990-93): 6.90%, 5th
Patents per 100,000 pop. (1993): 9.09, 46th
Public aid recipients (percent of resident pop. 1993): 6.3%, 29th
Medicaid recipients per 1,000 pop. (1993): 94.34, 42nd
Medicare recipients per 1,000 pop. (1993): 120.93, 43rd

TRAVEL AND TRANSPORTATION

Motor vehicle registrations (1993): 763,000
Per 1,000 pop.: 654.37, 47th
Motorcycle registrations (1993): 24,000
Per 1,000 pop.: 20.58, 16th
Licensed drivers per 1,000 pop. (1993): 629.5, 46th
Deaths from motor vehicle accidents per 100,000 pop. (1993): 11.49, 44th

Public roads & streets (1993):
Total mileage: 4,106
Per 1,000 pop.: 3.52, 50th
Rural mileage: 2,307
Per 1,000 pop.: 1.98, 47th
Urban mileage: 1,799
Per 1,000 pop.: 1.54, 51st
Interstate mileage: 44
Per 1,000 pop.: 0.04, 50th
Annual vehicle-mi. of travel per person (1993): 6,947, 48th
Mean travel time for workers age 16+ who work away from home: 23.8 min., 8th

GOVERNMENT

Percent of voting age pop. registered (1994): 51.5%, 50th
Percent of voting age pop. voting (1994): 46.0%, 27th
Percent of voting age pop. voting for U.S. representatives (1994): 39.3%, 24th
State legislators, total (1995): 76, 46th
Women members (1992): 21
Percent of legislature: 27.6%, 8th
U.S. Congress, House members (1995): 2
Change (1985-95): 0
Revenues (1993):
State govt.: $5,543,000,000
Per capita: $4,753.86, 2nd
Expenditures (1993):
State govt.: $5,605,000,000
Per capita: $4,807.89, 2nd
Debt outstanding (1993): $5,023,000,000
Per capita: $4,307.89, 6th

LAWS AND REGULATIONS

Legal driving age: 15
Marriage age without parental consent: 16
Divorce residence requirement: 6 mo.

ATTRACTIONS (1995)

Major opera companies: 1
State appropriations for arts agencies per capita: $7.34, 1st
State Fair in June at Honolulu

SPORTS AND COMPETITION

NCAA teams (Division I): Univ. of Hawaii Rainbow Warriors

IDAHO

"Dice 'em, hash 'em, boil 'em, mash 'em! Idaho, Idaho, Idaho!"

An Idaho football cheer

Idaho is a land of dramatic natural features, with towering, snow-capped mountain ranges, swirling white rapids, deep canyons, and peaceful lakes that deserve to be ranked among the world's most beautiful. The Snake River rushes through Hells Canyon, which is deeper than the Grand Canyon. Idaho's Shoshone Falls, on the Snake River, are higher than Niagara Falls. Known the world round for its potatoes, the state also possesses vast and unique mineral resources and forest reserves. Idahoans believe they live in a state where life is still unmatched for serenity and harmony, despite some recent social concerns.

SUPERLATIVES

• The tiny Malad River, said to be the shortest river in the world.
• Largest prehistoric art work in the United States, near Nampa.
• Hells Canyon—the deepest gorge in North America.
• World's largest stands of white pine.
• World's largest reserves of phosphate.
• First in silver production.
• Two-thirds of all U.S. processed potatoes produced.

MOMENTS IN HISTORY

• The great exploration of Meriwether Lewis and William Clark provided the first record of the area as the explorers crossed it in 1805.

So They Say

"...after brakfast I began to administer eye water and in a few minits had near 40 applicants with sore eyes and maney others with other complaints most common rhumatic disorders & weaknesses in the back and loins perticulary the womin."

William Clark

• Waiting for the snows to melt on their way home in 1806, Lewis and Clark performed many kindnesses for the Indians.
• Representing the Hudson Bay Company, noted explorer David Thompson set up the first trading post in present-day Idaho in 1809, Kullyspell House on Pend Oreille Lake.
• In 1810, Andrew Henry built Fort Henry, the first American trading post in the Pacific Northwest, but it was later abandoned.
• In 1818-1819, Donald Mackenzie firmly established the Idaho fur trade and began what became the great annual fur "rendezvous," attracting some of the most rowdy gatherings of the West.

So They Say

"I have again to repeat to you the advice which I before gave you not to come with a small party to the American rendezvous. There are here a great collection of scoundrels."

Nathaniel Wyeth

• Fort Hall on the Snake River was built by Nathaniel Wyeth in 1834 and sold two years later to Dr. John McLaughlin, "ruler" of the Hudson Bay Company in the region.
• In 1834 the first missionaries arrived, and at Fort Hall the Reverend Jason Lee conducted the first Christian religious service in present-day Idaho.
• The Reverend and Mrs. Henry H. Spalding established Lapwai Mission in Nez Percé country near Lewiston in 1836. He served his Indian congregation until his death in 1874.
• By the mid-1840s, a stream of settlers was crossing over the Oregon Trail, and many turned off to settle in present-day Idaho.
• Beginning in 1849, more thousands crossed the region on their way to California gold.
• Indian wars followed until 1855, when the tribes agreed to move to other tracts.

• Franklin, the first permanent European-style town in Idaho, was founded by the Mormons on April 14, 1860.

• Also in 1860, gold discoveries led to a boom, and the town that sprang up at the site was named for E. D. Pierce, a pioneer gold prospector.

• On June 17, 1877, the longtime friendship between the Nez Percé and the whites ended in the Battle of White Bird Canyon, during which the government forces lost a third of their men. Then, under the superb leadership of Chief Joseph, the Nez Percé tribe began its bitter flight from its ancestral lands.

• With the defeat of the Sheepeater tribe in 1879, Indian wars ended in Idaho.

• The 1870s brought rich gold strikes.

• Even greater was the strike of 1883 in silver, lead, and zinc in the Coeur d'Alene district.

• Idaho became a state on July 3, 1890.

• A particularly bitter miners' strike took place in 1899.

• In December 1905, Frank Steunenberg, governor at the time of the miners' strike, was killed in a bomb explosion; his murder trial gained international prominence.

• Craters of the Moon National Monument became a reality in 1924.

• Development of Sun Valley began in 1936.

• During World War II, the mammoth naval training base of Farragut Park was one of the principal centers of its kind.

• The world's first usable atomic-powered electricity was generated in 1951 at the National Reactor Testing Station.

• More than 460 miles from the sea, remote inland Lewiston became an "ocean port" with the opening of the Snake River Navigation Project in 1975.

• The collapse of the Teton Dam in June 1976 caused vast property damage, particularly to the cattle industry.

• The grasshopper infestation of 1985 devastated the state's farmlands.

• In 1994, Larry Echo-Hawk won the state's Democratic primary in his effort to become the nation's first American Indian governor, but he lost the general election.

THAT'S INTERESTING

• Thirsty travelers on the brink of Hells Canyon could look down on the waters of the Snake River but had no way to get down to drink.

• Wood River is known as the Upside Down River. At one place it flows through a gorge 4 feet wide and 104 feet deep. At another point the gorge is 104 feet wide and the river 4 feet deep.

• A pioneer family of Palouse country once gave an Indian family a meal. From that time on, the pioneer family found a large salmon left at their door at the same time each year.

• During the gold boom in the early 1860s, Idaho City was a large, rip-roaring boom town, where crime and "frontier justice" ran rampant. Of the 200 people buried in the pioneer cemetery of Idaho City, only 28 died of natural causes.

• A unique Idaho attraction is Thousand Springs. Each spring spouts out from the side of a single cliff.

• The 1980 eruption of Mt. St. Helens in Washington State brought great clouds of ash to Idaho, and the Palouse crop the next year increased 30%.

IDAHO NOTABLES

William Edgar Borah (Fairfield, IL, 1865-1940), public official/political leader. **William Dudley (Big Bill) Haywood** (Salt Lake City, UT, 1869-1928), labor leader. **Chief Joseph** (Wallowa Valley, near Idaho/Oregon/Washington border, 1840?-1904), Indian leader. **Ezra Loomis Pound** (Hailey, 1885-1972), poet. **Sacajawea** (in either eastern Idaho or western Montana, 1787?-1812?), Indian guide.

GENERAL

Admitted to statehood: July 3, 1890
Origin of name: A coined name with an invented Indian meaning: "gem of the mountains"; was originally suggested for the Pikes Peak mining territory (Colorado), then applied to the new mining territory of the Pacific Northwest. Another theory suggests Idaho may be a Kiowa Apache term for the Comanche.
Capital: Boise
Nickname: Gem State
Motto: *Esto Perpetua*—It is perpetual
Bird: Mountain bluebird
Flower: Syringa
Gem: Star garnet

Song: "Here We Have Idaho"
Tree: White pine

THE LAND

Area: 83,574 sq. mi., 14th
  Land: 82,751 sq. mi., 11th
  Water: 823 sq. mi., 31st
    Inland water: 823 sq. mi., 25th
Topography: Snake River plains in the S; central region of mountains, canyons, gorges (Hells Canyon, 7,900 ft., deepest in North America); subalpine northern region
Number of counties: 44
Geographic center: Custer SW of Challis
Length: 570 mi.; width: 300 mi.
Highest point: 12,662 ft. (Borah Peak), 11th
Lowest point: 710 ft. (Snake River), 44th
Mean elevation: 5,000 ft., 6th

CLIMATE AND ENVIRONMENT

Temp., highest: 118 deg. on July 28, 1934, at Orofino; lowest: –60 deg. on Jan. 16, 1943, at Island Park Dam
Monthly average: highest: 90.6 deg., 18th; lowest: 15.1 deg., 17th; spread (high to low): 75.5 deg., 14th
Hazardous waste sites (1993): 10, 36th
Endangered species: Mammals: 2—Woodland Caribou, Northern Rocky Mountain Gray wolf; birds: 2—Whooping crane, American peregrine falcon; reptiles: none; amphibians: none; fishes: none; invertebrates: none; plants: 1

MAJOR CITIES
POPULATION, 1990
PERCENTAGE INCREASE, 1980-90

Boise, 125,738—22.97%
Idaho Falls, 43,929—10.54%
Lewiston, 28,082—0.34%
Nampa, 28,365—12.95%
Pocatello, 46,080— –0.56%

THE PEOPLE

Population (1995): 1,163,261 41st
  Percent change (1990-95): 15.5%, 2nd
Population (2000 proj.): 1,290,000, 40th
  Percent change (1990-2000): 28.14%, 2nd
Per sq. mi. (1994): 13.7, 44th
Percent in metro. area (1992): 30.0%, 48th
Foreign born: 29,000, 40th
  Percent: 2.9%, 28th

Top three ancestries reported:
  English, 28.90%
  German, 27.71%
  Irish, 14.10%
White: 950,451, 94.41%, 7th
Black: 3,370, 0.33%, 50th
Native American: 13,780, 1.37%, 12th
Asian, Pacific Isle: 9,365,0. 93%, 31st
Other races: 29,783, 2.96%, 10th
Hispanic origin: 52,927, 5.26%, 15th
Percent over 5 yrs. speaking language other than English at home: 6.4%, 30th
Percent males: 49.76%, 7th; percent females: 50.24%, 45th
Percent never married: 21.2%, 49th
Marriages per 1,000 (1993): 12.7, 6th
Divorces per 1,000 (1993): 6.3, 6th
Median age: 31.5
Under 5 years (1994): 7.68%, 13th
Under 18 years (1994): 29.92%, 4th
65 years & older (1994): 11.6%, 38th
Percent increase among the elderly (1990-94): 8.85%, 13th

OF VITAL IMPORTANCE

Live births per 1,000 pop. (1993): 15.6, 13th
Infant mortality rate per 1,000 births (1992): 8.8, 20th
  Rate for blacks (1990): 10.9, 43rd
  Rate for whites (1990): 8.7, 8th
Births to unmarried women, % of total (1992): 18.3%, 49th
Births to teenage mothers, % of total (1992): 13.0%, 21st
Abortions (1992): 1,710, 48th
  Rate per 1,000 women 14-44 years old: 7.2, 49th
  Percent change (1988-92): –12%, 32nd
Average lifetime (1979-81): 75.19, 8th
Deaths per 1,000 pop. (1993): 7.6, 42nd
Causes of death per 100,000 pop.:
  Accidents & adverse effects (1992): 44.7, 9th
  Atherosclerosis (1991): 6.5, 29th
  Cancer (1991): 169 1, 44th
  Cerebrovascular diseases (1992): 59.1, 24th
  Chronic liver diseases & cirrhosis (1991): 6.7, 45th
  Chronic obstructive pulmonary diseases (1992): 40.2, 18th
  Diabetes mellitus (1992): 17.8, 37th
  Diseases of heart (1992): 218.1, 43rd
  Pneumonia, flu (1991): 28.5, 32nd
  Suicide (1992): 15.8, 8th

KEEPING WELL

Active nonfederal physicians per 100,000 pop. (1993): 131, 50th

Dentists per 100,000 (1991): 54, 24th

Nurses per 100,000 (1992): 537, 48th

Hospitals per 100,000 (1993): 3.73, 8th

Admissions per 1,000 (1993): 90.00, 48th

Occupancy rate per 100 beds (1993): 55.4, 44th

Average cost per patient per day (1993): $659, 43rd

Average cost per stay (1993): $4,635, 49th

Average stay (1992): 6.6 days, 41st

AIDS cases (adult, 1993): 77; per 100,000: 7.0, 46th

HIV infection, not yet AIDS (1993): 201

Other notifiable diseases:

Gonorrhea: 15.7, 48th

Measles: 2.6, 32nd

Syphilis: 2.7, 44th

Tuberculosis: 1.4, 50th

Pop. without health insur. (1991-93): 16.4%, 15th

HOUSEHOLDS BY TYPE

Total households (1994): 405,000

Percent change (1990-94): 12.2%, 2nd

Per 1,000 pop.: 357.46, 44th

Percent of households 65 yrs. and over: 20.74%, 37th

Persons per household (1994): 2.75, 6th

Family households: 263,194

Percent of total: 72.96%, 8th

Nonfamily households: 97,529

Percent of total: 27.04%, 44th

Pop. living in group quarters: 21,490

Percent of pop.: 2.13%, 47th

LIVING QUARTERS

Total housing units: 413,327

Persons per unit: 2.44, 17th

Occupied housing units: 360,723

Percent of total units: 87.27%, 36th

Persons per unit: 2.67, 9th

Percent of units with over 1 person per room: 4.21%, 14th

Owner-occupied units: 252,734

Percent of total units: 61.15%, 17th

Percent of occupied units: 70.06%, 10th

Persons per unit: 2.82, 10th

Median value: $58,200, 38th

Renter-occupied units: 107,989

Percent of total units: 26.13%, 43rd

Percent of occupied units: 29.94%, 42nd

Persons per unit: 2.51, 9th

Median contract rent: $261, 41st

Rental vacancy rate: 7.3%, 38th

Mobile home, trailer & other as a percent of occupied housing units: 16.70%, 8th

Persons in emergency shelters for homeless persons: 461, 0.046%, 27th

Persons visible in street locations: 19, 0.0019%, 45th

Persons in shelters for abused women: 78, 0.0077%, 5th

Nursing home population: 6,318, 0.63%, 32nd

CRIME INDEX PER 100,000 (1992-93)

Total reported: 3,845.1, 44th

Violent: 281.8, 42nd

Murder and nonnegligent manslaughter: 2.9, 47th

Aggravated assault: 226.7, 38th

Robbery: 16.9, 48th

Forcible rape: 35.3, 30th

Property: 3,563.3, 43rd

Burglary: 668.8, 42nd

Larceny, theft: 2,711.1, 33rd

Motor vehicle theft: 183.4, 45th

Drug abuse violations (1990): 174.6, 39th

Child-abuse rate per 1,000 children (1993): 20.70, 11th

TEACHING AND LEARNING

Pop. 3 and over enrolled in school: 295,638

Percent of pop.: 30.8%, 3rd

Public elementary & secondary schools (1992-93): 605

Total enrollment (1992): 231,668

Percent of total pop.: 21.73%, 2nd

Teachers (1992): 11,827

Percent of pop.: 1.11%, 16th

Pupil/teacher ratio (fall 1992): 19.6, 4th

Teachers' avg. salary (1992-93): $28,898, 46th

Expenditure per capita (1990-91): $2,852.09, 47th

Expenditure per pupil (1991-92): $3,556, 49th

Percent of graduates taking SAT (1993): 18%, 30th

Mean SAT verbal scores: 465, 20th

Mean SAT mathematical scores: 507, 22nd

Percent of graduates taking ACT (1995): 61%, 19th

Mean ACT scores: 21.2, 20th

Percent of pop. over 25 completing:
Less than 9th grade: 7.4%, 42nd
High school: 79.7%, 16th
College degree(s): 17.7%, 35th
Higher education, institutions (1993-94): 11
Enrollment (1992): 57,798
    Percent of pop.: 5.42%, 29th
    White non-Hispanic (1992): 52,914
        Percent of enroll.: 91.55%, 5th
    Black non-Hispanic (1992): 333
        Percent of enroll.: 0.58%, 49th
    Hispanic (1992): 1,305
        Percent of enroll.: 2.26%, 20th
    Asian/Pacific Islander (1992): 833
        Percent of enroll.: 1.44%, 37th
    American Indian/AK native (1992): 630
        Percent of enroll.: 1.09%, 16th
    Nonresident alien (1992): 1,783
        Percent of enroll.: 3.08%, 16th
    Female (1992): 31,546
        Percent of enroll.: 54.58%, 35th
Pub. institutions (1993-94): 6
    Enrollment (1992): 46,607
        Percent of enroll.: 80.64%, 33rd
Private institutions (1993-94): 5
    Enrollment (1992): 11,191
        Percent of enroll.: 19.36%, 19th
Tuition, public institution (avg., 1993-94):
    $4,983, 43rd
Tuition, private institution (avg., 1993-94):
    $12,751, 26th
Public library systems: 107
    Books & serial vol. per capita: 3.37, 15th
    Govt. expenditure per capita: $12.33, 35th

LAW ENFORCEMENT, COURTS, AND PRISONS

Police protection, corrections, judicial and
    legal functions expenditures (1992):
    $234,000,000
    Per capita: $220, 35th
Police per 10,000 pop. (1993): 18.36, 34th
Prisoners (state & fed.) per 100,000 pop.
    (1993): 2,369.09, 33rd
    Percent change (1992-93): 15.5%, 3rd
Death penalty: yes, by firing squad or lethal
    injection
    Under sentence of death (1993): 22, 22nd
    Executed (1993): 0

RELIGION, NUMBER AND PERCENT OF POPULATION

Agnostic: 7,682—1.10%, 6th
Buddhist: 1,397—0.20%, 11th
Christian: 571,944—81.90%, 41st
Hindu: NA
Jewish: NA
Muslim: NA
Unitarian: 2,793—0.40%, 8th
Other: 9,777—1.40%, 20th
None: 83,103—11.90%, 7th
Refused to answer: 21,649—3.10%, 7th

MAKING A LIVING

Personal income per capita (1994): $18,231,
    40th
    Percent increase (1993-94): 4.1%, 41st
Disposable personal income per capita (1994):
    $16,293, 40th
Median income of households (1993):
    $31,010, 25th
Percent of pop. below poverty level (1993):
    13.1%, 27th
    Percent 65 and over (1990): 11.5%, 27th
Expenditure for energy per person (1992):
    $1,811, 34th

ECONOMY

Civilian labor force (1994): 591,000
    Percent of total pop.: 52.16%, 19th
    Percent 65 and over (1990): 2.42%,
        35th
    Percent female: 44.84%, 45th
Percent job growth (1980-90): 16.89%,
    33rd
Major employer industries (1994):
    Agriculture: 31,000—6.1%, 7th
    Construction: 29,000—5.7%, 5th
    Finance, insurance, & real estate: 20,000—
        3.8%, 49th
    Government: 83,000—16.3%, 23rd
    Manufacturing: 78,000—15.2%, 26th
    Service: 90,000—17.6%, 46th
    Trade: 96,000—18.8%, 31st
    Transportation, communications, public
        utilities: 26,000—5.0%, 32nd
Unemployment rate (1994): 5.58%, 25th
    Male: 5.6%, 26th
    Female: 5.6%, 22nd
Total businesses (1991): 46,787
    New business incorps. (1991): 1,944
        Percent of total businesses: 4.16%,
            43rd
    Business failures (1991): 312
        Percent of total businesses: 0.67%
Agriculture farm income:
    Marketing (1993): $2,847,000,000, 25th
    Average per farm: $135,571.43, 8th

Leading products (1993): Cattle, potatoes, dairy products, wheat

Average value land & build. per acre (1994): $784, 32nd

Percent increase (1990-94): 18.61%, 12th

Govt. payments (1993): $159,000,000, 24th

Average per farm: $7,571.43, 15th

Construction, value of all: $824,000,000

Per capita: $818.48, 10th

Manufactures:

Value added: $3,928,000,000

Per capita: $3,901.67, 36th

Leading products: Processed foods, lumber and wood products, chemical products, primary metals, fabricated metal products, machinery, electronic parts

Value of nonfuel mineral production (1994): $343,000,000, 32nd

Leading mineral products: Silver, phosphate, gold

Retail sales (1993): $8,147,000,000, 42nd

Per household: $20,256, 41st

Percent increase (1992-93): 10.0%, 7th

Tourism revenues (1994): $1.4 bil.

Foreign exports, in total value (1994): $1,466,000,000, 39th

Per capita: $1,293.91, 24th

Gross state product per person (1993): $18,286.81, 46th

Percent change (1990-93): 5.56%, 9th

Patents per 100,000 pop. (1993): 32.36, 8th

Public aid recipients (percent of resident pop. 1993): 3.2%, 51st

Medicaid recipients per 1,000 pop. (1993): 90.91, 45th

Medicare recipients per 1,000 pop. (1993): 129.09, 38th

TRAVEL AND TRANSPORTATION

Motor vehicle registrations (1993): 1,023,000

Per 1,000 pop.: 930.00, 7th

Motorcycle registrations (1993): 32,000

Per 1,000 pop.: 29.09, 6th

Licensed drivers per 1,000 pop. (1993): 700.0, 20th

Deaths from motor vehicle accidents per 100,000 pop. (1993): 21.18, 11th

Public roads & streets (1993):

Total mileage: 58,835

Per 1,000 pop.: 53.49, 6th

Rural mileage: 55,419

Per 1,000 pop.: 50.38, 6th

Urban mileage: 3,416

Per 1,000 pop.: 3.11, 26th

Interstate mileage: 611

Per 1,000 pop.: 0.56, 7th

Annual vehicle-mi. of travel per person (1993): 10,455, 8th

Mean travel time for workers age 16+ who work away from home: 17.3 min., 43rd

GOVERNMENT

Percent of voting age pop. registered (1994): 63.0%, 30th

Percent of voting age pop. voting (1994): 50.7%, 16th

Percent of voting age pop. voting for U.S. representatives (1994): 49.0%, 9th

State legislators, total (1995): 105, 39th

Women members (1992): 36

Percent of legislature: 28.6%, 7th

U.S. Congress, House members (1995): 2

Change (1985-95): 0

Revenues (1993):

State govt.: $3,408,000,000

Per capita: $3,098.18, 25th

Parimutuel & amusement taxes & lotteries, revenue per capita: $52.73, 32nd

Expenditures (1993):

State govt.: $2,776,000,000

Per capita: $2,523.64, 33rd

Debt outstanding (1993): $1,290,000,000

Per capita: $1,172.73, 30th

LAWS AND REGULATIONS

Legal driving age: 17

Marriage age without parental consent: 18

Divorce residence requirement: 6 wks.

ATTRACTIONS (1995)

State appropriations for arts agencies per capita: $0.71, 27th

State Fair in late August at Boise and early September at Blackfoot

SPORTS AND COMPETITION

NCAA teams (Division I): Boise State Univ. Broncos, Idaho State Univ. Bengals, Univ. of Idaho Vandals

ILLINOIS

"Illinois is perhaps the most American of all the states. It's the U.S.A. in capsule....The capacity for greatness is as limitless as the sweep of the undulating corn fields."

Clyde Brion Davis, journalist and author

The Land of Lincoln nourished the future president and gave him his start toward world fame. The state is rich in archaeological treasures, including the unique Piasa bird and the largest primitive earthworks anywhere. Because of its central location and access to both the Mississippi and the Great Lakes, Illinois has the world's greatest concentration of transportation facilities by land, water, and air. The Chicago area ranks as the nation's major center of manufacture, and the state often leads the nation in production of foodstuffs, particularly corn and soybeans. Three of the world's five tallest buildings rise above a Chicago skyline that contains many architectural masterpieces and has been praised as the world's most beautiful. The concentration of attractions on the northern section of Chicago's Michigan Avenue has given it the nickname of the "Magnificent Mile."

So They Say

"We will enter upon a state government with better prospects than any state ever did—the best soil in the world, a mild climate, a large state with the most ample funds to educate every child in the state."

Nathaniel Pope, Illinois territorial delegate to Congress

SUPERLATIVES

• World center of transportation.
• The world's busiest airport—Chicago's O'Hare.
• World's first skyscraper.
• World's tallest building—Sears Tower in Chicago.
• A principal center of printing.
• Pioneer in commercial television.
• Leader in mail order sales.

MOMENTS IN HISTORY

• The expedition of Louis Jolliet and Father Jacques Marquette brought the first Europeans to Illinois in 1673.

So They Say

"Most beautiful and suitable for settlement...a settler would not there spend ten years in cutting down and burning trees; on the very day of his arrival, he could put his plow into the ground. Thus he would easily find in the country his food and clothing."

Louis Jolliet

• French priests founded Cahokia in 1699—oldest European settlement in the state.
• After the French surrendered North America, their flag at Fort de Chartres in 1765 was the last to be lowered on the continent.
• From 1765 to 1778, British rule was weak, and Illinois became a lawless "wild west."
• During the Revolution, American General George Rogers Clark and 175 men captured Kaskaskia on July 4, 1778.
• In 1809 the Territory of Illinois was created, with popular Ninian Edwards as its governor.
• During the War of 1812, tiny Fort Dearborn (Chicago) was ordered evacuated, and the people were massacred by the Potawatomi Indians.
• On December 3, 1818, Illinois became the 21st state.
• When Chief Black Hawk of the Sauk and Fox tried to reclaim the tribal lands in 1832, the Black Hawk War began. His forces won the small Battle of Stillman's Run in April, but he was later defeated in Wisconsin.
• Chicago was incorporated in 1837 with a population of 4,000.

• Nauvoo was the largest city in Illinois when Joseph Smith, the Mormon leader, was killed there in 1844. The Mormons left for the West, and Nauvoo became a ghost town.

• By 1845 the Galena area had become the nation's leading supplier of lead, and Galena had become the largest city in the state. The mining boom had almost died out by 1850.

• In 1858, Abraham Lincoln and Stephen Douglas engaged in a series of debates that gave Lincoln national prominence.

• In 1861, President-elect Lincoln left Springfield for the last time.

• On February 14, 1865, only days after Lee had surrendered at Appomattox, victorious President Lincoln was shot; he died the next day. His body was returned to a sorrowing Springfield.

• Galena's Ulysses S. Grant was elected president in 1868 and reelected in 1872.

• The great Chicago fire of 1871 destroyed much of the city, but rebuilding began before the ashes had died down.

• In 1893 the magnificent World's Columbian Exposition at Chicago dazzled visitors from around the world.

• In one of the great engineering feats of all time, in 1900, the Chicago River was reversed to dispose of sewage and to create a water route from the Great Lakes to the Gulf of Mexico.

So They Say

As the Marquette/Jolliet party rested near present Chicago, Marquette proposed the theory that creating a short canal at their campsite on the watershed would provide a waterway to connect Lake Michigan with the Gulf of Mexico. Centuries later this brilliant theory became a reality.

The Enchantment of Illinois

• Beginning in 1917, 351,153 Illinois residents served in U.S. armed forces in World War I.

• On December 2, 1942, the power of the atom was mastered at the University of Chicago, when the first nuclear chain reaction was produced.

• Riots at the Democratic National Convention at Chicago in 1968 brought the city notoriety.

• Sears Tower opened in 1974, the world's tallest building.

• In 1978, Hannah Gray became the first woman president of a major U.S. university, the University of Chicago.

• On November 25, 1987, Harold Washington, Chicago's first black mayor, died of a heart attack at his desk.

• Carol Moseley-Braun was elected to the U.S. Senate in 1992, the first African-American woman elected to that body.

• In 1992, violent natural gas explosions ripped up city streets, destroyed 18 buildings, and killed two people; and the business district was flooded after workers accidentally breached a tunnel beneath the Chicago River.

• In 1995, Congressman Mel Reynolds of Chicago was convicted of sexual assault of a young campaign worker.

THAT'S INTERESTING

• One of the most mysterious of all prehistoric remains is the huge figure of a monster, known as the Piasa Bird, painted high on the bluff near Alton. Its origin has never been determined.

• Lincoln, Illinois, was the only town named for Abraham Lincoln during his lifetime. Invited to dedicate the town, he christened it with watermelon juice and provided watermelon for the crowd.

• When a gang of counterfeiters tried to steal Abraham Lincoln's body from his tomb in exchange for a jailed member's freedom, quick Secret Service work foiled the bizarre ransom attempt.

NOTABLE NATIVES

Jane Addams (Cedarville, 1860-1935), social reformer. Jack Benny (Chicago, 1894-1974), comedian. Black Hawk (near Rockford, 1767-1838), Indian leader. William Jennings Bryan (Salem, 1860-1925), political leader. Charles Edgar Duryea (near Canton, 1861-1938), inventor. Betty Naomi Goldstein Friedan (Peoria, 1921-   ), author/social reformer. Benjamin David (Benny) Goodman (Chicago, 1909-1986), musician. Ernest Miller Hemingway (Oak Park, 1899-1961), author. James Butler (Wild Bill) Hickock (Troy Grove, 1837-1876), scout/frontiersman. Harriet Monroe (Chicago, 1860-1936), editor/poet. Ronald Wilson Reagan (Tampico, 1911-), U.S. president. Carl

Sandburg (Galesburg, 1878-1967), poet. **Charles Rudolph Walgreen** (Knox County, 1873-1939), pharmacist/merchant. **Florenz Ziegfeld** (Chicago, 1869-1932), theatrical producer.

GENERAL

Admitted to statehood: December 3, 1818
Origin of name: French for the *Illini* or "land of *Illini*," Algonquin word meaning men or warriors
Capital: Springfield
Nickname: Prairie State
Motto: State sovereignty, national union
Bird: Cardinal
Insect: Monarch butterfly
Fish: Bluegill
Flower: Native violet
Mineral: Fluorite
Song: "Illinois"
Tree: White oak

THE LAND

Area: 57,918 sq. mi., 25th
  Land: 55,593 sq. mi., 24th
  Water: 2,325 sq. mi., 17th
    Inland water: 750 sq. mi., 29th
    Great Lakes: 1,575 sq. mi., 6th
Topography: Prairies and fertile plains throughout; open hills in the southern region
Number of counties: 102
Geographic center: Logan, 28 mi. NE of Springfield
Length: 390 mi.; width: 210 mi.
Highest point: 1,235 ft. (Charles Mound), 45th
Lowest point: 279 ft. (Mississippi River), 33rd
Mean elevation: 600 ft., 38th

CLIMATE AND ENVIRONMENT

Temp., highest: 117 deg. on July 14, 1954, at East St. Louis; lowest: –35 deg. on Jan. 22, 1930, at Mount Carroll
Monthly average: highest: 87.1 deg., 26th; lowest: 9.8 deg., 11th; spread (high to low): 77.3 deg., 11th
Hazardous waste sites (1993): 37, 10th
Endangered species: Mammals: 2—Gray bat, Indiana bat; birds: 3—American peregrine falcon, Piping plover, Least tern; reptiles: none; amphibians: none; fishes: 1; invertebrates: 8; plants: 1

MAJOR CITIES
POPULATION, 1990
PERCENTAGE INCREASE, 1980-90

Aurora, 99,581—22.50%
Chicago, 2,783,726— -7.37%
Peoria, 113,504— -8.58%
Rockford, 139,426— -0.20%
Springfield, 105,227—5.17%

THE PEOPLE

Population (1995): 11,829,940, 6th
  Percent change (1990-95): 3.5%, 35th
Population (2000 proj.): 12,168,000, 6th
  Percent change (1990-2000): 6.45%, 34th
Per sq. mi. (1994): 211.4, 12th
Percent in metro. area (1992): 84.0%, 13th
Foreign born: 952,000, 6th
  Percent: 8.3%, 12th
Top three ancestries reported:
  German, 29.10%
  Irish, 16.28%
  African, 12.47%
White: 8,952,978, 78.32%, 36th
Black: 1,694,273, 14.82%, 14th
Native American: 21,836, 0.19%, 47th
Asian, Pacific Isle: 285,311, 2.50%, 10th
Other races: 476,204, 4.17%, 8th
Hispanic origin: 904,446, 7.91%, 10th
Percent over 5 yrs. speaking language other than English at home: 14.2%, 12th
Percent males: 48.57%, 26th; percent females: 51.43%, 26th
Percent never married: 28.8%, 10th
Marriages per 1,000 (1993): 7.8, 35th
Divorces per 1,000 (1993): 3.7, 36th
Median age: 32.8
Under 5 years (1994): 7.79%, 10th
Under 18 years (1994): 26.23%, 22nd
65 years & older (1994): 12.6%, 29th
Percent increase among the elderly (1990-94): 3.09%, 46th

OF VITAL IMPORTANCE

Live births per 1,000 pop. (1993): 16.3, 9th
Infant mortality rate per 1,000 births (1992): 10.1, 8th
  Rate for blacks (1990): 21.5, 2nd
  Rate for whites (1990): 7.7, 30th
Births to unmarried women, % of total (1992): 33.4%, 11th
Births to teenage mothers, % of total (1992): 12.9%, 23rd
Abortions (1992): 68,420, 5th

Rate per 1,000 women 14-44 years old: 25.4, 14th
Percent change (1988-92): –4%, 19th
Average lifetime (1979-81): 73.37, 36th
Deaths per 1,000 pop. (1993): 9.2, 20th
Causes of death per 100,000 pop.:
  Accidents & adverse effects (1992): 30.2, 42nd
  Atherosclerosis (1991): 5.9, 37th
  Cancer (1991): 212.0, 23rd
  Cerebrovascular diseases (1992): 58.4, 26th
  Chronic liver diseases & cirrhosis (1991): 11.4, 8th
  Chronic obstructive pulmonary diseases (1992): 33.3, 37th
  Diabetes mellitus (1992): 20.6, 26th
  Diseases of heart (1992): 296.8, 20th
  Pneumonia, flu (1991): 34.3, 16th
  Suicide (1992): 9.8, 44th

KEEPING WELL

Active nonfederal physicians per 100,000 pop. (1993): 230, 13th
Dentists per 100,000 (1991): 67, 10th
Nurses per 100,000 (1992): 804, 20th
Hospitals per 100,000 (1993): 1.78, 34th
  Admissions per 1,000 (1993): 125.60, 18th
  Occupancy rate per 100 beds (1993): 63.5, 22nd
  Average cost per patient per day (1993): $912, 17th
  Average cost per stay (1993): $6,318, 13th
  Average stay (1992): 7.2 days, 23rd
AIDS cases (adult, 1993): 2,959; per 100,000: 25.3, 23rd
HIV infection, not yet AIDS (1993): NA
Other notifiable diseases:
  Gonorrhea: 334.5, 14th
  Measles: 11.9, 6th
  Syphilis: 36.1, 19th
  Tuberculosis: 9.8, 16th
Pop. without health insur. (1991-93): 12.5%, 30th

HOUSEHOLDS BY TYPE

Total households (1994): 4,308,000
  Percent change (1990-94): 2.5%, 33rd
  Per 1,000 pop.: 366.58, 38th
  Percent of households 65 yrs. and over: 21.73%, 27th
  Persons per household (1994): 2.66, 14th
Family households: 2,924,880
  Percent of total: 69.60%, 34th
Nonfamily households: 1,277,360
  Percent of total: 30.40%, 17th

Pop. living in group quarters: 286,956
  Percent of pop.: 2.51%, 33rd

LIVING QUARTERS

Total housing units: 4,506,275
  Persons per unit: 2.54, 5th
Occupied housing units: 4,202,240
  Percent of total units: 93.25%, 2nd
  Persons per unit: 2.59, 14th
  Percent of units with over 1 person per room: 3.97%, 17th
Owner-occupied units: 2,699,182
  Percent of total units: 59.90%, 24th
  Percent of occupied units: 64.23%, 39th
  Persons per unit: 2.81, 12th
  Median value: $80,900, 19th
Renter-occupied units: 1,503,058
  Percent of total units: 33.35%, 13th
  Percent of occupied units: 35.77%, 15th
  Persons per unit: 2.37, 24th
  Median contract rent: $369, 19th
  Rental vacancy rate: 8.0%, 29th
Mobile home, trailer & other as a percent of occupied housing units: 4.50%, 44th
Persons in emergency shelters for homeless persons: 7,481, 0.065%, 16th
Persons visible in street locations: 1,755, 0.0154%, 12th
Persons in shelters for abused women: 536, 0.0047%, 28th
Nursing home population: 93,662, 0.82%, 20th

CRIME INDEX PER 100,000 (1992-93)

Total reported: 5,617.9, 16th
  Violent: 959.7, 8th
    Murder and nonnegligent manslaughter: 11.4, 10th
    Aggravated assault: 532.6, 10th
    Robbery: 381.2, 5th
    Forcible rape: 34.6, 33rd
  Property: 4,658.2, 21st
    Burglary: 1,015.5, 24th
    Larceny, theft: 3,084.0, 19th
    Motor vehicle theft: 558.7, 18th
Drug abuse violations (1990): 101.0, 47th
Child-abuse rate per 1,000 children (1993): 14.18, 26th

TEACHING AND LEARNING

Pop. 3 and over enrolled in school: 3,031,673
  Percent of pop.: 27.8%, 19th

Public elementary & secondary schools (1992-93): 4,185
Total enrollment (1992): 1,873,567
  Percent of total pop.: 16.13%, 40th
Teachers (1992): 111,461
  Percent of pop.: 0.96%, 35th
Pupil/teacher ratio (fall 1992): 16.8, 26th
Teachers' avg. salary (1992-93): $40,935, 11th
Expenditure per capita (1990-91): $3,293.58, 30th
Expenditure per pupil (1991-92): $5,670, 18th
Percent of graduates taking SAT (1993): 15%, 32nd
  Mean SAT verbal scores: 475, 18th
  Mean SAT mathematical scores: 541, 9th
Percent of graduates taking ACT (1995): 67%, 8th
  Mean ACT scores: 21.1, 26th
Percent of pop. over 25 completing:
  Less than 9th grade: 10.3%, 19th
  High school: 76.2%, 29th
  College degree(s): 21.0%, 20th
Higher education, institutions (1993-94): 169
  Enrollment (1992): 748,033
    Percent of pop.: 6.44%, 11th
  White non-Hispanic (1992): 543,108
    Percent of enroll.: 72.60%, 39th
  Black non-Hispanic (1992): 93,641
    Percent of enroll.: 12.52%, 12th
  Hispanic (1992): 54,582
    Percent of enroll.: 7.30%, 9th
  Asian/Pacific Islander (1992): 36,270
    Percent of enroll.: 4.85%, 9th
  American Indian/AK native (1992): 2,428
    Percent of enroll.: 0.32%, 35th
  Nonresident alien (1992): 18,004
    Percent of enroll.: 2.41%, 27th
  Female (1992): 411,698
    Percent of enroll.: 55.04%, 30th
  Pub. institutions (1993-94): 62
    Enrollment (1992): 565,889
    Percent of enroll.: 75.65%, 39th
  Private institutions (1993-94): 107
    Enrollment (1992): 182,144
    Percent of enroll.: 24.35%, 13th
  Tuition, public institution (avg., 1993-94): $6,964, 16th
  Tuition, private institution (avg., 1993-94): $14,299, 50th
Public library systems: 603
  Books & serial vol. per capita: 3.13, 17th
  Govt. expenditure per capita: $22.15, 11th

LAW ENFORCEMENT, COURTS, AND PRISONS

Police protection, corrections, judicial and legal functions expenditures (1992): $3,255,000,000
  Per capita: $280, 22nd
Police per 10,000 pop. (1993): 25.70, 9th
Prisoners (state & fed.) per 100,000 pop. (1993): 2,951.82, 25th
  Percent change (1992-93): 9.0%, 10th
Death penalty: yes, by lethal injection
  Under sentence of death (1993): 152, 5th
  Executed (1993): 0

RELIGION, NUMBER AND PERCENT OF POPULATION

Agnostic: 50,905—0.60%, 19th
Buddhist: 8,484—0.10%, 17th
Christian: 7,262,506—85.60%, 27th
Hindu: 16,969—0.20%, 3rd
Jewish: 127,264—1.50%, 13th
Muslim: 33,937—0.40%, 5th
Unitarian: 33,937—0.40%, 8th
Other: 118,779—1.40%, 20th
None: 593,897—7.00%, 23rd
Refused to answer: 237,559—2.80%, 12th

MAKING A LIVING

Personal income per capita (1994): $23,784, 10th
  Percent increase (1993-94): 5.4%, 17th
Disposable personal income per capita (1994): $20,587, 10th
Median income of households (1993): $32,875, 18th
Percent of pop. below poverty level (1993): 13.6%, 23rd
Percent 65 and over (1990): 10.7%, 34th
Expenditure for energy per person (1992): $1,832, 32nd

ECONOMY

Civilian labor force (1994): 6,000,000
  Percent of total pop.: 51.06%, 25th
  Percent 65 and over (1990): 2.82%, 24th
  Percent female: 46.25%, 27th
Percent job growth (1980-90): 13.49%, 40th
Major employer industries (1994):
  Agriculture: 103,000—1.9%, 36th
  Construction: 215,000—3.9%, 33rd
  Finance, insurance, & real estate: 399,000—7.2%, 6th
  Government: 734,000—13.3%, 41st

Manufacturing: 967,000—17.5%, 16th

Service: 1,278,000—23.1%, 16th

Trade: 1,094,000—19.7%, 11th

Transportation, communications, public utilities: 324,000—5.8%, 15th

Unemployment rate (1994): 5.67%, 24th

Male: 5.8%, 21st

Female: 5.5%, 23rd

Total businesses (1991): 441,411

New business incorps. (1991): 29,068

Percent of total businesses: 6.59%, 18th

Business failures (1991): 2,149

Percent of total businesses: 0.49%

Agriculture farm income:

Marketing (1993): $8,082,000,000, 5th

Average per farm: $101,025.00, 14th

Leading products (1993): Corn, soybeans, hogs, cattle

Average value land & build. per acre (1994): $1,645, 11th

Percent increase (1990-94): 18.43%, 13th

Govt. payments (1993): $851,000,000, 3rd

Average per farm: $10,637.50, 10th

Construction, value of all: $6,711,000,000

Per capita: $587.11, 21st

Manufactures:

Value added: $70,784,000,000

Per capita: $6,192.50, 11th

Leading products: Machinery, electric and electronic equipment, primary and fabricated metals, chemical products, printing and publishing, food and food products

Value of nonfuel mineral production (1994): $770,000,000, 16th

Leading mineral products: Coal, petroleum, stone

Retail sales (1993): $95,828,000,000, 6th

Per household: $22,274, 22nd

Percent increase (1992-93): 0.4%, 47th

Tourism revenues (1993): $15 bil.

Foreign exports, in total value (1994): $19,097,000,000, 6th

Per capita: $1,625.00, 14th

Gross state product per person (1993): $24,208.24, 12th

Percent change (1990-93): 2.95%, 28th

Patents per 100,000 pop. (1993): 28.34, 12th

Public aid recipients (percent of resident pop. 1993): 7.9%, 14th

Medicaid recipients per 1,000 pop. (1993): 119.46, 25th

Medicare recipients per 1,000 pop. (1993): 136.32, 32nd

TRAVEL AND TRANSPORTATION

Motor vehicle registrations (1993): 8,070,000

Per 1,000 pop.: 690.57, 44th

Motorcycle registrations (1993): 201,000

Per 1,000 pop.: 17.20, 24th

Licensed drivers per 1,000 pop. (1993): 638.54, 44th

Deaths from motor vehicle accidents per 100,000 pop. (1993): 11.91, 42nd

Public roads & streets (1993):

Total mileage: 136,965

Per 1,000 pop.: 11.72, 37th

Rural mileage: 101,784

Per 1,000 pop.: 8.71, 37th

Urban mileage: 35,181

Per 1,000 pop.: 3.01, 30th

Interstate mileage: 2,051

Per 1,000 pop.: 0.18, 32nd

Annual vehicle-mi. of travel per person (1993): 7,676, 44th

Mean travel time for workers age 16+ who work away from home: 25.1 min., 5th

GOVERNMENT

Percent of voting age pop. registered (1994): 63.0%, 30th

Percent of voting age pop. voting (1994): 42.8%, 36th

Percent of voting age pop. voting for U.S. representatives (1994): 34.9%, 38th

State legislators, total (1995): 177, 13th

Women members (1992): 33

Percent of legislature: 18.6%, 22nd

U.S. Congress, House members (1995): 20

Change (1985-95): –2

Revenues (1993):

State govt.: $30,351,000,000

Per capita: $2,597.21, 42nd

Parimutuel & amusement taxes & lotteries, revenue per capita: $132.12, 9th

Expenditures (1993):

State govt.: $28,133,000,000

Per capita: $2,407.41, 40th

Debt outstanding (1993): $19,893,000,000

Per capita: $1,702.29, 19th

LAWS AND REGULATIONS

Legal driving age: 18, 16 if completed driver education course

Marriage age without parental consent: 18

Divorce residence requirement: 90 days

ATTRACTIONS (1995)

Major opera companies: 2

Major symphony orchestras: 3

Major dance companies: 4

Major professional theater companies (non-profit): 1

State appropriations for arts agencies per capita: $0.57, 33rd

State Fair in early August at Springfield and late August at DuQuoin

SPORTS AND COMPETITION

NCAA teams (Division I): Bradley Univ. Braves, Chicago State Univ. Cougars, DePaul Univ. Blue Demons, Eastern Illinois Univ. Panthers, Illinois State Univ. Redbirds, Loyola Univ. Ramblers, Northeastern Illinois Univ. Golden Eagles, Northern Illinois Univ. Huskies, Northwestern Univ. Wildcats, Southern Illinois Univ. Salukis, Univ. of Illinois-Champaign Fighting Illini, Univ. of Illinois-Chicago Flames, Western Illinois Univ. Leathernecks

Major league baseball teams: Chicago White Sox (AL Central), Comiskey Park; Chicago Cubs (NL Central), Wrigley Field

NBA basketball teams: Chicago Bulls, United Center

NFL football teams: Chicago Bears (NFC), Soldier Field

NHL hockey teams: Chicago Blackhawks, United Center

INDIANA

"Blest Indiana....Find here the best retreat on earth."

John Finley, explorer

The Hoosier State provided a natural route between Canada and Louisiana for French explorers, trappers, and traders. Captured by the United States in the Revolution and secured by the War of 1812, Indiana soon greeted large numbers of settlers who came floating down the Ohio River in flatboats. The area has nurtured an extraordinary number of notables, including Indian leaders, future presidents, and four vice presidents. An impressive number of American literary figures, musicians, inventors, industrialists, and other personalities proudly lay claim to "My Indiana Home." The state also enjoys frequent leadership in sports, particularly in basketball.

SUPERLATIVES

• Wabash—the first electrically lighted city.
• The first U.S. industrial union, founded by Eugene V. Debs at Terre Haute.
• National leader in production of musical instruments.
• Produces 80% of the nation's dimensional limestone.

MOMENTS IN HISTORY

• In 1673, Robert Cavelier, Sieur de La Salle, entered the St. Joseph River near present-day Benton Harbor, the first recorded European visit.
• Records are unclear, but it is thought that Vincennes took shape between 1727 and 1732, when French fur trappers and traders plied their trade.
• In 1749, Pierre Joseph, Celeron de Bienville, led a colorful expedition down the Ohio River. He buried a series of lead plates along the way as evidence of French ownership of the region.
• In 1763 the British took over.
• During the American Revolution in 1779, American General George Rogers Clark, with only a handful of men, captured Vincennes and its hated leader, Henry Hamilton, the "Hair Buyer."

So They Say

"The capture of Vincennes by George Rogers Clark has been called ...one of the most heroic episodes in U.S. history...one of the greatest exploits of American arms."

Anonymous

• The Northwest Ordinance of 1787 paved the way for settlement in Indiana.
• Alarmed at the prospect of losing their lands, the Indians took up arms. But Revolutionary hero General "Mad Anthony" Wayne overcame Indian resistance and in 1795 forced the Indian leaders to sign a treaty giving up much of the region.
• After a period of relative peace, the Indians—led by Chief Tecumseh and his brother, The Prophet—again threatened the growing settlements. On November 7, 1811, territorial Governor William Henry Harrison decisively defeated the Indian confederation at their Prophetstown headquarters near present-day Lafayette, in the Battle of Tippecanoe.
• With the Indian threat diminished, the population quickly exceeded 60,000, and Indiana became the 19th state on December 11, 1816.

So They Say

The area of Buffaloville was "...a wild region with bears and other wild animals still in the woods. The clearing away of surplus wood was the great task ahead."

Abraham Lincoln in 1816

• In 1825, four wagons moved the government of Indiana to the new capital at Indianapolis, still much in its wilderness condition.

• Many Indiana cities became "stations" on the Underground Railroad in the years before the Civil War. More than 2,000 slaves found refuge at Levi Coffin's house in Fountain City on their way to freedom in Canada.

So They Say

"...A gentle rap at the door....Outside in the cold or rain, there would be a two horse wagon loaded with fugitives, perhaps the greater part of them women and children...the cold and hungry fugitives would be made comfortable."

Levi Coffin

• The Civil War reached Indiana in 1863 when Confederate raider John Hunt Morgan swept through the state.
• The state capitol was completed in 1878.
• In 1917, James Gresham of Evansville became one of the first three U.S. casualties in World War I. The war called 130,670 from Indiana into service.
• The worst-yet Ohio River floods in history occurred in 1937.
• World War II called 338,000 Indiana men and women into service.
• Burns Harbor opened for shipping in 1970, giving Indiana a much-needed major Great Lakes shipping port.
• In 1976, Indiana Dunes National Lakeshore was substantially expanded.
• The 1994 crash of a commuter plane near Gary helped focus increasing attention on small-plane safety.

THAT'S INTERESTING

• The British governor of Indiana, Henry Hamilton, was known as the "Hair Buyer" because he encouraged Indians friendly to the British to take American scalps, for which they were paid.
• Indiana's Lost River travels 22 miles underground.
• Indiana General Ambrose Burnside's bushy whiskers were originally called "burnsides" and now are known as "sideburns."

• Indiana is known for its many unusual place names, such as Gnaw Bone and Bean Blossom.

NOTABLE NATIVES

George Ade (Kentland, 1866-1944), humorist/playwright. Charles Austin Beard (near Knightstown, 1874-1948), political scientist/historian. Albert Jeremiah Beveridge (Highland County, 1862-1927), public official/historian. Larry Joe Bird (West Baden, 1956-), basketball player. Ambrose Everett Burnside (Liberty, 1824-1881), soldier/public official. Theodore Dreiser (Terre Haute, 1871-1945), author. Edward Eggleston (Vevay, 1837-1902), religious leader/historian. John Milton Hay (Salem, 1838-1905), diplomat/author. James (Jimmy) Riddle Hoffa (Brazil, 1913-1975?), labor leader. Robert Staughton Lind (New Albany, 1892-1970), sociologist. Thomas Riley Marshall (North Manchester, 1854-1925), U.S. vice president. John Tinney McCutcheon (Tippecanoe County, 1870-1949), cartoonist. Oliver Perry Morton (Salisbury, 1823-1877), public official. Cole Porter (Peru, 1893-1964), lyricist/composer. Gene Stratton Porter (Wabash County, 1863-1924), author. Ernest (Ernie) Taylor Pyle (Dana, 1900-1945), journalist. James Danforth (Dan) Quayle (Indianapolis, 1947-), U.S. vice president. James Whitcomb Riley (Greenfield, 1849-1916), poet. Newton Booth Tarkington (Indianapolis, 1869-1946), author. Lewis (Lew) Wallace (Brookville, 1827-1905), U.S. general/diplomat/author. Wendell L. Willkie (Elwood, 1892-1944), industrialist/political leader. Orville Wright (Dayton, 1871-1948), inventor/pioneer aviator. Wilbur Wright (Millville, 1867-1912), inventor/pioneer aviator.

GENERAL

Admitted to statehood: December 11, 1816
Origin of name: From the Latin for "land of the Indians"
Capital: Indianapolis
Nickname: Hoosier State
Motto: The crossroads of America
Bird: Cardinal
Flower: Peony

Stone: Limestone
Song: "On the Banks of the Wabash, Far Away"
Tree: Tulip poplar

THE LAND

Area: 36,420 sq. mi., 38th
  Land: 35,870 sq. mi., 38th
  Water: 550 sq. mi., 38th
    Inland water: 315 sq. mi., 42nd
  Great Lakes: 235 sq. mi., 8th
Topography: Hilly southern region; fertile rolling plains of central region; flat, heavily glaciated N; dunes along Lake Michigan shore
Number of counties: 92
Geographic center: Boone, 14 mi. NNW of Indianapolis
Length: 270 mi.; width: 140 mi.
Highest point: 1,257 ft. (Franklin Township), 44th
Lowest point: 320 ft. (Ohio River), 35th
Mean elevation: 700 ft., 34th

CLIMATE AND ENVIRONMENT

Temp., highest: 116 deg. on July 14, 1936, at Collegeville; lowest: –35 deg. on Feb. 2, 1951, at Greensburg
Monthly average: highest: 88.8 deg., 21st; lowest: 15.8 deg., 21st; spread (high to low): 73.0 deg., 19th
Hazardous waste sites (1993): 33, 12th
Endangered species: Mammals: 2—Gray bat, Indiana bat; birds: 3—American peregrine falcon, Piping plover, Least tern; reptiles: none; amphibians: none; fishes: none; invertebrates: 6; plants: 2

MAJOR CITIES
POPULATION, 1990
PERCENTAGE INCREASE, 1980-90

Evansville, 126,272— –3.24%
Fort Wayne, 173,072—0.40%
Gary, 116,646— –23.24%
Indianapolis, 731,327—4.35%
South Bend, 105,511— –3.84%

THE PEOPLE

Population (1995): 5,803,471, 14th
  Percent change (1990-95): 4.7%, 26th
Population (2000 proj.): 6,045,000, 14th
  Percent change (1990-2000): 9.03%, 29th

Per sq. mi. (1994): 160.4, 17th
Percent in metro. area (1992): 71.6%, 24th
Foreign born: 94,000, 25th
  Percent: 1.7%, 37th
Top three ancestries reported:
  German, 37.61%
  Irish, 17.41%
  English, 13.83%
White: 5,020,700, 90.56%, 18th
Black: 432,092, 7.79%, 23rd
Native American: 12,720, 0.23%, 40th
Asian, Pacific Isle: 37,617, 0. 68%, 38th
Other races: 41,030, 0.74%, 31st
Hispanic origin: 98,788, 1.78%, 32nd
Percent over 5 yrs. speaking language other than English at home: 4.8%, 39th
Percent males: 48.49%, 31st; percent females: 51.51%, 21st
Percent never married: 24.3%, 35th
Marriages per 1,000 (1993): 8.7, 24th
Median age: 32.8
Under 5 years (1994): 7.08%, 33rd
Under 18 years (1994): 25.61%, 31st
65 years & older (1994): 12.8%, 25th
Percent increase among the elderly (1990-94): 5.43%, 27th

OF VITAL IMPORTANCE

Live births per 1,000 pop. (1993): 14.8, 24th
Infant mortality rate per 1,000 births (1992): 9.4, 12th
  Rate for blacks (1990): 16.0, 25th
  Rate for whites (1990): 8.9, 6th
Births to unmarried women, % of total (1992): 29.5%, 23rd
Births to teenage mothers, % of total (1992): 14.1%, 17th
Abortions (1992): 15,840, 24th
  Rate per 1,000 women 14-44 years old: 12.0, 42nd
  Percent change (1988-92): 01%, 12th
Average lifetime (1979-81): 73.84, 26th
Deaths per 1,000 pop. (1993): 9.1, 23rd
Causes of death per 100,000 pop.:
  Accidents & adverse effects (1992): 34.1, 29th
  Atherosclerosis (1991): 9.1, 10th
  Cancer (1991): 212.6, 21st
  Cerebrovascular diseases (1992): 63.1, 18th
  Chronic liver diseases & cirrhosis (1991): 7.6, 42nd

Chronic obstructive pulmonary diseases (1992): 40.1, 19th

Diabetes mellitus (1992): 22.2, 16th

Diseases of heart (1992): 295.2, 21st

Pneumonia, flu (1991): 30 9, 27th

Suicide (1992): 12.3, 28th

KEEPING WELL

Active nonfederal physicians per 100,000 pop. (1993): 168, 42nd

Dentists per 100,000 (1991): 48, 35th

Nurses per 100,000 (1992): 700, 31st

Hospitals per 100,000 (1993): 2.02, 29th

Admissions per 1,000 (1993): 124.83, 19th

Occupancy rate per 100 beds (1993): 58.7, 35th

Average cost per patient per day (1993): $898, 20th

Average cost per stay (1993): $5,677, 26th

Average stay (1992): 6.8 days, 34th

AIDS cases (adult, 1993): 954; per 100,000: 16.7, 33rd

HIV infection, not yet AIDS (1993): 2,170

Other notifiable diseases:

Gonorrhea: 205.0, 24th

Measles: 7.3, 13th

Syphilis: 6.6, 36th

Tuberculosis: 4.9, 34th

Pop. without health insur. (1991-93): 12.0%, 33rd

HOUSEHOLDS BY TYPE

Total households (1994): 2,161,000

Percent change (1990-94): 4.6%, 23rd

Per 1,000 pop.: 375.70, 23rd

Percent of households 65 yrs. and over: 21.75%, 26th

Persons per household (1994): 2.59, 26th

Family households: 1,480,351

Percent of total: 71.68%, 16th

Nonfamily households: 585,004

Percent of total: 28.32%, 36th

Pop. living in group quarters: 161,992

Percent of pop.: 2.92%, 22nd

LIVING QUARTERS

Total housing units: 2,246,046

Persons per unit: 2.47, 12th

Occupied housing units: 2,065,355

Percent of total units: 91.96%, 9th

Persons per unit: 2.52, 28th

Percent of units with over 1 person per room: 2.20%, 40th

Owner-occupied units: 1,450,898

Percent of total units: 64.60%, 3rd

Percent of occupied units: 70.25%, 8th

Persons per unit: 2.73, 26th

Median value: $53,900, 40th

Renter-occupied units: 614,457

Percent of total units: 27.36%, 37th

Percent of occupied units: 29.75%, 44th

Persons per unit: 2.30, 32nd

Median contract rent: $291, 32nd

Rental vacancy rate: 8.3%, 26th

Mobile home, trailer & other as a percent of occupied housing units: 8.53%, 30th

Persons in emergency shelters for homeless persons: 2,251, 0.041%, 33rd

Persons visible in street locations: 268, 0.0048%, 29th

Persons in shelters for abused women: 279, 0.0050%, 25th

Nursing home population: 50,845, 0.92%, 16th

CRIME INDEX PER 100,000 (1992-93)

Total reported: 4,465.1, 35th

Violent: 489.1, 30th

Murder and nonnegligent manslaughter: 7.5, 24th

Aggravated assault: 322.6, 27th

Robbery: 119.8, 33rd

Forcible rape: 39.1, 25th

Property: 3,976.0, 37th

Burglary: 852.0, 34th

Larceny, theft: 2,695.9, 35th

Motor vehicle theft: 428.1, 27th

Drug abuse violations (1990): 109.9, 45th

Child-abuse rate per 1,000 children (1993): 19.83, 13th

TEACHING AND LEARNING

Pop. 3 and over enrolled in school: 1,436,188

Percent of pop.: 27.1%, 26th

Public elementary & secondary schools (1992-93): 1,902

Total enrollment (1992): 960,630

Percent of total pop.: 16.98%, 31st

Teachers (1992): 54,552

Percent of pop.: 0.96%, 35th

Pupil/teacher ratio (fall 1992): 17.6, 14th

Teachers' avg. salary (1992-93): $37,042, 21st

Expenditure per capita (1990-91): $2,993.85, 40th

Expenditure per pupil (1991-92): $5,074, 29th

Percent of graduates taking SAT (1993): 61%, 15th

Mean SAT verbal scores: 409, 46th

Mean SAT mathematical scores: 460, 46th

Percent of graduates taking ACT (1995): 22%, 31st

Mean ACT scores: 21.2, 20th

Percent of pop. over 25 completing:

Less than 9th grade: 8.5%, 33rd

High school: 75.6%, 31st

College degree(s): 15.6%, 46th

Higher education, institutions (1993-94): 77

Enrollment (1992): 296,912

Percent of pop.: 5.25%, 35th

White non-Hispanic (1992): 260,263

Percent of enroll.: 87.66%, 15th

Black non-Hispanic (1992): 17,466

Percent of enroll.: 5.88%, 26th

Hispanic (1992): 5,354

Percent of enroll.: 1.80%, 27th

Asian/Pacific Islander (1992): 4,600

Percent of enroll.: 1.55%, 34th

American Indian/AK native (1992): 1,015

Percent of enroll.: 0.34%, 32nd

Nonresident alien (1992): 8,124

Percent of enroll.: 6.06%, 3rd

Female (1992): 159,356

Percent of enroll.: 53.67%, 45th

Pub. institutions (1993-94): 28

Enrollment (1992): 234,624

Percent of enroll.: 79.02%, 36th

Private institutions (1993-94): 49

Enrollment (1992): 62,288

Percent of enroll.: 20.98%, 16th

Tuition, public institution (avg., 1993-94): $6,639, 18th

Tuition, private institution (avg., 1993-94): $14,196, 19th

Public library systems: 238

Books & serial vol. per capita: 3.39, 13th

Govt. expenditure per capita: $22.43, 10th

LAW ENFORCEMENT, COURTS, AND PRISONS

Police protection, corrections, judicial and legal functions expenditures (1992): $1,026,000,000

Per capita: $181, 45th

Police per 10,000 pop. (1993): 15.90, 46th

Prisoners (state & fed.) per 100,000 pop. (1993): 2,535.93, 30th

Percent change (1992-93): 3.8%, 33rd

Death penalty: yes, by electrocution

Under sentence of death (1993): 47, 16th

Executed (1993): 0

RELIGION, NUMBER AND PERCENT OF POPULATION

Agnostic: 12,265—0.30%, 37th

Buddhist: 4,088—0.10%, 17th

Christian: 3,577,171—87.50%, 21st

Hindu: NA

Jewish: 12,265—0.30%, 35th

Muslim: 4,089—0.10%, 22nd

Unitarian: 4,088—0.10%, 31st

Other: 77,676—1.90%, 12th

None: 302,526—7.40%, 17th

Refused to answer: 94,029—2.30%, 21st

MAKING A LIVING

Personal income per capita (1994): $20,378, 29th

Percent increase (1993-94): 6.1%, 10th

Disposable personal income per capita (1994): $17,801, 28th

Median income of households (1993): $29,475, 30th

Percent of pop. below poverty level (1993): 12.2%, 31st

Percent 65 and over (1990): 10.8%, 30th

Expenditure for energy per person (1992): $2,051, 11th

ECONOMY

Civilian labor force (1994): 3,056,000

Percent of total pop.: 53.13%, 13th

Percent 65 and over (1990): 2.26%, 39th

Percent female: 47.61%, 8th

Percent job growth (1980-90): 17.67%, 32nd

Major employer industries (1994):

Agriculture: 62,000—2.2%, 31st

Construction: 125,000—4.5%, 21st

Finance, insurance, & real estate: 152,000—5.5%, 20th

Government: 349,000—12.6%, 47th

Manufacturing: 675,000—24.3%, 2nd

Service: 548,000—19.7%, 34th

Trade: 499,000—17.9%, 42nd

Transportation, communications, public utilities: 142,000—5.1%, 30th
Unemployment rate (1994): 4.94%, 37th
  Male: 4.5%, 41st
  Female: 5.4%, 24th
Total businesses (1991): 160,619
  New business incorps. (1991): 10,205
    Percent of total businesses: 6.35%, 20th
  Business failures (1991): 1,171
  Percent of total businesses: 0.73%
Agriculture farm income:
  Marketing (1993): $5,118,000,000, 11th
    Average per farm: $81,238.10, 24th
  Leading products (1993): Corn, soybeans, hogs, cattle
  Average value land & build. per acre (1994): $1,473, 12th
    Percent increase (1990-94): 18.41%, 15th
  Govt. payments (1993): $379,000,000, 13th
    Average per farm: $6,015.87, 17th
Construction, value of all: $3,453,000,000
  Per capita: $622.82, 20th
Manufactures:
  Value added: $44,924,000,000
    Per capita: $8,102.94, 2nd
  Leading products: Primary and fabricated metals, transportation equipment, electric and electronic equipment, nonelectrical machinery, plastics, chemical products, foods
Value of nonfuel mineral production (1994): $517,000,000, 21st
Leading mineral products: Coal, petroleum, stone
Retail sales (1993): $45,787,000,000, 14th
  Per household: $21,346, 33rd
    Percent increase (1992-93): 8.7%, 14th
Tourism revenues (1993): $4.4 bil.
Foreign exports, in total value (1994): $8,256,000,000, 15th
  Per capita: $1,435.33, 19th
Gross state product per person (1993): $20,346.24, 31st
  Percent change (1990-93): 2.70%, 34th
Patents per 100,000 pop. (1993): 19.40, 25th
Public aid recipients (percent of resident pop. 1993): 5.1%, 39th
Medicaid recipients per 1,000 pop. (1993): 99.02, 36th
Medicare recipients per 1,000 pop. (1993): 140.73, 26th

TRAVEL AND TRANSPORTATION

Motor vehicle registrations (1993): 4,670,000
  Per 1,000 pop.: 818.44, 20th
Motorcycle registrations (1993): 96,000
  Per 1,000 pop.: 16.82, 25th
Licensed drivers per 1,000 pop. (1993): 664.39, 37th
Deaths from motor vehicle accidents per 100,000 pop. (1993): 15.62, 30th
Public roads & streets (1993):
  Total mileage: 92,374
    Per 1,000 pop.: 16.19, 29th
  Rural mileage: 73,112
    Per 1,000 pop.: 12.81, 28th
  Urban mileage: 19,262
    Per 1,000 pop.: 3.38, 13th
  Interstate mileage: 1,138
    Per 1,000 pop.: 0.20, 26th
Annual vehicle-mi. of travel per person (1993): 10,603, 6th
Mean travel time for workers age 16+ who work away from home: 20.4 min., 29th

GOVERNMENT

Percent of voting age pop. registered (1994): 55.6%, 46th
  Percent of voting age pop. voting (1994): 38.7%, 45th
  Percent of voting age pop. voting for U.S. representatives (1994): 36.0%, 34th
State legislators, total (1995): 150, 19th
  Women members (1992): 26
    Percent of legislature: 17.3%, 26th
U.S. Congress, House members (1995): 10
  Change (1985-95): 0
Revenues (1993):
  State govt.: $14,653,000,000
    Per capita: $2,568.00, 43rd
  Parimutuel & amusement taxes & lotteries, revenue per capita: $81.84, 23rd
Expenditures (1993):
  State govt.: $14,136,000,000
    Per capita: $2,477.39, 35th
Debt outstanding (1993): $5,458,000,000
  Per capita: $956.54, 38th

LAWS AND REGULATIONS

Legal driving age: 18, 16 if completed driver education course

Marriage age without parental consent: 18
Divorce residence requirement: 6 mo., for
    qualifications check local statutes

ATTRACTIONS (1995)

Major opera companies: 1
Major symphony orchestras: 2
Major dance companies: 1
Major professional theater companies (non-
    profit): 1
State appropriations for arts agencies per capita:
    $0.48, 39th
State Fair in mid-August at Indianapolis

SPORTS AND COMPETITION

NCAA teams (Division I): Ball State Univ.
    Cardinals, Butler Univ. Bulldogs, Indi-
    ana State Univ. Sycamores, Indiana
    Univ.-Bloomington Fightin' Hoosiers,
    Purdue Univ. Boilermakers, Univ. of
    Evansville Aces, Univ. of Notre Dame
    Fighting Irish, Valparaiso Univ. Cru-
    saders
NBA basketball teams: Indiana Pacers, Market
    Square Arena
NFL football teams: Indianapolis Colts
    (AFC), Hoosier Dome

I O W A

"The people who have lived on the land between the two great rivers have fought, struggled, labored, laughed, and grown in wealth and culture through the years. No other similar area has produced so much to feed the world—Iowa, an often neglected treasure!"

Allan Carpenter, native of Waterloo, Iowa

Many think of Iowa as a land of huge farms and small cities populated by people right out of Meredith Willson's *The Music Man*. True, it is one of the greatest farming states in the country, producing about one-fifth of the nation's corn supply and containing about a quarter of the country's richest farmlands. But it is also a leader in manufacturing cereals, tractors, and washing machines. Iowa also has one of the finest writing schools in the country (the University of Iowa), and among Iowa's notables are many authors and artists, including Grant Wood. The state is known as the "Hartford of the West" because of its many insurance company headquarters. The state is experiencing rapidly increasing growth in the manufacturing and service industries.

SUPERLATIVES

• Birthplace of Herbert Hoover, first U.S. president born west of the Mississippi River.
• The first state ever to produce a billion-dollar harvest from a single crop.
• Produced the first "traction machine" (tractor).
• World's largest tractor plant, at Waterloo.
• The mechanical washing machine, first manufactured in Iowa.

MOMENTS IN HISTORY

• In 1673, European explorers first glimpsed present-day Iowa as Father Jacques Marquette and Louis Jolliet marveled at the Iowa bluffs above the Mississippi River.
• The French claimed the region, and explorer Joseph Des Noyelles fought a little-known battle with the Fox and Sauk Indians in 1735, at the junction of the Raccoon and Des Moines rivers.
• In 1762, France turned over to Spain its claims west of the Mississippi, including Iowa.

• In 1788, Julian Dubuque settled at Cat-fish Creek on the Mississippi, founding the community of Dubuque, where he mined the plentiful lead of the region.

So They Say

"The Indians treated the exploring party [Marquette and Jolliet] with great respect, preparing a huge feast of dog meat and other delicacies. The hosts, as a sign of honor, insisted on placing the food in the mouths of the guests, much to the visitors' discomfort."

The Palimpsest

• In 1800, Spain secretly returned the Louisiana Territory to France. The Louisiana Purchase of 1803 brought Iowa to the United States.
• In 1804, Sergeant Floyd of the famed Lewis and Clark expedition died and was buried at the site of Sioux City; he was the only member of the party to die during the journey.
• At present-day Burlington, explorer Zebulon Pike hoisted the first U.S. flag to fly over Iowa, in 1805. The bluff near McGregor was named Pike's Peak but is less prominent than the Colorado peak bearing his name.
• In 1819 the first steamer, the *Western Engineer*, reached the area of Council Bluffs on the Missouri River.
• On December 28, 1846, Iowa became the first free state in the old Louisiana Territory.
• Progress continued rapidly with the first state fair, at Fairfield in 1854, at the University of Iowa at Iowa City in 1855, and at the new capital at Des Moines in 1856.
• In 1856 the bridge between Davenport and Rock Island was the first to span the mighty Mississippi River.

• Notorious abolitionist John Brown headquartered for a time at Tabor as he helped slaves escape to freedom over the Underground Railroad.

• Iowa Civil War troops were especially prominent in the Battle of Wilson's Creek (August 20, 1861) and Iuka (September 19, 1862).

• In 1869, Council Bluffs became the eastern terminus of the Central Pacific Railroad.

• In 1889, Grinnell College and the University of Iowa played the first intercollegiate football game west of the Mississippi.

• In the 1890s, Independence became famous as a center for trotting races.

• In 1917, Iowa serviceman Merle Hay was one of the first three Americans to be killed during World War I. Iowan J. C. Sabin is said to have fired the first U.S. shot of that war.

• During World War II, 260,000 Iowans served, and 8,398 lost their lives.

• The 1980s brought increasing problems to Iowa farmers, with rising costs, falling prices and values, and overextended debt, but the 1990s brought an upturn.

• In 1994, Representative Fred Grandy (remembered for his role as "Gopher" on the television show *The Loveboat*) failed in his bid for the Iowa governorship.

• Iowa celebrated its sesquicentennial of statehood in 1996.

THAT'S INTERESTING

• When the Fox Indians refused to do a favor for Julian Dubuque, he threatened to burn the Mississippi. At the mouth of Catfish Creek, Dubuque set fire to oil poured into the creek upstream by an assistant. The frightened Indians quickly came to terms, and Dubuque called on the fire to die just as the oil gave out.

• The honey trees of a region disputed between Iowa and Missouri were so prized that the two states almost came to blows in a territorial dispute called the Honey War.

• Iowa's Civil War Greybeard Regiment, made up of men over the legal age of 45, was the only one of its kind ever authorized.

• The first "road" in Iowa consisted of a furrow plowed by Lyman Dillon from Dubuque to Iowa City, thought to be the longest continuous furrow ever plowed.

• James "Tama Jim" Wilson of Traer holds the all-time record for service in any cabinet office—16 years as secretary of agriculture.

So They Say

When James Wilson went to Congress, there were two James Wilsons from Iowa. Asked how they might be distinguished, he suggested that because he was from Tama County, Iowa, he should be known as "Tama Jim." From that moment the name Tama Jim Wilson went on to worldwide fame.

The Enchantment of Iowa

• One Iowan traveling in Scotland was so taken with the local oatmeal that he ordered a barrel of it sent to him in Iowa. When it arrived from Scotland, it bore the legend "Quaker Oats, made in Cedar Rapids, Iowa."

• The popular delicious apple originated in Iowa.

NOTABLE NATIVES

Adrian Constantine (Cap) Anson (Marshalltown, 1851-1922), baseball player/manager. **William Frederick "Buffalo Bill" Cody** (Scott County, 1846-1917), frontiersman/showman. **Robert William Andrew Feller** (Van Meter, 1918-   ), baseball player. **George Horace Gallup** (Jefferson, 1901-1984), statistician/public opinion analyst. **James Norman Hall** (Colfax, 1887-1951), author. **Herbert Clark Hoover** (West Branch, 1874-1964), U.S. president. **MacKinlay Kantor** (Webster City, 1904-1977), author. **Glenn Miller** (Clarinda, 1904-1944), bandleader. **Lillian Russell** (Clinton, 1861-1922), singer/actress. **William Ashley (Billy) Sunday** (Ames, 1862-1935), baseball player/evangelist. **James Alfred Van Allen** (Mount Pleasant, 1914-), astrophysicist. **Henry Agard Wallace** (Adair County, 1888-1965), U.S. vice president. **John Wayne** (Winterset, 1907-1979), actor. **Margaret Wilson** (Traer, 1882-1976), author. **Grant Wood** (near Anamosa, 1892-1942), artist.

GENERAL

Admitted to statehood: December 28, 1846

Origin of name: Indian word variously translated as "one who puts to sleep" or "beautiful land"

Capital: Des Moines

Nickname: Hawkeye State

Motto: Our liberties we prize and our rights we will maintain

Bird: Eastern goldfinch
Flower: Wild rose
Stone: Geode
Song: "Song of Iowa"
Tree: Oak

THE LAND

Area: 56,276 sq. mi., 26th
  Land: 55,875 sq. mi., 23rd
  Water: 401 sq. mi., 42nd
    Inland water: 401 sq. mi., 36th
Topography: Watershed from NW to SE; soil especially rich and land level in the N central counties
Number of counties: 99
Geographic center: Story, 5 mi. NE of Ames
Length: 310 mi.; width: 200 mi.
Highest point: 1,670 ft. (Sec. 29, T100N, R41W, Osceola County), 42nd
Lowest point: 480 ft. (Mississippi River), 38th
Mean elevation: 1,100 ft., 22nd

CLIMATE AND ENVIRONMENT

Temp., highest: 118 deg. on July 20, 1934, at Keokuk; lowest: −47 deg. on Jan. 12, 1912, at Washta
Monthly average: highest: 86.2 deg., 32nd; lowest: 6.3 deg., 6th; spread (high to low): 79.9 deg., 7th
Hazardous waste sites (1993): 20, 19th
Endangered species: Mammals: 1—Indiana bat; birds: 2—American peregrine falcon, Least tern; reptiles: none; amphibians: none; fishes: 1; invertebrates: 3; plants: 1

MAJOR CITIES
POPULATION, 1990
PERCENTAGE INCREASE, 1980-90

Cedar Rapids, 108,751— −1.35%
Davenport, 95,333— −7.68%
Des Moines, 193,187—1.14%
Sioux City, 80,505— −1.83%
Waterloo, 66,467— −12.53%

THE PEOPLE

Population (1995): 2,841,764, 30th
  Percent change (1990-95): 2.3%, 43rd
Population (2000 proj.): 2,930,000, 30th
  Percent change (1990-2000): 5.52%, 38th
Per sq. mi. (1994): 50.6, 34th
Percent in metro. area (1992): 43.8%, 41st
Foreign born: 43,000, 36th
  Percent: 1.6%, 41st

Top three ancestries reported:
  German, 50.23%
  Irish, 18.98%
  English, 14.01%
White: 2,683,090, 96.63%, 4th
Black: 48,090, 1.73%, 41st
Native American: 7,349, 0.26%, 36th
Asian, Pacific Isle: 25,476, 0.92%, 32nd
Other races: 12,750, 0.46%, 37th
Hispanic origin: 32,647, 1.18%, 38th
Percent over 5 yrs. speaking language other than English at home: 3.9%, 42nd
Percent males: 48.43%, 35th; percent females: 51.57%, 17th
Percent never married: 23.7%, 39th
Marriages per 1,000 (1993): 8.9, 20th
Divorces per 1,000 (1993): 3.9, 34th
Median age: 34
Under 5 years (1994): 6.65%, 47th
Under 18 years (1994): 25.77%, 28th
65 years & older (1994): 15.4%, 4th
Percent increase among the elderly (1990-94): 2.56%, 49th

OF VITAL IMPORTANCE

Live births per 1,000 pop. (1993): 13.2, 47th
Infant mortality rate per 1,000 births (1992): 8.0, 31st
  Rate for blacks (1990): 18.0, 10th
  Rate for whites (1990): 7.8, 27th
Births to unmarried women, % of total (1992): 23.5%, 43rd
Births to teenage mothers, % of total (1992): 10.2%, 37th
Abortions (1992): 6,970, 37th
  Rate per 1,000 women 14-44 years old: 11.4, 44th
  Percent change (1988-92): −22%, 47th
Average lifetime (1979-81): 75.18, 9th
Deaths per 1,000 pop. (1993): 9.9, 8th
Causes of death per 100,000 pop.:
  Accidents & adverse effects (1992): 36.4, 22nd
  Atherosclerosis (1991): 13.8, 2nd
  Cancer (1991): 229.5, 9th
  Cerebrovascular diseases (1992): 72.5, 4th
  Chronic liver diseases & cirrhosis (1991): 6.2, 48th
  Chronic obstructive pulmonary diseases (1992): 41.8, 14th
  Diabetes mellitus (1992): 18.1, 35th
  Diseases of heart (1992): 327.5, 10th
  Pneumonia, flu (1991): 44.0, 2nd
  Suicide (1992): 10.2, 43rd

KEEPING WELL

Active nonfederal physicians per 100,000 pop.
  (1993): 159, 44th
Dentists per 100,000 (1991): 54, 24th
Nurses per 100,000 (1992): 922, 8th
Hospitals per 100,000 (1993): 4.22, 7th
  Admissions per 1,000 (1993): 123.50, 22nd
  Occupancy rate per 100 beds (1993): 57.9,
    38th
  Average cost per patient per day (1993):
    $612, 46th
  Average cost per stay (1993): $4,980, 44th
  Average stay (1992): 7.6 days, 16th
AIDS cases (adult, 1993): 202; per 100,000:
  7.2, 45th
HIV infection, not yet AIDS (1993): NA
Other notifiable diseases:
  Gonorrhea: 83.9, 38th
  Measles: 0.9, 41st
  Syphilis: 5.3, 38th
  Tuberculosis: 2.6, 42nd
Pop. without health insur. (1991-93): 9.5%,
  46th

HOUSEHOLDS BY TYPE

Total households (1994): 1,082,000
  Percent change (1990-94): 1.6%, 44th
  Per 1,000 pop.: 382.47, 7th
  Percent of households 65 yrs. and over:
    25.60%, 6th
  Persons per household (1994): 2.52, 48th
Family households: 740,819
  Percent of total: 69.60%, 35th
Nonfamily households: 323,506
  Percent of total: 30.40%, 18th
Pop. living in group quarters: 99,520
  Percent of pop.: 3.58%, 7th

LIVING QUARTERS

Total housing units: 1,143,669
  Persons per unit: 2.43, 19th
Occupied housing units: 1,064,325
  Percent of total units: 93.06%, 4th
  Persons per unit: 2.44, 48th
  Percent of units with over 1 person per
    room: 1.50%, 51st
Owner-occupied units: 745,377
  Percent of total units: 65.17%, 2nd
  Percent of occupied units: 70.03%, 11th
  Persons per unit: 2.63, 44th
  Median value: $15,900, 51st
Renter-occupied units: 318,948
  Percent of total units: 27.89%, 31st
  Percent of occupied units: 29.97%, 41st

Persons per unit: 2.25, 39th
  Median contract rent: $216, 50th
  Rental vacancy rate: 6.4%, 45th
Mobile home, trailer & other as a percent of
  occupied housing units: 6.43%, 41st
Persons in emergency shelters for homeless
  persons: 989, 0.036%, 43rd
Persons visible in street locations: 148,
  0.0053%, 27th
Persons in shelters for abused women: 164,
  0.0059%, 13th
Nursing home population: 36,455, 1.31%,
  2nd

CRIME INDEX PER 100,000 (1992-93)

Total reported: 3,846.4, 43rd
  Violent: 325.5, 39th
    Murder and nonnegligent manslaughter:
      2.3, 48th
    Aggravated assault: 244.8, 34th
    Robbery: 53.9, 42nd
    Forcible rape: 24.4, 48th
  Property: 3,521.0, 44th
    Burglary: 730.7, 39th
    Larceny, theft: 2,599.4, 40th
    Motor vehicle theft: 190.8, 44th
Drug abuse violations (1990): 116.1, 44th
Child-abuse rate per 1,000 children (1993):
  12.04, 33rd

TEACHING AND LEARNING

Pop. 3 and over enrolled in school: 737,729
  Percent of pop.: 27.7%, 22nd
Public elementary & secondary schools (1992-
  93): 1,560
  Total enrollment (1992): 494,839
    Percent of total pop.: 17.65%, 18th
  Teachers (1992): 31,405
    Percent of pop.: 1.12%, 15th
  Pupil/teacher ratio (fall 1992): 15.8, 33rd
  Teachers' avg. salary (1992-93): $31,991,
    33rd
  Expenditure per capita (1990-91):
    $3,416.89, 25th
  Expenditure per pupil (1991-92): $5,096,
    28th
Percent of graduates taking SAT (1993): 5%,
  49th
  Mean SAT verbal scores: 520, 1st
  Mean SAT mathematical scores: 583, 1st
Percent of graduates taking ACT (1995):
  64%, 12th
  Mean ACT scores: 21.8, 6th

Percent of pop. over 25 completing:
  Less than 9th grade: 9.2%, 28th
  High school: 80.1%, 14th
  College degree(s): 16.9%, 41st
Higher education, institutions (1993-94): 61
  Enrollment (1992): 177,813
    Percent of pop.: 6.33%, 14th
    White non-Hispanic (1992): 158,393
      Percent of enroll.: 89.08%, 13th
    Black non-Hispanic (1992): 5,179
      Percent of enroll.: 2.91%, 39th
    Hispanic (1992): 2,534
      Percent of enroll.: 1.43%, 33rd
    Asian/Pacific Islander (1992): 3,051
      Percent of enroll.: 1.72%, 32nd
    American Indian/AK native (1992): 552
      Percent of enroll.: 0.31%, 40th
    Nonresident alien (1992): 8,104
      Percent of enroll.: 4.56%, 6th
    Female (1992): 95,869
      Percent of enroll.: 53.92%, 43rd
  Pub. institutions (1993-94): 20
    Enrollment (1992): 127,849
      Percent of enroll.: 71.90%, 41st
  Private institutions (1993-94): 41
    Enrollment (1992): 49,964
      Percent of enroll.: 28.10%, 11th
  Tuition, public institution (avg., 1993-94): $5,440, 30th
  Tuition, private institution (avg., 1993-94): $13,566, 21st
Public library systems: 500
  Books & serial vol. per capita: 3.82, 8th
  Govt. expenditure per capita: $18.55, 19th

LAW ENFORCEMENT, COURTS, AND PRISONS

Police protection, corrections, judicial and legal functions expenditures (1992): $452,000,000
  Per capita: $161, 47th
Police per 10,000 pop. (1993): 15.92, 44th
Prisoners (state & fed.) per 100,000 pop. (1993): 1,736.26, 43rd
  Percent change (1992-93): 8.4%, 11th
Death penalty: no

RELIGION, NUMBER AND PERCENT OF POPULATION

Agnostic: 22,637—1.10%, 6th
Buddhist: NA
Christian: 1,837,682—89.30%, 15th
Hindu: 2,058—0.10%, 10th
Jewish: NA
Muslim: NA

Unitarian: 2,058—0.10%, 31st
Other: 41,158—2.00%, 10th
None: 121,415—5.90%, 34th
Refused to answer: 30,868—1.50%, 42nd

MAKING A LIVING

Personal income per capita (1994): $20,265, 30th
  Percent increase (1993-94): 10.9%, 1st
Disposable personal income per capita (1994): $17,529, 34th
Median income of households (1993): $28,663, 35th
Percent of pop. below poverty level (1993): 10.3%, 40th
  Percent 65 and over (1990): 11.2%, 28th
Expenditure for energy per person (1992): $1,889, 24th

ECONOMY

Civilian labor force (1994): 1,565,000
  Percent of total pop.: 55.32%, 3rd
  Percent 65 and over (1990): 4.34%, 3rd
  Percent female: 46.07%, 31st
Percent job growth (1980-90): 7.04%, 47th
Major employer industries (1994):
  Agriculture: 116,000—7.8%, 4th
  Construction: 56,000—3.8%, 36th
  Finance, insurance, & real estate: 82,000—5.5%, 20th
  Government: 226,000—15.2%, 27th
  Manufacturing: 253,000—17.0%, 19th
  Service: 270,000—18.2%, 44th
  Trade: 292,000—19.6%, 13th
  Transportation, communications, public utilities: 61,000—4.1%, 45th
Unemployment rate (1994): 3.71%, 48th
  Male: 3.9%, 48th
  Female: 3.4%, 48th
Total businesses (1991): 168,153
  New business incorps. (1991): 4,531
    Percent of total businesses: 2.69%, 49th
  Business failures (1991): 553
    Percent of total businesses: 0.33%
Agriculture farm income:
  Marketing (1993): $10,001,000,000, 3rd
    Average per farm: $100,010.00, 15th
  Leading products (1993): Hogs, corn, cattle, soybeans
  Average value land & build. per acre (1994): $1,316, 16th
    Percent increase (1990-94): 19.42%, 10th

Govt. payments (1993): $1,230,000,000, 2nd

Average per farm: $12,300.00, 8th

Construction, value of all: $1,249,000,000

Per capita: $449.81, 38th

Manufactures:

Value added: $19,503,000,000

Per capita: $7,023.67, 6th

Leading products: Tires, farm machinery, electronic products, appliances, office furniture, chemicals, fertilizers, auto accessories

Value of nonfuel mineral production (1994): $426,000,000, 28th

Leading mineral products: Stone, cement, sand/gravel

Retail sales (1993): $24,293,000,000, 29th

Per household: $22,324, 21st

Percent increase (1992-93): 9.7%, 11th

Tourism revenues (1994): $6.8 bil.

Foreign exports, in total value (1994): $3,214,000,000, 29th

Per capita: $1,136.09, 30th

Gross state product per person (1993): $20,057.31, 34th

Percent change (1990-93): 1.82%, 40th

Patents per 100,000 pop. (1993): 15.38, 28th

Public aid recipients (percent of resident pop. 1993): 4.9%, 41st

Medicaid recipients per 1,000 pop. (1993): 102.45, 30th

Medicare recipients per 1,000 pop. (1993): 166.25, 5th

TRAVEL AND TRANSPORTATION

Motor vehicle registrations (1993): 2,738,000

Per 1,000 pop.: 970.58, 6th

Motorcycle registrations (1993): 149,000

Per 1,000 pop.: 52.82, 1st

Licensed drivers per 1,000 pop. (1993): 673.17, 31st

Deaths from motor vehicle accidents per 100,000 pop. (1993): 15.49, 31st

Public roads & streets (1993):

Total mileage: 112,708

Per 1,000 pop.: 39.95, 8th

Rural mileage: 103,490

Per 1,000 pop.: 36.69, 8th

Urban mileage: 9,218

Per 1,000 pop.: 3.27, 18th

Interstate mileage: 783

Per 1,000 pop.: 0.28, 17th

Annual vehicle-mi. of travel per person (1993): 8,898, 34th

Mean travel time for workers age 16+ who work away from home: 16.2 min., 46th

GOVERNMENT

Percent of voting age pop. registered (1994): 71.7%, 13th

Percent of voting age pop. voting (1994): 52.5%, 12th

Percent of voting age pop. voting for U.S. representatives (1994): 46.3%, 12th

State legislators, total (1995): 150, 19th

Women members (1992): 22

Percent of legislature: 14.7%, 31st

U.S. Congress, House members (1995): 5

Change (1985-95): −1

Revenues (1993):

State govt.: $8,224,000,000

Per capita: $2,915.28, 29th

Parimutuel & amusement taxes & lotteries, revenue per capita: $70.54, 27th

Expenditures (1993):

State govt.: $7,766,000,000

Per capita: $2,752.92, 28th

Debt outstanding (1993): $1,837,000,000

Per capita: $651.19, 45th

LAWS AND REGULATIONS

Legal driving age: 18, 16 if completed driver education course

Marriage age without parental consent: 18

Divorce residence requirement: 1 yr., for qualifications check local statutes

ATTRACTIONS (1995)

Major opera companies: 1

Major symphony orchestras: 1

State appropriations for arts agencies per capita: $0.50, 36th

State Fair in mid-August at Des Moines

SPORTS AND COMPETITION

NCAA teams (Division I): Drake Univ. Bulldogs, Iowa State Univ. Cyclones, Univ. of Iowa Hawkeyes, Univ. of Northern Iowa Panthers

KANSAS

"There is no monument under heaven on which I would rather have my name inscribed than on this goodly state of Kansas."

Henry Ward Beecher, clergyman

Kansas is known as a world breadbasket and Hutchinson as a world grain center. At the same time, the state is also famous for aviation manufacture, with Wichita a major leader in private aircraft production. Kansas's historic trails were critical in the opening of the West. Dodge City, "the cowboy capital of the world," was once the world's largest cattle-market town—a dusty, brawling crossroads that was home to Wyatt Earp, Bat Masterson, and Wild Bill Hickock. Perhaps unexpectedly, this prairie state is also a world center of psychiatric study and practice, thanks to the Menninger family of Topeka. William Allen White's pioneer leadership as a Kansas newspaper editor anticipated many features of present-day journalism.

SUPERLATIVES

• Geographic center of the 48 conterminous states—in Smith County, Kansas.
• The world's greatest salt deposits, located at Hutchinson.
• Largest primary hard wheat market in the world.
• Long a major transportation crossroads of the nation.
• Claims more newspapers per capita than any other state.
• World leader in the manufacture of personal aircraft.

MOMENTS IN HISTORY

• In 1541, Spanish explorer Francisco Vásquez de Coronado came overland from Mexico, reaching what is now Junction City before turning back.

So They Say

"The plains are full of crooked necked oxen."

Francisco Vásquez de Coronado's description of the buffalo

• In 1719, French explorer Claude du Tisne crossed the southeastern border of present-day Kansas, but aside from a few other explorers, the region remained Indian country in the early days.
• Explorer Zebulon Pike crossed the length of Kansas in 1806. At a "grand council" with the Pawnees, he raised the U.S. flag for the first time in Kansas territory.

So They Say

"...I stood on a hill and in one view below me saw buffalo, elk, deer, cabrie [antelope] and panthers....I prevented the men shooting at the game, not merely because of the scarcity of ammunition, but, as I conceived, the laws of morality forbade it also."

Zebulon Pike

• In 1822, Captain William H. Becknell pioneered the Santa Fe Trail, and before long thousands of wagons used the trail, crossing 500 miles of Kansas to carry on very profitable trade with New Mexico. Fortunes were sometimes made in a single round trip.
• In 1824, Benton Pixley established a mission to the Osage Indians in present Neosho County, and in the years that followed, the Kansas plains were dotted with mission stations of many denominations.
• Fort Leavenworth was established in 1827.
• In 1854, Kansas was opened to settlement by the Kansas-Nebraska Act. This act permitted the residents of the territory to decide whether the territory would be free or slave, setting the stage for a frantic period when both sides came to blows over slavery, and Kansas became "Bleeding Kansas."
• The population grew, and Kansas became a free state on January 29, 1861.
• During the Civil War, Confederate raiders made many attacks on Kansas communities.

Notorious raider William Clarke Quantrill raided Lawrence on August 21, 1863, burned 200 buildings, and killed 150 civilians.

So They Say

"...During all this time citizens were being murdered everywhere. Germans and Negroes...were shot immediately....In many instances [women] placed themselves between their husbands and fathers...when the drunken fiends held cocked pistols at them."

A Kansas newspaper reporting on Quantrill's raid on Lawrence

• In the Battle of Mine Creek on October 25, 1864, Union forces were victorious, and the threat of Confederate invasion was ended. Kansas sent to the war the highest percentage of its eligible men of all the states.
• In 1867 the first cattle were driven up the Chisholm Trail to Abilene, where the railroad had arrived.
• As the railroad moved west, other communities became the principal cow towns, including famed Dodge City, which was established in 1872.
• In 1887, Susanna Salter was elected mayor of Argonia; she was said to be the first woman mayor in the United States.
• Kansas sent four regiments into the Spanish-American War in 1898.
• During World War I, thousands of Kansas acres were plowed for the first time to provide food. Later, during the drought of the 1930s, dirt from these fields was carried up into terrible dust storms.
• During 1951, Kansas experienced great floods, with damage amounting to about $2.5 billion.
• Kansas's adopted son, Dwight David Eisenhower, won the 1952 and 1956 presidential elections.
• In 1954 the U.S. Supreme Court struck down the segregation policies of the Topeka school system in a far-reaching decision.
• In 1987, former Governor Alf Landon celebrated his 100th birthday, but within a few weeks of the celebration Kansas lost its beloved centenarian.
• The largest remaining stretch of virgin Kansas prairie was plowed under in 1990.
• Kansas elected its first woman governor, Joan Finney, in 1991.

THAT'S INTERESTING

• The legendary lawmen of Dodge City, such as Bat Masterson and Wyatt Earp, were not always as heroic as they have been portrayed. On one occasion, Earp was said to have "amateurishly loaded all six chambers of his revolver and blasted a hole through his coat."
• Pioneering the Santa Fe Trail, the Becknell party almost died of thirst on the dry bed of the Cimarron River until they discovered by accident that the river was "flowing" beneath the sand.
• With the slaughter of the buffalo, the scattered bones became so valuable that they were collected by the tons, and Dodge City bankers and businesses accepted them as legal tender.

NOTABLE NATIVES

Gwendolyn Elizabeth Brooks (Topeka, born 1917), poet. Walter Percy Chrysler (Wamego, 1875-1940), automobile manufacturer. John Steuart Curry (Jefferson County, 1897-1946), painter. Charles Curtis (Topeka, 1860-1936), U.S. vice president. Amelia Mary Earhart (Atchison, 1897-1937), aviator. William Inge (Independence, 1913-1973), playwright. Emmett Kelly (Sedan, 1898-1979), clown. Edgar Lee Masters (Garnett, 1869-1950), poet/biographer. Karl Menninger (Topeka, 1893-1990), psychiatrist. Damon Runyon (Manhattan, KS, 1884-1946), journalist/author.

GENERAL

Admitted to statehood: January 29, 1861
Origin of name: Sioux word for "south wind people"
Capital: Topeka
Nickname: Sunflower State, Jayhawk State
Motto: Ad Astra per Aspera—To the stars through difficulties
Animal: American buffalo
Bird: Western meadowlark
Insect: Honeybee
Flower: Wild native sunflower
Song: "Home on the Range"
Tree: Cottonwood

THE LAND

Area: 82,282 sq. mi., 15th
   Land: 81,823 sq. mi., 13th

Water: 459 sq. mi., 40th
  Inland water: 459 sq. mi., 34th
Topography: Hilly Osage plains in the E; central region level prairie and hills; high plains in the W
Number of counties: 105
Geographic center: Barton, 15 mi. NE of Great Bend
Length: 400 mi.; width: 210 mi.
Highest point: 4,039 ft. (Mount Sunflower), 28th
Lowest point: 679 ft. (Verdigris River), 43rd
Mean elevation: 2,000 ft., 14th

CLIMATE AND ENVIRONMENT

Temp., highest: 121 deg. on July 24, 1936, near Alton; lowest: –40 deg. on Feb. 13, 1905, at Lebanon
Monthly average: highest: 92.9 deg., 9th; lowest: 15.7 deg., 20th; spread (high to low): 77.2 deg., 12th
Hazardous waste sites (1993): 10, 36th
Endangered species: Mammals: 2—Gray bat, Indiana bat; birds: 5—Whooping crane, Eskimo curlew, American peregrine falcon, Least tern, Black-capped vireo; reptiles: none; amphibians: none; fishes: 1; invertebrates: none; plants: 2

MAJOR CITIES
POPULATION, 1990
PERCENTAGE INCREASE, 1980-90

Kansas City, 149,767— -7.06%
Lawrence, 65,608—24.40%
Overland Park, 111,790—36.69%
Topeka, 119,883—1.01%
Wichita, 304,011—8.64%

THE PEOPLE

Population (1995): 2,565,328, 32nd
  Percent change (1990-95): 3.5%, 35th
Population (2000 proj.): 2,722,000, 32nd
  Percent change (1990-2000): 9.87%, 27th
Per sq. mi. (1994): 31.2, 41st
Percent in metro. area (1992): 54.6%, 37th
Foreign born: 63,000, 30th
  Percent: 2.5%, 32nd
Top three ancestries reported:
  German, 39.06%
  Irish, 17.59%
  English, 16.38%
White: 2,231,986, 90.09%, 19th
Black: 143,076, 5.77%, 28th
Native American: 21,965, 0.89%, 16th
Asian, Pacific Isle: 31,750, 1.28%, 22nd
Other races: 48,797, 1.97%, 18th
Hispanic origin: 93,670, 3.78%, 21st
Percent over 5 yrs. speaking language other than English at home: 5.7%, 33rd
Percent males: 49.03%, 19th; percent females: 50.97%, 33rd
Percent never married: 22.7%, 43rd
Marriages per 1,000 (1993): 8.3, 30th
Divorces per 1,000 (1993): 4.8, 22nd
Median age: 32.9
Under 5 years (1994): 7.20%, 26th
Under 18 years (1994): 27.02%, 15th
65 years & older (1994): 13.9%, 13th
Percent increase among the elderly (1990-94): 3.34%, 41st

OF VITAL IMPORTANCE

Live births per 1,000 pop. (1993): 15.0, 23rd
Infant mortality rate per 1,000 births (1992): 8.7, 24th
  Rate for blacks (1990): 15.4, 29th
  Rate for whites (1990): 7.7, 30th
Births to unmarried women, % of total (1992): 24.3%, 40th
Births to teenage mothers, % of total (1992): 12.4%, 24th
Abortions (1992): 12,570, 29th
  Rate per 1,000 women 14-44 years old: 22.4, 22nd
  Percent change (1988-92): 11%, 4th
Average lifetime (1979-81): 75.31, 7th
Deaths per 1,000 pop. (1993): 9.2, 20th
Causes of death per 100,000 pop.:
  Accidents & adverse effects (1992): 34.6, 26th
  Atherosclerosis (1991): 10.2, 7th
  Cancer (1991): 200.1, 36th
  Cerebrovascular diseases (1992): 64.6, 15th
  Chronic liver diseases & cirrhosis (1991): 6.1, 49th
  Chronic obstructive pulmonary diseases (1992): 37.8, 24th
  Diabetes mellitus (1992): 20.5, 28th
  Diseases of heart (1992): 295.1, 22nd
  Pneumonia, flu (1991): 35.6, 12th
  Suicide (1992): 12.4, 26th

KEEPING WELL

Active nonfederal physicians per 100,000 pop. (1993): 185, 34th
Dentists per 100,000 (1991): 51, 31st
Nurses per 100,000 (1992): 794, 22nd
Hospitals per 100,000 (1993): 5.29, 6th

Admissions per 1,000 (1993): 114.32, 26th

Occupancy rate per 100 beds (1993): 54.2, 47th

Average cost per patient per day (1993): $666, 42nd

Average cost per stay (1993): $5,108, 41st

Average stay (1992): 7.6 days, 17th

AIDS cases (adult, 1993): 356; per 100,000: 14.1, 38th

HIV infection, not yet AIDS (1993): NA

Other notifiable diseases:

Gonorrhea: 195.6, 26th

Measles: 9.4, 8th

Syphilis: 7.1, 35th

Tuberculosis: 3.1, 38th

Pop. without health insur. (1991-93): 11.7%, 35th

HOUSEHOLDS BY TYPE

Total households (1994): 966,000

Percent change (1990-94): 2.2%, 39th

Per 1,000 pop.: 378.23, 17th

Percent of households 65 yrs. and over: 23.29%, 13th

Persons per household (1994): 2.56, 35th

Family households: 658,600

Percent of total: 69.71%, 32nd

Nonfamily households: 286,126

Percent of total: 30.29%, 20th

Pop. living in group quarters: 82,765

Percent of pop.: 3.34%, 13th

LIVING QUARTERS

Total housing units: 1,044,112

Persons per unit: 2.37, 32nd

Occupied housing units: 944,726

Percent of total units: 90.48%, 19th

Persons per unit: 2.48, 38th

Percent of units with over 1 person per room: 2.51%, 36th

Owner-occupied units: 641,762

Percent of total units: 61.46%, 14th

Percent of occupied units: 67.93%, 22nd

Persons per unit: 2.64, 43rd

Median value: $52,200, 42nd

Renter-occupied units: 302,964

Percent of total units: 29.02%, 27th

Percent of occupied units: 32.07%, 30th

Persons per unit: 2.31, 30th

Median contract rent: $285, 33rd

Rental vacancy rate: 11.1%, 12th

Mobile home, trailer & other as a percent of occupied housing units: 8.30%, 31st

Persons in emergency shelters for homeless persons: 940, 0.038%, 39th

Persons visible in street locations: 158, 0.0064%, 26th

Persons in shelters for abused women: 60, 0.0024%, 49th

Nursing home population: 26,155, 1.06%, 7th

CRIME INDEX PER 100,000 (1992-93)

Total reported: 4,975.3, 25th

Violent: 496.4, 29th

Murder and nonnegligent manslaughter: 6.4, 28th

Aggravated assault: 326.3, 26th

Robbery: 123.6, 30th

Forcible rape: 40.1, 23rd

Property: 4,478.8, 23rd

Burglary: 1,132.2, 17th

Larceny, theft: 3,024.0, 23rd

Motor vehicle theft: 322.7, 34th

Drug abuse violations (1990): 223.4, 31st

Child-abuse rate per 1,000 children (1993): 18.02, 16th

TEACHING AND LEARNING

Pop. 3 and over enrolled in school: 668,365

Percent of pop.: 28.2%, 15th

Public elementary & secondary schools (1992-93): 1,483

Total enrollment (1992): 451,536

Percent of total pop.: 17.95%, 14th

Teachers (1992): 29,753

Percent of pop.: 1.18%, 12th

Pupil/teacher ratio (fall 1992): 15.2, 40th

Teachers' avg. salary (1992-93): $35,157, 25th

Expenditure per capita (1990-91): $3,199.99, 33rd

Expenditure per pupil (1991-92): $5,007, 30th

Percent of graduates taking SAT (1993): 9%, 42nd

Mean SAT verbal scores: 494, 5th

Mean SAT mathematical scores: 548, 7th

Percent of graduates taking ACT (1995): 72%, 5th

Mean ACT scores: 21.2, 20th

Percent of pop. over 25 completing:

Less than 9th grade: 7.7%, 41st

High school: 81.3%, 10th

College degree(s): 21.1%, 19th

Higher education, institutions (1993-94): 51

Enrollment (1992): 169,419
Percent of pop.: 6.73%, 9th
White non-Hispanic (1992): 145,577
Percent of enroll.: 85.93%, 18th
Black non-Hispanic (1992): 7,888
Percent of enroll.: 4.66%, 29th
Hispanic (1992): 4,185
Percent of enroll.: 2.47%, 17th
Asian/Pacific Islander (1992): 3,152
Percent of enroll.: 1.86%, 27th
American Indian/AK native (1992): 2,270
Percent of enroll.: 1.34%, 12th
Nonresident alien (1992): 6,347
Percent of enroll.: 3.75%, 12th
Female (1992): 93,430
Percent of enroll.: 55.15%, 28th
Pub. institutions (1993-94): 29
Enrollment (1992): 153,399
Percent of enroll.: 90.54%, 7th
Private institutions (1993-94): 22
Enrollment (1992): 16,202
Percent of enroll.: 9.56%, 45th
Tuition, public institution (avg., 1993-94): $5,236, 35th
Tuition, private institution (avg., 1993-94): $10,398, 37th
Public library systems: 318
Books & serial vol. per capita: 4.04, 6th
Govt. expenditure per capita: $12.42, 34th

LAW ENFORCEMENT, COURTS, AND PRISONS

Police protection, corrections, judicial and legal functions expenditures (1992): $604,000,000
Per capita: $240, 32nd
Police per 10,000 pop. (1993): 23.86, 13th
Prisoners (state & fed.) per 100,000 pop. (1993): 2,259.17, 34th
Percent change (1992-93): –5.0%, 50th
Death penalty: no

RELIGION, NUMBER AND PERCENT OF POPULATION

Agnostic: 10,896—0.60%, 19th
Buddhist: 5,448—0.30%, 8th
Christian: 1,632,548—89.90%, 12th
Hindu: 1,816.0—0.10%, 10th
Jewish: 5,448—0.30%, 35th
Muslim: 1,816—0.10%, 22nd
Unitarian: 7,264—0.40%, 8th
Other: 16,344—0.90%, 35th
None: 103,510—5.70%, 37th
Refused to answer: 30,871—1.70%, 35th

MAKING A LIVING

Personal income per capita (1994): $20,869, 24th
Percent increase (1993-94): 5.3%, 20th
Disposable personal income per capita (1994): $18,140, 26th
Median income of households (1993): $29,770, 29th
Percent of pop. below poverty level (1993): 13.1%, 27th
Percent 65 and over (1990): 12.0%, 24th
Expenditure for energy per person (1992): $2,103, 6th

ECONOMY

Civilian labor force (1994): 1,331,000
Percent of total pop.: 52.11%, 20th
Percent 65 and over (1990): 4.46%, 2nd
Percent female: 46.88%, 17th
Percent job growth (1980-90): 14.47%, 38th
Major employer industries (1994):
Agriculture: 66,000—5.2%, 8th
Construction: 47,000—3.7%, 39th
Finance, insurance, & real estate: 75,000—6.0%, 14th
Government: 215,000—17.2%, 17th
Manufacturing: 196,000—15.7%, 23rd
Service: 239,000—19.1%, 39th
Trade: 227,000—18.1%, 39th
Transportation, communications, public utilities: 77,000—8.1%, 1st
Unemployment rate (1994): 5.26%, 31st
Male: 5.6%, 26th
Female: 5.0%, 34th
Total businesses (1991): 107,489
New business incorps. (1991): 3,930
Percent of total businesses: 3.66%, 46th
Business failures (1991): 763
Percent of total businesses: 0.71%
Agriculture farm income:
Marketing (1993): $7,363,000,000, 6th
Average per farm: $113,276.92, 13th
Leading products (1993): Cattle, wheat, corn, soybeans
Average value land & build. per acre (1994): $537, 37th
Percent increase (1990-94): 16.23%, 21st
Govt. payments (1993): $784,000,000, 6th
Average per farm: $12,061.54, 9th
Construction, value of all: $1,185,000,000
Per capita: $478.29, 34th

Manufactures:
  Value added: $12,998,000,000
    Per capita: $5,246.26, 24th
  Leading products: Transportation equipment, industrial machinery, food and food products, printing and publishing products
Value of nonfuel mineral production (1994): $495,000,000, 11th
Leading mineral products: Petroleum, natural gas, cement
Retail sales (1993): $21,338,000,000, 30th
  Per household: $21,861, 28th
    Percent increase (1992-93): 9.9%, 9th
Tourism revenues (1991): $2.1 bil.
Foreign exports, in total value (1994): $3,028,000,000, 30th
  Per capita: $1,185.59, 27th
Gross state product per person (1993): $21,268.06, 25th
  Percent change (1990-93): 1.92%, 39th
Patents per 100,000 pop. (1993): 12.47, 37th
Public aid recipients (percent of resident pop. 1993): 4.7%, 44th
Medicaid recipients per 1,000 pop. (1993): 95.86, 41st
Medicare recipients per 1,000 pop. (1993): 148.32, 17th

TRAVEL AND TRANSPORTATION

Motor vehicle registrations (1993): 1,922,000
  Per 1,000 pop.: 758.19, 29th
Motorcycle registrations (1993): 53,000
  Per 1,000 pop.: 20.91, 14th
Licensed drivers per 1,000 pop. (1993): 699.80, 21st
Deaths from motor vehicle accidents per 100,000 pop. (1993): 16.88, 24th
Public roads & streets (1993):
  Total mileage: 133,256
    Per 1,000 pop.: 52.57, 7th
  Rural mileage: 123,676
    Per 1,000 pop.: 48.79, 7th
  Urban mileage: 9,580
    Per 1,000 pop.: 3.78, 8th

Interstate mileage: 871
  Per 1,000 pop.: 0.34, 11th
Annual vehicle-mi. of travel per person (1993): 9,507, 24th
Mean travel time for workers age 16+ who work away from home: 17.2 min., 44th

GOVERNMENT

Percent of voting age pop. registered (1994): 65.3%, 24th
  Percent of voting age pop. voting (1994): 50.5%, 18th
  Percent of voting age pop. voting for U.S. representatives (1994): 43.3%, 15th
State legislators, total (1995): 165, 17th
  Women members (1992): 45
    Percent of legislature: 27.3%, 9th
U.S. Congress, House members (1995): 4
  Change (1985-95): −1
Revenues (1993):
  State govt.: $6,730,000,000
    Per capita: $2,654.83, 41st
  Parimutuel & amusement taxes & lotteries, revenue per capita: $43.39, 34th
Expenditures (1993):
  State govt.: $5,742,000,000
    Per capita: $2,265.09, 45th
Debt outstanding (1993): $935,000,000
  Per capita: $368.84, 50th

LAWS AND REGULATIONS

Legal driving age: 16
Marriage age without parental consent: 18
Divorce residence requirement: 60 days

ATTRACTIONS (1995)

Major symphony orchestras: 1
State appropriations for arts agencies per capita: $0.53, 35th
State Fair mid-September at Hutchinson

SPORTS AND COMPETITION

NCAA teams (Division I): Kansas State Univ. Wildcats, Univ. of Kansas Jayhawks, Wichita State Univ. Shockers

KENTUCKY

"The moonlight is the softest in Kentucky.
Summer days come oftenest.
Love's fire glows the longest,
Yet a wrong is always wrongest in Kentucky."

James H. Mulligan

"I gained the summit of a commanding ridge . . . with astonishing delight, beheld the ample plains, the beauteous tracts below. . .the famous Ohio River, that rolled in silent dignity, marking the western boundary of Kentucky with inconceivable grandeur."

Daniel Boone, frontiersman

The Bluegrass State is famed for its fine horses, the renowned Kentucky Derby, its bourbon, and its fine tobacco, but it deserves greater fame for the extraordinary personalities who have been associated with it and for a state park system that has been called "the finest in the nation." Louisville's symphony is renowned as a leader in first performances of classical music, and the baseball world could not survive without "Louisville Slugger" bats. Among the numerous natural attractions, Mammoth Cave contains three rivers, two lakes, and one "sea." Millions around the world sing of the joys of "My Old Kentucky Home." When statesman Henry Clay stood at Cumberland Gap, he said, "I am listening to the tread of the coming millions," and they have indeed followed in his footsteps.

SUPERLATIVES

- Kentucky's Cave Region—world unique.
- First in pedigreed horses.
- World's largest loose-leaf tobacco market.
- First in fine grass seed.
- World's largest producer of bourbon.
- Leader in fluorspar production.
- First in bituminous coal production.
- First daily newspaper published west of the Alleghenies.

MOMENTS IN HISTORY

- The first recorded exploration of Kentucky was made by Virginia Colonel Abram Wood in 1654.
- By 1690 most of the native Indian people had been driven from the region by the Iro-quois. Then a few scattered groups of Native Americans returned.
- The whole vast region west of the Allegheny Mountains was claimed by France, and around 1729, Lower Shawneetown was begun by French traders and groups of Delaware, Shawnee, and Mingo tribes. It was abandoned before the French and Indian War.
- The British did not recognize French claims, and in 1750, Dr. Thomas Walker explored the region for the British Loyal Land Company of Virginia.
- In 1751 explorer Christopher Gist traveled the Ohio River country and visited Lower Shawneetown, as noted in his journal.
- The British were triumphant in the French and Indian War in 1763.
- In 1769, John Findley and Daniel Boone crossed the pass now known as the Cumberland Gap.

So They Say

"...returned to my family, being determined to reside in Kentucky which I esteemed a second paradise."

Daniel Boone in 1771

- James Harrod and a group of 31 settlers founded present-day Harrodsburg in 1774. It became the state's oldest permanent European settlement.
- After leading a party over "Boone's Trace" on April 5, 1775, Boone and 30 men began to build Fort Boonesborough.
- As the Revolutionary War approached, the British stirred up the Indians of the region

against the settlers, and in July 1776, Indians attacked Boonesborough and captured Daniel Boone's daughter and two other young women. They were rescued by a party led by Boone.

• Indian attacks continued after the Revolution, but settlement grew and on June 1, 1792, Kentucky became the first state to be carved from the great wilderness west.

• In 1799 a hunter tracking a wounded animal discovered Mammoth Cave.

So They Say

"...200 acres of second-rate land lying on the Green River, including two petre caves."

A land grant description of the Mammoth Cave region

• The terrible earthquake of 1811 shook western Kentucky, but progress came that year with the arrival of the first steamboat on the Ohio River.

• In 1833, Kentucky prohibited the importation of slaves.

• With the 1850 repeal of the slave ban, Kentucky became an important center of the slave trade.

• The state was bitterly divided over slavery during the Civil War. By 1862, Union forces controlled the state, but costly guerrilla warfare continued. At war's end in 1865, 90,000 from Kentucky had served in Union forces; 45,000 had fought for the Confederacy.

• The nation's first great suspension bridge, across the Ohio River between Covington, KY, and Cincinnati, Ohio, was completed in 1867.

• The Kentucky Derby began at Louisville in 1875.

• In 1900, William Goebel, candidate for governor, was murdered; the mystery of his death was never solved.

• A total of 75,043 Kentuckians served in World War I. But Breathitt County was the one county in the United States in which no one was drafted.

• In 1937 the Ohio River floods were the worst yet in the river's history.

• Fort Knox was a major training center for tank operations during World War II.

• The terrible supper club fire at Southgate in 1977 took 164 lives.

• Frankfort celebrated its 200th anniversary in 1986.

THAT'S INTERESTING

• Captured by the Indians at Boonesborough, Elizabeth Calloway broke off pieces of brush and twigs and tore off pieces of her clothing to leave a trail for possible rescue. Following this trail, a party led by Daniel Boone caught up with her captives, who fled.

• Prehistoric bones were not so highly regarded in 1773, when explorer James Douglas used the ribs of mastodons for tent poles.

• Confederate President Jefferson Davis and Union President Abraham Lincoln were both Kentucky natives.

• The admirers of a large sycamore tree at Pippa Passes bought 36 square feet of land on which it stood and registered the tree as the landowner.

• Handicapped U.S. Senate candidate John Pope received one man's vote because "he has only one arm to thrust into the treasury."

• Because Mammoth Cave has a constant 54°F temperature, it "breathes" in when the outside temperature is high and "exhales" when the temperature is lower.

NOTABLE NATIVES

Muhammad Ali (Louisville, 1942-), boxer. **Alben William Barkley** (Graves County, 1877-1956), U.S. vice president. **Christopher (Kit) Carson** (Madison County, 1809-1868), trapper, soldier. **Louis Dembitz Brandeis** (Louisville, 1856-1941), Supreme Court justice. **Jefferson Davis** (Fairview, 1808-1889), president of the Confederate States of America. **Abraham Lincoln** (near Hodgenville, 1809-1865), U.S. president. **Carry Amelia Moore Nation** (Gerrard County, 1846-1911), social reformer. **Frederick Moore Vinson** (Louisa, 1890-1953), chief justice of the United States.

GENERAL

Admitted to statehood: June 1, 1792
Origin of name: Indian word variously translated as "dark and bloody ground," "meadowland," "land of tomorrow"
Capital: Frankfort
Nickname: Bluegrass State
Motto: United we stand, divided we fall
Bird: Cardinal
Fish: Bass

Flower: Goldenrod
Song: "My Old Kentucky Home"
Tree: Kentucky coffee tree

THE LAND

Area: 40,411 sq. mi., 37th
   Land: 39,732 sq. mi., 36th
   Water: 679 sq. mi., 37th
   Inland water: 679 sq. mi., 32nd
Topography: Mountainous in E; rounded hills of the Knobs in the N; Bluegrass, heart of state; wooded rocky hillsides of the Pennyroyal; western coal field; the fertile Purchase in the SW
Number of counties: 120
Geographic center: Marion, 3 mi. NNW of Lebanon
Length: 380 mi.; width: 140 mi.
Highest point: 4,139 ft. (Black Mountain), 27th
Lowest point: 257 ft. (Mississippi River), 32nd
Mean elevation: 750 ft., 33rd

CLIMATE AND ENVIRONMENT

Temp., highest: 114 deg. on July 28, 1930, at Greensburg; lowest: −34 deg. on Jan. 28, 1963, at Cynthiana
Monthly average: highest: 87.6 deg., 25th; lowest: 23.1 deg., 31st; spread (high to low): 64.5 deg., 32nd
Hazardous waste sites (1993): 20, 19th
Endangered species: Mammals: 3—Gray bat, Indiana bat, Virginia big-eared bat; birds: 3—American peregrine falcon, Least tern, Red-cockaded woodpecker; reptiles: none; amphibians: none; fishes: 1; invertebrates: 16; plants: 3

MAJOR CITIES
POPULATION, 1990
PERCENTAGE INCREASE, 1980-90

Bowling Green, 40,641—0.47%
Covington, 43,264— −12.75%
Lexington-Fayette, 225,366—10.38%
Louisville, 269,063— −9.92%
Owensboro, 53,549— −1.65%

THE PEOPLE

Population (1995): 3,860,219, 24th
   Percent change (1990-95): 4.7%, 26th
Population (2000 proj.): 3,989,000, 25th
   Percent change (1990-2000): 8.24%, 30th
Per sq. mi. (1994): 96.3, 24th

Percent in metro. area (1992): 48.5%, 39th
Foreign born: 34,000, 39th
   Percent: 0.9%, 49th
Top three ancestries reported:
   German, 21.64%
   Irish, 18.88%
   American, 15.89%
White: 3,391,832, 92.04%, 15th
Black: 262,907, 7.13%, 26th
Native American: 5,769, 0.16%, 49th
Asian, Pacific Isle: 17,812, 0.48%, 49th
Other races: 6,976, 0.19%, 45th
Hispanic origin: 21,984, 0.60%, 49th
Percent over 5 yrs. speaking language other than English at home: 2.5%, 51st
Percent males: 48.44%, 34th; percent females: 51.56%, 18th
Percent never married: 22.6%, 44th
Marriages per 1,000 (1993): 12.0, 7th
Divorces per 1,000 (1993): 5.8, 10th
Median age: 33
Under 5 years (1994): 6.82%, 44th
Under 18 years (1994): 25.35%, 34th
65 years & older (1994): 12.8%, 25th
Percent increase among the elderly (1990-94): 4.75%, 33rd

OF VITAL IMPORTANCE

Live births per 1,000 pop. (1993): 13.8, 41st
Infant mortality rate per 1,000 births (1992): 8.3, 30th
   Rate for blacks (1990): 13.6, 34th
   Rate for whites (1990): 8.0, 22nd
Births to unmarried women, % of total (1992): 26.3%, 34th
Births to teenage mothers, % of total (1992): 16.5%, 10th
Abortions (1992): 10,000, 32nd
   Rate per 1,000 women 14-44 years old: 11.4, 44th
   Percent change (1988-92): −12%, 32nd
Average lifetime (1979-81): 73.06, 41st
Deaths per 1,000 pop. (1993): 9.7, 10th
Causes of death per 100,000 pop.:
   Accidents & adverse effects (1992): 44.2, 10th
   Atherosclerosis (1991): 6.2, 35th
   Cancer (1991): 227.7, 11th
   Cerebrovascular diseases (1992): 61.6, 20th
   Chronic liver diseases & cirrhosis (1991): 9.5, 21st
   Chronic obstructive pulmonary diseases (1992): 45.2, 7th
   Diabetes mellitus (1992): 21.8, 18th

Diseases of heart (1992): 313.8, 14th
Pneumonia, flu (1991): 38.4, 5th
Suicide (1992): 13.1, 16th

KEEPING WELL

Active nonfederal physicians per 100,000 pop.
(1993): 179, 37th
Dentists per 100,000 (1991): 54, 24th
Nurses per 100,000 (1992): 659, 36th
Hospitals per 100,000 (1993): 2.79, 16th
Admissions per 1,000 (1993): 140.38, 9th
Occupancy rate per 100 beds (1993): 62.2,
25th
Average cost per patient per day (1993):
$703, 38th
Average cost per stay (1993): $4,749, 46th
Average stay (1992): 6.8 days, 33rd
AIDS cases (adult, 1993): 323; per 100,000:
8.5, 44th
HIV infection, not yet AIDS (1993): NA
Other notifiable diseases:
Gonorrhea: 15.7, 48th
Measles: 1.2, 39th
Syphilis: 7.8, 34th
Tuberculosis: 9.8, 16th
Pop. without health insur. (1991-93): 13.4%,
22nd

HOUSEHOLDS BY TYPE

Total households (1994): 1,440,000
Percent change (1990-94): 4.3%, 26th
Per 1,000 pop.: 376.27, 22nd
Percent of households 65 yrs. and over:
22.29%, 25th
Persons per household (1994): 2.59, 26th
Family households: 1,015,998
Percent of total: 73.63%, 5th
Nonfamily households: 363,784
Percent of total: 26.37%, 47th
Pop. living in group quarters: 101,176
Percent of pop.: 2.75%, 25th

LIVING QUARTERS

Total housing units: 1,506,845
Persons per unit: 2.45, 16th
Occupied housing units: 1,379,782
Percent of total units: 91.57%, 12th
Persons per unit: 2.54, 22nd
Percent of units with over 1 person per
room: 2.60%, 33rd
Owner-occupied units: 960,469
Percent of total units: 63.74%, 7th
Percent of occupied units: 69.61%, 13th
Persons per unit: 2.69, 35th

Median value: $50,500, 44th
Renter-occupied units: 419,313
Percent of total units: 27.83%, 33rd
Percent of occupied units: 30.39%, 39th
Persons per unit: 2.39, 18th
Median contract rent: $250, 45th
Rental vacancy rate: 8.2%, 27th
Mobile home, trailer & other as a percent
of occupied housing units: 14.46%,
17th
Persons in emergency shelters for homeless
persons: 1,284, 0.035%, 44th
Persons visible in street locations: 118,
0.0032%, 35th
Persons in shelters for abused women: 190,
0.0052%, 21st
Nursing home population: 27,874, 0.76%,
22nd

CRIME INDEX PER 100,000 (1992-93)

Total reported: 3,259.7, 46th
Violent: 462.7, 31st
Murder and nonnegligent manslaughter:
6.6, 27th
Aggravated assault: 331.4, 25th
Robbery: 90.4, 39th
Forcible rape: 34.3, 34th
Property: 2,797.0, 47th
Burglary: 740.1, 38th
Larceny, theft: 1,840.7, 49th
Motor vehicle theft: 216.2, 41st
Drug abuse violations (1990): 315.3, 16th
Child-abuse rate per 1,000 children (1993):
26.04, 7th

TEACHING AND LEARNING

Pop. 3 and over enrolled in school: 918,315
Percent of pop.: 26.0%, 40th
Public elementary & secondary schools (1992-
93): 1,395
Total enrollment (1992): 655,041
Percent of total pop.: 17.45%, 25th
Teachers (1992): 37,868
Percent of pop.: 1.01%, 29th
Pupil/teacher ratio (fall 1992): 17.3, 19th
Teachers' avg. salary (1992-93): $33,187,
29th
Expenditure per capita (1990-91):
$2,946.69, 42nd
Expenditure per pupil (1991-92): $4,719,
35th
Percent of graduates taking SAT (1993): 11%,
35th

Mean SAT verbal scores: 476, 17th

Mean SAT mathematical scores: 522, 17th

Percent of graduates taking ACT (1995): 63%, 16th

Mean ACT scores: 20.1, 42nd

Percent of pop. over 25 completing:

Less than 9th grade: 19.0%, 1st

High school. 64.6%, 50th

College degree(s): 13.6%, 49th

Higher education, institutions (1993-94): 62

Enrollment (1992): 188,320

Percent of pop.: 5.02%, 39th

White non-Hispanic (1992): 170,235

Percent of enroll.: 90.40%, 10th

Black non-Hispanic (1992): 12,026

Percent of enroll.: 6.39%, 25th

Hispanic (1992): 977

Percent of enroll.: 0.52%, 47th

Asian/Pacific Islander (1992): 1,589

Percent of enroll.: 0.84%, 46th

American Indian/AK native (1992): 592

Percent of enroll.: 0.31%, 40th

Nonresident alien (1992): 2,901

Percent of enroll.: 1.54%, 49th

Female (1992): 109,978

Percent of enroll.: 58.40%, 2nd

Pub. institutions (1993-94): 22

Enrollment (1992): 157,836

Percent of enroll.: 83.81%, 25th

Private institutions (1993-94): 40

Enrollment (1992): 30,484

Percent of enroll.: 16.19%, 27th

Tuition, public institution (avg., 1993-94): $5,027, 41st

Tuition, private institution (avg., 1993-94): $9,559, 42nd

Public library systems: 115

Books & serial vol. per capita: 1.87, 42nd

Govt. expenditure per capita: $9.69, 42nd

LAW ENFORCEMENT, COURTS, AND PRISONS

Police protection, corrections, judicial and legal functions expenditures (1992): $722,000,000

Per capita: $192, 44th

Police per 10,000 pop. (1993): 18.31, 35th

Prisoners (state & fed.) per 100,000 pop. (1993): 2,751.71, 27th

Percent change (1992-93): 0.7%, 37th

Death penalty: yes, by electrocution

Under sentence of death (1993): 30, 21st

Executed (1993): 0

RELIGION, NUMBER AND PERCENT OF POPULATION

Agnostic: 8,194—0.30%, 37th

Buddhist: 2,731—0.10%, 17th

Christian: 2,452,619—89.80%, 13th

Hindu: NA

Jewish: 5,462—0.20%, 40th

Muslim: NA

Unitarian: 5,462—0.20%, 23rd

Other: 32,774—1.20%, 29th

None: 177,528—6.50%, 25th

Refused to answer: 46,430—1.70%, 35th

MAKING A LIVING

Personal income per capita (1994): $17,807, 43rd

Percent increase (1993-94): 5.4%, 17th

Disposable personal income per capita (1994): $15,446, 46th

Median income of households (1993): $24,376, 48th

Percent of pop. below poverty level (1993): 20.4%, 5th

Percent 65 and over (1990): 20.6%, 6th

Expenditure for energy per person (1992): $1,935, 18th

ECONOMY

Civilian labor force (1994): 1,825,000

Percent of total pop.: 47.69%, 45th

Percent 65 and over (1990): 2.77%, 25th

Percent female: 46.74%, 20th

Percent job growth (1980-90): 18.85%, 27th

Major employer industries (1994):

Agriculture: 57,000—3.4%, 16th

Construction: 86,000—5.1%, 9th

Finance, insurance, & real estate: 83,000—4.9%, 32nd

Government: 248,000—14.7%, 32nd

Manufacturing: 274,000—16.3%, 20th

Service: 321,000—19.0%, 41st

Trade: 320,000—19.0%, 26th

Transportation, communications, public utilities: 99,000—5.9%, 13th

Unemployment rate (1994): 5.37%, 30th

Male: 5.8%, 21st

Female: 4.9%, 37th

Total businesses (1991): 111,784

New business incorps. (1991): 6,782

Percent of total businesses: 6.07%, 24th

Business failures (1991): 1,063

Percent of total businesses: 0.95%

Agriculture farm income:
Marketing (1993): $3,376,000,000, 20th
Average per farm: $37,098.90, 47th
Leading products (1993): Tobacco, cattle, horses, dairy products
Average value land & build. per acre (1994): $1,144, 20th
Percent increase (1990-94): 16.62%, 19th
Govt. payments (1993): $97,000,000, 30th
Average per farm: $1,065.93, 41st
Construction, value of all: $1,424,000,000
Per capita: $386.40, 41st
Manufactures:
Value added: $23,629,000,000
Per capita: $6,411.70, 9th
Leading products: Nonelectrical machinery, food products, electric and electronic products, apparel, printing and publishing
Value of nonfuel mineral production (1994): $431,000,000, 26th
Leading mineral products: Coal, petroleum, stone
Retail sales (1993): $27,507,000,000, 28th
Per household: $19,267, 44th
Percent increase (1992-93): 6.3%, 32nd
Tourism revenues (1993): $6.8 bil.
Foreign exports, in total value (1994): $4,803,000,000, 25th
Per capita: $1,255.03, 25th
Gross state product per person (1993): $18,842.53, 40th
Percent change (1990-93): 4.48%, 16th
Patents per 100,000 pop. (1993): 8.51, 47th
Public aid recipients (percent of resident pop. 1993): 9.5%, 7th
Medicaid recipients per 1,000 pop. (1993): 162.89, 7th
Medicare recipients per 1,000 pop. (1993): 148.92, 15th

TRAVEL AND TRANSPORTATION

Motor vehicle registrations (1993): 2,629,000
Per 1,000 pop.: 692.94, 43rd
Motorcycle registrations (1993): 32,000
Per 1,000 pop.: 8.43, 45th
Licensed drivers per 1,000 pop. (1993): 650.76, 41st
Deaths from motor vehicle accidents per 100,000 pop. (1993): 23.09, 8th
Public roads & streets (1993):
Total mileage: 72,632
Per 1,000 pop.: 19.14, 24th
Rural mileage: 62,493
Per 1,000 pop.: 16.47, 24th

Urban mileage: 10,139
Per 1,000 pop.: 2.67, 41st
Interstate mileage: 761
Per 1,000 pop.: 0.20, 29th
Annual vehicle-mi. of travel per person (1993): 10,438, 9th
Mean travel time for workers age 16+ who work away from home: 20.7 min., 24th

GOVERNMENT

Percent of voting age pop. registered (1994): 62.5%, 32nd
Percent of voting age pop. voting (1994): 34.5%, 49th
Percent of voting age pop. voting for U.S. representatives (1994): 27.5%, 48th
State legislators, total (1995): 138, 30th
Women members (1992): 8
Percent of legislature: 5.8%, 49th
U.S. Congress, House members (1995): 6
Change (1985-95): –1
Revenues (1993):
State govt.: $11,011,000,000
Per capita: $2,902.21, 30th
Parimutuel & amusement taxes & lotteries, revenue per capita: $121.24, 15th
Expenditures (1993):
State govt.: $10,543,000,000
Per capita: $2,778.86, 27th
Debt outstanding (1993): $6,820,000,000
Per capita: $1,797.58, 17th

LAWS AND REGULATIONS

Legal driving age: 16
Marriage age without parental consent: 18
Divorce residence requirement: 180 days

ATTRACTIONS (1995)

Major opera companies: 1
Major symphony orchestras: 1
Major dance companies: 1
Major professional theater companies (non-profit): 1
State appropriations for arts agencies per capita: $0.84, 21st
State Fair in mid-August at Louisville

SPORTS AND COMPETITION

NCAA teams (Division I): Eastern Kentucky Univ. Colonels, Morehead State Univ. Eagles, Murray State Univ. Racers, Univ. of Kentucky Wildcats, Univ. of Louisville Cardinals, Western Kentucky Univ. Hilltoppers

L O U I S I A N A

"But where is that favored Land?—It is in this great continent.—It is, reader, in Louisiana that these bounties of nature are in the greatest perfection."

John James Audubon, ornithologist and artist

Louisiana is the home of the famous Mardi Gras held in New Orleans, that charming old city with its rich French heritage. Many people from southern Louisiana are descended from the French settlers who left the Acadia region of eastern Canada. Louisiana is one of the nation's busiest commercial areas. Shipping is important, as are fishing, petroleum production, and farming. White-columned mansions, built before the Civil War, symbolize Louisiana's past glory. Louisiana has been called "an unparalleled combination of beauty, historic charm, and bountiful resources." New Orleans continues to flourish as a major tourist center.

SUPERLATIVES

- Claimed at one time by more nations than any other state.
- Birthplace of jazz.
- Nation's leading port.
- Four major deep-water harbors.
- Largest U.S. iron ore reserves.
- First in sulfur production.
- First in production of fur pelts.

MOMENTS IN HISTORY

- In 1519, Spanish explorer Alonso de Pineda claimed to have reached the mouth of the Mississippi, calling it Rio del Espiritu Santo (River of the Holy Spirit).
- Despite Pineda's claims, Hernando de Soto is generally thought of as the Mississippi's discoverer, in his 1541-1542 expedition to the region.
- Few visitors touched the present state until 1682, when Robert Cavalier, Sieur de La Salle, claimed the entire Mississippi watershed for France and named it for King Louis XIV.
- In 1699, explorations of the brothers Pierre Le Moyne, Sieur d'Iberville, and the Sieur de Bienville strengthened French claims, and France made Louisiana a crown colony that year.

- Juchereau de St. Denis founded what is now Natchitoches in 1714; it was the first permanent European settlement in Louisiana.
- Bienville founded New Orleans in 1718.
- In 1743, Marquis de Vaudreuil became governor of French Louisiana.

So They Say

"His administration...was for Louisiana...what the reign of Louis XIV had been for France.... He loved to keep up a miniature court, a distant imitation of that of Versailles...old people were fond of talking of the exquisitely refined manner, the magnificent balls, the splendidly uniformed troops...and many other unparalleled things they had seen in the day of the great Marquis."

Historian Charles Gayarre, on the Marquis de Vaudreuil

- In 1762, King Louis XV gave his cousin Charles II of Spain all the land west of the Mississippi, to keep it out of British hands.
- In 1768, colonists of Louisiana rebelled against Spanish rule and governed an independent republic for almost a year.
- Spanish rule was reestablished in 1769.
- On Good Friday 1788, much of the city of New Orleans was destroyed by fire.
- The Treaty of San Ildefonso in 1801 returned Louisiana to France.
- On November 30, 1803, the United States took over the Cabildo (capitol) at New Orleans, after buying the entire Louisiana territory from France in one of history's best real estate deals.
- Spain continued to claim eastern Louisiana, but it was taken by the United States in 1810.
- Despite eastern fears of the "foreigners" in Louisiana, the territory became the 18th state on April 30, 1812.

• On January 8, 1815, Andrew Jackson scored a sweeping victory at the Battle of New Orleans. He had not heard that the War of 1812 had already ended.

• The 1840 census showed New Orleans to be the nation's fourth largest city, the informal capital of the great plantation region.

• One of the states most dependent on slavery, Louisiana moved quickly to join the Confederacy on January 26, 1861.

• On April 29, 1862, Union Admiral David Farragut captured New Orleans.

• When Confederate General Edmund Kirby-Smith surrendered at Shreveport on June 2, 1865, his was the last major army of the South to lay down arms.

• Chaos reigned in Louisiana for 12 years after war's end. Then in 1877, state control was returned.

• In 1892, New Orleans was hit by a general strike, the first in the nation.

• In 1901 the state's first oil flowed from a "monster" well near Jennings.

• In 1915, New Orleans jazz spread to Chicago and was soon popularized around the world.

• Huey Long was elected governor in 1928 and soon became one of the nation's best-known and most powerful politicians.

• In 1935, Huey Long—by then a U.S. senator—was assassinated on the steps of the state capitol.

• Of the 260,000 Louisianans who served in World War II, 5,015 died.

• In the mid-1990s New Orleans retained its longtime position as the nation's busiest port.

THAT'S INTERESTING

• When the Bonnet Carre Spillway was completed, 6,000 goats were put to work keeping the grass down so that flood waters could flow without resistance.

• Shipwrecked explorer Marcos de Mena was wounded by the Indians and buried alive; a small airhole permitted him to breathe. After his followers were killed, he managed to wriggle out and make his way back to Mexico.

• Jean Lafitte and his pirate crew were pardoned as reward for their services in the War of 1812, but soon returned to their ways.

• Huey Long was noted for his brilliant mind and often spellbound his opponents with apt quotations from the Bible, Shakespeare, and innumerable other sources, related with his great eloquence.

• Membership in the Live Oak Society was limited to the trees themselves. There was a senior membership of trees 100 years old, and a junior group. The society died out with the death of its founder—a man, not a tree.

• The Indians painted a conspicuous tree bright red as a marker. The French called this tree "baton rouge" (red stick), giving the Louisiana capital its name.

NOTABLE NATIVES

Louis Daniel Armstrong (New Orleans, 1900-1971), musician. **Pierre Gustave Toutant Beauregard** (New Orleans, 1818-1893), soldier. **Truman Capote** (New Orleans, 1924-1984), author. **Louis Moreau Gottschalk** (New Orleans, 1829-1869), pianist and composer. **Lillian Hellman** (New Orleans, 1905-1984), playwright. **Mahalia Jackson** (New Orleans, 1911-1972), gospel singer. **Huddie (Leadbelly) Ledbetter** (near Shreveport, 1888?-1949), folk singer/composer. **Huey Pierce Long** (Winnfield, 1893-1935), public official. **Edward Douglass White** (Lafourche Parish, 1845-1921), Supreme Court justice.

GENERAL

Admitted to statehood: April 30, 1812
Origin of name: Part of territory called Louisiana by Sieur de La Salle for French King Louis XIV
Capital: Baton Rouge
Nickname: Pelican State
Motto: Union, justice, and confidence
Bird: Eastern (Louisiana) brown pelican
Insect: Honeybee
Flower: Magnolia bloom
Song: "Give Me Louisiana" and "You Are My Sunshine"
Tree: Bald cypress

THE LAND

Area: 49,650 sq. mi., 31st
  Land: 43,566 sq. mi., 33rd
  Water: 6,084 sq. mi., 6th
    Inland water: 4,153 sq. mi., 5th
    Coastal water: 1,931 sq. mi., 3rd
Topography: Lowlands of the marshes and Mississippi River flood plain; Red River Valley lowlands; upland hills in the Florida parishes

Number of counties: 64 parishes
Geographic center: Avoyelles, 3 mi. SE of Marksville
Length: 380 mi.; width: 130 mi.
Highest point: 535 ft. (Driskill Mountain), 48th
Lowest point: –8 ft. (New Orleans), 2nd
Mean elevation: 100 ft., 50th
Coastline: 397 mi., 5th
Shoreline: 7,721 mi., 3rd

CLIMATE AND ENVIRONMENT

Temp., highest: 114 deg. on Aug. 10, 1936, at Plain Dealing; lowest: –16 deg. on Feb. 13, 1899, at Minden
Monthly average: highest: 93.3 deg., 7th; lowest: 36.2 deg., 47th; spread (high to low): 57.1 deg., 48th
Hazardous waste sites (1993): 12, 30th
Endangered species: Mammals: 1—West Indian manatee; birds: 4—American peregrine falcon, Brown pelican, Least tern, Red-cockaded woodpecker; reptiles: 3; amphibians: none; fishes: 1; invertebrates: 1; plants: 1

MAJOR CITIES POPULATION, 1990 PERCENTAGE INCREASE, 1980-90

Baton Rouge, 219,531— –0.39%
Lafayette, 94,440—17.19%
Metairie, 149,428— –8.97%
New Orleans, 496,938— –10.93%
Shreveport, 198,525— –3.62%

THE PEOPLE

Population (1995): 4,342,334, 21st
Percent change (1990-95): 2.9%, 38th
Population (2000 proj.): 4,478,000, 22nd
Percent change (1990-2000): 6.11%, 36th
Per sq. mi. (1994): 99.0, 23rd
Percent in metro. area (1992): 75.0%, 22nd
Foreign born: 87,000, 26th
Percent: 2.1%, 34th
Top three ancestries reported:
African, 26.00%
French, 13.03%
Irish, 12.27%
White: 2,839,138, 67.28%, 48th
Black: 1,299,281, 30.79%, 3rd
Native American: 18,541, 0.44%, 25th
Asian, Pacific Isle: 41,099, 0.97%, 29th
Other races: 21,914, 0.52%, 34th

Hispanic origin: 93,044, 2.20%, 28th
Percent over 5 yrs. speaking language other than English at home: 10.1%, 17th
Percent males: 48.14%, 43rd; percent females: 51.86%, 9th
Percent never married: 27.4%, 14th
Marriages per 1,000 (1993): 8.4, 27th
Median age: 31
Under 5 years (1994): 7.81%, 9th
Under 18 years (1994): 28.62%, 8th
65 years & older (1994): 11.4%, 40th
Percent increase among the elderly (1990-94): 5.33%, 28th

OF VITAL IMPORTANCE

Live births per 1,000 pop. (1993): 16.3, 9th
Infant mortality rate per 1,000 births (1992): 9.4, 12th
Rate for blacks (1990): 16.5, 20th
Rate for whites (1990): 7.3, 38th
Births to unmarried women, % of total (1992): 40.2%, 3rd
Births to teenage mothers, % of total (1992): 18.1%, 4th
Abortions (1992): 13,600, 26th
Rate per 1,000 women 14-44 years old: 13.4, 39th
Percent change (1988-92): –18%, 45th
Average lifetime (1979-81): 71.74, 49th
Deaths per 1,000 pop. (1993): 9.3, 17th
Causes of death per 100,000 pop.:
Accidents & adverse effects (1992): 41.5, 15th
Atherosclerosis (1991): 8.3, 16th
Cancer (1991): 207.0, 27th
Cerebrovascular diseases (1992): 56.5, 29th
Chronic liver diseases & cirrhosis (1991): 8.3, 37th
Chronic obstructive pulmonary diseases (1992): 29.6, 46th
Diabetes mellitus (1992): 27.9, 4th
Diseases of heart (1992): 284.1, 26th
Pneumonia, flu (1991): 24.5, 43rd
Suicide (1992): 12.4, 26th

KEEPING WELL

Active nonfederal physicians per 100,000 pop. (1993): 201, 24th
Dentists per 100,000 (1991): 47, 38th
Nurses per 100,000 (1992): 570, 44th
Hospitals per 100,000 (1993): 3.08, 15th
Admissions per 1,000 (1993): 139.39, 11th
Occupancy rate per 100 beds (1993): 57.0, 41st

Average cost per patient per day (1993): $875, 23rd

Average cost per stay (1993): $5,781, 25th

Average stay (1992): 6.5 days, 42nd

AIDS cases (adult, 1993): 1,464; per 100,000: 34.1, 16th

HIV infection, not yet AIDS (1993): 1,723

Other notifiable diseases:
Gonorrhea: 312.8, 16th
Measles: 0.2, 47th
Syphilis: 125.1, 3rd
Tuberculosis: 8.7, 18th

Pop. without health insur. (1991-93): 22.4%, 3rd

HOUSEHOLDS BY TYPE

Total households (1994): 1,543,000
Percent change (1990-94): 2.9%, 32nd
Per 1,000 pop.: 357.59, 43rd
Percent of households 65 yrs. and over: 20.80%, 36th
Persons per household (1994): 2.72, 9th
Family households: 1,089,882
Percent of total: 72.69%, 10th
Nonfamily households: 409,387
Percent of total: 27.31%, 42nd
Pop. living in group quarters: 112,578
Percent of pop.: 2.67%, 30th

LIVING QUARTERS

Total housing units: 1,716,241
Persons per unit: 2.46, 13th
Occupied housing units: 1,499,269
Percent of total units: 87.36%, 35th
Persons per unit: 2.70, 6th
Percent of units with over 1 person per room: 5.95%, 10th
Owner-occupied units: 987,919
Percent of total units: 57.56%, 33rd
Percent of occupied units: 65.89%, 33rd
Persons per unit: 2.83, 9th
Median value: $58,500, 36th
Renter-occupied units: 511,250
Percent of total units: 29.79%, 23rd
Percent of occupied units: 34.10%, 20th
Persons per unit: 2.57, 6th
Median contract rent: $260, 42nd
Rental vacancy rate: 12.5%, 5th
Mobile home, trailer & other as a percent of occupied housing units: 14.51%, 16th
Persons in emergency shelters for homeless persons: 1,559, 0.037%, 42nd
Persons visible in street locations: 184, 0.0044%, 31st

Persons in shelters for abused women: 244, 0.0058%, 15th

Nursing home population: 32,072, 0.76%, 22nd

CRIME INDEX PER 100,000 (1992-93)

Total reported: 6,846.6, 4th
Violent: 1,061.7, 5th
Murder and nonnegligent manslaughter: 20.3, 2nd
Aggravated assault: 715.4, 5th
Robbery: 283.6, 9th
Forcible rape: 42.3, 22nd
Property: 5,784.9, 5th
Burglary: 1,368.3, 6th
Larceny, theft: 3,802.9, 7th
Motor vehicle theft: 613.7, 13th
Drug abuse violations (1990): 309.4, 17th
Child-abuse rate per 1,000 children (1993): 12.27, 32nd

TEACHING AND LEARNING

Pop. 3 and over enrolled in school: 1,185,759
Percent of pop.: 29.5%, 8th
Public elementary & secondary schools (1992-93): 1,453
Total enrollment (1992): 797,985
Percent of total pop.: 18.65%, 11th
Teachers (1992): 47,024
Percent of pop.: 1.10%, 17th
Pupil/teacher ratio (fall 1992): 16.6, 30th
Teachers' avg. salary (1992-93): $29,914, 41st
Expenditure per capita (1990-91): $3,350.68, 28th
Expenditure per pupil (1991-92): $4,354, 42nd
Percent of graduates taking SAT (1993): 9%, 42nd
Mean SAT verbal scores: 481, 10th
Mean SAT mathematical scores: 527, 14th
Percent of graduates taking ACT (1995): 75%, 1st
Mean ACT scores: 19.4, 48th
Percent of pop. over 25 completing:
Less than 9th grade: 14.7%, 7th
High school: 68.3%, 44th
College degree(s): 16.1%, 43rd
Higher education, institutions (1993-94): 33
Enrollment (1992): 204,379
Percent of pop.: 4.78%, 44th
White non-Hispanic (1992): 139,873
Percent of enroll.: 68.44%, 46th

Black non-Hispanic (1992): 50,181
  Percent of enroll.: 24.55%, 3rd
Hispanic (1992): 4,348
  Percent of enroll.: 2.13%, 22nd
Asian/Pacific Islander (1992): 3,446
  Percent of enroll.: 1.69%, 33rd
American Indian/AK native (1992): 1,054
  Percent of enroll.: 0.52%, 24th
Nonresident alien (1992): 5,477
  Percent of enroll.: 2.68%, 24th
Female (1992): 116,450
  Percent of enroll.: 56.98%, 7th
Pub. institutions (1993-94): 20
  Enrollment (1992): 177,373
  Percent of enroll.: 86.79%, 16th
Private institutions (1993-94): 13
  Enrollment (1992): 27,006
  Percent of enroll.: 13.21%, 36th
Tuition, public institution (avg., 1993-94): $5,225, 37th
Tuition, private institution (avg., 1993-94): $15,785, 13th
Public library systems: 64
  Books & serial vol. per capita: 2.03, 37th
  Govt. expenditure per capita: $12.56, 33rd

LAW ENFORCEMENT, COURTS, AND PRISONS

Police protection, corrections, judicial and legal functions expenditures (1992): $1,096,000,000
  Per capita: $256, 27th
Police per 10,000 pop. (1993): 31.47, 4th
Prisoners (state & fed.) per 100,000 pop. (1993): 5,237.30, 3rd
  Percent change (1992-93): 7.1%, 17th
Death penalty: yes, by electrocution
  Under sentence of death (1993): 45, 18th
  Executed (1993): 1

RELIGION, NUMBER AND PERCENT OF POPULATION

Agnostic: NA
Buddhist: 2,993—0.10%, 17th
Christian: 2,834,091—94.70%, 1st
Hindu: NA
Jewish: 5,985—0.20%, 40th
Muslim: 2,993—0.10%, 22nd
Unitarian: NA
Other: 23,942—0.80%, 37th
None: 86,788—2.90%, 46th
Refused to answer: 35,912—1.20%, 46th

MAKING A LIVING

Personal income per capita (1994): $17,651, 46th
  Percent increase (1993-94): 6.3%, 9th
Disposable personal income per capita (1994): $15,754, 42nd
Median income of households (1993): $26,312, 43rd
Percent of pop. below poverty level (1993): 26.4%, 2nd
  Percent 65 and over (1990): 24.1%, 2nd
Expenditure for energy per person (1992): $2,893, 3rd

ECONOMY

Civilian labor force (1994): 1,939,000
  Percent of total pop.: 44.94%, 50th
  Percent 65 and over (1990): 2.93%, 19th
  Percent female: 46.26%, 25th
Percent job growth (1980-90): 2.46%, 49th
Major employer industries (1994):
  Agriculture: 44,000—2.5%, 23rd
  Construction: 101,000—5.8%, 4th
  Finance, insurance, & real estate: 85,000—4.9%, 32nd
  Government: 328,000—18.9%, 10th
  Manufacturing: 182,000—10.5%, 41st
  Service: 351,000—20.2%, 32nd
  Trade: 345,000—19.8%, 10th
  Transportation, communications, public utilities: 104,000—6.0%, 11th
Unemployment rate (1994): 8.05%, 4th
  Male: 7.3%, 8th
  Female: 9.0%, 1st
Total businesses (1991): 127,163
  New business incorps. (1991): 8,973
    Percent of total businesses: 7.06%, 14th
  Business failures (1991): 1,152
    Percent of total businesses: 0.91%
Agriculture farm income:
  Marketing (1993): $1,757,000,000, 33rd
    Average per farm: $60,586.21, 40th
  Leading products (1993): Cotton, sugar, cattle, soybeans
  Average value land & build. per acre (1994): $973, 25th
    Percent increase (1990-94): 6.34%, 33rd
  Govt. payments (1993): $367,000,000, 14th
    Average per farm: $12,655.17, 6th
Construction, value of all: $1,101,000,000
  Per capita: $260.90, 49th

Manufactures:

Value added: $22,617,000,000

Per capita: $5,359.51, 20th

Leading products: Chemical products, foods, transportation equipment, electronic equipment, petroleum products, lumber, wood and paper

Value of nonfuel mineral production (1994): $328,000,000, 34th

Leading mineral products: Petroleum, natural gas, sulfur

Retail sales (1993): $31,410,000,000, 23rd

Per household: $20,457, 40th

Percent increase (1992-93): 1.5%, 45th

Tourism revenues (1992): $5.2 bil.

Foreign exports, in total value (1994): $14,549,000,000, 9th

Per capita: $3,371.73, 3rd

Gross state product per person (1993): $22,400.38, 19th

Percent change (1990-93): 3.26%, 23rd

Patents per 100,000 pop. (1993): 11.19, 40th

Public aid recipients (percent of resident pop. 1993): 9.9%, 4th

Medicaid recipients per 1,000 pop. (1993): 175.06, 6th

Medicare recipients per 1,000 pop. (1993): 131.24, 37th

TRAVEL AND TRANSPORTATION

Motor vehicle registrations (1993): 3,166,000

Per 1,000 pop.: 738.00, 35th

Motorcycle registrations (1993): 35,000

Per 1,000 pop.: 8.16, 47th

Licensed drivers per 1,000 pop. (1993): 600.70, 49th

Deaths from motor vehicle accidents per 100,000 pop. (1993): 20.54, 13th

Public roads & streets (1993):

Total mileage: 59,599

Per 1,000 pop.: 13.89, 33rd

Rural mileage: 45,833

Per 1,000 pop.: 10.68, 34th

Urban mileage: 13,766

Per 1,000 pop.: 3.21, 22nd

Interstate mileage: 871

Per 1,000 pop.: 0.20, 28th

Annual vehicle-mi. of travel per person (1993): 8,485, 40th

Mean travel time for workers age 16+ who work away from home: 22.3 min., 11th

GOVERNMENT

Percent of voting age pop. registered (1994): 70.6%, 17th

Percent of voting age pop. voting (1994): 34.2%, 50th

Percent of voting age pop. voting for U.S. representatives (1994): NA

State legislators, total (1995): 144, 27th

Women members (1992): 10

Percent of legislature: 6.9%, 47th

U.S. Congress, House members (1995): 7

Change (1985-95): –1

Revenues (1993):

State govt.: $13,348,000,000

Per capita: $3,111.42, 24th

Parimutuel & amusement taxes & lotteries, revenue per capita: $108.86, 17th

Expenditures (1993):

State govt.: $12,893,000,000

Per capita: $3,005.36, 19th

Debt outstanding (1993): $9,585,000,000

Per capita: $2,234.27, 14th

LAWS AND REGULATIONS

Legal driving age: 17, 15 if completed driver education course

Marriage age without parental consent: 18

Divorce residence requirement: 6 mo., for qualifications check local statutes

ATTRACTIONS (1995)

Major opera companies: 1

Major symphony orchestras: 2

State appropriations for arts agencies per capita: $0.97, 15th

State Fair in October at Shreveport

SPORTS AND COMPETITION

NCAA teams (Division I): Centenary College Gentlemen, Grambling State Univ. Tigers, Louisiana State Univ. Fighting Tigers, Louisiana Tech Univ. Bulldogs, McNeese State Univ. Cowboys, Nicholls State Univ. Colonels, Northeast Louisiana Univ. Indians, Northwestern State Univ. Demons, Southeastern Louisiana Univ. Lions, Southern Univ.-Baton Rouge Jaguars, Tulane Univ. Green Wave, Univ. of New Orleans Privateers, Univ. of Southwestern Louisiana Ragin' Cajuns

NFL football teams: New Orleans Saints (NFC), Louisiana Superdome

MAINE

"Did you ever see a place that looks like it was built just to enjoy? Well this whole state of Maine looks that way."

Will Rogers, humorist

Potatoes, lobsters, and submarines make an unusual combination, but Maine has been famous for all of these. The seacoast of "hundred-harbor Maine," with its lighthouses, sandy beaches, quiet fishing villages, and thousands of off-shore islands, is one of the world's most notable for its beauty. It is also noted for tremendous catches of fish, many outstanding ports, and shipbuilding—boasting the first ship built in the Western Hemisphere. Although not primarily farming land, Maine has farms that are world famous for the wonderful white potatoes grown there. The lack of natural resources has been overcome by the courage, ingenuity, and persistence of the Maine character.

SUPERLATIVES

- World's highest tides.
- First ship launched in the Western Hemisphere—the *Virginia*, in 1607.
- First atomic submarine, the *Swordfish*, built in Maine.
- Leader in canoe manufacture.
- Holds clipper ship sailing record.
- First sawmill in the United States.
- Produces one-fourth of all U.S feldspar.
- Leader in lobster catch.
- World's first steel sailing vessel.

MOMENTS IN HISTORY

- In 1604 Pierre du Guast of France landed at Dochet Island and began a place he called St. Croix.
- In 1607 the primeval forests of Maine provided timber, the 120 settlers at the mouth of the Kennebec River provided the labor, and the *Virginia*, the first ship ever to be launched in the hemisphere, went down the primitive ways.
- Captain John Smith visited present-day Maine in 1614.
- In 1622, Maine's first permanent European settlement, Monhegan, was established.
- During King Philip's War, Saco was attacked on September 18, 1675, and a long period of war with the Indians continued in Maine.
- Peace came to Maine in 1760 in a treaty made with the Indians during the French and Indian War.

> ## So They Say
>
> "Those barren Isles are so furnished with good woods, springs, fruits, fish and foule, that it makes me think though the coast be rocky, and thus affrightable, the valleys, plains, and interior parts may well be very fertile."
>
> Captain John Smith

- The British King had claimed most of the area's best trees for masts. In 1775, when a British ship attempted to take the trees, the people of Machiasport rose up under Foster and Jeremiah O'Brien, captured the boat, and killed the commander. This engagement has been called the first naval battle of the Revolution, and it took place just five days before the Battle of Bunker Hill.
- During the Revolution, the coastal towns of Maine endured much destruction, but the British were not able to remove the needed mast trees for their navy.
- Maine suffered again during the War of 1812. Bangor was captured, and Britain seized sizable portions of Maine, but the state's boundaries remained unchanged after the war.
- Based on an ancient map by explorer Samuel de Champlain, the border with Canada was decided in Maine's favor in 1815, keeping much of present-day eastern Maine in U.S. hands.
- Maine became the 23rd state on March 15, 1820.
- Another boundary dispute was settled by the Webster-Ashburton Treaty of 1842, with Canada receiving a substantial area claimed by the United States.

- There never had been much slavery in Maine. In 1857, Republican Hannibal Hamlin became governor on an antislavery platform.
- By the end of the Civil War in 1865, a fifth of all Maine residents had served in the military, and 8,800 lost their lives.
- Portland suffered a destructive fire in 1866.

So They Say

"I have been in Portland since the fire. Desolation, desolation, desolation! It reminds me of Pompeii."

Poet Henry Wadsworth Longfellow

- Of the 35,000 from Maine who saw World War I service, special tribute for heroism was awarded to Passamaquody Indian Charles Nola.
- Shipbuilding in Maine played a prominent part in World War II, in which 95,000 men and women served in U.S. forces.
- In 1948, Margaret Chase Smith became the first Republican woman elected to the U.S. Senate.
- Schoolgirl Samantha Smith of Maine gained world fame in 1983 when she wrote a letter to Soviet leader Yuri Andropov expressing her fear of nuclear war, and then visited the Soviet Union at his invitation. She died tragically on August 25, 1985, in a private plane crash.

THAT'S INTERESTING

- The first European settlers in Maine brought timber in their ships to build houses and were astonished that their new home had its own magnificent forests.
- Because Cushnoc Island in the Kennebec River at Augusta was a navigation hazard, the people there hitched 200 oxen to the island, but they failed to move it an inch.
- Thanksgiving in Maine predated the Pilgrims. The Etchimin Indians celebrated for two weeks in autumn. Their feasts included turkey, cranberries, popcorn, and other familiar delicacies.
- Barney Beal of Beal's Island was a noted strongman who could knock out a horse with one blow and who once bested 15 men in a tavern dispute.

- During the Revolution, 19-year-old Aaron Burr fell in love with Indian Princess Jacataqua; Burr moved on to later fame and notoriety.
- Samuel Francis Smith of Waterville gave the nation "America" ("My Country, 'Tis of Thee"), which many believe should be the national anthem.

NOTABLE NATIVES

Cyrus H. K. Curtis (Portland, 1850-1933), publisher. **Dorothea Lynde Dix** (Hampden, 1802-1887), educator and social reformer. **Melville Weston Fuller** (Augusta, 1833-1910), chief justice of the United States. **Hannibal Hamlin** (Paris Hill, 1809-1891), U.S. vice president. **Stephen King** (Portland, 1947-), author. **Henry Wadsworth Longfellow** (Portland, 1807-1882), poet. **Hiram Stevens Maxim** (near Sangerville, 1840-1916), inventor. **Edna St. Vincent Millay** (Rockland, 1892-1950), poet. **Lillian Nordica** (Farmington, 1857-1914), opera singer. **John Knowles Paine** (Portland, 1839-1906), composer/educator. **Sir William Phips** (the Maine frontier, 1651-1695), colonial governor. **Thomas Brackett Reed** (Portland, 1839-1902), public official. **Kenneth Lewis Roberts** (Kennebunkport, 1885-1957), author. **Edwin Arlington Robinson** (Head Tide, 1869-1935), poet. **Nelson Aldrich Rockefeller** (Bar Harbor, 1908-1979), public official, U.S. vice president. **Nathaniel Parker Willis** (Portland, 1806-1867), poet.

GENERAL

Admitted to statehood: March 15, 1820
Origin of name: From Maine, ancient French province. Also descriptive, referring to the mainland as distinct from the many coastal islands.
Capital: Augusta
Nickname: Pine Tree State
Motto: *Dirigo*—I direct
Bird: Chickadee
Fish: Landlocked salmon
Flower: White pine coneand tassel
Gem: Tourmaline
Song: "State of Maine Song"
Tree: Eastern white pine

THE LAND

Area: 33,741 sq. mi., 39th
   Land: 30,865 sq. mi., 39th

Water: 2,876 sq. mi., 13th
  Inland water: 2,263 sq. mi., 9th
  Coastal water: 613 sq. mi., 9th
Topography: Appalachian Mountains extend through state; western borders have rugged terrain; long sand beaches on southern coast; northern coast mainly rocky promontories, peninsulas, fjords
Number of counties: 16
Geographic center: Piscataquis, N of Dover
Length: 320 mi.; width: 190 mi.
Highest point: 5,267 ft. (Mount Katahdin), 22nd
Lowest point: sea level (Atlantic Ocean), 3rd
Mean elevation: 600 ft., 39th
Coastline: 228 mi., 9th
Shoreline: 3,478 mi., 4th

CLIMATE AND ENVIRONMENT

Temp., highest: 105 deg. on July 10, 1911, at North Bridgton; lowest: –48 deg. on Jan. 19, 1925, at Van Buren
Monthly average: highest: 78.9 deg., 50th; lowest: 11.9 deg., 12th; spread (high to low): 67.0 deg., 28th
Hazardous waste sites (1993): 10, 36th
Endangered species: Mammals: none; birds: 2—American peregrine falcon, Roseate tern; reptiles: none; amphibians: none; fishes: none; invertebrates: none; plants: 2

MAJOR CITIES
POPULATION, 1990
PERCENTAGE INCREASE, 1980-90

Auburn, 24,309—5.11%
Bangor, 33,181—4.86%
Lewiston, 39,757— –1.79%
Portland, 64,358—4.52%
South Portland, 23,163—1.99%

THE PEOPLE

Population (1995): 1,241,382, 39th
  Percent change (1990-95): 0.9%, 45th
Population (2000 proj.): 1,240,000, 41st
  Percent change (1990-2000): 0.98%, 46th
Per sq. mi. (1994): 40.2, 37th
Percent in metro. area (1992): 35.7%, 45th
Foreign born: 36,000, 38th
  Percent: 3.0%, 27th
Top three ancestries reported:
  English, 30.29%
  French, 18.24%
  Irish, 17.67%

White: 1,208,360, 98.41%, 2nd
Black: 5,138, 0.42%, 48th
Native American: 5,998, 0.49%, 23rd
Asian, Pacific Isle: 6,683, 0.54%, 43rd
Other races: 1,749, 0.14%, 49th
Hispanic origin: 6,829, 0.56%, 50th
Percent over 5 yrs. speaking language other than English at home: 9.2%, 18th
Percent males: 48.69%, 24th; percent females: 51.31%, 28th
Percent never married: 24.0%, 36th
Marriages per 1,000 (1993): 8.8, 23rd
Divorces per 1,000 (1993): 4.3, 29th
Median age: 33.9
Under 5 years (1994): 6.29%, 50th
Under 18 years (1994): 24.68%, 41st
65 years & older (1994): 13.9%, 13th
Percent increase among the elderly (1990-94): 5.28%, 29th

OF VITAL IMPORTANCE

Live births per 1,000 pop. (1993): 12.1, 50th
Infant mortality rate per 1,000 births (1992): 5.6, 51st
  Rate for blacks (1990): 6.1, 47th
  Rate for whites (1990): 6.2, 50th
Births to unmarried women, % of total (1992): 25.3%, 38th
Births to teenage mothers, % of total (1992): 10.2%, 37th
Abortions (1992): 4,200, 41st
  Rate per 1,000 women 14-44 years old: 14.7, 34th
  Percent change (1988-92): –9%, 28th
Average lifetime (1979-81): 74.59, 18th
Deaths per 1,000 pop. (1993): 9.3, 17th
Causes of death per 100,000 pop.:
  Accidents & adverse effects (1992): 32.8, 33rd
  Atherosclerosis (1991): 8.9, 11th
  Cancer (1991): 237.8, 7th
  Cerebrovascular diseases (1992): 60.3, 22nd
  Chronic liver diseases & cirrhosis (1991): 11.0, 11th
  Chronic obstructive pulmonary diseases (1992): 50.8, 3rd
  Diabetes mellitus (1992): 25.9, 8th
  Diseases of heart (1992): 280.0, 28th
  Pneumonia, flu (1991): 30.4, 25th
  Suicide (1992): 12.7, 20th

KEEPING WELL

Active nonfederal physicians per 100,000 pop. (1993): 192, 29th

Dentists per 100,000 (1991): 47, 38th
Nurses per 100,000 (1992): 861, 14th
Hospitals per 100,000 (1993): 3.15, 14th
   Admissions per 1,000 (1993): 117.02, 24th
   Occupancy rate per 100 beds (1993): 68.0, 12th
   Average cost per patient per day (1993): $738, 37th
   Average cost per stay (1993): $5,543, 32nd
   Average stay (1992): 7.8 days, 15th
AIDS cases (adult, 1993): 149; per 100,000: 12.0, 40th
HIV infection, not yet AIDS (1993): NA
Other notifiable diseases:
   Gonorrhea: 16.3, 47th
   Measles: 2.4, 33rd
   Syphilis: 1.7, 47th
   Tuberculosis: 2.8, 40th
Pop. without health insur. (1991-93): 11.1%, 39th

HOUSEHOLDS BY TYPE

Total households (1994): 474,000
   Percent change (1990-94): 2.0%, 41st
   Per 1,000 pop.: 382.26, 8th
   Percent of households 65 yrs. and over: 22.36%, 23rd
   Persons per household (1994): 2.54, 43rd
Family households: 328,685
   Percent of total: 70.64%, 26th
Nonfamily households: 136,627
   Percent of total: 29.36%, 26th
Pop. living in group quarters: 37,169
   Percent of pop.: 3.03%, 16th

LIVING QUARTERS

Total housing units: 587,045
   Persons per unit: 2.09, 50th
Occupied housing units: 465,312
   Percent of total units: 79.26%, 50th
   Persons per unit: 2.46, 44th
   Percent of units with over 1 person per room: 1.72%, 48th
Owner-occupied units: 327,888
   Percent of total units: 55.85%, 38th
   Percent of occupied units: 70.47%, 7th
   Persons per unit: 2.71, 29th
   Median value: $87,400, 17th
Renter-occupied units: 137,424
   Percent of total units: 23.41%, 50th
   Percent of occupied units: 29.53%, 46th
   Persons per unit: 2.20, 47th
   Median contract rent: $358, 21st
   Rental vacancy rate: 8.4%, 25th

Mobile home, trailer & other as a percent of occupied housing units: 14.62%, 15th
Persons in emergency shelters for homeless persons: 419, 0.034%, 45th
Persons visible in street locations: 7, 0.0006%, 51st
Persons in shelters for abused women: 43, 0.0035%, 40th
Nursing home population: 9,855, 0.80%, 21st

CRIME INDEX PER 100,000 (1992-93)

Total reported: 3,153.9, 47th
   Violent: 125.7, 49th
      Murder and nonnegligent manslaughter: 1.6, 51st
      Aggravated assault: 76.3, 48th
      Robbery: 21.3, 46th
      Forcible rape: 26.6, 45th
   Property: 3,028.2, 45th
      Burglary: 719.0, 40th
      Larceny, theft: 2,174.7, 46th
      Motor vehicle theft: 134.4, 49th
Drug abuse violations (1990): 186.6, 37th
Child-abuse rate per 1,000 children (1993): 16.14, 22nd

TEACHING AND LEARNING

Pop. 3 and over enrolled in school: 304,868
   Percent of pop.: 25.9%, 41st
Public elementary & secondary schools (1992-93): 742
   Total enrollment (1992): 216,453
      Percent of total pop.: 17.51%, 23rd
   Teachers (1992): 15,375
      Percent of pop.: 1.24%, 5th
   Pupil/teacher ratio (fall 1992): 14.1, 48th
   Teachers' avg. salary (1992-93): $32,650, 30th
   Expenditure per capita (1990-91): $3,628.44, 19th
   Expenditure per pupil (1991-92): $5,652, 19th
Percent of graduates taking SAT (1993): 69%, 9th
   Mean SAT verbal scores: 422, 38th
   Mean SAT mathematical scores: 463, 45th
Percent of graduates taking ACT (1995): 2%, 49th
   Mean ACT scores: 21.5, 12th
Percent of pop. over 25 completing:
   Less than 9th grade: 8.8%, 30th
   High school: 78.8%, 18th

College degree(s): 18.8%, 29th
Higher education, institutions (1993-94): 31
  Enrollment (1992): 57,977
    Percent of pop.: 4.69%, 47th
    White non-Hispanic (1992): 54,777
      Percent of enroll.: 94.48%, 1st
    Black non-Hispanic (1992): 666
      Percent of enroll.: 1.15%, 44th
    Hispanic (1992): 352
      Percent of enroll.: 0.61%, 45th
    Asian/Pacific Islander (1992): 632
      Percent of enroll.: 1.09%, 42nd
    American Indian/AK native (1992): 854
      Percent of enroll.: 1.47%, 10th
    Nonresident alien (1992): 696
      Percent of enroll.: 1.20%, 51st
    Female (1992): 33,754
      Percent of enroll.: 58.22%, 3rd
  Pub. institutions (1993-94): 14
    Enrollment (1992): 40,846
      Percent of enroll.: 70.45%, 42nd
  Private institutions (1993-94): 17
    Enrollment (1992): 17,131
      Percent of enroll.: 29.55%, 10th
  Tuition, public institution (avg., 1993-94): $7,521, 13th
  Tuition, private institution (avg., 1993-94): $18,754, 3rd
Public library systems: 238
  Books & serial vol. per capita: 4.88, 1st
  Govt. expenditure per capita: $12.20, 36th

LAW ENFORCEMENT, COURTS, AND PRISONS

Police protection, corrections, judicial and legal functions expenditures (1992): $248,000,000
  Per capita: $201, 39th
Police per 10,000 pop. (1993): 16.15, 41st
Prisoners (state & fed.) per 100,000 pop. (1993): 1,184.68, 48th
  Percent change (1992-93): –3.3%, 49th
Death penalty: no

RELIGION, NUMBER AND PERCENT OF POPULATION

Agnostic: 8,270—0.90%, 14th
Buddhist: 919—0.10%, 17th
Christian: 780,168—84.90%, 35th
Hindu: 919—0.10%, 10th
Jewish: 3,676—0.40%, 31st
Muslim: NA
Unitarian: 5,514—0.60%, 5th
Other: 7,351—0.80%, 37th

None: 91,893—10.00%, 11th
Refused to answer: 20,216—2.20%, 23rd

MAKING A LIVING

Personal income per capita (1994): $19,663, 35th
  Percent increase (1993-94): 4.7%, 31st
Disposable personal income per capita (1994): $17,559, 33rd
Median income of households (1993): $27,438, 39th
Percent of pop. below poverty level (1993): 15.4%, 17th
Percent 65 and over (1990): 14.0%, 19th
Expenditure for energy per person (1992): $2,077, 9th

ECONOMY

Civilian labor force (1994): 613,000
  Percent of total pop.: 49.44%, 38th
  Percent 65 and over (1990): 3.15%, 17th
  Percent female: 47.31%, 13th
Percent job growth (1980-90): 29.08%, 14th
Major employer industries (1994):
  Agriculture: 13,000—2.2%, 31st
  Construction: 20,000—3.4%, 46th
  Finance, insurance, & real estate: 30,000—5.2%, 26th
  Government: 77,000—13.3%, 41st
  Manufacturing: 102,000—17.5%, 16th
  Service: 127,000—21.9%, 21st
  Trade: 120,000—20.6%, 4th
  Transportation, communications, public utilities: 24,000—4.1%, 45th
Unemployment rate (1994): 7.34%, 6th
  Male: 8.3%, 4th
  Female: 6.3%, 14th
Total businesses (1991): 45,619
  New business incorps. (1991): 2,326
    Percent of total businesses: 5.10%, 37th
  Business failures (1991): 199
    Percent of total businesses: 0.44%
Agriculture farm income:
  Marketing (1993): $427,000,000, 45th
    Average per farm: $61,000.00, 39th
  Leading products (1993): Eggs, potatoes, dairy products, aquaculture
  Average value land & build. per acre (1994): $1,081, 21st
    Percent increase (1990-94): 6.08%, 38th
  Govt. payments (1993): $20,000,000, 39th
    Average per farm: $2,857.14, 30th

Construction, value of all: $569,000,000
  Per capita: $463.38, 37th
Manufactures:
  Value added: $5,886,000,000
    Per capita: $4,793.44, 31st
  Leading products: Paper and wood products, leather goods
Value of nonfuel mineral production (1994): $58,000,000, 45th
Leading mineral products: Sand/gravel, cement, stone
Retail sales (1993): $11,992,000,000, 40th
  Per household: $25,407, 5th
    Percent increase (1992-93): 4.2%, 37th
Tourism revenues (1991): $2.75 bil.
Foreign exports, in total value (1994): $1,090,000,000, 41st
  Per capita: $879.03, 39th
Gross state product per person (1993): $18,593.37, 43rd
  Percent change (1990-93): 0.00%, 45th
Patents per 100,000 pop. (1993): 11.45, 39th
Public aid recipients (percent of resident pop. 1993): 7.6%, 16th
Medicaid recipients per 1,000 pop. (1993): 136.29, 14th
Medicare recipients per 1,000 pop. (1993): 156.45, 9th

TRAVEL AND TRANSPORTATION

Motor vehicle registrations (1993): 1,028,000
  Per 1,000 pop.: 829.03, 18th
Motorcycle registrations (1993): 31,000
  Per 1,000 pop.: 25.00, 11th
Licensed drivers per 1,000 pop. (1993): 730.65, 7th
Deaths from motor vehicle accidents per 100,000 pop. (1993): 15.00, 32nd
Public roads & streets (1993):
  Total mileage: 22,510
    Per 1,000 pop.: 18.15, 25th
  Rural mileage: 19,927
    Per 1,000 pop.: 16.07, 25th
  Urban mileage: 2,583
    Per 1,000 pop.: 2.08, 48th

Interstate mileage: 366
  Per 1,000 pop.: 0.30, 15th
Annual vehicle-mi. of travel per person (1993): 9,839, 21st
Mean travel time for workers age 16+ who work away from home: 19.0 min., 39th

GOVERNMENT

Percent of voting age pop. registered (1994): 81.6%, 4th
  Percent of voting age pop. voting (1994): 58.2%, 8th
  Percent of voting age pop. voting for U.S. representatives (1994): 54.0%, 4th
State legislators, total (1995): 186, 10th
  Women members (1992): 60
    Percent of legislature: 32.3%, 3rd
U.S. Congress, House members (1995): 2
  Change (1985-95): 0
Revenues (1993):
  State govt.: $3,926,000,000
    Per capita: $3,166.13, 22nd
    Parimutuel & amusement taxes & lotteries, revenue per capita: $95.97, 20th
Expenditures (1993):
  State govt.: $3,889,000,000
    Per capita: $3,136.29, 18th
Debt outstanding (1993): $2,999,000,000
  Per capita: $2,418.55, 13th

LAWS AND REGULATIONS

Legal driving age: 17, 16 if completed driver education course
Marriage age without parental consent: 18
Divorce residence requirement: 6 mo., for qualifications check local statutes

ATTRACTIONS (1995)

Major symphony orchestras: 1
State appropriations for arts agencies per capita: $0.43, 43rd
State Fair in mid-August at Skowhegan

SPORTS AND COMPETITION

NCAA teams (Division I): Univ. of Maine Black Bears

MARYLAND

"...a delightsome land!"

Captain John Smith, explorer

"America in miniature—a small state, it offers a large part of the variety of attractions found in the United States as a whole."

Theodore McKeldin, governor of Maryland (1951-59)

Chesapeake Bay, which divides Maryland into two parts, furnishes the state with several excellent harbors as well as fine seafood, especially crabs. The defense of Fort McHenry in the War of 1812 inspired the national anthem, "The Star-Spangled Banner," and some experts believe that the success there indeed "preserved us a nation," as the anthem proclaims. Maryland was given to the lords Baltimore for the annual rent of two Indian arrows a year plus complete loyalty to the King. Although Maryland was a slave-holding southern state, it remained loyal to the Union during the Civil War. Among its many contributions, it donated the site of the national capital. The state continues to benefit from its location, with increasing government and commercial activities making it a growing population magnet.

SUPERLATIVES

• Narrowest width of any state—1 mile wide, near Hancock.
• Most navigable rivers of any state.
• One of the foremost sources of marine fossils.
• First military highway in the United States.
• First railway locomotive in the United States.
• World's first telegraph line: Baltimore—Washington, D.C.
• First U.S. manufacture of umbrellas.

MOMENTS IN HISTORY

• In 1524, Giovanni de Verrazano described an estuary believed to be Chincoteague Bay.
• The first recorded European visit to what is now Maryland was made by Captain John Smith in 1608.

• William Claiborne's trading post on Kent Island in 1631 became the first permanent European settlement in Maryland.
• Cecilius Calvert, the second Lord Baltimore, arrived on November 22, 1633, to take possession of his great grant.
• Conflicting claims made for unsettled times during the Cromwell period, but in 1660 the new King, Charles II, affirmed the Baltimore lords' titles.
• In 1692 a royal governor took over the Maryland colony.
• The capital was moved to newly incorporated Annapolis in 1694.
• Baltimore was founded in 1729, and the colony's boundaries with Pennsylvania and Maryland were settled that year.
• Fort Mt. Pleasant was begun in 1754 by a youthful George Washington, to discourage French claims in the western area.
• In 1774, Maryland had its own "tea party" protesting the mother country's tax on tea, and delegates were chosen for the Continental Congress.
• On August 27, 1776, Maryland troops played a key role in the Battle of Long Island, saving Washington's forces from destruction.

• During the Revolution the Maryland Navy also had a key role, and in 1778, Count Casimir Pulaski organized his independent "legion" of fighting men at Baltimore.

• Because of mob action at Philadelphia, the capital of the infant United States was moved to Annapolis on November 26, 1783.

• Maryland became the seventh state on April 28, 1788.

• During the War of 1812, the bells of Baltimore warned that a British fleet was approaching. The fleet attacked Fort McHenry with advanced weapons, including new rockets. The British defeat outside of Baltimore was a turning point in the war.

So They Say

"Sir—I have the honor of informing you that the enemy...appears to be retiring. We have a force hanging on their rear....P.S. The enemy's vessels in the Patapsco are all under way going down the river."

U.S. Commander Samuel Smith
at the Battle of Baltimore

• Baltimore became a center of the slave trade, but there also was much opposition to slavery, especially in the west.

• When the Civil War came, President Abraham Lincoln placed Maryland under military control.

• The Battle of Antietam Creek near Sharpsburg on September 17, 1862, is known as the most costly single day of battle in the country, with some 23,000 dead or wounded.

• In 1872 the Radical Republicans held their national convention at Baltimore.

• In 1889 the Johns Hopkins Hospital opened.

• A disastrous fire swept Baltimore in 1904, bringing fire companies from as far away as New York City.

• Woodrow Wilson was nominated for president at the Democratic National Convention of 1912 in Baltimore.

• World War I brought 62,568 Marylanders into the armed services.

• In 1927, Maryland created the nation's first permanent interracial commission.

• World War II took a toll of 6,454 of the 250,787 Marylanders who served in that conflict.

• In 1984, Maryland celebrated the 350th anniversary of its founding.

• In 1992 the state required some form of public service to qualify for high school graduation.

• In 1992, in a controversial move, the city of Baltimore became the first U.S. city to contract with a private firm to manage a group of city schools.

THAT'S INTERESTING

• Near the town of Hancock, Maryland is only about 1 mile wide, the narrowest width of any state.

• The British attack on Fort McHenry during the War of 1812, with its "rockets' red glare," inspired onlooker Francis Scott Key to write the poem that is now the national anthem.

• Jan Frazier of the Cumberland area was expecting a child when she was captured by the Indians. The Indians raided another settlement to get clothes for the infant, who nevertheless died. The mother escaped, walking for 300 miles and living on herbs and bark until she reached a house of friends, only to find her husband had remarried.

• One of the king's colonial grants was known as the Thumb Grant, because the grantee was given as much land as his thumb could cover on a map.

• Maryland is the only state to have developed a distinct breed of dog—the Chesapeake Bay retriever.

• Maryland has the only official state sport — jousting.

NOTABLE NATIVES

Benjamin Banneker (Ellicott, 1731-1806), mathematician. **Anna Ellis Carroll** (Pocomoke City, 1815-1893), political science writer. **Charles Carroll** (Annapolis, 1737-1832), Revolutionary leader/public official. **Samuel Chase** (Somerset County, 1741-1811), Supreme Court justice. **Stephen Decatur** (Sineppuxent, 1779-1820), naval officer. **John Dickinson** (Talbot County, 1732-1808), colonial figure/public official. **Frederick Douglass** (Tuckahoe, 1817-1895), social reformer. **John Hanson** (Charles County, 1721-1783), president under the Articles of Confederation. **Billie Holiday** (Baltimore, 1915-1959), singer. **Francis Scott Key** (Carroll County, 1779-1843), lawyer/poet.

Thurgood Marshall (Baltimore, 1908-1993), Supreme Court justice. Henry Louis Mencken (Baltimore, 1880-1956), journalist/editor/critic. Charles Willson Peale (Queen Anne's County, 1741-1827), artist/naturalist. Anne Newport Royall (in Maryland, 1769-1854), author. James Rumsey (Cecil County, 1743-1792), inventor. George Herman (Babe) Ruth (Baltimore, 1895-1948), baseball player. Upton Beall Sinclair (Baltimore, 1878-1968), author/social reformer. Roger Brooke Taney (Calvert County, 1777-1864), chief justice of the United States. Harriet Tubman (Dorchester County, 1820?-1913), abolitionist. Leon Uris (Baltimore, 1924-), author. Mason Locke (Parson) Weems (Anne Arundel County, 1759-1825), author.

GENERAL

Admitted to statehood: April 28, 1788
Origin of name: For Queen Henrietta Maria, wife of Charles I of England
Capital: Annapolis
Nickname: Old Line State, Free State, Pine Tree State, Lumber State
Motto: *Fatti Maschii, Parole Femine*—Manly deeds, womanly words
Dog: Chesapeake Bay retriever
Bird: Baltimore oriole
Insect: Baltimore checkerspot butterfly
Fish: Striped bass, or rockfish
Flower: Black-eyed Susan
Song: "Maryland, My Maryland"
Tree: White oak

THE LAND

Area: 12,297 sq. mi., 42nd
  Land: 9,775 sq. mi., 42nd
  Water: 2,522 sq. mi., 16th
    Inland water: 680 sq. mi., 31st
    Coastal water: 1,842 sq. mi., 4th
Topography: Eastern Shore of coastal plain and Maryland Main of coastal plain, piedmont plateau, and the Blue Ridge, separated by Chesapeake Bay
Number of counties: 23
Geographic center: Prince Georges, 4.5 mi. NW of Davidsonville
Length: 250 mi.; width: 90 mi.
Highest point: 3,360 ft. (Backbone Mountain), 32nd
Lowest point: sea level (Atlantic Ocean), 3rd
Mean elevation: 350 ft., 43rd

Coastline: 31 mi., 20th
Shoreline: 3,190 mi., 9th

CLIMATE AND ENVIRONMENT

Temp., highest: 109 deg. on July 10, 1936, at Cumberland and Frederick; lowest: −40 deg. on Jan. 13, 1912, at Oakland
Monthly average: highest: 87.1 deg., 26th; lowest: 24.3 deg., 35th; spread (high to low): 62.8 deg., 35th
Hazardous waste sites (1993): 12, 30th
Endangered species: Mammals: 2—Indiana bat, Delmarva Peninsula fox squirrel; birds: 1—American peregrine falcon; reptiles: 2; amphibians: none; fishes: 1; invertebrates: 1; plants: 4

MAJOR CITIES
POPULATION, 1990
PERCENTAGE INCREASE, 1980-90

Baltimore, 736,014— −6.45%
Bethesda, 62,936—0.32%
Dundalk, 65,800— −7.70%
Silver Spring, 76,046—4.33%
Wheaton-Glenmont, 53,720—10.54%

THE PEOPLE

Population (1995): 5,042,438, 19th
  Percent change (1990-95): 5.5%, 22nd
Population (2000 proj.): 5,322,000, 19th
  Percent change (1990-2000): 11.30%, 23rd
Per sq. mi. (1994): 512.1, 6th
Percent in metro. area (1992): 92.8%, 8th
Foreign born: 313,000, 11th
  Percent: 6.6%, 14th
Top three ancestries reported:
  German, 25.48%
  African, 20.20%
  Irish, 16.08%
White: 3,393,964, 70.98%, 45th
Black: 1,189,899, 24.89%, 7th
Native American: 12,972, 0.27%, 35th
Asian, Pacific Isle: 139,719, 2.92%, 8th
Other races: 44,914, 0.94%, 28th
Hispanic origin: 125,102, 2.62%, 24th
Percent over 5 yrs. speaking language other than English at home: 8.9%, 20th
Percent males: 48.49%, 29th; percent females: 51.51%, 23rd
Percent never married: 29.1%, 7th
Marriages per 1,000 (1993): 8.5, 25th
Divorces per 1,000 (1993): 3.4, 40th
Median age: 33
Under 5 years (1994): 7.57%, 15th

Under 18 years (1994): 25.23%, 35th
65 years & older (1994): 11.2%, 42nd
Percent increase among the elderly (1990-94):
    8.22%, 18th

OF VITAL IMPORTANCE

Live births per 1,000 pop. (1993): 15.2, 17th
Infant mortality rate per 1,000 births (1992):
    9.8, 10th
    Rate for blacks (1990): 16.3, 22nd
    Rate for whites (1990): 6.5, 48th
Births to unmarried women, % of total
    (1992): 30.5%, 21st
Births to teenage mothers, % of total (1992):
    9.8%, 42nd
Abortions (1992): 31,260, 15th
    Rate per 1,000 women 14-44 years old:
    26.4, 12th
    Percent change (1988-92): −8%, 26th
Average lifetime (1979-81): 73.32, 37th
Deaths per 1,000 pop. (1993): 8.7, 29th
Causes of death per 100,000 pop.:
    Accidents & adverse effects (1992): 26.2,
        46th
    Atherosclerosis (1991): 4.2, 45th
    Cancer (1991): 202.4, 33rd
    Cerebrovascular diseases (1992): 42.8, 46th
    Chronic liver diseases & cirrhosis (1991):
        9.0, 26th
    Chronic obstructive pulmonary diseases
        (1992): 29.4, 47th
    Diabetes mellitus (1992): 22.5, 14th
    Diseases of heart (1992): 241.6, 37th
    Pneumonia, flu (1991): 24.5, 43rd
    Suicide (1992): 9.4, 45th

KEEPING WELL

Active nonfederal physicians per 100,000 pop.
    (1993): 335, 3rd
Dentists per 100,000 (1991): 71, 7th
Nurses per 100,000 (1992): 783, 23rd
Hospitals per 100,000 (1993): 1.01, 51st
    Admissions per 1,000 (1993): 112.81, 29th
    Occupancy rate per 100 beds (1993): 75.3,
        4th
    Average cost per patient per day (1993):
        $889, 21st
    Average cost per stay (1993): $5,632, 28th
    Average stay (1992): 7.0 days, 30th
AIDS cases (adult, 1993): 2,528; per 100,000:
    50.9, 8th
HIV infection, not yet AIDS (1993): NA
Other notifiable diseases:
    Gonorrhea: 489.7, 6th

Measles: 4.5, 25th
Syphilis: 66.4, 9th
Tuberculosis: 8.0, 19th
Pop. without health insur. (1991-93): 12.7%,
    25th

HOUSEHOLDS BY TYPE

Total households (1994): 1,831,000
    Percent change (1990-94): 4.7%, 22nd
    Per 1,000 pop.: 365.76, 40th
    Percent of households 65 yrs. and over:
        18.79%, 44th
    Persons per household (1994): 2.67, 12th
Family households: 1,245,814
    Percent of total: 71.23%, 19th
Nonfamily households: 503,177
    Percent of total: 28.77%, 33rd
Pop. living in group quarters: 113,856
    Percent of pop.: 2.38%, 38th

LIVING QUARTERS

Total housing units: 1,891,917
    Persons per unit: 2.53, 6th
Occupied housing units: 1,748,991
    Percent of total units: 92.45%, 6th
    Persons per unit: 2.62, 12th
    Percent of units with over 1 person per
        room: 3.04%, 24th
Owner-occupied units: 1,137,296
    Percent of total units: 60.11%, 22nd
    Percent of occupied units: 65.03%, 36th
    Persons per unit: 2.79, 15th
    Median value: $116,500, 10th
Renter-occupied units: 661,695
    Percent of total units: 34.97%, 9th
    Percent of occupied units: 37.83%, 10th
    Persons per unit: 2.45, 13th
    Median contract rent: $473, 8th
    Rental vacancy rate: 6.8%, 44th
Mobile home, trailer & other as a percent of
    occupied housing units: 3.20%, 45th
Persons in emergency shelters for homeless
    persons: 2,507, 0.052%, 22nd
Persons visible in street locations: 523,
    0.0109%, 17th
Persons in shelters for abused women: 199,
    0.0042%, 35th
Nursing home population: 26,884, 0.56%,
    41st

CRIME INDEX PER 100,000 (1992-93)

Total reported: 6,106.5, 11th
    Violent: 997.8, 7th

Murder and nonnegligent manslaughter: 12.7, 6th
Aggravated assault: 506.4, 11th
Robbery: 434.7, 3rd
Forcible rape: 44.0, 19th
Property: 5,108.7, 13th
Burglary: 1,132.8, 16th
Larceny, theft: 3,292.5, 16th
Motor vehicle theft: 683.4, 10th
Drug abuse violations (1990): 599.1, 5th

TEACHING AND LEARNING

Pop. 3 and over enrolled in school: 1,212,333
Percent of pop.: 26.6%, 32nd
Public elementary & secondary schools (1992-93): 1,263
Total enrollment (1992): 751,850
Percent of total pop.: 15.29%, 42nd
Teachers (1992): 44,495
Percent of pop.: 0.90%, 41st
Pupil/teacher ratio (fall 1992): 16.9, 24th
Teachers' avg. salary (1992-93): $41,071, 9th
Expenditure per capita (1990-91): $3,716.45, 16th
Expenditure per pupil (1991-92): $6,679, 7th
Percent of graduates taking SAT (1993): 66%, 12th
Mean SAT verbal scores: 431, 32nd
Mean SAT mathematical scores: 478, 32nd
Percent of graduates taking ACT (1995): 12%, 38th
Mean ACT scores: 20.6, 33rd
Percent of pop. over 25 completing:
Less than 9th grade: 7.9%, 38th
High school: 78.4%, 22nd
College degree(s): 26.5%, 5th
Higher education, institutions (1993-94): 57
Enrollment (1992): 268,399
Percent of pop.: 5.46%, 28th
White non-Hispanic (1992): 188,771
Percent of enroll.: 70.33%, 44th
Black non-Hispanic (1992): 51,623
Percent of enroll.: 19.23%, 7th
Hispanic (1992): 5,229
Percent of enroll.: 1.95%, 24th
Asian/Pacific Islander (1992): 13,254
Percent of enroll.: 4.94%, 8th
American Indian/AK native (1992): 863
Percent of enroll.: 0.32%, 35th
Nonresident alien (1992): 8,659
Percent of enroll.: 3.23%, 15th
Female (1992): 152,943

Percent of enroll.: 56.98%, 7th
Pub. institutions (1993-94): 33
Enrollment (1992): 227,987
Percent of enroll.: 84.94%, 20th
Private institutions (1993-94): 24
Enrollment (1992): 40,412
Percent of enroll.: 15.06%, 32nd
Tuition, public institution (avg., 1993-94): $8,171, 6th
Tuition, private institution (avg., 1993-94): $18,275, 6th
Public library systems: 24
Books & serial vol. per capita: 2.34, 30th
Govt. expenditure per capita: $23.84, 6th

LAW ENFORCEMENT, COURTS, AND PRISONS

Police protection, corrections, judicial and legal functions expenditures (1992): $1,709,000,000
Per capita: $348, 11th
Police per 10,000 pop. (1993): 26.27, 7th
Prisoners (state & fed.) per 100,000 pop. (1993): 4,087.13, 12th
Percent change (1992-93): 1.4%, 36th
Death penalty: yes, by lethal gas
Under sentence of death (1993): 15, 23rd
Executed (1993): 0

RELIGION, NUMBER AND PERCENT OF POPULATION

Agnostic: 25,335—0.70%, 17th
Buddhist: 3,619—0.10%, 17th
Christian: 3,069,105—84.80%, 36th
Hindu: 7,239—0.20%, 3rd
Jewish: 101,338—2.80%, 5th
Muslim: 7,239—0.20%, 13th
Unitarian: 10,858—0.30%, 15th
Other: 50,669—1.40%, 20th
None: 260,584—7.20%, 20th
Refused to answer: 83,242—2.30%, 21st

MAKING A LIVING

Personal income per capita (1994): $24,933, 6th
Percent increase (1993-94): 4.3%, 37th
Disposable personal income per capita (1994): $21,293, 6th
Median income of households (1993): $39,939, 4th
Percent of pop. below poverty level (1993): 9.7%, 47th
Percent 65 and over (1990): 10.5%, 38th

Expenditure for energy per person (1992): $1,670, 45th

ECONOMY

Civilian labor force (1994): 2,691,000
  Percent of total pop.: 53.76%, 10th
  Percent 65 and over (1990): 2.64%, 29th
  Percent female: 48.01%, 5th
Percent job growth (1980-90): 31.22%, 11th
Major employer industries (1994):
  Agriculture: NA—1.3%, 43rd
  Construction: 111,000—4.4%, 22nd
  Finance, insurance, & real estate: 155,000—6.2%, 11th
  Government: 594,000—23.7%, 3rd
  Manufacturing: 182,000—7.3%, 43rd
  Service: 632,000—25.2%, 8th
  Trade: 473,000—18.9%, 29th
  Transportation, communications, public utilities: 141,000—5.6%, 20th
Unemployment rate (1994): 5.09%, 34th
  Male: 5.7%, 24th
  Female: 4.5%, 42nd
Total businesses (1991): 148,454
  New business incorps. (1991): 16,463
    Percent of total businesses: 11.09%, 5th
  Business failures (1991): 693
    Percent of total businesses: 0.47%
Agriculture farm income:
  Marketing (1993): $1,366,000,000, 35th
    Average per farm: $91,066.67, 20th
  Leading products (1993): Broilers, greenhouse, dairy products, soybeans
  Average value land & build. per acre (1994): $2,866, 5th
    Percent increase (1990-94): 18.43%, 14th
  Govt. payments (1993): $26,000,000, 38th
    Average per farm: $1,733.33, 39th
Construction, value of all: $3,623,000,000
  Per capita: $757.72, 14th
Manufactures:
  Value added: $15,724,000,000
    Per capita: $3,288.53, 40th
  Leading products: Electric and electronic equipment, food and food products, chemicals and allied products
Value of nonfuel mineral production (1994): $324,000,000, 35th
Leading mineral products: Coal, stone, cement
Retail sales (1993): $40,364,000,000, 19th
  Per household: $22,091, 25th
    Percent increase (1992-93): 4.6%, 36th

Tourism revenues (1994): $5.7 bil.
Foreign exports, in total value (1994): $4,874,000,000, 24th
  Per capita: $973.63, 32nd
Gross state product per person (1993): $23,050.01, 16th
  Percent change (1990-93): 2.75%, 33rd
Patents per 100,000 pop. (1993): 21.60, 21st
Public aid recipients (percent of resident pop. 1993): 5.9%, 34th
Medicaid recipients per 1,000 pop. (1993): 89.75, 46th
Medicare recipients per 1,000 pop. (1993): 116.58, 45th

TRAVEL AND TRANSPORTATION

Motor vehicle registrations (1993): 3,560,000
  Per 1,000 pop.: 718.03, 39th
Motorcycle registrations (1993): 41,000
  Per 1,000 pop.: 8.27, 46th
Licensed drivers per 1,000 pop. (1993): 660.35, 39th
Deaths from motor vehicle accidents per 100,000 pop. (1993): 13.55, 36th
Public roads & streets (1993):
  Total mileage: 29,313
    Per 1,000 pop.: 5.91, 46th
  Rural mileage: 15,642
    Per 1,000 pop.: 3.15, 44th
  Urban mileage: 13,671
    Per 1,000 pop.: 2.76, 38th
  Interstate mileage: 482
    Per 1,000 pop.: 0.10, 42nd
Annual vehicle-mi. of travel per person (1993): 8,733, 38th
Mean travel time for workers age 16+ who work away from home: 27.0 min., 3rd

GOVERNMENT

Percent of voting age pop. registered (1994): 62.6%, 31st
  Percent of voting age pop. voting (1994): 46.2%, 26th
  Percent of voting age pop. voting for U.S. representatives (1994): 35.9%, 35th
State legislators, total (1995): 188, 8th
  Women members (1992): 44
    Percent of legislature: 23.4%, 14th
U.S. Congress, House members (1995): 8
  Change (1985-95): 0
Revenues (1993):
  State govt.: $14,842,000,000
    Per capita: $2,993.55, 27th

Parimutuel & amusement taxes & lotteries,
revenue per capita: $170.23, 6th
Expenditures (1993):
State govt.: $13,537,000,000
Per capita: $2,730.33, 29th
Debt outstanding (1993): $8,731,000,000
Per capita: $1,760.99, 18th

LAWS AND REGULATIONS

Legal driving age: 18, 16 if completed driver
education course
Marriage age without parental consent: 18
Divorce residence requirement: Check local
statutes

ATTRACTIONS (1995)

Major opera companies: 1
Major symphony orchestras: 1
Major professional theater companies (non-
profit): 1
State appropriations for arts agencies per capita:
$1.57, 10th
State Fair in late August–early September at
Timonium

SPORTS AND COMPETITION

NCAA teams (Division I): Coppin State Col-
lege Eagles, Loyola College Grey-
hounds, Morgan State Univ. Bears,
Mount St. Mary's College Mountain-
eers, Towson State Univ. Tigers, U.S.
Naval Academy Midshipmen, Univ. of
Maryland-Baltimore County Retrievers,
Univ. of Maryland-College Park Ter-
rapins, Univ. of Maryland-Eastern
Shore Hawks
Major league baseball teams: Baltimore Ori-
oles (AL East), Oriole Park at Camden
Yards
NBA basketball teams: Washington Bullets
(nickname will change to Wizards in
1997), USAir Arena
NFL football teams: Former Cleveland
Browns relocated to Baltimore (AFC)
in 1996, Memorial Stadium
NHL hockey teams: Washington Capitals,
USAir Arena

MASSACHUSETTS

"A spirit that's as American as apple pie. For the spirit of Massachusetts truly is the spirit of America."

Governor Michael S. Dukakis

"Massachusetts—the cornerstone of a nation!"

Henry Wadsworth Longfellow, poet

"I shall enter on no encomium upon Massachusetts; she needs none. There she is. Behold her and judge for yourselves."

Daniel Webster, statesman/orator

Even though it is the 44th state in terms of area, the commonwealth of Massachusetts has always been a national leader. The first printing press, regularly published newspaper, college, and secondary school in the country were established here. Massachusetts has also given the nation four presidents. It has long been one of the top manufacturing states. The historic city of Boston is a major seaport and airline terminal, and the many universities in and around Boston make this area one of the world's greatest educational, research, and cultural centers. The Revolutionary War really began in Massachusetts with the Boston Massacre, the Boston Tea Party, the battles of Lexington and Concord, and the Battle of Bunker Hill. The state has been home to more than its share of writers and statesmen. The city of Boston continues its progress in political diversity.

SUPERLATIVES

• The Mayflower Compact, model for future governments.
• First popular U.S. election.
• Institution of the town meeting.
• First Thanksgiving, 1621.
• Gave birth to the American Revolution.
• Birthplace of the iron/steel industry.
• First U.S. public school.
• Home of Harvard University, the oldest American college/university.
• Oldest U.S. private secondary school, the Mather School in Boston.
• Oldest boys' boarding school, Phillips Academy in Andover.
• First pipe organ in America.

MOMENTS IN HISTORY

• On his voyage of 1497-1498, John Cabot made the first record of European presence in what is now Massachusetts.
• In 1602, Bartholomew Gosnold noted so many codfish in the area that he named the nearby land Cape Cod.
• Church of England dissenters landed at Cape Cod near present-day Provincetown in November 11, 1620, to become the Pilgrims in this new land. A month later they reached their new home and named it Plymouth.

So They Say

A Harvard historian contends that the Mayflower could not have landed at Plymouth Rock because of the direction of the current.

• In April 1621, the Pilgrims and the Wampanoag chief Massasoit made a treaty regarding the settlement, kept by the chief for the rest of his life.
• In the fall of 1621, the Pilgrims and their Indian friends celebrated what became known as the first Thanksgiving.

So They Say

"In colonial Massachusetts it was illegal to observe Christmas. Anyone observing the day was fined five shillings."

One Night Stands
With American History

• The Royal Charter of 1629 provided the foundation for democratic government in the Massachusetts Bay Colony.
• Boston was founded by a Puritan group in 1630.
• Only six years later, Harvard was founded.
• Beginning in 1662, trouble with the Indian leaders brought on a protracted period of conflict.

So They Say

"Your patent from King James is but idle parchment. James has no more right to give away or sell Massasoit's lands...than Massasoit has to sell King James' kingdom...."

Roger Williams, founder of the colony of Rhode Island

• The terrible witchcraft hysteria reached its darkest period about 1692 with the trials at Salem, as a result of which 19 accused witches were hanged and one was crushed to death.
• By the mid-1700s, the colony prospered with fishing and trade in lumber, carried by ships built locally and manned by local sailors.
• Increasing laws and regulations imposed on the colony by Britain brought growing resistance. On March 5, 1770, British troops fired on a Boston mob and five died in the Boston Massacre.
• Protesting the British tax on tea, Bostonians dressed as Indians boarded a tea ship and threw its cargo into the harbor in December 1773—the famed Boston Tea Party.
• Alerted by Paul Revere and others, patriots in April 1775 harried British troops in the region of Lexington and Concord. The patriots' shots "heard round the world" heralded the coming Revolution.

So They Say

"Here once the embattled farmers stood, and fired the shot heard round the world."

Ralph Waldo Emerson, on the encounter at Concord Bridge

• On June 17, 1775, one of the first Revolutionary struggles took place on Breed's Hill; it was mistakenly called the Battle of Bunker Hill.

• The British laid siege to Boston, but on March 17, 1776, they were forced to withdraw, in the first great American victory of the war.

So They Say

"Stand your ground. Don't fire unless fired upon. But if they mean to have war, let it begin here."

Captain John Parker, at Lexington, April 1775

• Massachusetts became a state on February 6, 1788.
• In 1796, John Adams of Massachusetts was elected president. The famed Adams family also contributed his son, John Quincy Adams, to the presidency, in 1824.
• As early as 1832, an antislavery society was founded in Boston.
• The Civil War called 160,000 to service from Massachusetts.
• There was a continuing growth in industry and commerce, which was accelerated by World War I.
• His handling of the Boston police strike of 1919 brought fame to Governor Calvin Coolidge, who in 1923 became the third president from Massachusetts. (He was born in Vermont but lived in the Bay State.)
• The Great Depression was followed by a recovery stimulated by World War II; 556,000 went into service from the state.
• In 1961, Massachusetts celebrated the inauguration of its fourth U.S. president, John Fitzgerald Kennedy, but all too soon mourned his assassination, in 1963.
• In 1986, Harvard University celebrated its 350th anniversary.
• In 1992 the luxury liner *Queen Elizabeth* ran aground off Cape Cod.
• In 1993, Thomas M. Menino was the first Italian-American to become mayor of Boston.

THAT'S INTERESTING

• Chief Massasoit brought 94 of his people to the first Thanksgiving, but they also brought much food. The men played games, while five Pilgrim women and a few girls labored over the feast of venison, geese, turkey, clam chowder, oysters, lobsters, fish, dried fruits and berries, corn biscuits, Indian pudding, and probably popcorn balls.

- Silversmith Paul Revere made some fine false teeth of silver.
- The lake with the Indian name Chargoggagoggagoggmanchuaggagoggchubunagungamaugg gives the English language its longest word.
- The first cargo ship sent out by the colony was seized by the French as a prize of war.
- Several religious movements were founded in the Bay State. Mary Baker Eddy founded the Church of Christ Scientist in 1879. Following the lead of William Ellery Channing, the American Unitarian Association was organized in 1825. Dwight L. Moody established his evangelistic headquarters at Northfield in the late 1870s.

NOTABLE NATIVES

John Adams (Braintree, later Quincy, 1735-1826), U.S. president. John Quincy Adams (Braintree, later Quincy, 1767-1848), U.S. president. Susan Brownwell Anthony (Adams, 1820-1906), reformer. Clara Harlow Barton (Oxford, 1821-1912), founder of the American Red Cross. Katharine Lee Bates (Falmouth, 1859-1929), educator/author. William Cullen Bryant (Cummington, 1794-1878), poet/editor. Charles Bulfinch (Boston, 1763-1844), architect. Luther Burbank (Lancaster, 1849-1926), horticulturist. Bette Davis (Lowell, 1908-1989), actress. Emily Elizabeth Dickinson (Amherst, 1830-1886), poet. Ralph Waldo Emerson (Boston, 1803-1882), poet/essayist. Benjamin Franklin (Boston, 1706-1790), public official/diplomat/scientist. Edward Everett Hale (Boston, 1822-1909), religious leader. John Hancock (Braintree, 1737-1793), merchant/public official. Nathaniel Hawthorne (Salem, 1804-1864), author. Oliver Wendell Holmes (Cambridge, 1809-1894), physician/author/educator. Oliver Wendell Holmes (Boston, 1841-1935), Supreme Court justice. Winslow Homer (Boston, 1836-1910), painter. Elias Howe (Spencer, 1819-1867), inventor. Helen Maria Hunt Jackson (Amherst, 1830-1885), author. James Jackson Jarves (Boston, 1818-1888), art critic/collector. William LeBaron Jenney (Fairhaven, 1832-1907), architect. John Fitzgerald Kennedy (Brookline, 1917-1963), U.S. president. Jack Lemmon (Boston, 1925-), actor. Henry Cabot Lodge (Boston, 1850-1924), author/public official. Horace Mann (Franklin, 1796-1859), educator. Dwight Lyman Moody (Northfield, 1837-1899), evangelist. Samuel Finley Breese Morse (Charlestown, 1791-1872), artist/inventor. George Peabody (South Danvers, 1795-1869), merchant/philanthropist. Edgar Allan Poe (Boston, 1809-1849), writer. Paul Revere (Boston, 1735-1818), patriot/silversmith. Henry David Thoreau (Concord, 1817-1862), philosopher/naturalist. James Abbott McNeill Whistler (Lowell, 1834-1903), artist. Eli Whitney (Westboro, 1765-1825), inventor. John Greenleaf Whittier (Haverhill, 1807-1892), poet/abolitionist.

GENERAL

Admitted to statehood: February 6, 1788
Origin of name: From Indian tribe named after "large hill place" identified by Captain John Smith as being near Milton, Massachusetts
Capital: Boston
Nickname: Bay State, Old Colony State
Motto: *Ense Petit Placidam Sub Libertate Quietem*—By the sword we seek peace, but peace only under liberty
Animal: Morgan horse
Bird: Chickadee
Insect: Ladybug
Fish: Cod
Flower: Mayflower, or trailing arbutus
Gem: Rhodonite
Mineral: Babingtonite
Song: "All Hail to Massachusetts"
Tree: American elm

THE LAND

Area: 9,241 sq. mi., 45th
  Land: 7,838 sq. mi., 45th
  Water: 1,403 sq. mi., 21st
    Inland water: 424 sq. mi., 35th
    Coastal water: 979 sq. mi., 7th
Topography: Jagged indented coast from Rhode Island around Cape Cod; flat land yields to stony upland pastures near central region and gentle hill country in W; except in W, land is rocky, sandy, and not fertile.
Number of counties: 14
Geographic center: Worcester, N part of city
Length: 190 mi.; width: 50 mi.
Highest point: 3,487 ft. (Mount Greylock), 31st
Lowest point: sea level (Atlantic Ocean), 3rd
Mean elevation: 500 ft., 42nd

Coastline: 192 mi., 10th
Shoreline: 1,519 mi., 15th

CLIMATE AND ENVIRONMENT

Temp., highest: 107 deg. on Aug. 2, 1975, at Chester and New Bedford; lowest: –35 deg. on Jan. 12, 1981, at Chester
Monthly average: highest: 81.8 deg., 47th; lowest: 15.6 deg., 19th; spread (high to low): 66.2 deg., 31st
Hazardous waste sites (1993): 31, 13th
Endangered species: Mammals: none; birds: 2—American peregrine falcon, Roseate tern; reptiles: 3; amphibians: none; fishes: none; invertebrates: 2; plants: 2

MAJOR CITIES
POPULATION, 1990
PERCENTAGE INCREASE, 1980-90

Boston, 574,283—2.01%
Lowell, 103,439—11.93%
New Bedford, 99,922—1.47%
Springfield, 156,983—3.06%
Worcester, 169,759—4.92%

THE PEOPLE

Population (1995): 6,073,550, 13th
Percent change (1990-95): 0.9%, 45th
Population (2000 proj.): 5,950,000, 15th
Percent change (1990-2000): –1.10%, 50th
Per sq. mi. (1994): 770.7, 4th
Percent in metro. area (1992): 96.2%, 4th
Foreign born: 574,000, 7th
Percent: 9.5%, 7th
Top three ancestries reported:
Irish, 26.11%
English, 15.31%
Italian, 14.03%
White: 5,405,374, 89.84%, 20th
Black: 300,130, 4.99%, 30th
Native American: 12,241, 0.20%, 43rd
Asian, Pacific Isle: 143,392, 2.38%, 12th
Other races: 155,288, 2.58%, 11th
Hispanic origin: 287,549, 4.78%, 17th
Percent over 5 yrs. speaking language other than English at home: 15.2%, 10th
Percent males: 48.01%, 45th; percent females: 51.99%, 7th
Percent never married: 32.8%, 2nd
Marriages per 1,000 (1993): 6.2, 50th
Divorces per 1,000 (1993): 2.7, 47th
Median age: 33.6
Under 5 years (1994): 7.00%, 39th
Under 18 years (1994): 23.57%, 47th

65 years & older (1994): 14.1%, 10th
Percent increase among the elderly (1990-94): 3.63%, 40th

OF VITAL IMPORTANCE

Live births per 1,000 pop. (1993): 14.4, 30th
Infant mortality rate per 1,000 births (1992): 6.5, 47th
Rate for blacks (1990): 10.4, 44th
Rate for whites (1990): 6.7, 45th
Births to unmarried women, % of total (1992): 25.9%, 37th
Births to teenage mothers, % of total (1992): 7.7%, 50th
Abortions (1992): 40,660, 10th
Rate per 1,000 women 14-44 years old: 28.4, 10th
Percent change (1988-92): –6%, 22nd
Average lifetime (1979-81): 75.01, 12th
Deaths per 1,000 pop. (1993): 9.4, 15th
Causes of death per 100,000 pop.:
Accidents & adverse effects (1992): 21.6, 51st
Atherosclerosis (1991): 6.5, 29th
Cancer (1991): 236.7, 8th
Cerebrovascular diseases (1992): 55.6, 30th
Chronic liver diseases & cirrhosis (1991): 10.1, 16th
Chronic obstructive pulmonary diseases (1992): 35.9, 28th
Diabetes mellitus (1992): 19.9, 29th
Diseases of heart (1992): 284.8, 25th
Pneumonia, flu (1991): 39.8, 4th
Suicide (1992): 8.9, 47th

KEEPING WELL

Active nonfederal physicians per 100,000 pop. (1993): 361, 2nd
Dentists per 100,000 (1991): 76, 6th
Nurses per 100,000 (1992): 1,066, 2nd
Hospitals per 100,000 (1993): 1.65, 40th
Admissions per 1,000 (1993): 135.81, 12th
Occupancy rate per 100 beds (1993): 71.5, 9th
Average cost per patient per day (1993): $1,036, 10th
Average cost per stay (1993): $6,843, 9th
Average stay (1992): 10.7 days, 7th
AIDS cases (adult, 1993): 2,703; per 100,000: 45.0, 10th
HIV infection, not yet AIDS (1993): NA
Other notifiable diseases:
Gonorrhea: 125.3, 31st
Measles: 0.5, 45th

Syphilis: 28.3, 23rd
Tuberculosis: 7.3, 24th
Pop. without health insur. (1991-93): 11.1%, 39th

HOUSEHOLDS BY TYPE

Total households (1994): 2,265,000
  Percent change (1990-94): 0.8%, 46th
  Per 1,000 pop.: 374.94, 26th
  Percent of households 65 yrs. and over: 23.31%, 11th
  Persons per household (1994): 2.57, 31st
Family households: 1,514,746
  Percent of total: 67.41%, 48th
Nonfamily households: 732,364
  Percent of total: 32.59%, 4th
Pop. living in group quarters: 214,307
  Percent of pop.: 3.56%, 8th

LIVING QUARTERS

Total housing units: 2,472,711
  Persons per unit: 2.43, 18th
Occupied housing units: 2,247,110
  Percent of total units: 90.88%, 17th
  Persons per unit: 2.53, 23rd
  Percent of units with over 1 person per room: 2.52%, 35th
Owner-occupied units: 1,331,493
  Percent of total units: 53.85%, 42nd
  Percent of occupied units: 59.25%, 45th
  Persons per unit: 2.82, 10th
  Median value: $162,800, 4th
Renter-occupied units: 915,617
  Percent of total units: 37.03%, 6th
  Percent of occupied units: 40.75%, 8th
  Persons per unit: 2.24, 42nd
  Median contract rent: $506, 5th
  Rental vacancy rate: 6.9%, 42nd
Mobile home, trailer & other as a percent of occupied housing units: 2.27%, 49th
Persons in emergency shelters for homeless persons: 6,207, 0.103%, 6th
Persons visible in street locations: 674, 0.0112%, 15th
Persons in shelters for abused women: 269, 0.0045%, 33rd
Nursing home population: 55,662, 0.93%, 14th

CRIME INDEX PER 100,000 (1992-93)

Total reported: 4,893.9, 26th
  Violent: 804.9, 11th

  Murder and nonnegligent manslaughter: 3.9, 37th
  Aggravated assault: 592.0, 7th
  Robbery: 175.7, 21st
  Forcible rape: 33.4, 38th
  Property: 4,089.0, 33rd
  Burglary: 1,001.7, 26th
  Larceny, theft: 2,271.3, 44th
  Motor vehicle theft: 816.1, 6th
Drug abuse violations (1990): 253.9, 25th
Child-abuse rate per 1,000 children (1993): 17.36, 19th

TEACHING AND LEARNING

Pop. 3 and over enrolled in school: 1,530,134
  Percent of pop.: 26.5%, 35th
Public elementary & secondary schools (1992-93): 1,772
  Total enrollment (1992): 859,948
    Percent of total pop.: 14.35%, 49th
  Teachers (1992): 57,225
    Percent of pop.: 0.95%, 39th
  Pupil/teacher ratio (fall 1992): 15.0, 44th
  Teachers' avg. salary (1992-93): $46,206, 4th
  Expenditure per capita (1990-91): $4,104.51, 8th
  Expenditure per pupil (1991-92): $6,408, 10th
Percent of graduates taking SAT (1993): 81%, 2nd
  Mean SAT verbal scores: 427, 35th
  Mean SAT mathematical scores: 476, 35th
Percent of graduates taking ACT (1995): 4%, 44th
  Mean ACT scores: 20.9, 30th
Percent of pop. over 25 completing:
  Less than 9th grade: 8.0%, 36th
  High school: 80.0%, 15th
  College degree(s): 27.2%, 2nd
Higher education, institutions (1993-94): 117
  Enrollment (1992): 422,976
    Percent of pop.: 7.05%, 6th
  White non-Hispanic (1992): 342,585
    Percent of enroll.: 80.99%, 30th
  Black non-Hispanic (1992): 20,491
    Percent of enroll.: 4.84%, 28th
  Hispanic (1992): 15,146
    Percent of enroll.: 3.58%, 13th
  Asian/Pacific Islander (1992): 20,299
    Percent of enroll.: 4.80%, 10th
  American Indian/AK native (1992): 1,709
    Percent of enroll.: 0.40%, 26th

Nonresident alien (1992): 22,746
  Percent of enroll.: 5.38%, 4th
Female (1992): 234,225
  Percent of enroll.: 55.38%, 26th
Pub. institutions (1993-94): 31
  Enrollment (1992): 183,119
  Percent of enroll.: 43.29%, 50th
Private institutions (1993-94): 86
  Enrollment (1992): 239,857
  Percent of enroll.: 56.71%, 2nd
Tuition, public institution (avg., 1993-94): $8,467, 3rd
Tuition, private institution (avg., 1993-94): $20,223, 1st
Public library systems: 374
  Books & serial vol. per capita: 4.32, 2nd
  Govt. expenditure per capita: $23.71, 7th

LAW ENFORCEMENT, COURTS, AND PRISONS

Police protection, corrections, judicial and legal functions expenditures (1992): $1,781,000,000
  Per capita: $297, 18th
Police per 10,000 pop. (1993): 24.60, 10th
Prisoners (state & fed.) per 100,000 pop. (1993): 1,667.33, 44th
Percent change (1992-93): –0.2%, 44th
Death penalty: no

RELIGION, NUMBER AND PERCENT OF POPULATION

Agnostic: 46,634—1.00%, 10th
Buddhist: 18,653—0.40%, 5th
Christian: 3,837,937—82.30%, 40th
Hindu: 4,663—0.10%, 10th
Jewish: 163,217—3.50%, 4th
Muslim: 18,653—0.40%, 5th
Unitarian: 37,307—0.80%, 3rd
Other: 51,297—1.10%, 32nd
None: 340,425—7.30%, 19th
Refused to answer: 144,564—3.10%, 7th

MAKING A LIVING

Personal income per capita (1994): $25,616, 5th
  Percent increase (1993-94): 4.9%, 26th
Disposable personal income per capita (1994): $21,649, 5th
Median income of households (1993): $37,064, 7th
Percent of pop. below poverty level (1993): 10.7%, 38th
  Percent 65 and over (1990): 9.4%, 43rd

Expenditure for energy per person (1992): $1,810, 35th

ECONOMY

Civilian labor force (1994): 3,179,000
  Percent of total pop.: 52.62%, 16th
  Percent 65 and over (1990): 3.06%, 18th
  Percent female: 46.62%, 21st
Percent job growth (1980-90): 17.77%, 31st
Major employer industries (1994):
  Agriculture: 21,000—0.7%, 49th
  Construction: 96,000—3.2%, 50th
  Finance, insurance, & real estate: 213,000—7.2%, 6th
  Government: 375,000—12.7%, 45th
  Manufacturing: 479,000—16.2%, 21st
  Service: 862,000—29.2%, 3rd
  Trade: 556,000—18.8%, 31st
  Transportation, communications, public utilities: 134,000—4.5%, 37th
Unemployment rate (1994): 6.01%, 19th
  Male: 6.6%, 12th
  Female: 5.4%, 24th
Total businesses (1991): 201,385
  New business incorps. (1991): 11,706
    Percent of total businesses: 5.81%, 26th
  Business failures (1991): 1,913
    Percent of total businesses: 0.95%
Agriculture farm income:
  Marketing (1993): $497,000,000, 42nd
    Average per farm: $71,000.00, 30th
  Leading products (1993): Greenhouse, cranberries, dairy products, eggs
  Average value land & build. per acre (1994): $3,992, 4th
    Percent increase (1990-94): 6.09%, 36th
  Govt. payments (1993): $4,000,000, 44th
    Average per farm: $571.43, 47th
Construction, value of all: $2,889,000,000
  Per capita: $480.19, 33rd
Manufactures:
  Value added: $35,102,000,000
    Per capita: $5,834.36, 16th
  Leading products: Electric and electronic equipment, machinery, industrial machinery and equipment, printing and publishing, fabricated metal products
Value of nonfuel mineral production (1994): $157,000,000, 40th
Leading mineral products: Stone, sand/gravel, lime

Retail sales (1993): $48,498,000,000, 13th
 Per household: $21,505, 30th
   Percent increase (1992-93): 2.0%, 43rd
Tourism revenues (1993): $7.35 bil.
Foreign exports, in total value (1994): $11,199,000,000, 12th
 Per capita: $1,853.83, 10th
Gross state product per person (1993): $25,991.34, 9th
 Percent change (1990-93): 1.30%, 43rd
Patents per 100,000 pop. (1993): 41.61, 3rd
Public aid recipients (percent of resident pop. 1993): 7.7%, 15th
Medicaid recipients per 1,000 pop. (1993): 127.12, 20th
Medicare recipients per 1,000 pop. (1993): 151.38, 12th

TRAVEL AND TRANSPORTATION

Motor vehicle registrations (1993): 3,837,000
 Per 1,000 pop.: 637.59, 48th
Motorcycle registrations (1993): 68,000
 Per 1,000 pop.: 11.30, 35th
Licensed drivers per 1,000 pop. (1993): 691.43, 25th
Deaths from motor vehicle accidents per 100,000 pop. (1993): 7.88, 49th
Public roads & streets (1993):
 Total mileage: 30,563
   Per 1,000 pop.: 5.08, 48th
 Rural mileage: 10,927
   Per 1,000 pop.: 1.82, 48th
 Urban mileage: 19,636
   Per 1,000 pop.: 3.26, 20th
 Interstate mileage: 565
   Per 1,000 pop.: 0.09, 44th
Annual vehicle-mi. of travel per person (1993): 7,760, 43rd
Mean travel time for workers age 16+ who work away from home: 22.7 min., 9th

GOVERNMENT

Percent of voting age pop. registered (1994): 65.6%, 23rd
 Percent of voting age pop. voting (1994): 51.6%, 14th
 Percent of voting age pop. voting for U.S. representatives (1994): 43.3%, 15th

State legislators, total (1995): 200, 6th
 Women members (1992): 37
   Percent of legislature: 18.5%, 23rd
U.S. Congress, House members (1995): 10
 Change (1985-95): −1
Revenues (1993):
 State govt.: $21,493,000,000
   Per capita: $3,571.45, 15th
 Parimutuel & amusement taxes & lotteries, revenue per capita: $318.21, 1st
Expenditures (1993):
 State govt.: $21,557,000,000
   Per capita: $3,582.09, 9th
Debt outstanding (1993): $25,415,000,000
 Per capita: $4,223.16, 7th

LAWS AND REGULATIONS

Legal driving age: 18, 17 if completed driver education course
Marriage age without parental consent: 18
Divorce residence requirement: 1 yr., for qualifications check local statutes

ATTRACTIONS (1995)

Major opera companies: 4
Major symphony orchestras: 2
Major dance companies: 1
Major professional theater companies (non-profit): 2
State appropriations for arts agencies per capita: $2.00, 5th

SPORTS AND COMPETITION

NCAA teams (Division I): Boston College Eagles, Boston Univ. Terriers, Harvard Univ. Crimson, College of the Holy Cross Crusaders, Northeastern Univ. Huskies, Univ. of Massachusetts-Amherst Minutemen
Major league baseball teams: Boston Red Sox (AL East), Fenway Park
NBA basketball teams: Boston Celtics, Fleet Center
NFL football teams: New England Patriots (AFC), Foxboro Stadium
NHL hockey teams: Boston Bruins, Fleet Center

MICHIGAN

"Michigan, handsome as a well made woman, and dressed and jewelled. It seemed to me that the earth was generous and outgoing here in the heartland, and, perhaps its people took a cue from it."

John Steinbeck, author

Michigan extends as far east as parts of South Carolina. Parts of Canada, the "northern" neighbor, actually lie south of northern Michigan. Michigan is the only state that is divided into two peninsulas—Upper and Lower. The Upper Peninsula is sparsely populated and quite rural, whereas the Lower Peninsula contains all the large cities and most of the industry and agriculture. Michigan is a state in which almost half its area is fresh water; with water and land combined it is the largest state east of the Mississippi River. Michigan had the imagination to create a capital in the wilderness and the courage to elect the youngest governor to serve anywhere in the United States. The world automobile industry was established there, and Michigan still leads the United States in auto production. Detroit continues to work toward improvement in its response to social problems.

SUPERLATIVES

• Longest siege in Indian warfare—175 days, by Chief Pontiac.
• First in U.S. automobile production.
• World's busiest ship canal.
• Detroit River carries the world's greatest tonnage.
• Most million-ton ports in the United States.
• Largest U.S. producer of salt, mint, navy beans, and sour cherries.
• First in baby food and carpet sweepers.
• Greatest variety of trees in the United States.
• Largest copper reserve in the United States.
• First university established by a state.

MOMENTS IN HISTORY

• Coming from French Canada, Etienne Brulé reached present-day Michigan during his journeys of 1618-1622.

• In 1668, Father Jacques Marquette and Father Claude Dablon founded the first permanent European settlement in what is now Michigan, Sault Sainte Marie—at the Soo.
• In 1679, Robert Cavalier, Sieur de La Salle, constructed the first French fort in lower Michigan, where St. Joseph now stands.
• Detroit was begun in 1701 by Antoine de la Mothe, Sieur de Cadillac; it became the first major city founded in the Midwest.
• In 1760, Major Robert Rogers and his Royal English Rangers captured Detroit without a struggle, and French rule came to an end.
• Angered by British mistreatment, Chief Pontiac laid siege to Detroit in 1763. Lasting for 175 days, it was the longest siege in Indian warfare, but he failed to take the city.
• The Treaty of Paris in 1783 gave Michigan to the young United States, but the British continued to occupy most of the area until General "Mad Anthony" Wayne asserted American control, confirmed by the Jay Treaty of 1795.
• In 1805 much of Detroit was destroyed by fire.
• During the War of 1812, the British retook Detroit, but the Americans returned in September 1813.
• The cholera epidemic of 1832 took many lives, including that of the beloved priest Father Gabriel Richard.

So They Say

"Father Gabriel Richard...might be seen clothed in the robes of his high calling, pale and emaciated...going from house to house...encouraging the well, and administering spiritual consolation to the sick and dying."

Anonymous

• In a "border war" both Michigan and Ohio claimed the area now occupied by Toledo. Finally, Michigan accepted the entire Upper Peninsula in exchange for giving up its claim.

• Michigan became the 26th U.S. state on January 26, 1837.

• In 1840 the rich copper lands in the Upper Peninsula were discovered.

• In 1847 the legislature chose an unoccupied woodland site as the state capital, and Lansing became the "capital in the forest."

• A Republican party was created at Jackson on July 6, 1854, and later the same year Michigan became the first state to elect a Republican governor.

• During the Civil War the Michigan Cavalry Brigade played a key role in the Battle of Gettysburg.

• By strange coincidence a terrible fire roared through Holland and other areas of Michigan on the same day of the great Chicago fire, October 8, 1871.

• Around the turn of the century, Detroit began its rise as the principal center of automobile production.

• In World War I, the 32nd Division, with many Michigan troops, was the first from America to reach German soil.

• During World War II, Michigan factories manufactured an eighth of all war materiel produced in the nation.

• In 1957, Big Mac, the bridge, linked the Upper and Lower peninsulas for the first time.

• The riots of 1967 destroyed much of the inner city of Detroit.

• During the 1980s, Michigan auto industries began to encounter stiff competition from Japanese automobiles.

• In 1992 scientists announced that the largest living thing in the world was a fungus, *Armillaria bulbosa*, growing beneath 37 acres near Crystal Falls. (However, an organism in Washington State was later claimed to be larger.)

THAT'S INTERESTING

• Chief Black Hawk passed through Detroit after the Black Hawk War, and the whole city turned out to see the well-dressed leader in a Fourth of July celebration.

• Michigan history took a peculiar turn when Mormon leader James Strang proclaimed himself King of Beaver Island. He was assassinated in 1856, and mainland forces took over the Mormon properties.

• Disguised as a man, Sarah Emma Edmonds fought through four major Civil War campaigns before her identity was discovered.

• Michigan's shoreline of 3,177 miles is second only to that of Alaska.

• Ann Arbor's name came from the habit of two wives named Ann chatting under a grape arbor. Their husbands named the town for them.

NOTABLE NATIVES

Avery Brundage (Detroit, 1887-1975), businessman/sportsman. **Ralph Johnson Bunche** (Detroit, 1904-1971), diplomat. **Thomas Edmund Dewey** (Owosso, 1902-1971), public official. **Edna Ferber** (Kalamazoo, 1887-1968), author. **Henry Ford** (near Dearborn, 1863-1947), industrialist/philanthropist. **Will Keith Kellogg** (Battle Creek, 1860-1951), businessman. **Ring Lardner** (Niles, 1885-1933), journalist/author. **Charles Augustus Lindbergh** (Detroit, 1902-1974), aviator. **Theodore Roethke** (Saginaw, 1908-1963), poet. **Glenn Theodore Seaborg** (Ishpeming, 1912-), chemist.

GENERAL

Admitted to statehood: January 26, 1837
Origin of name: From Chippewa words *mici gama,* meaning "great water," after the lake of the same name
Capital: Lansing
Nickname: Wolverine State, Great Lakes State, Water Wonderland
Motto: *Si Quaeris Peninsulam Amoenam Circumspice*—If you seek a pleasant peninsula, look about you
Bird: Robin
Fish: Brook trout
Flower: Apple blossom
Gem: Isle Royal greenstone
Stone: Petoskey stone
Song: "Michigan, My Michigan"
Tree: White pine

THE LAND

Area: 96,705 sq. mi., 11th
  Land: 56,809 sq. mi., 22nd
  Water: 39,896 sq. mi., 2nd
    Inland water: 1,704 sq. mi., 13th
    Great Lakes: 38,192 sq. mi., 1st
Topography: Low rolling hills give way to northern tableland of hilly belts in

Lower Peninsula; Upper Peninsula is level in E, with swampy areas; western region is higher and more rugged.

Number of counties: 83

Geographic center: Wexford, 5 mi. NNW of Cadillac

Length: 490 mi.; width: 240 mi.

Highest point: 1,979 ft. (Mount Arvon), 38th

Lowest point: 572 ft. (Lake Erie), 40th

Mean elevation: 900 ft., 29th

CLIMATE AND ENVIRONMENT

Temp., highest: 112 deg. on July 13, 1936, at Mio; lowest: −51 deg. on Feb. 9, 1934, at Vanderbilt

Monthly average: highest: 83.1 deg., 43rd; lowest: 14.0 deg., 15th; spread (high to low): 69.1 deg., 24th

Hazardous waste sites (1993): 76, 5th

Endangered species: Mammals: 2—Indiana bat, Eastern timber wolf; birds: 3— American peregrine falcon, Piping plover, Kirtland's warbler; reptiles: none; amphibians: none; fishes: none; invertebrates: none; plants: 2

MAJOR CITIES
POPULATION, 1990
PERCENTAGE INCREASE, 1980-90

Detroit, 1,027,974— −14.58%

Flint, 140,761— −11.81%

Grand Rapids, 189,126—4.01%

Lansing, 127,321— −2.37%

Warren, 144,864— −10.10%

THE PEOPLE

Population (1995): 9,549,353, 8th
  Percent change (1990-95): 2.7%, 42nd
Population (2000 proj.): 9,759,000, 8th
  Percent change (1990-2000): 4.99%, 41st
Per sq. mi. (1994): 167.2, 15th
Percent in metro. area (1992): 82.7%, 16th
Foreign born: 355,000, 9th
  Percent: 3.8%, 21st
Top three ancestries reported:
  German, 28.68%
  Irish, 14.20%
  English, 14.15%
White: 7,756,086, 83.44%, 28th
Black: 1,291,706, 13.90%, 15th
Native American: 55,638, 0.60%, 21st
Asian, Pacific Isle: 104,983, 1.13%, 26th
Other races: 86,884, 0.93%, 29th
Hispanic origin: 201,596, 2.17%, 29th

Percent over 5 yrs. speaking language other than English at home: 6.6%, 28th

Percent males: 48.55%, 27th; percent females: 51.45%, 25th

Percent never married: 27.8%, 11th

Marriages per 1,000 (1993): 7.5, 39th

Divorces per 1,000 (1993): 4.1, 31st

Median age: 32.6

Under 5 years (1994): 7.38%, 20th

Under 18 years (1994): 16.06%, 51st

65 years & older (1994): 12.4%, 33rd

Percent increase among the elderly (1990-94): 3.12%, 44th

OF VITAL IMPORTANCE

Live births per 1,000 pop. (1993): 15.1, 19th

Infant mortality rate per 1,000 births (1992): 10.2, 7th
  Rate for blacks (1990): 21.0, 3rd
  Rate for whites (1990): 7.9, 25th

Births to unmarried women, % of total (1992): 26.8%, 30th

Births to teenage mothers, % of total (1992): 13.0%, 21st

Abortions (1992): 55,580, 6th
  Rate per 1,000 women 14-44 years old: 25.2, 15th
  Percent change (1988-92): −11%, 30th

Average lifetime (1979-81): 73.67, 30th

Deaths per 1,000 pop. (1993): 8.7, 29th

Causes of death per 100,000 pop.:
  Accidents & adverse effects (1992): 30.6, 38th
  Atherosclerosis (1991): 8.8, 12th
  Cancer (1991): 204.6, 30th
  Cerebrovascular diseases (1992): 54.1, 33rd
  Chronic liver diseases & cirrhosis (1991): 11.3, 10th
  Chronic obstructive pulmonary diseases (1992): 32.7, 39th
  Diabetes mellitus (1992): 22.5, 14th
  Diseases of heart (1992): 285.1, 24th
  Pneumonia, flu (1991): 29.7, 28th
  Suicide (1992): 11.3, 38th

KEEPING WELL

Active nonfederal physicians per 100,000 pop. (1993): 195, 27th

Dentists per 100,000 (1991): 62, 16th

Nurses per 100,000 (1992): 694, 33rd

Hospitals per 100,000 (1993): 1.77, 35th
  Admissions per 1,000 (1993): 119.99, 23rd
  Occupancy rate per 100 beds (1993): 64.7, 16th

Average cost per patient per day (1993): $902, 18th

Average cost per stay (1993): $6,147, 17th

Average stay (1992): 13.2 days, 2nd

AIDS cases (adult, 1993): 1,840; per 100,000: 19.4, 28th

HIV infection, not yet AIDS (1993): 1,104

Other notifiable diseases:
  Gonorrhea: 336.0, 13th
  Measles: 5.1, 21st
  Syphilis: 28.2, 24th
  Tuberculosis: 5.4, 31st

Pop. without health insur. (1991-93): 10.1%, 42nd

HOUSEHOLDS BY TYPE

Total households (1994): 3,502,000
  Percent change (1990-94): 2.4%, 36th
  Per 1,000 pop.: 368.79, 35th
  Percent of households 65 yrs. and over: 21.53%, 29th
  Persons per household (1994): 2.65, 17th
Family households: 2,439,171
  Percent of total: 71.33%, 18th
Nonfamily households: 980,160
  Percent of total: 28.67%, 34th
Pop. living in group quarters: 211,692
  Percent of pop.: 2.28%, 43rd

LIVING QUARTERS

Total housing units: 3,847,926
  Persons per unit: 2.42, 23rd
Occupied housing units: 3,419,331
  Percent of total units: 88.86%, 30th
  Persons per unit: 2.56, 19th
  Percent of units with over 1 person per room: 2.65%, 32nd
Owner-occupied units: 2,427,643
  Percent of total units: 63.09%, 9th
  Percent of occupied units: 71.00%, 4th
  Persons per unit: 2.80, 13th
  Median value: $60,600, 33rd
Renter-occupied units: 991,688
  Percent of total units: 25.77%, 45th
  Percent of occupied units: 29.00%, 48th
  Persons per unit: 2.31, 30th
  Median contract rent: $343, 25th
  Rental vacancy rate: 7.2%, 40th
Mobile home, trailer & other as a percent of occupied housing units: 6.69%, 39th
Persons in emergency shelters for homeless persons: 3,784, 0.041%, 33rd
Persons visible in street locations: 262, 0.0028%, 41st

Persons in shelters for abused women: 506, 0.0054%, 17th

Nursing home population: 57,622, 0.62%, 33rd

CRIME INDEX PER 100,000 (1992-93)

Total reported: 5,452.5, 20th
  Violent: 791.5, 12th
    Murder and nonnegligent manslaughter: 9.8, 17th
    Aggravated assault: 472.1, 14th
    Robbery: 238.5, 12th
    Forcible rape: 71.1, 3rd
  Property: 4,661.0, 19th
    Burglary: 982.7, 28th
    Larceny, theft: 3,063.2, 21st
    Motor vehicle theft: 615.0, 12th
Drug abuse violations (1990): 296.8, 18th
Child-abuse rate per 1,000 children (1993): 7.79, 44th

TEACHING AND LEARNING

Pop. 3 and over enrolled in school: 2,581,042
  Percent of pop.: 29.1%, 10th
Public elementary & secondary schools (1992-93): 3,340
  Total enrollment (1992): 1,603,610
    Percent of total pop.: 17.00%, 30th
  Teachers (1992): 82,301
    Percent of pop.: 0.87%, 45th
  Pupil/teacher ratio (fall 1992): 19.5, 5th
  Teachers' avg. salary (1992-93): $44,956, 6th
  Expenditure per capita (1990-91): $3,603.62, 20th
  Expenditure per pupil (1991-92): $6,268, 11th
Percent of graduates taking SAT (1993): 11%, 35th
  Mean SAT verbal scores: 469, 19th
  Mean SAT mathematical scores: 528, 13th
Percent of graduates taking ACT (1995): 64%, 12th
  Mean ACT scores: 21.1, 26th
Percent of pop. over 25 completing:
  Less than 9th grade: 7.8%, 40th
  High school: 76.8%, 25th
  College degree(s): 17.4%, 37th
Higher education, institutions (1993-94): 106
  Enrollment (1992): 559,729
    Percent of pop.: 5.94%, 19th
  White non-Hispanic (1992): 460,953
    Percent of enroll.: 82.35%, 26th

Black non-Hispanic (1992): 57,086
    Percent of enroll.: 10.20%, 17th
Hispanic (1992): 9,996
    Percent of enroll.: 1.79%, 29th
Asian/Pacific Islander (1992): 12,060
    Percent of enroll.: 2.15%, 23rd
American Indian/AK native (1992): 4,147
    Percent of enroll.: 0.74%, 21st
Nonresident alien (1992): 15,487
    Percent of enroll.: 2.77%, 20th
Female (1992): 310,544
    Percent of enroll.: 55.48%, 22nd
Pub. institutions (1993-94): 45
    Enrollment (1992): 473,322
    Percent of enroll.: 84.56%, 22nd
Private institutions (1993-94): 61
    Enrollment (1992): 86,407
    Percent of enroll.: 15.44%, 30th
Tuition, public institution (avg., 1993-94): $7,642, 12th
Tuition, private institution (avg., 1993-94): $11,411, 31st
Public library systems: 376
    Books & serial vol. per capita: 2.43, 28th
    Govt. expenditure per capita: $14.03, 28th

LAW ENFORCEMENT, COURTS, AND PRISONS

Police protection, corrections, judicial and legal functions expenditures (1992): $2,985,000,000
    Per capita: $316, 15th
Police per 10,000 pop. (1993): 19.79, 30th
Prisoners (state & fed.) per 100,000 pop. (1993): 4,156.24, 11th
    Percent change (1992-93): 0.5%, 38th
Death penalty: no

RELIGION, NUMBER AND PERCENT OF POPULATION

Agnostic: 34,183—0.50%, 27th
Buddhist: 6,837—0.10%, 17th
Christian: 5,790,543—84.70%, 37th
Hindu: 13,673—0.20%, 3rd
Jewish: 54,692—0.80%, 20th
Muslim: 20,510—0.30%, 9th
Unitarian: 20,510—0.30%, 15th
Other: 157,240—2.30%, 6th
None: 594,778—8.70%, 13th
Refused to answer: 143,567—2.10%, 28th

MAKING A LIVING

Personal income per capita (1994): $22,333, 17th
    Percent increase (1993-94): 8.5%, 4th

Disposable personal income per capita (1994): $19,517, 15th
Median income of households (1993): $32,662, 19th
Percent of pop. below poverty level (1993): 15.4%, 17th
    Percent 65 and over (1990): 10.8%, 30th
Expenditure for energy per person (1992): $1,775, 39th

ECONOMY

Civilian labor force (1994): 4,753,000
    Percent of total pop.: 50.05%, 34th
    Percent 65 and over (1990): 2.14%, 41st
    Percent female: 45.89%, 34th
Percent job growth (1980-90): 18.31%, 29th
Major employer industries (1994):
    Agriculture: 85,000—2.0%, 35th
    Construction: 166,000—3.8%, 36th
    Finance, insurance, & real estate: 204,000—4.7%, 36th
    Government: 626,000—14.3%, 36th
    Manufacturing: 1,018,000—23.3%, 4th
    Service: 920,000—21.0%, 25th
    Trade: 886,000—20.2%, 7th
    Transportation, communications, public utilities: 191,000—4.4%, 38th
Unemployment rate (1994): 5.89%, 22nd
    Male: 5.9%, 19th
    Female: 5.9%, 19th
Total businesses (1991): 320,693
    New business incorps. (1991): 20,099
        Percent of total businesses: 6.27%, 22nd
    Business failures (1991): 2,109
        Percent of total businesses: 0.66%
Agriculture farm income:
    Marketing (1993): $3,367,000,000, 21st
        Average per farm: $64,750.00, 36th
    Leading products (1993): Dairy products, corn, greenhouse, soybeans
    Average value land & build. per acre (1994): $1,212, 19th
        Percent increase (1990-94): 20.60%, 7th
    Govt. payments (1993): $241,000,000, 20th
        Average per farm: $4,634.62, 22nd
Construction, value of all: $5,075,000,000
    Per capita: $545.98, 25th
Manufactures:
    Value added: $64,799,000,000
        Per capita: $6,971.16, 7th

Leading products: Transportation equipment, machinery, primary and fabricated metals, food products, rubber and plastic

Value of nonfuel mineral production (1994): $1,621,000,000, 4th

Leading mineral products: Petroleum, iron ore, natural gas, clay

Retail sales (1993): $79,236,000,000, 8th
Per household: $22,624, 18th
Percent increase (1992-93): 7.5%, 23rd

Tourism revenues: $16.5 bil.

Foreign exports, in total value (1994): $25,830,000,000, 4th
Per capita: $2,720.09, 5th

Gross state product per person (1993): $20,170.76, 33rd
Percent change (1990-93): 1.07%, 44th

Patents per 100,000 pop. (1993): 32.90, 7th

Public aid recipients (percent of resident pop. 1993): 9.3%, 9th

Medicaid recipients per 1,000 pop. (1993): 123.89, 22nd

Medicare recipients per 1,000 pop. (1993): 138.37, 29th

TRAVEL AND TRANSPORTATION

Motor vehicle registrations (1993): 7,399,000
Per 1,000 pop.: 782.14, 26th

Motorcycle registrations (1993): 137,000
Per 1,000 pop.: 14.48, 27th

Licensed drivers per 1,000 pop. (1993): 689.96, 27th

Deaths from motor vehicle accidents per 100,000 pop. (1993): 14.89, 33rd

Public roads & streets (1993):
Total mileage: 117,659
Per 1,000 pop.: 12.44, 36th
Rural mileage: 89,485
Per 1,000 pop.: 9.46, 36th
Urban mileage: 28,174
Per 1,000 pop.: 2.98, 32nd
Interstate mileage: 1,240
Per 1,000 pop.: 0.13, 39th

Annual vehicle-mi. of travel per person (1993): 9,059, 33rd

Mean travel time for workers age 16+ who work away from home: 21.2 min., 20th

GOVERNMENT

Percent of voting age pop. registered (1994): 73.7%, 7th

Percent of voting age pop. voting (1994): 52.2%, 13th

Percent of voting age pop. voting for U.S. representatives (1994): 43.0%, 17th

State legislators, total (1995): 148, 24th
Women members (1992): 22
Percent of legislature: 14.9%, 30th

U.S. Congress, House members (1995): 16
Change (1985-95): –2

Revenues (1993):
State govt.: $28,760,000,000
Per capita: $3,040.17, 26th
Parimutuel & amusement taxes & lotteries, revenue per capita: $122.83, 13th

Expenditures (1993):
State govt.: $27,051,000,000
Per capita: $2,859.51, 25th

Debt outstanding (1993): $8,849,000,000
Per capita: $935.41, 39th

LAWS AND REGULATIONS

Legal driving age: 18, 16 if completed driver education course

Marriage age without parental consent: 18

Divorce residence requirement: 180 days, for qualifications check local statutes

ATTRACTIONS (1995)

Major opera companies: 2

Major symphony orchestras: 2

State appropriations for arts agencies per capita: $3.25, 2nd

State Fair in mid-August at Escanaba for the Upper Peninsula and late-August–early September at Detroit

SPORTS AND COMPETITION

NCAA teams (Division I): Central Michigan Univ. Chippewas, Eastern Michigan Univ. Eagles, Michigan State Univ. Spartans, Univ. of Detroit Titans, Univ. of Michigan Wolverines, Western Michigan Univ. Broncos

Major league baseball teams: Detroit Tigers (AL East), Tiger Stadium

NBA basketball teams: Detroit Pistons, The Palace of Auburn Hills

NFL football teams: Detroit Lions (NFC), Pontiac Silverdome

NHL hockey teams: Detroit Red Wings, Joe Louis Arena

MINNESOTA

"Minnesotans are just different, that's all...with the wind chill hovering at fifty-seven below...there were all these Minnesotans running around outdoors, happy as lambs in the spring."

Charles Kuralt, broadcaster

Minnesota modestly boasts of its 10,000 lakes, but in reality there are more than 15,000. Its history is said by some experts to hark back to Viking explorers in the 1300s, and the state has long been a haven for Scandinavian immigrants. Almost 3 million cattle graze on its rich pastures. The state makes more butter than any other, and it is a leading milk and cheese producer. It cherishes a world-renowned facility for medical care and research, the Mayo Clinic, and its state university system ranks among the largest and best. It is a principal world center of milling concerns. Today, the Twin Cities of Minneapolis and St. Paul are a leading center of music, theater, and shopping. Minneapolis has been ranked as the nation's most liveable city. Enhancing the attraction of the Twin Cities is the nation's largest shopping mall.

SUPERLATIVES

• Source of the Mississippi River.
• Only state with source of three main river systems (Mississippi, St. Lawrence, Red River of the North).
• Principal U.S. source of manganese.
• Lady's slipper, unique among the state flowers.
• Pioneer in open-pit mining.
• Pioneer in overland bus travel.

MOMENTS IN HISTORY

• Some experts believe that European explorers reached Minnesota in the 1300s. This belief is based on artifacts such as a carving called the Kensington Runestone, found near Kensington. But other experts call this find a hoax.
• The first authenticated record of European visitors was made by explorer Daniel Greysolon, Sieur de Lhut (Duluth), in 1679.
• Beginning in 1727, French trading posts were established, and in 1763 the British took control from the French.

> **So They Say**
>
> "We had a camp by two islands. We were out fishing one day. When we returned home, we found ten men red of blood and dead...Save us from evil."
>
> From a translation of the Kensington Runestone

• The Northwest Ordinance of 1787 included most of eastern Minnesota, and the Louisiana Purchase of 1803 brought most of the western region of Minnesota under U.S. control.
• In 1805, Zebulon Pike raised the U.S. flag over Minnesota for the first time, but the British paid little attention to U.S. claims.
• The War of 1812 finally settled the ownership of Minnesota.
• In 1820, Colonel Josiah Snelling started the fort bearing his name, erected at the site where the Minnesota and Mississippi rivers join together.
• In 1832, Henry R. Schoolcraft discovered the long-sought source of the Mississippi River and named it Lake Itasca.

> **So They Say**
>
> "...Unexpectedly, the outlet [source of the Mississippi] proved quite a brisk brook....Ten feet wide in most places, reached from bank, and the depth would probably average over a foot."
>
> Henry R. Schoolcraft

• In 1838 both St. Paul and Minneapolis were begun separately.
• Most of Minnesota's northern boundary was established by the Webster-Ashburton Treaty of 1842.
• On May 11, 1858, Minnesota became the 32nd state, with Henry H. Sibley as the first governor.

• During the Civil War, Minnesota was the first state to offer troops, and the first Minnesota Regiment played a key role in the Battle of Gettysburg.

• In 1862 the Sioux Indians went on a rampage. The warfare finally was put down by Henry H. Sibley, who took approximately 2,000 prisoners.

• The boundary line of the Lake of the Woods, extending into Canada, was not settled until 1873.

• The capitol was dedicated in 1905 and boasts the world's largest unsupported marble dome.

• World War I found 123,325 Minnesotans in uniform.

• The election of 1936 brought a dramatic victory to the Farmer-Labor party.

• More than 300,000 from Minnesota served in World War II, and over 6,000 lost their lives.

• The opening of the St. Lawrence Seaway in 1959 brought ocean traffic to the great port of Duluth.

• From 1965 to 1969, beloved Minnesota political figure Hubert H. Humphrey served as vice president under Lyndon B. Johnson.

• From 1977 to 1981, Minnesota's Walter F. Mondale was the U.S. vice president under Jimmy Carter.

• In 1992 the Duluth-Superior harbor continued to be the busiest on the Great Lakes.

• In 1993, Minneapolis elected its first African-American mayor, Sharon Sayles Belton, a Democrat.

THAT'S INTERESTING

• There are so many lakes in Minnesota that novel names are scarce. There are 91 Long Lakes, and other bodies of water also have identical names.

• In 1838 an unsavory character built a cabin at present-day St. Paul and called the place Pig's Eye. Fortunately, Father Lucian Galtier renamed the place after St. Paul when he built a chapel there in 1841.

• The execution of 37 Sioux for their part in the Sioux War was the largest official wholesale execution in U.S. history. The Indians went to the scaffold singing a war song.

• The Falls of St. Anthony have "traveled." Their waters have continued to cut into the soft limestone, causing them to move upstream about 4 miles since their discovery.

• Charles Mayo, of the famed Mayo medical family, began his career at age nine by administering ether during operations.

• The great Cuyuna iron range was named for Cuyler Adams and his dog Una (Cuy-Una).

• The red-colored stone of Pipestone National Monument is found nowhere else. It was a sacred place to the Indians, who carved their peace pipes from its soft redstone.

NOTABLE NATIVES

William Orville Douglas (Maine, 1898-1980), Supreme Court justice. **Francis Scott Fitzgerald** (St. Paul, 1896-1940), author. **James Earle Fraser** (Winona, 1876-1953), sculptor. **Judy Garland** (Grand Rapids, 1922-1969), actress/singer. **Jean Paul Getty** (Minneapolis, 1892-1976), businessman. **Garrison Keillor** (Anoka, 1942-), humorist. **Sinclair Lewis** (Sauk Centre, 1885-1951), author. **Charles Horace Mayo** (Rochester, 1865-1939), physician. **William James Mayo** (Le Sueur, 1861-1939), physician. **Charles Monroe Schultz** (Minneapolis, 1922-), cartoonist. **Harold Edward Stassen** (West St. Paul, 1907-) public official. **DeWitt Wallace** (St. Paul, 1889-1981), editor/publisher.

GENERAL

Admitted to statehood: May 11, 1858
Origin of name: From Dakota Sioux word meaning "cloudy water" or "sky-tinted water" of the Minnesota River
Capital: St. Paul
Nickname: North Star State, Gopher State
Motto: *L'Etoile du Nord*—The star of the North
Bird: Common loon
Fish: Walleye
Flower: Pink and white lady's slipper
Gem: Lake Superior agate
Song: "Hail! Minnesota"
Tree: Red (Norway) pine

THE LAND

Area: 86,943 sq. mi., 12th
  Land: 79,617 sq. mi., 14th
  Water: 7,326 sq. mi., 4th
    Inland water: 4,780 sq. mi., 3rd
  Great Lakes: 2,546 sq. mi., 5th
Topography: Central hill and lake region covering approximately half the state; to the NE, rocky ridges and deep lakes; to

the NW, flat plain; to the S, rolling plains and deep river valleys

Number of counties: 87

Geographic center: Crow Wing, 10 mi. SW of Brainerd

Length: 400 mi.; width: 250 mi.

Highest point: 2,301 ft. (Eagle Mountain), 37th

Lowest point: 602 ft. (Lake Superior), 42nd

Mean elevation: 1,200 ft., 21st

CLIMATE AND ENVIRONMENT

Temp., highest: 114 deg. on July 6, 1936, at Moorhead; lowest: –59 deg. on Feb. 16, 1903, at Pokegama Dam

Monthly average: highest: 83.4 deg., 42nd; lowest: –2.9 deg., 3rd; spread (high to low): 86.3 deg., 3rd

Hazardous waste sites (1993): 41, 8th

Endangered species: Mammals: none; birds: 2—American peregrine falcon, Piping plover; reptiles: none; amphibians: none; fishes: none; invertebrates: 1; plants: 1

MAJOR CITIES
POPULATION, 1990
PERCENTAGE INCREASE, 1980-90

Bloomington, 86,335—5.50%

Duluth, 85,493— –7.88%

Minneapolis, 368,383— –0.69%

Rochester, 70,745—22.17%

St. Paul, 272,235—0.74%

THE PEOPLE

Population (1995): 4,609,548, 20th
  Percent change (1990-95): 5.3%, 24th

Population (2000 proj.): 4,824,000, 20th
  Percent change (1990-2000): 10.26%, 25th

Per sq. mi. (1994): 57.4, 32nd

Percent in metro. area (1992): 69.3%, 27th

Foreign born: 113,000, 22nd
  Percent: 2.6%, 30th

Top three ancestries reported:
  German, 46.18%
  Norwegian, 17.30%
  Irish, 13.12%

White: 4,130,395, 94.41%, 8th

Black: 94,944, 2.17%, 39th

Native American: 49,909, 1.14%, 15th

Asian, Pacific Isle: 77,886, 1.78%, 18th

Other races: 21,965, 0.50%, 35th

Hispanic origin: 53,884, 1.23%, 36th

Percent over 5 yrs. speaking language other than English at home: 5.6%, 35th

Percent males: 49.03%, 18th; percent females: 50.97%, 34th

Percent never married: 27.4%, 14th

Marriages per 1,000 (1993): 7.0, 44th

Divorces per 1,000 (1993): 3.7, 36th

Median age: 32.5

Under 5 years (1994): 7.16%, 27th

Under 18 years (1994): 27.17%, 14th

65 years & older (1994): 12.5%, 30th

Percent increase among the elderly (1990-94): 4.77%, 32nd

OF VITAL IMPORTANCE

Live births per 1,000 pop. (1993): 14.1, 35th

Infant mortality rate per 1,000 births (1992): 7.1, 42nd
  Rate for blacks (1990): 19.7, 4th
  Rate for whites (1990): 6.7, 45th

Births to unmarried women, % of total (1992): 23.0%, 45th

Births to teenage mothers, % of total (1992): 8.1%, 47th

Abortions (1992): 16,180, 22nd
  Rate per 1,000 women 14-44 years old: 15.6, 33rd
  Percent change (1988-92): –14%, 36th

Average lifetime (1979-81): 76.15, 2nd

Deaths per 1,000 pop. (1993): 8.0, 37th

Causes of death per 100,000 pop.:
  Accidents & adverse effects (1992): 33.3, 31st
  Atherosclerosis (1991): 7.8, 17th
  Cancer (1991): 191.3, 39th
  Cerebrovascular diseases (1992): 63.1, 18th
  Chronic liver diseases & cirrhosis (1991): 6.6, 46th
  Chronic obstructive pulmonary diseases (1992): 33.5, 36th
  Diabetes mellitus (1992): 17.4, 38th
  Diseases of heart (1992): 229.4, 41st
  Pneumonia, flu (1991): 35.1, 14th
  Suicide (1992): 11.5, 37th

KEEPING WELL

Active nonfederal physicians per 100,000 pop. (1993): 232, 12th

Dentists per 100,000 (1991): 66, 11th

Nurses per 100,000 (1992): 893, 12th

Hospitals per 100,000 (1993): 3.21, 12th
  Admissions per 1,000 (1993): 109.66, 32nd
  Occupancy rate per 100 beds (1993): 66.0, 15th

Average cost per patient per day (1993): $652, 44th

Average cost per stay (1993): $5,867, 22nd

Average stay (1992): 10.3 days, 8th

AIDS cases (adult, 1993): 659; per 100,000: 14.6, 34th

HIV infection, not yet AIDS (1993): 1,863

Other notifiable diseases:

Gonorrhea: 95.6, 36th

Measles: 10.6, 7th

Syphilis: 4.8, 39th

Tuberculosis: 2.6, 42nd

Pop. without health insur. (1991-93): 9.2%, 47th

HOUSEHOLDS BY TYPE

Total households (1994): 1,711,000

Percent change (1990-94): 3.8%, 29th

Per 1,000 pop.: 374.64, 27th

Percent of households 65 yrs. and over: 21.16%, 33rd

Persons per household (1994): 2.60, 23rd

Family households: 1,130,683

Percent of total: 68.62%, 42nd

Nonfamily households: 517,170

Percent of total: 31.38%, 10th

Pop. living in group quarters: 117,621

Percent of pop.: 2.69%, 28th

LIVING QUARTERS

Total housing units: 1,848,445

Persons per unit: 2.37, 33rd

Occupied housing units: 1,647,853

Percent of total units: 89.15%, 28th

Persons per unit: 2.43, 50th

Percent of units with over 1 person per room: 2.07%, 42nd

Owner-occupied units: 1,183,673

Percent of total units: 64.04%, 6th

Percent of occupied units: 71.83%, 2nd

Persons per unit: 2.78, 17th

Median value: $74,000, 22nd

Renter-occupied units: 464,180

Percent of total units: 25.11%, 48th

Percent of occupied units: 28.17%, 50th

Persons per unit: 2.08, 51st

Median contract rent: $348, 22nd

Rental vacancy rate: 7.9%, 30th

Mobile home, trailer & other as a percent of occupied housing units: 6.77%, 38th

Persons in emergency shelters for homeless persons: 2,253, 0.051%, 23rd

Persons visible in street locations: 138, 0.0032%, 35th

Persons in shelters for abused women: 230, 0.0053%, 19th

Nursing home population: 47,051, 1.08%, 6th

CRIME INDEX PER 100,000 (1992-93)

Total reported: 4,386.2, 37th

Violent: 327.2, 38th

Murder and nonnegligent manslaughter: 3.4, 42nd

Aggravated assault: 175.8, 42nd

Robbery: 112.7, 36th

Forcible rape: 35.2, 31st

Property: 4,059.0, 34th

Burglary: 844.5, 35th

Larceny, theft: 2,872.0, 27th

Motor vehicle theft: 342.6, 31st

Drug abuse violations (1990): 126.2, 42nd

Child-abuse rate per 1,000 children (1993): 8.58, 42nd

TEACHING AND LEARNING

Pop. 3 and over enrolled in school: 1,175,027

Percent of pop.: 28.1%, 17th

Public elementary & secondary schools (1992-93): 1622

Total enrollment (1992): 793,724

Percent of total pop.: 17.76%, 16th

Teachers (1992): 45,050

Percent of pop.: 1.01%, 29th

Pupil/teacher ratio (fall 1992): 17.6, 14th

Teachers' avg. salary (1992-93): $37,160, 20th

Expenditure per capita (1990-91): $4,250.02, 7th

Expenditure per pupil (1991-92): $5,409, 22nd

Percent of graduates taking SAT (1993): 10%, 39th

Mean SAT verbal scores: 489, 6th

Mean SAT mathematical scores: 556, 4th

Percent of graduates taking ACT (1995): 59%, 21st

Mean ACT scores: 21.9, 5th

Percent of pop. over 25 completing:

Less than 9th grade: 8.6%, 32nd

High school: 82.4%, 6th

College degree(s): 21.8%, 16th

Higher education, institutions (1993-94): 98

Enrollment (1992): 272,918

Percent of pop.: 6.10%, 18th

White non-Hispanic (1992): 248,519

Percent of enroll.: 91.06%, 6th

Black non-Hispanic (1992): 5,588
Percent of enroll.: 2.05%, 41st
Hispanic (1992): 2,919
Percent of enroll.: 1.07%, 39th
Asian/Pacific Islander (1992): 7,062
Percent of enroll.: 2.59%, 18th
American Indian/AK native (1992): 2,548
Percent of enroll.: 0.93%, 18th
Nonresident alien (1992): 6,284
Percent of enroll.: 2.30%, 28th
Female (1992): 149,670
Percent of enroll.: 54.84%, 33rd
Pub. institutions (1993-94): 54
Enrollment (1992): 212,156
Percent of enroll.: 77.74%, 37th
Private institutions (1993-94): 44
Enrollment (1992): 60,762
Percent of enroll.: 22.26%, 15th
Tuition, public institution (avg., 1993-94): $5,904, 24th
Tuition, private institution (avg., 1993-94): $14,569, 17th
Public library systems: 130
Books & serial vol. per capita: 2.58, 25th
Govt. expenditure per capita: $18.42, 20th

LAW ENFORCEMENT, COURTS, AND PRISONS

Police protection, corrections, judicial and legal functions expenditures (1992): $1,078,000,000
Per capita: $241, 29th
Police per 10,000 pop. (1993): 15.94, 42nd
Prisoners (state & fed.) per 100,000 pop. (1993): 928.38, 50th
Percent change (1992-93): 9.9%, 6th
Death penalty: no

RELIGION, NUMBER AND PERCENT OF POPULATION

Agnostic: 19,250—0.60%, 19th
Buddhist: 3,208—0.10%, 17th
Christian: 2,865,026—89.30%, 15th
Hindu: 3,208—0.10%, 10th
Jewish: 25,667—0.80%, 20th
Muslim: 3,208—0.10%, 22nd
Unitarian: 12,833—0.40%, 8th
Other: 25,667—0.80%, 37th
None: 179,666—5.60%, 38th
Refused to answer: 70,583—2.20%, 23rd

MAKING A LIVING

Personal income per capita (1994): $22,453, 16th

Percent increase (1993-94): 7.0%, 6th
Disposable personal income per capita (1994): $18,919, 21st
Median income of households (1993): $33,682, 15th
Percent of pop. below poverty level (1993): 11.6%, 34th
Percent 65 and over (1990): 12.1%, 23rd
Expenditure for energy per person (1992): $1,721, 42nd

ECONOMY

Civilian labor force (1994): 2,565,000
Percent of total pop.: 56.16%, 1st
Percent 65 and over (1990): 2.41%, 36th
Percent female: 47.25%, 14th
Percent job growth (1980-90): 19.26%, 24th
Major employer industries (1994):
Agriculture: 110,000—4.7%, 9th
Construction: 81,000—3.4%, 46th
Finance, insurance, & real estate: 131,000—5.6%, 18th
Government: 361,000—15.4%, 25th
Manufacturing: 359,000—15.3%, 25th
Service: 538,000—23.0%, 18th
Trade: 454,000—19.4%, 14th
Transportation, communications, public utilities: 109,000—4.6%, 36th
Unemployment rate (1994): 4.02%, 46th
Male: 4.6%, 40th
Female: 3.4%, 48th
Total businesses (1991): 176,738
New business incorps. (1991): 9,564
Percent of total businesses: 5.41%, 33rd
Business failures (1991): 529
Percent of total businesses: 0.30%
Agriculture farm income:
Marketing (1993): $6,574,000,000, 7th
Average per farm: $75,563.22, 26th
Leading products (1993): Dairy products, cattle, hogs, corn
Average value land & build. per acre (1994): $900, 28th
Percent increase (1990-94): 11.80%, 29th
Govt. payments (1993): $823,000,000, 4th
Average per farm: $9,459.77, 13th
Construction, value of all: $3,628,000,000
Per capita: $829.24, 8th
Manufactures:
Value added: $25,804,000,000
Per capita: $5,897.92, 14th

Leading products: Food processing, non-electrical machinery, chemicals, paper, electric and electronic equipment, printing and publishing, instruments, fabricated metal products

Value of nonfuel mineral production (1994): $1,352,000,000, 9th

Leading mineral products: Iron ore, sand/gravel, stone

Retail sales (1993): $39,583,000,000, 20th
Per household: $23,020, 15th
Percent increase (1992-93): 9.8%, 10th

Tourism revenues (1994): $7 bil.

Foreign exports, in total value (1994): $6,621,000,000, 19th
Per capita: $1,449.75, 18th

Gross state product per person (1993): $23,255.81, 14th
Percent change (1990-93): 3.00%, 26th

Patents per 100,000 pop. (1993): 39.06, 5th

Public aid recipients (percent of resident pop. 1993): 5.5%, 36th

Medicaid recipients per 1,000 pop. (1993): 93.94, 43rd

Medicare recipients per 1,000 pop. (1993): 135.94, 33rd

TRAVEL AND TRANSPORTATION

Motor vehicle registrations (1993): 3,716,000
Per 1,000 pop.: 821.40, 19th

Motorcycle registrations (1993): 126,000
Per 1,000 pop.: 27.85, 8th

Licensed drivers per 1,000 pop. (1993): 582.89, 50th

Deaths from motor vehicle accidents per 100,000 pop. (1993): 11.89, 43rd

Public roads & streets (1993):
Total mileage: 129,959
Per 1,000 pop.: 28.73, 14th
Rural mileage: 115,073
Per 1,000 pop.: 25.44, 14th
Urban mileage: 14,886
Per 1,000 pop.: 3.29, 16th
Interstate mileage: 914
Per 1,000 pop.: 0.20, 27th

Annual vehicle-mi. of travel per person (1993): 9,328, 26th

Mean travel time for workers age 16+ who work away from home: 19.1 min., 36th

GOVERNMENT

Percent of voting age pop. registered (1994): 80.9%, 3rd
Percent of voting age pop. voting (1994): 58.4%, 7th
Percent of voting age pop. voting for U.S. representatives (1994): 52.0%, 5th

State legislators, total (1995): 201, 5th
Women members (1992): 42
Percent of legislature: 20.9%, 17th

U.S. Congress, House members (1995): 8
Change (1985-95): 0

Revenues (1993):
State govt.: $16,245,000,000
Per capita: $3,590.85, 14th
Parimutuel & amusement taxes & lotteries, revenue per capita: $81.56, 25th

Expenditures (1993):
State govt.: $14,295,000,000
Per capita: $3,159.81, 17th

Debt outstanding (1993): $4,145,000,000
Per capita: $916.22, 40th

LAWS AND REGULATIONS

Legal driving age: 18, 16 if completed driver education course
Marriage age without parental consent: 18
Divorce residence requirement: 180 days

ATTRACTIONS (1995)

Major opera companies: 1
Major symphony orchestras: 2
Major dance companies: 1
Major professional theater companies (non-profit): 2
State appropriations for arts agencies per capita: $1.46, 11th
State Fair in late August–early September at St. Paul

SPORTS AND COMPETITION

NCAA teams (Division I): Univ. of Minnesota Golden Gophers
Major league baseball teams: Minnesota Twins (AL Central), Hubert H. Humphrey Metrodome
NBA basketball teams: Minnesota Timberwolves, Target Center
NFL football teams: Minnesota Vikings (NFC), Hubert H. Humphrey Metrodome

MISSISSIPPI

"It is in Mississippi, more than any other state, that the character of the Old South remains apparent today. Once the very heartland of plantation society, the state remains the leading cotton producer of the states that once relied on such a one-crop economy....As a result, Mississippi has yet to show the effects of urbanization which have changed the character of the neighboring states."

Robert O'Brien

Mississippi is a land where a beetle (the boll weevil) changed the way of life. Before the Civil War the planters of Mississippi, with their "Little Cotton Kingdoms" and mansions, enjoyed the brilliant plantation culture, which was based on slave labor. During that war the state suffered greatly; it suffered still more during the brutal period of Reconstruction. At one time, Mississippi was the home of one of the largest Indian populations, but the Indians, known for their civilized lifestyle, were forced to leave their property to travel west over the "Trail of Tears." As the native state of some of the nation's best-known authors, composers, and playwrights, Mississippi has a well-earned reputation for culture, combined with a notable blending of rural and cosmopolitan backgrounds.

So They Say

"By far the most prominent feature of the geography is the mighty river called Meact Chassipi by the Indians, roughly translated as 'ancient father of Water.' For 400 miles along the state's western boundary, the mighty Mississippi River swells and courses, ebbs and flows, gleams and glistens, twists and turns."

The Enchantment of Mississippi

SUPERLATIVES

• First European settlement in the southern Mississippi Valley — Ocean Springs.
• One of the earliest and best reforestation programs.
• Natchez, boasting more than 500 pre-Civil War mansions.
• Biloxi, which has had record eight flags flying over it.

• Celebrated the first "Decoration Day," now Memorial Day.
• First U.S. state-operated university for women, at Columbus.
• Pioneer in state system of junior colleges.

MOMENTS IN HISTORY

• In 1540, Hernando de Soto and his expedition entered present-day Mississippi near where Columbus now stands, and his party may have been the first Europeans to see the Mississippi River. Their cruelty to the Indians was well-known.
• In 1682, Robert Cavelier, Sieur de La Salle, claimed the vast region drained by the Mississippi for the King of France.
• The first European settlement in the entire Mississippi Valley—Fort Maurepas, now Ocean Springs—was founded in 1699 by Pierre Le Moyne, Sieur d'Iberville.
• In 1720 at the command of King Louis XV, John Law was sent with 200 settlers to the Pascagoula area. Although other settlers arrived, Law's "Mississippi Bubble" burst, almost bringing France to financial collapse.
• After years of Indian attacks, in 1736, French forces under the Sieur de Bienville were defeated by the Chickasaw, hastening the French decline in North America.
• With the French withdrawal in 1763, the British made their headquarters at present-day Natchez, and most of the area now Mississippi became part of British West Florida. During the American Revolution, the Spanish attacked the area, and by 1781 they had seized British West Florida.
• After a long dispute with Spain over the ownership of the region, in 1798, Spanish forces left the upper area, and Congress created the Mississippi Territory, with its capital at Natchez. It also included much of Alabama.

• On December 10, 1817, Mississippi was admitted as the 20th state.

• By 1832 the last of the Indian tribes had their substantial property seized. Forced to leave the state, they trudged in desperation over the "Trail of Tears" on their way to western lands.

• The great plantations of Mississippi depended on their slave labor, and on January 9, 1861, Mississippi became the second state to secede from the Union.

• The 47-day siege of Vicksburg during the Civil War ended on July 4, 1863, and the battle for that city was one of the most crucial of the entire conflict. The Union success cut the Confederacy in two and opened the entire Mississippi to Union forces.

So They Say

"For five days 10,000 men worked hard with a will in that work of destruction with axes, crowbars, sledges, clawbars, and fire, and I have no hesitation in pronouncing the work well done. Meridian...no longer exists."

General William Tecumseh Sherman, on the destruction of Meridian

---

• Civil War battles raged across the state, ending with the Battle of Tupelo in early 1865. The state lost 60,000 soldiers.

• Mississippi was readmitted to the Union in 1870, but the terrible hardships of Reconstruction endured until about 1875.

• An epidemic of yellow fever swept the state in 1878, and thousands died.

• In 1904, James K. Vardaman became governor with the support of small farmers and others, ending the control of the plantation "planter class."

• During World War I, 66,000 men and women served in the armed forces, and Camp Shelby was a principal training center.

• The Mississippi River floods of 1927 were the worst in memory.

• During World War II, more Mississippians won the Medal of Honor than those of any other state.

• In 1967 the space age came to the state with the opening of what became the National Space Technology Laboratories.

• The 1990 census indicated that Mississippi continued a slow increase in population.

THAT'S INTERESTING

• Among geographic curiosities is the so-called Singing River, the Pascagoula. It sometimes makes a sound like the humming of bees, and this has never been explained.

• When Hernando de Soto died, his followers were so afraid of the Indians that they slipped his body into the Mississippi in the dead of night, at a spot thought to have been near present-day Natchez.

• The mother-daughter combination of Maria and Miranda Younghans manned the Biloxi lighthouse for a total of 62 years.

• The five sons of the William Henry Cox family all died tragic deaths. Among the tragedies were one son who was killed riding his horse up a stairway, one who killed his bride and committed suicide, and another who died in a wagon as it crashed over a cliff.

• Mississippi is the only state whose state flower is the blossom of the state tree.

NOTABLE NATIVES

Theodore Bilbo (near Poplarville, 1877-1947), public official. **William Cuthbert Faulkner** (New Albany, 1897-1962), author. **James Earl Jones** (Arkabutla, 1931-), actor. **Elvis Aaron Presley** (Tupelo, 1935-1977), entertainer. **Leontyne Price** (Laurel, 1927-), opera singer. **William Grant Still** (Woodville, 1895-1978), composer. **Eudora Welty** (Jackson, 1909-), author. **Tennessee Williams** (Columbus, 1911-1983), playwright.

GENERAL

Admitted to statehood: December 10, 1817
Origin of name: Probably Chippewa; *mici zibi*, "great river" or "gathering-in of all the waters"
Capital: Jackson
Nickname: Magnolia State
Motto: *Virtute et Armis*—By valor and arms
Bird: Mockingbird
Flower: Magnolia
Song: "Go, Mississippi"
Tree: Magnolia

THE LAND

Area: 48,286 sq. mi., 32nd
   Land: 46,914 sq. mi., 31st
   Water: 1,372 sq. mi., 22nd
      Inland water: 781 sq. mi., 27th
      Coastal water: 591 sq. mi., 10th

Topography: Low, fertile delta between Yazoo and Mississippi rivers; loess bluffs stretching around delta border; sandy gulf coastal terraces followed by piney woods and prairie; rugged, high sandy hills in extreme NE, followed by black prairie belt, Pontotoc Ridge, and flatwoods into the N central highlands

Number of counties: 82

Geographic center: Leake, 9 mi. WNW of Carthage

Length: 340 mi.; width: 170 mi.

Highest point: 806 ft. (Woodall Mountain), 47th

Lowest point: sea level (Gulf of Mexico), 3rd

Mean elevation: 300 ft., 45th

Coastline: 44 mi., 18th

Shoreline: 359 mi., 22nd

CLIMATE AND ENVIRONMENT

Temp., highest: 115 deg. on July 29, 1930, at Holly Springs; lowest: –19 deg. on Jan. 30, 1966, at Corinth

Monthly average: highest: 92.5 deg., 11th; lowest: 34.9 deg., 46th; spread (high to low): 57.6 deg., 47th

Hazardous waste sites (1993): 4, 45th

Endangered species: Mammals: 2—Indiana bat, West Indian manatee; birds: 5—Mississippi sandhill crane, American peregrine falcon, Brown pelican, Least tern, Red-cockaded woodpecker; reptiles: 3; amphibians: none; fishes: 1; invertebrates: 5; plants: 1

MAJOR CITIES
POPULATION, 1990
PERCENTAGE INCREASE, 1980-90

Biloxi, 46,319— –6.07%

Greenville, 45,226—11.36%

Hattiesburg, 41,882—2.58%

Jackson, 196,637— –3.08%

Meridian, 41,036— –11.90%

THE PEOPLE

Population (1995): 2,697,243, 31st
  Percent change (1990-95): 4.7%, 26th
Population (2000 proj.): 2,750,000, 31st
  Percent change (1990-2000): 6.9%, 33rd
Per sq. mi. (1994): 56.9, 33rd
Percent in metro. area (1992): 30.7%, 47th
Foreign born: 20,000, 45th
  Percent: 0.8%, 51st

Top three ancestries reported:
  African, 30.10%
  Irish, 15.26%
  American, 12.31%
White: 1,633,461, 63.48%, 49th
Black: 915,057, 35.56%, 2nd
Native American: 8,525, 0.33%, 31st
Asian, Pacific Isle: 13,016, 0.51%, 48th
Other races: 3,157, 0.12%, 50th
Hispanic origin: 15,931, 0.62%, 47th
Percent over 5 yrs. speaking language other than English at home: 2.8%, 48th
Percent males: 47.82%, 50th; percent females: 52.18%, 2nd
Percent never married: 26.7%, 20th
Marriages per 1,000 (1993): 8.9, 20th
Divorces per 1,000 (1993): 5.0, 20th
Median age: 31.2
Under 5 years (1994): 7.76%, 12th
Under 18 years (1994): 28.33%, 9th
65 years & older (1994): 12.5%, 30th
Percent increase among the elderly (1990-94): 3.34%, 42nd

OF VITAL IMPORTANCE

Live births per 1,000 pop. (1993): 16.0, 12th
Infant mortality rate per 1,000 births (1992): 11.9, 2nd
  Rate for blacks (1990): 16.1, 24th
  Rate for whites (1990): 8.5, 11th
Births to unmarried women, % of total (1992): 42.9%, 2nd
Births to teenage mothers, % of total (1992): 21.4%, 1st
Abortions (1992): 7,550, 34th
  Rate per 1,000 women 14-44 years old: 12.4, 41st
  Percent change (1988-92): 48%, 1st
Average lifetime (1979-81): 71.98, 48th
Deaths per 1,000 pop. (1993): 10.1, 6th
Causes of death per 100,000 pop.:
  Accidents & adverse effects (1992): 58.7, 2nd
  Atherosclerosis (1991): 5.8, 39th
  Cancer (1991): 212.6, 24th
  Cerebrovascular diseases (1992): 66.1, 13th
  Chronic liver diseases & cirrhosis (1991): 7.5, 43rd
  Chronic obstructive pulmonary diseases (1992): 33.6, 35th
  Diabetes mellitus (1992): 18.2, 34th
  Diseases of heart (1992): 349.1, 5th
  Pneumonia, flu (1991): 30.6, 24th
  Suicide (1992): 12.7, 20th

KEEPING WELL

Active nonfederal physicians per 100,000 pop. (1993): 130, 51st

Dentists per 100,000 (1991): 38, 51st

Nurses per 100,000 (1992): 516, 51st

Hospitals per 100,000 (1993): 3.67, 9th
  Admissions per 1,000 (1993): 140.45, 8th
  Occupancy rate per 100 beds (1993): 59.3, 33rd
  Average cost per patient per day (1993): $555, 47th
  Average cost per stay (1993): $4,053, 51st
  Average stay (1992): 7.0 days, 28th

AIDS cases (adult, 1993): 461; per 100,000: 17.4, 31st

HIV infection, not yet AIDS (1993): 2,314

Other notifiable diseases:
  Gonorrhea: 555.8, 3rd
  Measles: 1.1, 40th
  Syphilis: 96.5, 5th
  Tuberculosis: 14.1, 6th

Pop. without health insur. (1991-93): 18.8%, 9th

HOUSEHOLDS BY TYPE

Total households (1994): 949,000
  Percent change (1990-94): 4.2%, 27th
  Per 1,000 pop.: 355.56, 46th
  Percent of households 65 yrs. and over: 23.29%, 13th
  Persons per household (1994): 2.74, 8th
Family households: 674,378
  Percent of total: 74.00%, 2nd
Nonfamily households: 236,996
  Percent of total: 26.00%, 50th
Pop. living in group quarters: 69,717
  Percent of pop.: 2.71%, 27th

LIVING QUARTERS

Total housing units: 1,010,423
  Persons per unit: 2.55, 4th
Occupied housing units: 911,374
  Percent of total units: 90.20%, 21st
  Persons per unit: 2.72, 5th
  Percent of units with over 1 person per room: 5.80%, 11th
Owner-occupied units: 651,587
  Percent of total units: 64.49%, 4th
  Percent of occupied units: 71.50%, 3rd
  Persons per unit: 2.78, 17th
  Median value: $45,600, 49th
Renter-occupied units: 259,787
  Percent of total units: 25.71%, 46th
  Percent of occupied units: 28.50%, 49th

Persons per unit: 2.65, 4th
Median contract rent: $215, 51st
Rental vacancy rate: 9.5%, 18th
Mobile home, trailer & other as a percent of occupied housing units: 16.38%, 9th
Persons in emergency shelters for homeless persons: 383, 0.015%, 51st
Persons visible in street locations: 83, 0.0032%, 35th
Persons in shelters for abused women: 125, 0.0049%, 26th
Nursing home population: 15,803, 0.61%, 35th

CRIME INDEX PER 100,000 (1992-93)

Total reported: 4,418.3, 36th
  Violent: 433.9, 33rd
    Murder and nonnegligent manslaughter: 13.5, 3rd
    Aggravated assault: 238.4, 35th
    Robbery: 139.3, 25th
    Forcible rape: 42.6, 20th
  Property: 3,984.4, 35th
    Burglary: 1,285.8, 11th
    Larceny, theft: 2,363.5, 43rd
    Motor vehicle theft: 335.1, 33rd
Drug abuse violations (1990): 177.5, 38th
Child-abuse rate per 1,000 children (1993): 11.63, 35th

TEACHING AND LEARNING

Pop. 3 and over enrolled in school: 727,486
  Percent of pop.: 29.6%, 7th
Public elementary & secondary schools (1992-93): 978
  Total enrollment (1992): 506,668
    Percent of total pop.: 19.38%, 8th
  Teachers (1992): 27,829
    Percent of pop.: 1.06%, 20th
  Pupil/teacher ratio (fall 1992): 18.2, 12th
  Teachers' avg. salary (1992-93): $25,876, 50th
  Expenditure per capita (1990-91): $2,695.57, 49th
  Expenditure per pupil (1991-92): $3,245, 50th
Percent of graduates taking SAT (1993): 4%, 50th
  Mean SAT verbal scores: 481, 10th
  Mean SAT mathematical scores: 521, 18th
Percent of graduates taking ACT (1995): 73%, 4th
  Mean ACT scores: 18.8, 51st

Percent of pop. over 25 completing:
  Less than 9th grade: 15.6%, 4th
  High school: 64.3%, 51st
  College degree(s): 14.7%, 48th
Higher education, institutions (1993-94): 47
  Enrollment (1992): 123,754
    Percent of pop.: 4.74%, 46th
  White non-Hispanic (1992): 85,331
    Percent of enroll.: 68.95%, 45th
  Black non-Hispanic (1992): 34,496
    Percent of enroll.: 27.87%, 2nd
  Hispanic (1992): 454
    Percent of enroll.: 0.37%, 51st
  Asian/Pacific Islander (1992): 849
    Percent of enroll.: 0.69%, 49th
  American Indian/AK native (1992): 398
    Percent of enroll.: 0.32%, 35th
  Nonresident alien (1992): 2,226
    Percent of enroll.: 1.80%, 45th
  Female (1992): 69,348
    Percent of enroll.: 56.04%, 14th
  Pub. institutions (1993-94): 31
    Enrollment (1992): 109,911
    Percent of enroll.: 88.81%, 9th
  Private institutions (1993-94): 16
    Enrollment (1992): 13,843
    Percent of enroll.: 11.19%, 43rd
  Tuition, public institution (avg., 1993-94):
    $5,093, 39th
  Tuition, private institution (avg., 1993-94):
    $8,125, 48th
Public library systems: 46
  Books & serial vol. per capita: 1.88, 41st
  Govt. expenditure per capita: $5.73, 51st

LAW ENFORCEMENT, COURTS, AND PRISONS

Police protection, corrections, judicial and
    legal functions expenditures (1992):
    $356,000,000
  Per capita: $136, 50th
Police per 10,000 pop. (1993): 17.68, 38th
Prisoners (state & fed.) per 100,000 pop.
    (1993): 3,752.65, 17th
  Percent change (1992-93): 11.3%, 4th
Death penalty: yes, by lethal gas if convicted
    after July 1, 1984
  Under sentence of death (1993): 50, 14th
  Executed (1993): 0

RELIGION, NUMBER AND PERCENT OF POPULATION

Agnostic: 9,132—0.50%, 27th
Buddhist: NA

Christian: 1,720,521—94.20%, 3rd
Hindu: NA
Jewish: 10,959—0.60%, 25th
Muslim: NA
Unitarian: NA
Other: 23,744—1.30%, 24th
None: 51,141—2.80%, 47th
Refused to answer: 10,959—0.60%, 49th

MAKING A LIVING

Personal income per capita (1994): $15,838,
    51st
  Percent increase (1993-94): 7.4%, 5th
Disposable personal income per capita (1994):
    $14,362, 51st
Median income of households (1993):
    $22,191, 51st
Percent of pop. below poverty level (1993):
    24.7%, 3rd
  Percent 65 and over (1990): 29.4%, 1st
Expenditure for energy per person (1992):
    $1,883, 27th

ECONOMY

Civilian labor force (1994): 1,254,000
  Percent of total pop.: 46.98%, 48th
  Percent 65 and over (1990): 2.36%, 38th
  Percent female: 46.09%, 30th
Percent job growth (1980-90): 8.85%, 45th
Major employer industries (1994):
  Agriculture: 41,000—3.6%, 14th
  Construction: 58,000—5.1%, 9th
  Finance, insurance, & real estate: 41,000—
    3.6%, 50th
  Government: 191,000—16.9%, 18th
  Manufacturing: 236,000—20.8%, 12th
  Service: 188,000—16.5%, 49th
  Trade: 194,000—17.1%, 47th
  Transportation, communications, public
    utilities: 69,000—6.1%, 10th
Unemployment rate (1994): 6.62%, 10th
  Male: 6.3%, 15th
  Female: 6.9%, 8th
Total businesses (1991): 79,509
  New business incorps. (1991): 3,602
    Percent of total businesses: 4.53%, 40th
  Business failures (1991): 453
    Percent of total businesses: 0.57%
Agriculture farm income:
  Marketing (1993): $2,605,000,000, 27th
    Average per farm: $66,794.87, 34th
  Leading products (1993): Broilers, cotton,
    soybeans, aquaculture

Average value land & build. per acre (1994): $814, 30th

Percent increase (1990-94): 11.81%, 28th

Govt. payments (1993): $384,000,000, 12th

Average per farm: $9,846.15, 11th

Construction, value of all: $592,000,000

Per capita: $230.06, 50th

Manufactures:

Value added: $12,793,000,000

Per capita: $4,971.60, 29th

Leading products: Apparel, furniture, lumber and wood products, foods and food products, electrical machinery and equipment, transportation equipment

Value of nonfuel mineral production (1994): $112,000,000, 43rd

Leading mineral products: Petroleum, natural gas, sand/gravel

Retail sales (1993): $15,336,000,000, 33rd

Per household: $16,306, 50th

Percent increase (1992-93): 5.6%, 34th

Tourism revenues (1993): $3.3 bil.

Foreign exports, in total value (1994): $1,846,000,000, 34th

Per capita: $691.64, 43rd

Gross state product per person (1993): $15,805.71, 51st

Percent change (1990-93): 5.13%, 12th

Patents per 100,000 pop. (1993): 5.30, 51st

Public aid recipients (percent of resident pop. 1993): 11.3%, 2nd

Medicaid recipients per 1,000 pop. (1993): 190.91, 3rd

Medicare recipients per 1,000 pop. (1993): 145.45, 23rd

TRAVEL AND TRANSPORTATION

Motor vehicle registrations (1993): 2,000,000

Per 1,000 pop.: 757.58, 30th

Motorcycle registrations (1993): 28,000

Per 1,000 pop.: 10.61, 39th

Licensed drivers per 1,000 pop. (1993): 621.21, 48th

Deaths from motor vehicle accidents per 100,000 pop. (1993): 30.80, 1st

Public roads & streets (1993):

Total mileage: 72,834

Per 1,000 pop.: 27.59, 15th

Rural mileage: 64,930

Per 1,000 pop.: 24.59, 15th

Urban mileage: 7,904

Per 1,000 pop.: 2.99, 31st

Interstate mileage: 685

Per 1,000 pop.: 0.26, 19th

Annual vehicle-mi. of travel per person (1993): 10,189, 14th

Mean travel time for workers age 16+ who work away from home: 20.6 min., 27th

GOVERNMENT

Percent of voting age pop. registered (1994): 72.8%, 9th

Percent of voting age pop. voting (1994): 44.3%, 33rd

Percent of voting age pop. voting for U.S. representatives (1994): 32.6%, 42nd

State legislators, total (1995): 174, 14th

Women members (1992): 12

Percent of legislature: 6.9%, 47th

U.S. Congress, House members (1995): 5

Change (1985-95): 0

Revenues (1993):

State govt.: $7,205,000,000

Per capita: $2,729.17, 35th

Expenditures (1993):

State govt.: $6,235,000,000

Per capita: $2,361.74, 42nd

Debt outstanding (1993): $1,659,000,000

Per capita: $628.41, 46th

LAWS AND REGULATIONS

Legal driving age: 15

Marriage age without parental consent: Male, 17; female, 15

Divorce residence requirement: 6 mo.

ATTRACTIONS (1995)

Major symphony orchestras: 1

State appropriations for arts agencies per capita: $0.39, 47th

State Fair early October at Jackson

SPORTS AND COMPETITION

NCAA teams (Division I): Alcorn State Univ. Braves, Jackson State Univ. Tigers, Mississippi State Univ. Bulldogs, Mississippi Valley State Univ. Delta Devils, Univ. of Mississippi Rebels, Univ. of Southern Mississippi Golden Eagles

MISSOURI

"I come from a state that raises corn and cotton and cockleburs and Democrats, and frothy eloquence neither convinces nor satisfies me. I am from Missouri. You have got to show me."

Representative Willard D. Vandiver

Missouri is the "Show Me" state, a nickname that stands for intelligent skepticism. The name came into being when Missouri Congressman Willard Duncan Vandiver, in an 1899 speech in Philadelphia, said, "Frothy eloquence neither convinces nor satisfies me. I am from Missouri. You have got to show me." Missouri is a center of transportation. The nation's two greatest rivers, the Mississippi on the eastern border and the Missouri winding through the state, lend themselves to shipping. Fifteen major railroads and many transcontinental airlines service Missouri. The state is sometimes called "the Mother of the West" because it supplied so many of the pioneers who moved on to settle the land between the Missouri and the Pacific Ocean. In recent years, both St. Louis and Kansas City have led the way toward making improvements in infrastructure and other aspects of city life.

SUPERLATIVES

• Nation's tallest monument, the Gateway Arch in St. Louis.
• The University of Missouri—the first state university west of the Mississippi and the first college in the world to grant a journalism degree.
• First in U.S. production of lead.
• Center of U.S. barite mining.
• World's largest shoe manufacturing center, St. Louis.
• First newspaper published west of the Mississippi.
• Home of the Missouri mule.
• First Pony Express run, starting from St. Joseph.
• World's first all-steel railroad bridge.

MOMENTS IN HISTORY

• Father Jacques Marquette and Louis Jolliet floated down the Mississippi in 1673 and found the mouth of the Missouri.

• In 1682, Robert Cavalier, Sieur de La Salle, claimed the entire Mississippi Valley watershed in the name of France.
• In 1735, Ste. Genevieve was founded, the first permanent European settlement in what is now Missouri.
• St. Louis was begun in March 1764 by René Auguste Chouteau.

So They Say

"...the first boat reached the mouth of the gully at the head of which were the marked trees....I put the men to work....They commenced the shed, and the little cabins for the men were built in the vicinity."

René Auguste Chouteau, on the founding of St. Louis

• After France relinquished the area to Spain in 1764, settlers flocked to St. Louis, and the fur trade flourished.
• In 1780, 50 defenders of St. Louis held off more than 1,000 Indians and 24 white traders, keeping the vital Mississippi open to the United States.
• Spain returned the Louisiana territory to France. Then the entire Louisiana territory was bought by the United States in 1803.
• On May 14, 1804, the great Lewis and Clark expedition left St. Louis to explore the country's new territory.
• On December 16, 1811, the area for hundreds of miles around New Madrid was rocked by what has been called the strongest earthquake in North American history.
• Indian wars occurred between 1811 and 1815, but Missouri defenders held out.
• In 1819 the *Western Engineer* was the first steamboat to sail up the Missouri River.
• Missouri was admitted as a slave state on August 10, 1821, after an agreement known as the Missouri Compromise.

• After William H. Becknell blazed the Santa Fe Trail in 1822, fortunes were made in the New Mexico trade.

• In 1831, Mormon leader Joseph Smith and his followers arrived. They founded the towns of Salem and Far West, becoming so powerful that they were persecuted and fled the state. Far West was destroyed, and its site is now a field; the town of Salem remains.

• The University of Missouri was founded in Columbia in 1839.

• By the 1840s, thousands of immigrants began their trips to the far west from various Missouri cities, principally St. Louis, the "Gateway to the West."

• In the conflict over slavery, many from Missouri moved to Kansas in an effort to make it a slave state. They fought with free-state settlers until about 1858.

• Missouri refused to join the Confederacy in the Civil War, and many bloody battles were fought there for this critical state. The last major conflict, the Battle of Westport, was won by the Union on October 13, 1864. But Missouri was the center of raids by Confederate guerrillas.

• By the war's end, Missouri counted 1,100 battles and skirmishes.

• On January 11, 1865, Missouri became the first slave state to free its slaves.

• Former guerrillas turned into bandits, robbed banks, held up trains, and plagued the Midwest until about 1882.

• A border dispute between Missouri and Iowa was settled by the U.S. Supreme Court in 1896.

• In 1904, St. Louis held the Louisiana Purchase Exposition, a great world's fair, celebrating that historic event just over a hundred years later.

• A Missouri native, General John J. Pershing, led the U.S. expeditionary force during World War I.

• On the death of President Franklin D. Roosevelt, Missouri's Harry S Truman became president on April 12, 1945.

• World War II ended in the Pacific when the Japanese signed the surrender on the battleship *Missouri* on September 2, 1945.

• In 1946, Winston Churchill coined the phrase "Iron Curtain" at Fulton.

• The Gateway Arch was dedicated in St. Louis in 1966.

• In the 1980s, Kansas City became Missouri's largest city.

• In 1992 the bones of Missouri native William Clarke Quantrill, the Confederate guerilla, were returned from Ohio and buried in Higginsville.

THAT'S INTERESTING

• From the first steamboat on the Missouri River, smoke poured out of a stack made like a dragon's head to frighten the Indians.

• St. Louis is perhaps the only major city to have been founded by a 14-year-old boy—Auguste Chouteau, who undertook the task at the request of his patron, Pierre Laclede Liguest.

• The ice cream cone is said by some to have originated at the St. Louis world's fair of 1904.

NOTABLE NATIVES

Josephine Baker (St. Louis, 1906-1975), entertainer. **Thomas Hart Benton** (Neosho, 1889-1975), painter. **Omar Nelson Bradley** (Clark, 1893-1981), soldier. **Dale Carnegie** (Maryville, 1888-1935), author/teacher of public speaking. **George Washington Carver** (near Diamond Grove, 1864?-1943), agronomist/chemist. **Winston Churchill** (St. Louis, 1871-1947), novelist. **Samuel Langhorne Clemens (Mark Twain)** (Florida, 1835-1910), humorist/author. **Walter Leland Cronkite, Jr.** (St. Joseph, 1916-), journalist/commentator. **Ginger Rogers (Virginia McMath)** (Independence, 1911-1995), actress/dancer. **Thomas Stearns (T. S.) Eliot** (St. Louis, 1888-1965), poet/critic. **Eugene**

Field (St. Louis, 1850-1895), author/poet.
James Langston Hughes (Joplin, 1902-1967),
author. James Cash Penney (Hamilton, 1875-
1971), merchant. John Joseph Pershing
(Laclede, 1860-1948), soldier. Harry S Truman (Lamar, 1884-1972), U.S. president.

GENERAL

Admitted to statehood: August 10, 1821
Origin of name: Algonquin Indian tribe
    named after Missouri River, meaning
    "muddy water"
Capital: Jefferson City
Nickname: Show Me State
Motto: *Salus Populi Suprema Lex Esto*—The
    welfare of the people shall be the su-
    preme law
Bird: Eastern bluebird
Flower: Hawthorn blossom
Mineral: Galena (lead)
Stone: Mozarkite
Song: "Missouri Waltz"
Tree: Flowering dogwood

THE LAND

Area: 69,709 sq. mi., 21st
  Land: 68,898 sq. mi., 18th
  Water: 811 sq. mi., 32nd
    Inland water: 811 sq. mi., 26th
Topography: Rolling hills, open, fertile plains,
    and well-watered prairie N of the Mis-
    souri River; S of the river land is rough
    and hilly with deep, narrow valleys; al-
    luvial plain in the SE; low elevation in
    the W
Number of counties: 114
Geographic center: Miller, 20 mi. SW of Jef-
    ferson City
Length: 300 mi.; width: 240 mi.
Highest point: 1,772 ft. (Taum Sauk Moun-
    tain), 41st
Lowest point: 230 ft. (St. Francis River), 30th
Mean elevation: 800 ft., 32nd

CLIMATE AND ENVIRONMENT

Temp., highest: 118 deg. on July 14, 1954, at
    Warsaw and Union; lowest: −40 deg.
    on Feb. 13, 1905, at Warsaw
Monthly average: highest: 90.5 deg., 19th;
    lowest: 19.4 deg., 24th; spread (high to
    low): 71.1 deg., 21st
Hazardous waste sites (1993): 23, 17th
Endangered species: Mammals: 3—Gray bat,
    Indiana bat, Ozark big-eared bat; birds:

3—American peregrine falcon, Least
tern, Alabama beach mouse; reptiles:
none; amphibians: none; fishes: 1; invertebrates: 4; plants: 3

MAJOR CITIES
POPULATION, 1990
PERCENTAGE INCREASE, 1980-90

Independence, 112,301—0.45%
Kansas City, 435,146— −2.88%
Saint Joseph, 71,852— −6.31%
St. Louis, 396,685— −12.39%
Springfield, 140,494—5.54%

THE PEOPLE

Population (1995): 5,323,523, 16th
    Percent change (1990-95): 4.0%, 32nd
Population (2000 proj.): 5,437,000, 17th
    Percent change (1990-2000): 6.3%, 35th
Per sq. mi. (1994): 76.6, 28th
Percent in metro. area (1992): 68.3%, 28th
Foreign born: 84,000, 27th
    Percent: 1.6%, 41st
Top three ancestries reported:
    German, 36.02%
    Irish, 20.29%
    English, 14.52%
White: 4,486,228, 87.67%, 25th
Black: 584,208, 11.42%, 19th
Native American: 19,835, 0.39%, 29th
Asian, Pacific Isle: 41,277, 0.81%, 35th
Other races: 21,525, 0.42%, 39th
Hispanic origin: 61,702, 1.21%, 37th
Percent over 5 yrs. speaking language other
    than English at home: 3.8%, 44th
Percent males: 48.16%, 42nd; percent fe-
    males: 51.84%, 10th
Percent never married: 23.9%, 37th
Marriages per 1,000 (1993): 8.4, 27th
Divorces per 1,000 (1993): 5.1, 18th
Median age: 33.5
Under 5 years (1994): 7.12%, 31st
Under 18 years (1994): 26.13%, 23rd
65 years & older (1994): 14.1%, 10th
Percent increase among the elderly (1990-94):
    3.81%, 38th

OF VITAL IMPORTANCE

Live births per 1,000 pop. (1993): 14.8,
    24th
Infant mortality rate per 1,000 births (1992):
    8.5, 27th
    Rate for blacks (1990): 17.5, 12th
    Rate for whites (1990): 7.8, 27th

Births to unmarried women, % of total (1992): 31.5%, 18th
Births to teenage mothers, % of total (1992): 14.5%, 16th
Abortions (1992): 13,510, 27th
Rate per 1,000 women 14-44 years old: 11.6, 43rd
Percent change (1988-92): –29%, 51st
Average lifetime (1979-81): 73.84, 26th
Deaths per 1,000 pop. (1993): 10.8, 3rd
Causes of death per 100,000 pop.:
Accidents & adverse effects (1992): 41.1, 16th
Atherosclerosis (1991): 7.6, 19th
Cancer (1991): 227.5, 12th
Cerebrovascular diseases (1992): 66.5, 11th
Chronic liver diseases & cirrhosis (1991): 8.5, 34th
Chronic obstructive pulmonary diseases (1992): 42.8, 10th
Diabetes mellitus (1992): 20.8, 25th
Diseases of heart (1992): 341.9, 7th
Pneumonia, flu (1991): 36.6, 10th
Suicide (1992): 12.1, 31st

KEEPING WELL

Active nonfederal physicians per 100,000 pop. (1993): 207, 22nd
Dentists per 100,000 (1991): 53, 29th
Nurses per 100,000 (1992): 812, 18th
Hospitals per 100,000 (1993): 2.48, 23rd
Admissions per 1,000 (1993): 134.69, 13th
Occupancy rate per 100 beds (1993): 58.9, 34th
Average cost per patient per day (1993): $863, 24th
Average cost per stay (1993): $6,161, 16th
Average stay (1992): 7.5 days, 18th
AIDS cases (adult, 1993): 1,745; per 100,000: 33.3, 17th
HIV infection, not yet AIDS (1993): 2,810
Other notifiable diseases:
Gonorrhea: 391.2, 10th
Measles: 2.0, 35th
Syphilis: 11.7, 31st
Tuberculosis: 6.1, 28th
Pop. without health insur. (1991-93): 13.0%, 24th

HOUSEHOLDS BY TYPE

Total households (1994): 2,008,000
Percent change (1990-94): 2.4%, 36th
Per 1,000 pop.: 380.45, 10th
Percent of households 65 yrs. and over: 23.80%, 10th
Persons per household (1994): 2.56, 35th
Family households: 1,368,334
Percent of total: 69.77%, 31st
Nonfamily households: 592,872
Percent of total: 30.23%, 21st
Pop. living in group quarters: 145,397
Percent of pop.: 2.84%, 24th

LIVING QUARTERS

Total housing units: 2,199,129
Persons per unit: 2.33, 37th
Occupied housing units: 1,961,206
Percent of total units: 89.18%, 27th
Persons per unit: 2.46, 44th
Percent of units with over 1 person per room: 2.46%, 37th
Owner-occupied units: 1,348,746
Percent of total units: 61.33%, 15th
Percent of occupied units: 68.77%, 16th
Persons per unit: 2.67, 38th
Median value: $59,800, 34th
Renter-occupied units: 612,460
Percent of total units: 27.85%, 32nd
Percent of occupied units: 31.23%, 36th
Persons per unit: 2.24, 42nd
Median contract rent: $282, 35th
Rental vacancy rate: 10.7%, 13th
Mobile home, trailer & other as a percent of occupied housing units: 9.28%, 29th
Persons in emergency shelters for homeless persons: 2,276, 0.044%, 29th
Persons visible in street locations: 215, 0.0042%, 33rd
Persons in shelters for abused women: 117, 0.0023%, 51st
Nursing home population: 52,060, 1.02%, 9th

CRIME INDEX PER 100,000 (1992-93)

Total reported: 5,095.4, 24th
Violent: 744.4, 17th
Murder and nonnegligent manslaughter: 11.3, 11th
Aggravated assault: 455.2, 18th
Robbery: 241.8, 11th
Forcible rape: 36.2, 28th
Property: 4,351.0, 26th
Burglary: 1,028.5, 22nd
Larceny, theft: 2,777.8, 31st
Motor vehicle theft: 547.7, 19th

Drug abuse violations (1990): 269.1, 23rd

Child-abuse rate per 1,000 children (1993): 15.02, 23rd

TEACHING AND LEARNING

Pop. 3 and over enrolled in school: 1,292,623
  Percent of pop.: 26.4%, 37th

Public elementary & secondary schools (1992-93): 2,188
  Total enrollment (1992): 859,357
    Percent of total pop.: 16.55%, 35th
  Teachers (1992): 52,994
    Percent of pop.: 1.02%, 28th
  Pupil/teacher ratio (fall 1992): 16.2, 31st
  Teachers' avg. salary (1992-93): $31,391, 36th
  Expenditure per capita (1990-91): $2,663.88, 50th
  Expenditure per pupil (1991-92): $4,830, 33rd

Percent of graduates taking SAT (1993): 11%, 35th
  Mean SAT verbal scores: 481, 10th
  Mean SAT mathematical scores: 532, 10th

Percent of graduates taking ACT (1995): 64%, 12th
  Mean ACT scores: 21.3, 17th

Percent of pop. over 25 completing:
  Less than 9th grade: 11.6%, 14th
  High school: 73.9%, 38th
  College degree(s): 17.8%, 34th

Higher education, institutions (1993-94): 98
  Enrollment (1992): 296,617
    Percent of pop.: 5.71%, 22nd
  White non-Hispanic (1992): 252,664
    Percent of enroll.: 85.18%, 21st
  Black non-Hispanic (1992): 25,484
    Percent of enroll.: 8.59%, 20th
  Hispanic (1992): 4,030
    Percent of enroll.: 1.36%, 34th
  Asian/Pacific Islander (1992): 5,496
    Percent of enroll.: 1.85%, 29th
  American Indian/AK native (1992): 1,253
    Percent of enroll.: 0.42%, 25th
  Nonresident alien (1992): 7,690
    Percent of enroll.: 2.59%, 26th
  Female (1992): 162,168
    Percent of enroll.: 54.67%, 34th
  Pub. institutions (1993-94): 30
    Enrollment (1992): 198,610
    Percent of enroll.: 66.96%, 43rd
  Private institutions (1993-94): 68
    Enrollment (1992): 98,007
    Percent of enroll.: 33.04%, 9th

Tuition, public institution (avg., 1993-94): $5,836, 26th

Tuition, private institution (avg., 1993-94): $12,417, 28th

Public library systems: 155
  Books & serial vol. per capita: 3.38, 14th
  Govt. expenditure per capita: $12.58, 32nd

LAW ENFORCEMENT, COURTS, AND PRISONS

Police protection, corrections, judicial and legal functions expenditures (1992): $1.020,000,000
  Per capita: $197, 41st

Police per 10,000 pop. (1993): 19.65, 31st

Prisoners (state & fed.) per 100,000 pop. (1993): 3,090.35, 23rd
  Percent change (1992-93): –0.1%, 42nd

Death penalty: yes, by lethal gas or lethal injection
  Under sentence of death (1993): 80, 13th
  Executed (1993): 4

RELIGION, NUMBER AND PERCENT OF POPULATION

Agnostic: 15,209—0.40%, 34th
Buddhist: 3,802—0.10%, 17th
Christian: 3,372,593—88.70%, 17th
Hindu: NA
Jewish: 22,814—0.60%, 25th
Muslim: NA
Unitarian: 7,605—0.20%, 23rd
Other: 49,429—1.30%, 24th
None: 247,146—6.50%, 25th
Refused to answer: 83,650—2.20%, 23rd

MAKING A LIVING

Personal income per capita (1994): $20,717, 25th
  Percent increase (1993-94): 5.9%, 12th

Disposable personal income per capita (1994): $18,226, 23rd

Median income of households (1993): $28,682, 34th

Percent of pop. below poverty level (1993): 16.1%, 16th

Percent 65 and over (1990): 14.8%, 16th

Expenditure for energy per person (1992): $1,779, 38th

ECONOMY

Civilian labor force (1994): 2,695,000
  Percent of total pop.: 51.06%, 25th

Percent 65 and over (1990): 2.62%, 30th
Percent female: 46.16%, 29th
Percent job growth (1980-90): 19.25%, 25th
Major employer industries (1994):
  Agriculture: 100,000—4.0%, 13th
  Construction: 99,000—4.0%, 29th
  Finance, insurance, & real estate: 119,000—4.8%, 34th
  Government: 318,000—12.8%, 44th
  Manufacturing: 435,000—17.5%, 16th
  Service: 559,000—22.5%, 20th
  Trade: 507,000—20.4%, 6th
  Transportation, communications, public utilities: 148,000—6.0%, 11th
Unemployment rate (1994): 4.86%, 39th
  Male: 4.9%, 36th
  Female: 4.8%, 38th
Total businesses (1991): 172,165
  New business incorps. (1991): 9,521
    Percent of total businesses: 5.53%, 29th
  Business failures (1991): 1,221
    Percent of total businesses: 0.71%
Agriculture farm income:
  Marketing (1993): $4,053,000,000, 17th
    Average per farm: $38,235.85, 46th
  Leading products (1993): Cattle, soybeans, hogs, corn
  Average value land & build. per acre (1994): $762, 33rd
    Percent increase (1990-94): 12.22%, 27th
  Govt. payments (1993): $455,000,000, 10th
    Average per farm: $4,292.45, 24th
Construction, value of all: $2,522,000,000
  Per capita: $492.86, 29th
Manufactures:
  Value added: $30,255,000,000
    Per capita: $5,912.56, 13th
  Leading products: Transportation equipment, food and food products, electric and electronic equipment, chemicals
Value of nonfuel mineral production (1994): $1,003,000,000, 10th
Leading mineral products: Lead, cement, stone
Retail sales (1993): $44,823,000,000, 15th
  Per household: $22,154, 23rd
    Percent increase (1992-93): 7.5%, 24th
Tourism revenues (1993): $5 bil.
Foreign exports, in total value (1994): $3,541,000,000, 28th
  Per capita: $670.90, 45th

Gross state product per person (1993): $20,550.60, 29th
  Percent change (1990-93): 2.91%, 31st
Patents per 100,000 pop. (1993): 14.27, 31st
Public aid recipients (percent of resident pop. 1993): 6.9%, 24th
Medicaid recipients per 1,000 pop. (1993): 116.33, 26th
Medicare recipients per 1,000 pop. (1993): 155.49, 10th

TRAVEL AND TRANSPORTATION

Motor vehicle registrations (1993): 4,066,000
  Per 1,000 pop.: 776.70, 27th
Motorcycle registrations (1993): 57,000
  Per 1,000 pop.: 10.89, 37th
Licensed drivers per 1,000 pop. (1993): 663.23, 38th
Deaths from motor vehicle accidents per 100,000 pop. (1993): 18.13, 22nd
Public roads & streets (1993):
  Total mileage: 121,787
    Per 1,000 pop.: 23.26, 17th
  Rural mileage: 105,637
    Per 1,000 pop.: 20.18, 18th
  Urban mileage: 16,150
    Per 1,000 pop.: 3.09, 27th
  Interstate mileage: 1,178
    Per 1,000 pop.: 0.23, 21st
Annual vehicle-mi. of travel per person (1993): 10,468, 7th
Mean travel time for workers age 16+ who work away from home: 21.6 min., 16th

GOVERNMENT

Percent of voting age pop. registered (1994): 72.3%, 12th
  Percent of voting age pop. voting (1994): 54.5%, 10th
  Percent of voting age pop. voting for U.S. representatives (1994): 45.2%, 13th
State legislators, total (1995): 197, 7th
  Women members (1992): 31
    Percent of legislature: 15.7%, 28th
U.S. Congress, House members (1995): 9
  Change (1985-95): 0
Revenues (1993):
  State govt.: $12,559,000,000
    Per capita: $2,399.04, 48th
  Parimutuel & amusement taxes & lotteries, revenue per capita: $46.04, 33rd
Expenditures (1993):
  State govt.: $10,809,000,000
    Per capita: $2,064.76, 50th

Debt outstanding (1993): $6,516,000,000
    Per capita: $1,244.70, 27th

LAWS AND REGULATIONS

Legal driving age: 16
Marriage age without parental consent: 18
Divorce residence requirement: 90 days

ATTRACTIONS (1995)

Major opera companies: 2
Major symphony orchestras: 2
Major dance companies: 1
Major professional theater companies (nonprofit): 2
State appropriations for arts agencies per capita: $0.86, 20th
State Fair in the 3rd week in August at Sedalia

SPORTS AND COMPETITION

NCAA teams (Division I): St. Louis Univ. Billikens, Southeast Missouri State Univ. Indians, Southwest Missouri State Univ. Bears, Univ. of Missouri-Columbia Tigers, Univ. of Missouri-Kansas City Kangaroos

Major league baseball teams: St. Louis Cardinals (NL Central), Busch Stadium; Kansas City Royals (AL Central), Ewing Kauffman Stadium

NFL football teams: Kansas City Chiefs (AFC), Arrowhead Stadium; St. Louis Rams (NFC), Trans World Dome

NHL hockey teams: St. Louis Blues, Kiel Center

MONTANA

"I am in love with Montana. Montana seems to me to be what a small boy would think Texas is like from hearing Texans."

John Steinbeck, novelist

Montana is "Big Sky Country," a land of tall, rugged mountains in the west and broad plains in the east. The mountains have produced a great wealth of gold and silver, and some of the peaks in Glacier National Park are so steep and remote that they have never been climbed. On the prairies, huge herds of cattle graze. Montana's history recounts one of the nation's most memorable events, the Battle of Little Bighorn. Tourists feel close to the old frontier days in Montana when they visit the mountains, the battlefields, the old gold-mining camps, and the vast, lonely plains. The Indians knew the area as the Shining Land, and, despite some societal problems, the name still fits.

SUPERLATIVES

- "Birthplace" of the Missouri River.
- First woman in U.S. House—Jeannette Rankin, 1917.
- Site of Custer's Last Stand.

> ### So They Say
>
> "You cannot afford not to vote. You represent the womanhood of the country in the American Congress." — "I cannot vote for war...I vote No."
>
> Representatives Joseph Cannon and Jeannette Rankin, on her vote against World War I

MOMENTS IN HISTORY

- The La Vérendrye brothers, Francis and Louis Joseph, are said to have reached Montana in 1742, before any other Europeans are known to have come.
- James Mackay paid a visit to the region about 1795 and named the Yellowstone River.
- Little was known about the area until the great exploration of Meriwether Lewis and William Clark reached what is now Montana in 1805.

- On July 25, 1805, Lewis and Clark made a dramatic discovery. After much searching and discussion they concluded that the place where three rivers met was the long-sought "ultimate source of the Missouri River."

> ### So They Say
>
> "We were now about to penetrate a country at least two thousand miles in width, on which the foot of civilized man had never trodden."
>
> Meriwether Lewis

- On their way back to St. Louis, Lewis and Clark again entered and passed through what is now Montana on June 29, 1806.
- Many traders took advantage of the explorers' discoveries. In 1807, Manuel Lisa built a trading post fort where the Yellowstone and Big Horn rivers meet.
- The first steamboat reached Fort Union in 1832.
- By means of infected blankets, the white "civilization" deliberately brought a terrible smallpox epidemic to the Indians in 1837.
- St. Mary's Mission was founded in 1842.
- The main beaver trapping period lasted until about 1843.
- In 1858, John Mullan began the Mullan Road, which became the first wagon road over the northern Rockies.

> ### So They Say
>
> "Out there every prairie dog hole is a gold mine, every hill a mountain, every creek a river, and everybody you meet is a liar."
>
> Anonymous

- The mid-1850s found some disappointed miners from the California gold fields coming to Montana in search of possible rich finds there.

• John White made the first real gold discovery in July 1862, and Camp Bannack reached a population of 500 within a few days. A number of other gold discoveries were made as time went on.

• Montana territory was created on May 26, 1864.

• Butte was founded in 1864, after it started as a gold camp.

• The best known battle with the Indians in the nation's history took place at the Little Bighorn River on June 25, 1876. Civil War hero George Armstrong Custer led his troops into a massacre, and he and his entire force were killed. One horse was the lone survivor of the Custer forces.

So They Say

"Every man kept fighting to the last. There were no cowards on either side....Long Hair [Custer] was not scalped. He was a great chief. My people did not want his scalp."

Chief Sitting Bull

• Another Indian battle with an entirely different ending occurred on August 7, 1877. Brave and brilliant Chief Joseph of the Nez Percé tribe surrendered after the Battle of Big Hole Prairie.

So They Say

"Our chiefs are dead; the little children are freezing. My people have no blankets, no food. From where the sun now stands, I will fight no more, forever."

Chief Joseph

• The Northern Pacific Railroad arrived on July 5, 1881.

• Statehood was achieved on November 8, 1889.

• The United States and Canada cooperated to create the International Peace Park in 1932, with Glacier National Park (established in 1910) as the U.S. portion.

• On August 17, 1959, a severe earthquake caused damage over a wide area. A mountainside collapsed across the Madison River, creating Earthquake Lake.

• The state adopted a new constitution in 1978.

• In 1985, Glacier National Park celebrated its 75th anniversary.

• In 1992 the House of Representatives voted to shelter 1.5 million acres of Montana wilderness from development.

THAT'S INTERESTING

• On the present site of Helena, a little party of gold miners agreed that they had reached their "last chance" to find wealth. Then they made a strike on what is now the city's main street, Last Chance Gulch.

• In 1867, Montana's territorial governor, Francis Meagher, a hero of the Civil War, boarded a Missouri River steamboat at Fort Benton, went to his stateroom, and was never seen again.

• Montana Indians believed that stealing a horse was the best way to show bravery.

• Early visitors to Montana prairies noted the many mounds of earth covered with flowers and were startled to learn that these were the sod houses of the settlers.

• In a house near Frenchtown, four brothers were born, but each was born in a different territory. Before statehood Montana had been a part of five territories.

• Montana shepherds spent many lonely hours piling rocks into high stacks called cairns. Some cairns can still be seen.

NOTABLE NATIVES

Gary Cooper (Helena, 1901-1961), actor. **Chet Huntley** (Cardwell, 1911-1974), journalist/commentator. **Myrna Loy** (Radersburg, 1905-1993), actress. **Jeannette Rankin** (near Missoula, 1880-1973), suffragist/public official. **Sacajawea** (in either western Montana or eastern Idaho, 1787?-1812?), Indian guide. **Washakie** (in what is now Montana, 1804?-1900), Indian leader.

GENERAL

Admitted to statehood: November 8, 1889
Origin of name: Latin or Spanish for "mountainous"
Capital: Helena
Nickname: Treasure State
Motto: *Oro y Plata*—Gold and silver
Bird: Western meadowlark
Flower: Bitterroot
Stone: Sapphire, agate

Song: "Montana"
Tree: Ponderosa pine

THE LAND

Area: 147,046 sq. mi., 4th
  Land: 145,556 sq. mi., 4th
  Water: 1,490 sq. mi., 19th
    Inland water: 1,490 sq. mi., 15th
Topography: Rocky Mountains in western
    third of the state; eastern two-thirds
    gently rolling northern Great Plains
Number of counties: 56
Geographic center: Fergus, 11 mi. W of
    Lewistown
Length: 630 mi.; width: 280 mi.
Highest point: 12,799 ft. (Granite Peak), 10th
Lowest point: 1,800 ft., (Kootenai River),
    47th
Mean elevation: 3,400 ft., 8th

CLIMATE AND ENVIRONMENT

Temp., highest: 117 deg. on July 5, 1937, at
    Medicine Lake; lowest: –7 deg. on Jan.
    20, 1954, at Rogers Pass
Monthly average: highest: 86.6 deg., 30th;
    lowest: 8.1 deg., 8th; spread (high to
    low): 78.5 deg., 8th
Hazardous waste sites (1993): 8, 41st
Endangered species: Mammals: 2—Black-
    footed ferret, Northern Rocky Moun-
    tain gray wolf; birds: 3—Whooping
    crane, American peregrine falcon, Least
    tern; reptiles: none; amphibians: none;
    fishes: 1; invertebrates: none; plants:
    none

MAJOR CITIES
POPULATION, 1990
PERCENTAGE INCREASE, 1980-90

Billings, 81,151—21.46%
Butte, 33,336— –10.40%
Great Falls, 55,097— –3.14%
Helena, 24,569—2.64%
Missoula, 42,918—28.69%

THE PEOPLE

Population (1995): 870,281, 44th
  Percent change (1990-95): 8.9%, 13th
Population (2000 proj.): 920,000, 44th
  Percent change (1990-2000): 15.13%, 16th
Per sq. mi. (1994): 5.9, 49th
Percent in metro. area (1992): 24.0%, 51st
Foreign born: 14,000, 48th
  Percent: 1.7%, 37th

Top three ancestries reported:
  German, 35.67%
  Irish, 17.40%
  English, 17.15%
White: 741,111, 92.75%, 13th
Black: 2,381, 0.30%, 51st
Native American: 47,679, 5.97%, 5th
Asian, Pacific Isle: 4,259, 0.53%, 46th
Other races: 3,635, 0.45%, 38th
Hispanic origin: 12,174, 1.52%, 34th
Percent over 5 yrs. speaking language other
    than English at home: 5.0%, 37th
Percent males: 49.53%, 10th; percent females:
    50.47%, 42nd
Percent never married: 22.3%, 46th
Marriages per 1,000 (1993): 8.4, 27th
Divorces per 1,000 (1993): 5.1, 18th
Median age: 33.8
Under 5 years (1994): 6.89%, 41st
Under 18 years (1994): 27.80%, 11th
65 years & older (1994): 13.3%, 22nd
Percent increase among the elderly (1990-94):
    7.05%, 21st

OF VITAL IMPORTANCE

Live births per 1,000 pop. (1993): 13.6, 44th
Infant mortality rate per 1,000 births (1992):
    7.5, 37th
  Rate for blacks (1990): 13.3, 36th
  Rate for whites (1990): 8.6, 9th
Births to unmarried women, % of total
    (1992): 26.4%, 32nd
Births to teenage mothers, % of total (1992):
    11.9%, 29th
Abortions (1992): 3,300, 44th
  Rate per 1,000 women 14-44 years old:
    18.2, 27th
  Percent change (1988-92): 11%, 4th
Average lifetime (1979-81): 73.93, 24th
Deaths per 1,000 pop. (1993): 8.9, 27th
Causes of death per 100,000 pop.:
  Accidents & adverse effects (1992): 49.5,
    6th
  Atherosclerosis (1991): 13.1, 3rd
  Cancer (1991): 207.6, 26th
  Cerebrovascular diseases (1992): 60.4, 21st
  Chronic liver diseases & cirrhosis (1991):
    9.0, 26th
  Chronic obstructive pulmonary diseases
    (1992): 55.5, 1st
  Diabetes mellitus (1992): 19.5, 32nd
  Diseases of heart (1992): 231.9, 40th
  Pneumonia, flu (1991): 30.3, 26th
  Suicide (1992): 18.6, 3rd

KEEPING WELL

Active nonfederal physicians per 100,000 pop. (1993): 169, 41st

Dentists per 100,000 (1991): 56, 20th

Nurses per 100,000 (1992): 715, 26th

Hospitals per 100,000 (1993): 6.18, 3rd
  Admissions per 1,000 (1993): 115.93, 25th
  Occupancy rate per 100 beds (1993): 64.2, 17th
  Average cost per patient per day (1993): $481, 51st
  Average cost per stay (1993): $4,953, 45th
  Average stay (1992): 18.7 days, 1st

AIDS cases (adult, 1993): 32; per 100,000: 3.8, 49th

HIV infection, not yet AIDS (1993): NA

Other notifiable diseases:
  Gonorrhea: 30.8, 44th
  Measles: 0.1, 49th
  Syphilis: 1.3, 48th
  Tuberculosis: 3.3, 37th

Pop. without health insur. (1991-93): 12.5%, 30th

HOUSEHOLDS BY TYPE

Total households (1994): 325,000
  Percent change (1990-94): 6.1%, 18th
  Per 1,000 pop.: 379.67, 12th
  Percent of households 65 yrs. and over: 22.46%, 21st
  Persons per household (1994): 2.56, 35th

Family households: 211,666
  Percent of total: 69.14%, 36th

Nonfamily households: 94,497
  Percent of total: 30.86%, 16th

Pop. living in group quarters: 23,747
  Percent of pop.: 2.97%, 20th

LIVING QUARTERS

Total housing units: 361,155
  Persons per unit: 2.21, 45th

Occupied housing units: 306,163
  Percent of total units: 84.77%, 43rd
  Persons per unit: 2.47, 42nd
  Percent of units with over 1 person per room: 2.90%, 27th

Owner-occupied units: 205,899
  Percent of total units: 57.01%, 35th
  Percent of occupied units: 67.25%, 26th
  Persons per unit: 2.65, 42nd
  Median value: $56,600, 39th

Renter-occupied units: 100,264
  Percent of total units: 27.76%, 34th
  Percent of occupied units: 32.75%, 26th

Persons per unit: 2.28, 35th
  Median contract rent: $251, 44th
  Rental vacancy rate: 9.6%, 16th

Mobile home, trailer & other as a percent of occupied housing units: 19.13%, 5th

Persons in emergency shelters for homeless persons: 445, 0.056%, 19th

Persons visible in street locations: 17, 0.0021%, 44th

Persons in shelters for abused women: 49, 0.0061%, 11th

Nursing home population: 7,764, 0.97%, 11th

CRIME INDEX PER 100,000 (1992-93)

Total reported: 4,790.0, 31st
  Violent: 177.5, 47th
    Murder and nonnegligent manslaughter: 3.0, 46th
    Aggravated assault: 114.2, 47th
    Robbery: 32.4, 44th
    Forcible rape: 27.9, 42nd
  Property: 4,612.5, 22nd
    Burglary: 714.2, 41st
    Larceny, theft: 3,652.1, 10th
    Motor vehicle theft: 246.2, 39th

Drug abuse violations (1990): 129.0, 41st

Child-abuse rate per 1,000 children (1993): 20.81, 10th

TEACHING AND LEARNING

Pop. 3 and over enrolled in school: 215,759
  Percent of pop.: 28.2%, 15th

Public elementary & secondary schools (1992-93): 899
  Total enrollment (1992): 160,011
    Percent of total pop.: 19.47%, 7th
  Teachers (1992): 10,135
    Percent of pop.: 1.23%, 8th
  Pupil/teacher ratio (fall 1992): 15.8, 33rd
  Teachers' avg. salary (1992-93): $29,590, 42nd
  Expenditure per capita (1990-91): $3,503.02, 22nd
  Expenditure per pupil (1991-92): $5,423, 20th

Percent of graduates taking SAT (1993): 24%, 28th
  Mean SAT verbal scores: 459, 22nd
  Mean SAT mathematical scores: 516, 20th

Percent of graduates taking ACT (1995): 56%, 24th
  Mean ACT scores: 21.8, 6th

Percent of pop. over 25 completing:
  Less than 9th grade: 8.1%, 35th
  High school: 81.0%, 11th
  College degree(s): 19.8%, 25th
Higher education, institutions (1993-94): 20
  Enrollment (1992): 39,644
    Percent of pop.: 4.82%, 42nd
  White non-Hispanic (1992): 33,501
    Percent of enroll.: 84.50%, 22nd
  Black non-Hispanic (1992): 133
    Percent of enroll.: 0.34%, 51st
  Hispanic (1992): 371
    Percent of enroll.: 0.94%, 40th
  Asian/Pacific Islander (1992): 214
    Percent of enroll.: 0.54%, 51st
  American Indian/AK native (1992): 4,240
    Percent of enroll.: 10.70%, 1st
  Nonresident alien (1992): 1,185
    Percent of enroll.: 2.99%, 17th
  Female (1992): 21,120
    Percent of enroll.: 53.27%, 47th
  Pub. institutions (1993-94): 14
    Enrollment (1992): 33,765
    Percent of enroll.: 85.17%, 19th
  Private institutions (1993-94): 6
    Enrollment (1992): 5,879
    Percent of enroll.: 14.83%, 33rd
  Tuition, public institution (avg., 1993-94): $5,665, 28th
  Tuition, private institution (avg., 1993-94): $9,944, 41st
Public library systems: 82
  Books & serial vol. per capita: 3.01, 20th
  Govt. expenditure per capita: $11.71, 38th

LAW ENFORCEMENT, COURTS, AND PRISONS

Police protection, corrections, judicial and legal functions expenditures (1992): $173,000,000
  Per capita: $210, 37th
Police per 10,000 pop. (1993): 15.94, 42nd
Prisoners (state & fed.) per 100,000 pop. (1993): 1,832.34, 41st
  Percent change (1992-93): –0.5%, 47th
Death penalty: yes, by hanging or lethal injection
  Under sentence of death (1993): 6, 30th
  Executed (1993): 0

RELIGION, NUMBER AND PERCENT OF POPULATION

Agnostic: 3,462—0.60%, 19th
Buddhist: NA

Christian: 490,417—85.00%, 33rd
Hindu: NA
Jewish: NA
Muslim: NA
Unitarian: 1,731—0.30%, 15th
Other: 6,924—1.20%, 29th
None: 58,850—10.20%, 10th
Refused to answer: 15,578—2.70%, 16th

MAKING A LIVING

Personal income per capita (1994): $17,865, 42nd
  Percent increase (1993-94): 2.8%, 49th
Disposable personal income per capita (1994): $15,615, 44th
Median income of households (1993): $26,470, 42nd
Percent of pop. below poverty level (1993): 14.9%, 20th
  Percent 65 and over (1990): 12.5%, 20th
Expenditure for energy per person (1992): $2,091, 7th

ECONOMY

Civilian labor force (1994): 437,000
  Percent of total pop.: 51.05%, 27th
  Percent 65 and over (1990): 3.98%, 5th
  Percent female: 46.91%, 16th
Percent job growth (1980-90): 9.42%, 44th
Major employer industries (1994):
  Agriculture: 39,000—9.8%, 3rd
  Construction: 16,000—4.0%, 29th
  Finance, insurance, & real estate: 14,000—3.4%, 51st
  Government: 82,000—20.5%, 6th
  Manufacturing: 24,000—5.9%, 45th
  Service: 73,000—18.2%, 44th
  Trade: 77,000—19.2%, 20th
  Transportation, communications, public utilities: 23,000—5.6%, 20th
Unemployment rate (1994): 5.03%, 35th
  Male: 5.3%, 31st
  Female: 4.8%, 38th
Total businesses (1991): 43,961
  New business incorps. (1991): 1,572
    Percent of total businesses: 3.58%, 47th
  Business failures (1991): 191
    Percent of total businesses: 0.43%
Agriculture farm income:
  Marketing (1993): $1,781,000,000, 32nd
    Average per farm: $71,240.00, 29th
  Leading products (1993): Cattle, wheat, barley, hay

Average value land & build. per acre
(1994): $302, 45th
Percent increase (1990-94): 26.89%, 4th
Govt. payments (1993): $338,000,000, 15th
Average per farm: $13,520.00, 5th
Construction, value of all: $282,000,000
Per capita: $352.91, 42nd
Manufactures:
Value added: $1,190,000,000
Per capita: $1,489.24, 48th
Leading products: Food products, wood
and paper products, primary metals,
printing and publishing, petroleum and
coal products
Value of nonfuel mineral production (1994):
$492,000,000, 24th
Leading mineral products: Petroleum, coal,
natural gas
Retail sales (1993): $7,220,000,000, 44th
Per household: $22,354, 20th
Percent increase (1992-93): 12.2%, 2nd
Tourism revenues (1994): $1.2 bil.
Foreign exports, in total value (1994):
$328,000,000, 49th
Per capita: $383.18, 49th
Gross state product per person (1993):
$17,326.73, 48th
Percent change (1990-93): 7.69%, 4th
Patents per 100,000 pop. (1993): 12.84, 34th
Public aid recipients (percent of resident pop.
1993): 5.6%, 35th
Medicaid recipients per 1,000 pop. (1993):
105.83, 29th
Medicare recipients per 1,000 pop. (1993):
148.63, 16th

TRAVEL AND TRANSPORTATION

Motor vehicle registrations (1993): 939,000
Per 1,000 pop.: 1,116.53, 3rd
Motorcycle registrations (1993): 22,000
Per 1,000 pop.: 26.16, 9th
Licensed drivers per 1,000 pop. (1993):
631.39, 45th
Deaths from motor vehicle accidents per
100,000 pop. (1993): 23.07, 9th
Public roads & streets (1993):
Total mileage: 69,768
Per 1,000 pop.: 82.96, 3rd
Rural mileage: 67,388
Per 1,000 pop.: 80.13, 3rd

Urban mileage: 2,380
Per 1,000 pop.: 2.83, 37th
Interstate mileage: 1,190
Per 1,000 pop.: 1.41, 3rd
Annual vehicle-mi. of travel per person
(1993): 10,345, 11th
Mean travel time for workers age 16+ who
work away from home: 14.8 min.,
49th

GOVERNMENT

Percent of voting age pop. registered (1994):
73.2%, 8th
Percent of voting age pop. voting (1994):
60.7%, 5th
Percent of voting age pop. voting for U.S.
representatives (1994): 56.5%, 3rd
State legislators, total (1995): 150, 19th
Women members (1992): 31
Percent of legislature: 20.7%, 19th
U.S. Congress, House members (1995): 1
Change (1985-95): −1
Revenues (1993):
State govt.: $3,023,000,000
Per capita: $3,594.53, 12th
Parimutuel & amusement taxes & lotteries,
revenue per capita: $41.62, 35th
Expenditures (1993):
State govt.: $2,663,000,000
Per capita: $3,166.47, 16th
Debt outstanding (1993): $1,749,000,000
Per capita: $2,079.67, 15th

LAWS AND REGULATIONS

Legal driving age: 16, 15 if completed driver
education course
Marriage age without parental consent: 18
Divorce residence requirement: 90 days

ATTRACTIONS (1995)

State appropriations for arts agencies per capita:
$1.16, 15th
State Fair in late July-early August at Great
Falls

SPORTS AND COMPETITION

NCAA teams (Division I): Montana State
Univ. Bobcats, Univ. of Montana
Grizzlies

NEBRASKA

"For more than a century the wide Platte Valley has been the high-road to the American West. But Nebraska is more than a mere pathway...a land where the West that was wild continues to mingle with evidences of the most modern civilization...great cattle herds, nuclear reactors power modern industry...superhighways...replacing the ruts of the Oregon trail....Up-to-date cities have grown from the tracks of the Mormon wagons...some of the finest museums, music and other cultural attractions anywhere."

Frank B. Morrison

Once referred to as part of "the great American desert," Nebraska was changed into a land of vast farms through the spirit and determination of its early settlers. In the west are wheat fields as far as the eye can see. In the north-central region, huge herds of beef cattle graze on enormous ranches. In the east, corn, grain, sorghum, and other crops are grown. Nebraska is the only state to bear a nickname based on a college football team—the University of Nebraska Cornhuskers. Football at the university is so popular that on Saturdays when there is a home game, the stadium in Lincoln becomes "the third largest city in the state," after Omaha and Lincoln. Athletic prowess is balanced by notable civic and cultural institutions.

SUPERLATIVES

• Nation's first Homestead grant claimed by a Nebraskan, 1862.
• Capitol ranked among world's ten greatest buildings.
• First in alfalfa and other hays.
• World's largest concentration of meat packing and processing.
• Home of the world's largest health and accident insurance company and headquarters for more than 35 other insurance companies.

MOMENTS IN HISTORY

• In 1699 a Navajo group returned to the Spanish Southwest, probably from the South Platte valley, and they carried trophies indicating that there were French settlers there.
• In an effort to drive the French out, Pedro de Villasur in 1720 attacked them and was killed somewhere along the Platte River, perhaps at the site of Columbus.

• The Platte River is said to have been given its present name by the French brothers Pierre and Paul Mallet during their visit of 1739.
• After the region came to the United States in 1803 as part of the Louisiana Purchase, the explorers Meriwether Lewis and William Clark reached the mouth of the Platte on July 21, 1804.
• Lewis and Clark made their last camp in Nebraska on September 7, 1804, and continued up the Missouri River. They returned back down the river in 1806.

So They Say

"Arrived at the mouth of the great Platte River...passing through different channels, none of them more than five or six feet deep... [the river] spreds very wide and...cannot be navigated with Boats or Perogues. The Indians pass this river in Skin Boats which [are] flat and will not turn over."

Meriwether Lewis

• The American fur trader Manuel Lisa followed the explorers and set up a fur trading operation in 1807.
• Zebulon Pike assembled 400 Indians along the Republican River and in a ceremony of lowering the Spanish flag made them swear allegiance to the United States.
• Bellevue was founded in 1823 by Peter Sarpy as an American Fur Company post, and it proved to be the first permanent European settlement in what is now Nebraska.
• On a visit to the Oto Indian village near Papillion in 1836, Father Pierre Jean de Smet

was served a meal "shining with grease, a stew of buffalo tongue floating in a gravy of bear fat, thickened with wild sweet potato flour." Surprisingly, he liked it.

• Nebraska soon became a highway to the West, and more than 6,000 Mormon faithful crossed the Nebraska plains in the winter of 1846-1847 on their way to the "promised land" of Utah.

• The next major crossing of the state came with the almost endless procession of 49ers hurrying to the California gold fields, beginning in 1849.

So They Say

"The onlookers witnessed sights ranging from the laughable to the alarming. In one place six men were assisted ashore by hanging to the tail of a mule, with a rider on him....The line of wagons stretched for two miles...busy as it ordinarily [is] in St. Louis...."

Emigrant's Journal of a 49er party crossing the Platte River

• During the Civil War, Nebraska had a population of only about 30,000. Of these, 3,307 served in the war.

• In 1862, Daniel Freeman of Beatrice was the nation's first recipient of land granted under the unique Homestead Act.

• President Andrew Johnson vetoed the Nebraska statehood bill of 1866, but Congress overrode his veto, and Nebraska became a state on March 1, 1867.

• President William McKinley opened the Mississippi International Exposition at Omaha in 1898.

• During World War I, 47,801 Nebraskans were called into service, and 1,000 lost their lives.

• In 1934, Nebraska became unique among the states when it installed its unicameral (one-house) legislature, consisting only of a Senate.

• Of the 120,000 Nebraskans in World War II service, 3,830 lost their lives.

• In 1992, Omaha claimed the title of "Telemarketing Capital of the U.S.A."

• On May 6, 1877, famed Chief Crazy Horse surrendered with 1,000 of his followers near Camp Robinson. On September 7, 1877, he was killed because he was said to have resisted his captors.

So They Say

"The wealthiest potentate on earth cannot hire one [tree] to speed its growth....What infinite beauty and loveliness we can add...by planting forest and fruit trees. Arbor Day, an invention of mine, has now become a public holiday, destined to become a blessing to posterity as well as to ourselves....Other holidays repose upon the past; Arbor Day proposes for the future."

Julius Sterling Morton of Nebraska City, founder of Arbor Day

---

NOTABLE NATIVES

Fred Astaire (Omaha, 1899-1987), dancer/actor. **Marlon Brando** (Omaha, 1924-), actor. **Henry Fonda** (Grand Island, 1905-1982), actor. **Gerald Rudolph Ford** (Omaha, 1913-), U.S. president. **Howard Hanson** (Wahoo, 1896-1981), composer/conductor. **Harold Lloyd** (Burchard, 1893-1971), actor/producer. **Malcolm X** (Omaha, 1925-1965), religious leader/reformer. **Roscoe Pound** (Lincoln, 1870-1964), educator/legal scholar. **Red Cloud** (in north-central Nebraska, 1822-1909), Indian leader.

GENERAL

Admitted to statehood: March 1, 1867
Origin of name: From Omaha or Otos Indian word meaning "broad water" or "flat river," describing the Platte River
Capital: Lincoln
Nickname: Cornhusker State, Tree Planters State
Motto: Equality before the law
Bird: Western meadowlark
Insect: Honeybee
Flower: Goldenrod
Gem: Blue chalcedony (agate)
Stone: Prairie agate
Song: "Beautiful Nebraska"
Tree: Cottonwood

THE LAND

Area: 77,359 sq. mi., 16th
Land: 76,878 sq. mi., 15th
Water: 481 sq. mi., 39th
Inland water: 481 sq. mi., 33rd

Topography: Till plains of the central lowland in the eastern third rising to the Great Plains and hill country of the N central and NW

Number of counties: 93

Geographic center: Custer, 10 mi. NW of Broken Bow

Length: 430 mi.; width: 210 mi.

Highest point: 5,424 ft. (Johnson Township), 20th

Lowest point: 480 ft. (Missouri River), 38th

Mean elevation: 2,600 ft., 12th

CLIMATE AND ENVIRONMENT

Temp., highest: 118 deg. on July 24, 1936, at Minden; lowest: −47 deg. on Feb. 12, 1899, at Camp Clarke

Monthly average: highest: 89.5 deg., 20th; lowest: 8.9 deg., 9th; spread (high to low): 80.6 deg., 6th

Hazardous waste sites (1993): 10, 36th

Endangered species: Mammals: none; birds: 4—Whooping crane, Eskimo curlew, American peregrine falcon, Least tern; reptiles: none; amphibians: none; fishes: 1; invertebrates: 2; plants: 1

MAJOR CITIES
POPULATION, 1990
PERCENTAGE INCREASE, 1980-90

Bellevue, 30,982—42.03%

Grand Island, 39,386—18.70%

Kearney, 24,396—15.30%

Lincoln, 191,972—11.66%

Omaha, 335,795—6.96%

THE PEOPLE

Population (1995): 1,637,112, 37th
  Percent change (1990-95): 3.7%, 34th
Population (2000 proj.): 1,704,000, 37th
  Percent change (1990-2000): 7.96%, 31st
Per sq. mi. (1994): 21.1, 43rd
Percent in metro. area (1992): 50.6%, 38th
Foreign born: 28,000, 41st
  Percent: 1.8%, 36th
Top three ancestries reported:
  German, 50.38%
  Irish, 17.24%
  English, 13.24%
White: 1,480,558, 93.80%, 10th
Black: 57,404, 3.64%, 34th
Native American: 12,410, 0.79%, 20th
Asian, Pacific Isle: 12,422, 0.79%, 37th
Other races: 15,591, 0.99%, 26th

Hispanic origin: 36,969, 2.34%, 27th
Percent over 5 yrs. speaking language other than English at home: 4.8%, 39th
Percent males: 48.75%, 23rd; percent females: 51.25%, 29th
Percent never married: 24.4%, 33rd
Marriages per 1,000 (1993): 7.7, 37th
Divorces per 1,000 (1993): 3.9, 34th
Median age: 33
Under 5 years (1994): 7.15%, 30th
Under 18 years (1994): 27.23%, 13th
65 years & older (1994): 14.1%, 10th
Percent increase among the elderly (1990-94): 3.11%, 45th

OF VITAL IMPORTANCE

Live births per 1,000 pop. (1993): 14.2, 33rd
Infant mortality rate per 1,000 births (1992): 7.4, 38th
  Rate for blacks (1990): 16.8, 17th
  Rate for whites (1990): 7.2, 40th
Births to unmarried women, % of total (1992): 22.6%, 46th
Births to teenage mothers, % of total (1992): 9.9%, 41st
Abortions (1992): 5,580, 40th
  Rate per 1,000 women 14-44 years old: 15.7, 32nd
  Percent change (1988-92): −11%, 30th
Average lifetime (1979-81): 75.49, 5th
Deaths per 1,000 pop. (1993): 9.6, 13th
Causes of death per 100,000 pop.:
  Accidents & adverse effects (1992): 34.9, 25th
  Atherosclerosis (1991): 12.1, 4th
  Cancer (1991): 202 4, 34th
  Cerebrovascular diseases (1992): 64.3, 16th
  Chronic liver diseases & cirrhosis (1991): 6.6, 46th
  Chronic obstructive pulmonary diseases (1992): 41.7, 15th
  Diabetes mellitus (1992): 16.6, 40th
  Diseases of heart (1992): 329 6, 9th
  Pneumonia, flu (1991): 41.6, 3rd
  Suicide (1992): 11.7, 34th

KEEPING WELL

Active nonfederal physicians per 100,000 pop. (1993): 189, 31st
Dentists per 100,000 (1991): 64, 15th
Nurses per 100,000 (1992): 834, 15th
Hospitals per 100,000 (1993): 5.58, 4th
  Admissions per 1,000 (1993): 108.56, 35th

Occupancy rate per 100 beds (1993): 55.2, 45th

Average cost per patient per day (1993): $626, 45th

Average cost per stay (1993): $6,024, 18th

Average stay (1992): 9.7 days, 10th

AIDS cases (adult, 1993): 179; per 100,000: 11.1, 41st

HIV infection, not yet AIDS (1993): NA

Other notifiable diseases:

Gonorrhea: 114.2, 33rd

Measles: 6.5, 15th

Syphilis: 2.3, 46th

Tuberculosis: 1.5, 49th

Pop. without health insur. (1991-93): 9.9%, 44th

HOUSEHOLDS BY TYPE

Total households (1994): 614,000

Percent change (1990-94): 2.0%, 41st

Per 1,000 pop.: 378.31, 16th

Percent of households 65 yrs. and over: 23.94%, 9th

Persons per household (1994): 2.56, 35th

Family households: 415,427

Percent of total: 68.97%, 38th

Nonfamily households: 186,936

Percent of total: 31.03%, 14th

Pop. living in group quarters: 47,553

Percent of pop.: 3.01%, 18th

LIVING QUARTERS

Total housing units: 660,621

Persons per unit: 2.39, 28th

Occupied housing units: 602,363

Percent of total units: 91.18%, 15th

Persons per unit: 2.48, 38th

Percent of units with over 1 person per room: 1.75%, 47th

Owner-occupied units: 400,394

Percent of total units: 60.61%, 21st

Percent of occupied units: 66.47%, 30th

Persons per unit: 2.68, 36th

Median value: $50,400, 45th

Renter-occupied units: 201,969

Percent of total units: 30.57%, 19th

Percent of occupied units: 33.53%, 23rd

Persons per unit: 2.27, 36th

Median contract rent: $282, 35th

Rental vacancy rate: 7.7%, 34th

Mobile home, trailer & other as a percent of occupied housing units: 6.98%, 37th

Persons in emergency shelters for homeless persons: 764, 0.048%, 24th

Persons visible in street locations: 20, 0.0013%, 49th

Persons in shelters for abused women: 41, 0.0026%, 47th

Nursing home population: 19,171, 1.21%, 4th

CRIME INDEX PER 100,000 (1992-93)

Total reported: 4,117.1, 39th

Violent: 339.1, 37th

Murder and nonnegligent manslaughter: 3.9, 37th

Aggravated assault: 252.0, 33rd

Robbery: 55.4, 41st

Forcible rape: 27.8, 43rd

Property: 3,778.0, 41st

Burglary: 663.5, 44th

Larceny, theft: 2,912.9, 26th

Motor vehicle theft: 201.6, 42nd

Drug abuse violations (1990): 252.9, 26th

Child-abuse rate per 1,000 children (1993): 13.04, 29th

TEACHING AND LEARNING

Pop. 3 and over enrolled in school: 433,409

Percent of pop.: 28.7%, 12th

Public elementary & secondary schools (1992-93): 1,454

Total enrollment (1992): 282,476

Percent of total pop.: 17.64%, 19th

Teachers (1992): 19,323

Percent of pop.: 1.21%, 10th

Pupil/teacher ratio (fall 1992): 14.6, 45th

Teachers' avg. salary (1992-93): $31,298, 38th

Expenditure per capita (1990-91): $3,266.98, 31st

Expenditure per pupil (1991-92): $5,263, 24th

Percent of graduates taking SAT (1993): 10%, 39th

Mean SAT verbal scores: 479, 14th

Mean SAT mathematical scores: 544, 8th

Percent of graduates taking ACT (1995): 75%, 1st

Mean ACT scores: 21.4, 13th

Percent of pop. over 25 completing:

Less than 9th grade: 8.0%, 36th

High school: 81.8%, 8th

College degree(s): 18.9%, 27th

Higher education, institutions (1993-94): 33

Enrollment (1992): 122,603

Percent of pop.: 7.64%, 3rd

White non-Hispanic (1992): 111,388
　Percent of enroll.: 90.85%, 8th
Black non-Hispanic (1992): 3,820
　Percent of enroll.: 3.12%, 37th
Hispanic (1992): 2,336
　Percent of enroll.: 1.91%, 25th
Asian/Pacific Islander (1992): 1,644
　Percent of enroll.: 1.34%, 39th
American Indian/AK native (1992): 800
　Percent of enroll.: 0.65%, 22nd
Nonresident alien (1992): 2,615
　Percent of enroll.: 2.13%, 37th
Female (1992): 66,769
　Percent of enroll.: 54.46%, 37th
Pub. institutions (1993-94): 16
　Enrollment (1992): 103,196
　Percent of enroll.: 84.17%, 23rd
Private institutions (1993-94): 17
　Enrollment (1992): 19,407
　Percent of enroll.: 15.83%, 29th
Tuition, public institution (avg., 1993-94): $4,927, 45th
Tuition, private institution (avg., 1993-94): $11,221, 34th
Public library systems: 264
　Books & serial vol. per capita: 3.75, 9th
　Govt. expenditure per capita: $12.59, 31st

LAW ENFORCEMENT, COURTS, AND PRISONS

Police protection, corrections, judicial and legal functions expenditures (1992): $310,000,000
Per capita: $194, 42nd
Police per 10,000 pop. (1993): 18.07, 36th
Prisoners (state & fed.) per 100,000 pop. (1993): 1,561.07, 46th
Percent change (1992-93): 0.2%, 41st
Death penalty: yes, by electrocution
　Under sentence of death (1993): 11, 26th
　Executed (1993): 0

RELIGION, NUMBER AND PERCENT OF POPULATION

Agnostic: 1,149—0.10%, 47th
Buddhist: 1,149—0.10%, 17th
Christian: 1,016,046—88.40%, 18th
Hindu: 2,299—0.20%, 3rd
Jewish: 5,747—0.50%, 27th
Muslim: NA
Unitarian: 5,747—0.50%, 6th
Other: 17,241—1.50%, 18th
None: 80,456—7.00%, 23rd
Refused to answer: 19,539—1.70%, 35th

MAKING A LIVING

Personal income per capita (1994): $20,488, 26th
　Percent increase (1993-94): 4.1%, 41st
Disposable personal income per capita (1994): $18,089, 27th
Median income of households (1993): $31,008, 26th
Percent of pop. below poverty level (1993): 10.3%, 40th
　Percent 65 and over (1990): 12.2%, 22nd
Expenditure for energy per person (1992): $1,889, 24th

ECONOMY

Civilian labor force (1994): 876,000
　Percent of total pop.: 53.97%, 9th
　Percent 65 and over (1990): 4.05%, 4th
　Percent female: 47.49%, 10th
Percent job growth (1980-90): 12.30%, 41st
Major employer industries (1994):
　Agriculture: 63,000—7.6%, 5th
　Construction: 31,000—3.7%, 39th
　Finance, insurance, & real estate: 46,000—5.6%, 18th
　Government: 130,000—15.6%, 24th
　Manufacturing: 106,000—12.8%, 35th
　Service: 167,000—20.1%, 33rd
　Trade: 170,000—20.5%, 5th
　Transportation, communications, public utilities: 44,000—5.3%, 25th
Unemployment rate (1994): 2.85%, 51st
　Male: 2.5%, 51st
　Female: 3.3%, 50th
Total businesses (1991): 71,814
　New business incorps. (1991): 3,093
　　Percent of total businesses: 4.31%, 41st
　Business failures (1991): 358
　　Percent of total businesses: 0.50%
Agriculture farm income:
　Marketing (1993): $8,909,000,000, 4th
　　Average per farm: $161,981.82, 4th
　Leading products (1993): Cattle, corn, hogs, soybeans
　Average value land & build. per acre (1994): $635, 36th
　　Percent increase (1990-94): 15.45%, 22nd
　Govt. payments (1993): $806,000,000, 5th
　　Average per farm: $14,654.55, 3rd
Construction, value of all: $739,000,000
　Per capita: $468.20, 36th

Manufactures:

Value added: $7,450,000,000

Per capita: $4,720.01, 33rd

Leading products: Foods, machinery, electric and electronic equipment, primary and fabricated metal products, transportation equipment, instruments and related products

Value of nonfuel mineral production (1994): $137,000,000, 42nd

Leading mineral products: Petroleum, cement, stone

Retail sales (1993): $13,266,000,000, 35th

Per household: $21,424, 31st

Percent increase (1992-93): 8.7%, 13th

Tourism revenues (1993): $1.9 bil.

Foreign exports, in total value (1994): $1,573,000,000, 37th

Per capita: $969.19, 33rd

Gross state product per person (1993): $21,984.92, 20th

Percent change (1990-93): 2.94%, 29th

Patents per 100,000 pop. (1993): 11.84, 38th

Public aid recipients (percent of resident pop. 1993): 4.2%, 46th

Medicaid recipients per 1,000 pop. (1993): 102.29, 32nd

Medicare recipients per 1,000 pop. (1993): 151.89, 11th

TRAVEL AND TRANSPORTATION

Motor vehicle registrations (1993): 1,439,000

Per 1,000 pop.: 892.13, 8th

Motorcycle registrations (1993): 19,000

Per 1,000 pop.: 11.78, 33rd

Licensed drivers per 1,000 pop. (1993): 707.38, 16th

Deaths from motor vehicle accidents per 100,000 pop. (1993): 15.75, 28th

Public roads & streets (1993):

Total mileage: 92,702

Per 1,000 pop.: 57.47, 5th

Rural mileage: 87,648

Per 1,000 pop.: 54.34, 5th

Urban mileage: 5,054

Per 1,000 pop.: 3.13, 23rd

Interstate mileage: 481

Per 1,000 pop.: 0.30, 14th

Annual vehicle-mi. of travel per person (1993): 9,175, 31st

Mean travel time for workers age 16+ who work away from home: 15.8 min., 47th

GOVERNMENT

Percent of voting age pop. registered (1994): 72.6%, 11th

Percent of voting age pop. voting (1994): 54.3%, 11th

Percent of voting age pop. voting for U.S. representatives (1994): 47.9%, 11th

State legislators, total (1995): 49, 50th

Women members (1992): 9

Percent of legislature: 18.4%, 24th

U.S. Congress, House members (1995): 3

Change (1985-95): 0

Revenues (1993):

State govt.: $3,890,000,000

Per capita: $2,411.66, 46th

Parimutuel & amusement taxes & lotteries, revenue per capita: $6.82, 38th

Expenditures (1993):

State govt.: $3,823,000,000

Per capita: $2,370.12, 41st

Debt outstanding (1993): $1,587,000,000

Per capita: $983.88, 37th

LAWS AND REGULATIONS

Legal driving age: 19

Marriage age without parental consent: 18

Divorce residence requirement: 1 yr., for qualifications check local statutes

ATTRACTIONS (1995)

Major opera companies: 1

Major symphony orchestras: 1

Major dance companies: 1

State appropriations for arts agencies per capita: $0.76, 24th

State Fair in late August–early September at Lincoln

SPORTS AND COMPETITION

NCAA teams (Division I): Creighton Univ. Bluejays, Univ. of Nebraska Cornhuskers

NEVADA

"I had previously seen some beautiful valleys, but I place none of these ahead of Carson."

Horace Greeley, journalist

E very year, Nevada has enough tourists coming to the state to outnumber the population of several states. Some come only for the gambling—it is home to the world's most popular gambling and entertainment center—but many come for the vast tracts of beautiful deserts, plains, and mountains. Nevada is a cattle- and sheep-raising state, and most of the grains grown there are used to feed livestock. Hoover Dam, on the Colorado River, created Lake Mead, one of the world's largest artificial lakes. All of this has come from the desert lands where no European was known until 1826. As the 1990s progressed, the "splendor" of Las Vegas assumed even more striking proportions, accompanied by growth of pleasant new suburbs and increasing opportunities for newcomers.

SUPERLATIVES

- Home of two world-famed entertainment centers.
- Kept the Union solvent in the Civil War.
- Major world supplier of turquoise.
- World center of rare opals.
- World's largest open-pit copper mine.
- First large-scale reclamation program in the United States.
- Claims first use of skis in the United States.

MOMENTS IN HISTORY

- Father Silvestre Vélez de Escalante may have visited the Nevada region in 1775, but records of European exploration do not begin until 1826, with the exploration of Peter Skene Ogden.
- Dat-So-La-Lee, the Indian basketmaker whose artistry is known worldwide, was born probably around the year 1826.
- Walker Pass and Walker Lake are named for Joseph Walker, who brought an expedition in 1833.
- More complete records on Nevada were made by John C. Frémont, who came to the area in 1843-1844 with his guide, the famed Kit Carson.
- In 1846 the Donner party was blocked by heavy snow in what is now Donner Pass, and only about half of the party of 87 survived to reach California.
- Beginning in 1849, thousands of 49ers crossed the bleak country, and by fall of 1850 at least 60,000 had passed through in covered wagons, on muleback and horseback, and even on foot.
- In 1859, one of the world's richest silver discoveries was made in the region that became known as the Comstock, named for one of the prospectors, and Virginia City sprang up almost overnight.
- In 1862, Samuel Clemens of later fame arrived at Virginia City and took the name Mark Twain while working on the *Territorial Enterprise*, poking fun at almost everyone.

So They Say

"It was...impossible to print his lectures in full, as the cases had run out of capital I's."

Mark Twain, on a local judge

- By 1863, Virginia City had become the second most important city in the West, with luxurious homes, four banks, an opera house, six churches, 110 saloons, and the only elevator between Chicago and the west coast.
- During the Civil War, the wealth of Nevada silver was critically important in keeping the North solvent.

So They Say

"...the gold and silver in the region...has made it possible for the government to maintain sufficient credit to continue this terrible war for the Union...."

President Abraham Lincoln

• On October 31, 1864, at the urging of President Abraham Lincoln, Nevada became a state. Only a short four years earlier, it had been a wilderness.

• New mineral finds occurred at Eureka in 1864 and Hamilton in 1869, but the wealth of the Comstock dwindled, and by 1880, Virginia City had become a sleepy village.

• In 1869 the transcontinental railroad was completed. In 1873 famed travel writer Isabella Bird left a vivid description of crossing Nevada.

So They Say

"...I sat for an hour on the rear platform of the rear car to enjoy the wonderful beauty of the sunset and the atmosphere...in the crystalline air. The bright metal track, purpling like all else in the cool distance, was all that linked one with eastern or western civilization."

Travel writer Isabella Bird

• The 1897 heavyweight championship boxing bout held at Carson City brought world attention to the state. Bob Fitzsimmons defeated James J. Corbett.

• New mineral booms occurred at Tonopah and Goldfield in 1906. Goldfield soon became a ghost town, but Tonopah continued.

• In 1931, gambling was made legal, laying the foundations for the future reputation of the state.

• Hoover Dam was finished in 1936.

• In 1951 the Atomic Energy Commission established the Nevada Proving Ground.

• In the late 1970s, Nevada ranchers launched the "Sagebrush Rebellion," in an effort to reduce federal control of ranch lands.

• The census of 1990 revealed Nevada as the state with the largest percentage growth of population.

THAT'S INTERESTING

• In order to meet a deadline for statehood, the entire constitution of Nevada was sent to Washington by telegram at a cost of $3,400.

• Virginia City was named for James Fenimore, whose nickname was "Old Virginy." He celebrated too much one night, fell, and broke a bottle of whisky. Not wishing to waste the liquid, he called out, "I baptize thee Virginia Town," and the name stuck.

• Mark Twain offended a local newspaper writer, who challenged him to a duel. The challenger backed out, but not before Twain had been charged with breaking the law and had to flee from Virginia City on his way to fame elsewhere.

• Many of the horses of Virginia City sported multicolored polka dots. Chemicals from the mineral crushing mills where they worked caused the unusual decorations.

• Once when Nevada Senator William Stewart asked to meet with President Lincoln, the president sent a note saying he would see him the next morning. Lincoln was assassinated that night, and the note probably contained Lincoln's last written words.

• The discovery of moccasins a foot and a half long caused archaeologists to consider that Nevada might at one time have been inhabited by a race of giants.

NEVADA NOTABLES

Henry Tompkins Paige Comstock (Canada, 1820-1870), trapper/prospector. **Dat-So-La-Lee** (Washoe tribal lands, 1826?-1925), artist/weaver. **James Graham Fair** (Ireland, 1831-1894), mining leader/public official. **George Hearst** (Sullivan, MO, 1820-1891), businessman/public official. **John William Mackay** (Ireland, 1831-1902), mining and business leader. **James Warren Nye** (DeRuyter, NY, 1814-1876), public official. **William Morris Stewart** (Galen, NY, 1827-1909), lawyer/public official. **Sarah Winnemucca** (Humboldt Lake, 1844?-1891), Indian guide/author.

GENERAL

Admitted to statehood: October 31, 1864
Origin of name: Spanish for "snow-clad"
Capital: Carson City
Nickname: Silver State, Sagebrush State, Battle Born State
Motto: All for our country
Bird: Mountain bluebird
Flower: Sagebrush
Song: "Home Means Nevada"
Tree: Single-leaf piñon

THE LAND

Area: 110,567 sq. mi., 7th
    Land: 109,806 sq. mi., 7th
    Water: 761 sq. mi., 34th
        Inland water: 761 sq. mi., 28th

Topography: Rugged N-S mountain ranges; southern area is within the Mojave Desert with the Colorado River Canyon

Number of counties: 16

Geographic center: Lander, located 26 mi. SE of Austin

Length: 490 mi.; width: 320 mi.

Highest point: 13,140 ft. (Boundary Peak), 9th

Lowest point: 479 ft. (Colorado River), 37th

Mean elevation: 5,500 ft., 5th

CLIMATE AND ENVIRONMENT

Temp., highest: 122 deg. on June 23, 1954, at Overton; lowest: –50 deg. on Jan. 8, 1937, at San Jacinto

Monthly average: highest: 104.5 deg., 2nd; lowest: 19.5 deg., 25th; spread (high to low): 85.0 deg., 4th

Hazardous waste sites (1993): 1, 50th

Endangered species: Mammals: none; birds: 1—American peregrine falcon; reptiles: none; amphibians: none; fishes: 16; invertebrates: none; plants: 2

MAJOR CITIES POPULATION, 1990 PERCENTAGE INCREASE, 1980-90

Henderson, 64,942—166.56%

Las Vegas, 258,295—56.85%

Paradise, 124,682—47.00%

Reno, 133,850—32.85%

Sunrise Manor, 95,362—115.97%

THE PEOPLE

Population (1995): 1,530,108, 38th
  Percent change (1990-95): 27.3%, 1st
Population (2000 proj.): 1,691,000, 38th
  Percent change (1990-2000): 40.7%, 1st
Per sq. mi. (1994): 13.3, 46th
Percent in metro. area (1992): 84.8%, 10th
Foreign born: 105,000, 23rd
  Percent: 8.7%, 10th
Top three ancestries reported:
  German, 23.29%
  English, 17.22%
  Irish, 16.64%
White: 1,012,695, 84.26%, 27th
Black: 78,771, 6.55%, 27th
Native American: 19,637, 1.63%, 10th
Asian, Pacific Isle: 38,127, 3.17%, 7th
Other races: 52,603, 4.38%, 7th
Hispanic origin: 124,419, 10.35%, 8th

Percent over 5 yrs. speaking language other than English at home: 13.2%, 13th

Percent males: 50.91%, 2nd; percent females: 49.09%, 50th

Percent never married: 23.7%, 39th

Marriages per 1,000 (1993): 88.7, 1st

Median age: 33.3

Under 5 years (1994): 7.89%, 8th

Under 18 years (1994): 25.81%, 26th

65 years & older (1994): 11.3%, 41st

Percent increase among the elderly (1990-94): 28.50%, 1st

OF VITAL IMPORTANCE

Live births per 1,000 pop. (1993): 15.2, 17th

Infant mortality rate per 1,000 births (1992): 6.7, 46th
  Rate for blacks (1990): 12.5, 40th
  Rate for whites (1990): 8.1, 20th

Births to unmarried women, % of total (1992): 33.3%, 12th

Births to teenage mothers, % of total (1992): 12.4%, 24th

Abortions (1992): 13,300, 28th
  Rate per 1,000 women 14-44 years old: 44.2, 4th
  Ratio per 1,000 live births: 591, 4th
  Percent change (1988-92): 10%, 6th

Average lifetime (1979-81): 72.64, 44th

Deaths per 1,000 pop. (1993): 7.8, 41st

Causes of death per 100,000 pop.:
  Accidents & adverse effects (1992): 30.8, 36th
  Atherosclerosis (1991): 3.7, 49th
  Cancer (1991): 200.4, 35th
  Cerebrovascular diseases (1992): 37.3, 50th
  Chronic liver diseases & cirrhosis (1991): 13.4, 3rd
  Chronic obstructive pulmonary diseases (1992): 47.6, 6th
  Diabetes mellitus (1992): 12.9, 48th
  Diseases of heart (1992): 232.1, 39th
  Pneumonia, flu (1991): 18.9, 50th
  Suicide (1992): 24.6, 1st

KEEPING WELL

Active nonfederal physicians per 100,000 pop. (1993): 148, 47th

Dentists per 100,000 (1991): 43, 45th

Nurses per 100,000 (1992): 538, 47th

Hospitals per 100,000 (1993): 1.52, 42nd
  Admissions per 1,000 (1993): 89.00, 49th
  Beds per 1,000 (1993): 2.68, 42nd

Occupancy rate per 100 beds (1993): 67.8, 13th

Average cost per patient per day (1993): $900, 19th

Average cost per stay (1993): $6,796, 10th

Average stay (1992): 6.4 days, 43rd

AIDS cases (adult, 1993): 638; per 100,000: 45.9, 9th

HIV infection, not yet AIDS (1993): 1,496

Other notifiable diseases:

Gonorrhea: 218.8, 23rd

Measles: 20.0, 3rd

Syphilis: 33.9, 22nd

Tuberculosis: 7.1, 25th

Pop. without health insur. (1991-93): 20.0%, 6th

HOUSEHOLDS BY TYPE

Total households (1994): 560,000

Percent change (1990-94): 20.1%, 1st

Per 1,000 pop.: 384.35, 6th

Percent of households 65 yrs. and over: 18.21%, 46th

Persons per household (1994): 2.56, 35th

Family households: 307,400

Percent of total: 65.92%, 50th

Nonfamily households: 158,897

Percent of total: 34.08%, 2nd

Pop. living in group quarters: 24,200

Percent of pop.: 2.01%, 49th

LIVING QUARTERS

Total housing units: 518,858

Persons per unit: 2.32, 38th

Occupied housing units: 466,297

Percent of total units: 89.87%, 22nd

Persons per unit: 2.51, 29th

Percent of units with over 1 person per room: 6.41%, 9th

Owner-occupied units: 255,388

Percent of total units: 49.22%, 48th

Percent of occupied units: 54.77%, 48th

Persons per unit: 2.67, 38th

Median value: $95,700, 12th

Renter-occupied units: 210,909

Percent of total units: 40.65%, 5th

Percent of occupied units: 45.23%, 5th

Persons per unit: 2.35, 25th

Median contract rent: $445, 9th

Rental vacancy rate: 9.1%, 21st

Mobile home, trailer & other as a percent of occupied housing units: 16.22%, 10th

Persons in emergency shelters for homeless persons: 1,013, 0.084%, 9th

Persons visible in street locations: 436, 0.0363%, 5th

Persons in shelters for abused women: 49, 0.0041%, 38th

Nursing home population: 3,605, 0.30%, 49th

CRIME INDEX PER 100,000 (1992-93)

Total reported: 6,180.1, 10th

Violent: 875.2, 10th

Murder and nonnegligent manslaughter: 10.4, 13th

Aggravated assault: 463.9, 17th

Robbery: 340.1, 7th

Forcible rape: 60.9, 5th

Property: 5,304.9, 11th

Burglary: 1,245.0, 12th

Larceny, theft: 3,321.6, 15th

Motor vehicle theft: 738.3, 7th

Drug abuse violations (1990): 559.8, 7th

Child-abuse rate per 1,000 children (1993): 20.13, 12th

TEACHING AND LEARNING

Pop. 3 and over enrolled in school: 280,411

Percent of pop.: 24.4%, 50th

Public elementary & secondary schools (1992-93): 383

Total enrollment (1992): 229,974

Percent of total pop.: 17.21%, 28th

Teachers (1992): 11,953

Percent of pop.: 0.89%, 44th

Pupil/teacher ratio (fall 1992): 18.7, 8th

Teachers' avg. salary (1992-93): $36,690, 22nd

Expenditure per capita (1990-91): $3,740.07, 15th

Expenditure per pupil (1991-92): $4,926, 31st

Percent of graduates taking SAT (1993): 28%, 25th

Mean SAT verbal scores: 432, 31st

Mean SAT mathematical scores: 488, 27th

Percent of graduates taking ACT (1995): 42%, 26th

Mean ACT scores: 21.3, 17th

Percent of pop. over 25 completing:

Less than 9th grade: 6.0%, 46th

High school: 78.8%, 19th

College degree(s): 15.3%, 47th

Higher education, institutions (1993-94): 9

Enrollment (1992): 63,877

Percent of pop.: 4.80%, 43rd

White non-Hispanic (1992): 50,783
  Percent of enroll.: 79.50%, 32nd
Black non-Hispanic (1992): 3,222
  Percent of enroll.: 5.04%, 27th
Hispanic (1992): 4,104
  Percent of enroll.: 6.42%, 10th
Asian/Pacific Islander (1992): 3,338
  Percent of enroll.: 5.23%, 5th
American Indian/AK native (1992): 995
  Percent of enroll.: 1.56%, 9th
Nonresident alien (1992): 1,435
  Percent of enroll.: 2.25%, 32nd
Female (1992): 35,420
  Percent of enroll.: 55.45%, 23rd
Pub. institutions (1993-94): 6
  Enrollment (1992): 63,192
  Percent of enroll.: 98.93%, 1st
Private institutions (1993-94): 3
  Enrollment (1992): 685
  Percent of enroll.: 1.07%, 51st
Tuition, public institution (avg., 1993-94):
  $6,403, 20th
Tuition, private institution (avg., 1993-94):
  $8,797, 45th
Public library systems: 26
  Books & serial vol. per capita: 1.51, 50th
  Govt. expenditure per capita: $23.99, 5th

LAW ENFORCEMENT, COURTS, AND PRISONS

Police protection, corrections, judicial and
    legal functions expenditures (1992):
    $607,000,000
  Per capita: $454, 4th
Police per 10,000 pop. (1993): 24.04, 12th
Prisoners (state & fed.) per 100,000 pop.
    (1993): 4,441.39, 9th
  Percent change (1992-93): 1.5%, 35th
Death penalty: yes, by lethal injection
  Under sentence of death (1993): 42, 19th
  Executed (1993): 0

RELIGION, NUMBER AND PERCENT OF POPULATION

Agnostic: 8,144—0.90%, 14th
Buddhist: 3,620—0.40%, 5th
Christian: 773,677—85.50%, 28th
Hindu: NA
Jewish: 8,144—0.90%, 18th
Muslim: NA
Unitarian: 8,144—0.90%, 2nd
Other: 11,764—1.30%, 24th
None: 73,296—8.10%, 14th
Refused to answer: 18,098—2.00%, 30th

MAKING A LIVING

Personal income per capita (1994): $24,023,
    8th
  Percent increase (1993-94): 4.9%, 26th
Disposable personal income per capita (1994):
    $20,815, 8th
Median income of households (1993):
    $35,814, 10th
Percent of pop. below poverty level (1993):
    9.8%, 46th
  Percent 65 and over (1990): 9.6%, 42nd
Expenditure for energy per person (1992):
    $1,894, 23rd

ECONOMY

Civilian labor force (1994): 779,000
  Percent of total pop.: 53.47%, 11th
  Percent 65 and over (1990): NA
  Percent female: 44.29%, 50th
Percent job growth (1980-90): 53.41%, 1st
Major employer industries (1994):
  Agriculture: NA—1.3%, 43rd
  Construction: 49,000—7.0%, 2nd
  Finance, insurance, & real estate: 37,000—
    5.3%, 24th
  Government: 91,000—13.1%, 43rd
  Manufacturing: 37,000—5.3%, 47th
  Service: 233,000—33.8%, 2nd
  Trade: 132,000—19.1%, 23rd
  Transportation, communications, public
    utilities: 39,000—5.6%, 20th
Unemployment rate (1994): 6.16%, 18th
  Male: 5.9%, 19th
  Female: 6.5%, 12th
Total businesses (1991): 38,593
  New business incorps. (1991): 11,030
    Percent of total businesses: 28.58%,
    2nd
  Business failures (1991): 255
    Percent of total businesses: 0.66%
Agriculture farm income:
  Marketing (1993): $289,000,000, 47th
    Average per farm: $144,500.00, 7th
  Leading products (1993): Cattle, hay, dairy
    products, potatoes
  Average value land & build. per acre
    (1994): $229, 47th
    Percent increase (1990-94): 18.04%,
    17th
  Govt. payments (1993): $7,000,000,
    40th
    Average per farm: $3,500.00, 27th
Construction, value of all: $2,256,000,000
  Per capita: $1,877.13, 2nd

Manufactures:
  Value added: $1,470,000,000
    Per capita: $1,223.13, 51st
  Leading products: Gaming devices, chemicals, aerospace products, lawn and garden irrigation equipment, seismic and machinery-monitoring devices
Value of nonfuel mineral production (1994): $2,761,000,000, 2nd
Leading mineral products: Gold, silver, diatomite
Retail sales (1993): $12,390,000,000, 38th
  Per household: $22,643, 17th
  Percent increase (1992-93): 7.5%, 22nd
Tourism revenues (1992): $15.4 bil.
Foreign exports, in total value (1994): $621,000,000, 44th
  Per capita: $426.22, 47th
Gross state product per person (1993): $25,680.93, 10th
  Percent change (1990-93): 3.13%, 24th
Patents per 100,000 pop. (1993): 13.17, 33rd
Public aid recipients (percent of resident pop. 1993): 3.7%, 48th
Medicaid recipients per 1,000 pop. (1993): 63.68, 51st
Medicare recipients per 1,000 pop. (1993): 123.01, 40th

TRAVEL AND TRANSPORTATION

Motor vehicle registrations (1993): 937,000
  Per 1,000 pop.: 678.00, 46th
Motorcycle registrations (1993): 20,000
  Per 1,000 pop.: 14.47, 28th
Licensed drivers per 1,000 pop. (1993): 706.22, 17th
Deaths from motor vehicle accidents per 100,000 pop. (1993): 19.03, 21st
Public roads & streets (1993):
  Total mileage: 45,778
    Per 1,000 pop.: 33.12, 11th
  Rural mileage: 41,181
    Per 1,000 pop.: 29.80, 11th
  Urban mileage: 4,597
    Per 1,000 pop.: 3.33, 14th
  Interstate mileage: 545
    Per 1,000 pop.: 0.39, 10th

Annual vehicle-mi. of travel per person (1993): 8,394, 41st
Mean travel time for workers age 16+ who work away from home: 19.8 min., 31st

GOVERNMENT

Percent of voting age pop. registered (1994): 49.5%, 51st
  Percent of voting age pop. voting (1994): 40.1%, 44th
  Percent of voting age pop. voting for U.S. representatives (1994): 34.6%, 39th
State legislators, total (1995): 63, 47th
  Women members (1992): 12
  Percent of legislature: 19.0%, 20th
U.S. Congress, House members (1995): 2
  Change (1985-95): 0
Revenues (1993):
  State govt.: $4,500,000,000
    Per capita: $3,256.15, 21st
  Parimutuel & amusement taxes & lotteries, revenue per capita: $282.92, 2nd
Expenditures (1993):
  State govt.: $4,051,000,000
    Per capita: $2,931.26, 21st
Debt outstanding (1993): $1,653,000,000
  Per capita: $1,196.09, 28th

LAWS AND REGULATIONS

Legal driving age: 16
Marriage age without parental consent: 18
Divorce residence requirement: 6 wks

ATTRACTIONS (1995)

Major opera companies: 2
Major dance companies: 1
State appropriations for arts agencies per capita: $0.33, 49th
State Fair in late August–early September at Reno

SPORTS AND COMPETITION

NCAA teams (Division I): Univ. of Nevada-Las Vegas Rebels, Univ. of Nevada-Reno Wolf Pack

NEW HAMPSHIRE

"Up in the mountains of New Hampshire God Almighty has hung out a sign to show that there he makes men."

Attributed to statesman Daniel Webster

New Hampshire was one of the leaders on the road to independence. The state adopted a constitution six months before the Declaration of Independence was signed. New Hampshire offers year-round tourist attractions. In the summer, visitors flock to the rugged mountains, the blue lakes, the sandy beaches, and the quiet villages. In the fall, the state is a riot of color as the leaves turn. In the winter, skiers arrive from all over the East. New Hampshire might well be nicknamed "the Preparedness State," because it has seemed to be ready for any emergency and quick to respond to opportunities. The state's early and important presidential primary attracts considerable public attention every four years.

SUPERLATIVES

• Windiest place on earth, top of Mt. Washington.
• Alpine zone unique in eastern United States.
• Home of the Concord stagecoach.
• Produced the world's first machine-made watches.
• World's largest blanket mill.
• Nation's first regular stage run, between Portsmouth and Boston.
• Cog railroad system pioneered on Mt. Washington.

MOMENTS IN HISTORY

• Martin Pring in 1603 and Samuel de Champlain in 1605 both ventured up the Piscataqua River.
• Portsmouth and Dover, each founded in 1623, are usually said to be the oldest permanent European settlements in what is now New Hampshire.
• In 1627 the great Indian leader Passaconaway (Child of the Bear) united about 17 Indian groups in the Penacook Confederacy.

So They Say

"The Great Spirit...whispers me now— Tell your people, Peace, peace, is the only hope of your race...these forests shall fall by the axe—the pale faces shall live upon your hunting grounds, and make their village upon your fishing places!...We are few and powerless before them.' "

Chief Passaconaway

• In 1642 the New Hampshire region came under Massachusetts rule.
• Indian leader King Philip responded to growing white intrusion with raids beginning in 1675, and the French and Indian War led to more frightful raids on settlements.
• Meanwhile, New Hampshire separated from Massachusetts in 1679 and became a royal colony in 1680.
• In 1764 the King placed the western boundary along the west bank of the Connecticut River, where it remains.
• No Revolutionary battles were fought in the state, but New Hampshire forces played a critical role in the Battle of Bunker Hill on June 17, 1775.
• On January 5, 1776, an independent provisional government was set up, the first in the 13 colonies.
• In a sense, New Hampshire "created" the new nation by becoming the ninth state on June 21, 1788, meeting the requirement for nine states to ratify the Constitution.
• The War of 1812 again found New Hampshire among the best prepared, with 35,000 in service and 14 successful privateers.
• In the case of New Hampshire against Dartmouth College in 1819, the U.S. Supreme Court held for the college in a landmark decision upholding private property.

- The Webster-Ashburton Treaty of 1842 (negotiated by the state's native Daniel Webster) finally decided the boundary between the state and Canada.
- The only native president from the state, Franklin Pierce, took that office in 1853.
- During the Civil War, the 18th New Hampshire regiment led Union troops into Richmond, Virginia, in April 1865.
- After 13 years of work, in 1869, Enos M. Clough of Sunapee developed a successful horseless carriage, but the city fathers made him give it up because of the noise it made.
- More than 20,000 from New Hampshire served in World War I, and 697 died.
- In 1964, New Hampshire began the first state lottery since 1894.
- A boundary dispute with Maine was decided by the U.S. Supreme Court in 1976, giving most of the coastal waters to Maine.
- The tragic 1986 destruction of the space shuttle *Challenger* had particular meaning for the state in the loss of New Hampshire school teacher Christa McAuliffe.

THAT'S INTERESTING

- One of the world's notable natural features is the Old Man of the Mountain. This granite profile looms 48 feet from chin to forehead.
- New Hampshire's state House is the largest of all the states, with a total of 400 members. If the U.S. Congress were in proportion, it would have 100,000 members.
- Horace Greeley learned to read while his mother read to him as he sat on her lap. But he learned upside down because of the angle at which she held the book. He was able to read the Bible by age four.

NOTABLE NATIVES

Lewis Cass (Exeter, 1782-1866), public official. Salmon Portland Chase (Cornish, 1808-1873), chief justice of the United States. Jonas Chickering (Mason Village, 1798-1853), piano manufacturer. Ralph Adams Cram (Hampton Falls, 1863-1942), architect. John Adams Dix (Boscawen, 1798-1879), soldier/public official. Mary Morse Baker Eddy (Bow, 1821-1910), religious leader. Sam Walter Foss (Candia, 1858-1911), poet/journalist. Daniel Chester French (Exeter, 1850-1931), sculptor. Horace Greeley (Amherst, 1811-1872), reformer/political leader. John Parker

Hale (Rochester, 1806-1873), public official. Sarah Josepha Buell Hale (Newport, 1788-1879), editor/author. John Irving (Exeter, 1942-), author. Thaddeus Sobieski Coulincourt Lowe (Riverton, 1832-1913), aeronaut/inventor. Franklin Pierce (Hillsboro, 1804-1869), U.S. president. John Stark (Londonderry, 1728-1822), Revolutionary soldier. John Sullivan (Somersworth, 1740-1795), Revolutionary soldier/public official. Daniel Webster (Salisbury, 1782-1852), lawyer/public official. Benning Wentworth, (Portsmouth, 1696-1770), merchant/public official. John Wentworth (Portsmouth, 1737-1820), merchant/public official. John (Long John) Wentworth (Sandwich, 1815-1888), editor/public official. Paul Wentworth (probably in New Hampshire, ?-1793), British spy. Henry Wilson (Farmington, 1812-1875), U.S. vice president.

So They Say

"As a young lawyer, Daniel Webster lost his first case. His client was so obviously guilty of murder that all the young attorney could do was to argue against the wickedness of capital punishment."

The Enchantment of New Hampshire

GENERAL

Admitted to statehood: June 21, 1788
Origin of name: Named 1629 by Captain John Mason of Plymouth Council for his home county in England
Capital: Concord
Nickname: Granite State
Motto: Live free or die
Bird: Purple finch
Flower: Purple lilac
Song: "Old New Hampshire," "New Hampshire, My New Hampshire," "New Hampshire Hills"
Tree: Paper (white) birch

THE LAND

Area: 9,283 sq. mi., 44th
   Land: 8,969 sq. mi., 44th
   Water: 314 sq. mi., 46th
   Inland water: 314 sq. mi., 43rd
Topography: Low, rolling coast followed by countless hills and mountains rising out of a central plateau

Number of counties: 10
Geographic center: Belknap, 3 mi. E of Ashland
Length: 190 mi.; width: 70 mi.
Highest point: 6,288 ft. (Mount Washington), 18th
Lowest point: sea level (Atlantic Ocean), 3rd
Mean elevation: 1,000 ft., 25th
Coastline: 13 mi., 22nd
Shoreline: 131 mi., 23rd

CLIMATE AND ENVIRONMENT

Temp., highest: 106 deg. on July 4, 1911, at Nashua; lowest: –46 deg. on Jan. 28, 1925, at Pittsburg
Monthly average: highest: 82.6 deg., 45th; lowest: 9.0 deg., 10th; spread (high to low): 73.6 deg., 16th
Hazardous waste sites (1993): 17, 23rd
Endangered species: Mammals: none; birds: 1—American peregrine falcon; reptiles: none; amphibians: none; fishes: none; invertebrates: 1; plants: 3

MAJOR CITIES
POPULATION, 1990
PERCENTAGE INCREASE, 1980-90

Concord, 36,006—18.44%
Derry, 29,603—56.84%
Manchester, 99,567—9.49%
Nashua, 79,662—17.38%
Rochester, 26,630—23.52%

THE PEOPLE

Population (1995): 1,148,253, 42nd
  Percent change (1990-95): 3.5%, 34th
Population (2000 proj.): 1,165,000, 42nd
  Percent change (1990-2000): 5.03%, 41st
Per sq. mi. (1994): 126.7, 19th
Percent in metro. area (1992): 59.4%, 35th
Foreign born: 41,000, 37th
  Percent: 3.7%, 22nd
Top three ancestries reported:
  English, 23.99%
  Irish, 20.92%
  French, 18.49%
White: 1,087,433, 98.03%, 3rd
Black: 7,198, 0.65%, 45th
Native American: 2,134, 0.19%, 46th
Asian, Pacific Isle: 9,343, 0.84%, 33rd
Other races: 3,144, 0.28%, 41st
Hispanic origin: 11,333, 1.02%, 40th
Percent over 5 yrs. speaking language other than English at home: 8.7%, 21st

Percent males: 49.00%, 20th; percent females: 51.00%, 32nd
Percent never married: 25.5%, 26th
Marriages per 1,000 (1993): 8.5, 25th
Divorces per 1,000 (1993): 4.5, 26th
Median age: 32.8
Under 5 years (1994): 7.04%, 37th
Under 18 years (1994): 25.68%, 30th
65 years & older (1994): 11.9%, 36th
Percent increase among the elderly (1990-94): 8.77%, 15th

OF VITAL IMPORTANCE

Live births per 1,000 pop. (1993): 13.3, 46th
Infant mortality rate per 1,000 births (1992): 5.9, 49th
  Rate for blacks (1990): 5.4, 48th
  Rate for whites (1990): 7.2, 40th
Births to unmarried women, % of total (1992): 19.2%, 48th
Births to teenage mothers, % of total (1992): 6.7%, 51st
Abortions (1992): 3,890, 43rd
  Rate per 1,000 women 14-44 years old: 14.6, 35th
  Percent change (1988-92): –17%, 44th
Average lifetime (1979-81): 74.98, 14th
Deaths per 1,000 pop. (1993): 7.9, 40th
Causes of death per 100,000 pop.:
  Accidents & adverse effects (1992): 22.8, 49th
  Atherosclerosis (1991): 7.3, 21st
  Cancer (1991): 204.7, 29th
  Cerebrovascular diseases (1992): 50.0, 38th
  Chronic liver diseases & cirrhosis (1991): 8.5, 34th
  Chronic obstructive pulmonary diseases (1992): 36.5, 27th
  Diabetes mellitus (1992): 21.5, 20th
  Diseases of heart (1992): 240.7, 38th
  Pneumonia, flu (1991): 24.8, 42nd
  Suicide (1992): 12.3, 28th

KEEPING WELL

Active nonfederal physicians per 100,000 pop. (1993): 211, 18th
Dentists per 100,000 (1991): 59, 19th
Nurses per 100,000 (1992): 964, 6th
Hospitals per 100,000 (1993): 2.49, 22nd
  Admissions per 1,000 (1993): 97.60, 41st
  Occupancy rate per 100 beds (1993): 63.7, 21st
  Average cost per patient per day (1993): $976, 13th

Average cost per stay (1993): $6,964, 7th
Average stay (1992): 6.8 days, 35th
AIDS cases (adult, 1993): 124; per 100,000:
11.0, 42nd
HIV infection, not yet AIDS (1993): NA
Other notifiable diseases:
Gonorrhea: 22.8, 46th
Measles: 0.8, 42nd
Syphilis: 3.6, 41st
Tuberculosis: 1.8, 48th
Pop. without health insur. (1991-93): 11.7%,
35th

HOUSEHOLDS BY TYPE

Total households (1994): 424,000
Percent change (1990-94): 3.0%, 31st
Per 1,000 pop.: 372.91, 31st
Percent of households 65 yrs. and over:
19.58%, 40th
Persons per household (1994): 2.61, 21st
Family households: 292,601
Percent of total: 71.16%, 20th
Nonfamily households: 118,585
Percent of total: 28.84%, 32nd
Pop. living in group quarters: 32,151
Percent of pop.: 2.90%, 23rd

LIVING QUARTERS

Total housing units: 503,904
Persons per unit: 2.20, 47th
Occupied housing units: 411,186
Percent of total units: 81.60%, 47th
Persons per unit: 2.52, 26th
Percent of units with over 1 person per
room: 1.61%, 50th
Owner-occupied units: 280,372
Percent of total units: 55.64%, 39th
Percent of occupied units: 68.19%, 17th
Persons per unit: 2.80, 13th
Median value: $129,400, 8th
Renter-occupied units: 130,814
Percent of total units: 25.96%, 44th
Percent of occupied units: 31.81%, 35th
Persons per unit: 2.24, 42nd
Median contract rent: $479, 7th
Rental vacancy rate: 11.8%, 8th
Mobile home, trailer & other as a percent of
occupied housing units: 10.20%, 28th
Persons in emergency shelters for homeless
persons: 377, 0.034%, 45th
Persons visible in street locations: 8, 0.0007%,
50th
Persons in shelters for abused women: 27,
0.0024%, 49th

Nursing home population: 8,202, 0.74%,
24th

CRIME INDEX PER 100,000 (1992-93)

Total reported: 2,905.0, 49th
Violent: 137.8, 48th
Murder and nonnegligent manslaughter:
2.0, 49th
Aggravated assault: 64.1, 49th
Robbery: 27.3, 45th
Forcible rape: 44.4, 18th
Property: 2,767.2, 48th
Burglary: 515.1, 50th
Larceny, theft: 2,058.0, 48th
Motor vehicle theft: 194.0, 43rd
Drug abuse violations (1990): 161.6, 40th
Child-abuse rate per 1,000 children (1993):
3.28, 47th

TEACHING AND LEARNING

Pop. 3 and over enrolled in school: 276,765
Percent of pop.: 26.1%, 38th
Public elementary & secondary schools (1992-
93): 450
Total enrollment (1992): 181,247
Percent of total pop.: 16.26%, 38th
Teachers (1992): 11,654
Percent of pop.: 1.05%, 23rd
Pupil/teacher ratio (fall 1992): 15.6, 36th
Teachers' avg. salary (1992-93): $37,400,
19th
Expenditure per capita (1990-91):
$3,057.74, 37th
Expenditure per pupil (1991-92): $5,790,
16th
Percent of graduates taking SAT (1993): 78%,
3rd
Mean SAT verbal scores: 442, 26th
Mean SAT mathematical scores: 487, 28th
Percent of graduates taking ACT (1995): 2%,
49th
Mean ACT scores: 22.3, 2nd
Percent of pop. over 25 completing:
Less than 9th grade: 6.7%, 44th
High school: 82.2%, 7th
College degree(s): 24.4%, 8th
Higher education, institutions (1993-94): 30
Enrollment (1992): 63,924
Percent of pop.: 5.74%, 21st
White non-Hispanic (1992): 59,521
Percent of enroll.: 93.11%, 3rd
Black non-Hispanic (1992): 722
Percent of enroll.: 1.13%, 46th

Hispanic (1992): 926
  Percent of enroll.: 1.45%, 32nd
Asian/Pacific Islander (1992): 1,539
  Percent of enroll.: 2.41%, 22nd
American Indian/AK native (1992): 238
  Percent of enroll.: 0.37%, 28th
Nonresident alien (1992): 978
  Percent of enroll.: 1.53%, 50th
Female (1992): 35,777
  Percent of enroll.: 55.97%, 15th
Pub. institutions (1993-94): 12
  Enrollment (1992): 35,255
  Percent of enroll.: 55.15%, 48th
Private institutions (1993-94): 18
  Enrollment (1992): 28,669
  Percent of enroll.: 44.85%, 4th
Tuition, public institution (avg., 1993-94): $7,800, 9th
Tuition, private institution (avg., 1993-94): $17,698, 9th
Public library systems: 228
  Books & serial vol. per capita: 3.98, 7th
  Govt. expenditure per capita: $16.47, 22nd

LAW ENFORCEMENT, COURTS, AND PRISONS

Police protection, corrections, judicial and legal functions expenditures (1992): $269,000,000
  Per capita: $241, 29th
Police per 10,000 pop. (1993): 20.46, 28th
Prisoners (state & fed.) per 100,000 pop. (1993): 1,579.18, 45th
  Percent change (1992-93): –0.1%, 42nd
Death penalty: yes, by lethal injection or hanging if lethal injection could not be given
  Under sentence of death (1993): 0, 35th
  Executed (1993): 0

RELIGION, NUMBER AND PERCENT OF POPULATION

Agnostic: 9,966—1.20%, 2nd
Buddhist: 4,153—0.50%, 2nd
Christian: 650,279—78.30%, 46th
Hindu: NA
Jewish: 8,305—1.00%, 17th
Muslim: 1,661—0.20%, 13th
Unitarian: 1,661—0.20%, 23rd
Other: 22,423—2.70%, 2nd
None: 111,287—13.40%, 4th
Refused to answer: 20,762—2.50%, 18th

MAKING A LIVING

Personal income per capita (1994): $23,434, 11th
  Percent increase (1993-94): 4.8%, 30th
Disposable personal income per capita (1994): $20,780, 9th
Median income of households (1993): $37,964, 6th
Percent of pop. below poverty level (1993): 9.9%, 44th
  Percent 65 and over (1990): 10.2%, 39th
Expenditure for energy per person (1992): $1,796, 37th

ECONOMY

Civilian labor force (1994): 628,000
  Percent of total pop.: 55.23%, 4th
  Percent 65 and over (1990): 2.22%, 40th
  Percent female: 45.70%, 37th
Percent job growth (1980-90): 36.67%, 6th
Major employer industries (1994):
  Agriculture: NA—1.6%, 40th
  Construction: 24,000—4.1%, 25th
  Finance, insurance, & real estate: 29,000—5.0%, 30th
  Government: 65,000—11.2%, 51st
  Manufacturing: 127,000—21.9%, 9th
  Service: 135,000—23.4%, 14th
  Trade: 112,000—19.3%, 18th
  Transportation, communications, public utilities: 25,000—4.3%, 42nd
Unemployment rate (1994): 4.62%, 43rd
  Male: 4.4%, 43rd
  Female: 4.8%, 38th
Total businesses (1991): 43,357
  New business incorps. (1991): 2,387
    Percent of total businesses: 5.51%, 30th
  Business failures (1991): 279
    Percent of total businesses: 0.64%
Agriculture farm income:
  Marketing (1993): $163,000,000, 48th
    Average per farm: $54,333.33, 43rd
  Leading products (1993): Dairy products, greenhouse, Christmas trees, apples
  Average value land & build. per acre (1994): $2,374, 7th
    Percent increase (1990-94): 6.12%, 34th
  Govt. payments (1993): $2,000,000, 49th
    Average per farm: $666.67, 46th
Construction, value of all: $609,000,000
  Per capita: $549.02, 23rd

Manufactures:
Value added: $5,569,000,000
Per capita: $5,020.50, 28th
Leading products: Machinery, electric and electronic products, plastics, fabricated metal products
Value of nonfuel mineral production (1994): $40,000,000, 47th
Leading mineral products: Sand/gravel, stone, clays
Retail sales (1993): $12,566,000,000, 37th
Per household: $30,056, 2nd
Percent increase (1992-93): 8.0%, 16th
Tourism revenues (1993): $3.4 bil.
Foreign exports, in total value (1994): $1,000,000,000, 42nd
Per capita: $879.51, 38th
Gross state product per person (1993): $21,660.65, 23rd
Percent change (1990-93): 0%, 45th
Patents per 100,000 pop. (1993): 35.94, 6th
Public aid recipients (percent of resident pop. 1993): 3.4%, 50th
Medicaid recipients per 1,000 pop. (1993): 70.28, 50th
Medicare recipients per 1,000 pop. (1993): 131.67, 36th

TRAVEL AND TRANSPORTATION

Motor vehicle registrations (1993): 959,000
Per 1,000 pop.: 853.20, 12th
Motorcycle registrations (1993): 36,000
Per 1,000 pop.: 32.03, 4th
Licensed drivers per 1,000 pop. (1993): 773.13, 3rd
Deaths from motor vehicle accidents per 100,000 pop. (1993): 10.85, 45th
Public roads & streets (1993):
Total mileage: 14,938
Per 1,000 pop.: 13.29, 35th
Rural mileage: 12,069
Per 1,000 pop.: 10.74, 32nd
Urban mileage: 2,869
Per 1,000 pop.: 2.55, 44th

Interstate mileage: 224
Per 1,000 pop.: 0.20, 30th
Annual vehicle-mi. of travel per person (1993): 9,164, 32nd
Mean travel time for workers age 16+ who work away from home: 21.9 min., 14th

GOVERNMENT

Percent of voting age pop. registered (1994): 64.3%, 26th
Percent of voting age pop. voting (1994): 41.2%, 41st
Percent of voting age pop. voting for U.S. representatives (1994): 36.7%, 30th
State legislators, total (1995): 424, 1st
Women members (1992): 131
Percent of legislature: 30.9%, 6th
U.S. Congress, House members (1995): 2
Change (1985-95): 0
Revenues (1993):
State govt.: $3,011,000,000
Per capita: $2,678.83, 39th
Parimutuel & amusement taxes & lotteries, revenue per capita: $96.09, 19th
Expenditures (1993):
State govt.: $2,970,000,000
Per capita: $2,642.35, 30th
Debt outstanding (1993): $5,242,000,000
Per capita: $4,663.70, 5th

LAWS AND REGULATIONS

Legal driving age: 18, 16 if completed driver education course
Marriage age without parental consent: 18
Divorce residence requirement: 1 yr.—for qualifications check local statutes

ATTRACTIONS (1995)

State appropriations for arts agencies per capita: $0.44, 41st

SPORTS AND COMPETITION

NCAA teams (Division I): Dartmouth College Big Green, Univ. of New Hampshire Wildcats

NEW JERSEY

"Like China, New Jersey absorbs the invaders."

Federal Writers' Project, New Jersey

New Jersey gave the world both football and baseball, as well as Thomas Nast's Democratic donkey, the Republican elephant, and Santa Claus. It was the home to at least three of the most important inventors in American history. It was here that Thomas A. Edison invented the electric light bulb, Samuel F. B. Morse the electric telegraph, and John P. Holland the submarine. Washington's famed crossing of the Delaware brought his forces to the Jersey shore. The state became the "pathway of the Revolution" and suffered through four major battles. New Jersey leads the nation in many areas of manufacture and science and has long proven it is more than a convenient route from North to South.

SUPERLATIVES

- Claims greatest variety of manufactured products.
- Major glass manufacturing center.
- Leader in flag manufacture.
- Chemistry industry leader.
- The national jewelry center—Newark.
- Leader in scientific/industrial research.
- World's first four-lane highway, constructed between Elizabeth and Newark.
- First U.S. charter for a railroad.

MOMENTS IN HISTORY

- Explorers John Cabot in 1497 and Giovanni de Verrazano in 1524 sailed past what is now the Jersey shore.
- The first record of a European on New Jersey soil belongs to Henry Hudson, in 1609.

> ### So They Say
> *"This is a very good Land to fall with, and a pleasant land to see."*
>
> Henry Hudson

- By 1618 the Dutch had set up a trading post at Bergen.
- New Sweden was organized on the lower Delaware in 1638.

- Johan Printz ("Big Tub"), a 7-foot giant of 400 pounds, took control of the Swedish settlement in 1643.
- In 1664, England took over the colony and the city of Elizabeth was founded.
- New Jersey became a crown colony in 1702, under the governor of New York.
- In 1738, New Jersey got its own government.
- William Franklin, son of Benjamin Franklin, became governor in 1763.
- Dissatisfaction with the crown led to the little-known New Jersey "tea party" on December 22, 1774.
- After the Declaration of Independence, a provincial Congress took control and arrested Governor Franklin.
- After the Revolution reached New Jersey, the state endured four major battles and 90 minor skirmishes, becoming known as the "pathway of the Revolution."
- General George Washington and his armies crossed and recrossed New Jersey four times.
- Washington made his famed crossing of the Delaware River to the Jersey shore, and his victory at the Battle of Trenton at Christmas time, 1776, gave hope to the American cause.

> ### So They Say
> *"Our hopes were blasted by that unhappy affair at Trenton."*
>
> Anonymous British officer

- By the close of the Revolution, 17,000 New Jersey men had fought for the new country, and New Jersey became known as the Garden State for supplying war provisions.
- In 1783, Princeton was the temporary capital of the new country.
- New Jersey became the third state on December 18, 1787.
- The new state constitution of 1844 granted many new rights, and slaves gained a degree of freedom in 1846.

• The first organized baseball game was played at Hoboken in 1846.

• Divided over slavery, New Jersey nevertheless was important in the Underground Railroad. After the Civil War broke out, the New Jersey Brigade in May 1861 became the first to reach Washington, D.C.'s defenses.

• By war's end, 88,000 from New Jersey had been in service. Because of overcrowding and disease, thousands of Confederate prisoners died at the prison camp at Fort Delaware.

So They Say

"...a thousand ill, 20 deaths a day from dysentery. ...Thus a Christian nation treats the captives of the sword."

Anonymous federal inspector
at Fort Delaware

• The nation's first intercollegiate football game was played at New Brunswick in 1869 between Rutgers and Princeton. Rutgers won.

• Opposition to the power of big business brought reforms in the period 1911-1913, under Governor Woodrow Wilson.

• Spurred by the inventions of Thomas Edison in New Jersey, the state reigned as motion picture capital of the world until about 1916.

• During World War I, the state led in shipbuilding and production of artillery shells, and Hoboken became the major embarkation point of the war.

• The Miss America contest began at Atlantic City in 1921.

• The great George Washington Bridge was opened in 1931, and Bergen County became "the bedroom of New York."

• The days of the passenger dirigible came to an end at Lakehurst with the spectacular destruction of the *Hindenburg* in 1937.

• In World War II, New Jersey was predominant in production of airplane engines and warships, among other war matériel; and Camp Kilmer was a major debarkation center.

• During the 1940s and 1950s, a series of hurricanes—including Diane, Donna, and Hazel—took many lives and destroyed hundreds of millions of dollars' worth of property.

• The great Meadowlands development opened in 1976 with games of major league teams.

• The 1980s were notable for the resumption of large-scale gambling at Atlantic City.

• In 1991, New Jersey terminated ocean dumping.

THAT'S INTERESTING

• Johan Printz, governor of New Sweden, was so heavy (400 pounds) that the gangplank almost collapsed when he arrived at his colony. The Indians called him "Big Tub."

• When American Revolutionary heroine Molly Pitcher's husband was killed, she fought in his place at his cannon.

• The first real game of baseball (played under the Cartwright rules) was played at Hoboken in 1846.

• The first derby in the country was run at Passaic in 1864.

• One William Campbell, a non-Indian, founded a wampum mint near Hackensack; it operated until 1889.

• Colonel John Stevens of Hoboken operated an experimental railroad track of 630 feet near there.

• Standard Time was devised in 1883 by William F. Allen of South Orange.

NOTABLE NATIVES

William (Count) Basie (Red Bank, 1904-1984), musician. **Aaron Burr** (Newark, 1756-1836), public official/political leader. **Grover Cleveland** (Caldwell, 1837-1908), U.S. president. **James Fenimore Cooper** (Burlington, 1789-1851), author. **Stephen Crane** (Newark, 1871-1900), author. **Alfred Joyce Kilmer** (New Brunswick, 1886-1918), poet. **James Lawrence** (Burlington, 1781-1813), naval officer. **Mary Ludwig Hays McCauley (Molly Pitcher)** (Trenton, 1754-1832), Revolutionary War heroine. **Jack Nicholson** (Neptune, 1937-), actor. **Dorothy Parker** (West End, 1893-1967), author. **Zebulon Montgomery Pike** (Trenton, 1779-1813), soldier/explorer. **Paul Bustill Robeson** (Princeton, 1898-1976), singer/actor. **Philip Milton Roth** (Newark, 1933-), author. **Francis Albert (Frank) Sinatra** (Hoboken, 1915-), singer/actor. **Amos Alonzo Stagg** (West Orange, 1862-1965), football coach. **Robert Field Stockman** (Princeton, 1834-1902), naval officer. **Meryl Streep** (Summit, 1949-), actress. **Albert Payson Terhune** (Newark, 1872-1942), author. **William Henry Vanderbilt** (New Brunswick, 1821-1865), financier. **William Carlos Williams** (Rutherford, 1883-1963), poet/physician.

GENERAL

Admitted to statehood: December 18, 1787
Origin of name: The Duke of York, 1664, gave a patent to John Berkely and Sir George Carteret to be called Nova Caesaria, or New Jersey, after England's Isle of Jersey
Capital: Trenton
Nickname: Garden State
Motto: Liberty and Prosperity
Animal: Horse
Bird: Eastern goldfinch
Insect: Honeybee
Colors: Buff and blue
Flower: Purple violet
Song: "New Jersey Loyalty" (unofficial)
Tree: Red oak

THE LAND

Area: 8,215 sq. mi., 46th
 Land: 7,419 sq. mi., 46th
 Water: 796 sq. mi., 33rd
  Inland water: 371 sq. mi., 39th
  Coastal water: 425 sq. mi., 13th
Topography: Appalachian Valley in the NW has highest elevation; Appalachian Highlands, flat-topped NE-SW mountain ranges; piedmont plateau, low plains broken by high ridges; coastal plain, covering three-fifths of state in SE, gradually rises to gentle slopes.
Number of counties: 21
Geographic center: Mercer, 5 mi. SE of Trenton
Length: 150 mi.; width: 70 mi.
Highest point: 1,803 ft. (High Point), 40th
Lowest point: sea level (Atlantic Ocean), 3rd
Mean elevation: 250 ft., 46th
Coastline: 130 mi., 13th
Shoreline: 1,792 mi., 14th

CLIMATE AND ENVIRONMENT

Temp., highest: 110 deg. on July 10, 1936, at Runyon; lowest: –34 deg. on Jan. 5, 1904, at River Vale
Monthly average: highest: 85.6 deg., 35th; lowest: 24.2 deg., 34th; spread (high to low): 61.4 deg., 41st
Hazardous waste sites (1993): 109, 1st
Endangered species: Mammals: 1—Indiana bat; birds: 1—American peregrine falcon; reptiles: 2; amphibians: none; fishes: none; invertebrates: none; plants: 1

MAJOR CITIES
POPULATION, 1990
PERCENTAGE INCREASE, 1980-90

Elizabeth, 110,002—3.58%
Jersey City, 228,537—2.24%
Newark, 275,221— –16.41%
Paterson, 140,891—2.12%
Trenton, 88,675— –3.74%

THE PEOPLE

Population (1995): 7,945,298, 9th
 Percent change (1990-95): 2.8%, 39th
Population (2000 proj.): 8,135,000, 9th
 Percent change (1990-2000): 5.24%, 39th
Per sq. mi. (1994): 1,065.4, 2nd
Percent in metro. area (1992): 100.0%, 1st
Foreign born: 967,000, 5th
 Percent: 12.5%, 5th
Top three ancestries reported:
 Italian, 18.85%
 Irish, 18.31%
 German, 18.21%
White: 6,130,465, 79.31%, 35th
Black: 1,036,825, 13.41%, 17th
Native American: 14,970, 0.19%, 45th
Asian, Pacific Isle: 272,521, 3.53%, 6th
Other races: 275,407, 3.56%, 9th
Hispanic origin: 739,861, 9.57%, 9th
Percent over 5 yrs. speaking language other than English at home: 19.5%, 7th
Percent males: 48.33%, 38th; percent females: 51.67%, 14th
Percent never married: 29.1%, 7th
Marriages per 1,000 (1993): 6.8, 46th
Divorces per 1,000 (1993): 3.1, 44th
Median age: 34.5
Under 5 years (1994): 7.33%, 22nd
Under 18 years (1994): 24.43%, 43rd
65 years & older (1994): 13.6%, 16th
Percent increase among the elderly (1990-94): 4.36%, 35th

OF VITAL IMPORTANCE

Live births per 1,000 pop. (1993): 15.6, 13th
Infant mortality rate per 1,000 births (1992): 8.4, 28th
 Rate for blacks (1990): 17.3, 14th
 Rate for whites (1990): 6.8, 44th
Births to unmarried women, % of total (1992): 26.4%, 32nd
Births to teenage mothers, % of total (1992): 8.0%, 48th
Abortions (1992): 55,320, 7th
 Rate per 1,000 women 14-44 years old: 31.0, 7th

Percent change (1988-92): −12%, 32nd
Average lifetime (1979-81): 74.00, 22nd
Deaths per 1,000 pop. (1993): 9.2, 20th
Causes of death per 100,000 pop.:
  Accidents & adverse effects (1992): 25.8, 47th
  Atherosclerosis (1991): 5.7, 40th
  Cancer (1991): 228.5, 10th
  Cerebrovascular diseases (1992): 49.6, 39th
  Chronic liver diseases & cirrhosis (1991): 11.4, 8th
  Chronic obstructive pulmonary diseases (1992): 31.0, 44th
  Diabetes mellitus (1992): 26.9, 5th
  Diseases of heart (1992): 304.5, 17th
  Pneumonia, flu (1991): 29 1, 29th
  Suicide (1992): 6.6, 50th

KEEPING WELL

Active nonfederal physicians per 100,000 pop. (1993): 263, 7th
Dentists per 100,000 (1991): 78, 4th
Nurses per 100,000 (1992): 827, 16th
Hospitals per 100,000 (1993): 1.23, 47th
  Admissions per 1,000 (1993): 140.37, 10th
  Occupancy rate per 100 beds (1993): 77.0, 3rd
  Average cost per patient per day (1993): $829, 29th
  Average cost per stay (1993): $6,540, 12th
  Average stay (1992): 11.6 days, 6th
AIDS cases (adult, 1993): 5,434; per 100,000: 69.0, 4th
HIV infection, not yet AIDS (1993): 5,162
Other notifiable diseases:
  Gonorrhea: 230.0, 22nd
  Measles: 6.1, 16th
  Syphilis: 56.7, 13th
  Tuberculosis: 12.5, 10th
Pop. without health insur. (1991-93): 12.7%, 25th

HOUSEHOLDS BY TYPE

Total households (1994): 2,845,000
  Percent change (1990-94): 1.8%, 43rd
  Per 1,000 pop.: 359.94, 42nd
  Percent of households 65 yrs. and over: 23.16%, 15th
  Persons per household (1994): 2.72, 9th
Family households: 2,021,346
  Percent of total: 72.33%, 13th
Nonfamily households: 773,365
  Percent of total: 27.67%, 39th

Pop. living in group quarters: 171,368
  Percent of pop.: 2.22%, 45th

LIVING QUARTERS

Total housing units: 3,075,310
  Persons per unit: 2.51, 7th
Occupied housing units: 2,794,711
  Percent of total units: 90.88%, 17th
  Persons per unit: 2.64, 10th
  Percent of units with over 1 person per room: 3.89%, 18th
Owner-occupied units: 1,813,381
  Percent of total units: 58.97%, 26th
  Percent of occupied units: 64.89%, 38th
  Persons per unit: 2.87, 4th
  Median value: $162,300, 5th
Renter-occupied units: 981,330
  Percent of total units: 31.91%, 16th
  Percent of occupied units: 35.11%, 16th
  Persons per unit: 2.40, 17th
  Median contract rent: $521, 3rd
  Rental vacancy rate: 7.4%, 37th
Mobile home, trailer & other as a percent of occupied housing units: 2.74%, 46th
Persons in emergency shelters for homeless persons: 7,470, 0.097%, 7th
Persons visible in street locations: 1,639, 0.0212%, 8th
Persons in shelters for abused women: 255, 0.0033%, 41st
Nursing home population: 47,054, 0.61%, 35th

CRIME INDEX PER 100,000 (1992-93)

Total reported: 4,800.8, 30th
  Violent: 626.9, 23rd
    Murder and nonnegligent manslaughter: 5.3, 32nd
    Aggravated assault: 297.5, 30th
    Robbery: 296.0, 8th
    Forcible rape: 28.1, 41st
  Property: 4,174.0, 30th
    Burglary: 974.0, 30th
    Larceny, theft: 2,486.1, 41st
    Motor vehicle theft: 714.0, 8th
Drug abuse violations (1990): 599.6, 4th
Child-abuse rate per 1,000 children (1993): 5.54, 46th

TEACHING AND LEARNING

Pop. 3 and over enrolled in school: 1,867,402
  Percent of pop.: 25.2%, 46th

Public elementary & secondary schools (1992-93): 2,292
  Total enrollment (1992): 1,130,560
    Percent of total pop.: 14.46%, 47th
  Teachers (1992): 83,057
    Percent of pop.: 1.06%, 20th
  Pupil/teacher ratio (fall 1992): 13.6, 50th
  Teachers' avg. salary (1992-93): $46,024, 5th
  Expenditure per capita (1990-91): $4,093.46, 9th
  Expenditure per pupil (1991-92): $9,317, 2nd
Percent of graduates taking SAT (1993): 76%, 4th
  Mean SAT verbal scores: 419, 39th
  Mean SAT mathematical scores: 473, 37th
Percent of graduates taking ACT (1995): 3%, 47th
  Mean ACT scores: 20.4, 37th
Percent of pop. over 25 completing:
  Less than 9th grade: 9.4%, 26th
  High school: 76.7%, 26th
  College degree(s): 24.9%, 6th
Higher education, institutions (1993-94): 61
  Enrollment (1992): 342,446
    Percent of pop.: 4.38%, 49th
  White non-Hispanic (1992): 247,458
    Percent of enroll.: 72.26%, 40th
  Black non-Hispanic (1992): 38,001
    Percent of enroll.: 11.10%, 16th
  Hispanic (1992): 25,702
    Percent of enroll.: 7.51%, 8th
  Asian/Pacific Islander (1992): 17,075
    Percent of enroll.: 4.99%, 6th
  American Indian/AK native (1992): 837
    Percent of enroll.: 0.24%, 47th
  Nonresident alien (1992): 13,373
    Percent of enroll.: 3.91%, 9th
  Female (1992): 190,598
    Percent of enroll.: 55.66%, 18th
  Pub. institutions (1993-94): 33
    Enrollment (1992): 277,599
    Percent of enroll.: 81.06%, 31st
  Private institutions (1993-94): 28
    Enrollment (1992): 64,847
    Percent of enroll.: 18.94%, 21st
  Tuition, public institution (avg., 1993-94): $8,252, 5th
  Tuition, private institution (avg., 1993-94): $17,855, 8th
Public library systems: 311
  Books & serial vol. per capita: 3.56, 11th
  Govt. expenditure per capita: $21.01, 15th

LAW ENFORCEMENT, COURTS, AND PRISONS

Police protection, corrections, judicial and legal functions expenditures (1992): $2,887,000,000
  Per capita: $369, 8th
Police per 10,000 pop. (1993): 35.74, 2nd
Prisoners (state & fed.) per 100,000 pop. (1993): 3,032.32, 24th
  Percent change (1992-93): 5.2%, 25th
Death penalty: yes, by lethal injection
  Under sentence of death (1993): 7, 28th
  Executed (1993): 0

RELIGION, NUMBER AND PERCENT OF POPULATION

Agnostic: 35,584—0.60%, 19th
Buddhist: 5,931—0.10%, 17th
Christian: 5,041,117—85.00%, 33rd
Hindu: 17,792—0.30%, 2nd
Jewish: 255,021—4.30%, 2nd
Muslim: 35,584—0.60%, 2nd
Unitarian: 5,931—0.10%, 31st
Other: 47,446—0.80%, 37th
None: 326,190—5.50%, 39th
Refused to answer: 160,130—2.70%, 16th

MAKING A LIVING

Personal income per capita (1994): $28,038, 3rd
  Percent increase (1993-94): 4.3%, 37th
Disposable personal income per capita (1994): $23,929, 3rd
Median income of households (1993): $40,500, 3rd
Percent of pop. below poverty level (1993): 10.9%, 37th
  Percent 65 and over (1990): 8.5%, 47th
Expenditure for energy per person (1992): $2,066, 10th

ECONOMY

Civilian labor force (1994): 3,991,000
  Percent of total pop.: 50.49%, 32nd
  Percent 65 and over (1990): 3.29%, 11th
  Percent female: 45.38%, 39th
Percent job growth (1980-90): 21.77%, 21st
Major employer industries (1994):
  Agriculture: 35,000—1.0%, 46th
  Construction: 134,000—3.6%, 42nd
  Finance, insurance, & real estate: 297,000—8.0%, 4th
  Government: 544,000—14.7%, 32nd

Manufacturing: 565,000—15.2%, 26th
Service: 911,000—24.6%, 10th
Trade: 709,000—19.1%, 23rd
Transportation, communications, public
    utilities: 273,000—7.4%, 3rd
Unemployment rate (1994): 6.82%, 9th
    Male: 6.8%, 11th
    Female: 6.8%, 10th
Total businesses (1991): 263,070
    New business incorps. (1991): 27,994
        Percent of total businesses: 10.64%, 6th
    Business failures (1991): 1,265
    Percent of total businesses: 0.48%
Agriculture farm income:
    Marketing (1993): $706,000,000, 39th
        Average per farm: $88,250.00, 23rd
    Leading products (1993): Greenhouse, dairy
        products, eggs, blueberries
    Average value land & build. per acre
        (1994): $4,840, 2nd
        Percent increase (1990-94): 4.45%,
        43rd
    Govt. payments (1993): $7,000,000, 41st
        Average per farm: $875.00, 43rd
Construction, value of all: $3,734,000,000
    Per capita: $483.04, 31st
Manufactures:
    Value added: $45,179,000,000
    Per capita: $5,844.49, 15th
    Leading products: Chemicals, electric and
        electronic equipment, nonelectrical ma-
        chinery, fabricated metals
Value of nonfuel mineral production (1994):
    $274,000,000, 37th
Leading mineral products: Stone, sand/gravel,
    zinc
Retail sales (1993): $67,277,000,000, 9th
    Per household: $23,626, 9th
    Percent increase (1992-93): -1.5%, 51st
Tourism revenues (1994): $22.6 bil.
Foreign exports, in total value (1994):
    $10,519,000,000, 13th
    Per capita: $1,330.85, 22nd
Gross state product per person (1993):
    $27,423.72, 6th
    Percent change (1990-93): 2.90%, 32nd
Patents per 100,000 pop. (1993): 41.07,
    4th
Public aid recipients (percent of resident pop.
    1993): 6.1%, 33rd
Medicaid recipients per 1,000 pop. (1993):
    101.03, 35th
Medicare recipients per 1,000 pop. (1993):
    145.57, 22nd

TRAVEL AND TRANSPORTATION

Motor vehicle registrations (1993): 5,641,000
    Per 1,000 pop.: 717.78, 40th
Motorcycle registrations (1993): 89,000
    Per 1,000 pop.: 11.32, 34th
Licensed drivers per 1,000 pop. (1993):
    694.62, 23rd
Deaths from motor vehicle accidents per
    100,000 pop. (1993): 10.01, 47th
Public roads & streets (1993):
    Total mileage: 35,097
        Per 1,000 pop.: 4.47, 49th
    Rural mileage: 11,068
        Per 1,000 pop.: 1.41, 49th
    Urban mileage: 24,029
        Per 1,000 pop.: 3.06, 29th
    Interstate mileage: 413
        Per 1,000 pop.: 0.05, 49th
Annual vehicle-mi. of travel per person
    (1993): 7,596, 45th
Mean travel time for workers age 16+ who
    work away from home: 25.3 min., 4th

GOVERNMENT

Percent of voting age pop. registered (1994):
    61.6%, 33rd
    Percent of voting age pop. voting (1994):
        40.3%, 43rd
    Percent of voting age pop. voting for U.S.
        representatives (1994): 33.6%, 41st
State legislators, total (1995): 120, 36th
    Women members (1992): 15
        Percent of legislature: 12.5%, 40th
U.S. Congress, House members (1995): 13
    Change (1985-95): -1
Revenues (1993):
    State govt.: $29,614,000,000
        Per capita: $3,768.16, 9th
    Parimutuel & amusement taxes & lotteries,
        revenue per capita: $198.12, 3rd
Expenditures (1993):
    State govt.: $28,923,000,000
        Per capita: $3,680.24, 7th
Debt outstanding (1993): $21,779,000,000
    Per capita: $2,771.22, 10th

LAWS AND REGULATIONS

Legal driving age: 17
Marriage age without parental consent: 18
Divorce residence requirement: 1 yr., for
    qualifications check local statutes

ATTRACTIONS (1995)

Major opera companies: 3
Major symphony orchestras: 1

Major dance companies: 1

Major professional theater companies (non-profit): 1

State appropriations for arts agencies per capita: $1.35, 13th

State Fair in August at Cherry Hill

SPORTS AND COMPETITION

NCAA teams (Division I): Fairleigh Dickinson Univ. Knights, Monmouth Univ. Hawks, Princeton Univ. Tigers, Rider Univ. Broncos, Seton Hall Univ. Pirates, St. Peter's College Peacocks, State Univ. of N.J.-Rutgers Scarlet Knights

NBA basketball teams: New Jersey Nets, Continental Airlines Arena

NFL football teams: New York Jets (AFC) Giants Stadium; New York Giants (NFC), Giants Stadium

NHL hockey teams: New Jersey Devils, Continental Airlines Arena

NEW MEXICO

"I think New Mexico was the greatest experience from the outside world that I ever had. It certainly changed me forever....The moment I saw the brilliant, proud morning shine high over the deserts of Santa Fe, something stood still in my soul....For a greatness of beauty I have never experienced anything like New Mexico....Just day itself is tremendous there."

D. H. Lawrence, novelist

Early explorers failed to find the fabled seven cities of gold in New Mexico, but the prehistoric cities of the Pueblo peoples far outshone the mythical ones. Among their more important contributions, these gave the state the nation's oldest "cooperative apartments." By contrast with its ancient history, New Mexico is the state where the atomic age became a reality. This land of sunshine is governed from the nation's oldest state capital, where visitors from around the world can experience superlative grand opera. Visitors may follow the course of the country's oldest highway, take in the unique sights of Taos Pueblo and the other pueblos, and enjoy the Indian festivals held around the state. The remarkable attraction of the state for authors, artists, and musicians, as well as the state's many other cultural assets, have long been evident.

SUPERLATIVES

• Oldest capital city in the United States—Santa Fe.
• Oldest highway in the United States—the King's Highway.
• Yucca, the only commercially valuable state flower.
• First in production of potash.
• Leads in dry ice production from carbon dioxide wells.
• Birthplace of the U.S. livestock industry.

MOMENTS IN HISTORY

• The Pueblo people are among the most remarkable and most studied of prehistoric Americans. They developed substantial cities of stone masonry—their "skyscrapers" are noted as a distinctive contribution to world architecture. They developed great skill in weaving, created complex systems of irrigation, and domesticated turkeys. They fabricated tools, and their jewelry featured fine silverwork with turquoise. Their golden age appears to have been about 950-1200 A.D. New Mexico boasts many fascinating pueblo ruins.
• The great expedition of Francisco Vásquez de Coronado crossed what is now New Mexico in 1540.
• On July 11, 1598, wealthy Don Juan de Onate established San Juan, the first European settlement in New Mexico (the second in the United States), at the Tewa pueblo of Yugeuingge. In 1605, Onate journeyed to the Gulf of California, and he carved his signature on famed Inscription Rock.
• Don Pedro de Peralta founded Santa Fe in the winter of 1609-1610.
• By 1626 the Franciscan Fathers had established 43 missions, with 34,000 Indian converts.
• Because the Spaniards treated them so harshly, the Indians revolted under Pope, a Tewa medicine man, in 1680 and captured Santa Fe.
• The Indians ruled Santa Fe until 1692, when Governor Don Diego de Vagas recaptured it.
• Albuquerque, named for the Duke of Albuquerque, was founded in 1706.
• On his expedition of 1806-1807, Zebulon Pike was captured and taken to Spanish Santa Fe.
• On November 6, 1822, William H. Becknell brought the first wagon loads of goods into Santa Fe from the Northeast, blazing the Santa Fe Trail and pioneering trade with the states.
• During the Mexican War of 1846, U.S. military forces brought New Mexico under U.S. control.

So They Say

On the merchants of the early 1800s:
"....My father saw them unload...and when their rawhide packages of silver dollars were dumped on the sidewalk one of the men cut the thongs, and the money spilled out and clinking on the stone pavement rolled into the gutter. Everyone was excited."

Anonymous

• During the Civil War, Confederate forces captured Santa Fe on March 10, 1862, but General Henry H. Sibley recaptured the capital on April 8.
• The Plains Indians carried on warfare with the settlers for nearly 50 years, until Indian leader Geronimo surrendered in 1886.

So They Say

"Everything is quiet in Cimarron. Nobody has been killed for three days."

Las Vegas Gazette, on the lawlessness of the frontier

• In 1901, cowboy Jim White discovered a "hole in the ground." This proved to be a vast underground wonderland, and it became known as Carlsbad Caverns.
• On January 6, 1912, New Mexico became the 47th state.
• Pancho Villa, the Mexican revolutionary, raided the border town of Columbus in 1916.
• During World War I, 17,157 New Mexicans served, and 500 lost their lives.
• The atomic age was born at Alamogordo on July 16, 1945, with the test explosion of the first atomic bomb.
• From 1940 to 1982, the population expanded by almost 300%, but the 1990 census indicated a much slower growth.
• In 1985 a major rating of American cities placed Albuquerque among the best places to live in the nation.
• The state was forbidden in court in 1991 to open the nation's first permanent nuclear-waste disposal site.

THAT'S INTERESTING

• In the Four Corners region, where four states touch (New Mexico, Arizona, Utah, and Colorado), visitors often sprawl out so they can say they have slept in all four at once.
• Pueblo Bonito housed as many as 1,500 people in its 800 rooms, becoming perhaps the first "condominium."
• Just before his sentence of hanging was carried out, the outlaw Black Jack Ketchum demanded of the hangman, "Hurry it up; I'm due in hell for dinner."
• One of the principal attractions of Carlsbad Caverns is the evening flight of millions of bats. Winging their way out of the cavern entrance, the swarm of bats look like a column of smoke.

NEW MEXICO NOTABLES

William Henry (Billy the Kid) Bonney (New York City, 1859-1881), outlaw. **Christopher (Kit) Carson** (Madison City, KY, 1809-1868), trapper/Indian agent/soldier. **John Simpson Chisum** (Hardeman County, TN, 1824-1868), cattleman. **Emerson Hough** (Newton, IA, 1857-1923), author. **Jean Baptiste Lamy** (France, 1814-1888), religious leader. **David Herbert (D. H.) Lawrence** (England, 1885-1930), author. **Mangas Coloradas** (in southwest New Mexico, 1770?-1863), Indian leader. **William Henry (Bill) Mauldin** (Mountain Park, 1921-), cartoonist. **Georgia O'Keeffe** (Sun Prairie, WI, 1887-1986), artist. **Albert Pike** (Boston, MA, 1809-1891), lawyer/soldier. **Eugene Manlove Rhodes** (Tecumseh, NE, 1869-1934), cowboy/author. **Ernest Thompson Seton** (England, 1860-1946), author/naturalist. **Frank Springer** (Wapella, IA, 1848-1927), lawyer/paleontologist.

GENERAL

Admitted to statehood: January 6, 1912
Origin of name: Spaniards in Mexico applied term to land north and west of Rio Grande in the 16th century.
Capital: Santa Fe
Nickname: Land of Enchantment
Motto: *Crescit Eundo*—It grows as it goes
Animal: Black bear
Bird: Roadrunner
Fish: Cutthroat trout
Flower: Yucca
Gem: Turquoise
Song: "Asi Es Nuevo Mejico" and "O, Fair New Mexico"
Tree: Piñon

THE LAND

Area: 121,598 sq. mi., 5th
  Land: 121,364 sq. mi., 5th
  Water: 234 sq. mi., 47th
    Inland water: 234 sq. mi., 44th
Topography: Eastern third, Great Plains; central third, Rocky Mountains (85% of the state is over 4,000 ft. elevation); western third, high plateau
Number of counties: 33
Geographic center: Torrance, 12 mi. SSW of Willard
Length: 370 mi.; width: 343 mi.
Highest point: 13,161 ft. (Wheeler Peak), 8th
Lowest point: 2,842 ft. (Red Bluff Reservoir), 49th
Mean elevation: 5,700 ft., 4th

CLIMATE AND ENVIRONMENT

Temp., highest: 116 deg. on July 14, 1934, at Orogrande; lowest: –50 deg. on Feb. 1, 1951, at Gavilan
Monthly average: highest: 92.8 deg., 10th; lowest: 22.3 deg., 30th; spread (high to low): 70.5 deg., 22nd
Hazardous waste sites (1993): 11, 34th
Endangered species: Mammals: 3—Mexican long-nosed bat, Sanborn's long-nosed bat, Mexican gray wolf; birds: 3—Whooping crane, American peregrine falcon, Least tern; reptiles: none; amphibians: none; fishes: 4; invertebrates: 1; plants: 7

MAJOR CITIES
POPULATION, 1990
PERCENTAGE INCREASE, 1980-90

Albuquerque, 384,736—15.56%
Las Cruces, 62,126—37.79%
Roswell, 44,654—12.55%
Santa Fe, 55,859—13.63%
South Valley, 35,701— –8.26%

THE PEOPLE

Population (1995): 1,685,401, 36th
  Percent change (1990-95): 11.2%, 7th
Population (2000 proj.): 1,823,000, 36th
  Percent change (1990-2000): 20.32%, 8th
Per sq. mi. (1994): 13.6, 45th
Percent in metro. area (1992): 56.0%, 36th
Foreign born: 81,000, 28th
  Percent: 5.3%, 16th

Top three ancestries reported:
  German, 15.45%
  Mexican, 14.26%
  Spanish, 12.61%
White: 1,146,028, 75.64%, 38th
Black: 30,210, 1.99%, 40th
Native American: 134,355, 8.87%, 2nd
Asian, Pacific Isle: 14,124, 0.93%, 30th
Other races: 190,352, 12.56%, 2nd
Hispanic origin: 597,224, 39.42%, 1st
Percent over 5 yrs. speaking language other than English at home: 35.5%, 1st
Percent males: 49.19%, 15th; percent females: 50.81%, 37th
Percent never married: 25.8%, 24th
Marriages per 1,000 (1993): 7.8, 35th
Divorces per 1,000 (1993): 6.2, 7th
Median age: 31.2
Under 5 years (1994): 8.46%, 5th
Under 18 years (1994): 30.11%, 3rd
65 years & older (1994): 11.0%, 45th
Percent increase among the elderly (1990-94): 11.00%, 7th

OF VITAL IMPORTANCE

Live births per 1,000 pop. (1993): 17.1, 6th
Infant mortality rate per 1,000 births (1992): 7.6, 34th
  Rate for blacks (1990): 12.8, 39th
  Rate for whites (1990): 9.3, 4th
Births to unmarried women, % of total (1992): 39.5%, 4th
Births to teenage mothers, % of total (1992): 17.0%, 6th
Abortions (1992): 6,410, 38th
  Rate per 1,000 women 14-44 years old: 17.7, 29th
  Percent change (1988-92): –7%, 23rd
Average lifetime (1979-81): 74.01, 21st
Deaths per 1,000 pop. (1993): 7.3, 45th
Causes of death per 100,000 pop.:
  Accidents & adverse effects (1992): 52.0, 3rd
  Atherosclerosis (1991): 6.5, 29th
  Cancer (1991): 157.4, 47th
  Cerebrovascular diseases (1992): 38.1, 49th
  Chronic liver diseases & cirrhosis (1991): 14.2, 2nd
  Chronic obstructive pulmonary diseases (1992): 33.8, 34th
  Diabetes mellitus (1992): 23.4, 9th
  Diseases of heart (1992): 187.5, 47th
  Pneumonia, flu (1991): 23.6, 45th
  Suicide (1992): 19.2, 2nd

KEEPING WELL

Active nonfederal physicians per 100,000 pop. (1993): 190, 30th
Dentists per 100,000 (1991): 41, 49th
Nurses per 100,000 (1992): 600, 41st
Hospitals per 100,000 (1993): 2.29, 26th
 Admissions per 1,000 (1993): 93.50, 45th
 Occupancy rate per 100 beds (1993): 54.0, 48th
 Average cost per patient per day (1993): $1,046, 9th
 Average cost per stay (1993): $5,600, 29th
 Average stay (1992): 5.9 days, 48th
AIDS cases (adult, 1993): 294; per 100,000: 18.2, 29th
HIV infection, not yet AIDS (1993): NA
Other notifiable diseases:
 Gonorrhea: 81.5, 40th
 Measles: 6.0, 17th
 Syphilis: 14.7, 28th
 Tuberculosis: 7.5, 21st
Pop. without health insur. (1991-93): 21.3%, 5th

HOUSEHOLDS BY TYPE

Total households (1994): 587,000
 Percent change (1990-94): 8.1%, 10th
 Per 1,000 pop.: 354.90, 47th
 Percent of households 65 yrs. and over: 19.76%, 39th
 Persons per household (1994): 2.77, 5th
Family households: 391,487
 Percent of total: 72.14%, 14th
Nonfamily households: 151,222
 Percent of total: 27.86%, 38th
Pop. living in group quarters: 28,807
 Percent of pop.: 1.90%, 50th

LIVING QUARTERS

Total housing units: 632,058
 Persons per unit: 2.40, 26th
Occupied housing units: 542,709
 Percent of total units: 85.86%, 40th
 Persons per unit: 2.69, 8th
 Percent of units with over 1 person per room: 7.89%, 6th
Owner-occupied units: 365,965
 Percent of total units: 57.90%, 31st
 Percent of occupied units: 67.43%, 25th
 Persons per unit: 2.85, 6th
 Median value: $70,100, 24th
Renter-occupied units: 176,744
 Percent of total units: 27.96%, 30th
 Percent of occupied units: 32.57%, 27th

 Persons per unit: 2.52, 8th
 Median contract rent: $312, 29th
 Rental vacancy rate: 11.4%, 11th
Mobile home, trailer & other as a percent of occupied housing units: 20.71%, 2nd
Persons in emergency shelters for homeless persons: 667, 0.044%, 29th
Persons visible in street locations: 164, 0.0108%, 18th
Persons in shelters for abused women: 108, 0.0071%, 7th
Nursing home population: 6,276, 0.41%, 46th

CRIME INDEX PER 100,000 (1992-93)

Total reported: 6,266.1, 8th
 Violent: 929.7, 9th
  Murder and nonnegligent manslaughter: 8.0, 23rd
  Aggravated assault: 731.1, 4th
  Robbery: 138.4, 26th
  Forcible rape: 52.1, 10th
 Property: 5,336.4, 10th
  Burglary: 1,421.2, 5th
  Larceny, theft: 3,510.1, 13th
  Motor vehicle theft: 405.1, 28th
Drug abuse violations (1990): 220.2, 32nd
Child-abuse rate per 1,000 children (1993): 14.30, 24th

TEACHING AND LEARNING

Pop. 3 and over enrolled in school: 435,989
 Percent of pop.: 30.2%, 4th
Public elementary & secondary schools (1992-93): 700
 Total enrollment (1992): 315,668
  Percent of total pop.: 19.95%, 6th
 Teachers (1992): 17,912
  Percent of pop.: 1.13%, 14th
 Pupil/teacher ratio (fall 1992): 17.6, 14th
 Teachers' avg. salary (1992-93): $28,090, 47th
 Expenditure per capita (1990-91): $3,358.76, 27th
 Expenditure per pupil (1991-92): $3,765, 46th
Percent of graduates taking SAT (1993): 11%, 35th
 Mean SAT verbal scores: 478, 15th
 Mean SAT mathematical scores: 525, 16th
Percent of graduates taking ACT (1995): 59%, 21st
 Mean ACT scores: 20.1, 42nd

Percent of pop. over 25 completing:
  Less than 9th grade: 11.4%, 15th
  High school: 75.1%, 33rd
  College degree(s): 20.4%, 22nd
Higher education, institutions (1993-94): 32
  Enrollment (1992): 99,276
    Percent of pop.: 6.28%, 15th
    White non-Hispanic (1992): 58,334
      Percent of enroll.: 58.96%, 48th
    Black non-Hispanic (1992): 2,933
      Percent of enroll.: 2.95%, 38th
    Hispanic (1992): 28,577
      Percent of enroll.: 28.79%, 1st
    Asian/Pacific Islander (1992): 1,462
      Percent of enroll.: 1.47%, 36th
    American Indian/AK native (1992): 5,675
      Percent of enroll.: 5.72%, 4th
    Nonresident alien (1992): 2,095
      Percent of enroll.: 2.11%, 38th
    Female (1992): 55,741
      Percent of enroll.: 56.15%, 13th
  Pub. institutions (1993-94): 23
    Enrollment (1992): 94,901
      Percent of enroll.: 95.59%, 3rd
  Private institutions (1993-94): 9
    Enrollment (1992): 4,375
      Percent of enroll.: 4.41%, 49th
  Tuition, public institution (avg., 1993-94): $5,094, 38th
  Tuition, private institution (avg., 1993-94): $13,126, 23rd
Public library systems: 68
  Books & serial vol. per capita: 2.41, 29th
  Govt. expenditure per capita: $12.89, 30th

LAW ENFORCEMENT, COURTS, AND PRISONS

Police protection, corrections, judicial and legal functions expenditures (1992): $463,000,000
  Per capita: $293, 20th
Police per 10,000 pop. (1993): 21.28, 22nd
Prisoners (state & fed.) per 100,000 pop. (1993): 2,163.37, 36th
  Percent change (1992-93): 6.9%, 20th
Death penalty: yes, by lethal injection
  Under sentence of death (1993): 1, 33rd
  Executed (1993): 0

RELIGION, NUMBER AND PERCENT OF POPULATION

Agnostic: 10,683—1.00%, 10th
Buddhist: 1,068—0.10%, 17th
Christian: 910,216—85.20%, 32nd

Hindu: NA
Jewish: 7,478—0.70%, 21st
Muslim: NA
Unitarian: 3,205—0.30%, 15th
Other: 11,752—1.10%, 32nd
None: 106,833—10.00%, 11th
Refused to answer: 17,093—1.60%, 39th

MAKING A LIVING

Personal income per capita (1994): $17,106, 48th
  Percent increase (1993-94): 4.6%, 34th
Disposable personal income per capita (1994): $15,308, 48th
Median income of households (1993): $26,758, 41st
Percent of pop. below poverty level (1993): 17.4%, 12th
  Percent 65 and over (1990): 16.5%, 14th
Expenditure for energy per person (1992): $1,899, 21st

ECONOMY

Civilian labor force (1994): 770,000
  Percent of total pop.: 46.55%, 49th
  Percent 65 and over (1990): NA
  Percent female: 44.42%, 48th
Percent job growth (1980-90): 25.65%, 17th
Major employer industries (1994):
  Agriculture: NA—2.5%, 23rd
  Construction: 36,000—5.1%, 9th
  Finance, insurance, & real estate: NA—4.4%, 38th
  Government: 153,000—21.9%, 4th
  Manufacturing: 43,000—6.1%, 44th
  Service: 143,000—20.5%, 30th
  Trade: 134,000—19.2%, 20th
  Transportation, communications, public utilities: 33,000—4.8%, 35th
Unemployment rate (1994): 6.23%, 16th
  Male: 7.1%, 9th
  Female: 5.3%, 29th
Total businesses (1991): 55,334
  New business incorps. (1991): 2,713
    Percent of total businesses: 4.90%, 38th
  Business failures (1991): 319
    Percent of total businesses: 0.58%
Agriculture farm income:
  Marketing (1993): $1,621,000,000, 34th
    Average per farm: $115,785.71, 12th
  Leading products (1993): Cattle, dairy products, hay, greenhouse

Average value land & build. per acre
(1994): $240, 46th
Percent increase (1990-94): 22.45%, 5th
Govt. payments (1993): $76,000,000, 32nd
Average per farm: $5,428.57, 19th
Construction, value of all: $786,000,000
Per capita: $518.79, 28th
Manufactures:
Value added: $2,252,000,000
Per capita: $1,486.40, 49th
Leading products: Foods, machinery, apparel, lumber, printing, transportation equipment
Value of nonfuel mineral production (1994): $914,000,000, 13th
Leading mineral products: Natural gas, petroleum, coal
Retail sales (1993): $12,337,000,000, 39th
Per household: $21,099, 36th
Percent increase (1992-93): 10.3%, 6th
Tourism revenues (1994): $2.75 bil.
Foreign exports, in total value (1994): $526,000,000, 46th
Per capita: $318.02, 50th
Gross state product per person (1993): $19,392.37, 36th
Percent change (1990-93): 11.11%, 1st
Patents per 100,000 pop. (1993): 16.03, 26th
Public aid recipients (percent of resident pop. 1993): 8.3%, 11th
Medicaid recipients per 1,000 pop. (1993): 149.13, 10th
Medicare recipients per 1,000 pop. (1993): 122.52, 41st

TRAVEL AND TRANSPORTATION

Motor vehicle registrations (1993): 1,421,000
Per 1,000 pop.: 879.33, 9th
Motorcycle registrations (1993): 31,000
Per 1,000 pop.: 19.18, 20th
Licensed drivers per 1,000 pop. (1993): 710.40, 14th
Deaths from motor vehicle accidents per 100,000 pop. (1993): 26.79, 2nd
Public roads & streets (1993):
Total mileage: 60,812
Per 1,000 pop.: 37.63, 9th
Rural mileage: 54,961
Per 1,000 pop.: 34.01, 9th
Urban mileage: 5,851
Per 1,000 pop.: 3.62, 9th

Interstate mileage: 998
Per 1,000 pop.: 0.62, 6th
Annual vehicle-mi. of travel per person (1993): 11,696, 2nd
Mean travel time for workers age 16+ who work away from home: 19.1 min., 36th

GOVERNMENT

Percent of voting age pop. registered (1994): 58.8%, 41st
Percent of voting age pop. voting (1994): 46.8%, 21st
Percent of voting age pop. voting for U.S. representatives (1994): 39.6%, 23rd
State legislators, total (1995): 112, 38th
Women members (1992): 16
Percent of legislature: 14.3%, 35th
U.S. Congress, House members (1995): 3
Change (1985-95): 0
Revenues (1993):
State govt.: $6,303,000,000
Per capita: $3,900.37, 6th
Parimutuel & amusement taxes & lotteries, revenue per capita: NA
Expenditures (1993):
State govt.: $5,599,000,000
Per capita: $3,464.73, 10th
Debt outstanding (1993): $1,597,000,000
Per capita: $4,701.11, 4th

LAWS AND REGULATIONS

Legal driving age: 16, 15 if completed driver education course
Marriage age without parental consent: 18
Divorce residence requirement: 6 mo.

ATTRACTIONS (1995)

Major opera companies: 2
Major symphony orchestras: 1
Major dance companies: 1
State appropriations for arts agencies per capita: $1.60, 9th
State Fair in mid-September at Albuquerque

SPORTS AND COMPETITION

NCAA teams (Division I): New Mexico State Univ. Aggies, Univ. of New Mexico Lobos

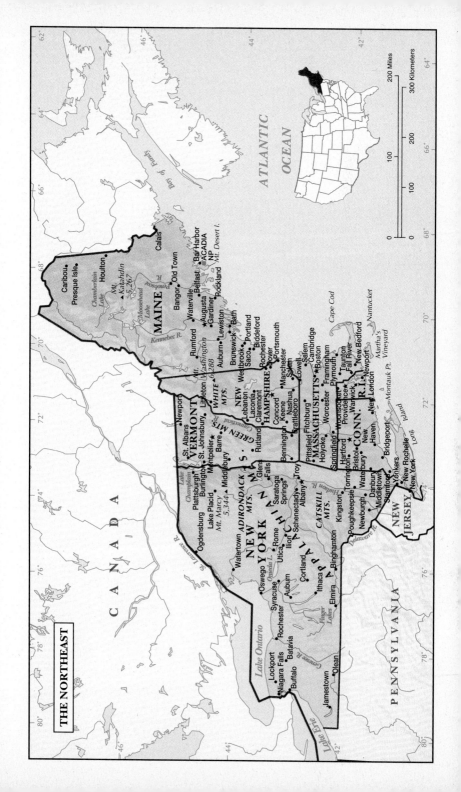

THE NORTHEAST

CANADA

MAINE

Caribou
Presque Isle
Houlton
Chamberlain Lake
Mt. Katahdin 5,267
Moosehead Lake
Bangor
Old Town
Calais

Penobscot R.
Kennebec R.

Waterville
Augusta
Gardiner
Belfast
Rockland
Bar Harbor
ACADIA NP
Mt. Desert I.

Rumford
Lewiston
Auburn
Brunswick
Bath
Saco
Portland
Biddeford
Westbrook
Portsmouth

NEW HAMPSHIRE
WHITE MTS.
Mt. Washington 6,288
Littleton
Lebanon
Claremont
Concord
Keene
Manchester
Rochester
Dover
Salem
Lowell

VERMONT
Newport
St. Albans
Burlington
St. Johnsbury
Barre
Montpelier
Middlebury
Rutland
Bennington
Brattleboro

GREEN MTS.
Lake Champlain
Connecticut R.

MASSACHUSETTS
Pittsfield
Fitchburg
Framingham
Worcester
Cambridge
Boston
Salem
Springfield
Holyoke
Taunton
Plymouth
Cape Cod
New Bedford
Fall River
Nantucket
Martha's Vineyard

CONN.
Torrington
Waterbury
Bristol
New Britain
Hartford
Middletown
New Haven
Bridgeport
Danbury
Stamford
Norwich
New London
R.I.
Providence
Woonsocket
Warwick
Newport

NEW YORK
ADIRONDACK MTS.
Mt. Marcy 5,344
Lake Placid
Plattsburgh
Ogdensburg
Watertown
Oswego
Rome
Utica
Ilion
Syracuse
Auburn
Rochester
Lockport
Niagara Falls
Buffalo
Batavia
Jamestown
Olean
Cortland
Ithaca
Elmira
Binghamton
Finger Lakes
Oneida L.
Lake Ontario
Lake Erie
Genesee R.
St. Lawrence R.

Glens Falls
Saratoga Springs
Schenectady
Troy
Albany
Kingston
Poughkeepsie
Newburgh
CATSKILL MTS.
Hudson R.

A P P A L A C H I A N M T S.

NEW JERSEY
Yonkers
New Rochelle
New York
Long Island
Montauk Pt.

Delaware R.

PENNSYLVANIA

ATLANTIC OCEAN

Bay of Fundy

200 Miles
300 Kilometers
100
200
100

62° 64° 66° 68° 70° 72° 74° 76° 78° 80°
46° 44° 42°

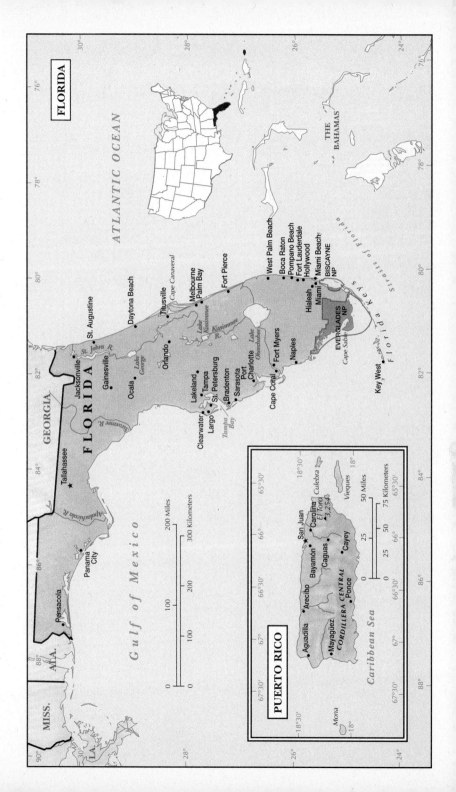

FLORIDA

ATLANTIC OCEAN

THE BAHAMAS

FLORIDA

GEORGIA

Jacksonville
St. Augustine
Daytona Beach
Titusville
Cape Canaveral
Melbourne
Palm Bay
Fort Pierce
West Palm Beach
Boca Raton
Pompano Beach
Fort Lauderdale
Hollywood
Miami Beach
Miami
BISCAYNE NP
Hialeah
EVERGLADES NP

Gainesville
Ocala
Lake George
Orlando
Lake Kissimmee
Kissimmee R.
Lake Okeechobee
St. Johns R.

Tallahassee
Apalachicola R.
Suwannee R.

Lakeland
Tampa
Clearwater
Largo
St. Petersburg
Tampa Bay
Bradenton
Sarasota
Port Charlotte
Cape Coral
Fort Myers
Naples
Cape Sable
Key West

Florida Keys
Straits of Florida

Panama City
Pensacola

MISS.
ALA.
LA.

Gulf of Mexico

200 Miles
300 Kilometers
100
200
100

PUERTO RICO

San Juan
Carolina
Culebra
Bayamón
El Toro 3,254
Vieques
Arecibo
Caguas
Cayey
Aguadilla
CORDILLERA CENTRAL
Mayagüez
Ponce

Mona

Caribbean Sea

50 Miles
75 Kilometers
25
50
25
50
25

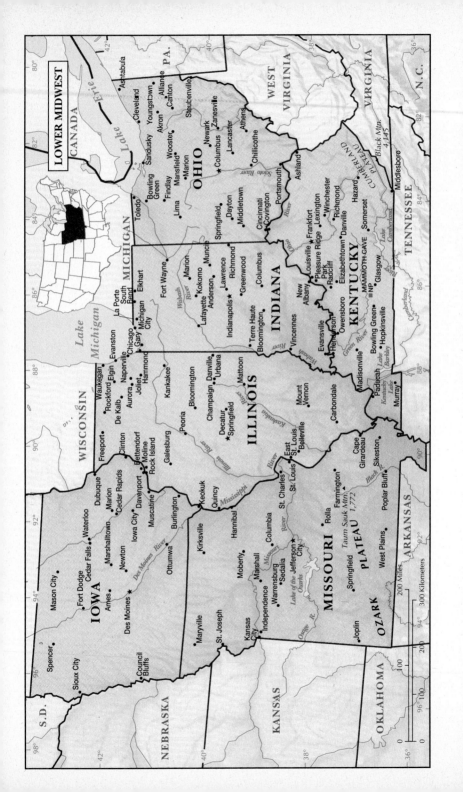

LOWER MIDWEST

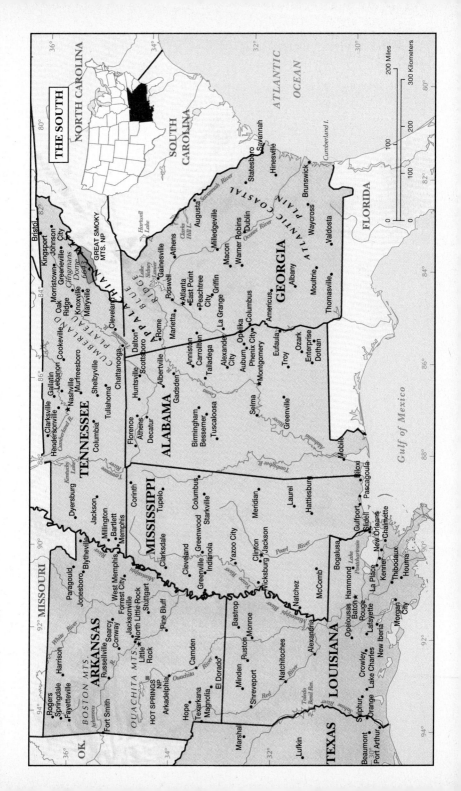

THE SOUTH

NORTH CAROLINA

SOUTH CAROLINA

ATLANTIC OCEAN

FLORIDA

Gulf of Mexico

GEORGIA

ATLANTIC COASTAL PLAIN

Savannah
Hinesville
Statesboro
Brunswick
Waycross
Valdosta
Thomasville
Moultrie
Albany
Americus
Dublin
Warner Robins
Macon
Milledgeville
Augusta
Athens
Gainesville
Roswell
Atlanta
East Point
Peachtree City
Griffin
La Grange
Marietta
Rome
Columbus
Phenix City
Opelika
Auburn
Alexander City
Eufaula
Troy
Ozark
Enterprise
Dothan
Montgomery

ALABAMA

APPALACHIAN

BLUE RIDGE

Clingmans Dome 6643

GREAT SMOKY MTS. NP

CUMBERLAND PLATEAU

Hartwell Lake
Clarks Hill L.
Savannah River
Oconee River
Ocmulgee River
Lake Sidney Lanier

Bristol
Kingsport
Johnson City
Greeneville
Morristown
Oak Ridge
Knoxville
Maryville
Cleveland
Dalton
Scottsboro
Albertville
Gadsden
Anniston
Carrollton
Talladega
Selma
Greenville
Mobile
Biloxi
Pascagoula

TENNESSEE

Clarksville
Hendersonville
Gallatin
Cookeville
Lebanon
Nashville
Murfreesboro
Shelbyville
Columbia
Tullahoma
Chattanooga
Huntsville
Florence
Athens
Decatur
Birmingham
Bessemer
Tuscaloosa

MISSISSIPPI

Corinth
Tupelo
Columbus
Starkville
Greenwood
Greenville
Indianola
Cleveland
Clarksdale
Yazoo City
Jackson
Clinton
Vicksburg
Meridian
Laurel
Hattiesburg
Natchez
McComb

Dyersburg
Jackson
Millington
Bartlett
Memphis
West Memphis
Forrest City
Stuttgart

ARKANSAS

BOSTON MTS
Rogers
Springdale
Fayetteville
Harrison
Paragould
Jonesboro
Blytheville
Searcy
Conway
Russellville
Jacksonville
North Little Rock
Little Rock
Pine Bluff
OUACHITA MTS
HOT SPRINGS NP
Arkadelphia
Camden
El Dorado
Hope
Texarkana
Magnolia

MISSOURI

OK.

White River
Arkansas River
Ouachita River
Red River
Kentucky Lake
Tennessee River
Cumberland R.
Mississippi River
Tombigbee R.
Alabama River
Pearl River
Tensas River
Yazoo River
Toledo Bend Res.
Sabine River
Lake Pontchartrain

LOUISIANA

Bastrop
Monroe
Ruston
Minden
Shreveport
Natchitoches
Alexandria
Opelousas
Baton Rouge
Hammond
Bogalusa
Lafayette
New Iberia
Crowley
Lake Charles
Morgan City
Thibodaux
Houma
Kenner
La Place
New Orleans
Chalmette
Slidell
Gulfport

TEXAS

Marshall
Lufkin
Beaumont
Port Arthur
Orange
Sulphur

200 Miles
300 Kilometers

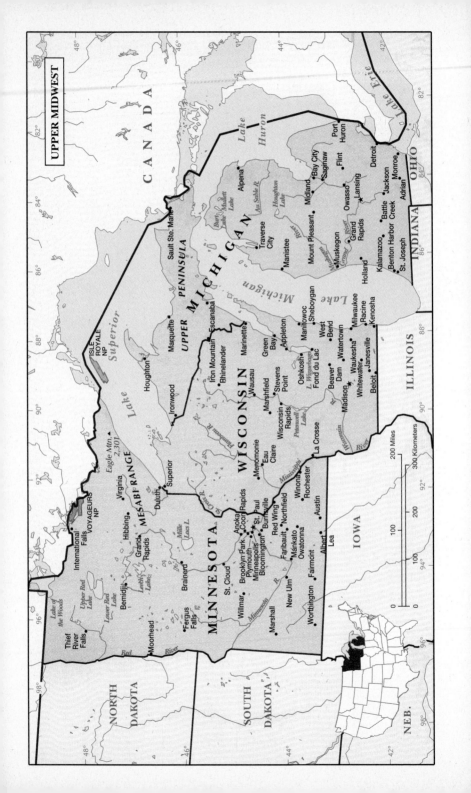

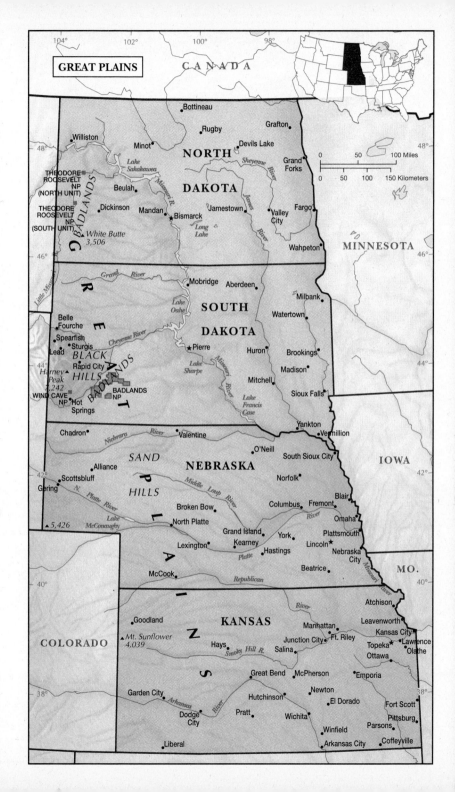

GREAT PLAINS

CANADA

NORTH DAKOTA

Bottineau
Rugby
Grafton
Williston
Minot
Devils Lake
Grand Forks
Lake Sakakawea
Sheyenne River
THEODORE ROOSEVELT NP (NORTH UNIT)
Beulah
THEODORE ROOSEVELT NP (SOUTH UNIT)
Dickinson
Mandan
Bismarck
Jamestown
James River
Valley City
Fargo
Long Lake
Missouri R.
White Butte 3,506
Wahpeton

MINNESOTA

SOUTH DAKOTA

Grand River
Mobridge
Aberdeen
Milbank
Lake Oahe
Watertown
Belle Fourche
Spearfish
Lead
Sturgis
Cheyenne River
BLACK HILLS
Rapid City
Pierre
Huron
Brookings
Harney Peak 7,242
Lake Sharpe
Madison
WIND CAVE NP
Hot Springs
BADLANDS
BADLANDS NP
Missouri River
Mitchell
Lake Francis Case
Sioux Falls

Little Missouri

G R E A T

P L A I N S

Yankton
Chadron
Niobrara River
Valentine
O'Neill
Vermillion
SAND HILLS
NEBRASKA
South Sioux City
IOWA
Alliance
Norfolk
Scottsbluff
Middle Loup River
Blair
Gering
N. Platte River
Broken Bow
Columbus
Fremont
Omaha
North Platte
Plattsmouth
Lake McConaughy
Grand Island
York
Lincoln
5,426
Lexington
Kearney
Hastings
Nebraska City
Platte
McCook
Beatrice
MO.
Republican

River
Atchison
Goodland
KANSAS
Leavenworth
Kansas City
COLORADO
Manhattan
Topeka
Lawrence
Mt. Sunflower 4,039
Hays
Junction City
Ft. Riley
Olathe
Smoky Hill R.
Salina
Ottawa
Great Bend
McPherson
Emporia
Garden City
Newton
Hutchinson
El Dorado
Fort Scott
Arkansas
River
Pratt
Wichita
Pittsburg
Dodge City
Winfield
Parsons
Liberal
Arkansas City
Coffeyville

0   50   100 Miles
0   50   100   150 Kilometers

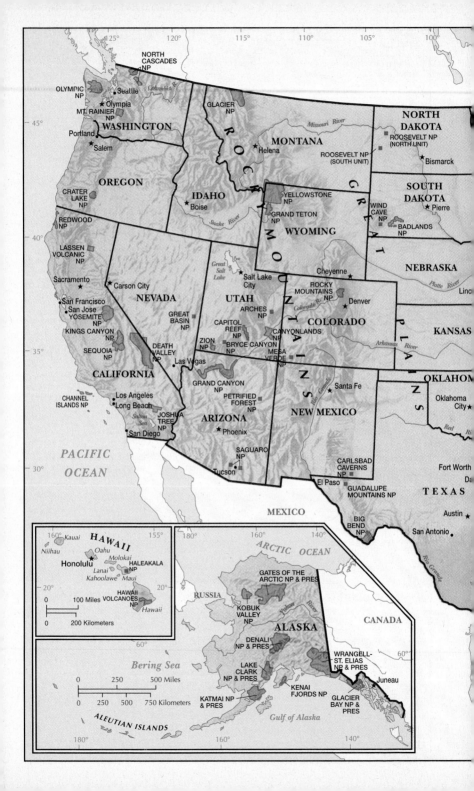

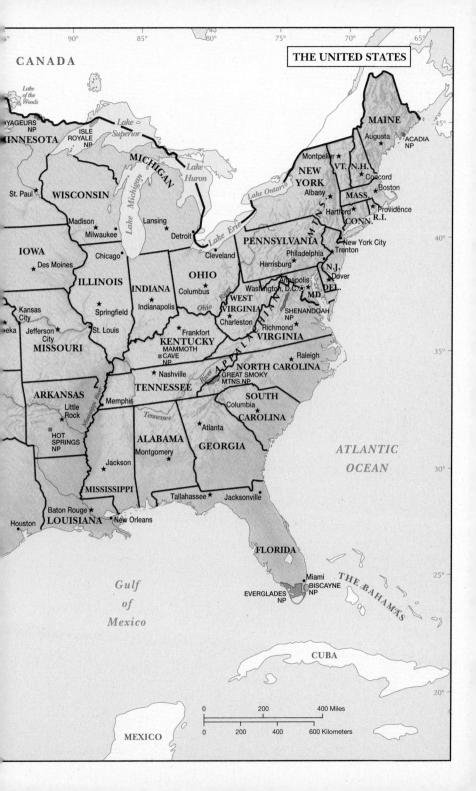

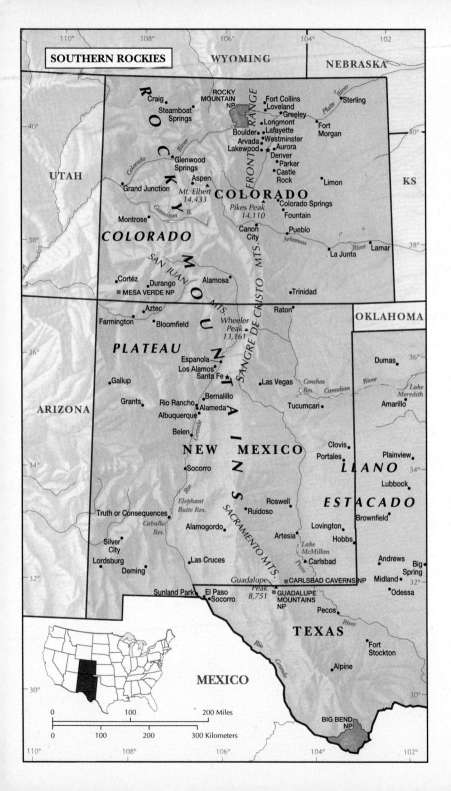

SOUTHERN ROCKIES

SOUTHERN PLAINS

KANSAS

100° 98° 96° 94°

MO.
ARK.

Guymon

GREAT

Woodward

Bartlesville

Miami

Ponca
City

Claremore

Arkansas R.

Neosho R.

36°

Dumas

Pampa

Lake
Meredith

Amarillo

P L A I N S

Enid

Keystone
Lake

Stillwater

Tulsa

Broken Arrow

Clinton

El Reno

Edmond

Sapulpa

Muskogee

Robert
S. Kerr
Lake

Oklahoma City

Okmulgee

Canadian

River

Shawnee

Eufaula
Lake

36°

Chickasha

Norman

McAlester

34°

Plainview

LLANO

ESTACADO

Brownfield

Altus

OKLAHOMA

Ada

Lawton

Duncan

Ardmore

Lake
Texoma

OUACHITA
MTS

Wichita Falls

Red

River

Durant

Paris

Sherman

Denison

Texarkana

34°

Lubbock

Denton

Plano

Greenville

Irving

Garland

Marshall

Andrews

Big Spring

Abilene

Fort Worth

Dallas

Arlington

Mesquite

Longview

Sabine

River

Tyler

32°

Midland

T E X A S

Brownwood

Corsicana

Nacogdoches

Lufkin

32°

Odessa

San Angelo

Colorado

River

Waco

Brazos

Sam
Rayburn
Res.

Pecos

EDWARDS

Killeen

Temple

River

Bryan

Huntsville

Lake
Livingston

Fort
Stockton

PLATEAU

River

Round Rock

College
Station

30°

Amistad
Res.

Austin

San Marcos

Houston

Baytown

30°

BIG BEND
NP

Del Rio

New Braunfels

Seguin

Pasadena

Texas City

Galveston

MEXICO

San Antonio

Victoria

Freeport

Galveston
Bay

Eagle Pass

Rio Grande

Nueces

River

Matagorda
Bay

28°

Laredo

Alice

Corpus
Christi

28°

Kingsville

Gulf

of

Mexico

Falcon
Res.

Padre
Island

26°

Edinburg

Mission

Pharr

Harlingen

McAllen

Weslaco

San Benito

Brownsville

26°

0   100   200 Miles

0   100   200   300 Kilometers

102° 100° 98° 96°

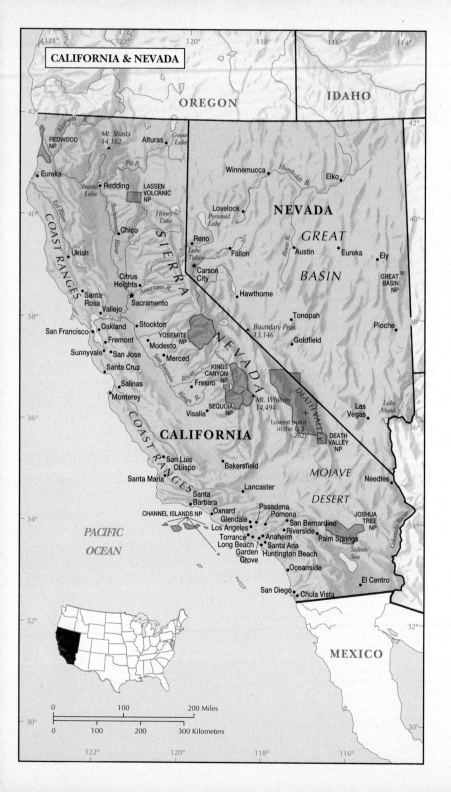

CALIFORNIA & NEVADA

OREGON

IDAHO

REDWOOD NP
Mt. Shasta 14,162
Alturas
Goose Lake
Eureka
Klamath R.
Pit R.
Shasta Lake
Redding
LASSEN VOLCANIC NP
Chico
Honey Lake
Ukiah
Sacramento River
Feather River
Sacramento River

NEVADA
Winnemucca
Humboldt R.
Elko

Lovelock
Pyramid Lake
GREAT
Reno
Lake Tahoe
Fallon
Reese R.
Austin
Eureka
Ely
Carson City
BASIN
GREAT BASIN NP

COAST RANGES

Citrus Heights
American R.
Hawthorne

Santa Rosa
Vallejo
Sacramento
SIERRA

Oakland
Stockton
Tonopah
Pioche

San Francisco
Fremont
YOSEMITE NP
Boundary Peak 13,146
Goldfield

Sunnyvale
San Jose
Modesto
Merced
San Joaquin River

Santa Cruz
KINGS CANYON NP
Salinas
Fresno
Kings R.
NEVADA

Monterey
SEQUOIA NP
Mt. Whitney 14,494
Las Vegas
Lake Mead

Visalia
Lowest point in the U.S. (-282)
DEATH VALLEY NP

CALIFORNIA

COAST RANGES

San Luis Obispo
Bakersfield
MOJAVE

Santa Maria
Lancaster
Needles

Santa Barbara
Oxnard
DESERT

CHANNEL ISLANDS NP
Glendale
Pasadena
Pomona
San Bernardino
JOSHUA TREE NP

PACIFIC OCEAN
Los Angeles
Torrance
Anaheim
Riverside
Palm Springs
Colorado River

Long Beach
Santa Ana
Garden Grove
Huntington Beach
Salton Sea

Oceanside

San Diego
Chula Vista
El Centro

MEXICO

0   100   200 Miles

0   100   200   300 Kilometers

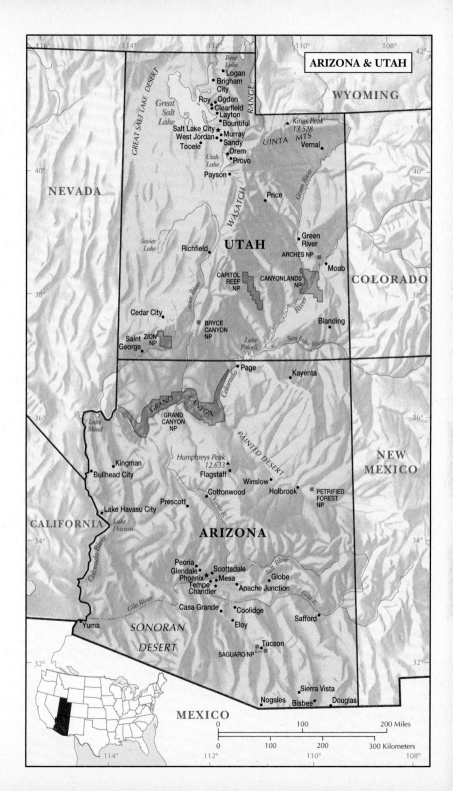

ARIZONA & UTAH

WYOMING

NEVADA

Bear Lake

Great Salt Lake Desert

Great Salt Lake

Logan
Brigham City
Roy Ogden
Clearfield
Layton
Bountiful
Salt Lake City ★
Murray
West Jordan Sandy
Tooele Orem
Provo
Utah Lake
Payson

Kings Peak 13,528 ▲ Vernal

UINTA MTS

WASATCH RANGE

Green River

Price

Sevier Lake

Richfield

UTAH

Green River
ARCHES NP Moab

CAPITOL REEF NP
CANYONLANDS NP

COLORADO

Cedar City

BRYCE CANYON NP

Sevier River

Colorado River

Blanding

Saint George
ZION NP
Lake Powell
San Juan River

Page
Kayenta

Lake Mead

GRAND CANYON
GRAND CANYON NP

Colorado

PAINTED DESERT

NEW MEXICO

Kingman
Bullhead City

Humphreys Peak 12,633 ▲
Flagstaff
Winslow
Holbrook
Cottonwood
PETRIFIED FOREST NP

CALIFORNIA

Lake Havasu City
Lake Havasu
Prescott

Verde R.

ARIZONA

Colorado River

Peoria
Glendale
Phoenix ★ Scottsdale
Tempe Mesa
Chandler
Apache Junction

Salt River
Globe

Gila R.

Gila River

Casa Grande
Coolidge
Safford
Eloy

Yuma

SONORAN DESERT

Tucson
SAGUARO NP

Sierra Vista
Nogales Bisbee Douglas

MEXICO

0   100   200 Miles

0   100   200   300 Kilometers

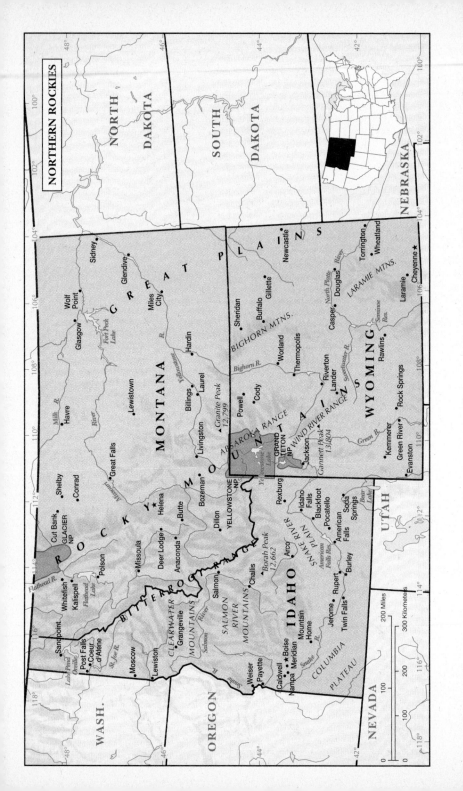

NORTHERN ROCKIES

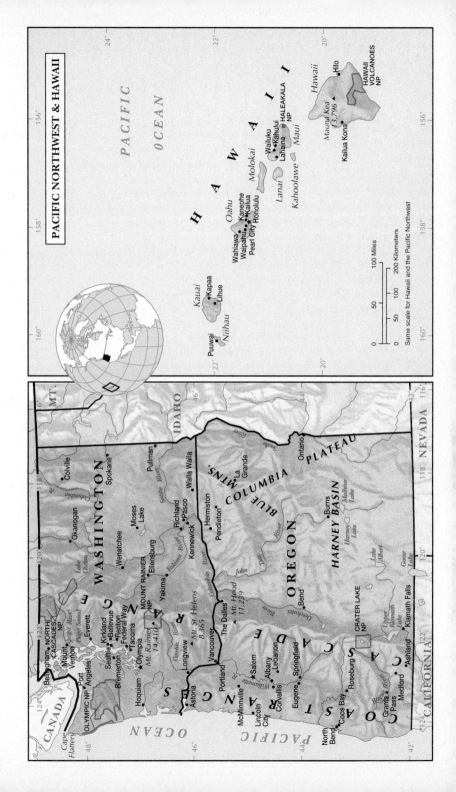

PACIFIC NORTHWEST & HAWAII

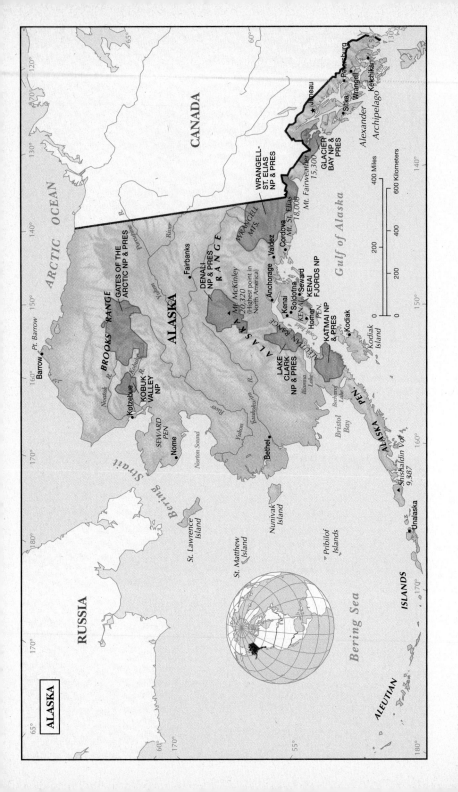

N E W   Y O R K

"We found a pleasant place between steep little hills...and from those hills a mighty, deep mouthed river ran into the sea."

Giovanni de Verrazano, explorer

Stretching from Niagara Falls in the west and the rugged Adirondacks in the northeast to the culturally rich and ethnically diverse "Big Apple"—Manhattan—in the southeast, New York is a state of dramatic contrasts. Although it no longer ranks first in population or manufacturing, New York State must still rank as the "Empire State" in its combination of historical tradition, cultural institutions, notable natives, commerce, industry, finance, and international influence, among other factors.

SUPERLATIVES

- World's most extensive deep water port.
- World's longest suspension bridge—the Verrazano-Narrows.
- World center of finance.
- First in publishing, the garment industry, and furs.
- First in the photographic industry.
- Historical center of Indian power.
- First capital of the United States—New York City.
- World center of tourism.
- Claims world's oldest chartered city—Albany.

MOMENTS IN HISTORY

- In 1524, Giovanni de Verrazano probably was the first European to set foot on New York soil, and in that same year black Portuguese explorer Estaban Gómez may also have done so.
- In 1609 explorer Henry Hudson entered the Hudson River, sailing up as far as present-day Albany, and Samuel de Champlain found Lake Champlain.

So They Say

"...large lake filled with beautiful islands and with a fine country around it."

Samuel de Champlain,
on Lake Champlain

- Hudson's discoveries supported Dutch claims. In 1614 the Dutch built Fort Nassau, near present-day Albany, and settlers arrived at what is now New York City in 1624.

So They Say

"...On our coming into the house, two mats were spread out to sit upon, and immediately some food was served in well-made red wooden bowls....They likewise killed a fat dog, and skinned it in great haste...."

Henry Hudson, on visiting
an Indian village

- In 1664 the Duke of York sent a large fleet to take over the area for England, and the Dutch surrendered.
- The acquittal of publisher John Peter Zenger in 1735 on libel charges was vital to the preservation of freedom of the press.
- A century of warfare between the French and British for control of the area finally ended in 1761, with the British taking full control.
- In 1775, more than a year before national independence was agreed upon, 225 residents of Coxsackie signed a declaration of independence.
- New York became one of the main Revolutionary battlegrounds, suffering 92 engagements—almost a third of the total.
- New York City fell in the battles of Long Island and Fort Washington, in August and October 1776.

So They Say

The Turtle, a submarine, was used in New York harbor in 1776, in an unsuccessful attempt to place an explosive on the hull of a British man-o'-war.

The Enchantment of New York

• The Battle of Saratoga is ranked as one of the most important in world history. The British General John Burgoyne surrendered there on October 17, 1777.

• Indian power in western New York was broken in 1779.

• On July 26, 1788, New York became the 11th state.

• New York City was the capital of the new nation when George Washington took the presidential oath on the balcony of Federal Hall on April 30, 1789.

• The steamboat era began when Robert Fulton's *Clermont* chugged up the Hudson in 1807.

• During the War of 1812, much land fighting took place along the Canadian border, and the British fleet was destroyed on Lake Champlain in 1814.

• The Erie Canal opened on October 26, 1825, bringing New York City commerce to and from the far reaches of the Great Lakes.

• New Yorkers made an important contribution to the work of the Underground Railroad, spiriting slaves to safety in Canada.

• New York forces comprised one-sixth of the entire Union Army during the Civil War.

• In 1883, New York became the first state with a civil service system for state employees.

• The Statue of Liberty was dedicated in 1886.

• President William McKinley received a fatal gunshot wound at the Pan-American Exposition at Buffalo in 1901.

• New York provided 10% of the U.S. servicemen and women in World War I.

• Lake Placid hosted the Winter Olympic Games in 1932 (and again in 1980).

• World War II brought death to 36,483 New York men and women in uniform, and New York produced 11.3% of all that war's matériel.

• In 1953 the United Nations moved to New York City.

• New York transportation advances continued with the opening of the New York State Thruway in 1954 and the St. Lawrence Seaway in 1959.

• In 1964 the Beatles gave their first U.S. concert, at New York City's Carnegie Hall.

• In 1986, New York City celebrated the 100th anniversary of the Statue of Liberty.

• In 1993 the World Trade Center was devastated by a terrorist bomb that killed six

people. A year later four terrorists tried for the crime were found guilty and received stiff prison sentences.

• Long Island was swept by a devastating brush fire in 1995.

THAT'S INTERESTING

• A giant "prehistoric" man uncovered in 1896 at the town of Cardiff drew worldwide attention, until the "Cardiff Giant" was found to be a hoax, one of the most notable of all time.

• Dutch leader Hendrick Brevoort insisted that his favorite tree be saved as the city grew, and Broadway at 10th Street still swings around the site of the now-long-vanished tree.

• Like a giant three-dimensional jigsaw puzzle, the Statue of Liberty was assembled from parts shipped to New York in 214 packing crates.

• Growing tired of his formal dinner clothes, a wealthy Hudson River man created another style that soon caught on. The new garment came to be known for the man's hometown—Tuxedo.

So They Say

Lord Cornbury, governor from 1702 to 1708, frequently appeared at public ceremonies in "drag," wearing a dress and silk stockings.

One Night Stands With American History

• After Washington's defeat at Long Island, patriot Mary Lindley Murray arranged for British leader Lord Howe to have tea with her, giving the Americans time to escape.

• To delay British General John Burgoyne on his march through New York, General Philip Schuyler's wife herself burned the wheat fields, slowing the enemy advance.

• Samuel Wilson, a Troy meat packer, was known as Uncle Sam as he furnished meat to the Army in the War of 1812. His reputation increased until the "real" Uncle Sam became the U.S. symbol.

• The world's first speed limit law was passed in New York City in 1652.

• Washington Square in New York City was once a potters' field, where the trees were used for hangings.

NOTABLE NATIVES

Humphrey Bogart (New York City, 1899-1957), actor. **James Cagney** (New York City, 1899-1986), actor/dancer. **William George Fargo** (Pompey, 1818-1881), businessman. **Millard Fillmore** (Summerhill, 1800-1874), U.S. president. **Henry Louis (Lou) Gehrig** (New York City, 1903-1941), baseball player. **George Gershwin** (Brooklyn, 1898-1837), composer. **Jackie Gleason** (Brooklyn, 1916-1987), actor/comedian. **Edward Henry Harriman** (Hempstead, 1848-1909), financier. **Julia Ward Howe** (New York City, 1819-1910), author/social reformer. **Charles Evans Hughes** (Glens Falls, 1862-1948), chief justice of the United States. **George Inness** (Newburgh, 1825-1894), artist. **Washington Irving** (New York City, 1783-1859), author. **Henry James** (New York City, 1843-1916), author. **William James** (New York City, 1842-1910), psychologist/philosopher. **Michael Jeffrey Jordan** (Brooklyn, 1963-), basketball player. **Herman Melville** (New York City, 1819-1891), author. **John Wesley Powell** (Mt. Morris, now part of New York City, 1834-1902), geologist/ethnologist. **George Mortimer Pullman** (Brocton, 1831-1897), inventor and industrialist. **Frederic Remington** (Canton, 1861-1909), artist. **John Davison Rockefeller** (Richford, 1839-1937), industrialist/philanthropist. **Anna Eleanor Roosevelt** (New York City, 1884-1962), author/diplomat/humanitarian/first lady. **Franklin Delano Roosevelt** (Hyde Park, 1882-1945), U.S. president. **Theodore Roosevelt** (New York City, 1858-1919), U.S. president. **William Henry Seward** (Florida, NY, 1801-1872), public official. **Shenandoah** (near Oneida Castle, 1706?-1816), Indian leader. **Alfred Emanuel Smith** (New York City, 1873-1944), political leader. **Elizabeth Cady Stanton** (Johnstown, 1815-1902), suffragist. **Barbra Streisand** (New York City, 1942-), actress/singer. **Kateri Tekakwitha** (what is now Auriesville, 1656-1680), religious figure. **Louis Comfort Tiffany** (New York City, 1848-1933), painter/craftsman/decorator. **Samuel Jones Tilden** (Lebanon, 1814-1886), public official. **Martin Van Buren** (Kinderhook, 1782-1862), U.S. president. **Walt Whitman** (West Hills, 1819-1892) poet/philosopher. **Frank Winfield Woolworth** (Rodman, 1852-1919), merchant. **Linus Yale** (Salisbury, 1821-1868), inventor.

GENERAL

Admitted to statehood: July 26, 1788
Origin of name: For Duke of York and Albany, who received patent to New Netherland from his brother Charles II and sent an expedition to capture the territory in 1664
Capital: Albany
Nickname: Empire State
Motto: *Excelsior*—Ever upward
Animal: Beaver
Bird: Bluebird
Fish: Brook trout (brookies or speckles)
Flower: Rose
Gem: Garnet
Song: "I Love New York"
Tree: Sugar maple

THE LAND

Area: 53,989 sq. mi., 27th
   Land: 47,224 sq. mi., 30th
   Water: 6,765 sq. mi., 5th
      Inland water: 1,888 sq. mi., 10th
      Coastal water: 976 sq. mi., 8th
   Great Lakes: 3,901 sq. mi., 3rd
Topography: Highest and most rugged mountains in the NE Adirondack upland; St. Lawrence-Champlain lowlands extend from Lake Ontario NE along the Canadian border; Hudson-Mohawk lowland follows the flows of the rivers N and W, 10-30 mi. wide; Atlantic coastal plain in the SE; Appalachian Highlands, covering half the state westward from the Hudson Valley, include the Catskill Mountains Finger Lakes; plateau of Erie-Ontario lowlands
Number of counties: 62
Geographic center: Madison, 12 mi. S of Oneida and 26 mi. SW of Utica
Length: 330 mi.; width: 283 mi.
Highest point: 5,344 ft. (Mount Marcy), 21st
Lowest point: sea level (Atlantic Ocean), 3rd
Mean elevation: 1,000 ft., 26th
Coastline: 127 mi., 14th
Shoreline: 1,850 mi., 13th

CLIMATE AND ENVIRONMENT

Temp., highest: 108 deg. on July 22, 1926, at Troy; lowest: −52 deg. on Feb. 18, 1979, at Old Forge
Monthly average: highest: 85.3 deg., 38th; lowest: 11.9 deg., 12th; spread (high to low): 73.4 deg., 18th

Hazardous waste sites (1993): 85, 4th

Endangered species: Mammals: 1—Indiana bat; birds: 3—American peregrine falcon, Piping plover, Roseate tern; reptiles: 2; amphibians: none; fishes: none; invertebrates: 1; plants: 2

MAJOR CITIES POPULATION, 1990 PERCENTAGE INCREASE, 1980-90

Buffalo, 328,123— –8.31%

New York City, 7,322,564—3.55%

Rochester, 231,636— –4.18%

Syracuse, 163,860— –3.67%

Yonkers, 188,082— –3.72%

THE PEOPLE

Population (1995): 18,136,081, 3rd
   Percent change (1990-95): 0.8%, 47th
Population (2000 proj.): 18,237,000, 3rd
   Percent change (1990-2000): 1.4%, 45th
Per sq. mi. (1994): 384.7, 7th
Percent in metro. area (1992): 91.7%, 9th
Foreign born: 2,852,000, 2nd
   Percent: 15.9%, 2nd
Top three ancestries reported:
   German, 16.11%
   Italian, 15.77%
   Irish, 15.56%
White: 13,385,255, 74.40%, 42nd
Black: 2,859,055, 15.89%, 13th
Native American: 62,651, 0.35%, 30th
Asian, Pacific Isle: 693,760, 3.86%, 4th
Other races: 989,734, 5.50%, 5th
Hispanic origin: 2,214,026, 12.31%, 6th
Percent over 5 yrs. speaking language other than English at home: 23.3%, 5th
Percent males: 47.95%, 47th; percent females: 52.05%, 5th
Percent never married: 32.1%, 3rd
Marriages per 1,000 (1993): 8.3, 30th
Divorces per 1,000 (1993): 3.1, 44th
Median age: 33.9
Under 5 years (1994): 7.61%, 14th
Under 18 years (1994): 24.83%, 39th
65 years & older (1994): 13.2%, 23rd
Percent increase among the elderly (1990-94): 1.24%, 50th

OF VITAL IMPORTANCE

Live births per 1,000 pop. (1993): 15.3, 16th
Infant mortality rate per 1,000 births (1992): 8.8, 20th

Rate for blacks (1990): 17.3, 14th
   Rate for whites (1990): 7.7, 30th
Births to unmarried women, % of total (1992): 34.8%, 8th
Births to teenage mothers, % of total (1992): 9.0%, 45th
Abortions (1992): 195,390, 2nd
   Rate per 1,000 women 14-44 years old: 46.2, 2nd
   Percent change (1988-92): 7%, 7th
Average lifetime (1979-81): 73.70, 29th
Deaths per 1,000 pop. (1993): 9.4, 15th
Causes of death per 100,000 pop.:
   Accidents & adverse effects (1992): 26.8, 45th
   Atherosclerosis (1991): 5.1, 44th
   Cancer (1991): 213.3, 20th
   Cerebrovascular diseases (1992): 46.0, 45th
   Chronic liver diseases & cirrhosis (1991): 10.7, 13th
   Chronic obstructive pulmonary diseases (1992): 32.3, 41st
   Diabetes mellitus (1992): 16.4, 41st
   Diseases of heart (1992): 354.0, 3rd
   Pneumonia, flu (1991): 37.8, 8th
   Suicide (1992): 8.5, 48th

KEEPING WELL

Active nonfederal physicians per 100,000 pop. (1993): 334, 4th
Dentists per 100,000 (1991): 79, 3rd
Nurses per 100,000 (1992): 881, 13th
Hospitals per 100,000 (1993): 1.27, 46th
   Admissions per 1,000 (1993): 130.00, 15th
   Occupancy rate per 100 beds (1993): 82.8, 2nd
   Average cost per patient per day (1993): $784, 32nd
   Average cost per stay (1993): $7,716, 2nd
   Average stay (1992): 10.2 days, 9th
AIDS cases (adult, 1993): 17,467; per 100,000: 96.0, 2nd
HIV infection, not yet AIDS (1993): NA
Other notifiable diseases:
   Gonorrhea: 287.8, 17th
   Measles: 9.4, 8th
   Syphilis: 51.7, 17th
   Tuberculosis: 23.2, 2nd
Pop. without health insur. (1991-93): 13.5%, 21st

HOUSEHOLDS BY TYPE

Total households (1994): 6,669,000
   Percent change (1990-94): 0.4%, 47th

Per 1,000 pop.: 367.05, 37th
Percent of households 65 yrs. and over: 22.40%, 22nd
Persons per household (1994): 2.64, 18th
Family households: 4,489,312
  Percent of total: 67.62%, 46th
Nonfamily households: 2,150,010
  Percent of total: 32.38%, 6th
Pop. living in group quarters: 545,265
  Percent of pop.: 3.03%, 15th

LIVING QUARTERS

Total housing units: 7,226,891
  Persons per unit: 2.49, 8th
Occupied housing units: 6,639,322
  Percent of total units: 91.87%, 10th
  Persons per unit: 2.62, 12th
  Percent of units with over 1 person per room: 6.50%, 8th
Owner-occupied units: 3,464,436
  Percent of total units: 47.94%, 49th
  Percent of occupied units: 52.18%, 50th
  Persons per unit: 2.86, 5th
  Median value: $131,600, 7th
Renter-occupied units: 3,174,886
  Percent of total units: 43.93%, 2nd
  Percent of occupied units: 47.82%, 2nd
  Persons per unit: 2.38, 22nd
  Median contract rent: $428, 11th
  Rental vacancy rate: 4.9%, 50th
Mobile home, trailer & other as a percent of occupied housing units: 4.56%, 43rd
Persons in emergency shelters for homeless persons: 32,472, 0.180%, 2nd
Persons visible in street locations: 10,732, 0.0597%, 3rd
Persons in shelters for abused women: 756, 0.0042%, 35th
Nursing home population: 126,175, 0.70%, 27th

CRIME INDEX PER 100,000 (1992-93)

Total reported: 5,551.3, 18th
  Violent: 1,073.5, 4th
    Murder and nonnegligent manslaughter: 13.3, 4th
    Aggravated assault: 471.5, 15th
    Robbery: 561.2, 2nd
    Forcible rape: 27.5, 44th
  Property: 4,477.8, 24th
    Burglary: 998.6, 27th
    Larceny, theft: 2,644.2, 38th
    Motor vehicle theft: 835.0, 5th
Drug abuse violations (1990): 683.1, 3rd

Child-abuse rate per 1,000 children (1993): 13.27, 28th

TEACHING AND LEARNING

Pop. 3 and over enrolled in school: 4,656,218
  Percent of pop.: 27.0%, 28th
Public elementary & secondary schools (1992-93): 4,032
  Total enrollment (1992): 2,689,686
    Percent of total pop.: 14.85%, 45th
  Teachers (1992): 176,375
    Percent of pop.: 0.97%, 34th
  Pupil/teacher ratio (fall 1992): 15.2, 40th
  Teachers' avg. salary (1992-93): $47,089, 2nd
  Expenditure per capita (1990-91): $5,457.12, 3rd
  Expenditure per pupil (1991-92): $8,527, 3rd
Percent of graduates taking SAT (1993): 74%, 6th
  Mean SAT verbal scores: 416, 42nd
  Mean SAT mathematical scores: 471, 39th
Percent of graduates taking ACT (1995): 18%, 32nd
  Mean ACT scores: 21.7, 9th
Percent of pop. over 25 completing:
  Less than 9th grade: 10.2%, 20th
  High school: 74.8%, 34th
  College degree(s): 23.1%, 11th
Higher education, institutions (1993-94): 314
  Enrollment (1992): 1,069,772
    Percent of pop.: 5.91%, 20th
    White non-Hispanic (1992): 753,717
      Percent of enroll.: 70.46%, 43rd
    Black non-Hispanic (1992): 128,966
      Percent of enroll.: 12.06%, 13th
    Hispanic (1992): 87,712
      Percent of enroll.: 8.20%, 7th
    Asian/Pacific Islander (1992): 56,395
      Percent of enroll.: 5.27%, 4th
    American Indian/AK native (1992): 3,564
      Percent of enroll.: 0.33%, 34th
    Nonresident alien (1992): 39,418
      Percent of enroll.: 3.68%, 13th
    Female (1992): 601,586
      Percent of enroll.: 56.23%, 12th
  Pub. institutions (1993-94): 88
    Enrollment (1992): 611,258
      Percent of enroll.: 57.14%, 47th
  Private institutions (1993-94): 226
    Enrollment (1992): 458,514
      Percent of enroll.: 42.86%, 5th
  Tuition, public institution (avg., 1993-94): $7,723, 11th

Tuition, private institution (avg., 1993-94): $17,637, 10th

Public library systems: 760

Books & serial vol. per capita: 3.70, 10th

Govt. expenditure per capita: $23.53, 8th

LAW ENFORCEMENT, COURTS, AND PRISONS

Police protection, corrections, judicial and legal functions expenditures (1992): $9,000,000,000

Per capita: $497, 3rd

Police per 10,000 pop. (1993): 31.66, 3rd

Prisoners (state & fed.) per 100,000 pop. (1993): 3,556.93, 19th

Percent change (1992-93): 4.6%, 27th

Death penalty: yes, by lethal injection

RELIGION, NUMBER AND PERCENT OF POPULATION

Agnostic: 82,385—0.60%, 19th

Buddhist: 27,462—0.20%, 11th

Christian: 10,957,263—79.80%, 44th

Hindu: 82,385—0.60%, 1st

Jewish: 947,433—6.90%, 1st

Muslim: 109,847—0.80%, 1st

Unitarian: 41,193—0.30%, 15th

Other: 205,964—1.50%, 18th

None: 878,778—6.40%, 28th

Refused to answer: 398,196—2.90%, 9th

MAKING A LIVING

Personal income per capita (1994): $25,999, 4th

Percent increase (1993-94): 4.7%, 31st

Disposable personal income per capita (1994): $22,047, 4th

Median income of households (1993): $31,697, 21st

Percent of pop. below poverty level (1993): 16.4%, 15th

Percent 65 and over (1990): 11.9%, 25th

Expenditure for energy per person (1992): $1,588, 48th

ECONOMY

Civilian labor force (1994): 8,571,000

Percent of total pop.: 47.17%, 47th

Percent 65 and over (1990): 3.42%, 9th

Percent female: 46.26%, 25th

Percent job growth (1980-90): 15.42%, 35th

Major employer industries (1994):

Agriculture: 89,000—1.1%, 45th

Construction: 288,000—3.6%, 42nd

Finance, insurance, & real estate: 657,000—8.2%, 3rd

Government: 1,466,000—18.4%, 15th

Manufacturing: 1,038,000—13.0%, 33rd

Service: 2,024,000—25.3%, 7th

Trade: 1,344,000—16.8%, 49th

Transportation, communications, public utilities: 417,000—5.2%, 28th

Unemployment rate (1994): 6.92%, 8th

Male: 7.5%, 7th

Female: 6.2%, 16th

Total businesses (1991): 605,384

New business incorps. (1991): 63,808

Percent of total businesses: 10.54%, 7th

Business failures (1991): 3,284

Percent of total businesses: 0.54%

Agriculture farm income:

Marketing (1993): $2,817,000,000, 26th

Average per farm: $74,131.58, 27th

Leading products (1993): Dairy products, greenhouse, cattle, apples

Average value land & build. per acre (1994): $1,251, 18th

Percent increase (1990-94): 28.44%, 3rd

Govt. payments (1993): $72,000,000, 33rd

Average per farm: $1,894.74, 37th

Construction, value of all: $5,947,000,000

Per capita: $330.56, 44th

Manufactures:

Value added: $85,532,000,000

Per capita: $4,754.30, 32nd

Leading products: Books and periodicals, apparel, pharmaceuticals, machinery, instruments, toys and sporting goods, electronic equipment, automotive and aircraft components

Value of nonfuel mineral production (1994): $871,000,000, 14th

Leading mineral products: Stone, cement, salt

Retail sales (1993): $127,516,000,000, 4th

Per household: $19,079, 45th

Percent increase (1992-93): 1.0%, 46th

Tourism revenues (1993): $20 bil.

Foreign exports, in total value (1994): $25,912,000,000, 3rd

Per capita: $1,426.17, 21st

Gross state product per person (1993): $26,384.35, 8th

Percent change (1990-93): 1.93%, 38th

Patents per 100,000 pop. (1993): 29.50, 11th

Public aid recipients (percent of resident pop. 1993): 9.6%, 5th

Medicaid recipients per 1,000 pop. (1993): 151.05, 9th

Medicare recipients per 1,000 pop. (1993): 142.90, 25th

TRAVEL AND TRANSPORTATION

Motor vehicle registrations (1993): 10,163,000
  Per 1,000 pop.: 559.85, 50th
Motorcycle registrations (1993): 195,000
  Per 1,000 pop.: 10.74, 38th
Licensed drivers per 1,000 pop. (1993): 568.89, 51st
Deaths from motor vehicle accidents per 100,000 pop. (1993): 9.67, 48th
Public roads & streets (1993):
  Total mileage: 111,882
    Per 1,000 pop.: 6.16, 44th
  Rural mileage: 72,589
    Per 1,000 pop.: 4.00, 43rd
  Urban mileage: 39,293
    Per 1,000 pop.: 2.16, 47th
  Interstate mileage: 1,500
    Per 1,000 pop.: 0.08, 46th
Annual vehicle-mi. of travel per person (1993): 6,181, 50th
Mean travel time for workers age 16+ who work away from home: 28.6 min., 1st

GOVERNMENT

Percent of voting age pop. registered (1994): 56.8%, 44th
  Percent of voting age pop. voting (1994): 44.6%, 32nd
  Percent of voting age pop. voting for U.S. representatives (1994): 33.8%, 40th
State legislators, total (1995): 211, 4th
  Women members (1992): 27
    Percent of legislature: 12.8%, 38th
U.S. Congress, House members (1995): 31
  Change (1985-95): –3
Revenues (1993):
  State govt.: $78,209,000,000
    Per capita: $4,308.32, 4th
  Parimutuel & amusement taxes & lotteries, revenue per capita: $123.07, 12th
Expenditures (1993):
  State govt.: $74,280,000,000
    Per capita: $4,091.89, 4th
Debt outstanding (1993): $59,219,000,000
  Per capita: $3,262.22, 9th

LAWS AND REGULATIONS

Legal driving age: 18, 17 if completed driver education course
Marriage age without parental consent: 18
Divorce residence requirement: 1 yr., for qualifications check local statutes

ATTRACTIONS (1995)

Major opera companies: 16
Major symphony orchestras: 11
Major dance companies: 35
Major professional theater companies (non-profit): 6
State appropriations for arts agencies per capita: $1.94, 6th
State Fair in late August–early September at Syracuse

SPORTS AND COMPETITION

NCAA teams (Division I): Canisius College Golden Griffins, Colgate Univ. Red Raiders, Columbia Univ. Lions, Cornell Univ. Big Red, Fordham Univ. Rams, Hofstra Univ. Flying Dutchmen, Iona College Gaels, Long Island Univ. Blackbirds, Manhattan College Jaspers, Marist College Red Foxes, Niagara Univ. Purple Eagles, Siena College Saints, St. Bonaventure Univ. Bonnies, St. Francis College Terriers, St. John's Univ. Red Storm, State Univ. of New York-Buffalo Bulls, Syracuse Univ. Orangemen, U.S. Military Academy Black Knights, Wagner College Seahawks
Major league baseball teams: New York Mets (NL East), Shea Stadium; New York Yankees (AL East), Yankee Stadium
NBA basketball teams: New York Knickerbockers, Madison Square Garden
NFL football teams: Buffalo Bills (AFC), Rich Stadium; New York Jets (AFC), Giants Stadium (NJ); New York Giants (NFC), Giants Stadium (NJ)
NHL hockey teams: New York Rangers, Madison Square Garden; Buffalo Sabres, Memorial Auditorium (scheduled to begin play at Marine Midland Arena in October 1996); New York Islanders, Veterans' Coliseum

NORTH CAROLINA

"In my honest and unbiased judgment, the Good Lord will place the Garden of Eden in North Carolina when He restores it to the earth. He will do this because He will have so few changes to make in order to achieve perfection."

Sam Irvin, Jr., local writer

North Carolina was the site of "mankind's single most significant event," as the Wright Brothers' first flight has been called. It also was the site of one of history's great mysteries—the disappearance of the Roanoke Island settlement. North Carolina is the "longest" state in the East, and Grandfather Mountain is said to be the world's oldest. The state's seacoast is unique in the country, and the Appalachian Mountains reach their highest levels in the state. Between the mountains and the sea lies a productive land—it is both an agricultural and a manufacturing state—of historic moment.

SUPERLATIVES

- World's first heavier-than-air flight.
- First radio SOS, sent off shores of Cape Hatteras.
- First U.S. school of forestry.
- Leader in fine furniture production.
- First in the nation in tobacco cultivation.
- Leads the nation in cigarette production.

MOMENTS IN HISTORY

- During his expedition of 1540, Hernando de Soto and his large party reached the western mountains, found no riches, and departed.
- After receiving rights to the North Carolina area, Sir Walter Raleigh sent Captains M. Philip Amadas and M. Arthur Barlowe to scout the area in 1584.

So They Say

"We found such plenty that I think in all the world the like abundance is not to be found."

Captain M. Arthur Barlowe

- Raleigh responded by sending seven ships that landed on Roanoke Island in 1585, but the settlement failed.
- Under Governor John White, in 1587 another group restored the Roanoke settlement and added to it. There, Virginia Dare became the first child of English parents to be born in America. White returned to England to bring help to the colony.
- Coming back to America in August 1590, White found one of the great mysteries of the continent. The colony had been abandoned without a trace except for two cryptic carvings. Nothing further was ever learned about the fate of little Virginia Dare or any of the other settlers.

So They Say

"As we entered up the sandy bank, upon a tree...were curiously carved ...Roman letters C R O....We passed toward the place where they were left in sundry houses, but we found the houses taken down...one of the chief trees...had the bark taken off, and five foot from the ground in fair capital letters, was graven CROATOAN, without any cross or sign of distress."

John White, on the abandonment of Roanoke

- In 1663, Charles II granted the Carolinas to eight "Lords Proprietors." A year later, Albemarle County was founded.
- Dissatisfied with their lot, in 1677 a group of Albemarle settlers led by John Culpeper took part in the short-lived "Culpeper's Rebellion," the first ever attempted by American colonists.

• The coasts were alive with pirates, and in 1718 the notorious pirate Blackbeard (real name, Edward Teach) was killed in a notable struggle.

So They Say

"Blackbeard....suddenly toppled over dead....Twenty-five wounds had sapped the life from his magnificent body. Edward Teach had died just as hard as he had lived."

Hugh F. Rankin, The Pirates of Colonial North Carolina

• The king bought out the Lords Proprietors in 1729.
• By 1765 there were 120,000 settlers in the new royal colony.
• The Regulators, a group protesting the injustice of British rule, were defeated in the Battle of Alamance. Although the movement collapsed in 1771, it has been called by some "the first battle of the Revolution."
• British Lord Cornwallis marched south, occupied Charlotte in 1780, and engaged in the battle of Guilford Court House in 1781.

So They Say

"I never saw such fighting since God made me. The Americans fought like demons."

Lord Cornwallis

• North Carolina became the 12th state on November 21, 1789.
• The state legislature met at the new capital city of Raleigh for the first time in 1794.
• In 1838 the government began to remove the Cherokee to the West, from their ancestral lands. On the "Trail of Tears," 4,000 died, but a few managed to escape into the mountains. Cherokee leader Tsali and all but one of his family were murdered, but finally those who remained bought a reservation, where their descendants continue to live today.
• The August 1861 capture of forts Clark and Hatteras was the first substantial Union victory in the Civil War.
• On May 6, 1865, the last Confederate army in the state laid down its arms. North Carolina troops suffered the greatest losses of all the states.

• After the tragedy of Reconstruction, the economy began to revive.
• The state took the lead in cigarette production in 1884.
• Cotton mills multiplied, and by 1900 the state had achieved leadership in the production of fine furniture.
• The Wright Brothers' plane lifted off the sands of Kitty Hawk on December 17, 1903.
• Some 86,000 people from North Carolina served in World War I, with more than 2,400 losing their lives.
• World War II called 362,000 to service from North Carolina, with nearly 8,000 losing their lives.
• When Hurricane Hazel struck in 1954, it was one of the most disastrous of such storms to hit the state.
• The year 1995 brought another tropical storm, this time carrying devastating floods.

THAT'S INTERESTING

• A prehistoric group known as the Early Farmers was notable for its careful burial of dogs.
• Trader John Lawson revealed that traders looked for the Indians with the smallest mouths. The Indians filled their mouths with as much rum as they could and spit it into a container before giving up a pelt.
• Colonel Benjamin Cleveland was noted not only for his courage in the Battle of Kings Mountain but also for his weight of 450 pounds.
• The women of Edenton opposed the British tax on tea by deciding not to drink it. A teapot-shaped monument pays tribute to this decision.
• Blowing Rock is a unique natural formation. When handkerchiefs are tossed over the ridge, the currents of air waft them back.
• In the course of the Civil War, General Bryan Grimes of Grimesville had six horses shot from under him.

NOTABLE NATIVES

Thomas Hart Benton (Hillsboro, 1782-1858), statesman. **Braxton Bragg** (Warrenton, 1817-1876), soldier. **Thomas Lanier Clingman** (Huntersville, 1812-1897), soldier/politician. **James Buchanan Duke** (Durham, 1856-1925), industrialist. **William Franklin (Billy) Graham** (Charlotte , 1918-), evangelist. **Jesse Louis Jackson** (Greenville,

1941-) civil rights leader. **Andrew Johnson** (Raleigh, 1808-1875), U.S. president. **Dolley Payne Madison** (Guilford City, 1768-1849), U.S. first lady. **Edward Roscoe Murrow** (Greensboro, 1908-1965), journalist/broadcaster. **James Knox Polk** (Mecklenburg County, 1795-1849), U.S. president. **William Sydney Porter (O. Henry)** (Greensboro, 1862-1910), author. **Matt Whittaker Ransom** (Warren County, 1826-1904), soldier/lawyer/legislator. **Zebulon Baird Vance** (Buncombe County, 1830-1894), lawyer/politician. **Thomas Clayton Wolfe** (Asheville, 1900-1938), author.

GENERAL

Admitted to statehood: November 21, 1789
Origin of name: Charles I gave a large patent to Sir Robert Heath, 1619, to be called Province of Carolana, from *Carolus*, Latin name for Charles. A new patent was granted by Charles II to Earl of Clarendon and others. Divided into North and South Carolina, 1710
Capital: Raleigh
Nickname: Tar Heel State, Old North State
Motto: *Esse Quam Videri*—To be, rather than to seem
Bird: Cardinal
Insect: Honeybee
Fish: Channel bass
Flower: Dogwood
Gem: Emerald
Song: "The Old North State"
Tree: Pine

THE LAND

Area: 52,672 sq. mi., 29th
  Land: 48,718 sq. mi., 29th
  Water: 3,954 sq. mi., 10th
    Inland water: 3,954 sq. mi., 6th
Topography: Coastal plain and tidewater, two-fifths of state, extending to the fall line of the rivers; piedmont plateau, another two-fifths, 200 mi. wide, of gentle to rugged hills; southern Appalachian Mountains contain Blue Ridge and Great Smoky Mountains
Number of counties: 100
Geographic center: Chatham, 10 mi. NW of Sanford
Length: 500 mi.; width: 150 mi.
Highest point: 6,684 ft. (Mount Mitchell), 16th

Lowest point: sea level (Atlantic Ocean), 3rd
Mean elevation: 700 ft., 35th
Coastline: 301 mi., 7th
Shoreline: 3,375 mi., 6th

CLIMATE AND ENVIRONMENT

Temp., highest: 110 deg. on Aug. 21, 1983, at Fayetteville; lowest: –34 deg. on Jan. 21, 1985, at Mount Mitchell
Monthly average: highest: 88.3 deg., 23rd; lowest: 27.3 deg., 39th; spread (high to low): 61.0 deg., 42nd
Hazardous waste sites (1993): 22, 18th
Endangered species: Mammals: 5—Indiana bat, Virginia big-eared bat, West Indian manatee, Carolina northern flying squirrel, Red wolf; birds: 2—American peregrine falcon, Red-cockaded woodpecker; reptiles: 3; amphibians: none; fishes: 1; invertebrates: 3; plants: 13

MAJOR CITIES
POPULATION, 1990
PERCENTAGE INCREASE, 1980-90

Charlotte, 395,934—25.50%
Durham, 136,611—35.06%
Greensboro, 183,521—17.91%
Raleigh, 207,951—38.40%
Winston-Salem, 143,485—8.80%

THE PEOPLE

Population (1995): 7,195,138, 11th
  Percent change (1990-95): 8.5%, 14th
Population (2000 proj.): 7,617,000, 11th
  Percent change (1990-2000): 14.91%, 17th
Per sq. mi. (1994): 145.1, 18th
Percent in metro. area (1992): 66.3%, 33rd
Foreign born: 115,000, 21st
  Percent: 1.7%, 37th
Top three ancestries reported:
  African, 18.52%
  German, 16.75%
  English, 14.88%
White: 5,008,491, 75.56%, 39th
Black: 1,456,323, 21.97%, 8th
Native American: 80,155, 1.21%, 14th
Asian, Pacific Isle: 52,166, 0.79%, 36th
Other races: 31,502, 0.48%, 36th
Hispanic origin: 76,726, 1.16%, 39th
Percent over 5 yrs. speaking language other than English at home: 3.9%, 42nd
Percent males: 48.49%, 30th; percent females: 51.51%, 22nd
Percent never married: 25.1%, 30th

Marriages per 1,000 (1993): 6.8, 46th
Divorces per 1,000 (1993): 5.0, 20th
Median age: 33.1
Under 5 years (1994): 7.21%, 25th
Under 18 years (1994): 24.84%, 38th
65 years & older (1994): 12.5%, 30th
Percent increase among the elderly (1990-94): 9.90%, 10th

OF VITAL IMPORTANCE

Live births per 1,000 pop. (1993): 14.5, 28th
Infant mortality rate per 1,000 births (1992): 10.0, 9th
  Rate for blacks (1990): 16.0, 27th
  Rate for whites (1990): 8.3, 14th
Births to unmarried women, % of total (1992): 31.3%, 19th
Births to teenage mothers, % of total (1992): 15.4%, 14th
Abortions (1992): 36,180, 12th
  Rate per 1,000 women 14-44 years old: 22.4, 22nd
Percent change (1988-92): −12%, 32nd
Average lifetime (1979-81): 72.96, 42nd
Deaths per 1,000 pop. (1993): 9.0, 25th
Causes of death per 100,000 pop.:
  Accidents & adverse effects (1992): 39.7, 17th
  Atherosclerosis (1991): 5.2, 43rd
  Cancer (1991): 204.0, 32nd
  Cerebrovascular diseases (1992): 66.9, 9th
  Chronic liver diseases & cirrhosis (1991): 9.8, 18th
  Chronic obstructive pulmonary diseases (1992): 35.1, 32nd
  Diabetes mellitus (1992): 20.9, 23rd
  Diseases of heart (1992): 277.8, 29th
  Pneumonia, flu (1991): 28.5, 32nd
  Suicide (1992): 12.6, 24th

KEEPING WELL

Active nonfederal physicians per 100,000 pop. (1993): 198, 25th
Dentists per 100,000 (1991): 42, 46th
Nurses per 100,000 (1992): 708, 28th
Hospitals per 100,000 (1993): 1.68, 39th
  Admissions per 1,000 (1993): 112.99, 28th
  Occupancy rate per 100 beds (1993): 69.6, 11th
  Average cost per patient per day (1993): $763, 35th
  Average cost per stay (1993): $5,571, 30th
  Average stay (1992): 7.2 days, 24th
AIDS cases (adult, 1993): 1,368; per 100,000: 19.7, 27th

HIV infection, not yet AIDS (1993): 3,949
Other notifiable diseases:
  Gonorrhea: 483.9, 7th
  Measles: 0.6, 43rd
  Syphilis: 51.2, 18th
  Tuberculosis: 10.0, 15th
Pop. without health insur. (1991-93): 14.3%, 19th

HOUSEHOLDS BY TYPE

Total households (1994): 2,679,000
  Percent change (1990-94): 6.4%, 14th
  Per 1,000 pop.: 378.93, 15th
  Percent of households 65 yrs. and over: 21.13%, 34th
  Persons per household (1994): 2.55, 42nd
Family households: 1,812,053
  Percent of total: 71.99%, 15th
Nonfamily households: 704,973
  Percent of total: 28.01%, 37th
Pop. living in group quarters: 224,470
  Percent of pop.: 3.39%, 10th

LIVING QUARTERS

Total housing units: 2,818,193
  Persons per unit: 2.35, 35th
Occupied housing units: 2,517,026
  Percent of total units: 89.31%, 26th
  Persons per unit: 2.51, 30th
  Percent of units with over 1 person per room: 2.89%, 28th
Owner-occupied units: 1,711,817
  Percent of total units: 60.74%, 20th
  Percent of occupied units: 68.01%, 21st
  Persons per unit: 2.62, 46th
  Median value: $65,800, 28th
Renter-occupied units: 805,209
  Percent of total units: 28.57%, 29th
  Percent of occupied units: 31.99%, 31st
  Persons per unit: 2.39, 18th
  Median contract rent: $284, 34th
  Rental vacancy rate: 9.2%, 20th
Mobile home, trailer & other as a percent of occupied housing units: 18.04%, 7th
Persons in emergency shelters for homeless persons: 2,637, 0.040%, 36th
Persons visible in street locations: 259, 0.0039%, 34th
Persons in shelters for abused women: 315, 0.0048%, 27th
Nursing home population: 47,014, 0.71%, 26th

CRIME INDEX PER 100,000 (1992-93)

Total reported: 5,652.3, 15th
  Violent: 679.3, 21st
    Murder and nonnegligent manslaughter: 11.3, 11th
    Aggravated assault: 441.3, 20th
    Robbery: 192.4, 17th
    Forcible rape: 34.3, 34th
  Property: 4,973.0, 14th
    Burglary: 1,515.8, 3rd
    Larceny, theft: 3,168.8, 18th
    Motor vehicle theft: 288.5, 37th
Drug abuse violations (1990): 383.4, 10th
Child-abuse rate per 1,000 children (1993): 17.49, 18th

TEACHING AND LEARNING

Pop. 3 and over enrolled in school: 1,624,913
  Percent of pop.: 25.6%, 44th
Public elementary & secondary schools (1992-93): 1,948
  Total enrollment (1992): 114,083
    Percent of total pop.: 16.30%, 36th
  Teachers (1992): 86,630
    Percent of pop.: 1.27%, 2nd
  Pupil/teacher ratio (fall 1992): 16.7, 28th
  Teachers' avg. salary (1992-93): $31,305, 37th
  Expenditure per capita (1990-91): $3,035.26, 38th
  Expenditure per pupil (1991-92): $4,555, 37th
Percent of graduates taking SAT (1993): 60%, 17th
  Mean SAT verbal scores: 406, 47th
  Mean SAT mathematical scores: 453, 48th
Percent of graduates taking ACT (1995): 12%, 38th
  Mean ACT scores: 19.6, 47th
Percent of pop. over 25 completing:
  Less than 9th grade: 12.7%, 12th
  High school: 70.0%, 43rd
  College degree(s): 17.4%, 38th
Higher education, institutions (1993-94): 122
  Enrollment (1992): 383,453
    Percent of pop.: 5.61%, 25th
  White non-Hispanic (1992): 291,861
    Percent of enroll.: 76.11%, 35th
  Black non-Hispanic (1992): 71,533
    Percent of enroll.: 18.65%, 8th
  Hispanic (1992): 3,552
    Percent of enroll.: 0.93%, 41st
  Asian/Pacific Islander (1992): 7,015
    Percent of enroll.: 1.83%, 30th

American Indian/AK native (1992): 3,338
    Percent of enroll.: 0.87%, 19th
  Nonresident alien (1992): 6,154
    Percent of enroll.: 1.60%, 48th
  Female (1992): 215,669
    Percent of enroll.: 56.24%, 11th
  Pub. institutions (1993-94): 75
    Enrollment (1992): 315,518
    Percent of enroll.: 82.28%, 29th
  Private institutions (1993-94): 47
    Enrollment (1992): 67,935
    Percent of enroll.: 17.72%, 23rd
  Tuition, public institution (avg., 1993-94): $4,704, 48th
  Tuition, private institution (avg., 1993-94): $12,743, 27th
Public library systems: 73
  Books & serial vol. per capita: 1.74, 45th
  Govt. expenditure per capita: $14.11, 27th

LAW ENFORCEMENT, COURTS, AND PRISONS

Police protection, corrections, judicial and legal functions expenditures (1992): $1,609,000,000
  Per capita: $235, 33rd
Police per 10,000 pop. (1993): 22.74, 18th
Prisoners (state & fed.) per 100,000 pop. (1993): 3,149.02, 22nd
  Percent change (1992-93): 7.0%, 18th
Death penalty: yes, by lethal gas or lethal injection
  Under sentence of death (1993): 99, 10th
  Executed (1993): 0

RELIGION, NUMBER AND PERCENT OF POPULATION

Agnostic: 15,068—0.30%, 37th
Buddhist: 5,023—0.10%, 17th
Christian: 4,550,374—90.60%, 8th
Hindu: NA
Jewish: 25,112—0.50%, 27th
Muslim: 10,045—0.20%, 13th
Unitarian: 5,023—0.10%, 31st
Other: 85,382—1.70%, 14th
None: 241,079—4.80%, 42nd
Refused to answer: 85,382—1.70%, 35th

MAKING A LIVING

Personal income per capita (1994): $19,669, 34th
  Percent increase (1993-94): 5.4%, 17th

Disposable personal income per capita (1994): $17,116, 37th

Median income of households (1993): $28,820, 32nd

Percent of pop. below poverty level (1993): 14.4%, 21st

Percent 65 and over (1990): 19.5%, 9th

Expenditure for energy per person (1992): $1,913, 20th

ECONOMY

Civilian labor force (1994): 3,609,000
Percent of total pop.: 51.05%, 27th
Percent 65 and over (1990): 2.88%, 22nd
Percent female: 47.71%, 7th

Percent job growth (1980-90): 28.18%, 15th

Major employer industries (1994):
Agriculture: 83,000—2.4%, 25th
Construction: 157,000—4.6%, 18th
Finance, insurance, & real estate: 140,000—4.1%, 45th
Government: 498,000—14.7%, 32nd
Manufacturing: 857,000—25.3%, 1st
Service: 593,000—17.5%, 47th
Trade: 620,000—18.3%, 37th
Transportation, communications, public utilities: 166,000—4.9%, 33rd

Unemployment rate (1994): 4.38%, 44th
Male: 4.0%, 47th
Female: 4.8%, 38th

Total businesses (1991): 209,770
New business incorps. (1991): 11,944
Percent of total businesses: 5.69%, 27th
Business failures (1991): 1,026
Percent of total businesses: 0.49%

Agriculture farm income:
Marketing (1993): $5,457,000,000, 9th
Average per farm: $92,491.53, 19th
Leading products (1993): Tobacco, broilers, hogs, turkeys
Average value land & build. per acre (1994): $1,349, 14th
Percent increase (1990-94): 6.81%, 31st
Govt. payments (1993): $132,000,000, 26th
Average per farm: $2,237.29, 34th

Construction, value of all: $5,227,000,000
Per capita: $788.55, 12th

Manufactures:
Value added: $57,674,000,000
Per capita: $8,700.73, 1st

Leading products: Textiles, tobacco products, electric and electronic equipment, chemical, furniture, food products, nonelectrical machinery

Value of nonfuel mineral production (1994): $705,000,000, 17th

Leading mineral products: Stone, phosphate, lithium

Retail sales (1993): $55,206,000,000, 11th
Per household: $20,621, 39th
Percent increase (1992-93): 6.7%, 29th

Tourism revenues (1994): $8 bil.

Foreign exports, in total value (1994): $11,863,000,000, 10th
Per capita: $1,677.93, 13th

Gross state product per person (1993): $21,919.43, 21st
Percent change (1990-93): 4.96%, 15th

Patents per 100,000 pop. (1993): 15.36, 29th

Public aid recipients (percent of resident pop. 1993): 7.3%, 17th

Medicaid recipients per 1,000 pop. (1993): 128.88, 17th

Medicare recipients per 1,000 pop. (1993): 139.67, 28th

TRAVEL AND TRANSPORTATION

Motor vehicle registrations (1993): 5,365,000
Per 1,000 pop.: 771.72, 28th

Motorcycle registrations (1993): 64,000
Per 1,000 pop.: 9.21, 44th

Licensed drivers per 1,000 pop. (1993): 679.66, 29th

Deaths from motor vehicle accidents per 100,000 pop. (1993): 19.91, 16th

Public roads & streets (1993):
Total mileage: 96,028
Per 1,000 pop.: 13.81, 34th
Rural mileage: 74,305
Per 1,000 pop.: 10.69, 33rd
Urban mileage: 21,723
Per 1,000 pop.: 3.12, 25th
Interstate mileage: 970
Per 1,000 pop.: 0.14, 37th

Annual vehicle-mi. of travel per person (1993): 9,997, 15th

Mean travel time for workers age 16+ who work away from home: 19.8 min., 31st

GOVERNMENT

Percent of voting age pop. registered (1994): 60.8%, 34th
Percent of voting age pop. voting (1994): 35.7%, 47th

Percent of voting age pop. voting for U.S. representatives (1994): 29.6%, 45th
State legislators, total (1995): 170, 15th
  Women members (1992): 25
  Percent of legislature: 14.7%, 31st
U.S. Congress, House members (1995): 12
  Change (1985-95): +1
Revenues (1993):
  State govt.: $19,377,000,000
  Per capita: $2,787.26, 33rd
Expenditures (1993):
  State govt.: $16,916,000,000
  Per capita: $2,433.26, 39th
Debt outstanding (1993): $4,002,000,000
  Per capita: $575.66, 47th

LAWS AND REGULATIONS

Legal driving age: 18, 16 if completed driver education course
Marriage age without parental consent: 18
Divorce residence requirement: 6 mo.

ATTRACTIONS (1995)

Major opera companies: 1
Major symphony orchestras: 3

Major dance companies: 2
State appropriations for arts agencies per capita: $0.76, 23rd
State Fair in mid-October at Raleigh

SPORTS AND COMPETITION

NCAA teams (Division I): Appalachian State Univ. Mountaineers, Campbell Univ. Fighting Camels, Davidson College Wildcats, Duke Univ. Blue Devils, East Carolina Univ. Pirates, North Carolina A&T State Univ. Aggies, North Carolina State Univ. Wolfpack, Univ. of North Carolina-Asheville Bulldogs, Univ. of North Carolina-Chapel Hill Tar Heels, Univ. of North Carolina-Charlotte 49ers, Univ. of North Carolina-Greensboro Spartans, Univ. of North Carolina-Wilmington Seahawks, Wake Forest Univ. Demon Deacons, Western Carolina Univ. Catamounts
NBA basketball teams: Charlotte Hornets, Charlotte Coliseum
NFL football teams: Carolina Panthers (NFC), Carolinas Stadium

NORTH DAKOTA

"I would never have been President if it had not been for my experiences in North Dakota."

President Theodore Roosevelt

"From pioneer hardships to the rich abundance of modern farms, mines, and factories in little more than a lifetime is the capsule history of North Dakota."

Arthur A. Link, local historian

North Dakota is a land where the great plains have been transformed into lake country by enormous modern reservoirs. Ancient lakes figured in the state's present by depositing the rich soil that brings agricultural abundance. North Dakota is the state where Theodore Roosevelt developed his dynamic image, and the nation dedicated its only National Memorial Park on a portion of the land he once owned. The state is small in population but rich in natural resources (for example, it has the world's greatest reserves of lignite) and in its wealth of tradition.

SUPERLATIVES

- Novel skyscraper capitol.
- "Capital" of the lignite industry.
- First in spring wheat, rye, and flax.

MOMENTS IN HISTORY

- Pierre Gaultier de Varennes, Sieur de La Vérendrye, and his two sons arrived in what is now North Dakota in 1738 and reached the Mandan Indian village near present-day Menoken.
- Braving an unusually bitter winter, in 1797 the party of British scientist David Thompson visited the Mandan towns on the Missouri River.
- After the Louisiana Purchase, the first true picture of the region came with the detailed reports of the Lewis and Clark expedition. Meriwether Lewis and William Clark spent the winter of 1804 at what they called Fort Mandan, near the Mandan and Arikara villages north of present Washburn. They lived in log cabins chinked with mud.

- As they left the winter camp on April 7, 1805, Lewis and Clark sent back to civilization a vast amount of information they had gathered to that point. This included numbers of new and unusual plants and animals and the most complete information on the Indian tribes yet noted.

So They Say

"I could but esteem this moment of my departure as among the most happy of my life. The party are in excellent health and spirits, zealously attached to the enterprise and anxious to proceed, not a whisper or murmur of discontent to be heard among them, but all act in unison, and with the most perfect harmony."

Meriwether Lewis

- On their way back in 1806, Lewis and Clark stopped again to visit their Indian friends at Fort Mandan. The expedition was enormously important in keeping peace with the western Indians for many years.
- Following the Lewis and Clark expedition, fur trading posts were opened, and in 1812, William Douglas established a Scottish settlement near present-day Pembina.
- David Thompson took part in the 1818 survey of the U.S.-Canadian border.
- In 1828 the American Fur Company began Fort Union on the North Dakota side of the Missouri River, and for about 40 years it remained the most important post in a vast region.

• Begun in 1857, Fort Abercrombie was the first federal stronghold located in what is now North Dakota.

• Dakota Territory was organized in 1861.

• Indian warfare went on over a long period, but by 1881 most of the Sioux people had turned to reservation life.

• One of the worst of many prairie fires swept the area on September 25, 1888.

So They Say

"...For at least 40 miles in width the fire burned off every vestige of grass unprotected by breaks. One could hardly recognize the charred land the next day. Thousands of bushels of grain were burned and many men lost all they had, grain, buildings and stock."

Newspaper account
of the 1888 prairie fires

• The first capitol's cornerstone was laid in 1883 by former President Ulysses S. Grant.

• Theodore Roosevelt arrived in North Dakota in 1883 and became a successful and popular rancher.

• Both Dakotas became states on November 2, 1889.

• After "Honest John" Burke was elected governor in 1906, child labor laws and other modern laws were enacted.

• Of 31,269 North Dakotans who served in World War I, 1,205 lost their lives.

• In 1919 the state began operating its own businesses, banks, and other formerly private enterprises—an action unique among the states.

• More than 60,000 people from North Dakota served in World War II, and 1,939 lost their lives.

• Discovery of oil in 1951 brought a new surge in the state's economy.

• Completion of vast artificial lakes and irrigation systems in the 1970s further enhanced the economy.

• By 1981, North Dakota had outstripped Kansas as the leading wheat state.

THAT'S INTERESTING

• When he signed the statehood bills for the two Dakotas on the same day, President Benjamin Harrison would not reveal which one he signed first. Consequently, no one knows whether North Dakota is technically the 39th or the 40th state.

• Seventeen years before Theodore Roosevelt was elected president, Medora storekeeper Joe Ferris publicly predicted the event.

• Among the state's interesting archaeological discoveries are the rows of carved turtles and the rings of boulders. The turtles were thought to have pointed to water sources, and the rocks probably held down the bottoms of tepees.

• A Crow Indian drew a message in the Missouri River sand. It consisted of a cluster of dots representing U.S. troops within a circle. Then he slashed out the dots with a stick. A river captain understood the message and carried the first news of the Custer massacre down the river to Bismarck.

• Inventor D. H. Houston named his new film Kodak, a variation of Dakota that became known around the world.

• A Portal golf course is probably the only place where a golfer might make a tee shot in the United States and end up in a hole in Canada.

NORTH DAKOTA NOTABLES

Maxwell Anderson (Atlantic, PA, 1888-1959), playwright. **George Catlin** (Wilkes-Barre, PA, 1796-1872), western Indian expert/artist. **John Bernard Flannagan** (Fargo, 1895-1942), sculptor. **Roger Eugene Maris** (Hibbing, MN, 1934-1985), baseball player. **Lawrence Welk** (Strasburg, 1903-1992), entertainer.

GENERAL

Admitted to statehood: November 2, 1889
Origin of name: *Dakota* is Sioux for "friend" or "ally"
Capital: Bismarck
Nickname: Peach Garden State, Sioux State
Motto: "Liberty and union, now and forever, one and inseparable"
Bird: Western meadowlark
Fish: Northern pike
Flower: Wild prairie rose
Stone: Teredo petrified wood
Song: "North Dakota Hymn"
Tree: American elm

THE LAND

Area: 70,704 sq. mi., 18th
    Land: 68,994 sq. mi., 17th

Water: 1,710 sq. mi., 18th
  Inland water: 1,710 sq. mi., 12th
Topography: Central lowland in the E comprises the flat Red River Valley and the rolling drift prairie; Missouri plateau of the Great Plains on the W
Number of counties: 53
Geographic center: Sheridan, 5 mi. SW of McClusky
Length: 340 mi.; width: 211 mi.
Highest point: 3,506 ft. (White Butte), 30th
Lowest point: 750 ft. (Red River), 45th
Mean elevation: 1,900 ft., 16th

CLIMATE AND ENVIRONMENT

Temp., highest: 121 deg. on July 6, 1936, at Steele; lowest: –60 deg. on Feb. 15, 1936, at Parshall
Monthly average: highest: 84.4 deg., 40th; lowest: –5.1 deg., 2nd; spread (high to low): 89.5 deg., 2nd
Hazardous waste sites (1993): 2, 49th
Endangered species: Mammals: 1—Black-footed ferret; birds: 3—Whooping crane, American peregrine falcon, Least tern; reptiles: none; amphibians: none; fishes: 1; invertebrates: none; plants: none

MAJOR CITIES
POPULATION, 1990
PERCENTAGE INCREASE, 1980-90

Bismarck, 49,256—10.72%
Dickinson, 16,097—1.09%
Fargo, 74,111—20.74%
Grand Forks, 49,425—12.93%
Minot, 34,544—5.18%

THE PEOPLE

Population (1995): 641,367, 47th
  Percent change (1990-95): 0.4%, 48th
Population (2000 proj.): 643,000, 48th
  Percent change (1990-2000): 0.7%, 47th
Per sq. mi. (1994): 9.2, 48th
Percent in metro. area (1992): 41.6%, 44th
Foreign born: 9,000, 49th
  Percent: 1.5%, 43rd
Top three ancestries reported:
  German, 50.86%
  Norwegian, 29.58%
  Irish, 8.45%
White: 604,142, 94.57%, 6th
Black: 3,524, 0.55%, 46th
Native American: 25,917, 4.06%, 7th

Asian, Pacific Isle: 3,462, 0.54%, 45th
Other races: 1,755, 0.27%, 42nd
Hispanic origin: 4,665, 0.73%, 44th
Percent over 5 yrs. speaking language other than English at home: 7.9%, 22nd
Percent males: 49.81%, 6th; females: 50.19%, 46th
Percent never married: 25.9%, 23rd
Marriages per 1,000 (1993): 7.7, 37th
Divorces per 1,000 (1993): 3.5, 38th
Median age: 32.4
Under 5 years (1994): 6.74%, 46th
Under 18 years (1994): 26.96%, 17th
65 years & older (1994): 14.7%, 7th
Percent increase among the elderly (1990-94): 3.23%, 43rd

OF VITAL IMPORTANCE

Live births per 1,000 pop. (1993): 13.8, 41st
Infant mortality rate per 1,000 births (1992): 7.8, 32nd
  Rate for blacks (1990): NA
  Rate for whites (1990): 7.9, 25th
Births to unmarried women, % of total (1992): 22.6%, 46th
Births to teenage mothers, % of total (1992): 9.3%, 44th
Abortions (1992): 1,490, 49th
  Rate per 1,000 women 14-44 years old: 10.7, 46th
  Percent change (1988-92): –28%, 50th
Average lifetime (1979-81): 75.71, 4th
Deaths per 1,000 pop. (1993): 9.3, 17th
Causes of death per 100,000 pop.:
  Accidents & adverse effects (1992): 36.6, 20th
  Atherosclerosis (1991): 15.3, 1st
  Cancer (1991): 215.0, 18th
  Cerebrovascular diseases (1992): 75.9, 2nd
  Chronic liver diseases & cirrhosis (1991): 8.8, 30th
  Chronic obstructive pulmonary diseases (1992): 36.9, 26th
  Diabetes mellitus (1992): 22.6, 13th
  Diseases of heart (1992): 300.0, 18th
  Pneumonia, flu (1991): 36.2, 11th
  Suicide (1992): 10.3, 42nd

KEEPING WELL

Active nonfederal physicians per 100,000 pop. (1993): 188, 32nd
Dentists per 100,000 (1991): 47, 38th
Nurses per 100,000 (1992): 1,007, 3rd
Hospitals per 100,000 (1993): 7.06, 2nd

Admissions per 1,000 (1993): 142.54, 6th

Occupancy rate per 100 beds (1993): 64.2, 17th

Average cost per patient per day (1993): $507, 49th

Average cost per stay (1993): $5,403, 35th

Average stay (1992): 13.0 days, 3rd

AIDS cases (adult, 1993): 11; per 100,000: 1.7, 51st

HIV infection, not yet AIDS (1993): 32

Other notifiable diseases:

Gonorrhea: 15.7, 48th

Measles: 0.0, 51st

Syphilis: 0.9, 50th

Tuberculosis: 2.8, 40th

Pop. without health insur. (1991-93): 9.7%, 45th

HOUSEHOLDS BY TYPE

Total households (1994): 241,000

Percent change (1990-94): 0.2%, 48th

Per 1,000 pop.: 377.74, 19th

Percent of households 65 yrs. and over: 24.90%, 8th

Persons per household (1994): 2.54, 43rd

Family households: 166,270

Percent of total: 69.03%, 37th

Nonfamily households: 74,608

Percent of total: 30.97%, 15th

Pop. living in group quarters: 24,234

Percent of pop.: 3.79%, 4th

LIVING QUARTERS

Total housing units: 276,340

Persons per unit: 2.31, 39th

Occupied housing units: 240,878

Percent of total units: 87.17%, 37th

Persons per unit: 2.46, 43rd

Percent of units with over 1 person per room: 1.98%, 43rd

Owner-occupied units: 157,950

Percent of total units: 57.16%, 34th

Percent of occupied units: 65.57%, 35th

Persons per unit: 2.74, 22nd

Median value: $50,800, 43rd

Renter-occupied units: 82,928

Percent of total units: 30.01%, 22nd

Percent of occupied units: 34.43%, 18th

Persons per unit: 2.18, 49th

Median contract rent: $266, 40th

Rental vacancy rate: 9.0%, 22nd

Mobile home, trailer & other as a percent of occupied housing units: 12.30%, 23rd

Persons in emergency shelters for homeless persons: 279, 0.044%, 29th

Persons visible in street locations: 30, 0.0047%, 30th

Persons in shelters for abused women: 36, 0.0056%, 16th

Nursing home population: 8,159, 1.28%, 3rd

CRIME INDEX PER 100,000 (1992-93)

Total reported: 2,820.3, 50th

Violent: 82.2, 51st

Murder and nonnegligent manslaughter: 1.7, 50th

Aggravated assault: 48.7, 51st

Robbery: 8.3, 51st

Forcible rape: 23.5, 50th

Property: 2,738.1, 50th

Burglary: 373.2, 51st

Larceny, theft: 2,216.2, 45th

Motor vehicle theft: 148.7, 48th

Drug abuse violations (1990): 66.2, 50th

Child-abuse rate per 1,000 children (1993): 23.31, 9th

TEACHING AND LEARNING

Pop. 3 and over enrolled in school: 177,543

Percent of pop.: 29.1%, 10th

Public elementary & secondary schools (1992-93): 642

Total enrollment (1992): 118,734

Percent of total pop.: 18.73%, 10th

Teachers (1992): 7,794

Percent of pop.: 1.23%, 8th

Pupil/teacher ratio (fall 1992): 15.2, 40th

Teachers' avg. salary (1992-93): $26,733, 49th

Expenditure per capita (1990-91): $3,541.28, 21st

Expenditure per pupil (1991-92): $4,441, 38th

Percent of graduates taking SAT (1993): 6%, 46th

Mean SAT verbal scores: 518, 2nd

Mean SAT mathematical scores: 583, 1st

Percent of graduates taking ACT (1995): 75%, 1st

Mean ACT scores: 21.2, 20th

Percent of pop. over 25 completing:

Less than 9th grade: 15.0%, 6th

High school: 76.7%, 27th

College degree(s): 18.1%, 31st

Higher education, institutions (1993-94): 20

Enrollment (1992): 40,470
  Percent of pop.: 6.37%, 13th
  White non-Hispanic (1992): 35,923
    Percent of enroll.: 88.76%, 14th
  Black non-Hispanic (1992): 311
    Percent of enroll.: 0.77%, 47th
  Hispanic (1992): 213
    Percent of enroll.: 0.53%, 46th
  Asian/Pacific Islander (1992): 281
    Percent of enroll.: 0.69%, 49th
  American Indian/AK native (1992): 2,019
    Percent of enroll.: 4.99%, 6th
  Nonresident alien (1992): 1,723
    Percent of enroll.: 4.26%, 7th
  Female (1992): 20,068
    Percent of enroll.: 49.59%, 50th
  Pub. institutions (1993-94): 15
    Enrollment (1992): 36,783
    Percent of enroll.: 90.89%, 6th
  Private institutions (1993-94): 5
    Enrollment (1992): 3,687
    Percent of enroll.: 9.11%, 46th
  Tuition, public institution (avg., 1993-94): $5,294, 32nd
  Tuition, private institution (avg., 1993-94): $8,768, 46th
Public library systems: 95
  Books & serial vol. per capita: 2.76, 22nd
  Govt. expenditure per capita: $9.98, 41st

LAW ENFORCEMENT, COURTS, AND PRISONS

Police protection, corrections, judicial and legal functions expenditures (1992): $98,000,000
  Per capita: $155, 48th
Police per 10,000 pop. (1993): 15.69, 48th
Prisoners (state & fed.) per 100,000 pop. (1993): 781.79, 51st
  Percent change (1992-93): 4.4%, 29th
Death penalty: no

RELIGION, NUMBER AND PERCENT OF POPULATION

Agnostic: 1,854—0.40%, 34th
Buddhist: NA
Christian: 437,927—94.50%, 2nd
Hindu: NA
Jewish: 1,854—0.40%, 31st
Muslim: NA
Unitarian: NA
Other: 2,781—0.60%, 46th
None: 7,415—1.60%, 49th
Refused to answer: 11,585—2.50%, 18th

MAKING A LIVING

Personal income per capita (1994): $18,546, 39th
  Percent increase (1993-94): 8.6%, 3rd
Disposable personal income per capita (1994): $16,664, 39th
Median income of households (1993): $28,118, 37th
Percent of pop. below poverty level (1993): 11.2%, 35th
  Percent 65 and over (1990): 14.6%, 17th
Expenditure for energy per person (1992): $2,471, 4th

ECONOMY

Civilian labor force (1994): 338,000
  Percent of total pop.: 52.98%, 14th
  Percent 65 and over (1990): 3.38%, 10th
  Percent female: 46.75%, 19th
Percent job growth (1980-90): 7.07%, 46th
Major employer industries (1994):
  Agriculture: 39,000—12.9%, 1st
  Construction: 11,000—3.6%, 42nd
  Finance, insurance, & real estate: 12,000—3.9%, 48th
  Government: 58,000—19.2%, 9th
  Manufacturing: 18,000—5.9%, 45th
  Service: 60,000—19.6%, 35th
  Trade: 67,000—22.1%, 1st
  Transportation, communications, public utilities: 13,000—4.3%, 42nd
Unemployment rate (1994): 3.85%, 47th
  Male: 4.4%, 43rd
  Female: 3.3%, 50th
Total businesses (1991): 32,361
  New business incorps. (1991): 820
    Percent of total businesses: 2.53%, 51st
  Business failures (1991): 144
    Percent of total businesses: 0.44%
Agriculture farm income:
  Marketing (1993): $2,933,000,000, 23rd
    Average per farm: $88,878.79, 22nd
  Leading products (1993): Wheat, cattle, barley, sugar beets
  Average value land & build. per acre (1994): $409, 42nd
    Percent increase (1990-94): 20.29%, 8th
  Govt. payments (1993): $565,000,000, 8th
    Average per farm: $17,121.21, 1st
Construction, value of all: $262,000,000
  Per capita: $410.14, 39th

Manufactures:
Value added: $1,110,000,000
Per capita: $1,737.63, 47th
Leading products: Farm equipment, processed foods
Value of nonfuel mineral production (1994): $26,000,000, 49th
Leading mineral products: Petroleum, coal, natural gas
Retail sales (1993): $5,921,000,000, 47th
Per household: $24,294, 6th
Percent increase (1992-93): 10.6%, 4th
Tourism revenues (1992): $826 mil.
Foreign exports, in total value (1994): $458,000,000, 47th
Per capita: $717.87, 42nd
Gross state product per person (1993): $18,927.44, 39th
Percent change (1990-93): 0%, 45th
Patents per 100,000 pop. (1993): 10.36, 42nd
Public aid recipients (percent of resident pop. 1993): 4.2%, 46th
Medicaid recipients per 1,000 pop. (1993): 97.33, 39th
Medicare recipients per 1,000 pop. (1993): 160.13, 7th

TRAVEL AND TRANSPORTATION

Motor vehicle registrations (1993): 662,000
Per 1,000 pop.: 1,039.25, 4th
Motorcycle registrations (1993): 18,000
Per 1,000 pop.: 28.26, 7th
Licensed drivers per 1,000 pop. (1993): 687.60, 28th
Deaths from motor vehicle accidents per 100,000 pop. (1993): 13.97, 34th
Public roads & streets (1993):
Total mileage: 86,727
Per 1,000 pop.: 136.15, 1st
Rural mileage: 84,909
Per 1,000 pop.: 133.30, 1st
Urban mileage: 1,818
Per 1,000 pop.: 2.85, 35th

Interstate mileage: 571
Per 1,000 pop.: 0.90, 5th
Annual vehicle-mi. of travel per person (1993): 9,733, 23rd
Mean travel time for workers age 16+ who work away from home: 13.0 min., 51st

GOVERNMENT

Percent of voting age pop. registered (1994): 93.3%, 1st
Percent of voting age pop. voting (1994): 61.1%, 3rd
Percent of voting age pop. voting for U.S. representatives (1994): 50.4%, 7th
State legislators, total (1995): 147, 25th
Women members (1992): 23
Percent of legislature: 14.5%, 33rd
U.S. Congress, House members (1995): 1
Change (1985-95): 0
Revenues (1993):
State govt.: $2,288,000,000
Per capita: $3,591.84, 13th
Parimutuel & amusement taxes & lotteries, revenue per capita: $10.99, 36th
Expenditures (1993):
State govt.: $2,129,000,000
Per capita: $3,342.23, 13th
Debt outstanding (1993): $830,000,000
Per capita: $1,302.98, 26th

LAWS AND REGULATIONS

Legal driving age: 16
Marriage age without parental consent: 18
Divorce residence requirement: 6 mo.

ATTRACTIONS (1995)

State appropriations for arts agencies per capita: $0.47, 40th
State Fair in third week in July at Minot

SPORTS AND COMPETITION

NCAA teams (Division II): North Dakota State Univ. Bison, Univ. of North Dakota Fighting Sioux

OHIO

"Ohio is the farthest west of the East and the farthest north of the South."

Attributed to Louis Bromfield, author

Without a historic agreement, Cleveland would have been in Connecticut. In another twist of history, Ohio did not enter the Union officially until 1953. Professional baseball got its start in Ohio. The hot dog was invented in the state, as well as floating soap (Ivory). On a more serious note, Ohio has long been one of the leaders in industry and cultural activities, and was the birthplace of seven U.S. presidents, along with a near record number of other figures of world acclaim. Ohio has more than 50 accredited colleges and universities; Oberlin College, established in 1833, was the first institution of higher education in the United States to enroll both men and women. In 1995, Cleveland celebrated the opening of the Rock and Roll Hall of Fame.

SUPERLATIVES

• First professional baseball team—the Cincinnati Red Stockings.
• First in clay products manufacture.
• Pioneer leader in rubber products.
• World leader in machine tools.

MOMENTS IN HISTORY

• The first known European explorer in the Ohio region was the French emissary Robert Cavalier, Sieur de La Salle, in 1669-1670. He claimed the entire vast region west of the Alleghenies for France.
• George Croghan, who operated in the area in the mid-1700s, was the most successful in promoting British claims to the area.
• Attempting to reassert French claims to the region, the Sieur de Bienville in 1749 planted a series of six lead plates along the banks of the Ohio River.
• On October 31, 1750, Ohio Company representative George Gist and his dog spent Christmas at the trading post of George Croghan. Gist and his faithful dog explored much of present-day Ohio, winning the Indians to the British cause.

> ### So They Say
> "The Ohio Country is fine, rich, level land, well-timbered with large walnut, ash, sugar trees...It is well watered...and full of beautiful natural...meadows, abounding with turkeys, deer, elk and most sorts of game, particularly buffaloes. In short, it wants nothing but cultivation to make it a most delightful country."
>
> George Gist

• In 1763 the French gave up all claims, and British claims were confirmed.
• Indian uprisings under chiefs including Pontiac and Cornstalk occupied British attention during most of the period before the Revolution.
• The Revolution brought no great battles to Ohio country. Most of the British cause was carried on by Indian raids. At war's end the new nation formally claimed the western lands after the Treaty of Paris in 1783.
• The claims to Ohio by Connecticut and Virginia were settled by agreements for Ohio to include the Western Reserve and the Virginia Military Survey.
• The Northwest Ordinance of 1787 established government in that whole region.
• In 1788 the first of many thousands of settlers floated down the Ohio River and founded Marietta.

> ### So They Say
> "No colony in America was settled under circumstances more favorable. There never were people better able to promote the welfare of the community."
>
> George Washington,
> on Marietta's founding

• In 12 months in 1788-1789, 10,000 settlers reached Ohio, most of them floating down the Ohio on flatboats, sometimes attacked by Indians or pirates.

• Indian troubles increased until, with the Treaty of Greenville in 1795, the Indians gave up much of their Ohio lands.

• In 1803, Ohio became the first state west of the Alleghenies.

• Many critical battles with British and Indian forces occurred in the state during the War of 1812.

• An American fleet led by Oliver Hazard Perry won a major victory over the British fleet at the Battle of Put-in-Bay off Ohio shores in September 1813.

So They Say

"We have met the enemy, and they are ours."

Oliver Hazard Perry's minimal report to his commander after his victory at Put-in-Bay

---

• The "border war" with Michigan in 1835 was settled, giving Ohio the area around Toledo.

• In the years before 1860, perhaps more slaves were spirited through Ohio on the Underground Railroad than through any other state.

• Several attacks by Confederate raiders plagued Ohio during the Civil War, which called 345,000 Ohioans into service.

• After the war, John D. Rockefeller founded the Standard Oil Company at Cleveland in 1870. National Cash Register was founded at Dayton in 1879, and, with many other industries, Ohio became one of the great industrial states.

• More than 200,000 Ohioans entered World War I service.

• In 1937 the Ohio River region suffered the worst floods in the history of the Ohio-Mississippi watershed.

• Ohioans in World War II uniform numbered 840,000.

• The Ohio Turnpike opened in 1955.

• Famed Ohio astronaut John Glenn was elected to the U.S. Senate in 1974.

• Cincinnati's Contemporary Arts Center in 1990 was acquitted in a widely publicized obscenity trial, reaffirming freedom of speech and expression.

THAT'S INTERESTING

• A part of one of the lead claim plates buried by Bienville in 1749 was found by small boys, and the historic relic went to a Massachusetts museum.

• If Connecticut claims in Ohio had not been settled, the present-day Ohio city might have been known as Cleveland, Connecticut.

• The design for the great seal of Ohio was inspired by the rising of the sun over the Ohio mountains after an all-night meeting of early Ohio officials.

• Technically, Ohio did not legally become a state until 1953 because Congress had up to then neglected to give its formal approval.

• Harry M. Stevens of Niles saw a cartoon of a dachshund dog as a wiener. He called his sandwich invention a "hot dog."

• The first cash register was named a "mechanical money drawer" by its inventor, James Ritty.

NOTABLE NATIVES

Sherwood Anderson (Camden, 1876-1941), author. **Neil Alden Armstrong** (Wapakoneta, 1930-), astronaut. **Arthur Holly Compton** (Wooster, 1892-1962), physicist. **Cornstalk** (Ohio-West Virginia frontier, 1720?-1777), Indian leader. **George Armstrong Custer** (New Rumley, 1839-1876), soldier. **Clarence Seward Darrow** (near Kinsman, 1857-1938), lawyer. **Paul Laurence Dunbar** (Dayton, 1872-1906), poet. **Thomas Alva Edison** (Milan, 1847-1931), inventor. **Daniel Decatur Emmett** (Mount Vernon, 1815-1904), entertainer/songwriter. **Frederick Funston** (New Carlisle, 1865-1917), soldier. **Clark Gable** (Cadiz, 1901-1960), actor. **James Abram Garfield** (Orange, 1831-1881), U.S. president. **John Herschel Glenn** (Cambridge, 1921-), astronaut/public official. **Ulysses Simpson Grant** (Point Pleasant, 1822-1885), soldier and U.S. president. **Zane Grey** (Zanesville, 1875-1939), author. **Warren Gamaliel Harding** (Blooming Grove, 1865-1923), U.S. president. **Benjamin Harrison** (North Bend, 1833-1901), U.S. president. **Rutherford Birchard Hayes** (Delaware, 1822-1893), U.S. president. **Dean Martin** (Steubenville, 1917-1995), singer and actor. **William McKinley** (Niles, 1843-1901), U.S. president. **Paul Newman** (Cleveland, 1925-), actor. **Jack William Nicklaus** (Columbus,

1940-), golfer. **Pontiac** (in northern Ohio, 1720?-1769), Indian leader. **Edward Vernon Rickenbacker** (Columbus, 1890-1973), aviator/businessman. **Philip Henry Sheridan** (Somerset?, 1831-1888), soldier. **William Tecumseh Sherman** (Lancaster, 1820-1891), soldier. **Steven Spielberg** (Cincinnati, 1947-), film director. **Robert Alphonso Taft** (Cincinnati, 1889-1953), public official. **William Howard Taft** (Cincinnati, 1857-1930), U.S. president. **James Grover Thurber** (Columbus, 1894-1961), humorist/cartoonist.

GENERAL

Admitted to statehood: March 1, 1803
Origin of name: Iroquois word for "fine or good river"
Capital: Columbus
Nickname: Buckeye State
Motto: With God, all things are possible
Bird: Cardinal
Insect: Ladybug
Flower: Scarlet carnation
Stone: Ohio flint
Song: "Beautiful Ohio"
Tree: Buckeye

THE LAND

Area: 44,828 sq. mi., 34th
  Land: 40,953 sq. mi., 35th
  Water: 3,875 sq. mi., 11th
    Inland water: 376 sq. mi., 37th
    Great Lakes: 3,499 sq. mi., 4th
Topography: Generally rolling plain; Allegheny plateau located in the E; Lake Erie plains extend southward; central plains in the W
Number of counties: 88
Geographic center: Delaware, 25 mi. NNE of Columbus
Length: 220 mi.; width: 220 mi.
Highest point: 1,549 ft. (Campbell Hill), 43rd
Lowest point: 455 ft. (Ohio River), 36th
Mean elevation: 850 ft., 31st

CLIMATE AND ENVIRONMENT

Temp., highest: 113 deg. on July 21, 1934, near Gallipolis; lowest: –39 deg. on Feb. 10, 1899, at Milligan
Monthly average: highest: 85.8 deg., 34th; lowest: 15.5 deg., 18th; spread (high to low): 70.3 deg., 23rd
Hazardous waste sites (1993): 36, 11th

Endangered species: Mammals: 1—Indiana bat; birds: 2—American peregrine falcon, Piping plover; reptiles: none; amphibians: none; fishes: 1; invertebrates: 3; plants: 1

MAJOR CITIES
POPULATION, 1990
PERCENTAGE INCREASE, 1980-90

Akron, 223,019— –5.97%
Cincinnati, 364,040— –5.54%
Cleveland, 505,616— –11.89%
Colombus, 632,910—12.02%
Toledo, 332,943— –6.12%

THE PEOPLE

Population (1995): 11,150,506, 7th
  Percent change (1990-95): 2.8%, 39th
Population (2000 proj.): 11,453,000, 7th
  Percent change (1990-2000): 5.59%, 37th
Per sq. mi. (1994): 271.1, 9th
Percent in metro. area (1992): 81.3%, 19th
Foreign born: 260,000, 15th
  Percent: 2.4%, 33rd
Top three ancestries reported:
  German, 37.50%
  Irish, 17.48%
  English, 13.36%
White: 9,521,756, 87.78%, 24th
Black: 1,154,826, 10.65%, 20th
Native American: 20,358, 0.19%, 48th
Asian, Pacific Isle: 91,179, 0.84%, 34th
Other races: 58,996, 0.54%, 33rd
Hispanic origin: 139,696, 1.29%, 35th
Percent over 5 yrs. speaking language other than English at home: 5.4%, 36th
Percent males: 48.18%, 40th; percent females: 51.82%, 12th
Percent never married: 25.5%, 26th
Marriages per 1,000 (1993): 8.0, 33rd
Divorces per 1,000 (1993): 4.6, 25th
Median age: 33.3
Under 5 years (1994): 7.06%, 35th
Under 18 years (1994): 25.71%, 29th
65 years & older (1994): 13.4%, 19th
Percent increase among the elderly (1990-94): 5.97%, 24th

OF VITAL IMPORTANCE

Live births per 1,000 pop. (1993): 14.1, 35th
Infant mortality rate per 1,000 births (1992): 9.4, 12th
  Rate for blacks (1990): 18.3, 8th
  Rate for whites (1990): 8.2, 18th

Births to unmarried women, % of total (1992): 31.6%, 16th

Births to teenage mothers, % of total (1992): 13.6%, 18th

Abortions (1992): 49,520, 9th
   Rate per 1,000 women 14-44 years old: 19.5, 25th
   Percent change (1988-92): –7%, 23rd

Average lifetime (1979-81): 73.49, 34th

Deaths per 1,000 pop. (1993): 9.1, 23rd

Causes of death per 100,000 pop.:
   Accidents & adverse effects (1992): 30.5, 40th
   Atherosclerosis (1991): 7.2, 22nd
   Cancer (1991): 220.7, 15th
   Cerebrovascular diseases (1992): 55.4, 31st
   Chronic liver diseases & cirrhosis (1991): 8.5, 34th
   Chronic obstructive pulmonary diseases (1992): 39.7, 21st
   Diabetes mellitus (1992): 26.3, 6th
   Diseases of heart (1992): 308 7, 16th
   Pneumonia, flu (1991): 28.9, 30th
   Suicide (1992): 10.8, 41st

KEEPING WELL

Active nonfederal physicians per 100,000 pop. (1993): 207, 22nd

Dentists per 100,000 (1991): 54, 24th

Nurses per 100,000 (1992): 816, 17th

Hospitals per 100,000 (1993): 1.74, 36th
   Admissions per 1,000 (1993): 127.81, 16th
   Occupancy rate per 100 beds (1993): 60.5, 31st
   Average cost per patient per day (1993): $940, 15th
   Average cost per stay (1993): $5,923, 21st
   Average stay (1992): 7.2 days, 22nd

AIDS cases (adult, 1993): 1,585; per 100,000: 14.3, 36th

HIV infection, not yet AIDS (1993): 965

Other notifiable diseases:
   Gonorrhea: 372.6, 11th
   Measles: 5.1, 21st
   Syphilis: 10.2, 33rd
   Tuberculosis: 3.5, 36th

Pop. without health insur. (1991-93): 10.8%, 41st

HOUSEHOLDS BY TYPE

Total households (1994): 4,190,000
   Percent change (1990-94): 2.5%, 33rd
   Per 1,000 pop.: 377.41, 21st

Percent of households 65 yrs. and over: 22.65%, 19th

Persons per household (1994): 2.59, 26th

Family households: 2,895,223
   Percent of total: 70.83%, 25th

Nonfamily households: 1,192,323
   Percent of total: 29.17%, 27th

Pop. living in group quarters: 261,451
   Percent of pop.: 2.41%, 36th

LIVING QUARTERS

Total housing units: 4,371,945
   Persons per unit: 2.48, 10th

Occupied housing units: 4,087,546
   Percent of total units: 93.49%, 1st
   Persons per unit: 2.51, 30th
   Percent of units with over 1 person per room: 1.76%, 46th

Owner-occupied units: 2,758,149
   Percent of total units: 63.09%, 10th
   Percent of occupied units: 67.48%, 24th
   Persons per unit: 2.74, 22nd
   Median value: $63,500, 29th

Renter-occupied units: 1,329,397
   Percent of total units: 30.41%, 20th
   Percent of occupied units: 32.52%, 28th
   Persons per unit: 2.27, 36th
   Median contract rent: $296, 31st
   Rental vacancy rate: 7.5%, 35th

Mobile home, trailer & other as a percent of occupied housing units: 6.03%, 42nd

Persons in emergency shelters for homeless persons: 4,277, 0.039%, 38th

Persons visible in street locations: 188, 0.0017%, 47th

Persons in shelters for abused women: 496, 0.0046%, 31st

Nursing home population: 93,769, 0.86%, 18th

CRIME INDEX PER 100,000 (1992-93)

Total reported: 4,485.3, 34th
   Violent: 504.1, 27th
      Murder and nonnegligent manslaughter: 6.0, 30th
      Aggravated assault: 256.3, 32nd
      Robbery: 192.7, 16th
      Forcible rape: 49.1, 14th
   Property: 3,981.2, 36th
      Burglary: 878.1, 32nd
      Larceny, theft: 2,667.7, 37th
      Motor vehicle theft: 435.3, 26th
Drug abuse violations (1990): 229.5, 29th

Child-abuse rate per 1,000 children (1993): 18.14, 15th

TEACHING AND LEARNING

Pop. 3 and over enrolled in school: 2,798,226
  Percent of pop.: 27.0%, 28th
Public elementary & secondary schools (1992-93): 3,821
  Total enrollment (1992): 1,796,418
    Percent of total pop.: 16.30%, 36th
  Teachers (1992): 106,233
    Percent of pop.: 0.96%, 35th
  Pupil/teacher ratio (fall 1992): 16.9, 24th
  Teachers' avg. salary (1992-93): $36,563, 23rd
  Expenditure per capita (1990-91): $3,194.63, 34th
  Expenditure per pupil (1991-92): $5,694, 17th
Percent of graduates taking SAT (1993): 22%, 29th
  Mean SAT verbal scores: 454, 23rd
  Mean SAT mathematical scores: 505, 24th
Percent of graduates taking ACT (1995): 59%, 21st
  Mean ACT scores: 21.2, 20th
Percent of pop. over 25 completing:
  Less than 9th grade: 7.9%, 38th
  High school: 75.7%, 30th
  College degree(s): 17.0%, 40th
Higher education, institutions (1993-94): 156
  Enrollment (1992): 573,183
    Percent of pop.: 5.21%, 37th
  White non-Hispanic (1992): 490,035
    Percent of enroll.: 85.49%, 19th
  Black non-Hispanic (1992): 49,884
    Percent of enroll.: 8.70%, 19th
  Hispanic (1992): 6,723
    Percent of enroll.: 1.17%, 37th
  Asian/Pacific Islander (1992): 8,862
    Percent of enroll.: 1.55%, 34th
  American Indian/AK native (1992): 1,827
    Percent of enroll.: 0.32%, 35th
  Nonresident alien (1992): 15,852
    Percent of enroll.: 2.77%, 20th
  Female (1992): 309,817
    Percent of enroll.: 54.05%, 42nd
  Pub. institutions (1993-94): 61
    Enrollment (1992): 437,027
    Percent of enroll.: 76.25%, 38th
  Private institutions (1993-94): 95
    Enrollment (1992): 136,156
    Percent of enroll.: 23.75%, 14th

Tuition, public institution (avg., 1993-94): $6,987, 15th
Tuition, private institution (avg., 1993-94): $14,361, 18th
Public library systems: 250
  Books & serial vol. per capita: 3.37, 15th
  Govt. expenditure per capita: $16.01, 23rd

LAW ENFORCEMENT, COURTS, AND PRISONS

Police protection, corrections, judicial and legal functions expenditures (1992): $2,883,000,000
  Per capita: $262, 25th
Police per 10,000 pop. (1993): 17.92, 37th
Prisoners (state & fed.) per 100,000 pop. (1993): 3,674.26, 18th
  Percent change (1992-93): 5.9%, 24th
Death penalty: yes, by electrocution
  Under sentence of death (1993): 129, 6th
  Executed (1993): 0

RELIGION, NUMBER AND PERCENT OF POPULATION

Agnostic: 40,237—0.50%, 27th
Buddhist: 8,047—0.10%, 17th
Christian: 6,928,786—86.10%, 26th
Hindu: 8,047—0.10%, 10th
Jewish: 56,332—0.70%, 23rd
Muslim: 32,190—0.40%, 5th
Unitarian: 8,047—0.10%, 31st
Other: 193,137—2.40%, 5th
None: 595,506—7.40%, 17th
Refused to answer: 177,042—2.20%, 23rd

MAKING A LIVING

Personal income per capita (1994): $20,928, 23rd
  Percent increase (1993-94): 6.3%, 8th
Disposable personal income per capita (1994): $18,195, 24th
Median income of households (1993): $31,285, 23rd
Percent of pop. below poverty level (1993): 13.0%, 29th
  Percent 65 and over (1990): 10.7%, 34th
Expenditure for energy per person (1992): $1,920, 19th

ECONOMY

Civilian labor force (1994): 5,537,000
  Percent of total pop.: 49.87%, 36th
  Percent 65 and over (1990): 2.69%, 27th
  Percent female: 46.27%, 24th

Percent job growth (1980-90): 13.71%, 39th

Major employer industries (1994):
  Agriculture: 93,000—1.8%, 37th
  Construction: 206,000—4.0%, 29th
  Finance, insurance, & real estate: 265,000—5.2%, 26th
  Government: 723,000—14.1%, 37th
  Manufacturing: 1,143,000—22.3%, 8th
  Service: 1,124,000—21.9%, 21st
  Trade: 992,000—19.3%, 18th
  Transportation, communications, public utilities: 252,000—4.9%, 33rd

Unemployment rate (1994): 5.54%, 27th
  Male: 5.6%, 26th
  Female: 5.4%, 24th

Total businesses (1991): 341,253
  New business incorps. (1991): 17,895
    Percent of total businesses: 5.24%, 36th
  Business failures (1991): 2,262
  Percent of total businesses: 0.66%

Agriculture farm income:
  Marketing (1993): $4,393,000,000, 13th
    Average per farm: $57,802.63, 41st
  Leading products (1993): Soybeans, corn, dairy products, greenhouse
  Average value land & build. per acre (1994): $1,386, 13th
    Percent increase (1990-94): 15.12%, 24th
  Govt. payments (1993): $265,000,000, 18th
    Average per farm: $3,486.84, 28th

Construction, value of all: $6,245,000,000
  Per capita: $575.73, 22nd

Manufactures:
  Value added: $80,377,000,000
    Per capita: $7,409.99, 4th
  Leading products: Transportation equipment, machinery, primary and fabricated metal products

Value of nonfuel mineral production (1994): $983,000,000, 11th
  Leading mineral products: Coal, natural gas, petroleum

Retail sales (1993): $92,428,000,000, 7th
  Per household: $21,970, 27th
    Percent increase (1992-93): 12.9%, 1st

Tourism revenues (1992): $8.8 bil.

Foreign exports, in total value (1994): $19,007,000,000, 7th
  Per capita: $1,712.03, 12th

Gross state product per person (1993): $20,856.20, 27th

Percent change (1990-93): 2.24%, 36th

Patents per 100,000 pop. (1993): 26.91, 15th

Public aid recipients (percent of resident pop. 1993): 8.3%, 11th

Medicaid recipients per 1,000 pop. (1993): 134.80, 15th

Medicare recipients per 1,000 pop. (1993): 147.00, 20th

TRAVEL AND TRANSPORTATION

Motor vehicle registrations (1993): 9,279,000
  Per 1,000 pop.: 838.89, 15th

Motorcycle registrations (1993): 233,000
  Per 1,000 pop.: 21.07, 13th

Licensed drivers per 1,000 pop. (1993): 690.26, 26th

Deaths from motor vehicle accidents per 100,000 pop. (1993): 13.42, 38th

Public roads & streets (1993):
  Total mileage: 113,823
    Per 1,000 pop.: 10.29, 39th
  Rural mileage: 82,255
    Per 1,000 pop.: 7.44, 39th
  Urban mileage: 31,568
    Per 1,000 pop.: 2.85, 35th
  Interstate mileage: 1,573
    Per 1,000 pop.: 0.14, 36th

Annual vehicle-mi. of travel per person (1993): 8,770, 36th

Mean travel time for workers age 16+ who work away from home: 20.7 min., 24th

GOVERNMENT

Percent of voting age pop. registered (1994): 64.6%, 24th
  Percent of voting age pop. voting (1994): 46.6%, 23rd
  Percent of voting age pop. voting for U.S. representatives (1994): 39.7%, 22nd

State legislators, total (1995): 132, 33rd
  Women members (1992): 20
    Percent of legislature: 15.2%, 29th

U.S. Congress, House members (1995): 19
  Change (1985-95): −2

Revenues (1993):
  State govt.: $38,341,000,000
    Per capita: $3,466.32, 18th
  Parimutuel & amusement taxes & lotteries, revenue per capita: $164.27, 7th

Expenditures (1993):
  State govt.: $31,665,000,000
    Per capita: $2,862.76, 23rd

Debt outstanding (1993): $12,486,000,000
  Per capita: $1,128.83, 32nd

LAWS AND REGULATIONS

Legal driving age: 18, 16 if completed driver education course

Marriage age without parental consent: 18

Divorce residence requirement: 6 mo.

ATTRACTIONS (1995)

Major opera companies: 7

Major symphony orchestras: 5

Major dance companies: 9

Major professional theater companies (non-profit): 2

State appropriations for arts agencies per capita: $0.97, 16th

State Fair in mid-August at Columbus

SPORTS AND COMPETITION

NCAA teams (Division I): Bowling Green State Univ. Falcons, Cleveland State Univ. Vi-kings, Kent State Univ. Golden Flashes, Miami Univ. Redskins, Ohio State Univ. Buckeyes, Ohio Univ. Bobcats, Univ. of Akron Zips, Univ. of Cincinnati Bearcats, Univ. of Dayton Flyers, Univ. of Toledo Rockets, Wright State Univ. Raiders, Xavier Univ. Musketeers, Youngstown State Univ. Penguins

Major league baseball teams: Cincinnati Reds (NL Central), Riverfront Stadium; Cleveland Indians (AL Central), Jacobs Field

NBA basketball teams: Cleveland Cavaliers, Gund Arena

NFL football teams: Cincinnati Bengals (AFC), Riverfront Stadium (Cleveland Browns relocated to Baltimore in 1996; replacement team, with same name, promised by 1999)

OKLAHOMA

"The state Oklahoma most resembles is of course Texas, if only because it too does everything with color and originality, but tell an Oklahoman that his state is a dependency of Texas and he will bite your eyes out."

John Gunther, writer

Thousands of oil and natural gas wells dot the Oklahoma landscape, and there are millions of beef cattle on its ranches. Oklahoma is the home of about a third of the nation's Indian people, who speak more than 50 languages. Oklahomans have demonstrated their genius in government and diplomacy, and celebrate such world-famous natives as humorist Will Rogers and the athlete Jim Thorpe. It is the state of the "Sooners" and the "Boomers." When the Oklahoma territory was opened up for settlement in 1889, those who entered the territory to stake their homestead claims before the official time were called "Sooners." Those who entered legally at the appointed time were called "Boomers." Oklahoma is also a center of cowboy culture and preserves notable collections of Western art and customs.

SUPERLATIVES

• Has the only county touching four states—Cimarron County.
• The former home of five separate Indian nations.
• "Oil capital of the world" —Tulsa.
• Finest collection of Western and cowboy art—Woolaroc Museum, in Bartlesville.

MOMENTS IN HISTORY

• Claimed variously by Spain and France, the territory that is now Oklahoma was the starting point of a trail to Spanish Santa Fe blazed by French traders in 1750.
• Control of the region came to the United States in 1803 with the Louisiana Purchase.
• In 1817, Pierre Chouteau of the famed Chouteau family founded Grand Saline (Salina), first permanent European settlement in what is now Oklahoma.
• One of the most shameful episodes in U.S. history began in 1817 with the first removal of scattered groups of Indians from their native lands to Indian Territory. Formal establishment of the lands known as Indian Territory was decided in 1834.
• The resettlement process intensified with the brutal removal of the groups known as the Five Civilized Tribes. When Congress in 1830 ordered the resettlement of the Creeks from their ancestral lands in parts of Georgia, Alabama, and Mississippi, and areas of the Appalachians, they fought back fiercely, and they executed Chief William McIntosh for having ceded the tribal land. But their resistance was beaten down, and they started their tragic march to Oklahoma.
• In the early 1830s, the Chickasaw people were moved to Oklahoma over the infamous route that became known as the "Trail of Tears."
• Forced by the federal government in 1831-1833, the Choctaw Indians also trudged over the "Trail of Tears." Before their removal there were about 20,000 Choctaws. By 1843 they numbered only about 12,000.
• By 1838, U.S. armed forces had begun the evacuation of the Cherokee people. About 15,000 were marched over the "Trail of Tears" to Indian Territory under conditions of extreme hardship, and nearly 4,000 perished on the way.
• The Seminole wars in Florida ended in 1842 without a surrender or peace treaty. After the war some of the few remaining Seminole agreed to move to Oklahoma, forming the fifth of the Civilized Tribes.
• The five tribes gathered in 1859 for an intertribal council, resulting in a progressive code of laws.
• When the Civil War came, the Five Nations embraced the Confederate cause.
• The first Civil War struggle in what is now Oklahoma was the Battle of Round Mountain near Keystone, on November 19, 1861.

• With the collapse of the Confederacy, the Five Nations faced ruin and the forfeiture of their lands and rights. However, the skill of the Indian negotiators in the late 1860s reduced the tribal losses to some of the western Oklahoma lands.

So They Say

Their [the Indian nations'] escape from Confederate losses "...constitutes a triumph of diplomacy almost unexampled in the history of the relations between a weak and a strong people."

Anonymous

• Beginning in the 1870s, more than 25 other tribes were forced to move to Oklahoma on land bought or leased by the federal government.

• The displaced Indians caused much unrest, but in 1875, George Armstrong Custer defeated Indian forces in the Battle of the Washita, and most of the Indian conflict ended.

• The Five Nations made remarkable progress in education, government, and commerce. Oklahoma's first telephone line was built by the Cherokee in 1885.

• One of the most remarkable events in U.S. history occurred when the government opened "unassigned lands" to settlement. At high noon on April 22, 1889, thousands rushed across the border, and by nightfall the formerly empty site of what is now Oklahoma City had become a tent community of 10,000 people. Other towns were also founded that day.

So They Say

"I saw excited men jump from the windows of crowded coaches even before the train came to a stop...and rush off to stake out claims in a field that by noon next day was a busy tent city of 10,000 people. ...Rivals shot it out over claim disputes."

Anonymous eyewitness, on settlers arriving in Oklahoma

• In all, ten land openings brought settlers to Oklahoma during the period from 1889 to 1906.

• In May 1890, Oklahoma Territory was created, coexisting with Indian Territory.

• Oklahoma became a state on November 6, 1907, with a population of 1,414,177, including residents in Indian Territory.

• During World War I, much of the virgin land was plowed for crops.

• In the drought of the 1930s, terrible dust storms swept the plowed lands and blanketed the skies. Thousands of "Okies" fled their devastated farms.

• During World War II, 13 Oklahomans won the Medal of Honor.

• In the 1970s, the McClellan-Kerr Arkansas River Navigation System opened. Tulsa and Muskogee became inland "seaports."

• On April 19, 1995, a federal office building center in Oklahoma City was bombed in the nation's worst terrorist attack; 169 people lost their lives.

THAT'S INTERESTING

• Because of its shape on the map, Oklahoma has been called "the nation's largest meat cleaver."

• With a mountain being defined as any elevation over 2,000 feet, Oklahoma claims that the 1,999-foot rise known as Cavanal is the world's highest hill.

• In an attempt to scalp an enemy, Chief Pawhuska once pulled at a man's white hair. The man's wig came off in his hand. The chief kept this powerful "magic" the rest of his life and took the name meaning "white hair."

• More languages are spoken in Oklahoma than in Europe. Each of the state's 55 Indian tribes has a separate language or its own distinctive dialect.

NOTABLE NATIVES

Acee Blue Eagle (near Anadarka, 1910-1959), artist. **Woodrow Wilson (Woody) Guthrie** (Okemah, 1912-1967), folk singer/composer. **Patrick Jay Hurley** (Indian Territory, 1883-1963), diplomat. **Karl Guthe Jansky** (Norman, 1905-1950), engineer. **Robert Samuel Kerr** (Ada, 1896-1963), political figure. **Mickey Charles Mantle** (Spavinaw, 1931-1995), baseball player. **Oral Roberts** (Ada, 1918-), evangelist. **William Penn Adair (Will) Rogers** (near Oologa, 1879-1935), humorist/actor. **Maria Tallchief** (Fairfax, 1925-), dancer. **James Francis (Jim) Thorpe** (Prague, 1888-1953), athlete.

Hazardous waste sites (1993): 11, 34th

Endangered species: Mammals: 3—Gray bat, Indiana bat, Ozark big-eared bat; birds: 6—Whooping crane, Eskimo curlew, American peregrine falcon, Least tern, Black-capped vireo, Red-cockaded woodpecker; reptiles: none; amphibians: none; fishes: none; invertebrates: 1; plants: none

---

So They Say

Will Rogers was born in Cherokee Territory in a comfortable two-story house of a well-to-do family, greatly enlarged from the earlier log structure. Before Will was born his mother moved into the earlier part of the house so that Will would be born in a log cabin.

The Enchantment of Oklahoma

GENERAL

Admitted to statehood: November 16, 1907

Origin of name: Choctaw word meaning "red man," proposed by Rev. Allen Wright, Choctaw-speaking Indian

Capital: Oklahoma City

Nickname: Sooner State

Motto: *Labor Omnia Vincit*—Labor conquers all things

Animal: Bison

Bird: Scissor-tailed flycatcher

Insect: Honeybee

Flower: Mistletoe

Stone: Rose rock (barite rose)

Song: "Oklahoma"

Tree: Redbud

THE LAND

Area: 69,903 sq. mi., 20th
    Land: 68,679 sq. mi., 19th
    Water: 1,224 sq. mi., 24th
        Inland water: 1,224 sq. mi., 17th

Topography: High plains predominate in the W, hills and small mountains in the E; the E central region is dominated by the Arkansas River Basin, and the Red River Plains are in the S

Number of counties: 77

Geographic center: 8 mi. N of Oklahoma City

Length: 400 mi.; width: 220 mi.

Highest point: 4,973 ft. (Black Mesa), 23rd

Lowest point: 289 ft. (Little River), 34th

Mean elevation: 1,300 ft., 20th

CLIMATE AND ENVIRONMENT

Temp., highest: 120 deg. on July 26, 1934, at Tishmoningo; lowest: –27 deg. on Jan. 18, 1930, at Watts

Monthly average: highest: 93.9 deg., 5th; lowest: 24.8 deg., 36th; spread (high to low): 69.1 deg., 24th

MAJOR CITIES
POPULATION, 1990
PERCENTAGE INCREASE, 1980-90

Broken Arrow, 58,043—62.31%

Lawton, 80,561—0.63%

Norman, 80,071—17.72%

Oklahoma City, 444,719—10.08%

Tulsa, 367,302—1.77%

THE PEOPLE

Population (1995): 3,277,687, 27th
    Percent change (1990-95): 4.2%, 31st

Population (2000 proj.): 3,382,000, 28th
    Percent change (1990-2000): 7.52%, 32nd

Per sq. mi. (1994): 47.4, 35th

Percent in metro. area (1992): 60.1%, 34th

Foreign born: 65,000, 29th
    Percent: 2.1%, 34th

Top three ancestries reported:
    German, 22.70%
    Irish, 20.41%
    American Indian, 14.91%

White: 2,583,512, 82.13%, 32nd

Black: 233,801, 7.43%, 24th

Native American: 252,420, 8.02%, 3rd

Asian, Pacific Isle: 33,563, 1.07%, 28th

Other races: 42,289, 1.34%, 22nd

Hispanic origin: 86,160, 2.74%, 23rd

Percent over 5 yrs. speaking language other than English at home: 5.0%, 37th

Percent males: 48.67%, 25th; percent females: 51.33%, 27th

Percent never married: 20.9%, 50th

Marriages per 1,000 (1993): 9.4, 17th

Divorces per 1,000 (1993): 7.1, 1st

Median age: 33.2

Under 5 years (1994): 7.27%, 23rd

Under 18 years (1994): 27.01%, 16th

65 years & older (1994): 13.6%, 16th

Percent increase among the elderly (1990-94): 4.43%, 34th

OF VITAL IMPORTANCE

Live births per 1,000 pop. (1993): 14.5, 28th
Infant mortality rate per 1,000 births (1992): 8.8, 20th
  Rate for blacks (1990): 13.2, 37th
  Rate for whites (1990): 9.4, 3rd
Births to unmarried women, % of total (1992): 28.4%, 25th
Births to teenage mothers, % of total (1992): 16.8%, 8th
Abortions (1992): 8,940, 33rd
  Rate per 1,000 women 14-44 years old: 12.5, 40th
  Percent change (1988-92): –23%, 48th
Average lifetime (1979-81): 73.67, 30th
Deaths per 1,000 pop. (1993): 10.1, 6th
Causes of death per 100,000 pop.:
  Accidents & adverse effects (1992): 39.5, 18th
  Atherosclerosis (1991): 11.2, 5th
  Cancer (1991): 211.3, 25th
  Cerebrovascular diseases (1992): 67.2, 8th
  Chronic liver diseases & cirrhosis (1991): 9.4, 23rd
  Chronic obstructive pulmonary diseases (1992): 43.0, 9th
  Diabetes mellitus (1992): 17.9, 36th
  Diseases of heart (1992): 339.1, 8th
  Pneumonia, flu (1991): 37.3, 9th
  Suicide (1992): 14.7, 11th

KEEPING WELL

Active nonfederal physicians per 100,000 pop. (1993): 153, 46th
Dentists per 100,000 (1991): 48, 35th
Nurses per 100,000 (1992): 534, 49th
Hospitals per 100,000 (1993): 3.40, 11th
  Admissions per 1,000 (1993): 112.34, 31st
  Occupancy rate per 100 beds (1993): 55.5, 42nd
  Average cost per patient per day (1993): $797, 31st
  Average cost per stay (1993): $5,093, 42nd
  Average stay (1992): 6.7 days, 39th
AIDS cases (adult, 1993): 725; per 100,000: 22.4, 26th
HIV infection, not yet AIDS (1993): 1,428
Other notifiable diseases:
  Gonorrhea: 198.3, 25th
  Measles: 5.5, 20th
  Syphilis: 19.5, 25th
  Tuberculosis: 7.7, 20th
Pop. without health insur. (1991-93): 21.4%, 4th

HOUSEHOLDS BY TYPE

Total households (1994): 1,236,000
  Percent change (1990-94): 2.5%, 33rd
  Per 1,000 pop.: 379.37, 13th
  Percent of households 65 yrs. and over: 23.30%, 12th
  Persons per household (1994): 2.56, 35th
Family households: 855,321
  Percent of total: 70.91%, 24th
Nonfamily households: 350,814
  Percent of total: 29.09%, 28th
Pop. living in group quarters: 93,677
  Percent of pop.: 2.98%, 19th

LIVING QUARTERS

Total housing units: 1,406,499
  Persons per unit: 2.24, 42nd
Occupied housing units: 1,206,135
  Percent of total units: 85.75%, 41st
  Persons per unit: 2.50, 34th
  Percent of units with over 1 person per room: 3.31%, 23rd
Owner-occupied units: 821,188
  Percent of total units: 58.39%, 28th
  Percent of occupied units: 68.08%, 19th
  Persons per unit: 2.59, 49th
  Median value: $48,100, 46th
Renter-occupied units: 384,947
  Percent of total units: 27.37%, 36th
  Percent of occupied units: 31.92%, 33rd
  Persons per unit: 2.41, 16th
  Median contract rent: $259, 43rd
  Rental vacancy rate: 14.7%, 2nd
Mobile home, trailer & other as a percent of occupied housing units: 11.91%, 24th
Persons in emergency shelters for homeless persons: 2,222, 0.071%, 14th
Persons visible in street locations: 340, 0.0108%, 18th
Persons in shelters for abused women: 113, 0.0036%, 39th
Nursing home population: 29,666, 0.94%, 12th

CRIME INDEX PER 100,000 (1992-93)

Total reported: 5,294.3, 21st
  Violent: 634.8, 22nd
    Murder and nonnegligent manslaughter: 8.4, 21st
    Aggravated assault: 455.3, 19th
    Robbery: 121.8, 32nd
    Forcible rape: 49.3, 13th

Property: 4,659.4, 20th
  Burglary: 1,235.0, 13th
  Larceny, theft: 2,943.7, 25th
  Motor vehicle theft: 480.7, 20th
Drug abuse violations (1990): 283.5, 20th
Child-abuse rate per 1,000 children (1993): 9.62, 38th

TEACHING AND LEARNING

Pop. 3 and over enrolled in school: 838,811
  Percent of pop.: 27.8%, 19th
Public elementary & secondary schools (1992-93): 1,829
  Total enrollment (1992): 597,096
    Percent of total pop.: 18.63%, 12th
  Teachers (1992): 38,433
    Percent of pop.: 1.20%, 11th
  Pupil/teacher ratio (fall 1992): 15.5, 37th
  Teachers' avg. salary (1992-93): $27,568, 48th
  Expenditure per capita (1990-91): $2,908.26, 44th
  Expenditure per pupil (1991-92): $4,078, 44th
  Percent of graduates taking SAT (1993): 9%, 42nd
    Mean SAT verbal scores: 482, 9th
    Mean SAT mathematical scores: 530, 12th
  Percent of graduates taking ACT (1995): 65%, 11th
    Mean ACT scores: 20.3, 38th
  Percent of pop. over 25 completing:
    Less than 9th grade: 9.8%, 22nd
    High school: 74.6%, 36th
    College degree(s): 17.8%, 33rd
  Higher education, institutions (1993-94): 46
    Enrollment (1992): 182,105
      Percent of pop.: 5.68%, 23rd
      White non-Hispanic (1992): 143,732
        Percent of enroll.: 78.93%, 33rd
      Black non-Hispanic (1992): 12,843
        Percent of enroll.: 7.05%, 23rd
      Hispanic (1992): 3,292
        Percent of enroll.: 1.81%, 26th
      Asian/Pacific Islander (1992): 3,306
        Percent of enroll.: 1.82%, 31st
      American Indian/AK native (1992): 11,832
        Percent of enroll.: 6.50%, 3rd
      Nonresident alien (1992): 7,100
        Percent of enroll.: 3.90%, 10th
      Female (1992): 99,077
        Percent of enroll.: 54.41%, 38th
    Pub. institutions (1993-94): 29

Enrollment (1992): 159,043
  Percent of enroll.: 87.34%, 15th
Private institutions (1993-94): 17
  Enrollment (1992): 23,062
  Percent of enroll.: 12.66%, 37th
Tuition, public institution (avg., 1993-94): $4,023, 49th
Tuition, private institution (avg., 1993-94): $10,096, 39th
Public library systems: 106
  Books & serial vol. per capita: 2.01, 38th
  Govt. expenditure per capita: $9.56, 43rd

LAW ENFORCEMENT, COURTS, AND PRISONS

Police protection, corrections, judicial and legal functions expenditures (1992): $623,000,000
  Per capita: $194, 42nd
Police per 10,000 pop. (1993): 19.09, 32nd
Prisoners (state & fed.) per 100,000 pop. (1993): 5,075.47, 5th
  Percent change (1992-93): 10.7%, 5th
Death penalty: yes, by lethal injection
  Under sentence of death (1993): 122, 7th
  Executed (1993): 0

RELIGION, NUMBER AND PERCENT OF POPULATION

Agnostic: 9,234—0.40%, 34th
Buddhist: 4,617—0.20%, 11th
Christian: 1,989,994—86.20%, 25th
Hindu: 2,309—0.10%, 10th
Jewish: 4,617—0.20%, 40th
Muslim: NA
Unitarian: 2,309—0.10%, 31st
Other: 48,480—2.10%, 9th
None: 150,058—6.50%, 25th
Refused to answer: 96,960—4.20%, 2nd

MAKING A LIVING

Personal income per capita (1994): $17,744, 44th
  Percent increase (1993-94): 4.2%, 40th
Disposable personal income per capita (1994): $15,575, 45th
Median income of households (1993): $26,260, 44th
Percent of pop. below poverty level (1993): 19.9%, 7th
  Percent 65 and over (1990): 17.9%, 11th
Expenditure for energy per person (1992): $1,887, 26th

ECONOMY

Civilian labor force (1994): 1,540,000
  Percent of total pop.: 47.27%, 46th
  Percent 65 and over (1990): 3.57%, 7th
  Percent female: 45.00%, 43rd
Percent job growth (1980-90): 6.51%, 48th
Major employer industries (1994):
  Agriculture: 64,000—4.5%, 10th
  Construction: 51,000—3.6%, 42nd
  Finance, insurance, & real estate: 64,000—4.4%, 38th
  Government: 265,000—18.5%, 14th
  Manufacturing: 205,000—14.3%, 31st
  Service: 280,000—19.6%, 35th
  Trade: 243,000—17.0%, 48th
  Transportation, communications, public utilities: 76,000—5.3%, 25th
Unemployment rate (1994): 5.84%, 23rd
  Male: 6.2%, 18th
  Female: 5.4%, 24th
Total businesses (1991): 119,162
  New business incorps. (1991): 7,073
    Percent of total businesses: 5.94%, 25th
  Business failures (1991): 1,597
    Percent of total businesses: 1.34%
Agriculture farm income:
  Marketing (1993): $3,869,000,000, 18th
    Average per farm: $54,492.96, 42nd
  Leading products (1993): Cattle, wheat, greenhouse, broilers
  Average value land & build. per acre (1994): $534, 38th
    Percent increase (1990-94): 7.44%, 30th
  Govt. payments (1993): $324,000,000, 16th
    Average per farm: $4,563.38, 23rd
Construction, value of all: $957,000,000
  Per capita: $304.24, 46th
Manufactures:
  Value added: $11,889,000,000
    Per capita: $3,779.58, 37th
  Leading products: Nonelectrical machinery, fabricated metal products, petroleum
Value of nonfuel mineral production (1994): $338,000,000, 33rd
Leading mineral products: Natural gas, petroleum, coal
Retail sales (1993): $20,818,000,000, 31st
  Per household: $16,740, 48th
    Percent increase (1992-93): 3.5%, 40th

Tourism revenues (1994): $3 bil.
Foreign exports, in total value (1994): $2,110,000,000, 33rd
  Per capita: $647.64, 46th
Gross state product per person (1993): $18,308.08, 45th
  Percent change (1990-93): 1.75%, 41st
Patents per 100,000 pop. (1993): 21.06, 22nd
Public aid recipients (percent of resident pop. 1993): 6.2%, 31st
Medicaid recipients per 1,000 pop. (1993): 119.70, 24th
Medicare recipients per 1,000 pop. (1993): 146.30, 21st

TRAVEL AND TRANSPORTATION

Motor vehicle registrations (1993): 2,771,000
  Per 1,000 pop.: 857.10, 11th
Motorcycle registrations (1993): 56,000
  Per 1,000 pop.: 17.32, 23rd
Licensed drivers per 1,000 pop. (1993): 722.55, 10th
Deaths from motor vehicle accidents per 100,000 pop. (1993): 20.79, 12th
Public roads & streets (1993):
  Total mileage: 112,467
    Per 1,000 pop.: 34.79, 10th
  Rural mileage: 99,673
    Per 1,000 pop.: 30.83, 10th
  Urban mileage: 12,794
    Per 1,000 pop.: 3.96, 6th
  Interstate mileage: 929
    Per 1,000 pop.: 0.29, 16th
Annual vehicle-mi. of travel per person (1993): 10,981, 5th
Mean travel time for workers age 16+ who work away from home: 19.3 min., 34th

GOVERNMENT

Percent of voting age pop. registered (1994): 65.8%, 21st
  Percent of voting age pop. voting (1994): 46.8%, 21st
  Percent of voting age pop. voting for U.S. representatives (1994): 40.5%, 20th
State legislators, total (1995): 149, 23rd
  Women members (1992): 13
    Percent of legislature: 8.7%, 45th
U.S. Congress, House members (1995): 6
Change (1985-95): 0
Revenues (1993):
  State govt.: $8,679,000,000
    Per capita: $2,684.50, 38th

Parimutuel & amusement taxes & lotteries, revenue per capita: $3.09, 40th
Expenditures (1993):
State govt.: $8,272,000,000
Per capita: $2,558.61, 32nd
Debt outstanding (1993): $3,919,000,000
Per capita: $987.01, 36th

LAWS AND REGULATIONS

Legal driving age: 16
Marriage age without parental consent: 18
Divorce residence requirement: 6 mo.

ATTRACTIONS (1995)

Major opera companies: 1
Major symphony orchestras: 2
Major dance companies: 1
State appropriations for arts agencies per capita: $0.96, 17th
State Fair in late August–early September at Oklahoma City

SPORTS AND COMPETITION

NCAA teams (Division I): Oklahoma State Univ. Cowboys, Oral Roberts Univ. Golden Eagles, Univ. of Oklahoma Sooners, Univ. of Tulsa Golden Hurricane

OREGON

"The cabins rise, the fields are sown, and Oregon is theirs! They will take, they will hold; by the spade in the mold; by the seed in the soil, by the sweat and the toil; by the plow in the loam; by the school and the home!"

Arthur Guiterman, poet

O regon stretches from one of the most spectacular coastlines, on the west, to Hells Canyon, the nation's deepest gorge, on the east. Crater Lake is the deepest in the United States and one of the loveliest. The state boasts the greatest extent of standing timber in the nation, the biggest sand dunes, and the largest geyser. Oregon was the goal of the many thousands of pioneers who traveled overland on the Oregon Trail. Harvesting of lumber, and the manufacturing industries based upon it, help keep Oregon vital today. The state has also long been a leader in sound ecological legislation and forward-looking public servants.

SUPERLATIVES

- Largest reserves of standing timber.
- Leading U.S. timber producer.
- Produces most U.S. plywood.
- Leads in nickel production.
- Greatest profusion of agates.
- First pheasants in United States, in Linn County.

MOMENTS IN HISTORY

- In 1543 the Spanish expedition of Bartolome Ferrello passed the present-day coast of Oregon, but it is not known how far he went to the north.
- Britain's Sir Francis Drake may have reached as far north as the southern Oregon coast in 1579.
- The prominent promontory called Cape Blanco by Martin d'Augilar in 1603 was the first Oregon feature to be given a name by Europeans.
- On August 17, 1775, the Spanish navigator Bruno Heceta discovered the mouth of the Columbia River.
- Famed English explorer Captain James Cook saw the Oregon coast and named Cape Foulweather in 1778.

- American Captain Robert Gray became the first white person known to have landed in Oregon, when he reached present-day Tillamook County in 1788. His men engaged in the first skirmish of white men with the Indians in Oregon. One sailor was killed.
- On May 11, 1792, Captain Gray became the first person to make the perilous entry into the Columbia River. He and his men sailed upstream about 15 miles and traded with the Indians, buying two salmon for one nail and a prime beaver skin for two spikes. He also bought 150 rare sea otters, worth $100 each in China. Gray named the river for his ship, the *Columbia*.
- As early as 1800, American ships controlled most of the fur trade of the northwest coast, but that trade diminished as they went into whaling.

So They Say

"...stately clippers of the China trade would leave New England ports, sail around Cape Horn and up to the Oregon coast. There they would trade their beads, trinkets, blankets, and a few tools or other items with the Indians for the precious sea otter, beaver and other furs. After taking on water and supplies, they would sail for China, usually stopping at the Hawaiian islands for more supplies. In China teas, spices, silks, and other goods of the Orient were acquired in exchange for furs. Sometimes as much as $250,000 was made in one voyage."

Anonymous

- The great expedition of Lewis and Clark reached its coveted goal of the Pacific and built Fort Clatsop on Young's Bay, spending the winter of 1805-1806 there.

• Lewis and Clark returned east in 1806, leaving behind certificates with Indian leaders that testified to their fair and hospitable treatment.

So They Say

"...the faithfulness, honesty, and devotion of the Indians when entrusted with any charge, as the care of horses or canoes—this character of the Indians was so marked that one can hardly avoid the conclusion that the subsequent troubles with the Indians were due largely to abuse by the whites."

Anonymous

• John Jacob Astor's Pacific Fur Company set up headquarters in 1811 and established Fort Astoria, the first permanent white settlement in Oregon.

• During the War of 1812, the British seized Astoria, but the Americans retook it in 1817.

• In 1824 the great Hudson's Bay Company took over Astoria, under the remarkable leadership of John McLoughlin.

• In 1834 the Reverend Jason Lee established a mission station and school near present-day Salem.

So They Say

"...with chimney of sticks and clay, Jason Lee had swung the broadaxe that hewed the logs. Danial Lee had calked the crevices with moss. There were Indian mats on the hewn-fir floors, home made stools and tables. The hearth was of baked clay and ashes, the batten doors hung on leather hinges and clicked with wooden latches. Four small windows let in the light through squares of dried deerskin set in sashes carved by the jack-knife of Jason Lee."

Description of Jason Lee's first mission in Oregon Territory

• In May 1843, the settlers at Champoeg voted in favor of government by the United States and set up a provisional government of their own.

• By 1846, thousands of settlers were coming over the Oregon Trail in numbers that increased until the railroad began to take over in the 1870s.

• On February 14, 1859, Oregon gained statehood.

• During the Civil War, Indian troubles plagued the new state.

• In 1877, Chief Joseph of the Nez Percé and his people were forced out of their homeland in Oregon, Washington, and parts of Idaho.

• The transcontinental railroad reached Portland in 1883.

• Oregon pioneered U.S. primary elections and initiated a presidential preference primary in 1911.

• The Third Oregon Infantry was the first of the country's national guards to be mobilized and ready for World War I.

• The great Bonneville Dam began to transmit power in 1938.

• In one of the few Japanese attacks on the mainland during World War II, a Japanese sub shelled Fort Stevens on June 21, 1942.

• Oregon attracted so many new residents that beginning in the 1970s the state discouraged newcomers.

• The much publicized effort of cult leader Bhagwan Shree Rajneesh to establish a stronghold in Oregon failed, and he left the state in 1985.

• In 1990, ten new active volcanoes were discovered on the seabed off the Oregon coast.

THAT'S INTERESTING

• The Indians thought the squeaks of the wheels of the settlers' wagons sounded like their words "chik-chik-chaile-kikash," and that became their name for wagon.

• At 1,932 feet, Oregon's Crater Lake is the nation's deepest lake—and one of the most beautiful.

• Oregon's madrona tree sheds its bark as well as its leaves.

• The giant insect-eating cobra lily is another unusual form of plant life.

• Oregon students earn money for school by picking up the innumerable pinecones for seed.

• More than two centuries ago, the ship *Manzanita* foundered on the coast; beachcombers are still picking up lumps of beeswax from its cargo.

NOTABLE NATIVES

Homer Davenport (Silverton, 1867-1912), cartoonist. **Chief Joseph** (Wallowa Valley, near the Oregon/Idaho/Washington border, 1840?-1904), Indian leader. **Edwin Markham** (Oregon City, 1852-1940), poet. **Linus Carl Pauling** (Portland, 1901-1994), chemist. **John Reed** (Portland, 1887-1920), journalist/political radical.

GENERAL

Admitted to statehood: February 14, 1859
Origin of name: Origin unknown. One theory holds that the name may have come from the French word *ouragon*, meaning "hurricane"
Capital: Salem
Nickname: Beaver State
Motto: "She flies with her own wings"
Animal: Beaver
Bird: Western meadowlark
Fish: Chinook salmon
Flower: Oregon grape
Stone: Thunderegg
Song: "Oregon, My Oregon"
Tree: Douglas fir

THE LAND

Area: 97,093 sq. mi., 10th
  Land: 96,002 sq. mi., 10th
  Water: 1,091 sq. mi., 26th
    Inland water: 1,050 sq. mi., 19th
    Coastal water: 41 sq. mi., 19th
Topography: Rugged coast range; fertile Willamette River Valley to E and S; Cascade Mountain range of volcanic peaks E of the valley; plateau E of Cascades, remaining two-thirds of state
Number of counties: 36
Geographic center: Crook, 25 mi. SSE of Prineville
Length: 360 mi.; width: 261 mi.
Highest point: 11,239 ft. (Mount Hood), 13th
Lowest point: sea level (Pacific Ocean), 3rd
Mean elevation: 3,300 ft., 9th
Coastline: 296 mi., 8th
Shoreline: 1,410 mi., 16th

CLIMATE AND ENVIRONMENT

Temp., highest: 119 deg. on Aug. 10, 1938, at Pendleton; lowest: –54 deg. on Feb. 10, 1933, at Seneca

Monthly average: highest: 82.6 deg., 46th; lowest: 32.8 deg., 45th; spread (high to low): 49.8 deg., 50th
Hazardous waste sites (1993): 12, 30th
Endangered species: Mammals: 1—Columbian white tailed deer; birds: 3—American peregrine falcon, Aleutian Canada goose, Brown pelican; reptiles: 1; amphibians: none; fishes: 3; invertebrates: 1; plants: 3

MAJOR CITIES
POPULATION, 1990
PERCENTAGE INCREASE, 1980-90

Beaverton, 53,310—66.79%
Eugene, 112,669—6.63%
Gresham, 68,235—106.74%
Portland, 437,319—18.79%
Salem, 107,786—20.98%

THE PEOPLE

Population (1995): 3,140,585, 29th
  Percent change (1990-95): 10.5%, 9th
Population (2000 proj.): 3,404,000, 27th
  Percent change (1990-2000): 19.76%, 9th
Per sq. mi. (1994): 32.1, 40th
Percent in metro. area (1992): 70.0%, 25th
Foreign born: 139,000, 19th
  Percent: 4.9%, 18th
Top three ancestries reported:
  German, 30.93%
  English, 20.23%
  Irish, 16.43%
White: 2,636,787, 92.77%, 12th
Black: 46,178, 1.62%, 42nd
Native American: 38,496, 1.35%, 13th
Asian, Pacific Isle: 69,269, 2.44%, 11th
Other races: 51,591, 1.82%, 21st
Hispanic origin: 112,707, 3.97%, 20th
Percent over 5 yrs. speaking language other than English at home: 7.3%, 24th
Percent males: 49.15%, 16th; percent females: 50.85%, 36th
Percent never married: 23.1%, 42nd
Marriages per 1,000 (1993): 8.0, 33rd
Divorces per 1,000 (1993): 5.3, 14th
Median age: 34.5
Under 5 years (1994): 6.77%, 45th
Under 18 years (1994): 25.37%, 33rd
65 years & older (1994): 13.7%, 15th
Percent increase among the elderly (1990-94): 7.84%, 19th

OF VITAL IMPORTANCE

Live births per 1,000 pop. (1993): 13.9, 40th
Infant mortality rate per 1,000 births (1992): 7.1, 42nd
Rate for blacks (1990): 15.1, 30th
Rate for whites (1990): 8.1, 20th
Births to unmarried women, % of total (1992): 27.0%, 29th
Births to teenage mothers, % of total (1992): 12.4%, 24th
Abortions (1992): 16,060, 23rd
Rate per 1,000 women 14-44 years old: 23.9, 18th
Percent change (1988-92): 00%, 13th
Average lifetime (1979-81): 74.99, 13th
Deaths per 1,000 pop. (1993): 9.0, 25th
Causes of death per 100,000 pop.:
Accidents & adverse effects (1992): 36.6, 20th
Atherosclerosis (1991): 10.4, 6th
Cancer (1991): 212.5, 22nd
Cerebrovascular diseases (1992): 70.7, 5th
Chronic liver diseases & cirrhosis (1991): 9.0, 26th
Chronic obstructive pulmonary diseases (1992): 42.2, 13th
Diabetes mellitus (1992): 18.9, 33rd
Diseases of heart (1992): 245.3, 33rd
Pneumonia, flu (1991): 27.5, 36th
Suicide (1992): 16.4, 7th

KEEPING WELL

Active nonfederal physicians per 100,000 pop. (1993): 210, 19th
Dentists per 100,000 (1991): 69, 9th
Nurses per 100,000 (1992): 808, 19th
Hospitals per 100,000 (1993): 2.08, 28th
Admissions per 1,000 (1993): 96.61, 42nd
Occupancy rate per 100 beds (1993): 54.7, 46th
Average cost per patient per day (1993): $1,053, 8th
Average cost per stay (1993): $5,309, 38th
Average stay (1992): 5.8 days, 51st
AIDS cases (adult, 1993): 778; per 100,000: 25.7, 22nd
HIV infection, not yet AIDS (1993): NA
Other notifiable diseases:
Gonorrhea: 89.5, 37th
Measles: 7.5, 12th
Syphilis: 11.3, 32nd
Tuberculosis: 5.2, 32nd
Pop. without health insur. (1991-93): 14.3%, 19th

HOUSEHOLDS BY TYPE

Total households (1994): 1,195,000
Percent change (1990-94): 8.3%, 9th
Per 1,000 pop.: 387.23, 4th
Percent of households 65 yrs. and over: 22.34%, 24th
Persons per household (1994): 2.53, 46th
Family households: 750,844
Percent of total: 68.05%, 45th
Nonfamily households: 352,469
Percent of total: 31.95%, 7th
Pop. living in group quarters: 66,205
Percent of pop.: 2.33%, 40th

LIVING QUARTERS

Total housing units: 1,193,567
Persons per unit: 2.38, 29th
Occupied housing units: 1,103,313
Percent of total: 92.44%, 7th
Persons per unit: 2.48, 38th
Percent of units with over 1 person per room: 3.64%, 21st
Owner-occupied units: 695,957
Percent of total units: 58.31%, 29th
Percent of occupied units: 63.08%, 41st
Persons per unit: 2.62, 46th
Median value: $67,100, 27th
Renter-occupied units: 407,356
Percent of total units: 34.13%, 11th
Percent of occupied units: 36.92%, 13th
Persons per unit: 2.33, 28th
Median contract rent: $344, 23rd
Rental vacancy rate: 5.3%, 49th
Mobile home, trailer & other as a percent of occupied housing units: 13.16%, 21st
Persons in emergency shelters for homeless persons: 3,254, 0.114%, 4th
Persons visible in street locations: 564, 0.0198%, 9th
Persons in shelters for abused women: 251, 0.0088%, 3rd
Nursing home population: 18,200, 0.64%, 31st

CRIME INDEX PER 100,000 (1992-93)

Total reported: 5,765.6, 14th
Violent: 503.1, 28th
Murder and nonnegligent manslaughter: 4.6, 35th
Aggravated assault: 317.6, 28th
Robbery: 129.6, 28th
Forcible rape: 51.3, 11th

Property: 5,262.5, 12th
  Burglary: 1,024.8, 23rd
  Larceny, theft: 3,656.9, 9th
  Motor vehicle theft: 580.7, 17th
Drug abuse violations (1990): 345.7, 13th
Child-abuse rate per 1,000 children (1993): NA

TEACHING AND LEARNING

Pop. 3 and over enrolled in school: 724,233
  Percent of pop.: 26.6%, 32nd
Public elementary & secondary schools (1992-93): 1,217
  Total enrollment (1992): 510,122
    Percent of total pop.: 17.16%, 29th
  Teachers (1992): 26,634
    Percent of pop.: 0.90%, 41st
  Pupil/teacher ratio (fall 1992): 19.2, 7th
  Teachers' avg. salary (1992-93): $38,164, 17th
  Expenditure per capita (1990-91): $3,631.26, 18th
  Expenditure per pupil (1991-92): $5,913, 14th
  Percent of graduates taking SAT (1993): 56%, 18th
  Mean SAT verbal scores: 441, 27th
  Mean SAT mathematical scores: 492, 26th
  Percent of graduates taking ACT (1995): 14%, 35th
  Mean ACT scores: 22.6, 1st
Percent of pop. over 25 completing:
  Less than 9th grade: 6.2%, 45th
  High school: 81.5%, 9th
  College degree(s): 20.6%, 21st
Higher education, institutions (1993-94): 44
  Enrollment (1992): 167,415
    Percent of pop.: 5.63%, 24th
  White non-Hispanic (1992): 143,921
    Percent of enroll.: 85.97%, 17th
  Black non-Hispanic (1992): 2,651
    Percent of enroll.: 1.58%, 42nd
  Hispanic (1992): 4,033
    Percent of enroll.: 2.41%, 18th
  Asian/Pacific Islander (1992): 8,285
    Percent of enroll.: 4.95%, 7th
  American Indian/AK native (1992): 2,184
    Percent of enroll.: 1.30%, 13th
  Nonresident alien (1992): 6,341
    Percent of enroll.: 3.79%, 11th
  Female (1992): 88,435
    Percent of enroll.: 52.82%, 49th
  Pub. institutions (1993-94): 21

Enrollment (1992): 144,902
  Percent of enroll.: 86.55%, 17th
Private institutions (1993-94): 23
  Enrollment (1992): 22,513
  Percent of enroll.: 13.45%, 35th
Tuition, public institution (avg., 1993-94): $6,648, 17th
Tuition, private institution (avg., 1993-94): $15,458, 14th
Public library systems: 125
  Books & serial vol. per capita: 2.32, 32nd
  Govt. expenditure per capita: $17.01, 21st

LAW ENFORCEMENT, COURTS, AND PRISONS

Police protection, corrections, judicial and legal functions expenditures (1992): $851,000,000
  Per capita: $286, 21st
Police per 10,000 pop. (1993): 15.73, 47th
Prisoners (state & fed.) per 100,000 pop. (1993): 2,160.46, 37th
  Percent change (1992-93): –0.4%, 46th
Death penalty: yes, by lethal injection
  Under sentence of death (1993): 12, 25th
  Executed (1993): 0

RELIGION, NUMBER AND PERCENT OF POPULATION

Agnostic: 25,418—1.20%, 2nd
Buddhist: 10,591—0.50%, 2nd
Christian: 1,611,943—76.10%, 49th
Hindu: NA
Jewish: 8,473—0.40%, 31st
Muslim: 2,118—0.10%, 22nd
Unitarian: 8,473—0.40%, 8th
Other: 36,009—1.70%, 14th
None: 364,329—17.20%, 1st
Refused to answer: 50,837—2.40%, 20th

MAKING A LIVING

Personal income per capita (1994): $20,419, 28th
  Percent increase (1993-94): 5.1%, 22nd
Disposable personal income per capita (1994): $17,419, 35th
Median income of households (1993): $33,138, 17th
Percent of pop. below poverty level (1993): 11.8%, 33rd
  Percent 65 and over (1990): 10.1%, 40th
Expenditure for energy per person (1992): $1,716, 43rd

ECONOMY

Civilian labor force (1994): 1,643,000
  Percent of total pop.: 53.24%, 12th
  Percent 65 and over (1990): 3.22%, 16th
  Percent female: 44.98%, 44th
Percent job growth (1980-90): 20.40%, 23rd
Major employer industries (1994):
  Agriculture: 51,000—3.5%, 15th
  Construction: 58,000—3.9%, 33rd
  Finance, insurance, & real estate: 88,000—5.9%, 15th
  Government: 248,000—16.9%, 18th
  Manufacturing: 199,000—13.5%, 32nd
  Service: 306,000—20.8%, 27th
  Trade: 280,000—19.0%, 26th
  Transportation, communications, public utilities: 64,000—4.4%, 38th
Unemployment rate (1994): 5.42%, 28th
  Male: 5.8%, 21st
  Female: 5.0%, 34th
Total businesses (1991): 127,176
  New business incorps. (1991): 8,375
    Percent of total businesses: 6.59%, 17th
  Business failures (1991): 591
    Percent of total businesses: 0.46%
Agriculture farm income:
  Marketing (1993): $2,476,000,000, 28th
    Average per farm: $66,918.92, 33rd
  Leading products (1993): Cattle, greenhouse, dairy products, wheat
  Average value land & build. per acre (1994): $740, 34th
    Percent increase (1990-94): 29.60%, 2nd
  Govt. payments (1993): $93,000,000, 31st
    Average per farm: $2,513.51, 33rd
Construction, value of all: $2,421,000,000
  Per capita: $851.77, 7th
Manufactures:
  Value added: $13,213,000,000
    Per capita: $4,648.67, 34th
  Leading products: Lumber and wood products, foods, machinery, primary and fabricated metals, paper, printing and publishing
Value of nonfuel mineral production (1994): $253,000,000, 38th
Leading mineral products: Stone, sand/gravel, cement
Retail sales (1993): $27,767,000,000, 27th
  Per household: $23,336, 13th
    Percent increase (1992-93): 7.0%, 28th

Tourism revenues (1992): $3.23 bil.
Foreign exports, in total value (1994): $6,103,000,000, 21st
  Per capita: $1,977.64, 9th
Gross state product per person (1993): $20,205.48, 32nd
  Percent change (1990-93): 5.36%, 11th
Patents per 100,000 pop. (1993): 26.99, 14th
Public aid recipients (percent of resident pop. 1993): 5.3%, 37th
Medicaid recipients per 1,000 pop. (1993): 107.08, 28th
Medicare recipients per 1,000 pop. (1993): 148.93, 14th

TRAVEL AND TRANSPORTATION

Motor vehicle registrations (1993): 2,624,000
  Per 1,000 pop.: 864.58, 10th
Motorcycle registrations (1993): 61,000
  Per 1,000 pop.: 20.10, 17th
Licensed drivers per 1,000 pop. (1993): 781.88, 2nd
Deaths from motor vehicle accidents per 100,000 pop. (1993): 17.20, 23rd
Public roads & streets (1993):
  Total mileage: 96,036
    Per 1,000 pop.: 31.64, 13th
  Rural mileage: 86,008
    Per 1,000 pop.: 28.34, 13th
  Urban mileage: 10,028
    Per 1,000 pop.: 3.30, 15th
  Interstate mileage: 727
    Per 1,000 pop.: 0.24, 20th
Annual vehicle-mi. of travel per person (1993): 9,357, 25th
Mean travel time for workers age 16+ who work away from home: 19.6 min., 33rd

GOVERNMENT

Percent of voting age pop. registered (1994): 72.7%, 9th
  Percent of voting age pop. voting (1994): 60.9%, 4th
  Percent of voting age pop. voting for U.S. representatives (1994): 51.6%, 6th
State legislators, total (1995): 90, 43rd
  Women members (1992): 22
    Percent of legislature: 24.4%, 12th
U.S. Congress, House members (1995): 5
  Change (1985-95): 0
Revenues (1993):
  State govt.: $10,826,000,000
    Per capita: $3,567.05, 16th
  Parimutuel & amusement taxes & lotteries, revenue per capita: $176.94, 5th

Expenditures (1993):
  State govt.: $9,013,000,000
    Per capita: $2,969.69, 20th
Debt outstanding (1993): $5,821,000,000
    Per capita: $1,917.96, 16th

LAWS AND REGULATIONS

Legal driving age: 16
Marriage age without parental consent: 18
Divorce residence requirement: 6 mo., for
    qualifications check local statutes

ATTRACTIONS (1995)

Major opera companies: 1
Major symphony orchestras: 1

Major dance companies: 2
Major professional theater companies (non-
    profit): 1
State appropriations for arts agencies per capita:
    $0.36, 48th
State Fair in late August–early September at
    Salem

SPORTS AND COMPETITION

NCAA teams (Division I): Oregon State
    Univ. Beavers, Univ. of Oregon Ducks,
    Univ. of Portland Pilots
NBA basketball teams: Portland Trail Blazers,
    Rose Garden

PENNSYLVANIA

"Nowhere in this country, from sea to sea, does nature comfort us with such assurance of plenty, such rich and tranquil beauty as in those unsung unpainted hills of Pennsylvania."

Richard Harding Davis, journalist and author

To many, Pennsylvania is the most historic state—the birthplace of independence and of the Constitution, with a claim to more historic events and historic firsts than perhaps any other state. It often is called the "Birthstate of the Nation." All of the hard coal in the country is mined in Pennsylvania, and Pittsburgh is famous for the production of pig iron and steel. Originally a refuge for persecuted Quakers, Pennsylvania is also home to the Amish and the Mennonites, religious groups characterized by their distinctive dress and simple lifestyle. Many still speak a variation of German called Pennsylvania Dutch.

SUPERLATIVES

• Nation's first museum of art—the Philadelphia Academy of Arts.
• First natural history museum.
• First hospital—the Pennsylvania Hospital.
• First scientific society—the Franklin Institute, endowed by Benjamin Franklin.
• First circulating library.
• First medical college, founded in 1765 by John Morgan.
• First chamber of commerce.
• Greatest anthracite reserves.
• First in magnetite ore.
• First regular steamboat run.
• First steam locomotive on rails.
• First computer, at the University of Pennsylvania in the 1940s.

MOMENTS IN HISTORY

• The first known visit to the area was by Captain John Smith of Virginia in 1608.
• Henry Hudson's voyage in 1609 gave the Dutch claim to the region.
• Johan Printz established the first permanent European settlement (Swedish), on Tinicum Island in 1643.
• The Dutch seized the Swedish settlements in 1655, and the British took over in turn in 1664.

• William Penn arrived in Pennsylvania in October 1682, aboard the *Welcome*, to take over his enormous grant that later became Pennsylvania and Delaware.

So They Say

"The air is sweet and clear, the Heavens serene...The country itself...is not to be despised...in some places a vast fat earth, like our best vales, in England."

William Penn

• In December 1682, Penn's "Great Law" became one of the first documents safeguarding life, liberty, and property through jury trial.
• The 1701 Charter of Privileges contained most of the principles of present constitutions.
• George Washington won the first skirmish of the French and Indian War, the Battle of Laurel Mountain, May 28, 1754, in present-day Fayette County.

So They Say

"The volley fired by a young Virginian [Washington] in the backwoods of America set the world on fire."

Robert Walpole, British leader

• In 1755, British General Edward Braddock's major defeat left much of Pennsylvania in French hands.
• After widespread losses, the French relinquished their claims in 1763.
• As Revolutionary tensions grew, James Smith in 1769 captured Fort Bedford, first stronghold to fall to American rebels.
• The first Continental Congress, meeting at Philadelphia in 1774, marked that city as a national capital.
• With the signing of the Declaration of Independence in Philadelphia on July 4,

1776, the process of Revolution formally began. Philadelphia fell to Lord William Howe on September 26, 1777.

• By the spring of 1778, the hardships of Valley Forge were left behind.

• Pennsylvania contributed to the Revolution in every way, with men, ordnance, and finance, even creating a state-financed and state-organized Navy in 1775.

So They Say

A group of settlers at Pine Creek was also meeting on July 4, 1776, under the "Tiadaghton Elm." Without any knowledge of the same action by the Continental Congress, they also declared their independence.

The Enchantment of Pennsylvania

• The first wagon trip westward in 1783 pioneered the way for the vast movement of settlers to western Pennsylvania.

• After the Articles of Confederation failed, delegates labored at Philadelphia from May to September 1787, to write a new Constitution. Held together, in part, by the will and skill of Benjamin Franklin, they brought forth a new nation.

• On December 12, 1787, Pennsylvania became the second state.

• During the War of 1812, Oliver Hazard Perry's eventually triumphant fleet was built in the wilds near present-day Erie.

So They Say

"But to appreciate his character, a person must have seen him, as I did, fitting out a fleet of six new vessels of war...at some hundreds of miles from the sea coast...almost abandoned by his country, toiling to fit out his fleet...."

Henry Eckford, on Perry's building of the Great Lakes war fleet

---

• In the 1830s, 1840s, and 1850s, Pennsylvania led the nation in science and culture.

• Pennsylvania played a key role in the Underground Railroad and gave Abraham Lincoln its vote in the 1860 election.

• Pennsylvania was the only Northern state in which a critical battle of the Civil War was fought. During the three days beginning on July 1, 1863, the Union successes in the Battle of Gettysburg marked a turning point of the war.

So They Say

"Troops under my command have repulsed the enemy's assault and we have gained a great victory. The enemy is now flying in all directions in my front."

Union General George Meade, at Gettysburg

• In 1876 the Centennial Exposition at Philadelphia celebrated the 100th birthday of the Declaration of Independence.

• The May 1889 flood at Johnstown was one of the nation's worst disasters, with 2,200 lives lost.

• More than 660,000 Pennsylvanians served in World War I.

• The record of 1.2 million Pennsylvania men and women in World War II service was surpassed only by New York.

• In 1972, Hurricane Agnes brought the state's worst-yet hurricane/flood damage.

• The returns from the 1990 census indicated that Pennsylvania had dropped from fourth to fifth place in population.

• In 1991, Harris Wofford became the first Democrat elected to the U.S. Senate from Pennsylvania since 1962.

THAT'S INTERESTING

• William Penn received the greatest land grant ever given an English subject, for which he was required to pay only two beaver skins per year to the king.

So They Say

"...he has been not only always just but very kind to us as well as our ancient Kings and Sachems deceased...not suffering us to receive any wrong...and freely entertaining us at his own cost and often filling us with many presents of necessary good."

Indian leader James Logan, on William Penn

- When houses were taxed according to the number of their windows, housewives poured hot water on the tax agents from those windows, spawning the "Hot Water War."
- The carp in Lake Pymatuning sometimes crowd so closely together that ducks walk across the backs of the fish.
- When the Ringing Rocks near Upper Black Eddy are struck, the pitch depends on the size of the rock.

NOTABLE NATIVES

Louisa May Alcott (Germantown, 1832-1888), author. **Richard Allen** (Philadelphia, 1760-1831), religious leader. **Marian Anderson** (Philadelphia, 1902-1993), opera singer. **Maxwell Anderson** (Atlantic, 1888-1959), playwright. **Samuel Barber** (West Chester, 1910-1981), composer. **James Buchanan** (Mercersburg, 1791-1868), U.S. president. **Charles Wakefield Cadman** (Johnstown, 1881-1946), composer. **Simon Cameron** (Maytown, 1799-1889), public official/political leader. **Mary Cassatt** (Allegheny, now Pittsburgh, 1845-1926), painter. **W. C. Fields** (Philadelphia, 1880-1946), entertainer. **Stephen Collins Foster** (Lawrenceville, 1826-1864), composer. **Henry Clay Frick** (West Overton, 1849-1919), industrialist and philanthropist. **Henry John Heinz** (Pittsburgh, 1845-1919), industrialist. **Milton Snavely Hershey** (Dauphin County, 1857-1945), industrialist/philanthropist. **Lido Anthony (Lee) Iacocca** (Allentown, 1924-), industrialist. **Harold LeClair Ickes** (Blair County, 1874-1952), public official. **Gene Kelly** (Pittsburgh, 1912-1996), actor and dancer. **Grace Kelly** (Philadelphia, 1929-1982), actress/princess of Monaco. **Walter Crawford Kelly** (Philadelphia, 1913-1973), cartoonist/illustrator. **George Catlett Marshall** (Uniontown, 1880-1959), soldier and public official. **George Brinton McClellan** (Philadelphia, 1826-1885), soldier. **William Holmes McGuffey** (near Claysville, 1800-1873), educator. **Andrew William Mellon** (Pittsburgh, 1855-1937), financier and art collector. **Ethelbert Woodbridge Nevin** (Edgeworth, 1862-1901), composer. **Maxfield Frederick Parrish** (Philadelphia, 1870-1966), artist. **Robert Edwin Peary** (Cresson, 1856-1920), explorer. **Mary Roberts Rinehart** (Pittsburgh, 1876-1958), author. **Washington Augustus Roebling** (Saxonburg, 1837-1926), engineer.

Charles Michael Schwab (Williamsburg, 1862-1939), industrialist. **James Stewart** (Indiana, 1908-), actor. **William Tatem (Big Bill) Tilden, Jr.** (Germantown, 1893-1953), tennis player. **John Wanamaker** (Philadelphia, 1838-1922), merchant. **Anthony Wayne** (Wayneboro, 1745-1796), soldier. **Benjamin West** (Springfield, 1738-1820), painter.

GENERAL

Admitted to statehood: December 12, 1787

Origin of name: William Penn, the Quaker who was made full proprietor by King Charles II in 1681, suggested "Sylvania," or "woodland," as the name for his tract. Charles II added "Penn" to "Sylvania", contrary to the desires of the modest proprietor, in honor of Penn's father.

Capital: Harrisburg

Nickname: Keystone State

Motto: Virtue, liberty, and independence

Animal: Whitetail deer

Bird: Ruffed grouse

Insect: Firefly

Fish: Brook trout

Flower: Mountain laurel

Song: "Pennsylvania"

Tree: Eastern hemlock

THE LAND

Area: 45,759 sq. mi., 33rd
　　Land: 44,820 sq. mi., 32nd
　　Water: 939 sq. mi., 29th
　　　　Inland water: 190 sq. mi., 45th
Great Lakes: 749 sq. mi., 7th

Topography: Allegheny Mountains run SW to NE, with piedmont and coastal plain in the SE triangle; Allegheny Front a diagonal spine across the state's center; NW rugged plateau falls to Lake Erie lowland.

Number of counties: 67

Geographic center: Centre, 2.5 mi. SW of Bellefonte

Length: 283 mi.; width: 160 mi.

Highest point: 3,213 ft. (Mount Davis), 33rd

Lowest point: sea level (Delaware River), 3rd

Mean elevation: 1,100 ft., 23rd

Coastline: 0 mi.

Shoreline: 89 mi., 24th

CLIMATE AND ENVIRONMENT

Temp., highest: 111 deg. on July 10, 1936, at Phoenixville; lowest: −42 deg. on Jan. 5, 1904, at Smethport

Monthly average: highest: 86.2 deg., 32nd; lowest: 18.0 deg., 23rd; spread (high to low): 68.2 deg., 26th

Hazardous waste sites (1993): 99, 2nd

Endangered species: Mammals: 1—Indiana bat; birds: 2—American peregrine falcon, Piping plover; reptiles: none; amphibians: none; fishes: none; invertebrates: 2; plants: 1

MAJOR CITIES
POPULATION, 1990
PERCENTAGE INCREASE, 1980-90

Allentown, 105,090—1.28%
Erie, 108,718— −8.73%
Philadelphia, 1,585,577— −6.08%
Pittsburgh, 369,879— −12.76%
Scranton, 81,805— −7.16%

THE PEOPLE

Population (1995): 12,071,842, 5th
  Percent change (1990-95): 1.6%, 44th
Population (2000 proj.): 12,296,000, 5th
  Percent change (1990-2000): 3.49%, 43rd
Per sq. mi. (1994): 268.9, 10th
Percent in metro. area (1992): 84.8%, 10th
Foreign born: 369,000, 8th
  Percent: 3.1%, 25th
Top three ancestries reported:
  German, 36.31%
  Irish, 18.99%
  Italian, 11.55%
White: 10,520,201, 88.54%, 21st
Black: 1,089,795, 9.17%, 21st
Native American: 14,733, 0.12%, 51st
Asian, Pacific Isle: 137,438, 1.16%, 25th
Other races: 119,476, 1.01%, 25th
Hispanic origin: 232,262, 1.95%, 30th
Percent over 5 yrs. speaking language other than English at home: 7.3%, 24th
Percent males: 47.92%, 48th; percent females: 52.08%, 4th
Percent never married: 27.3%, 16th
Marriages per 1,000 (1993): 6.4, 49th
Divorces per 1,000 (1993): 3.3, 43rd
Median age: 35
Under 5 years (1994): 6.63%, 48th
Under 18 years (1994): 24.05%, 46th
65 years & older (1994): 15.9%, 2nd

Percent increase among the elderly (1990-94): 4.86%, 31st

OF VITAL IMPORTANCE

Live births per 1,000 pop. (1993): 13.2, 47th
Infant mortality rate per 1,000 births (1992): 9.0, 18th
  Rate for blacks (1990): 18.8, 6th
  Rate for whites (1990): 7.8, 27th
Births to unmarried women, % of total (1992): 31.6%, 16th
Births to teenage mothers, % of total (1992): 10.5%, 35th
Abortions (1992): 49,740, 8th
  Rate per 1,000 women 14-44 years old: 18.6, 26th
  Percent change (1988-92): −2%, 16th
Average lifetime (1979-81): 73.58, 33rd
Deaths per 1,000 pop. (1993): 10.5, 5th
Causes of death per 100,000 pop.:
  Accidents & adverse effects (1992): 34.3, 28th
  Atherosclerosis (1991): 6.3, 34th
  Cancer (1991): 252.7, 4th
  Cerebrovascular diseases (1992): 64.1, 17th
  Chronic liver diseases & cirrhosis (1991): 10.2, 14th
  Chronic obstructive pulmonary diseases (1992): 39.8, 20th
  Diabetes mellitus (1992): 26.2, 7th
  Diseases of heart (1992): 360.2, 2nd
  Pneumonia, flu (1991): 32.8, 18th
  Suicide (1992): 11.6, 36th

KEEPING WELL

Active nonfederal physicians per 100,000 pop. (1993): 254, 9th
Dentists per 100,000 (1991): 66, 11th
Nurses per 100,000 (1992): 907, 10th
Hospitals per 100,000 (1993): 1.94, 31st
  Admissions per 1,000 (1993): 152.18, 3rd
  Occupancy rate per 100 beds (1993): 72.6, 8th
  Average cost per patient per day (1993): $861, 25th
  Average cost per stay (1993): $6,564, 11th
  Average stay (1992): 13.0 days, 4th
AIDS cases (adult, 1993): 3,214; per 100,000: 26.7, 21st
HIV infection, not yet AIDS (1993): NA
Other notifiable diseases:
  Gonorrhea: 258.9, 19th
  Measles: 4.6, 24th

Syphilis: 64.7, 10th
Tuberculosis: 6.5, 27th
Pop. without health insur. (1991-93): 9.2%, 47th

HOUSEHOLDS BY TYPE

Total households (1994): 4,551,000
Percent change (1990-94): 1.2%, 45th
Per 1,000 pop.: 377.61, 20th
Percent of households 65 yrs. and over: 26.61%, 3rd
Persons per household (1994): 2.57, 31st
Family households: 3,155,989
Percent of total: 70.20%, 29th
Nonfamily households: 1,339,977
Percent of total: 29.80%, 23rd
Pop. living in group quarters: 348,424
Percent of pop.: 2.93%, 21st

LIVING QUARTERS

Total housing units: 4,938,140
Persons per unit: 2.41, 25th
Occupied housing units: 4,495,966
Percent of total units: 91.05%, 16th
Persons per unit: 2.46, 44th
Percent of units with over 1 person per room: 1.84%, 45th
Owner-occupied units: 3,176,121
Percent of total units: 64.32%, 5th
Percent of occupied units: 70.64%, 5th
Persons per unit: 2.72, 28th
Median value: $69,700, 25th
Renter-occupied units: 1,319,845
Percent of total units: 26.73%, 39th
Percent of occupied units: 29.36%, 47th
Persons per unit: 2.19, 48th
Median contract rent: $322, 28th
Rental vacancy rate: 7.2%, 40th
Mobile home, trailer & other as a percent of occupied housing units: 7.12%, 35th
Persons in emergency shelters for homeless persons: 8,237, 0.069%, 15th
Persons visible in street locations: 1,312, 0.0110%, 16th
Persons in shelters for abused women: 603, 0.0051%, 23rd
Nursing home population: 106,454, 0.90%, 17th

CRIME INDEX PER 100,000 (1992-93)

Total reported: 3,271.4, 45th
Violent: 417.5, 34th
Murder and nonnegligent manslaughter: 6.8, 26th
Aggravated assault: 205.1, 39th

Robbery: 179.0, 20th
Forcible rape: 26.5, 46th
Property: 2,853.9, 46th
Burglary: 582.0, 48th
Larceny, theft: 1,831.7, 50th
Motor vehicle theft: 440.2, 25th
Drug abuse violations (1990): 233.0, 28th
Child-abuse rate per 1,000 children (1993): 2.72, 48th

TEACHING AND LEARNING

Pop. 3 and over enrolled in school: 2,829,553
Percent of pop.: 24.8%, 49th
Public elementary & secondary schools (1992-93): 3,197
Total enrollment (1992): 1,717,613
Percent of total pop.: 14.32%, 50th
Teachers (1992): 100,192
Percent of pop.: 0.84%, 49th
Pupil/teacher ratio (fall 1992): 17.0, 21st
Teachers' avg. salary (1992-93): $43,220, 7th
Expenditure per capita (1990-91): $3,192.89, 35th
Expenditure per pupil (1991-92): $6,613, 8th
Percent of graduates taking SAT (1993): 70%, 8th
Mean SAT verbal scores: 418, 41st
Mean SAT mathematical scores: 460, 46th
Percent of graduates taking ACT (1995): 7%, 41st
Mean ACT scores: 20.6, 33rd
Percent of pop. over 25 completing:
Less than 9th grade: 9.4%, 26th
High school: 74.7%, 35th
College degree(s): 17.9%, 32nd
Higher education, institutions (1993-94): 219
Enrollment (1992): 629,832
Percent of pop.: 5.25%, 35th
White non-Hispanic (1992): 536,620
Percent of enroll.: 85.20%, 20th
Black non-Hispanic (1992): 46,317
Percent of enroll.: 7.35%, 21st
Hispanic (1992): 11,109
Percent of enroll.: 1.76%, 30th
Asian/Pacific Islander (1992): 17,951
Percent of enroll.: 2.85%, 16th
American Indian/AK native (1992): 1,326
Percent of enroll.: 0.21%, 50th
Nonresident alien (1992): 16,509
Percent of enroll.: 2.62%, 25th
Female (1992): 342,281
Percent of enroll.: 54.34%, 40th

Pub. institutions (1993-94): 65
  Enrollment (1992): 362,784
  Percent of enroll.: 57.60%, 45th
Private institutions (1993-94): 154
  Enrollment (1992): 267,048
  Percent of enroll.: 42.40%, 7th
Tuition, public institution (avg., 1993-94): $8,278, 4th
Tuition, private institution (avg., 1993-94): $16,642, 12th
Public library systems: 445
  Books & serial vol. per capita: 2.08, 36th
  Govt. expenditure per capita: $8.39, 45th

LAW ENFORCEMENT, COURTS, AND PRISONS

Police protection, corrections, judicial and legal functions expenditures (1992): $2,944,000,000
  Per capita: $245, 28th
Police per 10,000 pop. (1993): 23.80, 14th
Prisoners (state & fed.) per 100,000 pop. (1993): 2,165.42, 35th
  Percent change (1992-93): 4.3%, 31st
Death penalty: yes, by electrocution
  Under sentence of death (1993): 169, 4th
  Executed (1993): 0

RELIGION, NUMBER AND PERCENT OF POPULATION

Agnostic: 63,608—0.70%, 17th
Buddhist: 9,087—0.10%, 17th
Christian: 7,987,326—87.90%, 19th
Hindu: 9,087—0.10%, 10th
Jewish: 154,476—1.70%, 10th
Muslim: 27,261—0.30%, 9th
Unitarian: 9,087—0.10%, 31st
Other: 208,997—2.30%, 6th
None: 445,255—4.90%, 40th
Refused to answer: 172,650—1.90%, 31st

MAKING A LIVING

Personal income per capita (1994): $22,324, 19th
  Percent increase (1993-94): 4.9%, 26th
Disposable personal income per capita (1994): $19,418, 17th
Median income of households (1993): $30,995, 27th
Percent of pop. below poverty level (1993): 13.2%, 26th
  Percent 65 and over (1990): 10.6%, 37th
Expenditure for energy per person (1992): $1,875, 28th

ECONOMY

Civilian labor force (1994): 5,829,000
  Percent of total pop.: 48.37%, 43rd
  Percent 65 and over (1990): 2.91%, 20th
  Percent female: 45.27%, 41st
Percent job growth (1980-90): 11.23%, 42nd
Major employer industries (1994):
  Agriculture: 87,000—1.6%, 40th
  Construction: 225,000—4.1%, 25th
  Finance, insurance, & real estate: 335,000—6.1%, 13th
  Government: 667,000—12.2%, 49th
  Manufacturing: 965,000—17.8%, 15th
  Service: 1,359,000—24.8%, 9th
  Trade: 1,102,000—20.1%, 8th
  Transportation, communications, public utilities: 306,000—5.6%, 20th
Unemployment rate (1994): 6.19%, 17th
  Male: 6.5%, 13th
  Female: 5.8%, 21st
Total businesses (1991): 367,348
  New business incorps. (1991): 17,340
    Percent of total businesses: 4.72%, 39th
  Business failures (1991): 2,228
    Percent of total businesses: 0.61%
Agriculture farm income:
  Marketing (1993): $3,712,000,000, 19th
    Average per farm: $72,784.31, 28th
  Leading products (1993): Dairy products, cattle, greenhouse, mushrooms
  Average value land & build. per acre (1994): $1,910, 9th
    Percent increase (1990-94): 5.70%, 42nd
  Govt. payments (1993): $45,000,000, 35th
    Average per farm: $882.35, 42nd
Construction, value of all: $5,662,000,000
  Per capita: $476.53, 35th
Manufactures:
  Value added: $64,065,000,000
    Per capita: $5,391.93, 19th
  Leading products: Primary metals, foods, fabricated metal products, nonelectrical machinery, electrical machinery
Value of nonfuel mineral production (1994): $964,000,000, 12th
Leading mineral products: Coal, natural gas, cement
Retail sales (1993): $96,464,000,000, 5th
  Per household: $21,007, 37th
    Percent increase (1992-93): 3.0%, 42nd
Tourism revenues (1992): $10.2 bil.

Foreign exports, in total value (1994):
$11,650,000,000, 11th
Per capita: $966.64, 34th
Gross state product per person (1993):
$21,344.27, 24th
Percent change (1990-93): 4.08%, 18th
Patents per 100,000 pop. (1993): 24.88, 19th
Public aid recipients (percent of resident pop.
1993): 7.0%, 20th
Medicaid recipients per 1,000 pop. (1993):
101.66, 34th
Medicare recipients per 1,000 pop. (1993):
169.49, 3rd

TRAVEL AND TRANSPORTATION

Motor vehicle registrations (1993): 8,282,000
Per 1,000 pop.: 688.45, 45th
Motorcycle registrations (1993): 172,000
Per 1,000 pop.: 14.30, 30th
Licensed drivers per 1,000 pop. (1993):
669.58, 33rd
Deaths from motor vehicle accidents per
100,000 pop. (1993): 12.71, 39th
Public roads & streets (1993):
Total mileage: 117,038
Per 1,000 pop.: 9.73, 40th
Rural mileage: 84,422
Per 1,000 pop.: 7.02, 40th
Urban mileage: 32,616
Per 1,000 pop.: 2.71, 39th
Interstate mileage: 1,588
Per 1,000 pop.: 0.13, 38th
Annual vehicle-mi. of travel per person
(1993): 7,539, 46th
Mean travel time for workers age 16+ who
work away from home: 21.6 min., 16th

GOVERNMENT

Percent of voting age pop. registered (1994):
58.9%, 40th
Percent of voting age pop. voting (1994):
42.7%, 37th
Percent of voting age pop. voting for U.S.
representatives (1994): 36.6%, 31st
State legislators, total (1995): 253, 2nd
Women members (1992): 24
Percent of legislature: 9.5%, 44th
U.S. Congress, House members (1995): 21
Change (1985-95): –2
Revenues (1993):
State govt.: $37,779,000,000
Per capita: $3,140.40, 23rd
Parimutuel & amusement taxes & lotteries,
revenue per capita: $111.89, 16th

Expenditures (1993):
State govt.: $34,359,000,000
Per capita: $2,856.11, 26th
Debt outstanding (1993): $12,989,000,000
Per capita: $1,079.72, 33rd

LAWS AND REGULATIONS

Legal driving age: 18, 17 if completed driver
education course
Marriage age without parental consent: 18
Divorce residence requirement: 6 mo.

ATTRACTIONS (1995)

Major opera companies: 5
Major symphony orchestras: 2
Major dance companies: 5
Major professional theater companies (non-
profit): 2
State appropriations for arts agencies per capita:
$0.75, 25th
State Fair during second week in January at
Harrisburg

SPORTS AND COMPETITION

NCAA teams (Division I): Bucknell Univ.
Bison, Drexel Univ. Dragons, Du-
quesne Univ. Dukes, Lafayette College
Leopards, La Salle Univ. Explorers,
Lehigh Univ. Engineers, Penn State
Univ. Nittany Lions, Robert Morris
College Colonials, St. Francis College
Red Flash, St. Joseph's Univ. Hawks,
Temple Univ. Owls, Univ. of Pennsyl-
vania Red & Blue/Quakers, Univ. of
Pittsburgh Panthers, Villanova Univ.
Wildcats
Major league baseball teams: Pittsburgh Pi-
rates (NL Central), Three Rivers Sta-
dium; Philadelphia Phillies (NL East),
Veterans Stadium
NBA basketball teams: Philadelphia 76ers,
CoreStates Spectrum (scheduled to be-
gin play at CoreStates Center in No-
vember 1996)
NFL football teams: Pittsburgh Steelers
(AFC), Three Rivers Stadium; Phila-
delphia Eagles (NFC), Veterans Sta-
dium
NHL hockey teams: Philadelphia Flyers,
CoreStates Spectrum (scheduled to
begin play at CoreStates Center in
October 1996); Pittsburgh Penguins,
Civic Arena

RHODE ISLAND

"One views it as placed there by some refinement in the scheme of nature, just a touchstone of taste—with a beautiful little sense to be read with it by a few persons and nothing at all to be made of it, as to its essence, by most others."

Henry James, novelist

The smallest state in area, Rhode Island could be fitted into enormous Alaska 425 times. However, despite its size, it has the longest official name. And it is an important industrial state, especially in textile and jewelry production. It lies on the beautiful Narragansett Bay—an arm of the Atlantic Ocean—and is a popular vacation area, to which boaters, fishermen, and other water-sports fans flock during the summer months. The big and the little have combined to weave the fascinating story of Rhode Island.

SUPERLATIVES

• Said to be the birthplace of the U.S. industrial revolution.
• Most heavily industrialized state in proportion to size.
• World's costume jewelry center.
• Birthplace of the poultry industry.
• Oldest synagogue in America—the Touro Synagogue in Newport.
• Largest unsupported dome in America, on the capitol.
• Nation's oldest indoor shopping center, at Providence.

MOMENTS IN HISTORY

• Giovanni de Verrazano made the first recorded European contact with what is now Rhode Island in 1524, at Narragansett Bay.
• In 1635, William Blackstone settled in Valley Falls, becoming the first European settler known in the Rhode Island area.
• Providence was founded by Roger Williams in 1636 on a grant of land ceded to him by the Narragansett Indians.
• In 1644 Williams obtained a charter for the colony; after the restoration of the English monarchy, a second, liberal charter for the colony was granted by King Charles II in 1663.

So They Say

"Having a sense of God's merciful providence unto me called this place Providence, desired it might be for a shelter for persons distressed for conscience."

Roger Williams

• The first law against slavery in North America was enacted by Rhode Island on May 18, 1652.
• King Philip, chief of the Wampanoag Indians, led his people in King Philip's War (1675-1676); he was captured and executed on August 12, 1676, crippling Indian power in the region.
• During the French and Indian War, in July of 1689, Block Island was attacked by privateers.

So They Say

The privateers at Block Island "...continued about a week on the island, plundering houses, stripping the people of their clothing, ripping up the beds, throwing out the feathers, and carrying away the ticking."

Reverend Samuel Niles

• Rhode Islanders were quick to protest the British tax laws. On June 9, 1772, the British sloop of war *Gaspee* was captured and burned in Narragansett Bay.
• Providence celebrated its own "tea party" on March 2, 1775, by burning a huge mound of captured tea.
• On May 4, 1776, Rhode Island "created the first free republic in the New World," ac-

cording to the Rhode Island Development Council.

• During the Revolutionary War many Rhode Island communities were captured. Heaviest fighting in the state was in the Battle of Rhode Island, August 28-29, 1778.

• Opposed to the new U.S. Constitution and its government, Rhode Island held out until May 29, 1790, when it became the last of the 13 original colonies to join.

• In 1824 women weavers of Pawtucket went on strike, in what was thought to be the first strike in the United States by women.

• More than 24,000 people from Rhode Island served during the Civil War, with 255 dying in combat and another 1,265 succumbing to disease.

• In 1876, President Rutherford B. Hayes made a historic conversation over the newly invented telephone, from Rocky Point to Providence, a distance of 8 miles.

• In 1895 the Cornelius Vanderbilt mansion, the Breakers, became perhaps the nation's most elegant private home, expanding Newport's high social position.

• World War I brought a total of 28,817 Rhode Island men and women into the armed services.

• The America's Cup yacht race came to Newport in 1930. In 1983, Americans lost the race for the first time, to Australia.

• The 300th anniversary of its founding by Roger Williams was celebrated by the state in 1936.

• During World War II, working at Quonset Point near Davisville, the Navy Seabees designed a structure that became world renowned, known as the Quonset hut.

• Newport held the first of its celebrated jazz festivals in 1954.

• The 1990 census showed a slight gain in the state's population during the preceding decade.

THAT'S INTERESTING

• The smallest state has the longest official name, the "State of Rhode Island and Providence Plantations."

• Gentlemanly Indian men would serenade an Indian woman. If interested, she would throw out her moccasin, then come out for an engagement walk. Less honorable braves sometimes knocked their prospective brides unconscious and carried them off.

• Samuel Gorton fled to Rhode Island after he was banished from Massachusetts for defending his maid, who had been punished for smiling in church.

• Many protests against the British tax on tea were made in Rhode Island. One man dashed around Providence crossing out the word "tea" on every sign he found.

• A lover of good jokes, Mrs. William Astor once invited Newport society to meet the Prince del Drago, who turned out to be a tiny monkey resplendent in a full dress suit.

NOTABLE NATIVES

Nelson Wilmarth Aldrich (Foster, 1841-1915), politician. Zachariah Allen (Providence, 1795-1882), inventor. Nicholas Brown (Providence, 1729-1791), manufacturer. William Ellery Channing (Newport, 1780-1842), clergyman. George Michael Cohan (Providence, 1878-1942), composer/actor. George William Curtis (Providence, 1824-1892), author/lecturer. Thomas Wilson Dorr (Providence, 1805-1854), political reformer. Robert Gray (Tiverton, 1755-1806), explorer. Nathanael Greene (Warwick, 1742-1786), Revolutionary soldier. Stephen Hopkins (Providence, 1707-1785), colonial adminstrator. Napoleon (Larry) Lajoie (Woonsocket, 1874-1959), baseball player. Matthew Calbraith Perry (Newport, 1794-1858), naval officer. Oliver Hazard Perry (South Kingston, 1785-1819), naval officer. Gilbert Charles Stuart (North Kingstown, 1755-1828), artist.

GENERAL

Admitted to statehood: May 29, 1790
Origin of name: Exact origin unknown. One theory notes that Giovanni de Verrazano recorded an island about the size of Rhodes in the Mediterranean in 1524, but others believe the state was named Roode Eylandt by Dutch explorer Adriaen Block because of its red clay.
Capital: Providence
Nickname: Little Rhody, Ocean State
Motto: Hope
Bird: Rhode Island red
Flower: Violet
Stone: Cumberlandite
Song: "Rhode Island"
Tree: Red maple

THE LAND

Area: 1,231 sq. mi., 50th
  Land: 1,045 sq. mi., 50th
  Water: 186 sq. mi., 48th
    Inland water: 168 sq. mi., 46th
    Coastal water: 18 sq. mi., 20th
Topography: Eastern lowlands of Narragansett Basin; western uplands of flat and rolling hills
Number of counties: 5
Geographic center: Kent, 1 mile SSW of Crompton
Length: 40 mi.; width: 30 mi.
Highest point: 812 ft. (Jerimoth Hill), 46th
Lowest point: sea level (Atlantic Ocean), 3rd
Mean elevation: 200 ft., 47th
Coastline: 40 mi., 19th
Shoreline: 384 mi., 20th

CLIMATE AND ENVIRONMENT

Temp., highest: 104 deg. on Aug. 2, 1975, at Providence; lowest: −23 deg. on Jan. 11, 1942, at Kingston
Monthly average: highest: 81.7 deg., 48th; lowest: 20.0 deg., 27th; spread (high to low): 61.7 deg., 39th
Hazardous waste sites (1993): 12, 30th
Endangered species: Mammals: none; birds: 2—American peregrine falcon, Roseate tern; reptiles: 2; amphibians: none; fishes: none; invertebrates: 1; plants: 2

MAJOR CITIES POPULATION, 1990 PERCENTAGE INCREASE, 1980-90

Cranston, 76,060—5.65%
East Providence, 50,380— −1.18%
Pawtucket, 72,644—2.02%
Providence, 160,728—2.50%
Warwick, 85,427— −1.95%

THE PEOPLE

Population (1995): 989,794, 43rd
  Percent change (1990-95): −1.4%, 50th
Population (2000 proj.): 998,000, 43rd
  Percent change (1990-2000): −0.54%, 48th
Per sq. mi. (1994): 953.8, 3rd
Percent in metro. area (1992): 93.6%, 6th
Foreign born: 95,000, 24th
  Percent: 9.5%, 7th
Top three ancestries reported:
  Irish, 21.34%
  Italian, 19.84%
  English, 16.05%

White: 917,375, 91.42%, 17th
Black: 38,861, 3.87%, 33rd
Native American: 4,071, 0.41%, 27th
Asian, Pacific Isle: 18,325, 1.83%, 16th
Other races: 24,832, 2.47%, 12th
Hispanic origin: 45,756, 4.56%, 18th
Percent over 5 yrs. speaking language other than English at home: 17.0%, 9th
Percent males: 47.98%, 46th; percent females: 52.02%, 6th
Percent never married: 29.6%, 6th
Marriages per 1,000 (1993): 7.1, 43rd
Divorces per 1,000 (1993): 3.4, 40th
Median age: 34
Under 5 years (1994): 7.12%, 31st
Under 18 years (1994): 24.07%, 44th
65 years & older (1994): 15.6%, 3rd
Percent increase among the elderly (1990-94): 2.96%, 47th

OF VITAL IMPORTANCE

Live births per 1,000 pop. (1993): 14.3, 32nd
Infant mortality rate per 1,000 births (1992): 7.4, 38th
  Rate for blacks (1990): 9.7, 45th
  Rate for whites (1990): 8.3, 14th
Births to unmarried women, % of total (1992): 29.6%, 22nd
Births to teenage mothers, % of total (1992): 9.8%, 42nd
Abortions (1992): 6,990, 36th
  Rate per 1,000 women 14-44 years old: 30.0, 8th
  Percent change (1988-92): −2%, 16th
Average lifetime (1979-81): 74.76, 17th
Deaths per 1,000 pop. (1993): 9.7, 10th
Causes of death per 100,000 pop.:
  Accidents & adverse effects (1992): 22.7, 50th
  Atherosclerosis (1991): 8.5, 14th
  Cancer (1991): 251 4, 5th
  Cerebrovascular diseases (1992): 58.5, 25th
  Chronic liver diseases & cirrhosis (1991): 11.9, 7th
  Chronic obstructive pulmonary diseases (1992): 37.6, 25th
  Diabetes mellitus (1992): 22.8, 11th
  Diseases of heart (1992): 323.0, 12th
  Pneumonia, flu (1991): 35.0, 15th
  Suicide (1992): 7.3, 49th

KEEPING WELL

Active nonfederal physicians per 100,000 pop. (1993): 271, 6th

Dentists per 100,000 (1991): 56, 20th
Nurses per 100,000 (1992): 971, 5th
Hospitals per 100,000 (1993): 1.10, 49th
  Admissions per 1,000 (1993): 126.80, 17th
  Occupancy rate per 100 beds (1993): 73.3, 6th
  Average cost per patient per day (1993): $885, 22nd
  Average cost per stay (1993): $5,672, 27th
  Average stay (1992): 7.3 days, 20th
AIDS cases (adult, 1993): 348; per 100,000: 34.8, 15th
HIV infection, not yet AIDS (1993): NA
Other notifiable diseases:
  Gonorrhea: 119.6, 32nd
  Measles: 3.2, 31st
  Syphilis: 16.7, 27th
  Tuberculosis: 7.5, 21st
Pop. without health insur. (1991-93): 10.0%, 43rd

HOUSEHOLDS BY TYPE

Total households (1994): 374,000
  Percent change (1990-94): –1.1%, 50th
  Per 1,000 pop.: 375.13, 25th
  Percent of households 65 yrs. and over: 25.67%, 4th
  Persons per household (1994): 2.57, 31st
Family households: 258,886
  Percent of total: 68.49%, 43rd
Nonfamily households: 119,091
  Percent of total: 31.51%, 9th
Pop. living in group quarters: 38,595
  Percent of pop.: 3.85%, 3rd

LIVING QUARTERS

Total housing units: 414,572
  Persons per unit: 2.42, 21st
Occupied housing units: 337,977
  Percent of total units: 81.52%, 48th
  Persons per unit: 2.51, 30th
  Percent of units with over 1 person per room: 2.57%, 34th
Owner-occupied units: 224,792
  Percent of total units: 54.22%, 40th
  Percent of occupied units: 66.51%, 29th
  Persons per unit: 2.78, 17th
  Median value: $133,500, 6th
Renter-occupied units: 153,185
  Percent of total units: 36.95%, 7th
  Percent of occupied units: 45.32%, 4th
  Persons per unit: 2.23, 45th
  Median contract rent: $416, 13th
  Rental vacancy rate: 7.9%, 30th

Mobile home, trailer & other as a percent of occupied housing units: 2.62%, 47th
Persons in emergency shelters for homeless persons: 469, 0.047%, 25th
Persons visible in street locations: 44, 0.0044%, 31st
Persons in shelters for abused women: 33, 0.0033%, 41st
Nursing home population: 10,156, 1.01%, 10th

CRIME INDEX PER 100,000 (1992-93)

Total reported: 4,499.0, 33rd
  Violent: 401.7, 35th
    Murder and nonnegligent manslaughter: 3.9, 37th
    Aggravated assault: 268.1, 31st
    Robbery: 101.1, 38th
    Forcible rape: 29.6, 40th
  Property: 4,097.3, 32nd
    Burglary: 1,040.9, 21st
    Larceny, theft: 2,410.1, 42nd
    Motor vehicle theft: 646.3, 11th
Drug abuse violations (1990): 281.1, 21st
Child-abuse rate per 1,000 children (1993): 13.32, 27th

TEACHING AND LEARNING

Pop. 3 and over enrolled in school: 254,635
  Percent of pop.: 26.5%, 35th
Public elementary & secondary schools (1992-93): 313
  Total enrollment (1992): 143,798
    Percent of total pop.: 14.37%, 48th
  Teachers (1992): 10,069
    Percent of pop.: 1.01%, 29th
  Pupil/teacher ratio (fall 1992): 14.3, 46th
  Teachers' avg. salary (1992-93): $39,641, 12th
  Expenditure per capita (1990-91): $3,867.15, 12th
  Expenditure per pupil (1991-92): $6,546, 9th
Percent of graduates taking SAT (1993): 71%, 7th
  Mean SAT verbal scores: 419, 39th
  Mean SAT mathematical scores: 464, 44th
Percent of graduates taking ACT (1995): 2%, 49th
  Mean ACT scores: 20.6, 33rd
Percent of pop. over 25 completing:
  Less than 9th grade: 11.1%, 18th
  High school: 72.0%, 41st
  College degree(s): 21.3%, 18th

Higher education, institutions (1993-94): 14
Enrollment (1992): 79,165
Percent of pop.: 7.90%, 2nd
White non-Hispanic (1992): 68,636
Percent of enroll.: 86.70%, 16th
Black non-Hispanic (1992): 2,976
Percent of enroll.: 3.76%, 31st
Hispanic (1992): 2,295
Percent of enroll.: 2.90%, 15th
Asian/Pacific Islander (1992): 2,289
Percent of enroll.: 2.89%, 15th
American Indian/AK native (1992): 273
Percent of enroll.: 0.34%, 32nd
Nonresident alien (1992): 2,696
Percent of enroll.: 3.41%, 14th
Female (1992): 43,614
Percent of enroll.: 55.09%, 29th
Pub. institutions (1993-94): 3
Enrollment (1992): 43,264
Percent of enroll.: 54.65%, 49th
Private institutions (1993-94): 11
Enrollment (1992): 35,901
Percent of enroll.: 45.35%, 3rd
Tuition, public institution (avg., 1993-94): $8,603, 2nd
Tuition, private institution (avg., 1993-94): $18,340, 4th
Public library systems: 51
Books & serial vol. per capita: 2.74, 23rd
Govt. expenditure per capita: $15.64, 25th

LAW ENFORCEMENT, COURTS, AND PRISONS

Police protection, corrections, judicial and legal functions expenditures (1992): $303,000,000
Per capita: $302, 17th
Police per 10,000 pop. (1993): 22.43, 20th
Prisoners (state & fed.) per 100,000 pop. (1993): 2,783.00, 26th
Percent change (1992-93): 0.3%, 39th
Death penalty: no

RELIGION, NUMBER AND PERCENT OF POPULATION

Agnostic: 3,889—0.50%, 27th
Buddhist: NA
Christian: 680,552—87.50%, 21st
Hindu: NA
Jewish: 12,444—1.60%, 11th
Muslim: 3,111—0.40%, 5th
Unitarian: 3,111—0.40%, 8th
Other: 5,444—0.70%, 43rd

None: 46,666—6.00%, 32nd
Refused to answer: 22,555—2.90%, 9th

MAKING A LIVING

Personal income per capita (1994): $22,251, 20th
Percent increase (1993-94): 4.7%, 31st
Disposable personal income per capita (1994): $19,544, 14th
Median income of households (1993): $33,509, 16th
Percent of pop. below poverty level (1993): 11.2%, 35th
Percent 65 and over (1990): 11.6%, 26th
Expenditure for energy per person (1992): $1,865, 30th

ECONOMY

Civilian labor force (1994): 505,000
Percent of total pop.: 50.65%, 30th
Percent 65 and over (1990): 3.29%, 11th
Percent female: 48.32%, 3rd
Percent job growth (1980-90): 15.26%, 37th
Major employer industries (1994):
Agriculture: NA—0.8%, 48th
Construction: 16,000—3.4%, 46th
Finance, insurance, & real estate: 27,000—5.7%, 17th
Government: 60,000—12.7%, 45th
Manufacturing: 101,000—21.5%, 11th
Service: 123,000—25.9%, 4th
Trade: 90,000—19.1%, 23rd
Transportation, communications, public utilities: 16,000—3.3%, 51st
Unemployment rate (1994): 7.13%, 7th
Male: 7.6%, 6th
Female: 6.5%, 12th
Total businesses (1991): 32,764
New business incorps. (1991): 2,458
Percent of total businesses: 7.50%, 13th
Business failures (1991): 183
Percent of total businesses: 0.56%
Agriculture farm income:
Marketing (1993): $79,000,000, 49th
Average per farm: $79,000.00, 25th
Leading products (1993): Greenhouse products, eggs, dairy products, potatoes
Average value land & build. per acre (1994): $5,334, 1st
Percent increase (1990-94): 6.09%, 37th
Govt. payments (1993): Less than $500,000, 50th

Construction, value of all: $328,000,000
  Per capita: $326.87, 45th
Manufactures:
  Value added: $5,149,000,000
    Per capita: $5,131.23, 25th
  Leading products: Costume jewelry, machinery, textiles, electronics
Value of nonfuel mineral production (1994): $27,000,000, 48th
Leading mineral products: Stone, sand/gravel, gemstones
Retail sales (1993): $7,593,000,000, 43rd
  Per household: $19,970, 43rd
    Percent increase (1992-93): 3.3%, 41st
Tourism revenues (1993): $1.4 bil.
Foreign exports, in total value (1994): $923,000,000, 43rd
  Per capita: $925.78, 36th
Gross state product per person (1993): $20,916.33, 26th
  Percent change (1990-93): 0%, 45th
Patents per 100,000 pop. (1993): 27.50, 13th
Public aid recipients (percent of resident pop. 1993): 8.3%, 11th
Medicaid recipients per 1,000 pop. (1993): 191.00, 2nd
Medicare recipients per 1,000 pop. (1993): 165.00, 6th

TRAVEL AND TRANSPORTATION

Motor vehicle registrations (1993): 695,000
  Per 1,000 pop.: 695.00, 42nd
Motorcycle registrations (1993): 20,000
  Per 1,000 pop.: 20.00, 19th
Licensed drivers per 1,000 pop. (1993): 675.00, 30th
Deaths from motor vehicle accidents per 100,000 pop. (1993): 7.40, 50th
Public roads & streets (1993):
  Total mileage: 6,057
    Per 1,000 pop.: 6.06, 45th
  Rural mileage: 1,334
    Per 1,000 pop.: 1.33, 50th
  Urban mileage: 4,723
    Per 1,000 pop.: 4.72, 2nd
  Interstate mileage: 70
    Per 1,000 pop.: 0.07, 47th

Annual vehicle-mi. of travel per person (1993): 7,200, 47th
Mean travel time for workers age 16+ who work away from home: 19.2 min., 35th

GOVERNMENT

Percent of voting age pop. registered (1994): 64.2%, 27th
  Percent of voting age pop. voting (1994): 50.6%, 17th
  Percent of voting age pop. voting for U.S. representatives (1994): 44.8%, 14th
State legislators, total (1995): 150, 19th
  Women members (1992): 25
    Percent of legislature: 16.7%, 27th
U.S. Congress, House members (1995): 2
  Change (1985-95): 0
Revenues (1993):
  State govt.: $3,765,000,000
    Per capita: $3,765.00, 10th
  Parimutuel & amusement taxes & lotteries, revenue per capita: $127.00, 11th
Expenditures (1993):
  State govt.: $4,176,000,000
    Per capita: $4,176.00, 3rd
Debt outstanding (1993): $5,147,000,000
  Per capita: $5,147.00, 2nd

LAWS AND REGULATIONS

Legal driving age: 18, 16 if completed driver education course
Marriage age without parental consent: 18
Divorce residence requirement: 1 yr.

ATTRACTIONS (1995)

Major symphony orchestras: 1
Major professional theater companies (nonprofit): 1
State appropriations for arts agencies per capita: $0.66, 30th
State Fair in mid-August at Richmond

SPORTS AND COMPETITION

NCAA teams (Division I): Brown Univ. Bears, Providence College Friars, Univ. of Rhode Island Rams

SOUTH CAROLINA

"South Carolina in many ways epitomizes the American South. Historically, it was central in the events that preceded the Civil War....Since the Civil War, South Carolina has endured some of the worst effects of the reconstruction era and subsequently negotiated the economic shift from agriculture to industry that has been crucial to the development of other states in the deep South."

Robert O'Brien, historian

Two of the most important battles in the history of the United States were fought in South Carolina. The British were defeated in 1780 in the Battle of King's Mountain, which was the turning point of the Revolutionary War in the South. And in 1861, Confederate batteries bombed Fort Sumter in Charleston Harbor, beginning the Civil War. The Palmetto State is the smallest in the Deep South and ranges from a lowland in the east, through sand hills, to the mountains in the west. Charleston, its first capital—much older than the nation—boasts a restored residential section which, with its historic homes, ironwork, courtyards, piazza, and gardens, is one of the country's most delightful.

SUPERLATIVES

• First European settlement on the North American coast, 1526.
• First American Protestant settlement, 1652.
• Site of the most Revolutionary battles of any state.
• First state to secede from the Union.
• First shots of the Civil War.
• Leader in vermiculite.
• First U.S. railroad designed for steam.
• Nation's first cotton mill.
• Leader in glass fiber production.
• Nation's oldest theater building—the Street Theater on Charleston's Old Dock.

MOMENTS IN HISTORY

• The short-lived settlement San Miguel de Guadalupe was founded at present-day Winyah Bay by Spanish Captain Lucas Vasquez de Ayllon in 1526. It is said to have been the first European settlement on the coast of North America.
• Near modern Silver Bluff, the destructive 1540-1541 expedition of Hernando de Soto entered present-day western South Carolina, leaving a trail of disease and misery upon its departure.
• The Parris Island settlement by Huguenots in 1652, under the leadership of Jean Ribaut, was the first Protestant settlement in America.
• Charles II granted the Carolina region to loyal friends, the Lords Proprietors, and Charles Towne was founded in 1670. The settlement was moved to its present location ten years later, and it eventually was named Charleston.
• Plantations flourished after the first importation of slaves in 1670.
• Alarmed by seizure of their lands, in 1715 the Indians attacked and massacred widely in a struggle known as the Yamassee War.
• Urged on by the French, the Cherokee began attacks on western settlements but were forced to surrender in 1761.
• Although prosperous, South Carolina resisted the despised British taxes and sent delegates to the Continental Congresses of 1774 and 1775.
• South Carolina experienced some of the fiercest fighting and suffering of the Revolutionary War, with 137 battles fought there, 103 of them without help from the other colonies.
• Francis Marion organized a guerrilla group in 1780. He became known as the "Swamp Fox" for his brilliant raids and disappearance into the swamps.

So They Say

"Our band is few, but true and tried,

Our leader frank and bold:

The British soldier trembles

When Marion's name is told."

William Cullen Bryant,
on Francis Marion

• A quickly assembled frontier force defeated the British at the Battle of King's Mountain on October 7, 1780—in a major turning point of the Revolution because it upset the British timetable.

• Another important American victory occurred on January 17, 1781, at the Battle of Cowpens.

• In December 1782, British forces withdrew from Charleston.

• On May 23, 1788, South Carolina became the eighth state.

• By 1827 state leaders were threatening to nullify U.S. laws, and it appeared that South Carolina might secede from the Union in opposition to high tariffs, but the tariff rates were lowered.

So They Say

"...they can talk and write resolutions and print threats to their heart's content. But if one drop of blood is shed there in defiance of the laws of the United States, I will hang the first man of them I can get my hands on, to the first tree I can find."

Andrew Jackson,
on nullification

• The country's divisions over slavery deepened, and on December 20, 1860, South Carolina became the first state to secede from the Union.

• On April 12, 1861, Fort Sumter in Charleston harbor was attacked. With that attack on the Union stronghold and the surrender of the fort, the Civil War had begun.

• The state suffered greatly during the war, and further suffering continued during Reconstruction until about 1876.

So They Say

"Thus began the darkest period in the State's history...from 1868 to 1874...the 'Rule of the Robbers.'...Votes in the legislature were bought. Furniture, jewelry, clothing, and groceries were purchased with public funds, while patients in the state hospital actually suffered for food, and threats were made to turn convicts out of the penitentiary because they could not be fed."

South Carolina: A Guide
to the Palmetto State

• The state constitution of 1895 deprived most of the state's blacks of the right to vote.

• World War I called 62,000 people to service from South Carolina; 2,085 died.

• Ervin David Shaw of Sumter was one of the first American pilots killed in action in World War II, when 173,642 served from South Carolina.

• During the period 1940 to 1960, the port of Charleston jumped from 57th place to 14th among the nation's ports.

• In 1975, Dr. James B. Edwards became the first Republican governor since Reconstruction days.

• The census of 1990 showed an almost 11% gain in the state's population.

• The first female student was admitted to the Citadel Military Academy in 1995, but she resigned after a short time.

THAT'S INTERESTING

• When the chief of an early Indian group died, his horse was buried alive with him. There were so many such burials that Indian Hill is known as a mountain.

• A group of Seewee Indians decided to take their grievances directly to the king of England. A pirate crew spotted their canoes at sea, and they were never heard from again.

• Corporal Jesse Gillespie was wounded, then recovered in a French hospital during World War I. Meanwhile, the U.S. Army had issued a death certificate. When he returned home he was made to sign an affidavit that he was not dead.

• On the way to a Lancaster cemetery, the body of Andrew Jackson's father was taken from bar to bar on a sled, until some mourner found it had disappeared. The body turned up in a snowbank and finally reached the intended burial place.

• Theodosia Burr Alston, Aaron Burr's daughter, was the wife of South Carolina Governor Joseph Alston. In 1812 she sailed from Charleston to New York and was never heard from again. Later, a pirate confessed that she had been made to walk the plank, but his story was never verified.

• The state's first steam locomotive produced such a hiss of steam that the fireman sat on the safety valve to reduce the noise; there was an explosion, and he was killed.

• Onlookers at Beaufort Bay thought that a man named Jones had finally reached his long-sought goal of perpetual motion, as his boat dashed about the bay. However, he had hooked a stingray, was being pulled by it, and could not cut the line.

NOTABLE NATIVES

Mary McLeod Bethune (Maysville, 1875-1955), educator. **James Francis Byrnes** (Charleston, 1879-1972), Supreme Court justice. **John Caldwell Calhoun** (Abbeville County, 1782-1850), public official/political leader. **Andrew Jackson** (Waxhaw's district, 1767-1845), U.S. president. **Henry Laurens** (Charleston, 1724-1792), political leader. **Francis (Swamp Fox) Marion** (Berkeley County, 1732?-1795), Revolutionary soldier. **Joel Roberts Poinsett** (Charleston, 1779-1851), diplomat.

GENERAL

Admitted to statehood: May 23, 1788
Origin of name: Charles I gave a large patent to Sir Robert Heath, 1619, to be called Province of Carolana, from *Carolus,* Latin name for Charles. A new patent was granted by Charles II to Earl of Clarendon and others. Divided into North and South Carolina, 1710
Capital: Columbia
Nickname: Palmetto State
Motto: *Animis Opibusque Parati*—Prepared in mind and resources; *Dum Spiro Spero*—While I breathe, I hope
Animal: White-tail deer
Bird: Carolina wren
Fish: Striped bass
Flower: Carolina (yellow) jessamine
Gem: Amethyst

Stone: Blue granite
Song: "Carolina" and "South Carolina on My Mind"
Tree: Palmetto

THE LAND

Area: 31,189 sq. mi., 40th
    Land: 30,111 sq. mi., 40th
    Water: 1,078 sq. mi., 27th
        Inland water: 1,006 sq. mi., 21st
        Coastal water: 72 sq. mi., 17th
Topography: Blue Ridge province in NW has highest peaks; piedmont lies between the mountains and the fall line; coastal plain covers two-thirds of the state.
Number of counties: 46
Geographic center: Richland, 13 mi. SE of Columbia
Length: 260 mi.; width: 200 mi.
Highest point: 3,560 ft. (Sassafras Mountain), 29th
Lowest point: sea level (Atlantic Ocean), 3rd
Mean elevation: 350 ft., 44th
Coastline: 187 mi.,1th
Shoreline: 2,876 mi., 11th

CLIMATE AND ENVIRONMENT

Temp., highest: 111 deg. on June 28, 1954, at Camden; lowest: –19 deg. on Jan. 21, 1985, at Caesar's Head
Monthly average: highest: 91.9 deg., 14th; lowest: 31.2 deg., 43rd; spread (high to low): 60.7 deg., 43rd
Hazardous waste sites (1993): 24, 15th
Endangered species: Mammals: 2—Indiana bat, West Indian manatee; birds: 3—American peregrine falcon, Wood stock, Red-cockaded woodpecker; reptiles: 3; amphibians: none; fishes: none; invertebrates: none; plants: 11

MAJOR CITIES
POPULATION, 1990
PERCENTAGE INCREASE, 1980-90

Charleston, 80,414—15.24%
Columbia, 98,052— –3.14%
Greenville, 58,282—0.07%
North Charleston, 70,218—12.39%
Spartanburg, 43,467— –0.82%

THE PEOPLE

Population (1995): 3,673,287, 26th
    Percent change (1990-95): 5.4%, 23rd

Population (2000 proj.): 3,932,000, 26th
  Percent change (1990-2000): 12.77%, 21st
Per sq. mi. (1994): 121.7, 22nd
Percent in metro. area (1992): 69.8%, 26th
Foreign born: 50,000, 34th
  Percent: 1.4%, 44th
Top three ancestries reported:
  African, 24.96%
  German, 14.34%
  Irish, 13.94%
White: 2,406,974, 69.03%, 46th
Black: 1,039,884, 29.82%, 4th
Native American: 8,246, 0.24%, 39th
Asian, Pacific Isle: 22,382, 0.64%, 40th
Other races: 9,217, 0.26%, 43rd
Hispanic origin: 30,551, 0.88%, 41st
Percent over 5 yrs. speaking language other
    than English at home: 3.5%, 45th
Percent males: 48.43%, 36th; percent females:
    51.57%, 16th
Percent never married: 26.4%, 21st
Marriages per 1,000 (1993): 14.4, 4th
Divorces per 1,000 (1993): 4.1, 31st
Median age: 32
Under 5 years (1994): 7.48%, 18th
Under 18 years (1994): 25.98%, 25th
65 years & older (1994): 11.9%, 36th
Percent increase among the elderly (1990-94):
    9.59%, 11th

OF VITAL IMPORTANCE

Live births per 1,000 pop. (1993): 14.8, 24th
Infant mortality rate per 1,000 births (1992):
    10.4, 4th
  Rate for blacks (1990): 17.1, 16th
  Rate for whites (1990): 8.3, 14th
Births to unmarried women, % of total
    (1992): 35.5%, 6th
Births to teenage mothers, % of total (1992):
    16.6%, 9th
Abortions (1992): 12,190, 30th
  Rate per 1,000 women 14-44 years old:
    14.2, 36th
  Percent change (1988-92): –15%, 38th
Average lifetime (1979-81): 71.58, 50th
Deaths per 1,000 pop. (1993): 8.6, 33rd
Causes of death per 100,000 pop.:
  Accidents & adverse effects (1992): 43.0,
    12th
  Atherosclerosis (1991): 4.1, 46th
  Cancer (1991): 194.1, 38th
  Cerebrovascular diseases (1992): 69.2, 6th
  Chronic liver diseases & cirrhosis (1991):
    11.0, 11th

Chronic obstructive pulmonary diseases
    (1992): 34.9, 33rd
Diabetes mellitus (1992): 21.7, 19th
Diseases of heart (1992): 268.0, 31st
Pneumonia, flu (1991): 23.0, 46th
Suicide (1992): 12.9, 17th

KEEPING WELL

Active nonfederal physicians per 100,000 pop.
    (1993): 173, 39th
Dentists per 100,000 (1991): 42, 46th
Nurses per 100,000 (1992): 584, 43rd
Hospitals per 100,000 (1993): 1.87, 33rd
  Admissions per 1,000 (1993): 108.60,
    34th
  Occupancy rate per 100 beds (1993): 67.3,
    14th
  Average cost per patient per day (1993):
    $838, 27th
  Average cost per stay (1993): $5,955,
    20th
  Average stay (1992): 6.7 days, 40th
AIDS cases (adult, 1993): 1,470; per 100,000:
    40.5, 12th
HIV infection, not yet AIDS (1993): 4,978
Other notifiable diseases:
  Gonorrhea: 402.2, 9th
  Measles: 0.1, 49th
  Syphilis: 62.5, 11th
  Tuberculosis: 13.0, 9th
Pop. without health insur. (1991-93): 15.8%,
    16th

HOUSEHOLDS BY TYPE

Total households (1994): 1,337,000
  Percent change (1990-94): 6.3%, 16th
  Per 1,000 pop.: 364.90, 41st
  Percent of households 65 yrs. and over:
    20.94%, 35th
  Persons per household (1994): 2.66, 14th
Family households: 928,206
  Percent of total: 73.78%, 4th
Nonfamily households: 329,838
  Percent of total: 26.22%, 48th
Pop. living in group quarters: 116,543
  Percent of pop.: 3.34%, 12th

LIVING QUARTERS

Total housing units: 1,424,155
  Persons per unit: 2.45, 15th
Occupied housing units: 1,258,044
  Percent of total units: 88.34%, 33rd
  Persons per unit: 2.50, 34th

Percent of units with over 1 person per room: 4.06%, 15th

Owner-occupied units: 878,704
Percent of total units: 61.70%, 13th
Percent of occupied units: 69.85%, 12th
Persons per unit: 2.75, 21st
Median value: $61,1000, 31st

Renter-occupied units: 379,340
Percent of total units: 26.64%, 41st
Percent of occupied units: 30.15%, 40th
Persons per unit: 2.25, 39th
Median contract rent: $276, 37th
Rental vacancy rate: 11.5%, 9th

Mobile home, trailer & other as a percent of occupied housing units: 20.14%, 3rd

Persons in emergency shelters for homeless persons: 973, 0.028%, 48th

Persons visible in street locations: 102, 0.0029%, 38th

Persons in shelters for abused women: 87, 0.0025%, 48th

Nursing home population: 18,228, 0.52%, 44th

CRIME INDEX PER 100,000 (1992-93)

Total reported: 5,903.4, 13th
Violent: 1,023.4, 6th
Murder and nonnegligent manslaughter: 10.3, 14th
Aggravated assault: 773.4, 3rd
Robbery: 187.3, 18th
Forcible rape: 52.3, 9th
Property: 4,880.0, 17th
Burglary: 1,309.2, 8th
Larceny, theft: 3,226.8, 17th
Motor vehicle theft: 344.0, 30th
Drug abuse violations (1990): 430.2, 9th
Child-abuse rate per 1,000 children (1993): 11.83, 34th

TEACHING AND LEARNING

Pop. 3 and over enrolled in school: 913,010
Percent of pop.: 27.4%, 23rd
Public elementary & secondary schools (1992-93): 1,104
Total enrollment (1992): 633,419
Percent of total pop.: 17.58%, 21st
Teachers (1992): 37,295
Percent of pop.: 1.04%, 24th
Pupil/teacher ratio (fall 1992): 17.0, 21st
Teachers' avg. salary (1992-93): $31,392, 35th
Expenditure per capita (1990-91): $3,138.01, 36th

Expenditure per pupil (1991-92): $4,436, 39th
Percent of graduates taking SAT (1993): 61%, 15th
Mean SAT verbal scores: 396, 51st
Mean SAT mathematical scores: 442, 50th
Percent of graduates taking ACT (1995): 14%, 35th
Mean ACT scores: 19.1, 49th
Percent of pop. over 25 completing:
Less than 9th grade: 13.6%, 9th
High school: 68.3%, 45th
College degree(s): 16.6%, 42nd
Higher education, institutions (1993-94): 59
Enrollment (1992): 171,443
Percent of pop.: 4.77%, 45th
White non-Hispanic (1992): 128,445
Percent of enroll.: 74.92%, 37th
Black non-Hispanic (1992): 36,268
Percent of enroll.: 21.15%, 6th
Hispanic (1992): 1,310
Percent of enroll.: 0.76%, 43rd
Asian/Pacific Islander (1992): 1,917
Percent of enroll.: 1.12%, 41st
American Indian/AK native (1992): 397
Percent of enroll.: 0.23%, 49th
Nonresident alien (1992): 3,106
Percent of enroll.: 1.81%, 44th
Female (1992): 97,770
Percent of enroll.: 57.03%, 6th
Pub. institutions (1993-94): 33
Enrollment (1992): 145,580
Percent of enroll.: 84.91%, 21st
Private institutions (1993-94): 26
Enrollment (1992): 25,863
Percent of enroll.: 15.09%, 31st
Tuition, public institution (avg., 1993-94): $6,203, 21st
Tuition, private institution (avg., 1993-94): $11,617, 30th
Public library systems: 40
Books & serial vol. per capita: 1.49, 51st
Govt. expenditure per capita: $10.14, 39th

LAW ENFORCEMENT, COURTS, AND PRISONS

Police protection, corrections, judicial and legal functions expenditures (1992): $869,000,000
Per capita: $241, 29th
Police per 10,000 pop. (1993): 20.55, 25th

Prisoners (state & fed.) per 100,000 pop. (1993): 5,152.62, 4th
  Percent change (1992-93): 0.3%, 39th
Death penalty: yes, by electrocution
  Under sentence of death (1993): 47, 16th
  Executed (1993): 0

RELIGION, NUMBER AND PERCENT OF POPULATION

Agnostic: 5,133—0.20%, 42nd
Buddhist: 2,567—0.10%, 17th
Christian: 2,386,841—93.00%, 6th
Hindu: NA
Jewish: 7,700—0.30%, 35th
Muslim: 5,133—0.20%, 13th
Unitarian: NA
Other: 30,798—1.20%, 29th
None: 82,128—3.20%, 45th
Refused to answer: 46,197—1.80%, 34th

MAKING A LIVING

Personal income per capita (1994): $17,695, 45th
  Percent increase (1993-94): 4.9%, 26th
Disposable personal income per capita (1994): $15,709, 43rd
Median income of households (1993): $26,053, 45th
Percent of pop. below poverty level (1993): 18.7%, 9th
  Percent 65 and over (1990): 20.5%, 7th
Expenditure for energy per person (1992): $1,869, 29th

ECONOMY

Civilian labor force (1994): 1,828,000
  Percent of total pop.: 49.89%, 35th
  Percent 65 and over (1990): 2.55%, 32nd
  Percent female: 47.76%, 6th
Percent job growth (1980-90): 27.41%, 16th
Major employer industries (1994):
  Agriculture: 38,000—2.3%, 29th
  Construction: 83,000—4.9%, 14th
  Finance, insurance, & real estate: 81,000—4.8%, 34th
  Government: 257,000—15.3%, 26th
  Manufacturing: 399,000—23.7%, 3rd
  Service: 289,000—17.1%, 48th
  Trade: 328,000—19.4%, 14th
  Transportation, communications, public utilities: 73,000—4.3%, 42nd
Unemployment rate (1994): 6.29%, 15th
  Male: 5.6%, 26th
  Female: 7.0%, 7th

Total businesses (1991): 103,796
  New business incorps. (1991): 5,700
    Percent of total businesses: 5.49%, 31st
  Business failures (1991): 415
    Percent of total businesses: 0.40%
Agriculture farm income:
  Marketing (1993): $1,221,000,000, 36th
    Average per farm: $50,875.00, 44th
  Leading products (1993): Tobacco, broilers, cattle, greenhouse
  Average value land & build. per acre (1994): $923, 27th
    Percent increase (1990-94): 1.54%, 44th
  Govt. payments (1993): $103,000,000, 29th
    Average per farm: $4,291.67, 25th
Construction, value of all: $2,503,000,000
  Per capita: $717.87, 17th
Manufactures:
  Value added: $21,075,000,000
    Per capita: $6,044.39, 12th
  Leading products: Textiles, chemicals and chemical products, machinery and fabricated metal products, apparel and related product
Value of nonfuel mineral production (1994): $415,000,000, 29th
Leading mineral products: Cement, stone, clays
Retail sales (1993): $27,914,000,000, 26th
  Per household: $20,955, 38th
    Percent increase (1992-93): 7.9%, 18th
Tourism revenues (1992): $6.5 bil.
Foreign exports, in total value (1994): $5,236,000,000, 23rd
  Per capita: $1,429.04, 20th
Gross state product per person (1993): $18,554.96, 44th
  Percent change (1990-93): 3.13%, 24th
Patents per 100,000 pop. (1993): 13.80, 32nd
Public aid recipients (percent of resident pop. 1993): 6.8%, 25th
Medicaid recipients per 1,000 pop. (1993): 129.48, 16th
Medicare recipients per 1,000 pop. (1993): 132.51, 35th

TRAVEL AND TRANSPORTATION

Motor vehicle registrations (1993): 2,684,000
  Per 1,000 pop.: 739.39, 34th
Motorcycle registrations (1993): 34,000
  Per 1,000 pop.: 9.37, 43rd

Licensed drivers per 1,000 pop. (1993): 669.70, 32nd

Deaths from motor vehicle accidents per 100,000 pop. (1993): 23.28, 7th

Public roads & streets (1993):
  Total mileage: 64,158
    Per 1,000 pop.: 17.67, 26th
  Rural mileage: 53,637
    Per 1,000 pop.: 14.78, 26th
  Urban mileage: 10,521
    Per 1,000 pop.: 2.90, 34th
  Interstate mileage: 810
    Per 1,000 pop.: 0.22, 22nd

Annual vehicle-mi. of travel per person (1993): 9,945, 16th

Mean travel time for workers age 16+ who work away from home: 20.5 min., 28th

GOVERNMENT

Percent of voting age pop. registered (1994): 60.8%, 35th
  Percent of voting age pop. voting (1994): 45.2%, 30th
  Percent of voting age pop. voting for U.S. representatives (1994): 31.7%, 43rd

State legislators, total (1995): 170, 15th
  Women members (1992): 22
    Percent of legislature: 12.9%, 36th

U.S. Congress, House members (1995): 6
  Change (1985-95): 0

Revenues (1993):
  State govt.: $10,637,000,000
    Per capita: $2,930.30, 28th

Parimutuel & amusement taxes & lotteries, revenue per capita: $6.61, 39th

Expenditures (1993):
  State govt.: $10,388,000,000
    Per capita: $2,861.71, 24th

Debt outstanding (1993): $4,901,000,000
  Per capita: $1,350.14, 24th

LAWS AND REGULATIONS

Legal driving age: 16

Marriage age without parental consent: 18

Divorce residence requirement: 1 yr., for qualifications check local statutes

ATTRACTIONS (1995)

Major opera companies: 1

Major symphony orchestras: 2

State appropriations for arts agencies per capita: $0.94, 18th

State Fair in mid-October at Columbia

SPORTS AND COMPETITION

NCAA teams (Division I): Charleston Southern Univ. Buccaneers, The Citadel Bulldogs, Clemson Univ. Tigers, College of Charleston Cougars, Coastal Carolina Univ. Chanticleers, Furman Univ. Paladins, South Carolina State Univ. Bulldogs, Univ. of South Carolina Fighting Gamecocks, Winthrop College Eagles, Wofford College Terriers

NFL football teams: Carolina Panthers, Carolinas Stadium (NC)

SOUTH DAKOTA

"Hard work is a legacy of the generations who settled the prairie, broke the soil, built the sod houses, fought the draughts and grasshoppers and penny-a-pound price for their products. It is a legacy that even those of us who leave carry with us. All of this work has produced what may be the largest collection of powerful hands in the world."

Tom Brokaw, newscaster

Visitors flock to South Dakota to see the world-famed "rock stars," the presidential faces of the Mount Rushmore Memorial. Dakota is a land where "the great lakes" were created on barren prairie and where the Homestake Mine has produced more gold than any other worldwide. The history of South Dakota reads like an adventure story, filled with daring fur trappers, battles between settlers and Indians, and such colorful characters as Calamity Jane, General George A. Custer, Sitting Bull, and Wild Bill Hickock. The state continues to gain as a center of financial and other service industries.

SUPERLATIVES

• Highest point east of the Rockies—Harney Peak.
• Longest nonnavigable river—James River.
• World's largest portrait busts—those on Mt. Rushmore.

So They Say

"This memorial will crown the height of land between the Rocky Mountains and the Atlantic seaboard, where coming generations may view it for all time ....On this towering wall...is to be inscribed a memorial which will represent some of the outstanding events of American history..."

President Calvin Coolidge, dedicating the Mount Rushmore Memorial

---

• World record total production of a single gold mine—Homestake Mine.
• Leader in bentonite production.

MOMENTS IN HISTORY

• On their expedition of 1743, brothers François and Louis-Joseph La Vérendrye are thought to have visited what is now South Dakota. On a hill overlooking the Missouri River, they buried a lead plate claiming the region for France.

So They Say

"Placed by the Chevalier de La Verendrye, Lo Jost Verendrye, Louis La Londette A Miotte, the 30th March 1743."

Legend on the lead plate left by the Vérendrye brothers, rediscovered February 16, 1913

• In 1794, Jean Baptiste Trudeau established a trading company in present-day Charles Mix County.
• On August 22, 1804, the great Meriwether Lewis and William Clark expedition camped at present-day Elk Point. The election they held for sergeant was the first in the entire Northwest.

So They Say

"This scenery already rich, pleasing and beautiful was still farther heightened by immense herds of buffalo, deer, elk and antelopes...I do not think I exaggerate when I estimate the number of buffalo, which could be comprehended at one view to amount to 3,000."

Meriwether Lewis

• Fort Pierre Chouteau (Pierre), founded in 1831, was the oldest permanently occupied European settlement in the state.

• The first "Puffing Canoe" (steamboat), the *Yellowstone*, reached Fort Pierre in 1831.

• When Father Pierre Jean de Smet visited the Black Hills in 1848, an Indian chief offered him a bag of glittering powder, which he recognized as gold but did not disclose to anyone, fearing for Indian rights.

So They Say

"Put it away and show it to nobody."

Father Pierre Jean de Smet, on being offered a bag of gold dust

---

• Dakota Territory was created on March 2, 1861.

• During the Civil War the Santee Sioux began an uprising called the War of the Outbreak, settled in 1865 at a great council with the Indians near present-day Pierre.

• Fort Sisseton was established in 1864 at the unheard of cost of $2 million.

• The great military expedition of George Armstrong Custer entered the Black Hills in 1874, and gold was discovered by the party. A Chicago newspaper carried the news, and the rush for gold was on.

• By midsummer 1876, Dead Tree Gulch (later Deadwood) harbored 25,000 gold seekers, squatters on Indian lands. Deadwood became a rip-roaring prospecting town.

• On August 2, 1876, Wild Bill Hickock was killed at Deadwood.

• The winter of 1880-1881 was the worst in history, followed by great floods, sweeping away villages.

• On the same day, November 2, 1889, South Dakota became a state along with North Dakota. President Benjamin Harrison never revealed which state he named first.

• Famed Chief Sitting Bull was killed by police action in 1890 at what is now Little Eagle.

• On December 28, 1890, the infamous "battle" at Wounded Knee resulted in the deaths of more than 200 Sioux men, women, and children, slain by government forces after an Indian shot an officer. This proved to be the country's last large-scale action between troops and Indians.

• After a contest between Mitchell and Pierre, the latter was chosen state capital by a vote in 1904.

• World War I called 32,719 people from South Dakota into service. It was noted that men from the state had the best health record of all who served.

• The visit of President Calvin Coolidge to the Black Hills captured world attention. On August 10, 1927, President Coolidge dedicated the unfinished Mount Rushmore Memorial. His speech there was said by some to have been the finest of a career not noted for public eloquence.

• The Great Depression was made worse by a terrible drought from 1933 through 1936. The Sioux planned to revive their rain dance, but no one remembered it.

• With the increase in gold prices in 1933, gold mining returned to the Black Hills.

• In 1948, South Dakota became the nation's leading gold producer.

• The disastrous flood of 1973 at Rapid City killed nearly 250 persons.

• In 1973, Indians occupied Wounded Knee in protest against the massacre of unarmed Sioux in that 1890 battle.

• A 1980 Supreme Court ruling ordered the United States to pay the Sioux Indians of South Dakota more than $100 million in compensation for the seizure of their lands in the 19th century.

• In the early 1980s, Citicorp moved its credit card operation to Sioux Falls, and other business followed, bringing many new jobs to the state.

• In 1992 federal agents seized a priceless tyrannosaurus rex skeleton from fossil collectors, claiming it had been illegally removed from U.S. land.

THAT'S INTERESTING

• In the floods of 1881, a church at Green Islands was swept away intact. The story was told that it was seen floating down the river with its bell tolling.

• During the skirmish at the murder of Sitting Bull, his horse performed many of the tricks his owner had taught him as they traveled with Buffalo Bill's Wild West Show.

• On his visit to the Black Hills, President Calvin Coolidge gained a reputation as a golfer. He did not know that the greens had been altered for his benefit, so as to slope toward the holes.

• The Nystrom Bank at Wall did not close during Franklin D. Roosevelt's 1933 bank holiday—the only one in the country not to. No one had thought to notify the owner.

NOTABLE NATIVES

Crazy Horse (Oglala Sioux tribal site, 1849?-1877), Indian leader. **Hubert Horatio Humphrey** (Wallace, 1911-1978), U.S. vice president. **Ernest Orlando Lawrence** (Canton, 1901-1958), physicist. **George Stanley McGovern** (Avon, 1922-), public official. **Sitting Bull** (Hunkpapa Sioux tribal site on Grand River, 1831?-1890), Indian leader.

GENERAL

Admitted to statehood: November 2, 1889
Origin of name: From the Sioux for "friend or ally"
Capital: Pierre
Nickname: Coyote State, Mount Rushmore State
Motto: Under God, the people rule
Animal: Coyote
Bird: Chinese ring-necked pheasant
Insect: Honeybee
Fish: Walleye
Flower: Pasqueflower
Gem: Fairburn agate
Mineral: Rose quartz
Stone: Black Hills gold
Song: "Hail, South Dakota"
Tree: Black Hills spruce

THE LAND

Area: 77,121 sq. mi., 17th
  Land: 75,896 sq. mi., 16th
  Water: 1,225 sq. mi., 23rd
  Inland water: 1,225 sq. mi., 16th
Topography: Prairie plains in the E; rolling hills of the Great Plains in the W; the Black Hills, rising 3,500 ft. in the SW corner
Number of counties: 67
Geographic center: Hughes, 8 mi. NE of Pierre
Length: 380 mi.; width: 210 mi.
Highest point: 7,242 ft. (Harney Peak), 15th
Lowest point: 966 ft. (Big Stone Lake), 46th
Mean elevation: 2,200 ft., 13th

CLIMATE AND ENVIRONMENT

Temp., highest: 120 deg. on July 5, 1936, at Gannvalley; lowest: –58 deg. on Feb. 17, 1936, at McIntosh

Monthly average: highest: 86.5 deg., 31st; lowest: 1.9 deg., 4th; spread (high to low): 84.6 deg., 5th
Hazardous waste sites (1993): 4, 45th
Endangered species: Mammals: 1—Black-footed ferret; birds: 4—Whooping crane, Eskimo curlew, American peregrine falcon, Least tern; reptiles: none; amphibians: none; fishes. 1; invertebrates: none; plants: none

MAJOR CITIES
POPULATION, 1990
PERCENTAGE INCREASE, 1980-90

Aberdeen, 24,927— –3.57%
Brookings, 16,270—8.82%
Rapid City, 54,523—17.27%
Sioux Falls, 100,814—23.94%
Watertown, 17,592—12.42%

THE PEOPLE

Population (1995): 729,034, 45th
  Percent change (1990-95): 4.7%, 26th
Population (2000 proj.): 770,000, 45th
  Percent change (1990-2000): 10.63%, 24th
Per sq. mi. (1994): 9.5, 47th
Percent in metro. area (1992): 32.6%, 46th
Foreign born: 8,000, 50th
  Percent: 1.1%, 46th
Top three ancestries reported:
  German, 51.01%
  Norwegian, 15.23%
  Irish, 12.64%
White: 637,515, 91.60%, 16th
Black: 3,258, 0.47%, 47th
Native American: 50,575, 7.27%, 4th
Asian, Pacific Isle: 3,123, 0.45%, 50th
Other races: 1,533, 0.22%, 44th
Hispanic origin: 5,252, 0.75%, 43rd
Percent over 5 yrs. speaking language other than English at home: 6.5%, 29th
Percent males: 49.21%, 14th; percent females: 50.79%, 38th
Percent never married: 24.4%, 33rd
Marriages per 1,000 (1993): 10.4, 11th
Divorces per 1,000 (1993): 4.0, 33rd
Median age: 32.5
Under 5 years (1994): 7.49%, 17th
Under 18 years (1994): 28.85%, 5th
65 years & older (1994): 14.7%, 8th
Percent increase among the elderly (1990-94): 2.61%, 48th

OF VITAL IMPORTANCE

Live births per 1,000 pop. (1993): 15.1, 19th
Infant mortality rate per 1,000 births (1992): 9.3, 16th
  Rate for blacks (1990): 7.4, 46th
  Rate for whites (1990): 8.6, 9th
Births to unmarried women, % of total (1992): 26.6%, 31st
Births to teenage mothers, % of total (1992): 11.4%, 31st
Abortions (1992): 1,040, 50th
  Rate per 1,000 women 14-44 years old: 6.8, 50th
  Percent change (1988-92): 19%, 2nd
Average lifetime (1979-81): 74.97, 15th
Deaths per 1,000 pop. (1993): 9.6, 13th
Causes of death per 100,000 pop.:
  Accidents & adverse effects (1992): 42.9, 13th
  Atherosclerosis (1991): 9.7, 8th
  Cancer (1991): 222.0, 14th
  Cerebrovascular diseases (1992): 67.9, 7th
  Chronic liver diseases & cirrhosis (1991): 8.3, 37th
  Chronic obstructive pulmonary diseases (1992): 42.5, 11th
  Diabetes mellitus (1992): 23.2, 10th
  Diseases of heart (1992): 323.8, 11th
  Pneumonia, flu (1991): 44.4, 1st
  Suicide (1992): 11.2, 39th

KEEPING WELL

Active nonfederal physicians per 100,000 pop. (1993): 156, 45th
Dentists per 100,000 (1991): 45, 42nd
Nurses per 100,000 (1992): 973, 4th
Hospitals per 100,000 (1993): 7.07, 1st
  Admissions per 1,000 (1993): 131.62, 14th
  Occupancy rate per 100 beds (1993): 60.6, 30th
  Average cost per patient per day (1993): $506, 50th
  Average cost per stay (1993): $5,052, 43rd
  Average stay (1992): 12.4 days, 5th
AIDS cases (adult, 1993): 29; per 100,000: 4.1, 48th
HIV infection, not yet AIDS (1993): 125
Other notifiable diseases:
  Gonorrhea: 44.4, 42nd
  Measles: 3.3, 29th
  Syphilis: 1.0, 49th
  Tuberculosis: 2.0, 46th
Pop. without health insur. (1991-93): 12.7%, 25th

HOUSEHOLDS BY TYPE

Total households (1994): 265,000
  Percent change (1990-94): 2.1%, 40th
  Per 1,000 pop.: 367.55, 36th
  Percent of households 65 yrs. and over: 25.66%, 5th
  Persons per household (1994): 2.63, 19th
Family households: 180,306
  Percent of total: 69.61%, 33rd
Nonfamily households: 78,728
  Percent of total: 30.39%, 19th
Pop. living in group quarters: 25,841
  Percent of pop.: 3.71%, 6th

LIVING QUARTERS

Total housing units: 292,436
  Persons per unit: 2.38, 30th
Occupied housing units: 259,034
  Percent of total units: 88.58%, 32nd
  Persons per unit: 2.53, 24th
  Percent of units with over 1 person per room: 2.96%, 26th
Owner-occupied units: 171,161
  Percent of total units: 58.53%, 27th
  Percent of occupied units: 66.08%, 32nd
  Persons per unit: 2.71, 29th
  Median value: $45,200, 50th
Renter-occupied units: 87,873
  Percent of total units: 30.05%, 21st
  Percent of occupied units: 33.92%, 21st
  Persons per unit: 2.34, 27th
  Median contract rent: $242, 46th
  Rental vacancy rate: 7.3%, 38th
Mobile home, trailer & other as a percent of occupied housing units: 13.21%, 20th
Persons in emergency shelters for homeless persons: 396, 0.057%, 18th
Persons visible in street locations: 71, 0.0102%, 20th
Persons in shelters for abused women: 41, 0.0059%, 13th
Nursing home population: 9,356, 1.34%, 1st

CRIME INDEX PER 100,000 (1992-93)

Total reported: 2,958.2, 48th
  Violent: 208.4, 45th
    Murder and nonnegligent manslaughter: 3.4, 42nd
    Aggravated assault: 145.6, 43rd
    Robbery: 15.0, 49th
    Forcible rape: 44.5, 17th
  Property: 2,749.8, 49th
    Burglary: 549.2, 49th

Larceny, theft: 2,086.0, 47th
Motor vehicle theft: 114.5, 51st
Drug abuse violations (1990): 61.4, 51st
Child-abuse rate per 1,000 children (1993):
11.38, 36th

TEACHING AND LEARNING

Pop. 3 and over enrolled in school: 185,246
Percent of pop.: 27.9%, 18th
Public elementary & secondary schools (1992-
93): 733
Total enrollment (1992): 134,573
Percent of total pop.: 19.01%, 9th
Teachers (1992): 8,787
Percent of pop.: 1.24%, 5th
Pupil/teacher ratio (fall 1992): 15.3, 39th
Teachers' avg. salary (1992-93): $24,918,
51st
Expenditure per capita (1990-91):
$2,949.43, 41st
Expenditure per pupil (1991-92): $4,173,
43rd
Percent of graduates taking SAT (1993): 6%,
46th
Mean SAT verbal scores: 502, 3rd
Mean SAT mathematical scores: 558, 3rd
Percent of graduates taking ACT (1995):
68%, 6th
Mean ACT scores: 21.2, 20th
Percent of pop. over 25 completing:
Less than 9th grade: 13.4%, 11th
High school: 77.1%, 24th
College degree(s): 17.2%, 39th
Higher education, institutions (1993-94): 20
Enrollment (1992): 37,596
Percent of pop.: 5.30%, 32nd
White non-Hispanic (1992): 33,998
Percent of enroll.: 90.43%, 9th
Black non-Hispanic (1992): 290
Percent of enroll.: 0.77%, 47th
Hispanic (1992): 146
Percent of enroll.: 0.39%, 50th
Asian/Pacific Islander (1992): 270
Percent of enroll.: 0.72%, 48th
American Indian/AK native (1992): 2,063
Percent of enroll.: 5.49%, 5th
Nonresident alien (1992): 829
Percent of enroll.: 2.21%, 34th
Female (1992): 20,905
Percent of enroll.: 55.60%, 19th
Pub. institutions (1993-94): 9
Enrollment (1992): 30,346
Percent of enroll.: 80.72%, 32nd
Private institutions (1993-94): 11

Enrollment (1992): 7,250
Percent of enroll.: 19.28%, 20th
Tuition, public institution (avg., 1993-94):
$4,874, 47th
Tuition, private institution (avg., 1993-94):
$10,927, 36th
Public library systems: 117
Books & serial vol. per capita: 4.13, 5th
Govt. expenditure per capita: $14.81, 26th

LAW ENFORCEMENT, COURTS, AND PRISONS

Police protection, corrections, judicial and
legal functions expenditures (1992):
$121,000,000
Per capita: $170, 46th
Police per 10,000 pop. (1993): 13.23, 51st
Prisoners (state & fed.) per 100,000 pop.
(1993): 2,153.95, 38th
Percent change (1992-93): 4.4%, 29th
Death penalty: yes, by lethal injection
Under sentence of death (1993): 2, 33rd
Executed (1993): 0

RELIGION, NUMBER AND PERCENT OF POPULATION

Agnostic: 4,975—1.00%, 10th
Buddhist: NA
Christian: 467,690—94.00%, 4th
Hindu: NA
Jewish: 995—0.20%, 40th
Muslim: 1,491—0.30%, 9th
Unitarian: 1,493—0.30%, 15th
Other: 3,483—0.70%, 43rd
None: 12,439—2.50%, 48th
Refused to answer: 4,975—1.00%, 47th

MAKING A LIVING

Personal income per capita (1994): $19,577,
36th
Percent increase (1993-94): 9.5%, 2nd
Disposable personal income per capita (1994):
$17,751, 30th
Median income of households (1993):
$27,737, 38th
Percent of pop. below poverty level (1993):
14.2%, 22nd
Percent 65 and over (1990): 15.5%, 15th
Expenditure for energy per person (1992):
$1,818, 33rd

ECONOMY

Civilian labor force (1994): 374,000
Percent of total pop.: 51.87%, 21st

Percent 65 and over (1990): 5.28%, 1st
Percent female: 46.79%, 18th
Percent job growth (1980-90): 15.30%, 36th
Major employer industries (1994):
  Agriculture: 39,000—11.3%, 2nd
  Construction: 13,000—3.8%, 36th
  Finance, insurance, & real estate: 15,000—4.4%, 38th
  Government: 60,000—17.4%, 16th
  Manufacturing: 40,000—11.4%, 39th
  Service: 64,000—18.5%, 42nd
  Trade: 67,000—19.4%, 14th
  Transportation, communications, public utilities: 13,000—3.7%, 50th
Unemployment rate (1994): 3.21%, 50th
  Male: 3.1%, 50th
  Female: 3.6%, 47th
Total businesses (1991): 39,038
  New business incorps. (1991): 1,040
    Percent of total businesses: 2.66%, 50th
  Business failures (1991): 271
    Percent of total businesses: 0.69%
Agriculture farm income:
  Marketing (1993): $3,320,000,000, 22nd
    Average per farm: $94,857.14, 17th
  Leading products (1993): Cattle, wheat, hogs, corn
  Average value land & build. per acre (1994): $388, 43rd
    Percent increase (1990-94): 18.29%, 16th
  Govt. payments (1993): $432,000,000, 11th
    Average per farm: $12,342.86, 7th
Construction, value of all: $363,000,000
  Per capita: $521.55, 27th
Manufactures:
  Value added: $1,630,000,000
    Per capita: $2,341.94, 44th
  Leading products: Food and food products, machinery, electric and electronic equipment
Value of nonfuel mineral production (1994): $322,000,000, 36th
Leading mineral products: Gold, cement, petroleum
Retail sales (1993): $6,276,000,000, 46th
  Per household: $23,330, 14th
    Percent increase (1992-93): 10.5%, 5th
Tourism revenues (1994): $1.24 bil.
Foreign exports, in total value (1994): $295,000,000, 51st
  Per capita: $409.15, 48th

Gross state product per person (1993): $19,943.02, 35th
  Percent change (1990-93): 7.69%, 3rd
Patents per 100,000 pop. (1993): 6.10, 50th
Public aid recipients (percent of resident pop. 1993): 4.5%, 45th
Medicaid recipients per 1,000 pop. (1993): 97.09, 40th
Medicare recipients per 1,000 pop. (1993): 159.50, 8th

TRAVEL AND TRANSPORTATION

Motor vehicle registrations (1993): 808,000
  Per 1,000 pop.: 1,120.67, 2nd
Motorcycle registrations (1993): 26,000
  Per 1,000 pop.: 36.06, 3rd
Licensed drivers per 1,000 pop. (1993): 703.19, 19th
Deaths from motor vehicle accidents per 100,000 pop. (1993): 19.42, 20th
Public roads & streets (1993):
  Total mileage: 83,305
    Per 1,000 pop.: 115.54, 2nd
  Rural mileage: 81,445
    Per 1,000 pop.: 112.96, 2nd
  Urban mileage: 1,860
    Per 1,000 pop.: 2.58, 43rd
  Interstate mileage: 678
    Per 1,000 pop.: 0.94, 4th
Annual vehicle-mi. of travel per person (1993): 10,264, 12th
Mean travel time for workers age 16+ who work away from home: 13.8 min., 50th

GOVERNMENT

Percent of voting age pop. registered (1994): 75.4%, 5th
  Percent of voting age pop. voting (1994): 63.9%, 1st
  Percent of voting age pop. voting for U.S. representatives (1994): 58.6%, 1st
State legislators, total (1995): 105, 39th
  Women members (1992): 26
    Percent of legislature: 24.8%, 10th
U.S. Congress, House members (1995): 1
  Change (1985-95): 0
Revenues (1993):
  State govt.: $1,942,000,000
    Per capita: $2,693.48, 37th
  Parimutuel & amusement taxes & lotteries, revenue per capita: $108.18, 18th

Expenditures (1993):
  State govt.: $1,686,000,000
    Per capita: $2,338.42, 43rd
  Debt outstanding (1993): $1,818,000,000
    Per capita: $2,521.50, 11th

LAWS AND REGULATIONS

Legal driving age: 16
Marriage age without parental consent: 18
Divorce residence requirement: For qualifications check local statutes

ATTRACTIONS (1995)

State appropriations for arts agencies per capita: $0.62, 32nd
State Fair in late August–September at Huron

SPORTS AND COMPETITION

NCAA teams (Division II): Augustana College Vikings, Northern State Univ. Wolves, South Dakota State Univ. Jackrabbits, Univ. of South Dakota Coyotes

TENNESSEE

> "With his good tempered easiness of manners, the Tennessean has democratic feeling of equality....Whether of farm, mountain or city, he is like the Tennessee farmer, who, after hearing Martin Van Buren speak, stepped up, took the President's hand and invited him 'to come out and r'ar around with the boys.' "
>
> Federal Writers' Project, Tennessee

Tennessee's borders touch eight other states, a record that is tied only by Missouri. Renowned for its scenery and natural wonders, Tennessee also has distinction in many other fields. In music it is known as the "Birthplace of the Blues" and the home of Elvis Presley. Nashville, with its Grand Ole Opry and its many recording studios, is the country music capital of the United States. The land in Tennessee slopes from its impressive mountains in the east to its lowlands along the Mississippi River in the west. The state has a long military tradition, and its famous military figures include John Sevier in the Revolutionary War, Andrew Jackson in the War of 1812, and Alvin C. York in World War I. More Civil War battles were fought in Tennessee than in any other state except for Virginia.

SUPERLATIVES

• Claims the greatest variety of birds in the United States.
• First in U.S. aluminum production.
• Leader in diverse hardwood products.
• The nation's largest, oldest, and most frequently visited national military park—Chickamauga-Chattanooga.
• Called "Birthplace of the Blues"—Memphis.
• Country music capital—Nashville.

MOMENTS IN HISTORY

• In April 1541, the great party of Spanish explorer Hernando de Soto reached the area of present-day Memphis and perhaps other Tennessee points.
• In 1673, Father Jacques Marquette and Louis Jolliet were greeted by Indians of the Memphis area, and in the same year, James Needham and Gabriel Arthur explored East Tennessee.

• Robert Cavelier, Sieur de La Salle, built primitive Fort Prudhomme in 1682.
• Spain, England, and France all claimed the region, but British interests seemed to prevail. In 1757, Fort Loudoun, near present-day Knoxville, was completed.
• In 1763 the French gave up all claims to the region.
• Defying a British ban on settlement, settlers arrived. Washington County was proclaimed, and Jonesboro was laid out in 1779 as its county seat, the oldest permanent European settlement in what is now Tennessee.
• No formal battles of the Revolution occurred in what is now Tennessee, but mountain men from the eastern section took an important part in the 1780 Battle of King's Mountain in northwestern South Carolina.
• In 1780, Fort Nashborough (Nashville) was founded.
• Ignored by the central government, settlers in 1784 in Jonesboro established what they called the (never-recognized) State of Franklin.

So They Say

Neglected by the central government, settlers met at Jonesboro in 1784, and three counties in present Tennessee attempted to form a new state, called the State of Franklin. They adopted a constitution, elected a governor and continued for four years until the action was repealed.

The Enchantment of Tennessee

• In 1790, North Carolina gave up its claim to the region, and the federal government established a territory including present-day Tennessee.
• Major Indian troubles began in 1792.

• Indian troubles diminished, population increased, and Tennessee became a state on June 1, 1796.

• The earthquake of 1811, said to be the most destructive in U.S. history, created Reelfoot Lake.

• Against their will, beginning in 1838, the Cherokee were driven from their ancestral lands in the mountain areas of Tennessee and other southern states and suffered the terrible hardships of the "Trail of Tears" on the journey west.

• Eastern Tennessee opposed slavery, but the central and western sections of the state favored the Confederate cause, and on June 8, 1861, Tennessee joined the Confederacy. The state became a major battleground of the Civil War.

• Nashville was captured by Union forces on February 23, 1862.

• By 1864 most of Tennessee was in Union hands, but there were destructive Confederate raids.

• On February 25, 1865, Tennessee adopted a state constitutional amendment freeing the slaves, the only state to do this by popular vote.

• By the end of the Civil War in 1865, 186,652 Tennesseans had joined the Confederates, with 31,092 on the Union side.

• After the Civil War, attacks of cholera and yellow fever took a heavy toll. The worst struck Memphis in 1878, with more than 5,000 dying.

• Nashville held the state's Centennial Exposition a year late, in 1897.

• Among the state's 91,180 serving in World War I, Sergeant Alvin C. York became one of the best known enlisted men, cited for outstanding bravery in that war.

• In 1925 world attention turned to Tennessee during the notorious "Monkey Trial" of Tennessee teacher John T. Scopes, who was convicted of teaching evolution.

• Begun in 1933, Norris Dam, near Andersonville, was the first of the great projects of the Tennessee Valley Authority.

• World War II called 315,501 from Tennessee to service, and 7,727 of these lost their lives.

• The progress in civil rights was shadowed by the murder of civil rights leader Dr. Martin Luther King, Jr., at Memphis on April 4, 1968.

• In 1977, Memphis mourned the death of a favorite son, Elvis Presley.

• The 1982 World's Fair at Knoxville attracted 11 million visitors.

• In 1985, Opryland launched the *General Jackson*, one of the nation's largest paddleboats.

THAT'S INTERESTING

• The only known defeat of a naval force by cavalry was carried out in a Civil War raid by Confederate General Nathan Bedford Forrest. On November 4, 1864, Forrest's cavalry attacked the federal supply base at Johnsonville on the Tennessee River. The base, with its fleet of 30 gunboats, transports, and barges, was virtually destroyed.

• When Tennessean Andrew Jackson won the Battle of New Orleans during the War of 1812, his fans in Tennessee spread the word that Jackson had left immediately to conquer England.

• Confederate heroine Antoinette Polk was so close to capture by Union forces that they managed to pluck a feather from her hat, but she escaped to warn Confederate troops of Union plans.

NOTABLE NATIVES

John Bell (Nashville, 1796-1869), public official. **Julian Bond** (Nashville, 1940-   ), civil rights leader/public official. **George Deforest Brush** (Shelbyville, 1855-1941), artist. **David (Davy) Crockett** (Greeneville, 1786-1836), frontiersman/public official. **David Glasgow Farragut** (near Knoxville, 1801-1870), naval officer. **Nathan Bedford Forrest** (Chapel Hill, 1821-1877), soldier. **Richard Halliburton** (Brownsville, 1900-1939), explorer/author. **Cordell Hull** (Overton County, 1871-1955), public official. **Opie Percival Read** (Nashville, 1842-1939), author. **Alvin Cullum York** (Pall Mall, 1887-1964), soldier.

GENERAL

Admitted to statehood: June 1, 1796
Origin of name: *Tanasi* was the name of Cherokee villages on the Little Tennessee River. From 1784 to 1788 this was the State of Franklin, or Frankland.
Capital: Nashville
Nickname: Volunteer State
Motto: Agriculture and commerce
Slogan: Tennessee—America at its best
Animal: Raccoon
Bird: Mockingbird
Insect: Firefly and ladybug
Flower: Iris
Gem: Tennessee River pearl
Rock: Limestone
Stone: Agate
Song: "When It's Iris Time in Tennessee," "Tennessee Waltz," "My Homeland Tennessee," "My Tennessee," and "Rocky Top"
Tree: Tulip poplar

THE LAND

Area: 42,145 sq. mi., 36th
  Land: 41,219 sq. mi., 34th
  Water: 926 sq. mi., 30th
    Inland water: 926 sq. mi., 24th
Topography: Rugged country in the E; Great Smoky Mountains of the Unakas; low ridges of the Appalachian Valley; the flat Cumberland Plateau; slightly rolling terrain and knobs of the interior low plateau, the largest region; Eastern Gulf coastal plain to the W, laced with meandering streams; Mississippi alluvial plain, a narrow strip of swamp and flood plain in the extreme W
Number of counties: 95
Geographic center: Rutherford, 5 mi. NE of Murfreesboro
Length: 440 mi.; width: 120 mi.
Highest point: 6,643 ft. (Clingmans Dome), 17th
Lowest point: 178 ft. (Mississippi River), 29th
Mean elevation: 900 ft., 30th

CLIMATE AND ENVIRONMENT

Temp., highest: 113 deg. on Aug. 9, 1930, at Perryville; lowest: –32 deg. on Dec. 30, 1917, at Mountain City
Monthly average: highest: 91.5 deg., 16th; lowest: 27.8 deg., 41st; spread (high to low): 63.7 deg., 34th
Hazardous waste sites (1993): 15, 24th
Endangered species: Mammals: 3—Gray bat, Indiana bat, Carolina northern flying squirrel; birds: 3—American peregrine falcon, Least tern, Red-cockaded woodpecker; reptiles: none; amphibians: none; fishes: 4; invertebrates: 24; plants: 7

MAJOR CITIES
POPULATION, 1990
PERCENTAGE INCREASE, 1980-90

Chattanooga, 152,466— –10.06%
Clarksville, 75,494—37.82%
Knoxville, 165,121— –5.67%
Memphis, 610,337— –5.55%
Nashville, 488,374—7.18%

THE PEOPLE

Population (1995): 5,256,051, 17th
  Percent change (1990-95): 7.8%, 15th
Population (2000 proj.): 5,538,000, 16th
  Percent change (1990-2000): 13.55%, 20th
Per sq. mi. (1994): 125.8, 20th
Percent in metro. area (1992): 67.7%, 30th
Foreign born: 59,000, 31st
  Percent: 1.2%, 45th
Top three ancestries reported:
  Irish, 17.94%
  German, 14.85%
  English, 14.19%
White: 4,048,068, 83.00%, 30th
Black: 778,035, 15.95%, 11th

Native American: 10,039, 0.21%, 42nd
Asian, Pacific Isle: 31,839, 0.65%, 39th
Other races: 9,204, 0.19%, 46th
Hispanic origin: 32,741, 0.67%, 45th
Percent over 5 yrs. speaking language other than English at home: 2.9%, 46th
Percent males: 48.16%, 41st; percent females: 51.84%, 11th
Percent never married: 23.2%, 41st
Marriages per 1,000 (1993): 14.3, 5th
Divorces per 1,000 (1993): 6.5, 3rd
Median age: 33.6
Under 5 years (1994): 7.07%, 34th
Under 18 years (1994): 25.06%, 37th
65 years & older (1994): 12.7%, 27th
Percent increase among the elderly (1990-94): 6.49%, 23rd

OF VITAL IMPORTANCE

Live births per 1,000 pop. (1993): 14.4, 30th
Infant mortality rate per 1,000 births (1992): 9.4, 12th
Rate for blacks (1990): 17.5, 12th
Rate for whites (1990): 8.0, 22nd
Births to unmarried women, % of total (1992): 32.7%, 13th
Births to teenage mothers, % of total (1992): 16.9%, 7th
Abortions (1992): 19,060, 20th
Rate per 1,000 women 14-44 years old: 16.2, 31st
Percent change (1988-92): –14%, 36th
Average lifetime (1979-81): 73.30, 38th
Deaths per 1,000 pop. (1993): 9.7, 10th
Causes of death per 100,000 pop.:
Accidents & adverse effects (1992): 43.9, 11th
Atherosclerosis (1991): 7.5, 20th
Cancer (1991): 214.4, 19th
Cerebrovascular diseases (1992): 73.6, 3rd
Chronic liver diseases & cirrhosis (1991): 9.6, 20th
Chronic obstructive pulmonary diseases (1992): 38.2, 23rd
Diabetes mellitus (1992): 19.9, 29th
Diseases of heart (1992): 298.8, 19th
Pneumonia, flu (1991): 34.2, 17th
Suicide (1992): 12.9, 17th

KEEPING WELL

Active nonfederal physicians per 100,000 pop. (1993): 210, 19th
Dentists per 100,000 (1991): 53, 29th

Nurses per 100,000 (1992): 706, 30th
Hospitals per 100,000 (1993): 2.55, 20th
Admissions per 1,000 (1993): 146.70, 4th
Occupancy rate per 100 beds (1993): 60.8, 28th
Average cost per patient per day (1993): $859, 26th
Average cost per stay (1993): $5,798, 23rd
Average stay (1992): 6.8 days, 32nd
AIDS cases (adult, 1993): 1,203; per 100,000: 23.6, 25th
HIV infection, not yet AIDS (1993): 1,783
Other notifiable diseases:
Gonorrhea: 408.6, 8th
Measles: 1.5, 36th
Syphilis: 89.1, 6th
Tuberculosis: 12.3, 12th
Pop. without health insur. (1991-93): 13.4%, 23rd

HOUSEHOLDS BY TYPE

Total households (1994): 1,966,000
Per 1,000 pop.: 379.90, 11th
Percent of households 65 yrs. and over: 21.57%, 28th
Percent change (1990-94): 6.0%, 19th
Persons per household (1994): 2.57, 31st
Family households: 1,348,019
Percent of total: 72.72%, 9th
Nonfamily households: 505,706
Percent of total: 27.28%, 43rd
Pop. living in group quarters: 129,129
Percent of pop.: 2.65%, 31st

LIVING QUARTERS

Total housing units: 2,026,067
Persons per unit: 2.41, 24th
Occupied housing units: 1,853,725
Percent of total units: 91.49%, 13th
Persons per unit: 2.51, 30th
Percent of units with over 1 person per room: 2.74%, 31st
Owner-occupied units: 1,261,118
Percent of total units: 62.24%, 11th
Percent of occupied units: 68.03%, 20th
Persons per unit: 2.66, 40th
Median value: $58,400, 37th
Renter-occupied units: 592,607
Percent of total units: 29.25%, 26th
Percent of occupied units: 31.97%, 32nd
Persons per unit: 2.35, 25th
Median contract rent: $273, 38th
Rental vacancy rate: 9.6%, 16th

Mobile home, trailer & other as a percent of occupied housing units: 11.19%, 25th

Persons in emergency shelters for homeless persons: 1,864, 0.038%, 39th

Persons visible in street locations: 357, 0.0073%, 23rd

Persons in shelters for abused women: 230, 0.0047%, 28th

Nursing home population: 35,192, 0.72%, 25th

CRIME INDEX PER 100,000 (1992-93)

Total reported: 5,239.5, 22nd
  Violent: 765.8, 14th
    Murder and nonnegligent manslaughter: 10.2, 15th
    Aggravated assault: 485.5, 13th
    Robbery: 220.1, 14th
    Forcible rape: 49.9, 12th
  Property: 4,473.8, 25th
    Burglary: 1,182.6, 14th
    Larceny, theft: 2,700.2, 34th
    Motor vehicle theft: 591.0, 16th
Drug abuse violations (1990): 240.7, 27th
Child-abuse rate per 1,000 children (1993): 9.56, 39th

TEACHING AND LEARNING

Pop. 3 and over enrolled in school: 1,171,640
  Percent of pop.: 25.0%, 48th
Public elementary & secondary schools (1992-93): 1,094
  Total enrollment (1992): 845,618
    Percent of total pop.: 16.83%, 32nd
  Teachers (1992): 43,586
    Percent of pop.: 0.87%, 45th
  Pupil/teacher ratio (fall 1992): 19.4, 6th
  Teachers' avg. salary (1992-93): $30,842, 40th
  Expenditure per capita (1990-91): $2,757.08, 48th
  Expenditure per pupil (1991-92): $3,692, 47th
  Percent of graduates taking SAT (1993): 13%, 33rd
  Mean SAT verbal scores: 486, 7th
  Mean SAT mathematical scores: 531, 11th
  Percent of graduates taking ACT (1995): 68%, 6th
  Mean ACT scores: 20.3, 38th
  Percent of pop. over 25 completing:
    Less than 9th grade: 16.0%, 3rd
    High school: 67.1%, 46th

College degree(s): 16.0%, 44th
Higher education, institutions (1993-94): 78
  Enrollment (1992): 242,970
    Percent of pop.: 4.84%, 41st
  White non-Hispanic (1992): 197,783
    Percent of enroll.: 81.40%, 29th
  Black non-Hispanic (1992): 35,459
    Percent of enroll.: 14.59%, 10th
  Hispanic (1992): 1,969
    Percent of enroll.: 0.81%, 42nd
  Asian/Pacific Islander (1992): 2,895
    Percent of enroll.: 1.19%, 40th
  American Indian/AK native (1992): 612
    Percent of enroll.: 0.25%, 45th
  Nonresident alien (1992): 4,252
    Percent of enroll.: 1.75%, 46th
  Female (1992): 133,544
    Percent of enroll.: 54.96%, 32nd
  Pub. institutions (1993-94): 24
    Enrollment (1992): 192,302
    Percent of enroll.: 79.15%, 35th
  Private institutions (1993-94): 54
    Enrollment (1992): 50,668
    Percent of enroll.: 20.85%, 17th
  Tuition, public institution (avg., 1993-94): $5,021, 42nd
  Tuition, private institution (avg., 1993-94): $11,267, 33rd
Public library systems: 135
  Books & serial vol. per capita: 1.56, 48th
  Govt. expenditure per capita: $8.01, 48th

LAW ENFORCEMENT, COURTS, AND PRISONS

Police protection, corrections, judicial and legal functions expenditures (1992): $1,135,000,000
  Per capita: $226, 34th
Police per 10,000 pop. (1993): 20.50, 27th
Prisoners (state & fed.) per 100,000 pop. (1993): 2,517.47, 31st
  Percent change (1992-93): 8.2%, 12th
Death penalty: yes, by electrocution
  Under sentence of death (1993): 98, 11th
  Executed (1993): 0

RELIGION, NUMBER AND PERCENT OF POPULATION

Agnostic: 7,321—0.20%, 42nd
Buddhist: 3,661—0.10%, 17th
Christian: 3,316,487—90.60%, 9th
Hindu: NA
Jewish: 10,982—0.30%, 35th
Muslim: 3,661—0.10%, 22nd

Unitarian: 3,661—0.10%, 31st
Other: 36,606—1.00%, 34th
None: 219,635—6.00%, 32nd
Refused to answer: 58,570—1.60%, 39th

MAKING A LIVING

Personal income per capita (1994): $19,482, 37th
Percent increase (1993-94): 5.7%, 13th
Disposable personal income per capita (1994): $17,387, 36th
Median income of households (1993): $25,102, 46th
Percent of pop. below poverty level (1993): 19.6%, 8th
Percent 65 and over (1990): 20.9%, 5th
Expenditure for energy per person (1992): $1,896, 22nd

ECONOMY

Civilian labor force (1994): 2,664,000
Percent of total pop.: 51.48%, 22nd
Percent 65 and over (1990): 3.25%, 13th
Percent female: 47.56%, 9th
Percent job growth (1980-90): 23.09%, 20th
Major employer industries (1994):
Agriculture: 69,000—2.9%, 19th
Construction: 92,000—3.9%, 33rd
Finance, insurance, & real estate: 96,000— 4.1%, 45th
Government: 323,000—13.7%, 39th
Manufacturing: 537,000—22.8%, 5th
Service: 462,000—19.6%, 35th
Trade: 438,000—18.6%, 34th
Transportation, communications, public utilities: 124,000—5.3%, 25th
Unemployment rate (1994): 4.77%, 40th
Male: 4.4%, 43rd
Female: 5.2%, 31st
Total businesses (1991): 151,392
New business incorps. (1991): 8,306
Percent of total businesses: 5.49%, 32nd
Business failures (1991): 1,475
Percent of total businesses: 0.97%
Agriculture farm income:
Marketing (1993): $2,039,000,000, 30th
Average per farm: $23,709.30, 49th
Leading products (1993): Cattle, dairy products, tobacco, soybeans
Average value land & build. per acre (1994): $1,054, 22nd
Percent increase (1990-94): 5.82%, 40th

Govt. payments (1993): $161,000,000, 23rd
Average per farm: $1,872.09, 38th
Construction, value of all: $2,667,000,000
Per capita: $546.83, 24th
Manufactures:
Value added: $30,245,000,000
Per capita: $6,201.32, 10th
Leading products: Chemicals and chemical products, food and food products, nonelectrical machinery, electric and electronic equipment, apparel, fabricated metal products, transportation equipment, rubber and misc. plastic products, paper and allied products
Value of nonfuel mineral production (1994): $577,000,000, 18th
Leading mineral products: Coal, stone, zinc
Retail sales (1993): $41,884,000,000, 18th
Per household: $21,399, 32nd
Percent increase (1992-93): 7.4%, 25th
Tourism revenues (1993): $5.15 bil.
Foreign exports, in total value (1994): $6,749,000,000, 18th
Per capita: $1,304.15, 23rd
Gross state product per person (1993): $20,404.04, 30th
Percent change (1990-93): 6.32%, 7th
Patents per 100,000 pop. (1993): 12.50, 35th
Public aid recipients (percent of resident pop. 1993): 9.4%, 8th
Medicaid recipients per 1,000 pop. (1993): 178.45, 5th
Medicare recipients per 1,000 pop. (1993): 144.88, 24th

TRAVEL AND TRANSPORTATION

Motor vehicle registrations (1993): 4,964,000
Per 1,000 pop.: 974.48, 5th
Motorcycle registrations (1993): 84,000
Per 1,000 pop.: 16.49, 26th
Licensed drivers per 1,000 pop. (1993): 695.52, 22nd
Deaths from motor vehicle accidents per 100,000 pop. (1993): 23.07, 9th
Public roads & streets (1993):
Total mileage: 85,037
Per 1,000 pop.: 16.69, 27th
Rural mileage: 68,516
Per 1,000 pop.: 13.45, 27th
Urban mileage: 16,521
Per 1,000 pop.: 3.24, 21st
Interstate mileage: 1,062
Per 1,000 pop.: 0.21, 25th

Annual vehicle-mi. of travel per person
(1993): 10,228, 13th
Mean travel time for workers age 16+ who
work away from home: 21.5 min., 19th

GOVERNMENT

Percent of voting age pop. registered (1994):
63.7%, 28th
Percent of voting age pop. voting (1994):
43.0%, 35th
Percent of voting age pop. voting for U.S.
representatives (1994): 36.2%, 33rd
State legislators, total (1995): 132, 33rd
Women members (1992): 15
Percent of legislature: 11.4%, 43rd
U.S. Congress, House members (1995): 9
Change (1985-95): 0
Revenues (1993):
State govt.: $11,864,000,000
Per capita: $2,329.01, 50th
Parimutuel & amusement taxes & lotteries,
revenue per capita: NA
Expenditures (1993):
State govt.: $11,028,000,000
Per capita: $2,164.90, 49th
Debt outstanding (1993): $2,632,000,000
Per capita: $516.69, 48th

LAWS AND REGULATIONS

Legal driving age: 16
Marriage age without parental consent: 18
Divorce residence requirement: 6 mo., for
qualifications check local statutes

ATTRACTIONS (1995)

Major opera companies: 2
Major symphony orchestras: 4
Major dance companies: 1
State appropriations for arts agencies per capita:
$0.74, 26th
State Fair in late September at Nashville

SPORTS AND COMPETITION

NCAA teams (Division I): Austin Peay State
Univ. Governors, East Tennessee State
Univ. Buccaneers, Middle Tennessee
State Univ. Blue Raiders, Tennessee
State Univ. Tigers, Tennessee Tech
Univ. Golden Eagles, Univ. of Memphis
Tigers, Univ. of Tennessee-
Chattanooga Moccasins, Univ. of Tennessee-Knoxville Volunteers, Univ. of
Tennessee-Martin Skyhawks, Vanderbilt Univ. Commodores

TEXAS

"The province of Techas will be the richest state of our union, without any exception."

President Thomas Jefferson

Novelist Edna Ferber labeled Texas as a giant, and she was right. The total wealth of its natural resources surpasses that of all the other states. As a separate country it would rank 11th in wealth among the nations. Texas leads the nation in total productivity, and its history retells one of the nation's most heroic events, the defense of the Alamo. Texans are friendly—indeed, "Friendship" is their state motto. Once the typical Texan was a frontier cowboy with a ten-gallon hat, but today the state's symbol might more appropriately be an oil field worker or a laboratory scientist. Texas is still a frontier state, but nowadays the frontier is the space program. Perhaps it is typical and appropriate that this giant state has constructed the largest of all the state capitols as a symbol of its strength.

SUPERLATIVES

- Greatest variety of flowers.
- Greatest variety of reptiles.
- Leader in helium production.
- First in petroleum refining.
- First in asphalt production.
- First in cotton production.
- Produces the greatest quantity of chemicals from seawater.
- Only state with five major ports.

MOMENTS IN HISTORY

- The shipwrecked party of Alvar Nuñez Cabéza de Vaca escaped from Indian captivity on an island off the Texas coast in 1535 and made an incredible journey across country back to Mexico.
- The renowned expedition of Francisco Vásquez de Coronado crossed the Rio Grande in 1541.
- The first permanent European settlement in what is now Texas was Ysleta, founded in 1682.
- In the first half of the 1700s about a dozen missions became outposts of civilization in Texas.

- The Sabine and Red rivers were established as northern and eastern boundaries in 1819.
- Moses and Stephen Austin established an American foothold in Texas before Moses died in the 1820s, and the American presence grew in the early 1830s.

So They Say

"When young folks danced in those days, they danced....They 'shuffled' and 'double-shuffled,' 'wired' and 'cut the pigeon's wing,' making the splinters fly...."

Noah Smithwick, on a wedding in 1828

- By 1835 the Americans in Texas realized that they must seek independence from Mexico, and they laid siege to San Antonio, which fell in December.
- Mexican leader Antonio López de Santa Anna arrived in February 1836 to recapture San Antonio, finding the defenders at an old mission called the Alamo. After a long siege, his forces overwhelmed and slaughtered them on March 6. Only one of the defenders managed to escape. Santa Ana then captured and murdered 330 Texans at Goliad.

So They Say

"The enemy has demanded a surrender at discretion, or otherwise, the garrison are to be put to the sword....I shall never surrender or retreat—victory or death."

Alamo Commander
William Barret Travis

- Texan dynamo Sam Houston led his forces eastward and lured Santa Anna into a difficult position. Santa Anna was defeated and captured at the decisive Battle of San Jacinto, on April 21, 1836.

So They Say

"This morning we are in preparation to meet Santa Anna. It is the only chance of saving Texas. Texas could have started 4,000 men. We will only have about seven hundred. We go to conquer."

Later—"Victory is certain. Trust in God and fear not. And remember the Alamo!"

Sam Houston

• Later that year, the people held an election and chose Sam Houston as the first president of the independent Republic of Texas.
• After ten years of independence, on December 29, 1845, Texas became the 28th state.
• As the divisions over slavery increased, Sam Houston became governor in 1859.

So They Say

"I cannot for a moment entertain that the masses of the people would be willing to precipitate the country into all the horrors of revolution and civil war. No human being could calculate the injury that would be inflicted upon mankind."

Sam Houston

• Despite Houston's objection, the state voted to secede on January 28, 1861, and Houston resigned as governor.
• During the Civil War, Texas furnished enormous quantities of essential materials and food.
• Texas was readmitted to the Union on March 30, 1870, and a new constitution became law on February 15, 1876.
• Between the years 1870 and 1890, 10 million cattle were shipped from Texas to the nation's markets.
• The terrible hurricane at Galveston on September 8, 1900, killed at least 6,000 and left 8,000 homeless.
• World War I called more than 200,000 Texans to service, and Texan E. M. House was a principal adviser to President Woodrow Wilson.

• Dallas celebrated the Texas Centennial in 1936.

So They Say

"I protest against surrendering the Federal Constitution, its government and its glorious flag to Northern abolition leaders and to accept in its stead a so-called Confederate Government whose constitution contains the germs and seeds of decay which must and will lead to its speedy ruin....The die has been cast by your secession leaders, whom you have permitted to sow and broadcast the seeds of secession, and you must before long reap the fearful harvest of conspiracy and revolution."

Sam Houston, on being forced to resign as governor

• An explosion at a New London school in 1937 brought death to more than 300 pupils and teachers.
• World War II called 750,000 Texans into the armed services, and 23,022 lost their lives.
• A border dispute with Mexico was settled in 1963.
• Texan Lyndon Baines Johnson succeeded to the presidency on the assassination of John F. Kennedy at Dallas on November 22, 1963.

So They Say

"All I have I would have given gladly not to be standing here today."

Lyndon Johnson, assuming the presidency after the assassination

• The year 1986 brought the 150th anniversary celebration of the founding of the Republic of Texas.
• A highly controversial federal raid on the Branch Davidian compound at Waco ended in a tragic fire on April 19, 1993; more than 70 cult members were killed.

THAT'S INTERESTING

• Texas even boasts some notable holes in the ground—Meteor Crater covers 10 acres near Odessa. The strange Hueco Tanks, where rainwater is held in natural cups carved into the granite, welcome thirsty travelers.

• In 1598 explorer Don Juan de Onate crossed the Rio Grande at present-day El Paso, bringing four purple and three yellow velvet coats, 11 pairs of satin trousers, 16 pairs of silk stockings, and five suits of armor.

• At statehood, Texas retained the right to divide itself into five new states. This could still be done if the people wished.

• In order to get to the Alamo to join his friend Colonel William B. Travis, who was in charge of the city of San Antonio, James Bonham had to borrow money. He did so, and met the fate of the other Alamo defenders.

• It's not a shrub but a full grown tree—Texas's own shin oak, only 12 inches high.

• Fifteen thousand carloads of Texas pink granite were required to build the Texas capitol, the largest outside Washington, DC. This material was donated by the owners of Granite Mountain, near Marble Falls.

NOTABLE NATIVES

Joan Crawford (San Antonio, 1908-1977), actress. **James Frank Dobie** (Live Oak County, 1888-1964), folklorist/educator. **Dwight David Eisenhower** (Denison, 1890-1969), military leader, U.S. president. **James Edward Ferguson** (Temple, 1871-1944), public official. **Miriam A. (Ma) Ferguson** (Bell County, 1875-1961), public official. **John Nance Garner** (Red River County, 1868-1967), U.S. vice president. **Howard Robard Hughes** (Houston, 1905-1976), industrialist/aviator/motion picture producer. **Lyndon Baines Johnson** (near Stonewall, 1908-1973), U.S. president. **Barbara Jordan** (Houston, 1936-1996), public official. **Audie Murphy** (Kingston, 1924-1971), soldier/actor. **Chester William Nimitz** (Fredericksburg, 1885-1966), naval officer. **Sandra Day O'Connor** (El Paso, 1930-), Supreme Court justice. **Katherine Anne Porter** (Indian Creek, 1890-1980), author. **Wiley Post** (near Grand Saline, 1899-1925), aviator. **Mildred Ella Didrikson (Babe) Zaharias** (Port Arthur, 1914-1956), athlete.

GENERAL

Admitted to statehood: December 29, 1845
Origin of name: Variant of word used by Caddo and other Indians meaning "friends" or "allies" and applied to them by the Spanish in eastern Texas. Also written *texias, tejas, teysas*

Capital: Austin
Nickname: Lone Star State
Motto: Friendship
Bird: Mockingbird
Flower: Bluebonnet
Gem: Topaz
Song: "Texas, Our Texas"
Stone: Petrified palmwood
Tree: Pecan

THE LAND

Area: 267,277 sq. mi., 2nd
    Land: 261,914 sq. mi., 2nd
    Water: 5,363 sq. mi., 8th
        Inland water: 4,959 sq. mi., 2nd
        Coastal water: 404 sq. mi., 14th
Topography: Gulf Coast Plain in the S and SE; North Central Plains slope upward with some hills; Great Plains extend over the Panhandle, are broken by low mountains; Trans-Pecos are southern extension of the Rockies.
Number of counties: 254
Geographic center: McCulloch, 15 mi. NE of Brady
Length: 790 mi.; width: 660 mi.
Highest point: 8,749 ft. (Guadalupe Peak), 14th
Lowest point: sea level (Gulf of Mexico), 3rd
Mean elevation: 1,700 ft., 17th
Coastline: 367 mi., 6th
Shoreline: 3,359 mi., 7th

CLIMATE AND ENVIRONMENT

Temp., highest: 120 deg. on Aug. 12, 1936, at Seymour; lowest: –23 deg. on Feb. 8, 1933, at Seminole
Monthly average: highest: 98.5 deg., 4th; lowest: 21.7 deg., 29th; spread (high to low): 76.8 deg., 13th
Hazardous waste sites (1993): 30, 14th
Endangered species: Mammals: 4—Mexican long-nosed bat, Jaguarundi, West Indian manatee, Ocelot; birds: 10—Whooping crane, Eskimo curlew, American peregrine falcon, Northern aplomado falcon, Brown pelican, Attwater's greater prairie-chicken, Least tern, Black-capped vireo, Golden-cheeked (wood) warbler, Red-cockaded woodpecker; reptiles: 3; amphibians: 2; fishes: 7; invertebrates: 5; plants: 16

MAJOR CITIES
POPULATION, 1990
PERCENTAGE INCREASE, 1980-90

Austin, 465,622—34.62%
Dallas, 1,006,877—11.31%
El Paso, 515,342—21.18%
Houston, 1,630,553—2.22%
San Antonio, 935,933—19.08%

THE PEOPLE

Population (1995): 18,723,991, 2nd
  Percent change (1990-95): 10.2%, 10th
Population (2000 proj.): 20,039,000, 2nd
  Percent change (1990-2000): 17.97%, 12th
Per sq. mi. (1994): 70.2, 30th
Percent in metro. area (1992): 83.9%, 14th
Foreign born: 1,524,000, 4th
  Percent: 9.0%, 9th
Top three ancestries reported:
  Mexican, 20.03%
  German, 17.37%
  Irish, 13.95%
White: 12,774,762, 75.21%, 41st
Black: 2,021,632, 11.90%, 18th
Native American: 65,877, 0.39%, 28th
Asian, Pacific Isle: 319,459, 1.88%, 14th
Other races: 1,804,780, 10.62%, 3rd
Hispanic origin: 4,339,905, 25.55%, 3rd
Percent over 5 yrs. speaking language other
  than English at home: 25.4%, 3rd
Percent males: 49.25%, 13th; percent females:
  50.75%, 39th
Percent never married: 25.1%, 30th
Marriages per 1,000 (1993): 10.3, 13th
Divorces per 1,000 (1993): 5.5, 11th
Median age: 30.8
Under 5 years (1994): 8.48%, 4th
Under 18 years (1994): 28.84%, 6th
65 years & older (1994): 10.2%, 47th
Percent increase among the elderly (1990-94):
  8.82%, 14th

OF VITAL IMPORTANCE

Live births per 1,000 pop. (1993): 18.3, 3rd
Infant mortality rate per 1,000 births (1992):
  7.8, 32nd
  Rate for blacks (1990): 13.9, 33rd
  Rate for whites (1990): 7.1, 43rd
Births to unmarried women, % of total
  (1992): 17.5%, 50th
Births to teenage mothers, % of total (1992):
  15.9%, 13th
Abortions (1992): 97,400, 3rd

Rate per 1,000 women 14-44 years old:
  23.1, 20th
Percent change (1988-92): –7%, 23rd
Average lifetime (1979-81): 73.64, 32nd
Deaths per 1,000 pop. (1993): 7.5, 43rd
Causes of death per 100,000 pop.:
  Accidents & adverse effects (1992): 34.5,
    27th
  Atherosclerosis (1991): 6.6, 26th
  Cancer (1991): 170.2, 43rd
  Cerebrovascular diseases (1992): 49.2, 40th
  Chronic liver diseases & cirrhosis (1991):
    10.2, 14th
  Chronic obstructive pulmonary diseases
    (1992): 30.4, 45th
  Diabetes mellitus (1992): 21.3, 22nd
  Diseases of heart (1992): 229.0, 42nd
  Pneumonia, flu (1991): 21.6, 49th
  Suicide (1992): 12.8, 19th

KEEPING WELL

Active nonfederal physicians per 100,000 pop.
  (1993): 177, 38th
Dentists per 100,000 (1991): 48, 35th
Nurses per 100,000 (1992): 528, 50th
Hospitals per 100,000 (1993): 2.30, 24th
  Admissions per 1,000 (1993): 108.97,
    33rd
  Occupancy rate per 100 beds (1993): 55.5,
    42nd
  Average cost per patient per day (1993):
    $1,010, 12th
  Average cost per stay (1993): $6,021, 19th
  Average stay (1992): 6.2 days, 45th
AIDS cases (adult, 1993): 7,543; per 100,000:
  41.8, 11th
HIV infection, not yet AIDS (1993): NA
Other notifiable diseases:
  Gonorrhea: 254.5, 20th
  Measles: 26.0, 2nd
  Syphilis: 77.5, 8th
  Tuberculosis: 13.2, 8th
Pop. without health insur. (1991-93): 22.6%,
  2nd

HOUSEHOLDS BY TYPE

Total households (1994): 6,539,000
  Percent change (1990-94): 7.7%, 11th
  Per 1,000 pop.: 355.81, 45th
  Percent of households 65 yrs. and over:
    18.11%, 47th
  Persons per household (1994): 2.75, 6th
Family households: 4,343,878
  Percent of total: 71.55%, 17th

Nonfamily households: 1,727,059
  Percent of total: 28.45%, 35th
Pop. living in group quarters: 393,447
  Percent of pop.: 2.32%, 41st

LIVING QUARTERS

Total housing units: 7,008,999
  Persons per unit: 2.42, 20th
Occupied housing units: 6,070,937
  Percent of total units: 86.62%, 39th
  Persons per unit: 2.70, 6th
  Percent of units with over 1 person per room: 8.15%, 5th
Owner-occupied units: 3,695,115
  Percent of total units: 52.72%, 45th
  Percent of occupied units: 60.87%, 44th
  Persons per unit: 2.85, 6th
  Median value: $59,600, 35th
Renter-occupied units: 2,375,822
  Percent of total units: 33.90%, 12th
  Percent of occupied units: 39.13%, 9th
  Persons per unit: 2.55, 7th
  Median contract rent: $328, 27th
  Rental vacancy rate: 13.0%, 4th
Mobile home, trailer & other as a percent of occupied housing units: 10.39%, 27th
Persons in emergency shelters for homeless persons: 7,816, 0.046%, 27th
Persons visible in street locations: 1,442, 0.0085%, 22nd
Persons in shelters for abused women: 1,049, 0.0062%, 10th
Nursing home population: 101,005, 0.59%, 38th

CRIME INDEX PER 100,000 (1992-93)

Total reported: 6,439.1, 6th
  Violent: 762.1, 15th
    Murder and nonnegligent manslaughter: 11.9, 7th
    Aggravated assault: 470.8, 16th
    Robbery: 224.4, 13th
    Forcible rape: 55.0, 7th
  Property: 5,677.0, 6th
    Burglary: 1,297.3, 10th
    Larceny, theft: 3,687.3, 8th
    Motor vehicle theft: 692.3, 9th
Drug abuse violations (1990): 366.3, 12th
Child-abuse rate per 1,000 children (1993): 11.25, 37th

TEACHING AND LEARNING

Pop. 3 and over enrolled in school: 4,805,895
  Percent of pop.: 29.7%, 6th

Public elementary & secondary schools (1992-93): 6,184
  Total enrollment (1992): 3,535,871
    Percent of total pop.: 20.00%, 5th
  Teachers (1992): 225,207
    Percent of pop.: 1.27%, 2nd
  Pupil/teacher ratio (fall 1992): 15.7, 35th
  Teachers' avg. salary (1992-93): $31,241, 39th
  Expenditure per capita (1990-91): $2,895.44, 45th
  Expenditure per pupil (1991-92): $4,632, 36th
Percent of graduates taking SAT (1993): 45%, 23rd
  Mean SAT verbal scores: 413, 45th
  Mean SAT mathematical scores: 472, 38th
Percent of graduates taking ACT (1995): 33%, 29th
  Mean ACT scores: 20.1, 42nd
Percent of pop. over 25 completing:
  Less than 9th grade: 13.5%, 10th
  High school: 72.1%, 40th
  College degree(s): 20.3%, 24th
Higher education, institutions (1993-94): 178
  Enrollment (1992): 938,526
    Percent of pop.: 5.31%, 31st
  White non-Hispanic (1992): 616,515
    Percent of enroll.: 65.69%, 47th
  Black non-Hispanic (1992): 89,213
    Percent of enroll.: 9.51%, 18th
  Hispanic (1992): 168,644
    Percent of enroll.: 17.97%, 2nd
  Asian/Pacific Islander (1992): 33,423
    Percent of enroll.: 3.56%, 13th
  American Indian/AK native (1992): 3,762
    Percent of enroll.: 0.40%, 26th
  Nonresident alien (1992): 26,969
    Percent of enroll.: 2.87%, 19th
  Female (1992): 504,067
    Percent of enroll.: 53.71%, 44th
  Pub. institutions (1993-94): 106
    Enrollment (1992): 832,458
    Percent of enroll.: 88.70%, 10th
  Private institutions (1993-94): 72
    Enrollment (1992): 106,068
    Percent of enroll.: 11.30%, 42nd
  Tuition, public institution (avg., 1993-94): $4,935, 44th
  Tuition, private institution (avg., 1993-94): $11,322, 32nd
Public library systems: 478
  Books & serial vol. per capita: 2.22, 33rd
  Govt. expenditure per capita: $9.11, 44th

LAW ENFORCEMENT, COURTS, AND PRISONS

Police protection, corrections, judicial and legal functions expenditures (1992): $4,596,000,000
Per capita: $260, 26th
Police per 10,000 pop. (1993): 21.59, 21st
Prisoners (state & fed.) per 100,000 pop. (1993): 3,891.19, 14th
Percent change (1992-93): 16.0%, 2nd
Death penalty: yes, by lethal injection
Under sentence of death (1993): 357, 2nd
Executed (1993): 17

RELIGION, NUMBER AND PERCENT OF POPULATION

Agnostic: 72,904—0.60%, 19th
Buddhist: 24,301—0.20%, 11th
Christian: 10,935,604—90.00%, 11th
Hindu: NA
Jewish: 85,055—0.70%, 23rd
Muslim: 24,301—0.20%, 13th
Unitarian: 24,301—0.20%, 23rd
Other: 194,411—1.60%, 17th
None: 595,383—4.90%, 40th
Refused to answer: 194,411—1.60%, 39th

MAKING A LIVING

Personal income per capita (1994): $19,857, 33rd
Percent increase (1993-94): 3.7%, 46th
Disposable personal income per capita (1994): $17,668, 32nd
Median income of households (1993): $28,727, 33rd
Percent of pop. below poverty level (1993): 17.4%, 12th
Percent 65 and over (1990): 18.4%, 10th
Expenditure for energy per person (1992): $2,454, 5th

ECONOMY

Civilian labor force (1994): 9,385,000
Percent of total pop.: 51.07%, 24th
Percent 65 and over (1990): 2.71%, 26th
Percent female: 44.39%, 49th
Percent job growth (1980-90): 21.07%, 22nd
Major employer industries (1994):
Agriculture: 202,000—2.4%, 25th
Construction: 435,000—5.1%, 9th
Finance, insurance, & real estate: 426,000—5.0%, 30th
Government: 1,397,000—16.4%, 22nd

Manufacturing: 1,077,000—12.7%, 36th
Service: 1,749,000—20.6%, 29th
Trade: 1,698,000—20.0%, 9th
Transportation, communications, public utilities: 568,000—6.7%, 4th
Unemployment rate (1994): 6.44%, 12th
Male: 6.3%, 15th
Female: 6.6%, 11th
Total businesses (1991): 844,821
New business incorps. (1991): 34,571
Percent of total businesses: 4.09%, 44th
Business failures (1991): 6,742
Percent of total businesses: 0.80%
Agriculture farm income:
Marketing (1993): $12,617,000,000, 2nd
Average per farm: $68,200.00, 32nd
Leading products (1993): Cattle, cotton, dairy products, greenhouse
Average value land & build. per acre (1994): $493, 40th
Percent increase (1990-94): –0.40%, 46th
Govt. payments (1993): $1,421,000,000, 1st
Average per farm: $7,681.08, 14th
Construction, value of all: $8,161,000,000
Per capita: $480.44, 32nd
Manufactures:
Value added: $83,630,000,000
Per capita: $4,923.32, 30th
Leading products: Machinery, transportation equipment, foods, electric and electronic equipment, chemicals and chemical products
Value of nonfuel mineral production (1994): $1,409,000,000, 18th
Leading mineral products: Petroleum, natural gas, cement
Retail sales (1993): $142,855,000,000, 2nd
Per household: $22,076, 26th
Percent increase (1992-93): 1.9%, 44th
Tourism revenues (1993): $22.8 bil.
Foreign exports, in total value (1994): $51,818,000,000, 2nd
Per capita: $2,819.57, 4th
Gross state product per person (1993): $22,832.10, 18th
Percent change (1990-93): 3.66%, 20th
Patents per 100,000 pop. (1993): 20.67, 23rd
Public aid recipients (percent of resident pop. 1993): 6.3%, 29th
Medicaid recipients per 1,000 pop. (1993): 128.07, 18th

Medicare recipients per 1,000 pop. (1993): 109.48, 49th

TRAVEL AND TRANSPORTATION

Motor vehicle registrations (1993): 13,118,000
  Per 1,000 pop.: 727.89, 38th
Motorcycle registrations (1993): 144,000
  Per 1,000 pop.: 7.99, 48th
Licensed drivers per 1,000 pop. (1993): 658.97, 40th
Deaths from motor vehicle accidents per 100,000 pop. (1993): 16.85, 25th
Public roads & streets (1993):
  Total mileage: 294,142
      Per 1,000 pop.: 16.32, 28th
  Rural mileage: 215,010
      Per 1,000 pop.: 11.93, 30th
  Urban mileage: 79,132
      Per 1,000 pop.: 4.39, 4th
  Interstate mileage: 3,234
      Per 1,000 pop.: 0.18, 31st
Annual vehicle-mi. of travel per person (1993): 9,300, 27th
Mean travel time for workers age 16+ who work away from home: 22.2 min., 12th

GOVERNMENT

Percent of voting age pop. registered (1994): 58.2%, 43rd
  Percent of voting age pop. voting (1994): 37.6%, 46th
  Percent of voting age pop. voting for U.S. representatives (1994): 31.3%, 44th
State legislators, total (1995): 181, 11th
  Women members (1992): 23
      Percent of legislature: 12.7%, 39th
U.S. Congress, House members (1995): 30
  Change (1985-95): +3
Revenues (1993):
  State govt.: $42,019,000,000
      Per capita: $2,331.54, 49th
  Parimutuel & amusement taxes & lotteries, revenue per capita: $94.38, 22nd
Expenditures (1993):
  State govt.: $39,091,000,000
      Per capita: $2,169.07, 48th
Debt outstanding (1993): $8,684,000,000
  Per capita: $481.86, 49th

LAWS AND REGULATIONS

Legal driving age: 18, 16 if completed driver education course
Marriage age without parental consent: 18
Divorce residence requirement: 6 mo., for qualifications check local statutes

ATTRACTIONS (1995)

Major opera companies: 5
Major symphony orchestras: 5
Major dance companies: 3
Major professional theater companies (non-profit): 2
State appropriations for arts agencies per capita: $0.18, 51st
State Fair in mid-October at Dallas

SPORTS AND COMPETITION

NCAA teams (Division I): Baylor Univ. Bears, Lamar Univ. Cardinals, Prairie View A&M Univ. Panthers, Rice Univ. Owls, Sam Houston State Univ. Bearkats, Southern Methodist Univ. Mustangs, Southwest Texas State Univ. Bobcats, Stephen F. Austin State Univ. Lumberjacks, Texas A&M Univ. Aggies, Texas Christian Univ. Horned Frogs, Texas Southern Univ. Tigers, Texas Tech Univ. Red Raiders, Univ. of Houston Cougars, Univ. of North Texas Eagles, Univ. of Texas-Arlington Mavericks, Univ. of Texas-Austin Longhorns, Univ. of Texas-El Paso Miners, Univ. of Texas-Pan American Broncos, Univ. of Texas-San Antonio Roadrunners
Major league baseball teams: Houston Astros (NL Central), The Astrodome; Texas Rangers (AL West), The Ballpark in Arlington
NBA basketball teams: San Antonio Spurs, Alamodome; Dallas Mavericks, Reunion Arena; Houston Rockets, The Summit
NFL football teams: Houston Oilers (AFC), Astrodome; Dallas Cowboys (NFC), Texas Stadium
NHL hockey teams: Dallas Stars, Reunion Arena

UTAH

"...that the physical obstacles to the occupation of a region so unpromising were sufficient to discourage the most sanguine imagination and to appall the stoutest heart, the mind is filled with wonder at witnessing the immense results which have been accomplished in so short a time, and from a beginning apparently so insignificant."

Howard Stansbury, explorer, civil engineer

U tah is a land that was settled because no one else wanted it, and it soon blossomed under the dedication of an unusual people, the Mormons. It is a "desert" land swarming with seagulls and pelicans, where the faithful erected a monument to a bird. Its broad expanses possess some of the nation's most spectacular natural formations, many found nowhere else. Today the capital, Salt Lake City, is the smallest city in the country to boast a top-ranked symphony, dance company, and opera company. Utah is a fascinating land described as "wonderful, outrageous, mysterious, and strange."

SUPERLATIVES

• Bear River, the continent's longest river not reaching the sea.
• Largest salt lake in North America—Great Salt Lake.
• Nation's only major east-west range—the Uintas.
• Highest and largest natural arch—Rainbow Bridge.
• Boasts 210 useful minerals.
• World center of genealogical research.

MOMENTS IN HISTORY

• Little was known of the region until Catholic priests Silvestre Velez de Escalante and Francisco Atanasio Dominguez passed through the area in 1776, looking for a route to California. They left present-day Utah at Padre Creek. Many Spanish expeditions followed the padres' route to California.
• The winter of 1824-1825 brought Jim Bridger, the first European explorer known to have arrived at the shores of Great Salt Lake. Bridger told of a terrible winter which "froze" all the buffalo there.

• In 1826 the fur business of Jackson and Sublette was organized in the region, and the great frontiersman Jedediah Strong Smith made a thorough exploration of the area.
• A "rendezvous" of fur traders and trappers was held in 1826 at present-day Ogden. These gatherings in the wilderness, which became annual events, took on a carnival atmosphere, with games, singing, storytelling, races, and other contests, brightened by the colorful Indian costumes or frontier garb of all the participants.
• The explorations of John C. Frémont in 1843, 1844, 1845, and 1854, did much to make the region known.
• In 1845, guided by Kit Carson, Frémont crossed the central Salt Desert.
• The first permanent European-style settlement in Utah was Fort Buenaventura (later Ogden), which was built in 1844-1845 by Miles Goodyear.
• Driven from their three prosperous settlements in the East, the first of vast numbers of members of the Church of Jesus Christ of the Latter-Day Saints (Mormons) reached their "Promised Land" on July 24, 1847. Their leader, Brigham Young, looked out from a hill over the site of present-day Salt Lake City and said, "This is the place"—a region so remote and forlorn he expected never again to be driven out.

So They Say

"When my husband said 'This is the place,' I cried, for it seemed to me the most desolate in all the world."

Clara Decker Young,
wife of Brigham Young

• The fall of 1847 found the Mormons ready to reap substantial crops, until a swarm of crickets threatened all. The crops were saved by the arrival of flights of seagulls, who ate the crickets and gave the Mormons their "symbol of deliverance."

• By 1849 the broad streets of Salt Lake City had been laid out; there were gristmills and sawmills run by waterpower, carding machines, and other advances. That year, the thousands of 49ers began to pass by on their way to the California gold fields, and the Mormons prospered by supplying their desperate needs.

• With incredible Mormon energy, by 1855, Ogden, Provo, Utah Valley, Manti, Sanpete Valley, Tooele, Nephi, Fillmore, Brigham City, Cedar City, and Santa Clara had been established in Utah, along with Las Vegas in Nevada, and Morgan, Moab, and Fort Lemhi in Idaho—all by the Mormons.

• From 1855 to 1860, more than 4,000 Mormon converts from Europe crossed the plains to Utah, pulling and pushing their handcarts from the eastern railheads, the only "transportation" the leaders at Salt Lake City could provide for them.

So They Say

"They are expected to walk and draw their carts across the plains. Sufficient teams will be furnished to haul the aged, infirm and those unable to walk. A few good cows will be sent along to furnish milk and some beef cattle."

Brigham Young

• Indian warfare plagued the settlers until about 1868.

• On January 4, 1896, Utah became the 45th state.

• The magnificent Rainbow Bridge was discovered in 1909.

• World War I called 21,000 Utahans to service, and the Mormon Relief Societies made substantial contributions to the starving of Europe.

• During World War II, 70,000 Utah men and women saw service.

• In 1983 the heaviest rains and snowfalls of record brought the most widespread flooding ever experienced there. Great Salt Lake rose 10 feet in two years.

• By the late 1980s, the lake level had fallen, confounding the doomsayers.

THAT'S INTERESTING

• The beautiful Seagull monument at Salt Lake City pays tribute to the bird that saved the first Mormon crops.

• The Navajo banned their ancient symbol of friendship during World War II because it resembled the Nazi swastika.

• Celebrating the completion of the first transcontinental railroad, Governor Leland Stanford of California swung his sledgehammer at the gold spike—and missed.

• Zion Narrows canyon is so narrow and deep that even in bright daylight stars are visible from the canyon bottom.

• When Bishop Whipple of Minnesota asked a Utah chief if his belongings were safe in his tent, the chief replied, "Yes, there is not a white man within a hundred miles."

• Brigham Young did not choose the Salt Lake valley for its beauty but rather because it was so desolate he thought no one would ever try to take it away from his Mormon people.

NOTABLE NATIVES

Maude Adams (Salt Lake City, 1872-1953), actress. **John Moses Browning** (Ogden, 1855-1926), inventor. **Bernard Augustine De Voto** (Ogden, 1897-1955), author. **Marriner Stoddard Eccles** (Logan, 1890-1977), banker. **Philo Taylor Farnsworth** (Beaver, 1906-1971), engineer/inventor. **Harvey Fletcher** (Provo, 1884-1981), physicist. **John Held, Jr.** (Salt Lake City, 1889-1958), illustrator/author. **Mahonri Mackintosh Young** (Salt Lake City, 1877-1957), sculptor/painter/etcher.

GENERAL

Admitted to statehood: January 4, 1896

Origin of name: From Navajo word meaning "upper," or "higher up," as applied to a Shoshone tribe called Ute. Spanish form is *Yutta*, English *Uta* or *Utah*. Proposed name *Deseret*, "land of honeybees," from Book of Mormon, was rejected by Congress.

Capital: Salt Lake City

Nickname: Beehive State

Motto: Industry

Bird: Seagull

Flower: Sego lily

Gem: Topaz
Song: "Utah, We Love Thee"
Tree: Blue spruce

THE LAND

Area: 84,904 sq. mi., 13th
  Land: 82,168 sq. mi., 12th
  Water: 2,736 sq. mi., 14th
    Inland water: 2,736 sq. mi., 7th
Topography: High Colorado plateau cut by brilliantly colored canyons of the SE; broad, flat, desert-like Great Basin of the W; the Great Salt Lake and Bonneville Salt Flats to the NW; Middle Rockies in the NE running E-W; valleys and plateaus of the Wasatch Front
Number of counties: 29
Geographic center: Sanpete, 3 mi. N of Manti
Length: 350 mi.; width: 270 mi.
Highest point: 13,528 ft. (Kings Peak), 7th
Lowest point: 2,000 ft. (Beaverdam Wash), 48th
Mean elevation: 6,100 ft., 3rd

CLIMATE AND ENVIRONMENT

Temp., highest: 117 deg. on July 5, 1985, at Saint George; lowest: –69 deg. on Feb. 1, 1985, at Peter's Sink
Monthly average: highest: 93.2 deg., 8th; lowest: 19.7 deg., 26th; spread (high to low): 73.5 deg., 17th
Hazardous waste sites (1993): 13, 27th
Endangered species: Mammals: 1—Black-footed ferret; birds: 2—Whooping crane, American peregrine falcon; reptiles: none; amphibians: none; fishes: 6; invertebrates: none; plants: 10

MAJOR CITIES
POPULATION, 1990
PERCENTAGE INCREASE, 1980-90

Orem, 67,561—28.94%
Provo, 86,835—17.17%
Salt Lake City, 159,936— –1.90%
Sandy, 75,058—43.76%
West Valley City, 86,976—19.95%

THE PEOPLE

Population (1995): 1,951,408, 34th
  Percent change (1990-95): 13.3%, 5th
Population (2000 proj.): 2,148,000, 34th
  Percent change (1990-2000): 24.68%, 4th
Per sq. mi. (1994): 23.2, 42nd
Percent in metro. area (1992): 77.5%, 20th

Foreign born: 59,000, 31st
  Percent: 3.4%, 23rd
Top three ancestries reported:
  English, 43.53%
  German, 17.35%
  Danish, 9.46%
White: 1,615,845, 93.79%, 11th
Black: 11,576, 0.67%, 44th
Native American: 24,283, 1.41%, 11th
Asian, Pacific Isle: 33,371, 1.94%, 13th
Other races: 37,775, 2.19%, 16th
Hispanic origin: 84,597, 4.91%, 16th
Percent over 5 yrs. speaking language other than English at home: 7.8%, 23rd
Percent males: 49.67%, 8th; percent females: 50.33%, 44th
Percent never married: 25.5%, 26th
Marriages per 1,000 (1993): 11.1, 8th
Divorces per 1,000 (1993): 4.8, 22nd
Median age: 26.2
Under 5 years (1994): 9.49%, 1st
Under 18 years (1994): 35.22%, 1st
65 years & older (1994): 8.8%, 50th
Percent increase among the elderly (1990-94): 12.70%, 5th

OF VITAL IMPORTANCE

Live births per 1,000 pop. (1993): 19.6, 1st
Infant mortality rate per 1,000 births (1992): 5.9, 49th
  Rate for blacks (1990): 13.0, 38th
  Rate for whites (1990): 7.4, 37th
Births to unmarried women, % of total (1992): 15.1%, 51st
Births to teenage mothers, % of total (1992): 10.5%, 35th
Abortions (1992): 3,940, 42nd
  Rate per 1,000 women 14-44 years old: 9.3, 47th
  Percent change (1988-92): –27%, 49th
Average lifetime (1979-81): 75.76, 3rd
Deaths per 1,000 pop. (1993): 5.5, 49th
Causes of death per 100,000 pop.:
  Accidents & adverse effects (1992): 30.6, 39th
  Atherosclerosis (1991): 3.9, 47th
  Cancer (1991): 108.3, 50th
  Cerebrovascular diseases (1992): 38.7, 48th
  Chronic liver diseases & cirrhosis (1991): 4.8, 51st
  Chronic obstructive pulmonary diseases (1992): 23.2, 49th
  Diabetes mellitus (1992): 19.8, 31st
  Diseases of heart (1992): 151.8, 50th

Pneumonia, flu (1991): 22.5, 48th
Suicide (1992): 14.1, 12th

KEEPING WELL

Active nonfederal physicians per 100,000 pop. (1993): 187, 33rd
Dentists per 100,000 (1991): 65, 13th
Nurses per 100,000 (1992): 545, 46th
Hospitals per 100,000 (1993): 2.26, 27th
    Admissions per 1,000 (1993): 93.28, 46th
    Occupancy rate per 100 beds (1993): 53.4, 49th
    Average cost per patient per day (1993): $1,081, 6th
    Average cost per stay (1993): $5,314, 37th
    Average stay (1992): 6.3 days, 44th
AIDS cases (adult, 1993): 264; per 100,000: 14.2, 37th
HIV infection, not yet AIDS (1993): 723
Other notifiable diseases:
    Gonorrhea: 23.0, 45th
    Measles: 8.5, 10th
    Syphilis: 2.8, 43rd
    Tuberculosis: 3.0, 39th
Pop. without health insur. (1991-93): 12.4%, 32nd

HOUSEHOLDS BY TYPE

Total households (1994): 599,000
    Percent change (1990-94): 11.6%, 3rd
    Per 1,000 pop.: 313.94, 51st
    Percent of households 65 yrs. and over: 17.86%, 48th
    Persons per household (1994): 3.13, 1st
Family households: 410,862
    Percent of total: 76.47%, 1st
Nonfamily households: 126,411
    Percent of total: 23.53%, 51st
Pop. living in group quarters: 29,048
    Percent of pop.: 1.69%, 51st

LIVING QUARTERS

Total housing units: 598,388
    Persons per unit: 2.88, 1st
Occupied housing units: 537,273
    Percent of total units: 89.79%, 23rd
    Persons per unit: 3.03, 1st
    Percent of units with over 1 person per room: 5.51%, 13th
Owner-occupied units: 365,979
    Percent of total units: 61.16%, 16th
    Percent of occupied units: 68.12%, 18th
    Persons per unit: 3.38, 1st
    Median value: $68,900, 26th

Renter-occupied units: 171,294
    Percent of total units: 28.63%, 28th
    Percent of occupied units: 31.88%, 34th
    Persons per unit: 2.67, 3rd
    Median contract rent: $300, 30th
    Rental vacancy rate: 8.6%, 23rd
Mobile home, trailer & other as a percent of occupied housing units: 7.64%, 34th
Persons in emergency shelters for homeless persons: 925, 0.054%, 21st
Persons visible in street locations: 276, 0.0160%, 10th
Persons in shelters for abused women: 49, 0.0028%, 46th
Nursing home population: 6,222, 0.36%, 48th

CRIME INDEX PER 100,000 (1992-93)

Total reported: 5,237.4, 23rd
    Violent: 301.0, 40th
        Murder and nonnegligent manslaughter: 3.1, 45th
        Aggravated assault: 194.7, 40th
        Robbery: 58.6, 40th
        Forcible rape: 44.6, 16th
    Property: 4,936.3, 16th
        Burglary: 790.8, 37th
        Larceny, theft: 3,903.4, 6th
        Motor vehicle theft: 242.2, 40th
Drug abuse violations (1990): 189.6, 35th
Child-abuse rate per 1,000 children (1993): 16.51, 20th

TEACHING AND LEARNING

Pop. 3 and over enrolled in school: 610,696
    Percent of pop.: 37.7%, 1st
Public elementary & secondary schools (1992-93): 714
    Total enrollment (1992): 463,870
        Percent of total pop.: 25.61%, 1st
    Teachers (1992): 19,191
        Percent of pop.: 1.06%, 20th
    Pupil/teacher ratio (fall 1992): 24.2, 1st
    Teachers' avg. salary (1992-93): $28,953, 44th
    Expenditure per capita (1990-91): $3,015.33, 39th
    Expenditure per pupil (1991-92): $3,040, 51st
Percent of graduates taking SAT (1993): 4%, 50th
    Mean SAT verbal scores: 500, 4th

Mean SAT mathematical scores: 549, 6th
Percent of graduates taking ACT (1995): 67%, 8th
Mean ACT scores: 21.4, 13th
Percent of pop. over 25 completing:
Less than 9th grade: 3.4%, 51st
High school: 85.1%, 2nd
College degree(s): 22.3%, 15th
Higher education, institutions (1993-94): 16
Enrollment (1992): 133,083
Percent of pop.: 7.35%, 4th
White non-Hispanic (1992): 119,979
Percent of enroll.: 90.15%, 11th
Black non-Hispanic (1992): 766
Percent of enroll.: 0.58%, 49th
Hispanic (1992): 2,905
Percent of enroll.: 2.18%, 21st
Asian/Pacific Islander (1992): 2,489
Percent of enroll.: 1.87%, 26th
American Indian/AK native (1992): 1,301
Percent of enroll.: 0.98%, 17th
Nonresident alien (1992): 5,643
Percent of enroll.: 4.24%, 8th
Female (1992): 65,516
Percent of enroll.: 49.23%, 51st
Pub. institutions (1993-94): 9
Enrollment (1992): 96,958
Percent of enroll.: 72.86%, 40th
Private institutions (1993-94): 7
Enrollment (1992): 36,125
Percent of enroll.: 27.14%, 12th
Tuition, public institution (avg., 1993-94): $5,227, 36th
Tuition, private institution (avg., 1993-94): $5,645, 49th
Public library systems: 69
Books & serial vol. per capita: 2.47, 27th
Govt. expenditure per capita: $15.86, 24th

LAW ENFORCEMENT, COURTS, AND PRISONS

Police protection, corrections, judicial and legal functions expenditures (1992): $396,000,000
Per capita: $219, 36th
Police per 10,000 pop. (1993): 18.58, 33rd
Prisoners (state & fed.) per 100,000 pop. (1993): 1,552.69, 47th
Percent change (1992-93): 7.0%, 18th
Death penalty: yes, by firing squad or lethal injection
Under sentence of death (1993): 9, 27th
Executed (1993): 0

RELIGION, NUMBER AND PERCENT OF POPULATION

Agnostic: 9,859—0.90%, 14th
Buddhist: 1,095—0.10%, 17th
Christian: 959,576—87.60%, 20th
Hindu: NA
Jewish: 7,668—0.70%, 23rd
Muslim: NA
Unitarian: 1,095—0.10%, 31st
Other: NA
None: 85,442—7.80%, 16th
Refused to answer: 31,767—2.90%, 9th

MAKING A LIVING

Personal income per capita (1994): $17,043, 49th
Percent increase (1993-94): 5.6%, 14th
Disposable personal income per capita (1994): $14,938, 50th
Median income of households (1993): $35,786, 11th
Percent of pop. below poverty level (1993): 10.7%, 38th
Percent 65 and over (1990): 8.8%, 46th
Expenditure for energy per person (1992): $1,580, 49th

ECONOMY

Civilian labor force (1994): 975,000
Percent of total pop.: 51.10%, 23rd
Percent 65 and over (1990): NA
Percent female: 44.62%, 47th
Percent job growth (1980-90): 30.88%, 12th
Major employer industries (1994):
Agriculture: 19,000—2.2%, 31st
Construction: 38,000—4.3%, 23rd
Finance, insurance, & real estate: 46,000—5.2%, 26th
Government: 176,000—20.2%, 8th
Manufacturing: 128,000—14.4%, 30th
Service: 179,000—20.5%, 30th
Trade: 168,000—19.2%, 20th
Transportation, communications, public utilities: 48,000—5.5%, 24th
Unemployment rate (1994): 3.69%, 49th
Male: 3.4%, 49th
Female: 4.2%, 44th
Total businesses (1991): 58,156
New business incorps. (1991): 4,973
Percent of total businesses: 8.55%, 11th
Business failures (1991): 372
Percent of total businesses: 0.64%

Agriculture farm income:
  Marketing (1993): $804,000,000, 38th
    Average per farm: $61,846.15, 38th
  Leading products (1993): Cattle, dairy
    products, hay, turkeys
  Average value land & build. per acre
    (1994): $508, 39th
    Percent increase (1990-94): 30.59%, 1st
  Govt. payments (1993): $37,000,000, 37th
    Average per farm: $2,846.15, 32nd
Construction, value of all: $1,271,000,000
  Per capita: $737.73, 15th
Manufactures:
  Value added: $6,111,000,000
    Per capita: $3,547.03, 38th
  Leading products: Guided missiles and parts,
    electronic components, food products,
    fabricated metals, steel, electric equipment
Value of nonfuel mineral production (1994):
  $1,428,000,000, 7th
Leading mineral products: Petroleum, coal,
  copper
Retail sales (1993): $13,390,000,000, 34th
  Per household: $22,995, 16th
  Percent increase (1992-93): 11.7%, 3rd
Tourism revenues: NA
Foreign exports, in total value (1994):
  $2,355,000,000, 32nd
  Per capita: $1,234.28, 26th
Gross state product per person (1993):
  $18,675.72, 42nd
  Percent change (1990-93): 6.45%, 6th
Patents per 100,000 pop. (1993): 25.32, 18th
Public aid recipients (percent of resident pop.
  1993): 3.7%, 48th
Medicaid recipients per 1,000 pop. (1993):
  79.57, 48th
Medicare recipients per 1,000 pop. (1993):
  95.16, 50th

TRAVEL AND TRANSPORTATION

Motor vehicle registrations (1993): 1,335,000
  Per 1,000 pop.: 717.74, 41st
Motorcycle registrations (1993): 23,000
  Per 1,000 pop.: 12.37, 32nd
Licensed drivers per 1,000 pop. (1993):
  639.78, 43rd
Deaths from motor vehicle accidents per
  100,000 pop. (1993): 16.29, 26th
Public roads & streets (1993):
  Total mileage: 40,508
    Per 1,000 pop.: 21.78, 22nd
  Rural mileage: 34,402
    Per 1,000 pop.: 18.50, 20th

Urban mileage: 6,106
  Per 1,000 pop.: 3.28, 17th
Interstate mileage: 937
  Per 1,000 pop.: 0.50, 9th
Annual vehicle-mi. of travel per person
  (1993): 9,194, 29th
Mean travel time for workers age 16+ who
  work away from home: 18.9 min., 40th

GOVERNMENT

Percent of voting age pop. registered (1994):
  59.4%, 39th
  Percent of voting age pop. voting (1994):
    44.1%, 34th
  Percent of voting age pop. voting for U.S.
    representatives (1994): 40.5%, 20th
State legislators, total (1995): 104, 41st
  Women members (1992): 12
    Percent of legislature: 11.5%, 42nd
U.S. Congress, House members (1995): 3
  Change (1985-95): 0
Revenues (1993):
  State govt.: $5,348,000,000
    Per capita: $2,875.27, 31st
  Parimutuel & amusement taxes & lotteries,
    revenue per capita: NA
Expenditures (1993):
  State govt.: $4,834,000,000
    Per capita: $2,598.92, 31st
Debt outstanding (1993): $2,193,000,000
  Per capita: $1,179.03, 29th

LAWS AND REGULATIONS

Legal driving age: 16
Marriage age without parental consent: 18,
  county to provide premarital counseling
  if under 19 or divorced
Divorce residence requirement: 3 mo., for
  qualifications check local statutes

ATTRACTIONS (1995)

Major opera companies: 1
Major symphony orchestras: 1
Major dance companies: 3
State appropriations for arts agencies per capita:
  $2.16, 4th
State Fair in early September at Salt Lake City

SPORTS AND COMPETITION

NCAA teams (Division I): Brigham Young Univ.
  Cougars, Southern Utah Univ. Thunder-
  birds, Univ. of Utah Utes, Utah State
  Univ. Aggies, Weber State Univ. Wildcats
NBA basketball teams: Utah Jazz, Delta Center

VERMONT

"Up where the north wind blows just a little keener,
Up where the grasses grow just a little greener,
Up where the mountain peaks rise a little higher
Up where the human kind draws just a little nigher,
That's where Vermont comes in."

Charles Hial Darling, poet

Vermont is known for the independent nature of its people. They were so opposed to slavery that the Georgia legislature once voted humorously that "...the whole state should be made into an island and towed out to sea." Vermonters are so "politically correct" that their legislature declared war on Germany before the United States did. Every year, the spectacular Green Mountains attract thousands of skiers and other tourists. Farming is more important in Vermont than in the other New England states. Three-fifths of the state is covered by forests, and lumbering and wood processing are major industries, as is the quarrying of granite, marble, and slate. Only about a third of the people reside in cities and towns.

SUPERLATIVES

- Claims only breed of horse produced in the United States.
- Leader in marble production.
- World granite center.
- First in maple syrup production.
- First U.S. patent issued.

MOMENTS IN HISTORY

- On July 4, 1609, during the first known European visit to present-day Vermont, French explorer Samuel de Champlain discovered a lake he named Champlain.
- In 1666, French Captain de La Motte built a fortress on present-day La Motte Island in Lake Champlain.
- In 1690 the English built a fort at Chimney Point.
- The outpost of Fort Dummer, begun in 1724, was the first permanent settlement in present-day Vermont.
- The 1741 proclamation of King George II of England appeared to include present-day Vermont in New Hampshire, but the boundaries were long disputed.

- In 1764, King George III set the boundary at the Connecticut River, leaving present-day Vermont in New York territory.
- The owners of New Hampshire grants contested the New York claims and were supported by Ethan Allen and his Green Mountain Boys. They withstood a New York attack in 1771.
- On May 10, 1775, Allen and Colonel Benedict Arnold captured Fort Ticonderoga in one of the early actions of the Revolution.

So They Say

"Ethan Allen demanded the surrender of Fort Ticonderoga '...in the name of the Great Jehovah and the Continental Congress' in spite of the fact that he held a commission from neither source."

Anonymous

- After British General John Burgoyne recaptured Fort Ticonderoga on July 6, 1777, he pursued American General Arthur St. Clair. The next day the Americans defeated Burgoyne in the Battle of Hubbardton, the only battle of the Revolution fought on Vermont soil.
- The Battle of Bennington, in August 1777, was fought just across the New York border but was led by General John Stark and Seth Warner of Vermont. Vermont men played the key role in this struggle.

So They Say

"There are the Red Coats and they are ours, or this night Molly Stark sleeps a widow!"

General John Stark

• Indian attacks terrorized the countryside during the Revolution; the worst saw plundering, burning, and taking of prisoners from Tunbridge to Royalton during October 1780.

• Vermont operated as an independent republic from 1777 to 1791, but this was not recognized by the Continental Congress or New York State.

• Various difficulties were settled and on March 4, 1791, Vermont became the first state added to the Union following the original 13 colonies.

• During the War of 1812, the Battle of Plattsburgh in September 1814 brought U.S. control to Lake Champlain and thwarted the British invasion of Vermont.

• The state legislature was converted to the two-house system in 1836.

• Vermonters were always opposed to slavery, and Senator Jacob Collamer of Woodstock introduced Lincoln's first war powers act in 1861.

• During the Civil War, Vermont forces played a key role in the Battle of Gettysburg.

• Vermont's Chester A. Arthur became president of the United States in 1881.

• Montpelier native Admiral George Dewey emerged the hero of the Spanish-American War of 1898.

• Admiral Henry T. Mayo of Burlington was the principal commander of the U.S. Atlantic fleet during World War I, the fourth leading "sea dog" from inland Vermont.

• On the death of President Warren G. Harding, in the flicker of kerosene lamps at Plymouth, Calvin Coolidge on August 3, 1923, took the oath of office as U.S. president, administered by his justice-of-the-peace father.

So They Say

"Never before or since has a president taken the oath of office from his own father, in his own home, and under such unique surroundings. It holds an appeal, in its uniqueness and moving simplicity, to all Americans."

Vermont Board of Historic Sites, on Coolidge's taking the oath of office

---

• In 1941 the good people of Vermont got so enraged at the Nazis that they declared war on Germany two months before the United States did. Of the 49,942 Vermonters who saw service in that war, 1,233 lost their lives.

• In 1985, Democrat Madeleine M. Kunin became the first woman governor of Vermont.

• The Vermont Supreme Court in 1992 ruled against a claim by Abenaki Indians to 150 square miles of the state.

• Floods of 1992 swept the city of Montpelier when ice floes dammed the Winooski River.

THAT'S INTERESTING

• In the late 1700s, schoolteacher Justin Morgan developed the Morgan horse, the only breed originating in the United States.

• The Indians were so devoted to the chapel they had built at Swanton that when the French were driven out, the faithful Indians went with them and took the chapel apart, rebuilding it stone by stone at their new home in Canada.

• In the 18th-century dispute between Vermont and New York, the Green Mountain Boys tore the roof from the home of New York supporter Benjamin Spencer. After he took an oath to support Vermont, the "boys" restored his roof.

• Although ridiculed by some as a do-nothing president, Calvin Coolidge had the support of many Vermonters who agreed that government should interfere as little as possible in the affairs of the people.

• James Johns of Huntington printed by hand every copy of every issue of the newspaper he published for 40 years.

• At the Haskell opera house at Derby Line, the audience sits in the United States and the stage is in Canada. According to one account, an American police officer once had to sit in the audience and watch a wanted criminal performing on the stage.

NOTABLE NATIVES

Chester Alan Arthur (Fairfield, 1829-1886), U.S. president. **Calvin Coolidge** (Plymouth, 1872-1933), U.S. president. **John Deere** (Rutland, 1804-1886), inventor/industrialist. **George Dewey** (Montpelier, 1837-1917), naval officer. **John Dewey** (Burlington, 1859-1952), philosopher/psychologist/educator. **Stephen Arnold Douglas** (Brandon, 1813-1861), public official/political leader. **James Fisk** (Bennington, 1834-1872), financier. **Joseph Smith** (Sharon, 1805-1844), religious leader. **Brigham Young** (Whitingham, 1801-1877), religious leader.

GENERAL

Admitted to statehood: March 4, 1791

Origin of name: From French words *vert* (green) and *mont* (mountain). The Green Mountains were said to have been named by Samuel de Champlain. When the state was formed, 1777, Dr. Thomas Young suggested combining *vert* and *mont* into Vermont

Capital: Montpelier

Nickname: Green Mountain State

Motto: Freedom and unity

Animal: Morgan horse

Bird: Hermit thrush

Insect: Honeybee

Fish: Brook trout, walleye pike

Flower: Red clover

Song: "Hail, Vermont"

Tree: Sugar maple

THE LAND

Area: 9,615 sq. mi., 43rd
  Land: 9,249 sq. mi., 43rd
  Water: 366 sq. mi., 44th
    Inland water: 366 sq. mi., 40th

Topography: Green Mountains create N-S backbone 20-36 mi. wide; average altitude, 1,000 ft.

Number of counties: 14

Geographic center: Washington, 3 mi. E of Roxbury

Length: 160 mi.; width: 80 mi.

Highest point: 4,393 ft. (Mount Mansfield), 26th

Lowest point: 95 ft. (Lake Champlain), 28th

Mean elevation: 1,000 ft., 27th

CLIMATE AND ENVIRONMENT

Temp., highest: 105 deg. on July 4, 1911, at Vernon; lowest: –50 deg. on Dec. 30, 1933, at Bloomfield

Monthly average: highest: 80.5 deg., 49th; lowest: 7.7 deg., 7th; spread (high to low): 72.8 deg., 20th

Hazardous waste sites (1993): 8, 41st

Endangered species: Mammals: 1—Indiana bat; birds: 1—American peregrine falcon; reptiles: none; amphibians: none; fishes: none; invertebrates: 1; plants: 3

MAJOR CITIES
POPULATION, 1990
PERCENTAGE INCREASE, 1980-90

Bennington, 16,451—4.02%

Burlington, 39,127—3.75%

Colchester, 14,731—16.64%

Essex, 16,498—14.63%

Rutland, 18,230— –1.12%

THE PEOPLE

Population (1995): 584,771, 49th
  Percent change (1990-95): 3.9%, 33rd

Population (2000 proj.): 592,000, 49th
  Percent change (1990-2000): 5.20%, 39th

Per sq. mi. (1994): 62.7, 31st

Percent in metro. area (1992): 27.0%, 50th

Foreign born: 18,000, 46th
  Percent: 3.1%, 25th

Top three ancestries reported:
  English, 26.11%
  French, 23.62%
  Irish, 17.94%

White: 555,088, 98.64%, 1st

Black: 1,951, 0.35%, 49th

Native American: 1,696, 0.30%, 33rd

Asian, Pacific Isle: 3,215, 0.57%, 42nd

Other races: 808, 0.14%, 47th

Hispanic origin: 3,661, 0.65%, 46th

Percent over 5 yrs. speaking language other than English at home: 5.8%, 31st

Percent males: 48.95%, 21st; percent females: 51.05%, 31st

Percent never married: 27.6%, 12th

Marriages per 1,000 (1993): 10.5, 9th

Divorces per 1,000 (1993): 4.8, 22nd

Median age: 33

Under 5 years (1994): 6.55%, 49th

Under 18 years (1994): 25.17%, 36th

65 years & older (1994): 12.1%, 34th

Percent increase among the elderly (1990-94): 5.80%, 25th

OF VITAL IMPORTANCE

Live births per 1,000 pop. (1993): 12.6, 49th

Infant mortality rate per 1,000 births (1992): 7.2, 40th
  Rate for blacks (1990): (NA)
  Rate for whites (1990): 6.5, 48th

Births to unmarried women, % of total (1992): 23.4%, 44th

Births to teenage mothers, % of total (1992): 8.5%, 46th

Abortions (1992): 2,900, 46th
  Rate per 1,000 women 14-44 years old: 21.2, 24th
  Percent change (1988-92): –18%, 45th

Average lifetime (1979-81): 74.79, 16th

Deaths per 1,000 pop. (1993): 8.5, 34th

Causes of death per 100,000 pop.:
  Accidents & adverse effects (1992): 29.8, 43rd

Atherosclerosis (1991): 5.3, 41st
Cancer (1991): 204.1, 31st
Cerebrovascular diseases (1992): 50.4, 37th
Chronic liver diseases & cirrhosis (1991): 8.1, 39th
Chronic obstructive pulmonary diseases (1992): 42.4, 12th
Diabetes mellitus (1992): 21.9, 17th
Diseases of heart (1992): 277.4, 30th
Pneumonia, flu (1991): 28.0, 34th
Suicide (1992): 14.0, 13th

KEEPING WELL

Active nonfederal physicians per 100,000 pop. (1993): 259, 8th
Dentists per 100,000 (1991): 56, 20th
Nurses per 100,000 (1992): 910, 9th
Hospitals per 100,000 (1993): 2.60, 19th
Admissions per 1,000 (1993): 99.83, 39th
Occupancy rate per 100 beds (1993): 64.2, 17th
Average cost per patient per day (1993): $676, 41st
Average cost per stay (1993): $5,241, 39th
Average stay (1992): 7.3 days, 21st
AIDS cases (adult, 1993): 74; per 100,000: 12.9, 39th
HIV infection, not yet AIDS (1993): NA
Other notifiable diseases:
Gonorrhea: 9.8, 51st
Measles: 0.2, 47th
Syphilis: 0.4, 51st
Tuberculosis: 2.3, 44th
Pop. without health insur. (1991-93): 11.4%, 37th

HOUSEHOLDS BY TYPE

Total households (1994): 220,000
Percent change (1990-94): 4.6%, 23rd
Per 1,000 pop.: 379.31, 14th
Percent of households 65 yrs. and over: 20.00%, 38th
Persons per household (1994): 2.54, 43rd
Family households: 144,895
Percent of total: 68.78%, 39th
Nonfamily households: 65,755
Percent of total: 31.22%, 13th
Pop. living in group quarters: 21,642
Percent of pop.: 3.85%, 2nd

LIVING QUARTERS

Total housing units: 271,241
Persons per unit: 2.07, 51st

Occupied housing units: 210,650
Percent of total units: 77.66%, 51st
Persons per unit: 2.48, 38th
Percent of units with over 1 person per room: 1.71%, 49th
Owner-occupied units: 145,368
Percent of total units: 53.59%, 43rd
Percent of occupied units: 69.01%, 15th
Persons per unit: 2.73, 26th
Median value: $95,500, 13th
Renter-occupied units: 65,282
Percent of total units: 24.07%, 49th
Percent of occupied units: 30.99%, 37th
Persons per unit: 2.22, 46th
Median contract rent: $374, 17th
Rental vacancy rate: 7.5%, 35th
Mobile home, trailer & other as a percent of occupied housing units: 13.57%, 19th
Persons in emergency shelters for homeless persons: 232, 0.041%, 33rd
Persons visible in street locations: 16, 0.0028%, 41st
Persons in shelters for abused women: 29, 0.0052%, 21st
Nursing home population: 4,809, 0.85%, 19th

CRIME INDEX PER 100,000 (1992-93)

Total reported: 3,972.4, 42nd
Violent: 114.2, 50th
Murder and nonnegligent manslaughter: 3.6, 41st
Aggravated assault: 61.8, 50th
Robbery: 9.0, 50th
Forcible rape: 39.8, 24th
Property: 3,858.2, 39th
Burglary: 874.3, 33rd
Larceny, theft: 2,851.2, 28th
Motor vehicle theft: 132.6, 50th
Drug abuse violations (1990): 85.6, 49th
Child-abuse rate per 1,000 children (1993): 9.06, 40th

TEACHING AND LEARNING

Pop. 3 and over enrolled in school: 145,988
Percent of pop.: 27.1%, 26th
Public elementary & secondary schools (1992-93): 399
Total enrollment (1992): 98,558
Percent of total pop.: 17.26%, 27th
Teachers (1992): 7,301
Percent of pop.: 1.28%, 1st
Pupil/teacher ratio (fall 1992): 14.0, 49th

Teachers' avg. salary (1992-93): $34,076, 26th
Expenditure per capita (1990-91): $3,864.55, 13th
Expenditure per pupil (1991-92): $6,944, 6th
Percent of graduates taking SAT (1993): 68%, 10th
Mean SAT verbal scores: 426, 36th
Mean SAT mathematical scores: 467, 41st
Percent of graduates taking ACT (1995): 4%, 44th
Mean ACT scores: 21.7, 9th
Percent of pop. over 25 completing:
Less than 9th grade: 8.7%, 31st
High school: 80.8%, 12th
College degree(s): 24.3%, 9th
Higher education, institutions (1993-94): 22
Enrollment (1992): 37,377
Percent of pop.: 6.55%, 10th
White non-Hispanic (1992): 35,108
Percent of enroll.: 93.93%, 2nd
Black non-Hispanic (1992): 429
Percent of enroll.: 1.15%, 44th
Hispanic (1992): 406
Percent of enroll.: 1.09%, 38th
Asian/Pacific Islander (1992): 522
Percent of enroll.: 1.40%, 38th
American Indian/AK native (1992): 97
Percent of enroll.: 0.26%, 42nd
Nonresident alien (1992): 815
Percent of enroll.: 2.18%, 36th
Female (1992): 21,346
Percent of enroll.: 57.11%, 5th
Pub. institutions (1993-94): 6
Enrollment (1992): 21,485
Percent of enroll.: 57.48%, 46th
Private institutions (1993-94): 16
Enrollment (1992): 15,980
Percent of enroll.: 42.75%, 6th
Tuition, public institution (avg., 1993-94): $10,057, 1st
Tuition, private institution (avg., 1993-94): $18,339, 5th
Public library systems: 205
Books & serial vol. per capita: 4.14, 4th
Govt. expenditure per capita: $12.06, 37th

LAW ENFORCEMENT, COURTS, AND PRISONS

Police protection, corrections, judicial and legal functions expenditures (1992): $118,000,000
Per capita: $207, 38th
Police per 10,000 pop. (1993): 14.50, 49th

Prisoners (state & fed.) per 100,000 pop. (1993): 2,123.26, 39th
Percent change (1992-93): –2.5%, 48th
Death penalty: no

RELIGION, NUMBER AND PERCENT OF POPULATION

Agnostic: 5,036—1.20%, 2nd
Buddhist: NA
Christian: 350,848—83.60%, 39th
Hindu: NA
Jewish: 4,616—1.10%, 15th
Muslim: NA
Unitarian: 4,616—1.10%, 1st
Other: 3,777—0.90%, 35th
None: 47,843—11.40%, 8th
Refused to answer: 2,938—0.70%, 48th

MAKING A LIVING

Personal income per capita (1994): $20,224, 32nd
Percent increase (1993-94): 4.0%, 43rd
Disposable personal income per capita (1994): $17,763, 29th
Median income of households (1993): $31,065, 24th
Percent of pop. below poverty level (1993): 10.0%, 43rd
Percent 65 and over (1990): 12.4%, 21st
Expenditure for energy per person (1992): $2,005, 13th

ECONOMY

Civilian labor force (1994): 321,000
Percent of total pop.: 55.34%, 2nd
Percent 65 and over (1990): 2.59%, 31st
Percent female: 48.29%, 4th
Percent job growth (1980-90): 30.60%, 13th
Major employer industries (1994):
Agriculture: 10,000—3.3%, 17th
Construction: 12,000—4.1%, 25th
Finance, insurance, & real estate: 13,000—4.2%, 42nd
Government: 40,000—13.4%, 40th
Manufacturing: 47,000—15.7%, 23rd
Service: 73,000—24.5%, 11th
Trade: 53,000—17.7%, 44th
Transportation, communications, public utilities: 12,000—3.9%, 48th
Unemployment rate (1994): 4.67%, 42nd
Male: 5.0%, 34th
Female: 4.4%, 43rd
Total businesses (1991): 26,339

New business incorps. (1991): 1,486
  Percent of total businesses: 5.64%, 28th
Business failures (1991): 78
  Percent of total businesses: 0.30%
Agriculture farm income:
  Marketing (1993): $484,000,000, 44th
    Average per farm: $69,142.86, 31st
  Leading products (1993): Dairy products, cattle, greenhouse, Christmas trees
  Average value land & build. per acre (1994): $1,262, 17th
    Percent increase (1990-94): 6.05%, 39th
  Govt. payments (1993): $3,000,000, 47th
    Average per farm: $428.57, 48th
Construction, value of all: $352,000,000
  Per capita: $625.49, 19th
Manufactures:
  Value added: $3,233,000,000
    Per capita: $5,744.92, 17th
  Leading products: Machine tools, furniture, scales, books, computer components, fishing rods
Value of nonfuel mineral production (1994): $48,000,000, 46th
Leading mineral products: Stone, asbestos, sand/gravel
Retail sales (1993): $5,090,000,000, 49th
  Per household: $23,382, 12th
    Percent increase (1992-93): −0.8%, 49th
Tourism revenues: $1.25 bil.
Foreign exports, in total value (1994): $1,371,000,000, 40th
  Per capita: $2,363.79, 6th
Gross state product per person (1993): $19,366.20, 37th
  Percent change (1990-93): 0%, 45th
Patents per 100,000 pop. (1993): 26.74, 16th
Public aid recipients (percent of resident pop. 1993): 7.0%, 20th
Medicaid recipients per 1,000 pop. (1993): 140.63, 11th
Medicare recipients per 1,000 pop. (1993): 137.15, 31st

TRAVEL AND TRANSPORTATION

Motor vehicle registrations (1993): 483,000
  Per 1,000 pop.: 838.54, 16th
Motorcycle registrations (1993): 17,000
  Per 1,000 pop.: 29.51, 5th
Licensed drivers per 1,000 pop. (1993): 748.26, 4th

Deaths from motor vehicle accidents per 100,000 pop. (1993): 19.44, 19th
Public roads & streets (1993):
  Total mileage: 14,166
    Per 1,000 pop.: 24.59, 16th
  Rural mileage: 12,842
    Per 1,000 pop.: 22.30, 16th
  Urban mileage: 1,324
    Per 1,000 pop.: 2.30, 46th
  Interstate mileage: 320
    Per 1,000 pop.: 0.56, 8th
Annual vehicle-mi. of travel per person (1993): 10,417, 10th
Mean travel time for workers age 16+ who work away from home: 18.0 min., 42nd

GOVERNMENT

Percent of voting age pop. registered (1994): 70.7%, 14th
  Percent of voting age pop. voting (1994): 48.8%, 20th
  Percent of voting age pop. voting for U.S. representatives (1994): 49.3%, 8th
State legislators, total (1995): 180, 12th
  Women members (1992): 56
    Percent of legislature: 31.1%, 4th
U.S. Congress, House members (1995): 1
  Change (1985-95): 0
Revenues (1993):
  State govt.: $1,953,000,000
    Per capita: $3,390.63, 19th
  Parimutuel & amusement taxes & lotteries, revenue per capita: $81.60, 24th
Expenditures (1993):
  State govt.: $1,849,000,000
    Per capita: $3,210.07, 15th
Debt outstanding (1993): $1,419,000,000
  Per capita: $2,463.54, 12th

LAWS AND REGULATIONS

Legal driving age: 18
Marriage age without parental consent: 18
Divorce residence requirement: 6 mo., for qualifications check local statutes

ATTRACTIONS (1995)

State appropriations for arts agencies per capita: $0.78, 22nd
State Fair in early September at Rutland

SPORTS AND COMPETITION

NCAA teams (Division I): Univ. of Vermont Catamounts

VIRGINIA

"Of all the states, but three will live in story,
Old Massachusetts with her Plymouth Rock,
And old Virginia with her noble stock,
And sunny Kansas with her woes and glory."

Eugene Fitch Ware, poet

Before the Europeans arrived, Virginia was the realm of a great Indian emperor, Powhatan. During its epic years, Virginia became both the "Mother of Presidents" (eight) and the "Mother of the Frontier." Having given up claims to Illinois, Indiana, Ohio, Michigan, Wisconsin, and parts of Minnesota, it also is known as "Mother of the States." Virginia was in the forefront of the Revolutionary War, which ended when Lord Cornwallis surrendered to Washington in Yorktown. In the Civil War, more battles were fought on Virginia soil than in any other state. Virginia is a land of stately mansions, battlefields, old churches, and colonial homes. In 1989 the state was the first since Reconstruction to elect an African-American governor, L. Douglas Wilder.

SUPERLATIVES

- Most native presidents—eight.
- First manufacturing in the United States—in a glass factory, 1608.
- First iron furnace, 1619.
- Leads in synthetic fiber production.
- Pioneer in tobacco farming.
- Country's first canal—in 1790, running the 7 miles between Richmond and Westham.

So They Say

"Here was buried Thomas Jefferson, author of the Declaration of American Independence, of the Statute of Virginia for religious freedom and father of the University of Virginia."

Thomas Jefferson,
author of his own epitaph

MOMENTS IN HISTORY

- Early explorers must have passed the shores of Virginia. By the 1580s, the Spanish

Jesuit missionaries had a mission on Aquia Creek in the Potomac region, but they were massacred by the Indians.

- On May 14, 1607, three English ships anchored in the James River and next day James Town (Jamestown) was begun, the first permanent English American settlement.

So They Say

The ships "...moored to the trees in 6 fathoms of water...." The Indians came "...creeping upon all foures from the Hills, like Beares with their Bowes in their mouthes." Next morning, May 15, 1607, the pioneers "...set to work about the fortifications."

Captain John Smith, on landing
and settling in Virginia

- Captain John Smith, leader of the settlement, made peace with powerful Chief Powhatan, probably with the somewhat legendary help of the chief's daughter, Pocahontas. Smith returned to England in October 1609, to care for an injury.
- The 65 survivors of the "starving time" of 1609-1610 were rescued by Lord De la Warr, who brought supplies and new settlers.
- In 1619 the colonists organized a House of Burgesses, claimed as the first democratically elected legislative body in the New World.
- After the death of Powhatan in 1618, Indian troubles began and continued until 1646, when King Opechancanough was shot.

So They Say

A Virginia law of 1658 "expelled all attorneys" from the colony.

- Nathaniel Bacon rallied the people against the government of Sir William Berkeley in

1676 with "America's first declaration of independence," but he died soon after, and Berkeley hanged some 20 of his followers.

• The frontiers pushed westward, and Augusta County was organized in 1738, claiming lands to the Mississippi.

• As discontent over taxes and other acts of the government grew, Patrick Henry entered the House of Burgesses in 1765 and became a leader in opposing the government.

So They Say

"The gentlemen may cry 'Peace! Peace!' but there is no peace. The war is actually begun!...Is life so dear or peace so sweet as to be purchased at the price of chains and slavery? Forbid it, Almighty God. I know not what course others may take...but as for me, give me liberty or give me death!"

Patrick Henry

• On May 6, 1776, the fifth Virginia Convention declared that the colony was free and independent.

So They Say

"Caesar had his Brutus, Charles I his Cromwell, and George the III..."At this point the speaker paused and his friends feared he might be committing treason, but he continued "...and George the III may profit from their example."

Patrick Henry

• Sponsored by Virginia, the work of General George Rogers Clark during the American Revolution kept the western area in the hands of the colonies.

• American armies laid siege to Yorktown, and General Lord Cornwallis surrendered in October 1781.

• After the failure of the Articles of Confederation, Virginian George Washington presided at the convention that finally created a new government, and Virginia became the tenth state on June 25, 1788.

• On April 30, 1789, Washington became the first of the long succession of Virginians who were to hold the office of president.

• As early as 1778, Virginia had made the slave trade a criminal offense, but most Virginians supported slavery, and Richmond became the capital of the Confederacy on May 29, 1861.

So They Say

"...slavery as an institution is a moral and political evil in any country...a greater evil to the white than to the black race."

General Robert E. Lee

• Many important battles of the Civil War were fought in Virginia until, on April 9, 1865, General Robert E. Lee surrendered his exhausted forces at Virginia's Appomattox Court House.

• On January 26, 1870, Virginia once more became a sovereign state.

• The great financial and human losses of the Civil War caused many hardships, but by the 1890s, prosperity was returning.

• World War I found Virginia a center of shipping, troop embarkation, ship building, and war training. Of 91,623 Virginians in service, 1,635 lost their lives.

• During the administration of Governor Harry Flood Byrd, in 1927 the government was simplified and improved, but segregation became law.

• World War II called 214,903 Virginians to service, and Newport News Shipyard built 185 ships for war purposes.

• Virginia's third constitution was approved in 1970, and the state elected its first Republican governor since 1886.

• In 1989, L. Douglas Wilder was elected as the first African-American governor since Reconstruction.

THAT'S INTERESTING

• Virginia might be considered a midwestern as well as an eastern state because it extends as far west as Detroit.

• George Washington was said to be as proud of his estate as of his public service. One of his many prizes was awarded for the largest jackass.

• The old apothecary shop in Alexandria, where Martha Washington bought castor oil in quarts, is still standing. One jokester said she probably used it to make her candy.

So They Say

"It openeth all the pores and passages of the body....[Users] are notably preserved in health and know not many greevous diseases wherewithal wee in England are oftentimes afflicted."

A 1588 Virginia report on tobacco

• As Lord Cornwallis surrendered at Yorktown, the band played "The World Turned Upside Down."

• The annual jousting tournament near Staunton is said to be the nation's oldest continuously operating sporting event.

NOTABLE NATIVES

Stephen Fuller Austin (Austinville, 1793-1836), colonizer/political leader. **Richard Evelyn Byrd** (Winchester, 1888-1957), naval officer/explorer. **Willa Sibert Cather** (Winchester, 1873-1947), author. **George Rogers Clark** (Charlottesville, 1752-1818), frontier leader/soldier. **William Clark** (Caroline County, 1770-1838), soldier/explorer. **Henry Clay** (Hanover County, 1777-1852), political leader. **William Henry Harrison** (Berkeley, 1773-1841), U.S. president. **Thomas Jefferson** (Goochland, now Albemarle County, 1743-1826), U.S. president. **Joseph Eggleston Johnston** (Farmville, 1807-1891), soldier. **Henry (Light-Horse Harry) Lee** (Prince William County, 1756-1818) soldier/public official. **Robert Edward Lee** (Westmoreland County, 1807-1870), soldier. **Meriwether Lewis** (Albemarle County, 1774-1809), soldier/explorer/public official. **Charles Lynch** (Lynchburg, 1736-1779), planter/patriot. **James Madison** (Port Conway, 1751-1836), U.S. president. **John Marshall** (Fauquier County, 1755-1835), chief justice of the U.S. **Cyrus Hall McCormick** (Rockbridge County, 1809-1884), inventor and industrialist. **James Monroe** (Westmoreland County, 1758-1831), U.S. president. **Pocahontas** (probably near Jamestown, 1595?-1617), Indian figure. **Powhatan** (in Virginia, 1550?-1618), Indian leader. **Peyton Randolph** (Williamsburg?, 1721?-1775), politician. **Walter Reed** (Gloucester County, 1851-1902), physician. **George Campbell Scott** (Wise, 1927-), actor. **William Clark Styron, Jr.** (Newport News, 1925-), author. **Zachary Taylor** (Orange County, 1784-1850), soldier and U.S. president. **John Tyler** (Greenway, 1790-1862), U.S. president. **Booker Taliaferro Washington** (Franklin County, 1856-1915), educator. **George Washington** (Westmoreland County, 1732-1799), soldier and first U.S. president. **Thomas Woodrow Wilson** (Staunton, 1856-1924), educator and U.S. president.

GENERAL

Admitted to statehood: June 25, 1788

Origin of name: Named by Sir Walter Raleigh, who fitted out the expedition of 1584 to the New World in honor of Queen Elizabeth, the Virgin Queen of England

Capital: Richmond

Nickname: Old Dominion, Mother of Presidents

Motto: *Sic Semper Tyrannis*—Thus always to tyrants

Animal: Fox hound

Bird: Cardinal

Flower: Dogwood

Song: "Carry Me Back to Old Virginia"

Tree: Dogwood

THE LAND

Area: 42,326 sq. mi., 35th
   Land: 39,598 sq. mi., 37th
   Water: 2,728 sq. mi., 15th
      Inland water: 1,000 sq. mi., 22nd
      Coastal water: 1,728 sq. mi., 5th
Topography: Mountain and valley region in the W, including the Blue Ridge Mountains; rolling piedmont plateau; tidewater, or coastal plain, including the eastern shore
Number of counties: 95
Geographic center: 5 mi. SW of Buckingham
Length: 430 mi.; width: 200 mi.
Highest point: 5,729 ft. (Mount Rogers), 19th
Lowest point: sea level (Atlantic Ocean), 3rd
Mean elevation: 950 ft., 28th
Coastline: 112 mi., 15th
Shoreline: 3,315 mi., 8th

CLIMATE AND ENVIRONMENT

Temp., highest: 110 deg. on July 15, 1954, at Balcony Falls; lowest: −30 deg. on Jan. 22, 1985, at Mountain Lake Biological Station

Monthly average: highest: 88.4 deg., 22nd; lowest: 26.2 deg., 37th; spread (high to low): 62.2 deg., 37th

Hazardous waste sites (1993): 24, 15th

Endangered species: Mammals: 5—Gray bat, Indiana bat, Virginia big-eared bat, Delmarva peninsula fox squirrel, Virginia northern flying squirrel; birds: 2—American peregrine falcon, Red-cockaded woodpecker; reptiles: 3; amphibians: 1; fishes: 1; invertebrates: 17; plants: 4

MAJOR CITIES
POPULATION, 1990
PERCENTAGE INCREASE, 1980-90

Arlington, 170,936—12.02%
Newport News, 170,045—17.35%
Norfolk, 261,229— –2.15%
Richmond, 203,056— –7.37%
Virginia Beach, 393,069—49.91%

THE PEOPLE

Population (1995): 6,618,358, 12th
  Percent change (1990-95): 6.9%, 18th
Population (2000 proj.): 7,048,000, 12th
  Percent change (1990-2000): 13.91%, 18th
Per sq. mi. (1994): 165.5, 16th
Percent in metro. area (1992): 77.5%, 20th
Foreign born: 312,000, 12th
  Percent: 5.0%, 17th
Top three ancestries reported:
  German, 19.16%
  English, 16.98%
  African, 15.67%
White: 4,791,739, 77.44%, 37th
Black: 1,162,994, 18.80%, 9th
Native American: 15,282, 0.25%, 37th
Asian, Pacific Isle: 159,053, 2.57%, 9th
Other races: 58,290, 0.94%, 27th
Hispanic origin: 160,288, 2.59%, 25th
Percent over 5 yrs. speaking language other than English at home: 7.3%, 24th
Percent males: 49.04%, 17th; percent females: 50.96%, 35th
Percent never married: 27.1%, 18th
Marriages per 1,000 (1993): 10.5, 9th
Divorces per 1,000 (1993): 4.5, 26th
Median age: 32.6
Under 5 years (1994): 7.16%, 27th
Under 18 years (1994): 24.47%, 42nd
65 years & older (1994): 11.1%, 43rd
Percent increase among the elderly (1990-94): 9.08%, 12th

OF VITAL IMPORTANCE

Live births per 1,000 pop. (1993): 14.7, 27th
Infant mortality rate per 1,000 births (1992): 9.5, 11th
  Rate for blacks (1990): 18.8, 6th
  Rate for whites (1990): 7.5, 36th
Births to unmarried women, % of total (1992): 28.3%, 26th
Births to teenage mothers, % of total (1992): 11.0%, 32nd
Abortions (1992): 35,020, 13th
  Rate per 1,000 women 14-44 years old: 22.7, 21st
  Percent change (1988-92): –5%, 20th
Average lifetime (1979-81): 73.43, 35th
Deaths per 1,000 pop. (1993): 8.0, 37th
Causes of death per 100,000 pop.:
  Accidents & adverse effects (1992): 30.3, 41st
  Atherosclerosis (1991): 5.3, 41st
  Cancer (1991): 187.8, 40th
  Cerebrovascular diseases (1992): 53.0, 35th
  Chronic liver diseases & cirrhosis (1991): 7.8, 41st
  Chronic obstructive pulmonary diseases (1992): 32.2, 42nd
  Diabetes mellitus (1992): 15.1, 44th
  Diseases of heart (1992): 242.4, 36th
  Pneumonia, flu (1991): 27.2, 37th
  Suicide (1992): 12.7, 20th

KEEPING WELL

Active nonfederal physicians per 100,000 pop. (1993): 215, 16th
Dentists per 100,000 (1991): 54, 24th
Nurses per 100,000 (1992): 684, 34th
Hospitals per 100,000 (1993): 1.48, 44th
  Admissions per 1,000 (1993): 105.16, 37th
  Occupancy rate per 100 beds (1993): 64.2, 17th
  Average cost per patient per day (1993): $830, 28th
  Average cost per stay (1993): $5,504, 34th
  Average stay (1992): 7.0 days, 31st
AIDS cases (adult, 1993): 1,625; per 100,000: 25.0, 24th
HIV infection, not yet AIDS (1993): 4,697
Other notifiable diseases:
  Gonorrhea: 285.2, 18th
  Measles: 1.4, 37th
  Syphilis: 34.5, 21st
  Tuberculosis: 6.6, 26th
Pop. without health insur. (1991-93): 14.7%, 17th

HOUSEHOLDS BY TYPE

Total households (1994): 2,439,000
  Percent change (1990-94): 6.4%, 14th
  Per 1,000 pop.: 372.25, 32nd
  Percent of households 65 yrs. and over:
    18.57%, 45th
  Persons per household (1994): 2.60, 23rd
Family households: 1,629,490
  Percent of total: 71.10%, 21st
Nonfamily households: 662,340
  Percent of total: 28.90%, 31st
Pop. living in group quarters: 209,300
  Percent of pop.: 3.38%, 11th

LIVING QUARTERS

Total housing units: 2,496,334
  Persons per unit: 2.48, 11th
Occupied housing units: 2,291,830
  Percent of total units: 91.81%, 11th
  Persons per unit: 2.57, 17th
  Percent of units with over 1 person per
    room: 2.84%, 29th
Owner-occupied units: 1,519,521
  Percent of total units: 60.87%, 19th
  Percent of occupied units: 66.30%, 31st
  Persons per unit: 2.70, 33rd
  Median value: $91,000, 16th
Renter-occupied units: 772,309
  Percent of total units: 30.94%, 18th
  Percent of occupied units: 33.70%, 22nd
  Persons per unit: 2.43, 15th
  Median contract rent: $411, 14th
  Rental vacancy rate: 8.1%, 28th
Mobile home, trailer & other as a percent of
    occupied housing units: 7.95%, 33rd
Persons in emergency shelters for homeless
    persons: 2,657, 0.043%, 32nd
Persons visible in street locations: 319,
    0.0052%, 28th
Persons in shelters for abused women: 185,
    0.0030%, 44th
Nursing home population: 37,762, 0.61%,
    35th

CRIME INDEX PER 100,000 (1992-93)

Total reported: 4,115.5, 40th
  Violent: 372.2, 36th
    Murder and nonnegligent manslaughter:
      8.3, 22nd
    Aggravated assault: 189.8, 41st
    Robbery: 142.0, 24th
    Forcible rape: 32.1, 39th
  Property: 3,743.3, 42nd
    Burglary: 667.7, 43rd
    Larceny, theft: 2,790.1, 30th
    Motor vehicle theft: 258.5, 38th
  Drug abuse violations (1990): 284.5, 19th
Child-abuse rate per 1,000 children (1993):
    8.86, 41st

TEACHING AND LEARNING

Pop. 3 and over enrolled in school: 1,546,257
  Percent of pop.: 26.1%, 38th
Public elementary & secondary schools (1992-
    93): 1,816
  Total enrollment (1992): 1,031,935
    Percent of total pop.: 16.14%, 39th
  Teachers (1992): 64,789
    Percent of pop.: 1.01%, 29th
  Pupil/teacher ratio (fall 1992): 15.9, 32nd
  Teachers' avg. salary (1992-93): $33,945,
    27th
  Expenditure per capita (1990-91):
    $3,318.70, 29th
  Expenditure per pupil (1991-92): $4,880,
    32nd
Percent of graduates taking SAT (1993): 63%,
    14th
  Mean SAT verbal scores: 425, 37th
  Mean SAT mathematical scores: 469, 40th
Percent of graduates taking ACT (1995): 6%,
    42nd
  Mean ACT scores: 20.6, 33rd
Percent of pop. over 25 completing:
  Less than 9th grade: 11.2%, 16th
  High school: 75.2%, 32nd
  College degree(s): 24.5%, 7th
Higher education, institutions (1993-94): 87
  Enrollment (1992): 354,172
    Percent of pop.: 5.54%, 27th
  White non-Hispanic (1992): 273,589
    Percent of enroll.: 77.25%, 34th
  Black non-Hispanic (1992): 52,881
    Percent of enroll.: 14.93%, 9th
  Hispanic (1992): 5,963
    Percent of enroll.: 1.68%, 31st
  Asian/Pacific Islander (1992): 14,128
    Percent of enroll.: 3.99%, 12th
  American Indian/AK native (1992): 1,127
    Percent of enroll.: 0.32%, 35th
  Nonresident alien (1992): 6,484
    Percent of enroll.: 1.83%, 43rd
  Female (1992): 197,645
    Percent of enroll.: 55.80%, 17th
  Pub. institutions (1993-94): 39
    Enrollment (1992): 297,522
      Percent of enroll.: 84.00%, 24th

Private institutions (1993-94): 48
　Enrollment (1992): 56,650
　Percent of enroll.: 16.00%, 28th
　Tuition, public institution (avg., 1993-94): $7,726, 10th
　Tuition, private institution (avg., 1993-94): $13,217, 22nd
Public library systems: 90
　Books & serial vol. per capita: 2.33, 31st
　Govt. expenditure per capita: $21.06, 14th

LAW ENFORCEMENT, COURTS, AND PRISONS

Police protection, corrections, judicial and legal functions expenditures (1992): $1,698,000,000
　Per capita: $266, 24th
Police per 10,000 pop. (1993): 20.89, 24th
Prisoners (state & fed.) per 100,000 pop. (1993): 3,530.05, 21st
　Percent change (1992-93): 7.8%, 14th
Death penalty: yes, by electrocution
　Under sentence of death (1993): 48, 15th
　Executed (1993): 5

RELIGION, NUMBER AND PERCENT OF POPULATION

Agnostic: 28,096—0.60%, 19th
Buddhist: 18,731—0.40%, 5th
Christian: 4,092,610—87.40%, 23rd
Hindu: 4,683—0.10%, 10th
Jewish: 51,509—1.10%, 15th
Muslim: 9,365—0.20%, 13th
Unitarian: 9,365—0.20%, 23rd
Other: 79,605—1.70%, 14th
None: 299,688—6.40%, 28th
Refused to answer: 88,970—1.90%, 31st

MAKING A LIVING

Personal income per capita (1994): $22,594, 14th
　Percent increase (1993-94): 4.3%, 37th
Disposable personal income per capita (1994): $19,501, 16th
Median income of households (1993): $36,433, 8th
Percent of pop. below poverty level (1993): 9.7%, 47th
　Percent 65 and over (1990): 14.1%, 18th
Expenditure for energy per person (1992): $1,761, 40th

ECONOMY

Civilian labor force (1994): 3,422,000
　Percent of total pop.: 52.23%, 18th

Percent 65 and over (1990): 2.85%, 23rd
Percent female: 47.40%, 11th
Percent job growth (1980-90): 34.17%, 8th
Major employer industries (1994):
　Agriculture: 56,000—1.7%, 39th
　Construction: 172,000—5.4%, 7th
　Finance, insurance, & real estate: 170,000—5.3%, 24th
　Government: 607,000—18.9%, 10th
　Manufacturing: 418,000—13.0%, 33rd
　Service: 759,000—23.7%, 13th
　Trade: 588,000—18.3%, 37th
　Transportation, communications, public utilities: 186,000—5.8%, 15th
Unemployment rate (1994): 4.88%, 38th
　Male: 4.7%, 37th
　Female: 5.1%, 33rd
Total businesses (1991): 193,800
　New business incorps. (1991): 16,883
　　Percent of total businesses: 8.71%, 9th
　Business failures (1991): 1,597
　　Percent of total businesses: 0.82%
Agriculture farm income:
　Marketing (1993): $2,068,000,000, 29th
　　Average per farm: $48,093.02, 45th
　Leading products (1993): Broilers, cattle, dairy products, tobacco
　Average value land & build. per acre (1994): $1,338, 15th
　　Percent increase (1990-94): –11.74%, 48th
　Govt. payments (1993): $46,000,000, 34th
　　Average per farm: $1,069.77, 40th
Construction, value of all: $4,979,000,000
　Per capita: $804.71, 11th
Manufactures:
　Value added: $32,511,000,000
　　Per capita: $5,254.42, 23rd
　Leading products: Textiles, transportation equipment, electric and electronic equipment, food processing, chemicals
Value of nonfuel mineral production (1994): $514,000,000, 22nd
Leading mineral products: Coal, stone, cement
Retail sales (1993): $58,251,000,000, 10th
　Per household: $24,096, 7th
　　Percent increase (1992-93): 7.5%, 21st
Tourism revenues (1992): $8.6 bil.
Foreign exports, in total value (1994): $9,573,000,000, 14th
　Per capita: $1,461.08, 17th

Gross state product per person (1993): $23,063.46, 15th

Percent change (1990-93): 3.57%, 21st

Patents per 100,000 pop. (1993): 15.19, 30th

Public aid recipients (percent of resident pop. 1993): 4.8%, 42nd

Medicaid recipients per 1,000 pop. (1993): 88.99, 47th

Medicare recipients per 1,000 pop. (1993): 120.35, 44th

TRAVEL AND TRANSPORTATION

Motor vehicle registrations (1993): 5,408,000
Per 1,000 pop.: 835.47, 17th

Motorcycle registrations (1993): 62,000
Per 1,000 pop.: 9.58, 41st

Licensed drivers per 1,000 pop. (1993): 707.55, 15th

Deaths from motor vehicle accidents per 100,000 pop. (1993): 13.52, 37th

Public roads & streets (1993):
Total mileage: 68,429
Per 1,000 pop.: 10.57, 38th
Rural mileage: 52,848
Per 1,000 pop.: 8.16, 38th
Urban mileage: 15,581
Per 1,000 pop.: 2.41, 45th
Interstate mileage: 1,106
Per 1,000 pop.: 0.17, 34th

Annual vehicle-mi. of travel per person (1993): 9,918, 18th

Mean travel time for workers age 16+ who work away from home: 24.0 min., 7th

GOVERNMENT

Percent of voting age pop. registered (1994): 60.0%, 37th
Percent of voting age pop. voting (1994): 45.7%, 29th
Percent of voting age pop. voting for U.S. representatives (1994): 38.4%, 28th

State legislators, total (1995): 140, 28th
Women members (1992): 17
Percent of legislature: 12.1%, 41st

U.S. Congress, House members (1995): 11
Change (1985-95): +1

Revenues (1993):
State govt.: $16,307,000,000
Per capita: $2,519.23, 44th
Parimutuel & amusement taxes & lotteries, revenue per capita: $127.14, 10th

Expenditures (1993):
State govt.: $14,721,000,000
Per capita: $2,274.22, 44th

Debt outstanding (1993): $7,438,000,000
Per capita: $1,149.08, 31st

LAWS AND REGULATIONS

Legal driving age: 18, 16 if completed driver education course

Marriage age without parental consent: 18

Divorce residence requirement: 6 mo., for qualifications check local statutes

ATTRACTIONS (1995)

Major opera companies: 2

Major symphony orchestras: 2

Major dance companies: 1

State appropriations for arts agencies per capita: $0.33, 50th

State Fair in late September–early October at Richmond

SPORTS AND COMPETITION

NCAA teams (Division I): College of William and Mary Tribe, George Mason Univ. Patriots, Hampton Univ. Pirates, James Madison Univ. Dukes, Liberty Univ. Flames, Old Dominion Univ. Monarchs, Radford Univ. Highlanders, Univ. of Richmond Spiders, Univ. of Virginia Cavaliers, Virginia Commonwealth Univ. Rams, Virginia Military Institute Keydets, Virginia Polytechnic Institute & State Univ. Gobblers/ Hokies

WASHINGTON

"But, however inviting may be the soil, the remote distance and savage aspect of the boundless wilderness along the Pacific seem to defer the colonization of such a region to a period far beyond the present generation [early 1800s] and yet, if we consider the rapid progress of civilization in other new and equally remote countries, we might still indulge the hope of seeing this, at no distant time, one of the most flourishing countries on the globe."

Alexander Ross, fur trader and chronicler

Smallest in area of the conterminous states west of Iowa, Washington is a state with a split personality—the rainy lands to the west and the desert land east of the Cascade Mountains, which stretch for miles without a single tree. Both sides are known for their production of major crops. Ships from all parts of the world dock in the ports of Washington, and fishing fleets catch salmon, halibut, and other fish in the Pacific Ocean. Washington is a lumbering state as well as a leader in dairy farming and flower-bulb production, cattle raising, and wheat, fruit, and vegetable crops. Grand Coulee Dam, on the Columbia River, is the mightiest piece of masonry in the world. Seattle has often been ranked as the "most livable" U.S. city.

SUPERLATIVES

• Provides 10% of all U.S. annual timber growth.
• Produces 30% of the nation's hydroelectric power.
• World leader in apple production.
• World's largest farm reclamation project.
• First in hops, rhubarb, edible peas, and sweet cherries.
• Leader in vegetable seed production.
• Unique temperate rain forest—Olympic Peninsula.

MOMENTS IN HISTORY

• Juan de Fuca may have sailed the Washington shores in 1592, but the first recorded visit was made by Juan Perez in 1774.
• Bruno Heceta and Juan de Bodega y Quadra in 1775 were the first Europeans known to have touched present-day Washington, and they claimed the land for the King of Spain.

• Captain George Vancouver discovered Puget Sound in 1792.
• In 1792, Captain Robert Gray reached the Columbia River, sailed into its treacherous mouth, and landed his ship the *Columbia* at present-day Fort Columbia.
• The great expedition of Meriwether Lewis and William Clark made the dangerous passage down the Snake and Columbia rivers and arrived at the coast in November 1805.

So They Say

"Great joy in camp, we are in view of the Ocean, this great Pacific Ocean which we been so long anxious to see, and the roreing or noise made by the waves...may be heard distinctly."

Meriwether Lewis

• Lewis and Clark began their return journey on March 23, 1806, trading with the Indians they encountered and considerately treating their ailments.
• David Thompson established the trading post of Spokane House in 1810.

So They Say

"...The Pierced nose Indians [Nez Percé] are stout likely men, handsom women, and verry dressey in their way, the dress of the men are a White Buffalow robe or Elk Skin dressed with Beeds...Sea Shells and the Mother of Pirl hung to their hair...The women dress in a shirt of Ibex or Goat Skins which reach quite down to their anckles."

Meriwether Lewis

• Several mergers extended the Hudson's Bay Company interests in the area, and they established Fort Vancouver in 1824. It became the first permanent European settlement in present-day Washington.

• By 1828, Fort Vancouver had become a civilization in the wilderness, under the direction of a British fur trader named Dr. John McLoughlin, who was known throughout the West for his hospitality and kindness to those in difficulty. McLoughlin's actions got him in trouble with both American and British authorities, and he ended up as a "man without a country."

• In 1836, Dr. Marcus Whitman established a mission called Waiilatpu, near present-day Walla Walla.
• The rival claims of Britain and the United States appeared to be leading to war, but in 1846 the present boundaries of Washington were settled.

• In 1847 the Cayuse Indians attacked the Waiilatpu mission and killed Dr. and Mrs. Whitman.
• Oregon Territory—Washington, Oregon, and parts of Idaho—was established in 1848, and development came rapidly.
• The Indian wars came to a virtual halt in 1858.
• The cities of Vancouver, Ellensburg, Spokane, and Seattle were all swept by fire in 1889.
• On November 11, 1889, Washington became a state.
• Seattle hosted the Alaska-Yukon-Pacific Exposition in 1909.
• World War I called 68,326 Washingtonians to service.
• The Golden Jubilee of statehood was celebrated in 1939.
• During World War II the super-secret installations at Richland turned out nuclear materials, and the state's production of airplanes and ships made a vital contribution to the war effort.
• Seattle (1962) and Spokane (1974) held world's fairs.
• The explosion of Mount St. Helens volcano, on May 18, 1980, was one of the worst disasters of an era.
• In 1988 state apple growers lost more than $145 million in wake of reports that alar, a growth-inducing chemical sprayed on apples, causes cancer.
• The 1991 collision of a Japanese fishing vessel and a Chinese freighter covered the beaches in Olympic National Park with oil from the resulting spill.
• In 1992 experts claimed the world's largest living organism, a 1,500-acre fungus, was growing south of Mount Adams.

THAT'S INTERESTING

• Point Roberts on the mainland is American territory but juts out from Canada and cannot be reached by land from the rest of the United States.
• The Indian custom of potlatch was observed at parties, when the host or hostess of the event gave away most of his or her possessions to the guests.
• The "Pig War" started when both the United States and Canada claimed the San Juan Islands, and the British threatened to place one Lyman Cutler on trial for shooting a

pig owned by a Briton. The matter was settled when arbitration gave the islands to the United States.

• Early Seattle had a shortage of females. Asa Mercer went east and persuaded 11 girls of good families to return to meet the many eligible bachelors. Several prominent families trace their roots back to the Mercer girls.

NOTABLE NATIVES

Harry Lillis (Bing) Crosby (Tacoma, 1904-1977), singer/actor. **Chief Joseph** (Wallowa Valley, near the Washington/Idaho/Oregon border, 1840?-1904), Indian leader. **Mary Therese McCarthy** (Seattle, 1912-1989), author. **Seattle or Seatlh** (near Seattle, 1786?-1866), Indian leader. **Minoru Yamasaki** (Seattle, 1912-1986), architect.

GENERAL

Admitted to statehood: November 11, 1889
Origin of name: Named after George Washington. When the bill creating the territory of Columbia was introduced in the 32nd Congress, the name was changed to Washington.
Capital: Olympia
Nickname: Evergreen State
Motto: *Al-ki*—By and by
Bird: Willow goldfinch
Fish: Steelhead trout
Flower: Western rhododendron
Song: "Washington, My Home"
Tree: Western hemlock

THE LAND

Area: 70,637 sq. mi., 19th
  Land: 66,581 sq. mi., 20th
  Water: 4,056 sq. mi., 9th
    Inland water: 1,545 sq. mi., 14th
    Coastal water: 2,511 sq. mi., 2nd
Topography: Olympic Mountains on NW peninsula; open land along coast to Columbia River; flat terrain of Puget Sound lowland; Cascade Mountains' high peaks to the E of lowland; Columbia Basin in central portion; highlands to the NE; mountains to the SE
Number of counties: 39
Geographic center: Chelan, 10 mi. WSW of Wenatchee
Length: 360 mi.; width: 240 mi.
Highest point: 14,410 ft. (Mount Rainier), 4th

Lowest point: sea level (Pacific Ocean), 3rd
Mean elevation: 1,700 ft., 18th
Coastline: 157 mi., 12th
Shoreline: 3,026 mi., 10th

CLIMATE AND ENVIRONMENT

Temp., highest: 118 deg. on Aug. 5, 1961, at Ice Harbor Dam; lowest: –48 deg. on Dec. 30, 1968, at Mazama and Winthrop
Monthly average: highest: 84.0 deg., 41st; lowest: 20.0 deg., 27th; spread (high to low): 64.0 deg., 33rd
Hazardous waste sites (1993): 55, 6th
Endangered species: Mammals: 3—Woodland caribou, Columbian white tailed deer, Northern Rocky Mountain gray wolf; birds: 3—American peregrine falcon, Aleutian Canada goose, Brown pelican; reptiles: 1; amphibians: none; fishes: none; invertebrates: 1; plants: none

MAJOR CITIES
POPULATION, 1990
PERCENTAGE INCREASE, 1980-90

Bellevue, 86,874—17.55%
Everett, 69,961—28.57%
Seattle, 516,259—4.54%
Spokane, 177,196—3.44%
Tacoma, 176,664—11.46%

THE PEOPLE

Population (1995): 5,430,940, 15th
  Percent change (1990-95): 11.6%, 6th
Population (2000 proj.): 6,070,000, 13th
  Percent change (1990-2000): 24.73%, 4th
Per sq. mi. (1994): 80.2, 27th
Percent in metro. area (1992): 83.0%, 15th
Foreign born: 322,000, 10th
  Percent: 6.6%, 14th
Top three ancestries reported:
  German, 28.56%
  English, 18.43%
  Irish, 15.78%
White: 4,308,937, 88.54%, 22nd
Black: 149,801, 3.08%, 36th
Native American: 81,483, 1.67%, 9th
Asian, Pacific Isle: 210,958, 4.33%, 3rd
Other races: 115,513, 2.37%, 14th
Hispanic origin: 214,570, 4.41%, 19th
Percent over 5 yrs. speaking language other than English at home: 9.0%, 19th
Percent males: 49.60%, 9th; percent females: 50.40%, 43rd

Percent never married: 24.8%, 32nd
Marriages per 1,000 (1993): 8.3, 30th
Divorces per 1,000 (1993): 5.2, 17th
Median age: 33.1
Under 5 years (1994): 7.37%, 21st
Under 18 years (1994): 26.35%, 21st
65 years & older (1994): 11.6%, 38th
Percent increase among the elderly (1990-94): 7.42%, 20th

OF VITAL IMPORTANCE

Live births per 1,000 pop. (1993): 13.6, 44th
Infant mortality rate per 1,000 births (1992): 6.8, 45th
  Rate for blacks (1990): 14.5, 31st
  Rate for whites (1990): 7.6, 33rd
Births to unmarried women, % of total (1992): 25.3%, 38th
Births to teenage mothers, % of total (1992): 10.6%, 34th
Abortions (1992): 33,190, 14th
  Rate per 1,000 women 14-44 years old: 27.7, 11th
  Percent change (1988-92): 0%, 13th
Average lifetime (1979-81): 75.13, 10th
Deaths per 1,000 pop. (1993): 8.0, 37th
Causes of death per 100,000 pop.:
  Accidents & adverse effects (1992): 33.4, 30th
  Atherosclerosis (1991): 8.7, 13th
  Cancer (1991): 184.0, 41st
  Cerebrovascular diseases (1992): 56.7, 28th
  Chronic liver diseases & cirrhosis (1991): 8.1, 39th
  Chronic obstructive pulmonary diseases (1992): 40.6, 17th
  Diabetes mellitus (1992): 15.8, 43rd
  Diseases of heart (1992): 217.5, 44th
  Pneumonia, flu (1991): 26.9, 38th
  Suicide (1992): 13.5, 14th

KEEPING WELL

Active nonfederal physicians per 100,000 pop. (1993): 220, 15th
Dentists per 100,000 (1991): 62, 16th
Nurses per 100,000 (1992): 761, 25th
Hospitals per 100,000 (1993): 1.71, 38th
  Admissions per 1,000 (1993): 93.97, 44th
  Occupancy rate per 100 beds (1993): 57.6, 39th
  Average cost per patient per day (1993): $1,143, 3rd
  Average cost per stay (1993): $5,792, 24th
  Average stay (1992): 5.8 days, 50th

AIDS cases (adult, 1993): 1,564; per 100,000: 29.8, 20th
HIV infection, not yet AIDS (1993): NA
Other notifiable diseases:
  Gonorrhea: 102.9, 35th
  Measles: 7.2, 14th
  Syphilis: 17.1, 26th
  Tuberculosis: 5.8, 29th
Pop. without health insur. (1991-93): 11.2%, 38th

HOUSEHOLDS BY TYPE

Total households (1994): 2,042,000
  Percent change (1990-94): 9.1%, 7th
  Per 1,000 pop.: 382.18, 9th
  Percent of households 65 yrs. and over: 19.15%, 41st
  Persons per household (1994): 2.56, 35th
Family households: 1,264,934
  Percent of total: 67.56%, 47th
Nonfamily households: 607,497
  Percent of total: 32.44%, 5th
Pop. living in group quarters: 120,531
  Percent of pop.: 2.48%, 35th

LIVING QUARTERS

Total housing units: 2,032,378
  Persons per unit: 2.39, 27th
Occupied housing units: 1,872,431
  Percent of total units: 92.13%, 8th
  Persons per unit: 2.49, 36th
  Percent of units with over 1 person per room: 3.89%, 19th
Owner-occupied units: 1,171,580
  Percent of total units: 57.65%, 32nd
  Percent of occupied units: 62.57%, 42nd
  Persons per unit: 2.68, 36th
  Median value: $93,400, 15th
Renter-occupied units: 700,851
  Percent of total units: 34.48%, 10th
  Percent of occupied units: 37.43%, 12th
  Persons per unit: 2.30, 32nd
  Median contract rent: $383, 16th
  Rental vacancy rate: 5.8%, 47th
Mobile home, trailer & other as a percent of occupied housing units: 11.07%, 26th
Persons in emergency shelters for homeless persons: 4,565, 0.094%, 8th
Persons visible in street locations: 772, 0.0159%, 11th
Persons in shelters for abused women: 297, 0.0061%, 11th
Nursing home population: 32,840, 0.67%, 30th

CRIME INDEX PER 100,000 (1992-93)

Total reported: 5,952.3, 12th
   Violent: 514.6, 26th
      Murder and nonnegligent manslaughter: 5.2, 33rd
      Aggravated assault: 307.9, 29th
      Robbery: 137.1, 27th
      Forcible rape: 64.4, 4th
   Property: 5,437.7, 8th
      Burglary: 1,067.2, 20th
      Larceny, theft: 3,914.4, 5th
      Motor vehicle theft: 456.1, 21st
Drug abuse violations (1990): 219.6, 33rd
Child-abuse rate per 1,000 children (1993): 29.87, 3rd

TEACHING AND LEARNING

Pop. 3 and over enrolled in school: 1,252,312
   Percent of pop.: 26.9%, 30th
Public elementary & secondary schools (1992-93): 2,017
   Total enrollment (1992): 896,475
      Percent of total pop.: 17.43%, 26th
   Teachers (1992): 44,295
      Percent of pop.: 0.86%, 48th
   Pupil/teacher ratio (fall 1992): 20.2, 3rd
   Teachers' avg. salary (1992-93): $38,371, 16th
   Expenditure per capita (1990-91): $3,810.26, 14th
   Expenditure per pupil (1991-92): $5,271, 23rd
Percent of graduates taking SAT (1993): 52%, 20th
   Mean SAT verbal scores: 435, 30th
   Mean SAT mathematical scores: 486, 29th
Percent of graduates taking ACT (1995): 17%, 34th
   Mean ACT scores: 22.2, 3rd
Percent of pop. over 25 completing:
   Less than 9th grade: 5.5%, 49th
   High school: 83.8%, 4th
   College degree(s): 22.9%, 13th
Higher education, institutions (1993-94): 62
   Enrollment (1992): 276,484
      Percent of pop.: 5.37%, 30th
   White non-Hispanic (1992): 230,176
      Percent of enroll.: 83.25%, 24th
   Black non-Hispanic (1992): 9,350
      Percent of enroll.: 3.38%, 34th
   Hispanic (1992): 7,528
      Percent of enroll.: 2.72%, 16th
   Asian/Pacific Islander (1992): 18,701

Percent of enroll.: 6.76%, 3rd
   American Indian/AK native (1992): 4,435
      Percent of enroll.: 1.60%, 8th
   Nonresident alien (1992): 6,294
      Percent of enroll.: 2.28%, 29th
   Female (1992): 153,250
      Percent of enroll.: 55.43%, 24th
   Pub. institutions (1993-94): 36
      Enrollment (1992): 238,763
      Percent of enroll.: 86.36%, 18th
   Private institutions (1993-94): 26
      Enrollment (1992): 37,721
      Percent of enroll.: 13.64%, 34th
   Tuition, public institution (avg., 1993-94): $6,438, 19th
   Tuition, private institution (avg., 1993-94): $15,357, 15th
Public library systems: 70
   Books & serial vol. per capita: 2.56, 26th
   Govt. expenditure per capita: $25.46, 4th

LAW ENFORCEMENT, COURTS, AND PRISONS

Police protection, corrections, judicial and legal functions expenditures (1992): $1,679,000,000
   Per capita: $327, 13th
Police per 10,000 pop. (1993): 15.92, 44th
Prisoners (state & fed.) per 100,000 pop. (1993): 1,981.18, 40th
   Percent change (1992-93): 4.6%, 27th
Death penalty: yes, by lethal injection or hanging
   Under sentence of death (1993): 7, 29th
   Executed (1993): 1

RELIGION, NUMBER AND PERCENT OF POPULATION

Agnostic: 50,474—1.40%, 1st
Buddhist: 18,027—0.50%, 2nd
Christian: 2,779,690—77.10%, 47th
Hindu: 3,605—0.10%, 10th
Jewish: 14,421—0.40%, 31st
Muslim: NA
Unitarian: 18,027—0.50%, 6th
Other: 97,343—2.70%, 2nd
None: 504,743—14.00%, 2nd
Refused to answer: 118,975—3.30%, 4th

MAKING A LIVING

Personal income per capita (1994): $22,610, 13th
   Percent increase (1993-94): 3.8%, 45th

Disposable personal income per capita (1994): $19,886, 12th

Median income of households (1993): $35,655, 12th

Percent of pop. below poverty level (1993): 12.1%, 32nd

Percent 65 and over (1990): 9.1%, 44th

Expenditure for energy per person (1992): $1,728, 41st

ECONOMY

Civilian labor force (1994): 2,708,000
  Percent of total pop.: 50.68%, 29th
  Percent 65 and over (1990): NA
  Percent female: 45.38%, 38th
Percent job growth (1980-90): 33.51%, 9th
Major employer industries (1994):
  Agriculture: NA—1.8%, 37th
  Construction: 115,000—4.6%, 18th
  Finance, insurance, & real estate: 165,000—6.6%, 9th
  Government: 464,000—18.6%, 13th
  Manufacturing: 298,000—12.0%, 38th
  Service: 517,000—20.8%, 27th
  Trade: 492,000—19.7%, 11th
  Transportation, communications, public utilities: 130,000—5.2%, 28th
Unemployment rate (1994): 6.43%, 13th
  Male: 6.5%, 13th
  Female: 6.3%, 14th
Total businesses (1991): 183,769
  New business incorps. (1991): 11,521
    Percent of total businesses: 6.27%, 21st
  Business failures (1991): 860
    Percent of total businesses: 0.47%
Agriculture farm income:
  Marketing (1993): $4,574,000,000, 12th
    Average per farm: $127,055.56, 10th
  Leading products (1993): Cattle, apples, dairy products, wheat
  Average value land & build. per acre (1994): $898, 29th
    Percent increase (1990-94): 15.28%, 23rd
  Govt. payments (1993): $207,000,000, 22nd
    Average per farm: $5,750.00, 18th
Construction, value of all: $4,794,000,000
  Per capita: $985.06, 3rd
Manufactures:
  Value added: $24,871,000,000
    Per capita: $5,110.45, 26th
  Leading products: Aircraft, pulp and paper, lumber and plywood, aluminum, processed fruits and vegetables

Value of nonfuel mineral production (1994): $556,000,000, 20th

Leading mineral products: Cement, sand and gravel, stone

Retail sales (1993): $43,370,000,000, 16th
  Per household: $21,332, 34th
    Percent increase (1992-93): 3.7%, 39th
Tourism revenues: $5.3 bil.
Foreign exports, in total value (1994): $23,629,000,000, 5th
  Per capita: $4,422.42, 1st
Gross state product per person (1993): $23,714.63, 13th
  Percent change (1990-93): 6.25%, 8th
Patents per 100,000 pop. (1993): 20.44, 24th
Public aid recipients (percent of resident pop. 1993): 7.1%, 19th
Medicaid recipients per 1,000 pop. (1993): 120.37, 23rd
Medicare recipients per 1,000 pop. (1993): 125.12, 39th

TRAVEL AND TRANSPORTATION

Motor vehicle registrations (1993): 4,413,000
  Per 1,000 pop.: 839.13, 14th
Motorcycle registrations (1993): 109,000
  Per 1,000 pop.: 20.73, 15th
Licensed drivers per 1,000 pop. (1993): 703.37, 18th
Deaths from motor vehicle accidents per 100,000 pop. (1993): 12.59, 40th
Public roads & streets (1993):
  Total mileage: 79,428
    Per 1,000 pop.: 15.10, 31st
  Rural mileage: 62,210
    Per 1,000 pop.: 11.83, 31st
  Urban mileage: 17,218
    Per 1,000 pop.: 3.27, 18th
  Interstate mileage: 763
    Per 1,000 pop.: 0.15, 35th
Annual vehicle-mi. of travel per person (1993): 8,766, 37th
Mean travel time for workers age 16+ who work away from home: 22.0 min., 13th

GOVERNMENT

Percent of voting age pop. registered (1994): 66.8%, 20th
  Percent of voting age pop. voting (1994): 46.3%, 25th
  Percent of voting age pop. voting for U.S. representatives (1994): 42.2%, 19th

State legislators, total (1995): 147, 25th
  Women members (1992): 48
    Percent of legislature: 32.7%, 2nd
U.S. Congress, House members (1995): 9
  Change (1985-95): +1
Revenues (1993):
  State govt.: $19,930,000,000
    Per capita: $3,789.69, 8th
  Parimutuel & amusement taxes & lotteries, revenue per capita: $70.36, 28th
Expenditures (1993):
  State govt.: $18,003,000,000
    Per capita: $3,423.27, 11th
Debt outstanding (1993): $7,848,000,000
    Per capita: $1,492.30, 22nd

LAWS AND REGULATIONS

Legal driving age: 18, 16 if completed driver education course
Marriage age without parental consent: 18
Divorce residence requirement: Bona fide resident

ATTRACTIONS (1995)

Major opera companies: 1
Major symphony orchestras: 2
Major dance companies: 1
Major professional theater companies (non-profit): 1
State appropriations for arts agencies per capita: $0.43, 44th
State fair: Western Washington, mid-August at Puyallup; Eastern Washington, late September at Ellensburg

SPORTS AND COMPETITION

NCAA teams (Division I): Eastern Washington Univ. Eagles, Gonzaga Univ. Bulldogs/Zags, Univ. of Washington Huskies, Washington State Univ. Cougars
Major league baseball teams: Seattle Mariners (AL West), The Kingdome
NBA basketball teams: Seattle SuperSonics, Key Arena
NFL football teams: Seattle Seahawks (AFC), The Kingdome

WEST
VIRGINIA

"We West Virginians are very tired of being considered inhabitants of just a dominion of Old Dominion....Some inhabitants take a very strong line about this and always refer to it in conversation as 'West—By God—Virginia!' "

John Knowles, novelist

West Virginia's "birth" during the Civil War, when the region refused to secede from the Union, made it unique among the states. Its mountains have given it the loftiest average height east of the Rockies. The state contains some of the most rugged land in the country: There are no large areas of level ground, except along major rivers. Its beautiful mountain scenery and mineral springs attract many tourists. Its surface shelters an unusual variety of plants, ranging from Arctic types to those of the semitropics. Beneath the surface lie minerals, including coal, in which the state has long been a leader. This war-born state suffered terribly during the Civil War. One city changed hands an incredible 56 times. But West Virginia is a state that always seems able to bounce back from disaster.

SUPERLATIVES

• "Highest state" east of the Mississippi.
• Only state carved from another without its permission.
• Pioneer in natural gas production and leads the eastern states.
• Noted for record sizes of individual trees.

MOMENTS IN HISTORY

• The earliest known Europeans in what is now West Virginia came with the party of Walter Austin in 1641.
• Noted for its heavy drinking, the party of Governor Alexander Spotswood of Virginia may have staggered as far as present-day Pendelton County in 1716.
• Laid out in 1732, Shepherdstown became the oldest permanent settlement in West Virginia.
• By 1753 settlers were arriving in substantial numbers.

• The French and Indian War caused great hardship, diminishing when the French lost the continent in 1763.

So They Say

"I am too little acquainted, Sir, with pathetic language to attempt a description of the people's distresses—I see inevitable destruction in so clear a light, that, unless vigorous measures are taken by the Assembly and speedy assistance sent...the poor inhabitants that are now in the Fort [Edwards] must unavoidably fall..."

George Washington,
on French and Indian War attacks

• In 1774 the entire family of Mingo Indian leader James Logan was murdered in his absence.

So They Say

"...in cold blood and unprovoked, [white men] cut off all the relatives of Logan, not sparing even my women and chilldren. There runs not a drop of my blood in the veins of any creature. This called on me for revenge. I have fully glutted my vengeance...."

Indian leader James Logan,
who reputedly took
some 30 white scalps in revenge

• A battle with the Indians at Point Pleasant in 1774 has been labeled "the first battle of the Revolution."
• During the Revolution, Indian wars again erupted in 1777. A principal cause was the cold-blooded murder of Chief Cornstalk, who was on a peaceful mission.

• The Battle of Fort Henry (Wheeling), called the "Last Battle of the Revolution," was fought in September 1782, long after war had ceased in the East.

• The most notorious episode of the growing hostility over slavery took place in 1859 when "Isaac Smith" led his followers across the Potomac and captured the federal arsenal at Harpers Ferry. Of course, he was really the abolitionist John Brown, who was quickly tried and executed.

So They Say

"Let no man pray that Brown be spared. Let Virginia make him a martyr. Now he has only blundered. His cause was noble, his work miserable. But a cord and a gibbet would redeem all that, and round up Brown's failure with a heroic success."

Henry Ward Beecher,
on John Brown

• When Virginia seceded in 1861, the West Virginia legislators voted against it but were overruled.

• The skirmish at Philippi on June 3, 1861, is considered to have been the first land battle of the Civil War. It was important because it shut off the Confederates from the coal fields of the region.

• On two different occasions, the people of West Virginia voted to separate from Virginia. On June 20, 1863, the wartime state of West Virginia was born by acceptance of the federal government.

• Civil War battles brought much destruction, especially to industry. The state's last major encounter of the war was the Battle of Droop Mountain, on November 6, 1863, but Confederate raids continued. Romney changed hands 56 times between Union and Confederate troops. Those in Union service totaled 36,530, with 7,000 in Confederate uniform.

• After much controversy, the capital was moved permanently to Charleston in 1885.

• A mine explosion in 1907 at Monongah was one of the worst in the state's history, causing 361 deaths.

• World War I called 46,648 West Virginians into the armed services, with 1,721 losing their lives.

• The state capitol burned on January 3, 1921, and that same year a miners' disagreement came to be known as the Battle of Blair Mountain.

• The 1937 Ohio River floods were the worst yet recorded, with some cities overwhelmed by water more than 20 feet above flood stage.

• During World War II the famed Greenbrier Hotel became an internment center for enemy diplomats, then a government hospital, serving more than 20,000 patients. The state's war casualties totaled 4,865 dead.

• The state's coal production reached its all-time high in 1947, declined, then was reborn in the mid-1970s.

• In the decade between 1980 and 1990, West Virginia lost a higher percentage of its population than any other state.

THAT'S INTERESTING

• The discovery of wild marijuana growing in Moorefield brought a marked increase in tourism to the town, but the weed was destroyed by officials.

• The West Virginia "panhandle" is so narrow that the city of Weirton stretches from border to border. The only U.S. city that extends from one state border to another, it is wedged in between Ohio and Pennsylvania.

• A touring circus is said to have decided the choice of Charleston as state capital. Its supporters lured voters statewide with a flamboyant circus and won handily.

• Ann Royall became the first woman journalist to interview a president. While John Quincy Adams was swimming, she stole his clothes and would not return them until he gave her a hearing.

• Entomologist Romeo D. Erdie gained fame for his bug factory. Uses for his model insects have ranged from exterminator ads to fine jewelry. He turned them out by the millions.

• The community of Shepherdstown was on George Washington's list for choice of a national capital, but it lost out in the final selection.

• Bluefield, 2,558 feet above sea level, is the highest city east of Denver.

NOTABLE NATIVES

Newton Diehl Baker (Martinsburg, 1871-1937), public official. **Pearl Sydenstricker Buck** (Hillsboro, 1892-1973), author. **Cornstalk** (Ohio-West Virginia frontier, 1720?-1777), Indian leader. **John William Davis** (Clarksburg, 1873-1955), politician. **Thomas Jonathan**

(Stonewall) Jackson (Clarksburg, 1824-1863), soldier. **Dwight Whitney Morrow** (Huntington, 1873-1931), banker/diplomat. **Walter Philip Reuther** (Wheeling, 1907-1970), labor leader.

GENERAL

Admitted to statehood: June 20, 1863
Origin of name: Virginia was named by Sir Walter Raleigh, who fitted out the expedition of 1584, in honor of Queen Elizabeth, the Virgin Queen of England. It became West Virginia when western counties of Virginia refused to secede from the United States in 1863
Capital: Charleston
Nickname: Mountain State
Motto: *Montani Semper Liberi*—Mountaineers are always free
Animal: Black bear
Bird: Cardinal
Fish: Brook trout
Flower: Big rhododendron
Song: "West Virginia, My Home Sweet Home," "The West Virginia Hills," and "This Is My West Virginia"
Tree: Sugar maple

THE LAND

Area: 24,232 sq. mi., 41st
  Land: 24,087 sq. mi., 41st
  Water: 145 sq. mi., 49th
    Inland water: 145 sq. mi., 48th
Topography: Ranging from hilly to mountainous; Allegheny plateau, in the W, covers two-thirds of the state; mountains here are the highest in the state, over 4,000 ft.
Number of counties: 55
Geographic center: Braxton, 4 mi. E of Sutton
Length: 240 mi.; width: 130 mi.
Highest point: 4,861 ft. (Spruce Knob), 24th
Lowest point: 240 ft. (Potomac River), 31st
Mean elevation: 1,500 ft., 19th

CLIMATE AND ENVIRONMENT

Temp., highest: 112 deg. on July 10, 1936, at Martinsburg; lowest: –37 deg. on Dec. 30, 1917, at Lewisburg
Monthly average: highest: 85.6 deg., 35th; lowest: 23.9 deg., 33rd; spread (high to low): 61.7 deg., 39th
Hazardous waste sites (1993): 6, 44th
Endangered species: Mammals: 3—Indiana bat, Virginia big-eared bat, Virginia

northern flying squirrel; birds: 1—American peregrine falcon; reptiles: none; amphibians: none; fishes: none; invertebrates: 5; plants: 3

MAJOR CITIES
POPULATION, 1990
PERCENTAGE INCREASE, 1980-90

Charleston, 57,287— –10.44%
Huntington, 54,844— –13.88%
Morgantown, 25,879— –6.25%
Parkersburg, 33,862— –15.23%
Wheeling, 34,882— –19.01%

THE PEOPLE

Population (1995): 1,828,140, 35th
  Percent change (1990-95): 1.9%, 43rd
Population (2000 proj.): 1,840,000, 35th
  Percent change (1990-2000): 2.59%, 44th
Per sq. mi. (1994): 75.6, 29th
Percent in metro. area (1992): 41.8%, 42nd
Foreign born: 16,000, 47th
  Percent: 0.9%, 49th
Top three ancestries reported:
  German, 26.16%
  Irish, 19.41%
  English, 15.06%
White: 1,725,523, 96.21%, 5th
Black: 56,295, 3.14%, 35th
Native American: 2,458, 0.14%, 50th
Asian, Pacific Isle: 7,459, 0.42%, 51st
Other races: 1,742, 0.10%, 51st
Hispanic origin: 8,489, 0.47%, 51st
Percent over 5 yrs. speaking language other than English at home: 2.6%, 50th
Percent males: 48.04%, 44th; percent females: 51.96%, 8th
Percent never married: 22.2%, 47th
Marriages per 1,000 (1993): 7.2, 40th
Divorces per 1,000 (1993): 5.3, 14th
Median age: 35.4
Under 5 years (1994): 5.93%, 51st
Under 18 years (1994): 23.55%, 48th
65 years & older (1994): 15.4%, 5th
Percent increase among the elderly (1990-94): 4.13%, 37th

OF VITAL IMPORTANCE

Live births per 1,000 pop. (1993): 12.1, 50th
Infant mortality rate per 1,000 births (1992): 9.2, 17th
  Rate for blacks (1990): 16.6, 19th
  Rate for whites (1990): 9.6, 2nd

Births to unmarried women, % of total (1992): 27.7%, 27th

Births to teenage mothers, % of total (1992): 17.2%, 5th

Abortions (1992): 3,140, 45th
Rate per 1,000 women 14-44 years old: 7.7, 48th
Percent change (1988-92): 2%, 10th

Average lifetime (1979-81): 72.84, 43rd

Deaths per 1,000 pop. (1993): 11.0, 1st

Causes of death per 100,000 pop.:
Accidents & adverse effects (1992): 46.7, 8th
Atherosclerosis (1991): 8.4, 15th
Cancer (1991): 255.1, 3rd
Cerebrovascular diseases (1992): 60.3, 22nd
Chronic liver diseases & cirrhosis (1991): 9.3, 24th
Chronic obstructive pulmonary diseases (1992): 54.3, 2nd
Diabetes mellitus (1992): 30.1, 1st
Diseases of heart (1992): 382.9, 1st
Pneumonia, flu (1991): 38.2, 6th
Suicide (1992): 13.3, 15th

KEEPING WELL

Active nonfederal physicians per 100,000 pop. (1993): 182, 35th

Dentists per 100,000 (1991): 45, 42nd

Nurses per 100,000 (1992): 657, 38th

Hospitals per 100,000 (1993): 3.19, 13th
Admissions per 1,000 (1993): 153.08, 2nd
Occupancy rate per 100 beds (1993): 61.9, 26th
Average cost per patient per day (1993): $701, 39th
Average cost per stay (1993): $4,712, 47th
Average stay (1992): 7.1 days, 26th

AIDS cases (adult, 1993): 106; per 100,000: 5.8, 47th

HIV infection, not yet AIDS (1993): 224

Other notifiable diseases:
Gonorrhea: 82.1, 39th
Measles: 0.3, 46th
Syphilis: 13.7, 29th
Tuberculosis: 4.9, 34th

Pop. without health insur. (1991-93): 16.5%, 14th

HOUSEHOLDS BY TYPE

Total households (1994): 705,000
Percent change (1990-94): 2.4%, 36th

Per 1,000 pop.: 386.94, 5th
Percent of households 65 yrs. and over: 26.67%, 2nd
Persons per household (1994): 2.53, 46th

Family households: 500,259
Percent of total: 72.65%, 11th

Nonfamily households: 188,298
Percent of total: 27.35%, 41st

Pop. living in group quarters: 36,911
Percent of pop.: 2.06%, 48th

LIVING QUARTERS

Total housing units: 781,295
Persons per unit: 2.30, 41st

Occupied housing units: 688,557
Percent of total units: 88.13%, 34th
Persons per unit: 2.48, 37th
Percent of units with over 1 person per room: 1.91%, 44th

Owner-occupied units: 510,058
Percent of total units: 65.28%, 1st
Percent of occupied units: 74.08%, 1st
Persons per unit: 2.63, 44th
Median value: $47,900, 47th

Renter-occupied units: 178,499
Percent of total units: 22.85%, 51st
Percent of occupied units: 25.92%, 51st
Persons per unit: 2.33, 28th
Median contract rent: $221, 49th
Rental vacancy rate: 10.1%, 15th

Mobile home, trailer & other as a percent of occupied housing units: 18.61%, 6th

Persons in emergency shelters for homeless persons: 451, 0.025%, 49th

Persons visible in street locations: 33, 0.0018%, 46th

Persons in shelters for abused women: 128, 0.0071%, 7th

Nursing home population: 12,591, 0.70%, 27th

CRIME INDEX PER 100,000 (1992-93)

Total reported: 2,532.6, 51st
Violent: 208.4, 45th
Murder and nonnegligent manslaughter: 6.9, 25th
Aggravated assault: 138.5, 44th
Robbery: 43.0, 43rd
Forcible rape: 20.1, 51st
Property: 2,324.2, 51st
Burglary: 599.1, 47th
Larceny, theft: 1,563.5, 51st
Motor vehicle theft: 161.5, 46th

Drug abuse violations (1990): 87.8, 48th
Child-abuse rate per 1,000 children (1993): NA

TEACHING AND LEARNING

Pop. 3 and over enrolled in school: 436,513
  Percent of pop.: 25.2%, 46th
Public elementary & secondary schools (1992-
    93): 949
  Total enrollment (1992): 318,296
    Percent of total pop.: 17.60%, 20th
  Teachers (1992): 20,861
    Percent of pop.: 1.15%, 13th
  Pupil/teacher ratio (fall 1992): 15.2, 40th
  Teachers' avg. salary (1992-93): $32,242,
    32nd
  Expenditure per capita (1990-91): $2,865.60,
    46th
  Expenditure per pupil (1991-92): $5,109,
    27th
Percent of graduates taking SAT (1993): 17%,
    31st
  Mean SAT verbal scores: 439, 28th
  Mean SAT mathematical scores: 485, 30th
Percent of graduates taking ACT (1995):
    56%, 24th
  Mean ACT scores: 20.0, 45th
Percent of pop. over 25 completing:
  Less than 9th grade: 16.8%, 2nd
  High school: 66.0%, 49th
  College degree(s): 12.3%, 51st
Higher education, institutions (1993-94):
    28
  Enrollment (1992): 90,252
    Percent of pop.: 4.99%, 40th
  White non-Hispanic (1992): 83,673
    Percent of enroll.: 92.71%, 4th
  Black non-Hispanic (1992): 3,384
    Percent of enroll.: 3.75%, 32nd
  Hispanic (1992): 451
    Percent of enroll.: 0.50%, 49th
  Asian/Pacific Islander (1992): 829
    Percent of enroll.: 0.92%, 44th
  American Indian/AK native (1992): 155
    Percent of enroll.: 0.17%, 51st
  Nonresident alien (1992): 1,760
    Percent of enroll.: 1.95%, 40th
  Female (1992): 50,009
    Percent of enroll.: 55.41%, 25th
  Pub. institutions (1993-94): 16
    Enrollment (1992): 79,284
    Percent of enroll.: 87.85%, 14th
  Private institutions (1993-94): 12
    Enrollment (1992): 10,968
    Percent of enroll.: 12.15%, 38th

Tuition, public institution (avg., 1993-94):
    $5,691, 27th
Tuition, private institution (avg., 1993-94):
    $12,281, 29th
Public library systems: 98
  Books & serial vol. per capita: 2.15, 34th
  Govt. expenditure per capita: $7.26, 49th

LAW ENFORCEMENT, COURTS, AND PRISONS

Police protection, corrections, judicial and
    legal functions expenditures (1992):
    $212,000,000
  Per capita: $117, 51st
Police per 10,000 pop. (1993): 17.07, 40th
Prisoners (state & fed.) per 100,000 pop.
    (1993): 992.85, 49th
  Percent change (1992-93): 7.8%, 14th
Death penalty: no

RELIGION, NUMBER AND PERCENT OF POPULATION

Agnostic: 2,700—0.20%, 42nd
Buddhist: 1,350—0.10%, 17th
Christian: 1,167,664—86.50%, 24th
Hindu: 1,350—0.10%, 10th
Jewish: 1,350—0.10%, 43rd
Muslim: 1,350—0.10%, 22nd
Unitarian: 1,350—0.10%, 31st
Other: 39,147—2.90%, 1st
None: 107,992—8.00%, 15th
Refused to answer: 25,648—1.90%, 31st

MAKING A LIVING

Personal income per capita (1994): $17,208,
    47th
  Percent increase (1993-94): 6.4%, 7th
Disposable personal income per capita (1994):
    $15,445, 47th
Median income of households (1993):
    $22,421, 50th
Percent of pop. below poverty level (1993):
    22.2%, 4th
  Percent 65 and over (1990): 16.7%, 13th
Expenditure for energy per person (1992):
    $2,079, 8th

ECONOMY

Civilian labor force (1994): 788,000
  Percent of total pop.: 43.25%, 51st
  Percent 65 and over (1990): NA
  Percent female: 44.80%, 46th

Percent job growth (1980-90): –1.13%, 50th
Major employer industries (1994):
  Agriculture: NA—1.5%, 42nd
  Construction: 26,000—3.7%, 39th
  Finance, insurance, & real estate: 28,000—4.0%, 47th
  Government: 132,000—18.8%, 12th
  Manufacturing: 104,000—14.8%, 28th
  Service: 134,000—19.1%, 39th
  Trade: 145,000—20.7%, 3rd
  Transportation, communications, public utilities: 45,000—6.4%, 8th
Unemployment rate (1994): 8.88%, 1st
  Male: 7.5%, 4th
  Female: 10.1%, 1st
Total businesses (1991): 51,655
  New business incorps. (1991): 2,219
    Percent of total businesses: 4.30%, 42nd
  Business failures (1991): 240
    Percent of total businesses: 0.46%
Agriculture farm income:
  Marketing (1993): $405,000,000, 46th
    Average per farm: $20,250.00, 50th
  Leading products (1993): Cattle, broilers, dairy products, turkeys
  Average value land & build. per acre (1994): $713, 35th
    Percent increase (1990-94): 16.31%, 20th
  Govt. payments (1993): $6,000,000, 43rd
    Average per farm: $300.00, 49th
Construction, value of all: $302,000,000
  Per capita: $168.39, 51st
Manufactures:
  Value added: $6,342,000,000
    Per capita: $3,536.15, 39th
  Leading products: Machinery, plastic and hardwood products, fabricated metals, basic organic and inorganic chemicals, aluminum, steel
Value of nonfuel mineral production (1994): $176,000,000, 39th
Leading mineral products: Coal, natural gas, petroleum
Retail sales (1993): $11,586,000,000, 41st
  Per household: $16,484, 49th
    Percent increase (1992-93): 7.7%, 19th
Tourism revenues (1992): $2.6 bil.
Foreign exports, in total value (1994): $1,586,000,000, 36th
  Per capita: $870.47, 40th

Gross state product per person (1993): $16,120.07, 50th
  Percent change (1990-93): 3.57%, 21st
Patents per 100,000 pop. (1993): 9.90, 44th
Public aid recipients (percent of resident pop. 1993): 9.6%, 5th
Medicaid recipients per 1,000 pop. (1993): 190.87, 4th
Medicare recipients per 1,000 pop. (1993): 177.12, 2nd

TRAVEL AND TRANSPORTATION

Motor vehicle registrations (1993): 1,345,000
  Per 1,000 pop.: 739.82, 33rd
Motorcycle registrations (1993): 19,000
  Per 1,000 pop.: 10.45, 40th
Licensed drivers per 1,000 pop. (1993): 716.17, 13th
Deaths from motor vehicle accidents per 100,000 pop. (1993): 23.60, 6th
Public roads & streets (1993):
  Total mileage: 35,045
    Per 1,000 pop.: 19.28, 23rd
  Rural mileage: 31,908
    Per 1,000 pop.: 17.55, 22nd
  Urban mileage: 3,137
    Per 1,000 pop.: 1.73, 50th
  Interstate mileage: 550
    Per 1,000 pop.: 0.30, 13th
Annual vehicle-mi. of travel per person (1993): 9,241, 28th
Mean travel time for workers age 16+ who work away from home: 21.0 min., 23rd

GOVERNMENT

Percent of voting age pop. registered (1994): 60.8%, 35th
  Percent of voting age pop. voting (1994): 33.9%, 51st
  Percent of voting age pop. voting for U.S. representatives (1994): 29.3%, 46th
State legislators, total (1995): 134, 32nd
  Women members (1992): 28
    Percent of legislature: 20.9%, 17th
U.S. Congress, House members (1995): 3
  Change (1985-95): –1
Revenues (1993):
  State govt.: $6,047,000,000
    Per capita: $3,326.18, 20th
  Parimutuel & amusement taxes & lotteries, revenue per capita: $60.51, 30th

Expenditures (1993):
  State govt.: $5,943,000,000
    Per capita: $3,268.98, 14th
  Debt outstanding (1993): $2,684,000,000
    Per capita: $1,476.35, 23rd

LAWS AND REGULATIONS

Legal driving age: 18, 16 if completed driver
  education course
Marriage age without parental consent: 18
Divorce residence requirement: 1 yr., for
  qualifications check local statutes

ATTRACTIONS (1995)

Major symphony orchestras: 1
State appropriations for arts agencies per capita:
  $0.87, 19th
State Fair during late August at Lewisburg
  (Fairlea)

SPORTS AND COMPETITION

NCAA teams (Division I): Marshall Univ.
  Thundering Herd, West Virginia Univ.
  Mountaineers

WISCONSIN

"Wisconsin is the soul of a great people. She manifests the spirit of the conqueror, whose strength has subdued the forest, quickened the soil, harnessed the forces of Nature and multiplied production. From her abundance she served food to the world."

Fred L. Holmes, author

Wisconsin is a state of progress and leadership in many areas. Spurred by Wisconsin native Robert La Follette, the state pioneered in progressive social legislation. It leads the nation in number of milk cows, in production of milk, and in value of milk products. It also produces 40% of the nation's cheese and 20% of its butter. But manufacturing is Wisconsin's chief industry. It is a leader in the manufacturing of machinery and produces more paper than any other state. The state's nickname (the Badger State) began with a group of burrowing miners—all adding to the state's many contrasts.

SUPERLATIVES

• First U.S. kindergarten—opened by Mrs. Carl Schurz in Waterton, 1865.
• Pioneer in social legislation.
• Leads nation in dairy products.
• First in paper, paper products, and paper-making machinery.
• Smallest city with a major pro football team—the Green Bay Packers.
• World's oldest continuously operating radio station, WHA, in Madison.

MOMENTS IN HISTORY

• In 1634, French explorer Jean Nicolet became the first European in the area.
• Pierre Esprit Radisson and Medart Chouart, Sieur de Groseillier, explored in 1654-1656, opening the area to fur trade.

So They Say

As he marveled at the Mississippi's great flow, Father Marquette felt *"...a joy that I cannot express."*

• After crossing the state and pioneering a route from the east, on June 17, 1673, the explorers Father Jacques Marquette and Louis Jolliet discovered the long-sought upper reaches of the Mississippi River at the mouth of the Wisconsin River.
• Daniel Greysolon, Sieur de Lhut, in 1678 explored the western end of Lake Superior and claimed the land in the name of France.
• With the 1763 Treaty of Paris, the British gained control.
• Augustin Monet de Langlade founded Green Bay in 1764, a thriving fur trading post and the first permanent European settlement.

So They Say

"I liked noe country as I have that wherein we wintered Washington Island, Wisconsin; for whatever a man could desire was to be had in great plenty; viz. staggs, fishes in abundance, and all sort of meat, corne enough."

Explorer Pierre Esprit Radisson, in later memoirs

• Prairie du Chien was founded in 1781 on the site of a large Indian village.
• The 1783 Treaty of Paris gave the area to the United States, but the British continued to claim the region until after the War of 1812.
• By 1822 lead mining was in full swing in southwest Wisconsin. Many miners burrowed into the hillside like badgers, giving the "Badger State" its nickname.
• During the Black Hawk War, Chief Black Hawk fled into Wisconsin. On August 2, 1832, the Battle of Bad Axe ended the war. Trying to escape across the Mississippi River, many of the men, women, and children were massacred.
• In 1835 the first steamboat arrived at the trading port that became Milwaukee.
• Madison was selected as the territorial capital in 1836, although still wilderness.

So They Say

"Bad, and cruel, as our people were treated by the whites, not one of them was hurt or molested by any of my band...This is a lesson worthy for the white man to learn...."

Chief Black Hawk

- After it became the 30th state on May 29, 1848, Wisconsin attracted waves of Scandinavian, German, and other immigrants.
- In 1851 the first train chugged over new tracks from Milwaukee to Waukesha.
- The October 8, 1871, forest fire devastated the lumber town of Peshtigo, killing nearly 1,200.
- In 1890, Stephen M. Babcock developed a machine and method of testing the amount of butterfat in milk, giving a new boost to the "Dairy State."
- Robert M. La Follette became the first native-born governor of Wisconsin in 1901, bringing many widely copied reforms.
- In 1904 fire partially destroyed the statehouse. The third capitol in Madison, the present one, was built between 1906 and 1917, as the state mobilized for World War I.
- During the Great Depression of the 1930s, Wisconsin passed the first unemployment compensation legislation.
- The Depression squeeze on dairy workers sparked the state's milk strikes of 1934, and thousands of gallons of milk were dumped in protest of conditions.
- The baseball Braves came to Milwaukee in 1953 and won the World Series in 1957. (They moved on to Atlanta in 1966.)
- The opening of the St. Lawrence Seaway in 1959 brought many benefits to Wisconsin's ports.
- The 1992 Wautoma tornado cut through the city, causing two deaths and heavy property damage.

THAT'S INTERESTING

- Believing that he had reached China and the Far East, Jean Nicolet stepped ashore near the Winnebago village of Red Bank, shooting pistols and wearing embroidered Chinese silk robes, to the astonishment of the Indians.
- Prairie du Chien (Prairie of the Dog) was named for Chief Alim, a prominent Indian whose native name means Dog.

- During pioneering days the Wisconsin region was so sparsely settled that Justice of the Peace Pat Kelly reputedly was sometimes forced to use trees as witnesses for wedding ceremonies.

NOTABLE NATIVES

Carrie Chapman Catt (Ripon, 1859-1947), social reformer. **Zona Gale** (Portage, 1874-1938), author. **Hamlin Garland** (West Salem, 1860-1940), author. **King Camp Gillette** (Fond du Lac, 1855-1932), industrialist. **Vinnie Ream Hoxie** (Madison, 1847-1914), sculptor. **Robert Marion La Follette** (Primrose, 1855-1925), political leader. **Spencer Tracy** (Milwaukee, 1900-1967), actor. **George Orson Welles** (Kenosha, 1915-1985), director/actor. **Thornton Niven Wilder** (Madison, 1897-1975), novelist and playwright. **Thomas James Walsh** (Two Rivers, 1859-1933), public official. **Frank Lloyd Wright** (Richland Center, 1867-1959), architect.

So They Say

"So she's young and poor, is she. Well that's nothing agin' her....You may tell her she can come."

Abraham Lincoln, on agreeing to sit for his sculpture by Vinnie Ream Hoxie, Madison native and first woman sculptor commissioned by Congress

GENERAL

Admitted to statehood: May 29, 1848
Origin of name: An Indian name, spelled *Ouisconsin* and *Mesconsing* by the early chroniclers. Believed to mean "grassy place" in Chippewa. Congress made it *Wisconsin*.
Capital: Madison
Nickname: Badger State
Motto: Forward
Animal: Badger
Bird: Robin
Fish: Muskellunge
Insect: Honeybee
Flower: Wood violet
Mineral: Galena
Stone: Red granite
Song: "On, Wisconsin!"
Tree: Sugar maple

THE LAND

Area: 65,500 sq. mi., 22nd
  Land: 54,314 sq. mi., 25th
  Water: 11,186 sq. mi., 3rd
    Inland water: 1,831 sq. mi., 11th
  Great Lakes: 9,355 sq. mi., 2nd
Topography: Narrow Lake Superior lowland plain met by Northern highland, which slopes gently to the sandy crescent central plain; Western upland in the SW; three broad parallel limestone ridges running N-S are separated by wide and shallow lowland in the SE
Number of counties: 72
Geographic center: Wood, 9 mi. SE of Marshfield
Length: 310 mi.; width: 260 mi.
Highest point: 1,951 ft. (Timms Hill), 39th
Lowest point: 581 ft. (Lake Michigan), 41st
Mean elevation: 1,050 ft., 24th

CLIMATE AND ENVIRONMENT

Temp., highest: 114 deg. on July 13, 1936, at Wisconsin Dells; lowest: –54 deg. on Jan. 24, 1922, at Danbury
Monthly average: highest: 82.8 deg., 44th; lowest: 5.4 deg., 5th; spread (high to low): 77.4 deg., 10th
Hazardous waste sites (1993): 40, 9th
Endangered species: Mammals: 2—Indiana bat, Eastern timber wolf; birds: 3—American peregrine falcon, Piping plover, Kirtland's warbler; reptiles: none; amphibians: none; fishes: none; invertebrates: 1; plants: none

MAJOR CITIES
POPULATION, 1990
PERCENTAGE INCREASE, 1980-90

Green Bay, 96,466—9.75%
Kenosha, 80,352—3.43%
Madison, 191,262—12.10%
Milwaukee, 628,088— -1.29%
Racine, 84,298— -1.66%

THE PEOPLE

Population (1995): 5,122,871, 18th
  Percent change (1990-95): 4.7%, 26th
Population (2000 proj.): 5,381,000, 18th
  Percent change (1990-2000): 10.00%, 26th
Per sq. mi. (1994): 93.6, 25th
Percent in metro. area (1992): 68.1%, 29th
Foreign born: 122,000, 20th
  Percent: 2.5%, 31st

Top three ancestries reported:
  German, 53.78%
  Irish, 12.51%
  Polish, 10.34%
White: 4,512,523, 92.25%, 14th
Black: 244,539, 5.00%, 29th
Native American: 39,387, 0.81%, 19th
Asian, Pacific Isle: 53,583, 1.10%, 27th
Other races: 41,737, 0.85%, 30th
Hispanic origin: 93,194, 1.91%, 31st
Percent over 5 yrs. speaking language other than English at home: 5.8%, 31st
Percent males: 48.92%, 22nd; percent females: 51.08%, 30th
Percent never married: 27.1%, 18th
Marriages per 1,000 (1993): 7.2, 40th
Divorces per 1,000 (1993): 3.5, 38th
Median age: 32.9
Under 5 years (1994): 6.89%, 41st
Under 18 years (1994): 26.51%, 20th
65 years & older (1994): 13.4%, 19th
Percent increase among the elderly (1990-94): 5.03%, 30th

OF VITAL IMPORTANCE

Live births per 1,000 pop. (1993): 13.8, 41st
Infant mortality rate per 1,000 births (1992): 7.2, 40th
  Rate for blacks (1990): 18.1, 9th
  Rate for whites (1990): 7.2, 42nd
Births to unmarried women, % of total (1992): 26.1%, 36th
Births to teenage mothers, % of total (1992): 10.2%, 37th
Abortions (1992): 15,450, 25th
  Rate per 1,000 women 14-44 years old: 13.6, 37th
  Percent change (1988-92): –15%, 38th
Average lifetime (1979-81): 75.35, 6th
Deaths per 1,000 pop. (1993): 8.7, 29th
Causes of death per 100,000 pop.:
  Accidents & adverse effects (1992): 31.8, 34th
  Atherosclerosis (1991): 7.2, 22nd
  Cancer (1991): 206.8, 28th
  Cerebrovascular diseases (1992): 66.5, 11th
  Chronic liver diseases & cirrhosis (1991): 7.2, 44th
  Chronic obstructive pulmonary diseases (1992): 32.8, 38th
  Diabetes mellitus (1992): 20.9, 23rd
  Diseases of heart (1992): 281.5, 27th
  Pneumonia, flu (1991): 35.3, 13th
  Suicide (1992): 11.7, 34th

KEEPING WELL

Active nonfederal physicians per 100,000 pop. (1993): 196, 26th

Dentists per 100,000 (1991): 62, 16th

Nurses per 100,000 (1992): 799, 21st

Hospitals per 100,000 (1993): 2.52, 21st

Admissions per 1,000 (1993): 112.69, 30th

Occupancy rate per 100 beds (1993): 63.4, 23rd

Average cost per patient per day (1993): $744, 36th

Average cost per stay (1993): $5,348, 36th

Average stay (1992): 8.2 days, 14th

AIDS cases (adult, 1993): 731; per 100,000: 14.5, 35th

HIV infection, not yet AIDS (1993): 1,733

Other notifiable diseases:

Gonorrhea: 176.6, 29th

Measles: 15.2, 4th

Syphilis: 12.7, 30th

Tuberculosis: 2.0, 46th

Pop. without health insur. (1991-93): 8.6%, 49th

HOUSEHOLDS BY TYPE

Total households (1994): 1,890,000

Percent change (1990-94): 3.7%, 30th

Per 1,000 pop.: 371.90, 33rd

Percent of households 65 yrs. and over: 22.75%, 18th

Persons per household (1994): 2.62, 20th

Family households: 1,275,172

Percent of total: 69.98%, 30th

Nonfamily households: 546,946

Percent of total: 30.02%, 22nd

Pop. living in group quarters: 133,598

Percent of pop.: 2.73%, 26th

LIVING QUARTERS

Total housing units: 2,055,774

Persons per unit: 2.38, 31st

Occupied housing units: 1,822,118

Percent of total units: 88.63%, 31st

Persons per unit: 2.53, 24th

Percent of units with over 1 person per room: 2.10%, 41st

Owner-occupied units: 1,215,350

Percent of total units: 59.12%, 25th

Percent of occupied units: 66.70%, 28th

Persons per unit: 2.79, 15th

Median value: $62,500, 30th

Renter-occupied units: 606,768

Percent of total units: 29.52%, 25th

Percent of occupied units: 33.30%, 24th

Persons per unit: 2.26, 38th

Median contract rent: $331, 26th

Rental vacancy rate: 4.7%, 51st

Mobile home, trailer & other as a percent of occupied housing units: 7.10%, 36th

Persons in emergency shelters for homeless persons: 1,555, 0.032%, 47th

Persons visible in street locations: 71, 0.0015%, 48th

Persons in shelters for abused women: 258, 0.0053%, 19th

Nursing home population: 50,345, 1.03%, 8th

CRIME INDEX PER 100,000 (1992-93)

Total reported: 4,054.1, 41st

Violent: 264.4, 43rd

Murder and nonnegligent manslaughter: 4.4, 36th

Aggravated assault: 121.4, 45th

Robbery: 113.4, 35th

Forcible rape: 25.2, 47th

Property: 3,789.7, 40th

Burglary: 663.0, 45th

Larceny, theft: 2,762.0, 32nd

Motor vehicle theft: 364.7, 29th

Drug abuse violations (1990): 192.4, 34th

Child-abuse rate per 1,000 children (1993): 14.30, 24th

TEACHING AND LEARNING

Pop. 3 and over enrolled in school: 1,302,230

Percent of pop.: 27.8%, 19th

Public elementary & secondary schools (1992-93): 2,030

Total enrollment (1992): 829,415

Percent of total pop.: 16.61%, 34th

Teachers (1992): 53,387

Percent of pop.: 1.07%, 19th

Pupil/teacher ratio (fall 1992): 15.5, 37th

Teachers' avg. salary (1992-93): $37,618, 18th

Expenditure per capita (1990-91): $3,672.24, 17th

Expenditure per pupil (1991-92): $6,139, 12th

Percent of graduates taking SAT (1993): 10%, 39th

Mean SAT verbal scores: 485, 8th

Mean SAT mathematical scores: 551, 5th

Percent of graduates taking ACT (1995): 64%, 12th

Mean ACT scores: 22.0, 4th
Percent of pop. over 25 completing:
Less than 9th grade: 9.5%, 24th
High school: 78.6%, 21st
College degree(s): 17.7%, 36th
Higher education, institutions (1993-94): 64
Enrollment (1992): 307,902
Percent of pop.: 6.16%, 17th
White non-Hispanic (1992): 274,875
Percent of enroll.: 89.27%, 12th
Black non-Hispanic (1992): 12,354
Percent of enroll.: 4.01%, 30th
Hispanic (1992): 5,545
Percent of enroll.: 1.80%, 27th
Asian/Pacific Islander (1992): 5,720
Percent of enroll.: 1.86%, 27th
American Indian/AK native (1992): 2,429
Percent of enroll.: 0.79%, 20th
Nonresident alien (1992): 6,979
Percent of enroll.: 2.27%, 30th
Female (1992): 170,243
Percent of enroll.: 55.29%, 27th
Pub. institutions (1993-94): 30
Enrollment (1992): 256,890
Percent of enroll.: 83.43%, 26th
Private institutions (1993-94): 34
Enrollment (1992): 51,012
Percent of enroll.: 16.57%, 26th
Tuition, public institution (avg., 1993-94): $5,252, 34th
Tuition, private institution (avg., 1993-94): $13,012, 25th
Public library systems: 377
Books & serial vol. per capita: 3.11, 19th
Govt. expenditure per capita: $21.53, 12th

LAW ENFORCEMENT, COURTS, AND PRISONS

Police protection, corrections, judicial and legal functions expenditures (1992): $1467,000,000
Per capita: $294, 19th
Police per 10,000 pop. (1993): 22.57, 19th
Prisoners (state & fed.) per 100,000 pop. (1993): 1,740.88, 42nd
Percent change (1992-93): 7.2%, 16th
Death penalty: no

RELIGION, NUMBER AND PERCENT OF POPULATION

Agnostic: 10,808—0.30%, 37th
Buddhist: 10,808—0.30%, 8th
Christian: 3,249,714—90.20%, 10th
Hindu: NA

Jewish: 14,411—0.40%, 31st
Muslim: 7,206—0.20%, 13th
Unitarian: 7,206—0.20%, 23rd
Other: 28,822—0.80%, 37th
None: 219,770—6.10%, 31st
Refused to answer: 54,042—1.50%, 42nd

MAKING A LIVING

Personal income per capita (1994): $21,019, 22nd
Percent increase (1993-94): 6.1%, 10th
Disposable personal income per capita (1994): $18,151, 25th
Median income of households (1993): $31,766, 20th
Percent of pop. below poverty level (1993): 12.6%, 30th
Percent 65 and over (1990): 9.1%, 44th
Expenditure for energy per person (1992): $1,630, 46th

ECONOMY

Civilian labor force (1994): 2,795,000
Percent of total pop.: 55.00%, 6th
Percent 65 and over (1990): 2.90%, 21st
Percent female: 46.48%, 22nd
Percent job growth (1980-90): 16.82%, 34th
Major employer industries (1994):
Agriculture: 117,000—4.5%, 10th
Construction: 106,000—4.1%, 25th
Finance, insurance, & real estate: 134,000—5.2%, 26th
Government: 359,000—13.9%, 38th
Manufacturing: 584,000—22.6%, 6th
Service: 543,000—21.0%, 25th
Trade: 455,000—17.6%, 45th
Transportation, communications, public utilities: 104,000—4.0%, 47th
Unemployment rate (1994): 4.72%, 41st
Male: 5.2%, 33rd
Female: 4.2%, 44th
Total businesses (1991): 175,870
New business incorps. (1991): 6,994
Percent of total businesses: 3.98%, 45th
Business failures (1991): 666
Percent of total businesses: 0.38%
Agriculture farm income:
Marketing (1993): $5,250,000,000, 10th
Average per farm: $66,455.70, 35th
Leading products (1993): Dairy products, cattle, corn, hogs

Average value land & build. per acre (1994): $975, 24th

Percent increase (1990-94): 21.42%, 6th

Govt. payments (1993): $310,000,000, 17th

Average per farm: $3,924.05, 26th

Construction, value of all: $3,412,000,000

Per capita: $697.50, 18th

Manufactures:

Value added: $37,090,000,000

Per capita: $7,582.12, 3rd

Leading products: Machinery, foods, fabricated metals, transportation equipment, paper and wood products

Value of nonfuel mineral production (1994): $344,000,000, 31st

Leading mineral products: Stone, sand/gravel, lime

Retail sales (1993): $41,948,000,000, 17th

Per household: $22,140, 24th

Percent increase (1992-93): 4.2%, 38th

Tourism revenues (1994): $5.7 bil.

Foreign exports, in total value (1994): $7,722,000,000, 17th

Per capita: $1,519.48, 16th

Gross state product per person (1993): $20,812.29, 28th

Percent change (1990-93): 3.00%, 26th

Patents per 100,000 pop. (1993): 26.49, 17th

Public aid recipients (percent of resident pop. 1993): 6.7%, 26th

Medicaid recipients per 1,000 pop. (1993): 93.38, 44th

Medicare recipients per 1,000 pop. (1993): 147.70, 19th

TRAVEL AND TRANSPORTATION

Motor vehicle registrations (1993): 3,815,000

Per 1,000 pop.: 756.34, 31st

Motorcycle registrations (1993): 197,000

Per 1,000 pop.: 39.06, 2nd

Licensed drivers per 1,000 pop. (1993): 694.29, 24th

Deaths from motor vehicle accidents per 100,000 pop. (1993): 13.94, 35th

Public roads & streets (1993):

Total mileage: 110,978

Per 1,000 pop.: 22.00, 21st

Rural mileage: 95,387

Per 1,000 pop.: 18.91, 19th

Urban mileage: 15,591

Per 1,000 pop.: 3.09, 27th

Interstate mileage: 638

Per 1,000 pop.: 0.13, 40th

Annual vehicle-mi. of travel per person (1993): 9,754, 22nd

Mean travel time for workers age 16+ who work away from home: 18.3 min., 41st

GOVERNMENT

Percent of voting age pop. registered (1994): 77.2%, 4th

Percent of voting age pop. voting (1994): 49.6%, 19th

Percent of voting age pop. voting for U.S. representatives (1994): 38.6%, 27th

State legislators, total (1995): 132, 33rd

Women members (1992): 32

Percent of legislature: 24.2%, 13th

U.S. Congress, House members (1995): 9

Change (1985-95): 0

Revenues (1993):

State govt.: $18,677,000,000

Per capita: $3,702.82, 11th

Parimutuel & amusement taxes & lotteries, revenue per capita: $95.16, 21st

Expenditures (1993):

State govt.: $14,621,000,000

Per capita: $2,898.69, 22nd

Debt outstanding (1993): $7,674,000,000

Per capita: $1,521.41, 21st

LAWS AND REGULATIONS

Legal driving age: 18, 16 if completed driver education course

Marriage age without parental consent: 18

Divorce residence requirement: 6 mo.

ATTRACTIONS (1995)

Major opera companies: 2

Major symphony orchestras: 1

Major dance companies: 1

Major professional theater companies (non-profit): 1

State appropriations for arts agencies per capita: $0.56, 34th

State Fair in early August at West Allis

SPORTS AND COMPETITION

NCAA teams (Division I): Marquette Univ. Warriors, Univ. of Wisconsin-Green Bay Phoenix, Univ. of Wisconsin-Madison Badgers, Univ. of Wisconsin-Milwaukee Panthers

Major league baseball teams: Milwaukee Brewers (AL Central), County Stadium

NBA basketball teams: Milwaukee Bucks, Bradley Center

NFL football teams: Green Bay Packers (NFC), Lambeau Field

WYOMING

September 20, 1852—"Here we reached the dividing height between the waters of the Pacific and those of the Atlantic. One universal shout arose at the announcement of this fact; and visions of home and all its joys floated before the imagination in vivid brightness."

September 23—"The scenery from the 'divide' was in beautiful contrast with that of the country left behind us. Broad and grassy valleys were spread out before us, bounded by low rounded hills covered with verdure, over which ranged bands of buffalo, while little flocks of antelope bounded gracefully around us. The low bottom of the Medicine-bow, upon which we are encamped, is thickly covered with excellent grass, and the stream has an extensive fringe of willows and rose-bushes, with occasional groves of cottonwood and aspens."

Howard Stansbury, Wyoming pioneer

Small in population, rich in history, Wyoming lives up to its nickname of "the Equality State." It boasts the nation's first elected woman official, as well as the first woman governor, and the greatest plainswoman of the West. It relishes such mysteries as the prehistoric Medicine Wheel. Among its notable scenic attractions, Wyoming claims the first national park (Yellowstone), the first national monuments (Devils Tower), and the first national forest (Shoshone). More than 80% of its land is used for cattle grazing, and thousands of oil wells dot the prairies. To emphasize its Western past, Wyoming celebrates with one of the nation's most notable annual festivals, Frontier Days at Cheyenne.

SUPERLATIVES

• World's largest elk (wapiti) herd—Jackson Elk Refuge.
• Largest U.S. coal reserves.
• First "dude ranch"—Eaton Brothers, near Dayton.

MOMENTS IN HISTORY

• The first white explorer of record in what is now Wyoming was John Colter, who discovered Yellowstone and the Tetons in 1807.
• In 1811, Wilson Price Hunt's party crossed much of the present state.

• General William H. Ashley established a trading center on the Yellowstone River in 1822.
• Wyoming's first substantial trading post was set up by Antonio Mateo in 1828, near the Powder River forks.
• In 1832 the expedition of Captain B. L. E. de Bonneville made tracks across Wyoming, pioneering parts of the Oregon Trail.
• Sponsored by General Ashley, a series of meetings known as rendezvous gathered annually in various locations from 1834 through the 1840s. These attracted a picturesque group of trappers, traders, and Indian families, who traded furs, frolicked, and brawled uproariously.
• Laramie was begun in 1834 to become the first permanent European-style settlement in Wyoming.
• During the California gold rush, in 1850 alone more than 60,000 people and 90,000 domestic animals crossed the state.
• A period of Indian troubles extended from about 1862 to 1868, with 1865 known as "the bloody year on the plains."
• The transcontinental railroad arrived at Cheyenne in 1867 and was completed two years later. Cities sprang up almost overnight.
• In the early 1870s the first scientific party reached Yellowstone and reported on its many natural wonders.

So They Say

"...All were killed. Within a small space most were found, horribly mutilated. I loaded the wagons with as many of the bodies as they could contain...the soldiers being so overcome with horror as almost unable to obey orders..."

Captain Tenadore Ten Eyck, on a bloody massacre of the 1860s

• On March 1, 1872, Yellowstone became the first national park.

So They Say

"All honor then to the United States for having bequeathed as a free gift to man the beauties and curiosities of Wonderland. It was an act worthy of the greatest nation."

Earl of Dunraven, on the establishment of Yellowstone National Park

---

• "Nesters" and rustlers vied for positions with ranchers in the so-called Johnson County Cattle War of 1892.
• Although the Wyoming population of 62,500 was not enough to qualify for statehood, on July 10, 1890, Wyoming nevertheless became a state.
• Devils Tower became the nation's first national monument in 1906.
• The 11,393 from Wyoming who served in World War I represented 7% of the state's population.
• The election of Nellie Tayloe Ross as governor in 1924 was a landmark in women's progress.
• The state's 75th anniversary was celebrated in 1965.
• The forest fires of 1988 swept through much of the timberland of Yellowstone National Park.
• In 1995 the dedication of the Chief Joseph Scenic Highway marked completion of the state's goal to pave every highway. Construction had begun 25 years earlier on the 46-mile route.

THAT'S INTERESTING

• When the Indians saw the first two white women in Wyoming, they were astonished that such pale creatures could survive the trip, and they killed the fattest dogs to prepare a feast for their guests.
• The Indian name for Bull Lake was "the lake that roars." The strange sound comes from the action of the wind on the ice.
• The prehistoric Medicine Wheel is similar to Stonehenge in England and one in the Gobi Desert. It remains a mystery to scholars.
• The first telephone poles in Wyoming made such attractive scratching posts for buffaloes that as many as 30 of the huge animals might sometimes be seen waiting their turn to rub against one.

WYOMING NOTABLES

James Bridger (Richmond, VA, 1804-1881), frontiersman/fur trader/scout. **Martha Jane (Calamity Jane) Cannary Burk** (Princeton, MO, 1852?-1903), frontiers-woman. **William Frederick (Buffalo Bill) Cody** (Scott County, IA, 1846-1917), frontiersman/entertainer. **Crazy Horse** (Oglala Sioux tribe site, 1849?-1877), Indian leader. **Emerson Hough** (Newton, IA, 1857-1923), author. **Thomas Moran** (England, 1837-1926), artist. **Edgar Wilson (Bill) Nye** (Shirley, ME, 1850-1896), humorist. **(Paul) Jackson Pollock** (Cody, 1912-1956), artist. **Red Cloud** (north-central Nebraska, 1822-1909), Indian leader. **Nellie Tayloe Ross** (St. Joseph, MO, 1880?-1977), public official. **Washakie** (in Montana, 1804-1900), Indian leader. **Owen Wister** (Philadelphia, PA, 1860-1938), author.

GENERAL

Admitted to statehood: July 10, 1890
Origin of name: Taken from Wyoming Valley, Pennsylvania, which was the site of an Indian massacre in 1778 and became widely known from Thomas Campbell's account in the poem "Gertrude of Wyoming." The Algonquin word means "large prairie place" and the Delaware Indian word means "mountains and valleys alternating."
Capital: Cheyenne
Nickname: Equality State
Motto: Equal rights
Bird: Meadowlark
Flower: Indian paintbrush
Stone: Jade
Song: "Wyoming"
Tree: Cottonwood

THE LAND

Area: 97,819 sq. mi., 9th
  Land: 97,105 sq. mi., 9th
  Water: 714 sq. mi., 35th
    Inland water: 714 sq. mi., 30th
Topography: Eastern Great Plains rise to the foothills of the Rocky Mountains; Continental Divide crosses the state from the NW to the SE.
Number of counties: 23
Geographic center: Fremont, 58 mi. ENE of Lander
Length: 360 mi.; width: 280 mi.
Highest point: 13,804 ft. (Gannett Peak), 5th
Lowest point: 3,099 ft. (Belle Fourche River), 50th
Mean elevation: 6,700 ft., 2nd

CLIMATE AND ENVIRONMENT

Temp., highest: 114 deg. on July 12, 1900, at Basin; lowest: –63 deg. on Feb. 9, 1933, at Moran
Monthly average: highest: 87.1 deg., 26th; lowest: 11.9 deg., 12th; spread (high to low): 75.2 deg., 15th
Hazardous waste sites (1993): 3, 47th
Endangered species: Mammals: 2—Black-footed ferret, Northern Rocky Mountain gray wolf; birds: 2—Whooping crane, American peregrine falcon; reptiles: none; amphibians: 1; fishes: 2; invertebrates: none; plants: none

MAJOR CITIES
POPULATION, 1990
PERCENTAGE INCREASE, 1980-90

Casper, 46,742— –8.38%
Cheyenne, 50,008—5.76%
Gillette, 17,635—45.34%
Laramie, 26,687—9.33%
Rock Springs, 19,050— –2.10%

THE PEOPLE

Population (1995): 480,184, 51st
  Percent change (1990-95): 5.9%, 21st
Population (2000 proj.): 522,000, 51st
  Percent change (1990-2000): 15.08%, 15th
Per sq. mi. (1994): 4.9, 50th
Percent in metro. area (1992): 29.7%, 49th
Foreign born: 8,000, 50th
  Percent: 1.7%, 37th

Top three ancestries reported:
  German, 34.80%
  English, 22.25%
  Irish, 16.08%
White: 427,061, 94.15%, 9th
Black: 3,606, 0.79%, 43rd
Native American: 9,479, 2.09%, 8th
Asian, Pacific Isle: 2,806, 0.62%, 41st
Other races: 10,636, 2.34%, 15th
Hispanic origin: 25,751, 5.68%, 13th
Percent over 5 yrs. speaking language other than English at home: 5.7%, 33rd
Percent males: 50.05%, 5th; percent females: 49.95%, 47th
Percent never married: 21.7%, 48th
Marriages per 1,000 (1993): 9.8, 15th
Divorces per 1,000 (1993): 6.5, 3rd
Median age: 32
Under 5 years (1994): 6.93%, 40th
Under 18 years (1994): 28.78%, 7th
65 years & older (1994): 11.1%, 43rd
Percent increase among the elderly (1990-94): 10.18%, 9th

OF VITAL IMPORTANCE

Live births per 1,000 pop. (1993): 14.2, 33rd
Infant mortality rate per 1,000 births (1992): 8.9, 19th
  Rate for blacks (1990): NA
  Rate for whites (1990): 8.8, 7th
Births to unmarried women, % of total (1992): 24.0%, 41st
Births to teenage mothers, % of total (1992): 13.2%, 20th
Abortions (1992): 460, 51st
  Rate per 1,000 women 14-44 years old: 4.3, 51st
  Percent change (1988-92): –16%, 41st
Average lifetime (1979-81): 73.85, 25th
Deaths per 1,000 pop. (1993): 7.5, 43rd
Causes of death per 100,000 pop.:
  Accidents & adverse effects (1992): 51.0, 4th
  Atherosclerosis (1991): 5.9, 37th
  Cancer (1991): 160.7, 46th
  Cerebrovascular diseases (1992): 52.3, 36th
  Chronic liver diseases & cirrhosis (1991): 8.9, 29th
  Chronic obstructive pulmonary diseases (1992): 49.5, 4th
  Diabetes mellitus (1992): 14.6, 46th
  Diseases of heart (1992): 194.1, 46th
  Pneumonia, flu (1991): 22.8, 47th
  Suicide (1992): 18.1, 4th

KEEPING WELL

Active nonfederal physicians per 100,000 pop. (1993): 137, 49th

Dentists per 100,000 (1991): 50, 33rd

Nurses per 100,000 (1992): 658, 37th

Hospitals per 100,000 (1993): 5.32, 5th

Admissions per 1,000 (1993): 91.06, 47th

Occupancy rate per 100 beds (1993): 48.4, 51st

Average cost per patient per day (1993): $537, 48th

Average cost per stay (1993): $4,706, 48th

Average stay (1992): 7.5 days, 19th

AIDS cases (adult, 1993): 46; per 100,000: 9.8, 43rd

HIV infection, not yet AIDS (1993): 64

Other notifiable diseases:

Gonorrhea: 34.4, 43rd

Measles: 3.3, 29th

Syphilis: 2.6, 45th

Tuberculosis: 1.1, 51st

Pop. without health insur. (1991-93): 12.6%, 29th

HOUSEHOLDS BY TYPE

Total households (1994): 178,000

Percent change (1990-94): 5.3%, 20th

Per 1,000 pop.: 373.95, 28th

Percent of households 65 yrs. and over: 19.10%, 42nd

Persons per household (1994): 2.68, 11th

Family households: 119,825

Percent of total: 70.97%, 23rd

Nonfamily households: 49,014

Percent of total: 29.03%, 29th

Pop. living in group quarters: 10,240

Percent of pop.: 2.26%, 44th

LIVING QUARTERS

Total housing units: 203,411

Persons per unit: 2.23, 44th

Occupied housing units: 168,839

Percent of total units: 83.00%, 45th

Persons per unit: 2.57, 17th

Percent of units with over 1 person per room: 2.78%, 30th

Owner-occupied units: 114,544

Percent of total units: 56.31%, 37th

Percent of occupied units: 67.84%, 23rd

Persons per unit: 2.74, 22nd

Median value: $61,600, 32nd

Renter-occupied units: 54,295

Percent of total units: 26.69%, 40th

Percent of occupied units: 32.16%, 29th

Persons per unit: 2.39, 18th

Median contract rent: $270, 39th

Rental vacancy rate: 14.4%, 3rd

Mobile home, trailer & other as a percent of occupied housing units: 21.24%, 1st

Persons in emergency shelters for homeless persons: 183, 0.040%, 36th

Persons visible in street locations: 13, 0.0029%, 38th

Persons in shelters for abused women: 45, 0.0099%, 2nd

Nursing home population: 2,679, 0.59%, 38th

CRIME INDEX PER 100,000 (1992-93)

Total reported: 4,163.0, 38th

Violent: 286.2, 41st

Murder and nonnegligent manslaughter: 3.4, 42nd

Aggravated assault: 231.3, 36th

Robbery: 17.2, 47th

Forcible rape: 34.3, 34th

Property: 3,876.8, 38th

Burglary: 643.2, 46th

Larceny, theft: 3,078.7, 20th

Motor vehicle theft: 154.9, 47th

Drug abuse violations (1990): 121.3, 43rd

Child-abuse rate per 1,000 children (1993): 12.33, 31st

TEACHING AND LEARNING

Pop. 3 and over enrolled in school: 134,739

Percent of pop.: 31.1%, 2nd

Public elementary & secondary schools (1992-93): 410

Total enrollment (1992): 100,313

Percent of total pop.: 21.57%, 3rd

Teachers (1992): 5,821

Percent of pop.: 1.25%, 4th

Pupil/teacher ratio (fall 1992): 17.2, 20th

Teachers' avg. salary (1992-93): $31,820, 34th

Expenditure per capita (1990-91): $5,063.84, 4th

Expenditure per pupil (1991-92): $5,812, 15th

Percent of graduates taking SAT (1993): 13%, 33rd

Mean SAT verbal scores: 463, 21st

Mean SAT mathematical scores: 507, 22nd

Percent of graduates taking ACT (1995): 66%, 10th

Mean ACT scores: 21.3, 17th
Percent of pop. over 25 completing:
 Less than 9th grade: 5.7%, 47th
 High school: 83.0%, 5th
 College degree(s): 18.8%, 28th
Higher education, institutions (1993-94): 9
 Enrollment (1992): 31,548
  Percent of pop.: 6.80%, 8th
 White non-Hispanic (1992): 28,691
  Percent of enroll.: 90.94%, 7th
 Black non-Hispanic (1992): 371
  Percent of enroll.: 1.18%, 43rd
 Hispanic (1992): 1,150
  Percent of enroll.: 3.65%, 12th
 Asian/Pacific Islander (1992): 268
  Percent of enroll.: 0.85%, 45th
 American Indian/AK native (1992): 454
  Percent of enroll.: 1.44%, 11th
 Nonresident alien (1992): 614
  Percent of enroll.: 1.95%, 40th
 Female (1992): 17,876
  Percent of enroll.: 56.66%, 10th
 Pub. institutions (1993-94): 8
  Enrollment (1992): 30,687
  Percent of enroll.: 97.27%, 2nd
 Private institutions (1993-94): 1
  Enrollment (1992): 861
  Percent of enroll.: 2.73%, 50th
 Tuition, public institution (avg., 1993-94): $4,900, 46th
Public library systems: 23
 Books & serial vol. per capita: 4.28, 3rd
 Govt. expenditure per capita: $23.32, 9th

LAW ENFORCEMENT, COURTS, AND PRISONS

Police protection, corrections, judicial and legal functions expenditures (1992): $148,000,000
 Per capita: $319, 14th
Police per 10,000 pop. (1993): 23.65, 15th
Prisoners (state & fed.) per 100,000 pop. (1993): 2,402.13, 32nd
 Percent change (1992-93): 6.2%, 23rd
Death penalty: yes, by lethal injection
 Under sentence of death (1993): 0, 35th
 Executed (1993): 0

RELIGION, NUMBER AND PERCENT OF POPULATION

Agnostic: 1,590—0.50%, 27th
Buddhist: NA
Christian: 260,494—81.90%, 41st
Hindu: 636—0.20%, 3rd
Jewish: NA
Muslim: NA
Unitarian: NA
Other: 1,908—0.60%, 46th
None: 42,939—13.50%, 3rd
Refused to answer: 10,496—3.30%, 4th

MAKING A LIVING

Personal income per capita (1994): $20,436, 27th
 Percent increase (1993-94): 3.6%, 47th
Disposable personal income per capita (1994): $18,271, 22nd
Median income of households (1993): $29,442, 31st
Percent of pop. below poverty level (1993): 13.3%, 25th
 Percent 65 and over (1990): 10.7%, 34th
Expenditure for energy per person (1992): $3,334, 1st

ECONOMY

Civilian labor force (1994): 249,000
 Percent of total pop.: 52.31%, 17th
 Percent 65 and over (1990): 3.25%, 13th
 Percent female: 45.78%, 36th
Percent job growth (1980-90): -4.34%, 51st
Major employer industries (1994):
 Agriculture: 15,000—6.8%, 6th
 Construction: 11,000—4.7%, 17th
 Finance, insurance, & real estate: 10,000—4.2%, 42nd
 Government: 49,000—21.7%, 5th
 Manufacturing: 10,000—4.3%, 47th
 Service: 35,000—15.4%, 51st
 Trade: 43,000—19.0%, 26th
 Transportation, communications, public utilities: 15,000—6.7%, 4th
Unemployment rate (1994): 5.22%, 32nd
 Male: 5.4%, 30th
 Female: 5.2%, 31st
Total businesses (1991): 26,383
 New business incorps. (1991): 1,386
  Percent of total businesses: 5.25%, 35th
 Business failures (1991): 178
  Percent of total businesses: 0.67%
Agriculture farm income:
 Marketing (1993): $817,000,000, 37th
  Average per farm: $90,777.78, 21st
 Leading products (1993): Cattle, sugar beets, hay, sheep

Average value land & build. per acre (1994): $169, 48th

Percent increase (1990-94): 13.42%, 26th

Govt. payments (1993): $43,000,000, 36th
Average per farm: $4,777.78, 21st

Construction, value of all: $135,000,000
Per capita: $297.63, 47th

Manufactures:

Value added: $844,000,000
Per capita: $1,860.72, 46th

Leading products: Refined petroleum products, foods, wood products, stone, clay and glass products

Value of nonfuel mineral production (1994): $781,000,000, 15th

Leading mineral products: Petroleum, coal, natural gas

Retail sales (1993): $3,531,000,000, 51st
Per household: $20,098, 42nd
Percent increase (1992-93): 8.8%, 12th

Tourism revenues (1992): $1.5 bil.

Foreign exports, in total value (1994): $360,000,000, 48th
Per capita: $756.30, 41st

Gross state product per person (1993): $28,384.28, 5th
Percent change (1990-93): 0%, 45th,

Patents per 100,000 pop. (1993): 9.15, 45th

Public aid recipients (percent of resident pop. 1993): 5.0%, 40th

Medicaid recipients per 1,000 pop. (1993): 97.87, 38th

Medicare recipients per 1,000 pop. (1993): 121.28, 42nd

TRAVEL AND TRANSPORTATION

Motor vehicle registrations (1993): 558,000
Per 1,000 pop.: 1187.23, 1st

Motorcycle registrations (1993): 12,000
Per 1,000 pop.: 25.53, 10th

Licensed drivers per 1,000 pop. (1993): 744.68, 5th

Deaths from motor vehicle accidents per 100,000 pop. (1993): 25.53, 53rd

Public roads & streets (1993):
Total mileage: 37,642
Per 1,000 pop.: 80.09, 4th

Rural mileage: 35,256
Per 1,000 pop.: 75.01, 4th

Urban mileage: 2,386
Per 1,000 pop.: 5.08, 1st

Interstate mileage: 914
Per 1,000 pop.: 1.94, 1st

Annual vehicle-mi. of travel per person (1993): 14,468, 1st

Mean travel time for workers age 16+ who work away from home: 15.4 min., 48th

GOVERNMENT

Percent of voting age pop. registered (1994): 69.0%, 17th

Percent of voting age pop. voting (1994): 63.5%, 2nd

Percent of voting age pop. voting for U.S. representatives (1994): 57.2%, 2nd

State legislators, total (1995): 94, 43rd
Women members (1992): 23
Percent of legislature: 24.5%, 11th

U.S. Congress, House members (1995): 1
Change (1985-95): 0

Revenues (1993):
State govt.: $21,181,000,000
Per capita: $4,640.43, 3rd

Parimutuel & amusement taxes & lotteries, revenue per capita: NA

Expenditures (1993):
State govt.: $1,887,000,000
Per capita: $4,014.89, 5th

Debt outstanding (1993): $781,000,000
Per capita: $1,661.70, 20th

LAWS AND REGULATIONS

Legal driving age: 16

Marriage age without parental consent: 18

Divorce residence requirement: 2 mo., for qualifications check local statutes

ATTRACTIONS (1995)

State appropriations for arts agencies per capita: $0.66, 28th

State Fair in late August at Douglas

SPORTS AND COMPETITION

NCAA teams (Division I): Univ. of Wyoming Cowboys

OUTLYING AREAS

CARIBBEAN ISLANDS

Commonwealth of Puerto Rico

Puerto Rico is the smallest of the islands known as the Greater Antilles. The Atlantic Ocean lies to the north and the Caribbean to the south. The Dominican Republic is the neighbor to the west; the American Virgin Islands lie to the east. Vieques is the largest of the outlying islands. The main island is mountainous, rising to massive El Yunque near the east coast. Puerto Rico's climate is ideal, with little variation year-round, making it a mecca for tourists, but Puerto Rico is also subject to destructive hurricanes.

Christopher Columbus reached the island in 1493, and by early 1511, the island became the first Spanish colony in the New World. It suffered many attacks by the English. After almost 400 years of Spanish rule, Spain ceded Puerto Rico to the United States after the Spanish-American War of 1898.

Puerto Ricans received U.S. citizenship in 1917, and the island became an internally self-governing commonwealth in 1952. Its relationship to the United States is a matter of continuing concern, with many Puerto Ricans preferring the present system, others desiring statehood, and others advocating independence. The people do not vote in national elections, except for primaries. Puerto Rico is represented in the U.S. House of Representatives by a nonvoting delegate.

General

Name: Commonwealth of Puerto Rico (Estado Libre Asociado de Puerto Rico)
Capital: San Juan
Motto: *Joannes Est Norman Eius* (John is his name)
Bird: Reinita
Flower: Maga
Song: "La Borinqueña"
Tree: Ceiba

The Land and Climate

Area: 3,508 sq. mi.
  Land: 3,427 sq. mi.

Topography: Mountainous area covering three-fourths of the rectangular island, surrounded by a broken coastal plain
Highest point: 4,389 ft. (Cerro de Punta)
Lowest point: Sea level (Atlantic Ocean)
Climate: Mildly tropical, with a mean temperature of 77 deg; rainfall is plentiful, except in some arid regions in the south

The People

Population (1994 est.): 3,801,977
Per sq. mi.: 1,035
Percent urban (1990): 66.8%

Principal Cities

Bayamón, Caguas, Carolina, Ponce, San Juan

Government

Chief of state: President of the United States
Head of government: Governor of Puerto Rico
Legislature: Bicameral legislature (Senate and House of Representatives)

Economy

Principal industries: Manufacturing
Manufactured goods: Pharmaceuticals, chemicals, machinery and metals, electric machinery and equipment, petroleum refining, food products, apparel
Agricultural products: Sugarcane, coffee, pineapples, plantains, bananas, yams, pigeon peas, peppers, pumpkins, coriander, lettuce, tobacco
Minerals: Cement, crushed stone
GDP in millions (1994): $39,265
Per capita income (1992): $6,360
Employment (1994):
  Labor force: 1,203,000
  Unemployment rate: 14.6%

Virgin Islands

In 1493, Columbus became the first European to reach the Virgin Islands, which he named in honor of the Virgins of St. Ursula. Before Columbus, the islands had been inhabited by the Siboney Indians, by the Arawak from South America, and by the fierce Caribes (whose name was given to the Caribbean).

Pirates swarmed over the islands, which have been claimed by Holland, Spain, France, England, and Denmark. In 1917 the United States bought its present portion of the Virgins from Denmark, to keep them from falling into German hands during World War I.

In 1927 the people became American nationals; they achieved limited self-government in 1936, and their rights were expanded in 1954. Today the Virgin Islands has a republican form of government, with an elected governor and lieutenant governor; the people elect a nonvoting member to the U.S. House of Representatives.

Luis, one of the strongest hurricanes of recent memory, swept the area in 1995.

General

Name: Virgin Islands of the United States
Capital: Charlotte Amalie, St. Thomas
Bird: Yellow breast
Flower: Yellow elder or yellow trumpet
Song: "Virgin Islands March"

The Land and Climate

Area: 151 sq. mi.
Topography: Mostly hilly to rugged and mountainous with little level land
Highest point: 1,556 ft. (Crown Mountain, St. Thomas)
Lowest Point: Sea level (Atlantic Ocean)
Climate: Subtropical, tempered by easterly trade winds; relatively low humidity; little seasonal temperature variation; rainy season from May to November

The People

Population (1994): 97,564
Per sq. mi.: 646.1

Principal Cities

Charlotte Amalie, Saint Croix, Saint Thomas

Government

Chief of state: President of the United States
Head of government: Governor of the Virgin Islands
Legislature: Unicameral

Economy

Principal industries: Tourism, rum, alumina production, petroleum refining, watch assembly, textiles, electronics
Manufactured goods: Rum, textiles, pharmaceuticals, perfume

Agricultural products: Truck garden produce, food crops (small scale), fruit, sorghum, cattle
Minerals: Sand, gravel
GDP (1987): $1.246 billion
Per capita income (1989): $11,052
Employment: 70% of those employed are engaged in tourism
Unemployment rate (1992): 7.8%

Other Caribbean Islands

Navassa, which is uninhabited, lies between Jamaica and Haiti and has an area of about 3 square miles. It is administered by the U.S. Coast Guard, which operates an automatic lighthouse.

The United States laid claim to the uninhabited islands of **Quita Sueno Bank, Roncador,** and **Serrana** until 1981, when the claim of Colombia to the islands was recognized.

PACIFIC ISLANDS

American Samoa

This unincorporated territory of seven small islands of the Samoan group is the most southerly region under U.S. jurisdiction. The islands lie 2,300 miles southwest of Honolulu, Hawaii. The main islands are mountainous and volcanic, surrounded by coral reefs. Swains Island came under U.S. control in 1925 and is organized as a part of the Samoan group.

Native Polynesians probably reached the islands about 1000 B.C. The Dutch explorer Jacob Roggeveen visited the islands in 1722. The United States, Britain, and France claimed trade and other privileges in the islands, and the United States established a naval station at Pago Pago in 1878. An agreement of 1899 recognized the U.S. right to govern present American Samoa. In 1978 a governor was popularly elected for the first time.

The islands retain much of their original Polynesian culture, clinging to traditional dress. Siva, the traditional dance, is popular with both locals and the increasing number of tourists. Pago Pago was the site of the famous short story "Rain" by Somerset Maugham.

Principal exports are fish products, mostly tuna, packed by leading producers. Copra, breadfruit, yams, coconuts, bananas, oranges and pineapples are other products of American Samoa. The cocoa of the island is ranked among the world's best. Most of the cultivated crops are grown near the coasts. The Samoan people are known for their fine craft work, particularly tapa cloth, pounded from the bark of the paper mulberry trees. Baskets and laufala floor mats are woven from palm leaves.

Some of the multi-oared longboats, known as *fautasi*, are hollowed from tree trunks, reaching 40 feet in length. Other craft are the smaller outrigger fishing boats.

General

Name: Territory of American Samoa
Capital: Pago Pago, Island of Tutuila
Motto: *Samoa Muamua le Atua* (In Samoa, God is first)
Flower: Paogo (Ula-fala)
Plant: Ava
Song: "Amerika Samoa"

The Land and Climate

Area: 84 sq. mi.
Topography: Five volcanic islands with rugged peaks and limited coastal plains; two coral atolls
Highest point: 3,160 ft. (Lata Mountain, Tau Island)
Lowest point: Sea level (Pacific Ocean)
Climate: Tropical marine, moderated by southeast tradewinds; little seasonal temperature variation; rainy season from November to April, dry season from May to October

The People

Population (1994): 55,223
Per sq. mi.: 657.4
Largest city: Pago Pago

Government

Chief of state: President of the United States
Head of government: Governor of American Samoa
Legislature: Bicameral legislative assembly (Fono)

Economy

Principal industries: Tuna fishing and processing, meat canning, handicrafts
Agricultural products: Bananas, coconuts, vegetables, taro, breadfruit, yams, copra, pineapples, papayas, dairy products
GDP (1991): $128 million
Unemployment rate (1991): 12%

Guam

The explorer Ferdinand Magellan reached Guam in the Marianas chain in 1521. Spanish missionaries began colonization in 1668.

After the Spanish-American War of 1898, Spain ceded the island to the United States. Its residents are U.S. citizens but do not vote for president. Guam is represented in the U.S. House of Representatives by a nonvoting delegate.

Guam is the largest and most southerly of the Marianas, with a tropical climate. The government is the principal employer, and tourism is important.

General

Name: Territory of Guam
Capital: Agana
Nickname: Where America's Day Begins
Bird: Toto (fruit dove)
Flower: Puti Tai Nobio (bougainvillea)
Song: "Stand Ye Guamanians"
Tree: Ifit (intsiabijuga)

The Land and Climate

Land area: 210 sq. mi.
Topography: Coralline limestone plateaus in the north, southern chain of low volcanic mountains sloping gently to the west, more steeply to coastal cliffs on the east
Highest point: 1,332 ft. (Mount Lamlam, Agat District)
Lowest point: Sea level (Pacific Ocean)
Climate: Tropical, with temperatures from 70 deg. to 90 deg.

The People

Population (1995 est.): 149,249
Per sq. mi. (1994): 631.6

Principal Cities

Dededo, Mangilao, Santa Rita, Tamuning, Yigo

Government

Chief of state: President of the United States
Head of Government: Governor of Guam
Legislature: Unicameral

Economy

Principal industries: Tourism, U.S. military construction, transshipment services, concrete products, printing and publishing, food processing, textiles

Manufactured goods: Textiles, foods
Agricultural products: Fruits, vegetables, eggs, pork, poultry, beef, copra
GDP in billions (1993): $2,917
Per capita income (1986): $7,116
Employment:
    Labor force (1993): 66,500
    Unemployment rate (1992): 2%

Small Pacific Islands

With its sister islands, Wilkes and Peale, **Wake Island** is an important outpost on the route from Hawaii to Hong Kong. These islands formally became a U.S. possession in 1899. Administered by the U.S. Air Force, they have a population mainly associated with the Air Force.

With Sand and Eastern Island in the North Pacific, 1,150 miles northwest of Hawaii, **Midway** came under U.S. control in 1867. The Midway Islands are administered by the U.S. Navy and occupied only by military personnel.

South of Hawaii, **Johnston Atoll** occupies only about 1 square mile and is under the U.S. Defense Nuclear Agency, Fish and Wildlife Service, and Department of the Interior. **Kingman Reef** was discovered in 1874 by American explorers. Less than half a mile square, it is under U.S. Navy control.

Howland, Jarvis, and **Baker Islands,** lying some 1,500 miles southwest of Hawaii, are uninhabited islets under control of the U.S. Interior Department.

Palmyra is a 2-square-mile island privately owned and administered by the U.S. Interior Department.

Micronesia

Several Pacific Island groups, collectively known as Micronesia, were placed under U.S. trusteeship after World War II. The trusteeship has since been dissolved. The Northern Mariana Islands is a U.S. commonwealth; the other island groups are now independent states, with close ties to the United States.

Commonwealth of the Northern Mariana Islands is an archipelago of 14 islands stretching for 300 miles, with a total land area of 179 square miles. The population, of Chamorro descent, is 49,799, concentrated on three main islands: Saipan, Rota, and Tinian. The group has been self-governing since 1978, under a constitution adopted by the people in free association with the United States. There is a governor and a bicameral legislature. Tourism is increasing and is the principal industry on these islands.

Stretching for 1,800 miles along the archipelago of the Caroline Islands are the four **Federated States of Micronesia.** The states are **Pohnpei** (population 52,000), with the capital city of Kolonia; **Kosrae** (16,500); **Truk** (31,000); and **Yap** (12,000)—each made up of several small islands. The island federation lies southwest of Honolulu and southeast of Guam. The population is diverse, with several languages. The Federated States of Micronesia is now a sovereign self-governing state, with guarantees of U.S. defense and aid. Major economic activities are subsistence farming and fishing. Geographical isolation and a poor infrastructure impede long-term growth.

Republic of the Marshall Islands is a sovereign, self-governing state consisting of two clusters of atolls. Each atoll is a cluster of a number of small islands surrounding a lagoon. The total land area is 70 square miles. The total population is 54,000, with 20,000 in the capital, Majuro. The main economic activities are agriculture (producing coconuts, tomatoes, melons, and breadfruit) and tourism. The United States remains responsible for defense and retains certain other responsibilities.

The 200 islands of the Caroline Island chain form the **Republic of Palau.** Eight are permanently inhabited, with a total population of 16,366, with more than 10,000 of these on the island of Koror. The economy consists of subsistence agriculture and farming, plus some tourism. The United States recognized the constitution of Palau, which became effective in 1980. There is a bicameral legislature and an elected president and vice president, advised by a council of chiefs.

Palau was the last remaining entity of the U.S. Trust Territory of the Pacific Islands, established in 1947. The government of Palau and the United States signed a compact of free association, which was eventually approved—by a plebiscite of Palau voters in 1993; Palau became independent in 1994.

WORLD WIDE WEB SITES

Listed below are sites on the Internet's World Wide Web for all 50 states and the District of Columbia. The list includes both official state government sites and unofficial sites that may have been created by a college or university, by a commercial enterprise, or by some other source. The sites listed here typically feature a message from the state governor; state symbols and facts; tourist information; state employee directories; access to state government documents and agencies; state scholarship and grant information; state employment information; relocation information; invitations for public bids for state contracts; election information; cultural events listings; and special student sections. They also may offer multimedia features such as up-to-date weather or traffic reports, interactive maps, photographs, sound, and trivia quizzes. A state's official home page often will have a World Wide Web address in the following format: http://www.state.<state postal abbreviation>.us/ (for example, http://www.state.ak.us/ is the address of Alaska's home page). When typing an address, be certain to type it exactly as it appears, including capital and lowercase letters, any nonalphanumeric characters, and spaces (generally none). You may be unable to connect with a site for the following reasons: (1) You have mistyped the address; (2) the site is busy; (3) the site has moved; (4) the site no longer exists.

ALABAMA
Alabama Department of Archives and
    History Homepage
    http://sgisrvr.asc.edu/archives/agis.html
AlaWeb
    http://alaweb.asc.edu/

ALASKA
The Alaskan Center
    http://alaskan.com/
State of Alaska's Home Page
    http://www.state.ak.us/

ARIZONA
Arizona Guide
    http://www.arizonaguide.com
State of Arizona Services via World Wide
    Web
    http://www.state.az.us/

ARKANSAS
Arkansas Home Page
    http://www.state.ar.us/

CALIFORNIA
California State Home Page
    http://www.ca.gov/

COLORADO
Colorado Virtual Tourist
    http://www.capcon.com/virtualtourist/
State of Colorado Home Page
    http://www.state.co.us/

CONNECTICUT
Connecticut Government Information
    Home Page
    http://www.state.ct.us/
Connecticut Tourism Guide
    http://www.atlantic.com/feldmann/
    vacguide
The Connecticut Homepage
    http://www.connecticut.com/

DELAWARE
State of Delaware
    http://www.state.de.us/

DISTRICT OF COLUMBIA
The Washington DC City Pages
    http://dcpages.ari.net/

FLORIDA
Florida Communities Network
    http://www.state.fl.us/
GuideNet Florida On-Line Guide and
    Directory
    http://www.GuideNet.com/GuideNet/
    states/fl

GEORGIA
Georgia DOAS Home Page Go Network
    http://www.state.ga.us/
Georgia-on-my-mind
    http://www.iarc.com/georgia/code/
    georgia.html

HAWAII
Hawaii Home Page
  http://www.hawaii.edu/
Hawaii, This Week Travel Magazines in Hawaii
  http://www.thisweek.com/
HINC Welcome Page
  http://hinc.hinc.hawaii.gov/soh_home.html

IDAHO
State of Idaho Home Page
  http://www.state.id.us/

ILLINOIS
The State of Illinois
  http://www.state.il.us/

INDIANA
Access Indiana Information Network
  http://www.state.in.us/

IOWA
Iowa Virtual Tourist
  http://www.jeonet.com/tourist
State of Iowa Home Page
  http://www.state.ia.us/

KANSAS
Kansas Sights
  http://falcon.cc.ukans.edu/~nsween/europa.html

KENTUCKY
Commonwealth of Kentucky Web Server
  http://name1.state.ky.us/
Kentucky Atlas & Gazetteer
  http://www.uky.edu/KentuckyAtlas/kentucky.html

LOUISIANA
Info Louisiana: Main Page
  http://www.state.la.us/
Welcome to Louisiana
  http://www.trans-actions.com/lamain.html

MAINE
Maine Map of WWW Resources
  http://www.destek.net/Maps/ME.html
Maine State Government (WWW) Home Page
  http://www.state.me.us/

MARYLAND
Governor of Maryland
  http://www.gov.state.md.us/

MASSACHUSETTS
Massachusetts Map of WWW Resources
  http://donald.phast.umass.edu/misc/mass.html
Massachusetts Vacation Information
  http://www.magnet.state.ma.us/travel/travel.html
Commonwealth of Massachusetts—MAGNet
  http://www.state.ma.us/

MICHIGAN
MDE–State Government Resources
  http://web.mde.state.mi.us/legis/state.html
RING!OnLine Michigan's Internet Super-Station
  http://www.ring.com/michigan.html

MINNESOTA
State of Minnesota—North Star Options
  http://www.state.mn.us/

MISSISSIPPI
State of Mississippi
  http://www.state.ms.us/

MISSOURI
State of Missouri Homepage
  http://www.ecodev.state.mo.us/

MONTANA
Montana Online: Homepage for the State of Montana
  http://www.mt.gov/

NEBRASKA
Nebraska Tourism Office
  http://www.ded.state.ne.us/tourism.html

NEVADA
The State of Nevada
  http://www.state.nv.us

NEW HAMPSHIRE
The New Hampshire State Government Online Information Center
  http://www.state.nh.us/
Vermont/New Hampshire Map of WWW Resources
  http://www.desktek.net/Maps/VT-NH.html

NEW JERSEY
State of New Jersey
  http://www.state.nj.us/

NEW MEXICO
Bienvenidos a Nuevo Mexico
  http://www.nets.com/newmextourism
State of New Mexico Services via World Wide Web
  http://www.state.nm.us/
VIVA New Mexico! Home Page
  http://www.viva.com/nm/nmhome.html

NEW YORK
Empire State Development Page
  http://empire.state.ny.us/
I Love NY—Tourism in the State of New York
  http://www.iloveny.state.ny.us/
Welcome to New York
  http://www.state.ny.us/

NORTH CAROLINA
State of North Carolina
  http://www.sips.state.nc.us/nchome.html
Welcome NCNetWorks
  http://www.webpress.net/ncnetworks/

NORTH DAKOTA
State of North Dakota
  http://www.state.nd.us/

OHIO
State of Ohio Government Front Page
  http://www.state.oh.us/

OKLAHOMA
Oklahoma Home Page
  http://www.oklaosf.state.ok.us/

OREGON
Welcome to Oregon On-Line!
  http://www.state.or.us/

PENNSYLVANIA
Commonwealth of Pennsylvania
  http://www.state.pa.us/

RHODE ISLAND
Rhode Island State Info
  http://www.ids.net/ri/ri.html
RI Secretary of State Jim Langevin
  http://www.state.ri.us/

SOUTH CAROLINA
Center for Carolina Living
  http://www.sunbelt.net/helios/ccl/ccl.html
South Carolina Extravaganza
  http://www.sunbelt.net/cni/statesc/schome.html

South Carolina Information
  http://www.state.sc.us/

SOUTH DAKOTA
State of South Dakota
  http://www.state.sd.us/

TENNESSEE
Tennessee Home Page
  http://www.tenn.net/
Tennessee's WWW Home Page
  http://www.state.tn.us/

TEXAS
State of Texas Government World Wide Web Server
  http://www.state.tx.us/

UTAH
State of Utah WWW Homepage
  http://www.state.ut.us/

VERMONT
State of Vermont Home Page
  http://www.state.vt.us/
Vermont/New Hampshire Map of WWW Resources
  http://www.desktek.net/Maps/VT-NH.html
Vermont: The Green Mountain State
  http://mole.uvm.edu/Vermont

VIRGINIA
Welcome to Virginia
  http://www.state.va.us/

WASHINGTON
Home Page Washington—Home
  http://www.wa.gov/wahome.html

WEST VIRGINIA
West Virginia K-12 Home Page
  http://access.K12.wv.us/

WISCONSIN
State of Wisconsin Web Page
  http://www.state.wi.us/
Wisconsin Information and Web Sites
  http://infomad.com/wisconsin
Wisconsin On-Line
  http://www.wistravel.com

WYOMING
Welcome to the State of Wyoming
  http://www.state.wy.us/

PART III:
THE STATES COMPARED

GENERAL

HISTORICAL HIGHLIGHTS

	1st Permanent European Settlement		Date Entered Union	Chron. Order
FL	1565	DE	Dec. 7, 1787	1
NM	1598	PA	Dec. 12, 1787	2
VA	1607	NJ	Dec. 18, 1787	3
NY	1614	GA	Jan. 2, 1788	4
NJ	1618	CT	Jan. 9, 1788	5
MA	1620	MA	Feb. 6, 1788	6
ME	1622	MD	April 28, 1788	7
NH	1623	SC	May 23, 1788	8
MD	1631	NH	June 21, 1788	9
CT	1634	VA	June 25, 1788	10
RI	1635	NY	July 26, 1788	11
DE	1638	NC	Nov. 21, 1789	12
PA	1643	RI	May 29, 1790	13
NC	1664	VT	March 4, 1791	14
MI	1668	KY	June 1, 1792	15
SC	1670	TN	June 1, 1796	16
TX	1682	OH	March 1, 1803	17
AR	1686	LA	April 30, 1812	18
IL	1699	IN	Dec. 11, 1816	19
MS	1699	MS	Dec. 10, 1817	20
AL	1702	IL	Dec. 3, 1818	21
LA	1714	AL	Dec. 14, 1819	22
VT	1724	ME	March 15, 1820	23
IN	1727?	MO	Aug. 10, 1821	24
WV	1732	AR	June 15, 1836	25
GA	1733	MI	Jan. 26, 1837	26
MO	1735	FL	March 3, 1845	27
DC	1751	TX	Dec. 29, 1845	28
AZ	1752	IA	Dec. 28, 1846	29
WI	1764	WI	May 29, 1848	30
CA	1769	CA	Sept. 9, 1850	31
KY	1774	MN	May 11, 1858	32
TN	1779	OR	Feb. 14, 1859	33
AK	1784	KS	Jan. 29, 1861	34
IA	1788	WV	June 20, 1863	35
OH	1788	NV	Oct. 31, 1864	36
MT	1807	NE	March 1, 1867	37
WA	1810	CO	Aug. 1, 1876	38
OR	1811	ND	Nov. 2, 1889	39
ND	1812	SD	Nov. 2, 1889	40
OK	1817	MT	Nov. 8, 1889	41
HI	1820	WA	Nov. 11, 1889	42
MN	1820	ID	July 3, 1890	43
NE	1823	WY	July 10, 1890	44
KS	1827	UT	Jan. 4, 1896	45
SD	1831	OK	Nov. 16, 1907	46
CO	1832	NM	Jan. 6, 1912	47
WY	1834	AZ	Feb. 14, 1912	48
UT	1844	AK	Jan. 3, 1959	49
NV	1849	HI	Aug. 21, 1959	50
ID	1860	DC	NA	51

THE LAND

AREA

	Total Area, Sq. Miles		Land, Sq. Miles		Water, Sq. Miles	Desc. Num. Order
AK	656,424	AK	570,374	AK	86,051	1
TX	268,601	TX	261,914	MI	40,001	2
CA	163,707	CA	155,973	FL	11,761	3
MT	147,046	MT	145,556	WI	11,190	4
NM	121,598	NM	121,365	LA	8,277	5
AZ	114,006	AZ	113,642	CA	7,734	6
NV	110,567	NV	109,806	MN	7,326	7
CO	104,100	CO	103,730	NY	7,251	8
OR	98,386	WY	97,105	TX	6,687	9
WY	97,818	OR	96,003	NC	5,103	10
MI	96,810	ID	82,751	WA	4,721	11
MN	86,943	UT	82,168	ME	4,523	12
UT	84,904	KS	81,823	HI	4,508	13
ID	83,574	MN	79,617	OH	3,875	14
KS	82,282	NE	76,878	VA	3,171	15
NE	77,358	SD	75,898	UT	2,736	16
SD	77,121	ND	68,994	MA	2,717	17
WA	71,303	MO	68,898	MD	2,633	18
ND	70,704	OK	68,679	OR	2,383	19
OK	69,903	WA	66,582	IL	2,325	20
MO	69,709	GA	57,919	SC	1,896	21
FL	65,758	MI	56,809	ND	1,710	22
WI	65,503	IA	55,875	AL	1,673	23
GA	59,441	IL	55,593	GA	1,522	24
IL	57,918	WI	54,314	MS	1,520	25
IA	56,276	FL	52,997	MT	1,490	26
NY	54,475	AR	52,075	NJ	1,303	27
NC	53,821	AL	50,750	PA	1,239	28
AR	53,182	NC	48,708	SD	1,224	29
AL	52,423	NY	47,224	OK	1,224	30
LA	51,843	MS	46,914	AR	1,107	31
MS	48,434	PA	44,820	TN	926	32
PA	46,058	LA	43,566	ID	823	33
OH	44,828	TN	41,220	MO	811	34
VA	42,769	OH	40,953	NV	761	35
TN	42,146	KY	39,732	WY	714	36
KY	40,411	VA	39,598	CT	698	37
IN	36,420	IN	35,870	KY	679	38
ME	35,387	ME	30,865	IN	550	39
SC	32,007	SC	30,111	DE	535	40
WV	24,231	WV	24,087	RI	500	41
MD	12,407	MD	9,775	NE	481	42
HI	10,932	VT	9,249	KS	459	43
MA	10,555	NH	8,969	IA	401	44
VT	9,615	MA	7,838	NH	382	45
NH	9,351	NJ	7,419	CO	371	46
NJ	8,722	HI	6,423	VT	366	47
CT	5,544	CT	4,845	AZ	364	48
DE	2,489	DE	1,955	NM	234	49
RI	1,545	RI	1,045	WV	145	50
DC	68	DC	61	DC	7	51

Source: U.S. Geological Survey, Dept. of the Interior

CLIMATE AND ENVIRONMENT

MONTHLY AVERAGE TEMPERATURES, IN DEG. F

	Highest		Lowest[1]		Spread (High to Low)		Greatest	Desc. Num. Order
AZ	105.0	AK	-21.6	AK	(71.8	-21.6)	93.4	1
NV	104.5	ND	-5.1	ND	(84.4	-5.1)	89.5	2
CA	98.8	MN	-2.9	MN	(83.4	-2.9)	86.3	3
TX	98.5	SD	1.9	NV	(104.5	19.5)	85.0	4
OK	93.9	WI	5.4	SD	(86.5	1.9)	84.6	5
AR	93.6	IA	6.3	NE	(89.5	8.9)	80.6	6
LA	93.3	VT	7.7	IA	(86.2	6.3)	79.9	7
UT	93.2	MT	8.1	MT	(86.6	8.1)	78.5	8
KS	92.9	NE	8.9	CO	(92.2	14.3)	77.9	9
NM	92.8	NH	9.0	WI	(82.8	5.4)	77.4	10
MS	92.5	IL	9.8	IL	(87.1	9.8)	77.3	11
CO	92.2	ME	11.9	KS	(92.9	15.7)	77.2	12
GA	92.2	NY	11.9	TX	(98.5	21.7)	76.8	13
SC	91.9	WY	11.9	ID	(90.6	15.1)	75.5	14
FL	91.7	MI	14.0	WY	(87.1	11.9)	75.2	15
AL	91.5	CO	14.3	NH	(82.6	9.0)	73.6	16
TN	91.5	ID	15.1	UT	(93.2	19.7)	73.5	17
ID	90.6	OH	15.5	NY	(85.3	11.9)	73.4	18
MO	90.5	MA	15.6	IN	(88.8	15.8)	73.0	19
NE	89.5	KS	15.7	VT	(80.5	7.7)	72.8	20
IN	88.8	IN	15.8	MO	(90.5	19.4)	71.1	21
VA	88.4	CT	16.7	NM	(92.8	22.3)	70.5	22
NC	88.3	PA	18.0	OH	(85.8	15.5)	70.3	23
DC	87.9	MO	19.4	MI	(83.1	14.0)	69.1	24
KY	87.6	NV	19.5	OK	(93.9	24.8)	69.1	25
HI	87.1	UT	19.7	PA	(86.2	18.0)	68.2	26
IL	87.1	RI	20.0	CT	(84.8	16.7)	68.1	27
MD	87.1	WA	20.0	AR	(93.6	26.6)	67.0	28
WY	87.1	TX	21.7	ME	(78.9	11.9)	67.0	29
MT	86.6	NM	22.3	AZ	(105.0	38.1)	66.9	30
SD	86.5	KY	23.1	MA	(81.8	15.6)	66.2	31
IA	86.2	DE	23.2	KY	(87.6	23.1)	64.5	32
PA	86.2	WV	23.9	WA	(84.0	20.0)	64.0	33
OH	85.8	NJ	24.2	TN	(91.5	27.8)	63.7	34
DE	85.6	MD	24.3	MD	(87.1	24.3)	62.8	35
NJ	85.6	OK	24.8	DE	(85.6	23.2)	62.4	36
WV	85.6	VA	26.2	VA	(88.4	26.2)	62.2	37
NY	85.3	AR	26.6	CA	(98.8	36.8)	62.0	38
CT	84.8	NC	27.3	RI	(81.7	20.0)	61.7	39
ND	84.4	DC	27.5	WV	(85.6	23.9)	61.7	40
WA	84.0	TN	27.8	NJ	(85.6	24.2)	61.4	41
MN	83.4	AL	31.0	NC	(88.3	27.3)	61.0	42
MI	83.1	SC	31.2	SC	(91.9	31.2)	60.7	43
WI	82.8	GA	32.6	AL	(91.5	31.0)	60.5	44
NH	82.6	OR	32.8	DC	(87.9	27.5)	60.4	45
OR	82.6	MS	34.9	GA	(92.2	32.6)	59.6	46
MA	81.8	LA	36.2	MS	(92.5	34.9)	57.6	47
RI	81.7	CA	36.8	LA	(93.3	36.2)	57.1	48
VT	80.5	AZ	38.1	FL	(91.7	39.9)	51.8	49
ME	78.9	FL	39.9	OR	(82.6	32.8)	49.8	50
AK	71.8	HI	65.3	HI	(87.1	65.3)	21.8	51

[1]Ranked lowest to highest.
Source: National Climatic Data Center, NOAA, U.S. Dept. of Commerce

HAZARDOUS WASTE SITES ON THE NATIONAL PRIORITY LIST[1] (1993)

Total Sites		Percent Distribution		Federal		Non-Federal		Desc. Num. Order
NJ	109	NJ	8.7	CA	22	NJ	103	1
PA	99	PA	7.9	WA	18	PA	95	2
CA	95	CA	7.6	MA	8	NY	81	3
NY	85	NY	6.8	AK	6	MI	76	4
MI	76	MI	6.0	NJ	6	CA	73	5
FL	55	FL	4.4	VA	5	FL	51	6
WA	55	WA	4.4	FL	4	WI	40	7
MN	41	MN	3.3	IL	4	MN	39	8
WI	40	WI	3.2	NY	4	WA	37	9
IL	37	IL	2.9	PA	4	IL	33	10
OH	36	OH	2.9	TX	4	OH	33	11
IN	33	IN	2.6	UT	4	IN	33	12
MA	31	MA	2.5	AL	3	TX	26	13
TX	30	TX	2.4	AZ	3	MA	23	14
SC	24	SC	1.9	CO	3	SC	23	15
VA	24	VA	1.9	ME	3	NC	21	16
MO	23	MO	1.8	MD	3	MO	20	17
NC	22	NC	1.7	MO	3	VA	19	18
IA	20	IA	1.6	OH	3	IA	19	19
KY	20	KY	1.6	TN	3	KY	19	20
DE	19	DE	1.5	GA	2	DE	18	21
CO	18	CO	1.4	HI	2	NH	16	22
NH	17	NH	1.4	ID	2	CO	15	23
CT	15	CT	1.2	MN	2	CT	14	24
TN	15	TN	1.2	NM	2	TN	12	25
AL	14	AL	1.1	OR	2	AR	12	26
GA	13	GA	1.0	RI	2	AL	11	27
UT	13	UT	1.0	CT	1	GA	11	28
AR	12	AR	1.0	DE	1	LA	11	29
LA	12	LA	1.0	IA	1	OR	10	30
MD	12	MD	1.0	KS	1	RI	10	31
OR	12	OR	1.0	KY	1	OK	10	32
RI	12	RI	1.0	LA	1	UT	9	33
NM	11	NM	0.9	NE	1	MD	9	34
OK	11	OK	0.9	NH	1	NM	9	35
AZ	10	AZ	0.8	NC	1	KS	9	36
ID	10	ID	0.8	OK	1	NE	9	37
KS	10	KS	0.8	SC	1	ID	8	38
ME	10	ME	0.8	SD	1	MT	8	39
NE	10	NE	0.8	WV	1	VT	8	40
AK	8	AK	0.6	WY	1	AZ	7	41
MT	8	MT	0.6	AR	0	ME	7	42
VT	8	VT	0.6	DC	0	WV	5	43
WV	6	WV	0.5	IN	0	MS	4	44
MS	4	MS	0.3	MI	0	SD	3	45
SD	4	SD	0.3	MS	0	AK	2	46
HI	3	HI	0.2	MT	0	WY	2	47
WY	3	WY	0.2	NV	0	ND	2	48
ND	2	ND	0.2	ND	0	HI	1	49
NV	1	NV	0.1	VT	0	NV	1	50
DC	0	DC	0.0	WI	0	DC	0	51

[1]Includes both proposed and final sites on National Priorities List for the federal Superfund program.
Source: U.S. Environmental Protection Agency

MAJOR CITIES

MOST POPULOUS CITIES IN EACH STATE

	Pop., 1990		Pop., % Inc., 1980-90		Pop. per Sq. Mi.	Desc. Num. Order
NY, NY City	7,322,564	NV, Las Vegas	56.85%	NY, NY City	23,698	1
CA, Los Angeles	3,485,398	VA, Virginia Beach	49.91%	NJ, Newark	15,766	2
IL, Chicago	2,783,726	AK, Anchorage	29.76%	IL, Chicago	12,252	3
TX, Houston	1,630,553	NC, Charlotte	25.50%	MA, Boston	11,865	4
PA, Philadelphia	1,585,577	AZ, Phoenix	24.53%	PA, Philadelphia	11,736	5
MI, Detroit	1,027,974	SD, Sioux Falls	23.94%	DC, Washington	9,884	6
AZ, Phoenix	983,403	ID, Boise	22.97%	MD, Baltimore	9,109	7
MD, Baltimore	736,014	MT, Billings	21.46%	CT, Bridgeport	8,855	8
IN, Indianapolis	731,327	ND, Fargo	20.74%	RI, Providence	8,688	9
FL, Jacksonville	635,230	OR, Portland	18.79%	CA, Los Angeles	7,427	10
OH, Columbus	632,910	FL, Jacksonville	17.44%	MI, Detroit	7,411	11
WI, Milwaukee	628,088	CA, Los Angeles	17.41%	MN, Minneapolis	6,710	12
TN, Memphis	610,337	NM, Albuquerque	15.56%	DE, Wilmington	6,623	13
DC, Washington	606,900	OH, Columbus	12.02%	WI, Milwaukee	6,536	14
MA, Boston	574,283	AR, Little Rock	10.45%	WA, Seattle	6,153	15
WA, Seattle	516,259	OK, Oklahoma City	10.08%	HI, Honolulu	4,411	16
LA, New Orleans	496,938	NH, Manchester	9.49%	KY, Louisville	4,333	17
CO, Denver	467,610	KS, Wichita	8.64%	VT, Burlington	3,691	18
OK, Oklahoma City	447,719	NE, Omaha	6.96%	OR, Portland	3,507	19
OR, Portland	437,319	WY, Cheyenne	5.76%	NE, Omaha	3,335	20
MO, Kansas City	435,146	WA, Seattle	4.54%	OH, Columbus	3,315	21
NC, Charlotte	395,934	ME, Portland	4.52%	NV, Las Vegas	3,101	22
GA, Atlanta	394,017	IN, Indianapolis	4.35%	CO, Denver	3,050	23
VA, Virginia Beach	393,069	VT, Burlington	3.75%	TX, Houston	3,020	24
NM, Albuquerque	384,736	NY, New York City	3.55%	NH, Manchester	3,017	25
NJ, Newark	375,221	RI, Providence	2.50%	GA, Atlanta	2,990	26
MN, Minneapolis	368,383	TX, Houston	2.22%	NM, Albuquerque	2,910	27
HI, Honolulu	365,272	MA, Boston	2.01%	ME, Portland	2,848	28
NE, Omaha	335,795	DE, Wilmington	1.90%	LA, New Orleans	2,750	29
KS, Wichita	304,011	IA, Des Moines	1.14%	ID, Boise	2,728	30
KY, Louisville	269,063	HI, Honolulu	0.06%	WY, Cheyenne	2,660	31
AL, Birmingham	265,968	CT, Bridgeport	-0.60%	KS, Wichita	2,641	32
NV, Las Vegas	258,295	MN, Minneapolis	-0.69%	IA, Des Moines	2,566	33
AK, Anchorage	226,338	WI, Milwaukee	-1.29%	MT, Billings	2,489	34
MS, Jackson	196,637	UT, Salt Lake City	-1.90%	ND, Fargo	2,487	35
IA, Des Moines	193,187	MO, Kansas City	-2.88%	TN, Memphis	2,384	36
AR, Little Rock	175,795	MS, Jackson	-3.08%	AZ, Phoenix	2,342	37
RI, Providence	160,728	SC, Columbia	-3.14%	SD, Sioux Falls	2,296	38
UT, Salt Lake City	159,936	DC, Washington	-4.94%	NC, Charlotte	2,272	39
CT, Bridgeport	141,686	CO, Denver	-5.09%	IN, Indianapolis	2,022	40
ID, Boise	125,738	TN, Memphis	-5.55%	WV, Charleston	1,942	41
SD, Sioux Falls	100,814	PA, Philadelphia	-6.08%	MS, Jackson	1,804	42
NH, Manchester	99,567	MD, Baltimore	-6.45%	AL, Birmingham	1,791	43
SC, Columbia	98,052	AL, Birmingham	-6.49%	AR, Little Rock	1,708	44
MT, Billings	81,151	GA, Atlanta	-7.29%	VA, VA Beach	1,583	45
ND, Fargo	74,111	IL, Chicago	-7.37%	UT, Salt Lake City	1,467	46
DE, Wilmington	71,529	KY, Louisville	-9.92%	MO, Kansas City	1,057	47
ME, Portland	64,358	WV, Charleston	-10.44%	SC, Columbia	837	48
WV, Charleston	57,287	LA, New Orleans	-10.93%	FL, Jacksonville	837	49
WY, Cheyenne	50,008	MI, Detroit	-14.58%	OK, Oklahoma City	736	50
VT, Burlington	39,127	NJ, Newark	-16.41%	AK, Anchorage	324	51

Source: Bureau of the Census, U.S. Dept. of Commerce

THE PEOPLE

POPULATION, 1995-2000

	July 1, 1995		% Inc., 1990-95		Proj. Pop., 2000		% Inc., 1990-2000	Desc. Num. Order
CA	31,589,153	NV	27.3	CA	34,888,000	NV	40.7	1
TX	18,723,991	ID	15.5	TX	20,039,000	ID	28.1	2
NY	18,136,081	AZ	15.1	NY	18,237,000	AK	27.1	3
FL	14,165,570	CO	13.7	FL	15,313,000	UT	24.7	4
PA	12,071,842	UT	13.3	PA	12,296,000	WA	24.7	5
IL	11,829,940	WA	11.6	IL	12,168,000	CO	23.2	6
OH	11,150,506	GA	11.2	OH	11,453,000	AZ	21.1	7
MI	9,549,353	NM	11.2	MI	9,759,000	NM	20.3	8
NJ	7,945,298	OR	10.5	NJ	8,135,000	OR	19.8	9
GA	7,200,882	TX	10.2	GA	7,637,000	HI	19.7	10
NC	7,195,138	AK	9.7	NC	7,617,000	FL	18.4	11
VA	6,618,358	FL	9.5	VA	7,048,000	TX	18.0	12
MA	6,073,550	MT	8.9	WA	6,070,000	GA	17.9	13
IN	5,803,471	NC	8.5	IN	6,045,000	CA	17.2	14
WA	5,430,940	TN	7.8	MA	5,950,000	MT	15.1	15
MO	5,323,523	DE	7.7	TN	5,538,000	WY	15.1	16
TN	5,256,051	HI	7.1	MO	5,437,000	NC	14.9	17
WI	5,122,871	VA	6.9	WI	5,381,000	DE	13.9	18
MD	5,042,438	CA	6.2	MD	5,322,000	VA	13.9	19
MN	4,609,548	WY	5.9	MN	4,824,000	TN	13.6	20
LA	4,342,334	AR	5.7	AL	4,485,000	SC	12.8	21
AL	4,252,982	MD	5.5	LA	4,478,000	MD	11.3	22
AZ	4,217,940	SC	5.4	AZ	4,437,000	AL	11.0	23
KY	3,860,219	AL	5.3	CO	4,059,000	SD	10.6	24
CO	3,746,585	MN	5.3	KY	3,989,000	MN	10.3	25
SC	3,673,287	IN	4.7	SC	3,932,000	WI	10.0	26
OK	3,277,687	KY	4.7	OR	3,404,000	KS	9.9	27
CT	3,274,662	MS	4.7	OK	3,382,000	AR	9.7	28
OR	3,140,585	SD	4.7	CT	3,271,000	IN	9.0	29
IA	2,841,764	WI	4.7	IA	2,930,000	KY	8.2	30
MS	2,697,243	OK	4.2	MS	2,750,000	NE	8.0	31
KS	2,565,328	MO	4.0	KS	2,722,000	OK	7.5	32
AR	2,483,769	VT	3.9	AR	2,578,000	MS	6.9	33
UT	1,951,408	NE	3.7	UT	2,148,000	IL	6.5	34
WV	1,828,140	IL	3.5	WV	1,840,000	MO	6.3	35
NM	1,685,401	KS	3.5	NM	1,823,000	LA	6.1	36
NE	1,637,112	NH	3.5	NE	1,704,000	OH	5.6	37
NV	1,530,108	LA	2.9	NV	1,691,000	IA	5.5	38
ME	1,241,382	NJ	2.8	HI	1,327,000	NJ	5.2	39
HI	1,186,815	OH	2.8	ID	1,290,000	VT	5.2	40
ID	1,163,261	MI	2.7	ME	1,240,000	MI	5.0	41
NH	1,148,253	IA	2.3	NH	1,165,000	NH	5.0	42
RI	989,794	WV	1.9	RI	998,000	PA	3.5	43
MT	870,281	PA	1.6	MT	920,000	WV	2.6	44
SD	729,034	ME	0.9	SD	770,000	NY	1.4	45
DE	717,197	MA	0.9	DE	759,000	ME	1.0	46
ND	641,367	NY	0.8	AK	699,000	ND	0.7	47
AK	603,617	ND	0.4	ND	643,000	CT	-0.5	48
VT	584,771	CT	-0.4	VT	592,000	RI	-0.5	49
DC	554,256	RI	-1.4	DC	537,000	MA	-1.1	50
WY	480,184	DC	-8.7	WY	522,000	DC	-11.5	51

Source: Bureau of the Census, U.S. Dept. of Commerce

POPULATION CHARACTERISTICS

Pop. per Sq. Mi., 1994		% of Pop. in Metro. Areas, 1990		Foreign-Born, 1990		% of Pop. Foreign-Born		Desc. Num. Order
DC	9,283.4	DC	100.0%	CA	6,459,000	CA	21.7%	1
NJ	1,065.4	NJ	100.0%	NY	2,852,000	NY	15.9%	2
RI	953.8	CA	96.7%	FL	1,663,000	HI	14.7%	3
MA	770.7	MA	96.2%	TX	1,524,000	FL	12.9%	4
CT	676.0	CT	95.7%	NJ	967,000	NJ	12.5%	5
MD	512.1	RI	93.6%	IL	952,000	DC	9.7%	6
NY	384.7	FL	93.0%	MA	574,000	MA	9.5%	7
DE	361.3	MD	92.8%	PA	369,000	RI	9.5%	8
OH	271.1	NY	91.7%	MI	355,000	TX	9.0%	9
PA	268.9	NV	84.8%	WA	322,000	NV	8.7%	10
FL	258.4	PA	84.8%	MD	313,000	CT	8.5%	11
IL	211.4	AZ	84.7%	VA	312,000	IL	8.3%	12
CA	201.5	IL	84.0%	CT	279,000	AZ	7.6%	13
HI	183.5	TX	83.9%	AZ	278,000	MD	6.6%	14
MI	167.2	WA	83.0%	OH	260,000	WA	6.6%	15
VA	165.5	DE	82.7%	GA	173,000	NM	5.3%	16
IN	160.4	MI	82.7%	HI	163,000	VA	5.0%	17
NC	145.1	CO	81.8%	CO	142,000	OR	4.9%	18
NH	126.7	OH	81.3%	OR	139,000	AK	4.5%	19
TN	125.8	UT	77.5%	WI	122,000	CO	4.3%	20
GA	121.8	VA	77.5%	NC	115,000	MI	3.8%	21
SC	121.7	LA	75.0%	MN	113,000	NH	3.7%	22
LA	99.0	HI	74.7%	NV	105,000	UT	3.4%	23
KY	96.3	IN	71.6%	RI	95,000	DE	3.3%	24
WI	93.6	OR	70.0%	IN	94,000	PA	3.1%	25
AL	83.1	SC	69.8%	LA	87,000	VT	3.1%	26
WA	80.2	MN	69.3%	MO	84,000	ME	3.0%	27
MO	76.6	MO	68.3%	NM	81,000	ID	2.9%	28
WV	75.6	WI	68.1%	OK	65,000	GA	2.7%	29
TX	70.2	GA	67.7%	KS	63,000	MN	2.6%	30
VT	62.7	TN	67.7%	DC	59,000	KS	2.5%	31
MN	57.4	AL	67.0%	TN	59,000	WI	2.5%	32
MS	56.9	NC	66.3%	UT	59,000	OH	2.4%	33
IA	50.6	OK	60.1%	SC	50,000	LA	2.1%	34
OK	47.4	NH	59.4%	AL	44,000	OK	2.1%	35
AR	47.1	NM	56.0%	IA	43,000	NE	1.8%	36
ME	40.2	KS	54.6%	NH	41,000	IN	1.7%	37
AZ	35.9	NE	50.6%	ME	36,000	MT	1.7%	38
CO	35.2	KY	48.5%	KY	34,000	NC	1.7%	39
OR	32.1	AR	44.7%	ID	29,000	WY	1.7%	40
KS	31.2	IA	43.8%	NE	28,000	IA	1.6%	41
UT	23.2	AK	41.8%	AK	25,000	MO	1.6%	42
NE	21.1	WV	41.8%	AR	25,000	ND	1.5%	43
ID	13.7	ND	41.6%	DE	22,000	SC	1.4%	44
NM	13.6	ME	35.7%	MS	20,000	TN	1.2%	45
NV	13.3	SD	32.6%	VT	18,000	AL	1.1%	46
SD	9.5	MS	30.7%	WV	16,000	AR	1.1%	47
ND	9.2	ID	30.0%	MT	14,000	SD	1.1%	48
MT	5.9	WY	29.7%	ND	9,000	KY	0.9%	49
WY	4.9	VT	27.0%	SD	8,000	WV	0.9%	50
AK	1.1	MT	24.0%	WY	8,000	MS	0.8%	51

Source: Bureau of the Census, U.S. Dept. of Commerce

RACIAL AND ETHNIC GROUPS, BY PERCENT OF POPULATION

Whites	Blacks	Amer. Inds.	Asian or Pacific Islanders	Those of Hispan. Origin	Desc. Num. Order
VT 98.64%	DC 65.84%	AK 15.58%	HI 61.83%	NM 39.42%	1
ME 98.41%	MS 35.56%	NM 8.87%	CA 9.56%	CA 25.83%	2
NH 98.03%	LA 30.79%	OK 8.02%	WA 4.33%	TX 25.55%	3
IA 96.63%	SC 29.82%	SD 7.27%	NY 3.86%	AZ 18.78%	4
WV 96.21%	GA 26.96%	MT 5.97%	AK 3.59%	CO 12.88%	5
ND 94.57%	AL 25.26%	AZ 5.55%	NJ 3.53%	NY 12.31%	6
ID 94.41%	MD 24.89%	ND 4.06%	NV 3.17%	FL 12.17%	7
MN 94.41%	NC 21.97%	WY 2.09%	MD 2.92%	NV 10.35%	8
WY 94.15%	VA 18.80%	WA 1.67%	VA 2.57%	NJ 9.57%	9
NE 93.80%	DE 16.88%	NV 1.63%	IL 2.50%	IL 7.91%	10
UT 93.79%	TN 15.95%	UT 1.41%	OR 2.44%	HI 7.34%	11
OR 92.77%	AR 15.91%	ID 1.37%	MA 2.38%	CT 6.48%	12
MT 92.75%	NY 15.89%	OR 1.35%	UT 1.94%	WY 5.68%	13
WI 92.25%	IL 14.82%	NC 1.21%	TX 1.88%	DC 5.39%	14
KY 92.04%	MI 13.90%	MN 1.14%	DC 1.85%	ID 5.26%	15
SD 91.60%	FL 13.60%	KS 0.89%	RI 1.83%	UT 4.91%	16
RI 91.42%	NJ 13.41%	CO 0.84%	CO 1.82%	MA 4.78%	17
IN 90.56%	TX 11.90%	CA 0.81%	MN 1.78%	RI 4.56%	18
KS 90.09%	MO 11.42%	WI 0.81%	CT 1.54%	WA 4.41%	19
MA 89.84%	OH 10.65%	NE 0.79%	AZ 1.51%	OR 3.97%	20
PA 88.54%	PA 9.17%	MI 0.60%	DE 1.36%	KS 3.78%	21
WA 88.54%	CT 8.34%	AR 0.54%	KS 1.28%	AK 3.24%	22
CO 88.19%	IN 7.79%	ME 0.49%	FL 1.19%	OK 2.74%	23
OH 87.78%	OK 7.43%	HI 0.46%	GA 1.17%	MD 2.62%	24
MO 87.67%	CA 7.42%	LA 0.44%	PA 1.16%	VA 2.59%	25
CT 86.99%	KY 7.13%	AL 0.41%	MI 1.13%	DE 2.37%	26
NV 84.26%	NV 6.55%	RI 0.41%	WI 1.10%	NE 2.34%	27
MI 83.44%	KS 5.77%	TX 0.39%	OK 1.07%	LA 2.20%	28
FL 83.08%	WI 5.00%	MO 0.39%	LA 0.97%	MI 2.17%	29
TN 83.00%	MA 4.99%	NY 0.35%	NM 0.93%	PA 1.95%	30
AR 82.73%	AK 4.08%	MS 0.33%	ID 0.93%	WI 1.91%	31
OK 82.13%	CO 4.04%	DE 0.30%	IA 0.92%	IN 1.78%	32
AZ 80.85%	RI 3.87%	VT 0.30%	NH 0.84%	GA 1.68%	33
DE 80.32%	NE 3.64%	FL 0.28%	OH 0.84%	MT 1.52%	34
NJ 79.31%	WV 3.14%	MD 0.27%	MO 0.81%	OH 1.29%	35
IL 78.32%	WA 3.08%	IA 0.26%	NC 0.79%	MN 1.23%	36
VA 77.44%	AZ 3.02%	VA 0.25%	NE 0.79%	MO 1.21%	37
NM 75.64%	HI 2.45%	DC 0.24%	IN 0.68%	IA 1.18%	38
NC 75.56%	MN 2.17%	SC 0.24%	TN 0.65%	NC 1.16%	39
AK 75.54%	NM 1.99%	IN 0.23%	SC 0.64%	NH 1.02%	40
TX 75.21%	IA 1.73%	GA 0.21%	WY 0.62%	SC 0.88%	41
NY 74.40%	OR 1.62%	TN 0.21%	VT 0.57%	AR 0.85%	42
AL 73.65%	WY 0.79%	MA 0.20%	ME 0.54%	SD 0.75%	43
GA 71.01%	UT 0.67%	CT 0.20%	AL 0.54%	ND 0.73%	44
MD 70.98%	NH 0.65%	NJ 0.19%	ND 0.54%	TN 0.67%	45
SC 69.03%	ND 0.55%	NH 0.19%	MT 0.53%	VT 0.65%	46
CA 68.97%	SD 0.47%	IL 0.19%	AR 0.53%	MS 0.62%	47
LA 67.28%	ME 0.42%	OH 0.19%	MS 0.51%	AL 0.61%	48
MS 63.48%	VT 0.35%	KY 0.16%	KY 0.48%	KY 0.60%	49
HI 33.35%	ID 0.33%	WV 0.14%	SD 0.45%	ME 0.56%	50
DC 29.60%	MT 0.30%	PA 0.12%	WV 0.42%	WV 0.47%	51

Source: Bureau of the Census, U.S. Dept. of Commerce

GENDER AND MARITAL STATUS

% Male		% Female		% of Pop. Never Married[1]		Marriage Rate per 1,000 Pop.[2]		Divorce Rate per 1,000 Pop.[2]		Desc. Num. Order
AK	52.70%	DC	53.37%	DC	47.6%	NV	88.7	OK	7.1	1
NV	50.91%	MS	52.18%	MA	32.8%	AR	15.0	AR	6.9	2
HI	50.88%	AL	52.08%	NY	32.1%	HI	14.9	AL	6.5	3
CA	50.06%	PA	52.08%	CA	30.1%	SC	14.4	TN	6.5	4
WY	50.05%	NY	52.05%	HI	29.8%	TN	14.3	WY	6.5	5
ND	49.81%	RI	52.02%	RI	29.6%	ID	12.7	ID	6.3	6
ID	49.76%	MA	51.99%	MD	29.1%	KY	12.0	AZ	6.2	7
UT	49.67%	WV	51.96%	NJ	29.1%	UT	11.1	NM	6.2	8
WA	49.60%	LA	51.86%	CT	29.0%	VT	10.5	FL	6.1	9
MT	49.53%	MO	51.84%	IL	28.8%	VA	10.5	KY	5.8	10
CO	49.52%	TN	51.84%	MI	27.8%	FL	10.4	GA	5.5	11
AZ	49.40%	OH	51.82%	DE	27.6%	SD	10.4	TX	5.5	12
TX	49.25%	AR	51.80%	VT	27.6%	TX	10.3	CO	5.4	13
SD	49.21%	NJ	51.67%	LA	27.4%	AZ	9.9	AK	5.3	14
NM	49.19%	FL	51.60%	MN	27.4%	WY	9.8	OR	5.3	15
OR	49.15%	SC	51.57%	PA	27.3%	CO	9.5	WV	5.3	16
VA	49.04%	IA	51.57%	AK	27.2%	AL	9.4	WA	5.2	17
MN	49.03%	KY	51.56%	VA	27.1%	OK	9.4	MO	5.1	18
KS	49.03%	CT	51.54%	WI	27.1%	AK	9.2	MT	5.1	19
NH	49.00%	DE	51.52%	MS	26.7%	GA	8.9	MS	5.0	20
VT	48.95%	IN	51.51%	SC	26.4%	IA	8.9	NC	5.0	21
WI	48.92%	NC	51.51%	GA	26.2%	MS	8.9	KS	4.8	22
NE	48.75%	MD	51.51%	ND	25.9%	ME	8.8	UT	4.8	23
ME	48.69%	GA	51.46%	CO	25.8%	IN	8.7	VT	4.8	24
OK	48.67%	MI	51.45%	NM	25.8%	MD	8.5	OH	4.6	25
IL	48.57%	IL	51.43%	AZ	25.5%	NH	8.5	DE	4.5	26
MI	48.55%	OK	51.33%	NH	25.5%	LA	8.4	NH	4.5	27
GA	48.54%	ME	51.31%	OH	25.5%	MO	8.4	VA	4.5	28
MD	48.49%	NE	51.25%	UT	25.5%	MT	8.4	ME	4.3	29
NC	48.49%	WI	51.08%	NC	25.1%	KS	8.3	HI	4.2	30
IN	48.49%	VT	51.05%	TX	25.1%	NY	8.3	MI	4.1	31
DE	48.48%	NH	51.00%	WA	24.8%	WA	8.3	SC	4.1	32
CT	48.46%	KS	50.97%	NE	24.4%	OH	8.0	SD	4.0	33
KY	48.44%	MN	50.97%	SD	24.4%	OR	8.0	IA	3.9	34
IA	48.43%	VA	50.96%	IN	24.3%	IL	7.8	NE	3.9	35
SC	48.43%	OR	50.85%	ME	24.0%	NM	7.8	IL	3.7	36
FL	48.40%	NM	50.81%	AL	23.9%	NE	7.7	MN	3.7	37
NJ	48.33%	SD	50.79%	MO	23.9%	ND	7.7	ND	3.5	38
AR	48.20%	TX	50.75%	IA	23.7%	MI	7.5	WI	3.5	39
OH	48.18%	AZ	50.60%	NV	23.7%	DE	7.2	DC	3.4	40
TN	48.16%	CO	50.48%	TN	23.2%	WV	7.2	MD	3.4	41
MO	48.16%	MT	50.47%	OR	23.1%	WI	7.2	RI	3.4	42
LA	48.14%	WA	50.40%	KS	22.7%	RI	7.1	PA	3.3	43
WV	48.04%	UT	50.33%	FL	22.6%	CT	7.0	CT	3.1	44
MA	48.01%	ID	50.24%	KY	22.6%	MN	7.0	NJ	3.1	45
RI	47.98%	ND	50.19%	MT	22.3%	NJ	6.8	NY	3.1	46
NY	47.95%	WY	49.95%	WV	22.2%	NC	6.8	MA	2.7	47
PA	47.92%	CA	49.94%	WY	21.7%	CA	6.5	CA	NA	48
AL	47.92%	HI	49.12%	ID	21.2%	PA	6.4	IN	NA	49
MS	47.82%	NV	49.09%	OK	20.9%	MA	6.2	LA	NA	50
DC	46.63%	AK	47.30%	AR	20.7%	DC	5.2	NV	NA	51

[1]Among those 15 years old or older.   [2]1993.
Source: Bureau of the Census, U.S. Dept. of Commerce

AGE (1994)

% of Pop. Under 5 Years		% of Pop. Under 18		% 65 Years & Over		% Inc. in the Elderly, 1990-94		Desc. Num. Order
UT	9.49%	UT	35.22%	FL	18.4%	NV	28.50%	1
AK	9.24%	AK	31.68%	PA	15.9%	AK	25.17%	2
CA	9.01%	NM	30.11%	RI	15.6%	AZ	14.04%	3
TX	8.48%	ID	29.92%	IA	15.4%	HI	12.80%	4
NM	8.46%	SD	28.85%	WV	15.4%	UT	12.70%	5
AZ	8.44%	TX	28.84%	AR	14.8%	CO	11.70%	6
HI	8.06%	WY	28.78%	ND	14.7%	NM	11.00%	7
NV	7.89%	LA	28.62%	SD	14.7%	DE	10.24%	8
LA	7.81%	MS	28.33%	CT	14.2%	WY	10.18%	9
IL	7.79%	AZ	27.95%	MA	14.1%	NC	9.90%	10
GA	7.78%	MT	27.80%	MO	14.1%	SC	9.59%	11
MS	7.76%	CA	27.61%	NE	14.1%	VA	9.08%	12
ID	7.68%	NE	27.23%	KS	13.9%	ID	8.85%	13
NY	7.61%	MN	27.17%	ME	13.9%	TX	8.82%	14
MD	7.57%	KS	27.02%	OR	13.7%	NH	8.77%	15
DC	7.54%	OK	27.01%	NJ	13.6%	GA	8.52%	16
SD	7.49%	ND	26.96%	OK	13.6%	FL	8.51%	17
SC	7.48%	GA	26.83%	DC	13.5%	MD	8.22%	18
CO	7.39%	CO	26.53%	AZ	13.4%	OR	7.84%	19
MI	7.38%	WI	26.51%	OH	13.4%	WA	7.42%	20
WA	7.37%	WA	26.35%	WI	13.4%	MT	7.05%	21
NJ	7.33%	IL	26.23%	MT	13.3%	CA	6.74%	22
OK	7.27%	MO	26.13%	NY	13.2%	TN	6.49%	23
DE	7.22%	AR	26.09%	AL	13.1%	OH	5.97%	24
NC	7.21%	SC	25.98%	IN	12.8%	VT	5.80%	25
KS	7.20%	NV	25.81%	KY	12.8%	AL	5.55%	26
AL	7.16%	HI	25.78%	DE	12.7%	IN	5.43%	27
MN	7.16%	IA	25.77%	TN	12.7%	LA	5.33%	28
VA	7.16%	OH	25.71%	IL	12.6%	ME	5.28%	29
NE	7.15%	NH	25.68%	MN	12.5%	WI	5.03%	30
MO	7.12%	IN	25.61%	MS	12.5%	PA	4.86%	31
RI	7.12%	AL	25.60%	NC	12.5%	MN	4.77%	32
IN	7.08%	OR	25.37%	MI	12.4%	KY	4.75%	33
TN	7.07%	KY	25.35%	HI	12.1%	OK	4.43%	34
OH	7.06%	MD	25.23%	VT	12.1%	NJ	4.36%	35
CT	7.05%	VT	25.17%	NH	11.9%	CT	4.28%	36
NH	7.04%	TN	25.06%	SC	11.9%	WV	4.13%	37
AR	7.01%	NC	24.84%	ID	11.6%	MO	3.81%	38
MA	7.00%	NY	24.83%	WA	11.6%	AR	3.70%	39
WY	6.93%	DE	24.79%	LA	11.4%	MA	3.63%	40
FL	6.89%	ME	24.68%	NV	11.3%	KS	3.34%	41
MT	6.89%	VA	24.47%	MD	11.2%	MS	3.34%	42
WI	6.89%	NJ	24.43%	VA	11.1%	ND	3.23%	43
KY	6.82%	RI	24.07%	WY	11.1%	MI	3.12%	44
OR	6.77%	CT	24.06%	NM	11.0%	NE	3.11%	45
ND	6.74%	PA	24.05%	CA	10.6%	IL	3.09%	46
IA	6.65%	MA	23.57%	TX	10.2%	RI	2.96%	47
PA	6.63%	WV	23.55%	CO	10.1%	SD	2.61%	48
VT	6.55%	FL	23.38%	GA	10.1%	IA	2.56%	49
ME	6.29%	DC	20.88%	UT	8.8%	NY	1.24%	50
WV	5.93%	MI	16.06%	AK	4.6%	DC	-1.09%	51

Source: Bureau of the Census, U.S. Dept. of Commerce

OF VITAL IMPORTANCE

BIRTH RATES; INFANT MORTALITY

Live Birth Rate per 1,000 Pop.[1]	Infant Mortality Rate[2]	Infant Mortality, Blacks[3]	Infant Mortality, Whites[3]	Births to Teenagers, % of Tot.[4]	Births to Unmarried, % of Tot.[4]	Desc. Num. Order
UT 19.6	DC 19.6	DC 24.4	DC 12.1	MS 21.4	DC 66.9	1
CA 18.9	MS 11.9	IL 21.5	WV 9.6	AR 19.4	MS 42.9	2
TX 18.3	AL 10.5	MI 21.0	OK 9.4	AL 18.2	LA 40.2	3
AZ 18.0	SC 10.4	MN 19.7	NM 9.3	LA 18.1	NM 39.5	4
AK 17.6	AR 10.3	DE 19.4	GA 9.1	WV 17.2	AZ 36.2	5
NM 17.1	GA 10.3	PA 18.8	IN 8.9	NM 17.0	SC 35.5	6
DC 16.9	MI 10.2	VA 18.8	WY 8.8	TN 16.9	GA 35.0	7
HI 16.7	IL 10.1	OH 18.3	ID 8.7	OK 16.8	NY 34.8	8
IL 16.3	NC 10.0	WI 18.1	MT 8.6	SC 16.6	CA 34.3	9
LA 16.3	MD 9.8	GA 18.0	SD 8.6	KY 16.5	FL 34.2	10
GA 16.2	VA 9.5	IA 18.0	AK 8.5	DC 16.3	IL 33.4	11
MS 16.0	IN 9.4	MO 17.5	MS 8.5	GA 16.2	NV 33.3	12
ID 15.6	LA 9.4	TN 17.5	CO 8.4	TX 15.9	TN 32.7	13
NJ 15.6	OH 9.4	NJ 17.3	AL 8.3	NC 15.4	AL 32.6	14
CO 15.4	TN 9.4	NY 17.3	NC 8.3	AZ 15.0	DE 32.6	15
NY 15.3	SD 9.3	SC 17.1	RI 8.3	MO 14.5	OH 31.6	16
MD 15.2	WV 9.2	NE 16.8	SC 8.3	IN 14.1	PA 31.6	17
NV 15.2	PA 9.0	AZ 16.7	AZ 8.2	OH 13.6	MO 31.5	18
AL 15.1	WY 8.9	WV 16.6	OH 8.2	FL 13.5	NC 31.3	19
DE 15.1	FL 8.8	CO 16.5	NV 8.1	WY 13.2	AR 31.0	20
MI 15.1	ID 8.8	LA 16.5	OR 8.1	ID 13.0	MD 30.5	21
SD 15.1	NY 8.8	MD 16.3	AR 8.0	MI 13.0	RI 29.6	22
KS 15.0	OK 8.8	FL 16.2	KY 8.0	IL 12.9	IN 29.5	23
IN 14.8	KS 8.7	MS 16.1	TN 8.0	DE 12.4	CT 28.7	24
MO 14.8	AK 8.6	CT 16.0	MI 7.9	KS 12.4	OK 28.4	25
SC 14.8	DE 8.6	IN 16.0	ND 7.9	NV 12.4	VA 28.3	26
VA 14.7	MO 8.5	NC 16.0	IA 7.8	OR 12.4	WV 27.7	27
NC 14.5	AZ 8.4	AL 15.9	MO 7.8	CO 12.0	AK 27.4	28
OK 14.5	NJ 8.4	KS 15.4	PA 7.8	MT 11.9	OR 27.0	29
MA 14.4	KY 8.3	OR 15.1	IL 7.7	CA 11.8	MI 26.8	30
TN 14.4	IA 8.0	WA 14.5	KS 7.7	SD 11.4	SD 26.6	31
RI 14.3	ND 7.8	CA 14.2	NY 7.7	VA 11.0	MT 26.4	32
NE 14.2	TX 7.8	TX 13.9	CA 7.6	AK 10.6	NJ 26.4	33
WY 14.2	CO 7.6	AR 13.6	FL 7.6	WA 10.6	KY 26.3	34
AR 14.1	CT 7.6	KY 13.6	WA 7.6	PA 10.5	HI 26.2	35
FL 14.1	NM 7.6	MT 13.3	VA 7.5	UT 10.5	WI 26.1	36
MN 14.1	MT 7.5	OK 13.2	UT 7.4	IA 10.2	MA 25.9	37
OH 14.1	NE 7.4	UT 13.0	DE 7.3	ME 10.2	ME 25.3	38
CT 14.0	RI 7.4	NM 12.8	LA 7.3	WI 10.2	WA 25.3	39
OR 13.9	VT 7.2	NV 12.5	NE 7.2	HI 10.0	KS 24.3	40
KY 13.8	WI 7.2	HI 11.5	NH 7.2	NE 9.9	WY 24.0	41
ND 13.8	MN 7.1	AK 11.2	WI 7.2	MD 9.8	CO 23.8	42
WI 13.8	OR 7.1	ID 10.9	TX 7.1	RI 9.8	IA 23.5	43
MT 13.6	CA 7.0	MA 10.4	NJ 6.8	ND 9.3	VT 23.4	44
WA 13.6	WA 6.8	RI 9.7	MA 6.7	NY 9.0	MN 23.0	45
NH 13.3	NV 6.7	SD 7.4	MN 6.7	VT 8.5	NE 22.6	46
IA 13.2	MA 6.5	ME 6.1	CT 6.6	MN 8.1	ND 22.6	47
PA 13.2	HI 6.3	NH 5.4	MD 6.5	CT 8.0	NH 19.2	48
VT 12.6	NH 5.9	ND NA	VT 6.5	NJ 8.0	ID 18.3	49
ME 12.1	UT 5.9	VT NA	ME 6.2	MA 7.7	TX 17.5	50
WV 12.1	ME 5.6	WY NA	HI 5.1	NH 6.7	UT 15.1	51

[1]1993 [2]Per 1,000 live births, 1992 [3]1990 [4]1992

Source: U.S. Dept. of Health and Human Services, National Center for Health Statistics

ABORTIONS (1992)

	Abortions Reported		Rate per 1,000 Women		Rate per 1,000 Live Births	Desc. Num. Order
CA	304,230	DC	138.4	DC	1,104	1
NY	195,390	NY	46.2	NY	694	2
TX	97,400	HI	46.0	HI	617	3
FL	84,680	NV	44.2	NV	591	4
IL	68,420	CA	42.1	CA	519	5
MI	55,580	DE	35.2	DE	502	6
NJ	55,320	NJ	31.0	MA	472	7
PA	49,740	FL	30.0	RI	461	8
OH	49,520	RI	30.0	NJ	460	9
MA	40,660	MA	28.4	MD	454	10
GA	39,680	WA	27.7	WA	447	11
NC	36,180	MD	26.4	CT	444	12
VA	35,020	CT	26.2	FL	438	13
WA	33,190	IL	25.4	MI	393	14
MD	31,260	MI	25.2	VT	393	15
DC	21,320	AZ	24.1	VA	373	16
AZ	20,600	GA	24.0	OR	372	17
CO	19,880	OR	23.9	CO	362	18
CT	19,720	CO	23.6	IL	361	19
TN	19,060	TX	23.1	NC	357	20
AL	17,450	VA	22.7	KS	353	21
MN	16,180	KS	22.4	GA	350	22
OR	16,060	NC	22.4	PA	302	23
IN	15,840	VT	21.2	MT	298	24
WI	15,450	OH	19.5	TX	297	25
LA	13,600	PA	18.6	AZ	295	26
MO	13,510	AL	18.2	OH	294	27
NV	13,300	MT	18.2	ME	282	28
KS	12,570	NM	17.7	AL	277	29
HI	12,190	AK	16.5	NH	269	30
SC	12,190	TN	16.2	MN	251	31
KY	10,000	NE	15.7	NE	246	32
OK	8,940	MN	15.6	TN	243	33
MS	7,550	ME	14.7	SC	229	34
AR	7,130	NH	14.6	NM	228	35
RI	6,990	SC	14.2	WI	223	36
IA	6,970	WI	13.6	AK	222	37
NM	6,410	AR	13.5	AR	213	38
DE	5,730	LA	13.4	LA	195	39
NE	5,580	OK	12.5	OK	193	40
ME	4,200	MS	12.4	KY	191	41
UT	3,940	IN	12.0	IN	185	42
NH	3,890	MO	11.6	IA	185	43
MT	3,300	IA	11.4	MS	176	44
WV	3,140	KY	11.4	MO	175	45
VT	2,900	ND	10.7	ND	149	46
AK	2,370	UT	9.3	WV	134	47
ID	1,710	WV	7.7	UT	104	48
ND	1,490	ID	7.2	ID	97	49
SD	1,040	SD	6.8	SD	92	50
WY	460	WY	4.3	WY	74	51

Source: The Alan Guttmacher Institute (copyright)

KEEPING WELL

PHYSICIANS, DENTISTS, AND NURSES

Physicians Per 100,000 Pop., 1993		Dentists Per 100,000 Pop., 1991		Nurses Per 100,000 Pop., 1992		Desc. Num. Order
DC	667	DC	122	DC	1,966	1
MA	361	CT	80	MA	1,066	2
MD	335	NY	79	ND	1,007	3
NY	334	HI	78	SD	973	4
CT	321	NJ	78	RI	971	5
RI	271	MA	76	NH	964	6
NJ	263	CO	71	CT	946	7
VT	259	MD	71	IA	922	8
PA	254	OR	69	VT	910	9
HI	244	IL	67	PA	907	10
CA	240	MN	66	DE	894	11
MN	232	PA	66	MN	893	12
IL	230	CA	65	NY	881	13
CO	222	UT	65	ME	861	14
WA	220	NE	64	NE	834	15
FL	215	MI	62	NJ	827	16
VA	215	WA	62	OH	816	17
NH	211	WI	62	MO	812	18
OR	210	NH	59	OR	806	19
TN	210	AK	56	IL	804	20
DE	209	MT	56	WI	799	21
MO	207	RI	56	KS	794	22
OH	207	VT	56	MD	783	23
LA	201	ID	54	CO	780	24
NC	198	IA	54	WA	761	25
WI	196	KY	54	MT	715	26
MI	195	OH	54	AZ	711	27
AZ	194	VA	54	NC	708	28
ME	192	MO	53	FL	707	29
NM	190	TN	53	TN	706	30
NE	189	FL	51	IN	700	31
ND	188	KS	51	HI	697	32
UT	187	AZ	50	MI	694	33
KS	185	WY	50	VA	684	34
GA	182	IN	48	AL	673	35
WV	182	OK	48	KY	659	36
KY	179	TX	48	WY	658	37
TX	177	LA	47	WV	657	38
SC	173	ME	47	GA	647	39
AL	170	ND	47	AK	637	40
MT	169	GA	46	NM	600	41
IN	168	DE	45	AR	587	42
AR	162	SD	45	SC	584	43
IA	159	WV	45	LA	570	44
SD	156	NV	43	CA	568	45
OK	153	AL	42	UT	545	46
NV	148	NC	42	ID	537	47
AK	142	SC	42	NV	536	48
WY	137	AR	41	OK	534	49
ID	131	NM	41	TX	528	50
MS	130	MS	38	MS	516	51

Source: American Medical Assoc. (copyright); American Dental Assoc.; Health Resources and Services Administration, U.S. Dept. of Health and Human Services

HOSPITALS (1993)

Hosp. per 100,000 Pop.		Patients Admitted per 1,000 Pop.		Occupancy Rate		Avg. Cost per Patient per Day		Avg. Cost per Patient per Stay		Avg. Days Stay, 1992		Desc. Num. Order
SD	7.07	DC	270.12	HI	83.1%	CA	$1,221	DC	$8,594	MT	18.7	1
ND	7.06	WV	153.08	NY	82.8%	DC	$1,201	NY	$7,716	MI	13.2	2
MT	6.18	PA	152.18	NJ	77.0%	WA	$1,143	HI	$7,633	ND	13.0	3
NE	5.58	TN	146.70	MD	75.3%	AK	$1,136	AK	$7,594	PA	13.0	4
WY	5.32	AL	144.68	CT	74.4%	AZ	$1,091	CT	$7,478	SD	12.4	5
KS	5.29	ND	142.54	RI	73.3%	UT	$1,081	DE	$7,307	NJ	11.6	6
IA	4.22	AR	141.01	DC	73.2%	CT	$1,058	NH	$6,964	MA	10.7	7
ID	3.73	MS	140.45	CT	73.2%	OR	$1,053	CA	$6,918	MN	10.3	8
MS	3.67	KY	140.38	PA	72.6%	NM	$1,046	MA	$6,843	NY	10.2	9
AR	3.59	NJ	140.37	MA	71.5%	MA	$1,036	NV	$6,796	NE	9.7	10
OK	3.40	LA	139.39	DE	70.9%	DE	$1,028	PA	$6,564	CT	8.6	11
MN	3.21	MA	135.81	NC	69.6%	TX	$1,010	NJ	$6,540	HI	8.5	12
WV	3.19	MO	134.69	ME	68.0%	NH	$976	IL	$6,318	DC	8.3	13
ME	3.15	SD	131.62	NV	67.8%	CO	$961	CO	$6,212	WI	8.2	14
LA	3.08	NY	130.00	SC	67.3%	FL	$940	FL	$6,169	ME	7.8	15
KY	2.79	OH	127.81	MN	66.0%	OH	$940	MO	$6,161	IA	7.6	16
AL	2.77	RI	126.80	MI	64.7%	IL	$912	MI	$6,147	KS	7.6	17
AK	2.68	IL	125.60	MT	64.2%	MI	$902	NE	$6,024	MO	7.5	18
VT	2.60	IN	124.83	ND	64.2%	NV	$900	TX	$6,021	WY	7.5	19
TN	2.55	FL	124.26	VT	64.2%	IN	$898	SC	$5,955	RI	7.3	20
WI	2.52	GA	123.60	VA	64.2%	MD	$889	OH	$5,923	VT	7.3	21
NH	2.49	IA	123.50	NH	63.7%	RI	$885	MN	$5,867	CO	7.2	22
MO	2.48	MI	119.99	IL	63.5%	LA	$875	TN	$5,798	IL	7.2	23
GA	2.30	ME	117.02	GA	63.4%	MO	$863	WA	$5,792	NC	7.2	24
TX	2.30	MT	115.93	WI	63.4%	PA	$861	LA	$5,781	OH	7.2	25
NM	2.29	KS	114.32	KY	62.2%	TN	$859	IN	$5,677	AL	7.1	26
UT	2.26	DE	113.61	WV	61.9%	SC	$838	RI	$5,672	WV	7.1	27
OR	2.08	NC	112.99	CA	61.2%	VA	$830	MD	$5,632	FL	7.0	28
CO	2.02	MD	112.81	TN	60.8%	NJ	$829	NM	$5,600	MD	7.0	29
IN	2.02	WI	112.69	AL	60.7%	HI	$823	NC	$5,571	MS	7.0	30
PA	1.94	OK	112.34	SD	60.6%	OK	$797	GA	$5,554	VA	7.0	31
DC	1.90	MN	109.66	OH	60.5%	NY	$784	ME	$5,543	IN	6.8	32
SC	1.87	TX	108.97	FL	60.4%	AL	$775	AZ	$5,528	KY	6.8	33
IL	1.78	SC	108.60	MS	59.3%	GA	$775	VA	$5,504	NH	6.8	34
MI	1.77	NE	108.56	MO	58.9%	NC	$763	ND	$5,403	TN	6.8	35
OH	1.74	CT	105.64	IN	58.7%	WI	$744	WI	$5,348	AR	6.7	36
HI	1.72	VA	105.16	CO	58.6%	ME	$738	UT	$5,314	DE	6.7	37
WA	1.71	AZ	102.31	AR	58.3%	KY	$703	OR	$5,309	GA	6.7	38
NC	1.68	VT	99.83	WA	57.6%	WV	$701	VT	$5,241	OK	6.7	39
MA	1.65	CA	97.77	AZ	57.1%	AR	$678	AL	$5,229	SC	6.7	40
FL	1.62	NH	97.60	LA	57.0%	VT	$676	KS	$5,108	ID	6.6	41
AZ	1.52	OR	96.61	OK	55.5%	KS	$666	OK	$5,093	LA	6.5	42
NV	1.52	CO	95.40	TX	55.5%	ID	$659	SD	$5,052	NV	6.4	43
VA	1.48	WA	93.97	ID	55.4%	MN	$652	IA	$4,980	UT	6.3	44
CA	1.37	NM	93.50	NE	55.2%	NE	$626	MT	$4,953	TX	6.2	45
NY	1.27	UT	93.28	OR	54.7%	IA	$612	KY	$4,749	CA	6.1	46
NJ	1.23	WY	91.06	KS	54.2%	MS	$555	WV	$4,712	AK	5.9	47
DE	1.15	ID	90.00	NM	54.0%	WY	$537	NM	$4,706	NM	5.9	48
RI	1.10	NV	89.00	UT	53.4%	ND	$507	ID	$4,635	AZ	5.8	49
CT	1.07	HI	83.10	AK	52.9%	SD	$506	AR	$4,585	OR	5.8	50
MD	1.01	AK	62.37	WY	48.4%	MT	$481	MS	$4,053	WA	5.8	51

Source: American Hospital Assoc. (copyright)

HOUSEHOLDS

NUMBER, SIZE, THOSE WITH ELDERLY (1994)

Households per 1,000 Pop.		% With Householder 65 or Older		Increase in Households, 1990-94		Persons per Household		Desc. Num. Order
DC	415.79	FL	28.98%	NV	20.1%	UT	3.13	1
FL	391.03	WV	26.67%	ID	12.2%	HI	2.99	2
CO	387.58	PA	26.61%	UT	11.6%	CA	2.83	3
OR	387.23	RI	25.67%	CO	10.5%	AK	2.81	4
WV	386.94	SD	25.66%	AK	10.3%	NM	2.77	5
NV	384.35	IA	25.60%	AZ	9.8%	ID	2.75	6
IA	382.47	AR	25.35%	GA	9.1%	TX	2.75	7
ME	382.26	ND	24.90%	WA	9.1%	MS	2.74	8
WA	382.18	NE	23.94%	OR	8.3%	LA	2.72	9
MO	380.45	MO	23.80%	NM	8.1%	NJ	2.72	10
TN	379.90	MA	23.31%	TX	7.7%	WY	2.68	11
MT	379.67	OK	23.30%	HI	7.1%	GA	2.67	12
OK	379.37	KS	23.29%	DE	6.8%	MD	2.67	13
VT	379.31	MS	23.29%	NC	6.4%	AZ	2.66	14
NC	378.93	CT	23.16%	VA	6.4%	IL	2.66	15
NE	378.31	NJ	23.16%	FL	6.3%	SC	2.66	16
KS	378.23	AL	22.93%	SC	6.3%	MI	2.65	17
AR	377.90	WI	22.75%	MT	6.1%	NY	2.64	18
ND	377.74	OH	22.65%	TN	6.0%	SD	2.63	19
PA	377.61	AZ	22.62%	WY	5.3%	WI	2.62	20
OH	377.41	MT	22.46%	AL	5.1%	AL	2.61	21
KY	376.27	NY	22.40%	MD	4.7%	NH	2.61	22
IN	375.70	ME	22.36%	IN	4.6%	CT	2.60	23
AL	375.21	OR	22.34%	VT	4.6%	MN	2.60	24
RI	375.13	KY	22.29%	CA	4.5%	VA	2.60	25
MA	374.94	IN	21.75%	KY	4.3%	DE	2.59	26
MN	374.64	IL	21.73%	MS	4.2%	IN	2.59	27
WY	373.95	TN	21.57%	AR	4.0%	KY	2.59	28
DE	373.94	MI	21.53%	MN	3.8%	OH	2.59	29
CT	373.13	DC	21.52%	WI	3.7%	AR	2.58	30
NH	372.91	HI	21.26%	NH	3.0%	MA	2.57	31
VA	372.25	DE	21.21%	LA	2.9%	PA	2.57	32
WI	371.90	MN	21.16%	IL	2.5%	RI	2.57	33
AZ	368.83	NC	21.13%	OH	2.5%	TN	2.57	34
MI	368.79	SC	20.94%	OK	2.5%	KS	2.56	35
SD	367.55	LA	20.80%	MI	2.4%	MO	2.56	36
NY	367.05	ID	20.74%	MO	2.4%	MT	2.56	37
IL	366.58	VT	20.00%	WV	2.4%	NE	2.56	38
GA	365.84	NM	19.76%	KS	2.2%	NV	2.56	39
MD	365.76	NH	19.58%	SD	2.1%	OK	2.56	40
SC	364.90	WA	19.15%	ME	2.0%	WA	2.56	41
NJ	359.94	WY	19.10%	NE	2.0%	NC	2.55	42
LA	357.59	CA	18.82%	NJ	1.8%	ME	2.54	43
ID	357.46	MD	18.79%	IA	1.6%	ND	2.54	44
TX	355.81	VA	18.57%	PA	1.2%	VT	2.54	45
MS	355.56	NV	18.21%	MA	0.8%	OR	2.53	46
NM	354.90	TX	18.11%	NY	0.4%	WV	2.53	47
CA	345.20	UT	17.86%	ND	0.2%	CO	2.52	48
AK	343.23	GA	17.47%	CT	-0.7%	IA	2.52	49
HI	323.16	CO	16.51%	RI	-1.1%	FL	2.50	50
UT	313.94	AK	8.17%	DC	-5.2%	DC	2.24	51

Source: Bureau of the Census, U.S. Dept. of Commerce

HOUSEHOLDS: FAMILY, NONFAMILY, GROUP (1994)

Family Households		Family Households % of Total		Nonfamily Households		Nonfamily Households % of Total		% of Total Pop. in Group Qtrs.		Desc. Num. Order
CA	7,139,394	UT	76.47%	CA	3,241,812	DC	51.09%	DC	6.87%	1
NY	4,489,312	MS	74.00%	NY	2,150,010	NV	34.08%	VT	3.85%	2
TX	4,343,878	HI	73.95%	TX	1,727,059	CO	33.39%	RI	3.85%	3
FL	3,511,825	SC	73.78%	FL	1,623,044	MA	32.59%	ND	3.79%	4
PA	3,155,989	KY	73.63%	PA	1,339,977	WA	32.44%	AK	3.76%	5
IL	2,924,880	AL	73.26%	IL	1,277,360	NY	32.38%	SD	3.71%	6
OH	2,895,223	AR	73.11%	OH	1,192,323	OR	31.95%	IA	3.58%	7
MI	2,439,171	ID	72.96%	MI	980,160	FL	31.61%	MA	3.56%	8
NJ	2,021,346	TN	72.72%	NJ	773,365	RI	31.51%	HI	3.40%	9
NC	1,812,053	LA	72.69%	MA	732,364	MN	31.38%	NC	3.39%	10
GA	1,713,072	WV	72.65%	NC	704,973	AZ	31.32%	VA	3.38%	11
VA	1,629,490	GA	72.38%	VA	662,340	CA	31.23%	SC	3.34%	12
MA	1,514,746	NJ	72.33%	GA	653,543	VT	31.22%	KS	3.34%	13
IN	1,480,351	NM	72.14%	WA	607,497	NE	31.03%	CT	3.08%	14
MO	1,368,334	NC	71.99%	MO	592,872	ND	30.97%	NY	3.03%	15
TN	1,348,019	IN	71.68%	IN	585,004	MT	30.86%	ME	3.03%	16
WI	1,275,172	TX	71.55%	WI	546,946	IL	30.40%	DE	3.01%	17
WA	1,264,934	MI	71.33%	MN	517,170	IA	30.40%	NE	3.01%	18
MD	1,245,814	MD	71.23%	TN	505,706	SD	30.39%	OK	2.98%	19
MN	1,130,683	NH	71.16%	MD	503,177	KS	30.29%	MT	2.97%	20
AL	1,103,835	VA	71.10%	AZ	428,737	MO	30.23%	PA	2.93%	21
LA	1,089,882	DE	71.06%	CO	428,275	WI	30.02%	IN	2.92%	22
KY	1,015,998	WY	70.97%	LA	409,387	PA	29.80%	NH	2.90%	23
AZ	940,106	OK	70.91%	AL	402,955	CT	29.74%	MO	2.84%	24
SC	928,206	OH	70.83%	CT	365,986	AK	29.68%	KY	2.75%	25
CT	864,493	ME	70.64%	KY	363,784	ME	29.36%	WI	2.73%	26
OK	855,321	AK	70.32%	OR	352,469	OH	29.17%	MS	2.71%	27
CO	854,214	CT	70.26%	OK	350,814	OK	29.09%	MN	2.69%	28
OR	750,844	PA	70.20%	SC	329,838	WY	29.03%	GA	2.68%	29
IA	740,819	WI	69.98%	IA	323,506	DE	28.94%	LA	2.67%	30
MS	674,378	MO	69.77%	KS	286,126	VA	28.90%	TN	2.65%	31
KS	658,600	KS	69.71%	AR	239,624	NH	28.84%	CA	2.53%	32
AR	651,555	SD	69.61%	MS	236,996	MD	28.77%	IL	2.51%	33
WV	500,259	IL	69.60%	WV	188,298	MI	28.67%	AR	2.48%	34
NE	415,427	IA	69.60%	NE	186,936	TX	28.45%	WA	2.48%	35
UT	410,862	MT	69.14%	NV	158,897	IN	28.32%	OH	2.41%	36
NM	391,487	ND	69.03%	NM	151,222	NC	28.01%	CO	2.41%	37
ME	328,685	NE	68.97%	ME	136,627	NM	27.86%	MD	2.38%	38
NV	307,400	VT	68.78%	DC	127,547	NJ	27.67%	FL	2.38%	39
NH	292,601	CA	68.77%	UT	126,411	GA	27.62%	OR	2.33%	40
HI	263,456	AZ	68.68%	RI	119,091	WV	27.35%	TX	2.32%	41
ID	263,194	MN	68.62%	NH	118,585	LA	27.31%	AL	2.29%	42
RI	258,886	RI	68.49%	ID	97,529	TN	27.28%	MI	2.28%	43
MT	211,666	FL	68.39%	MT	94,497	ID	27.04%	WY	2.26%	44
SD	180,306	OR	68.05%	HI	92,811	AR	26.89%	NJ	2.22%	45
DE	175,867	NY	67.62%	SD	78,728	AL	26.74%	AZ	2.20%	46
ND	166,270	WA	67.56%	ND	74,608	KY	26.37%	ID	2.13%	47
VT	144,895	MA	67.41%	DE	71,630	SC	26.22%	WV	2.06%	48
AK	132,837	CO	66.61%	VT	65,755	HI	26.05%	NV	2.01%	49
DC	122,087	NV	65.92%	AK	56,078	MS	26.00%	NM	1.90%	50
WY	119,825	DC	48.91%	WY	49,014	UT	23.53%	UT	1.69%	51

Source: Bureau of the Census, U.S. Dept. of Commerce

LIVING QUARTERS

RENTAL HOUSING UNITS

As % of Housing Units		As % of Occupied Units		Persons per Unit		Median Contract Rent		Vacancy Rate		Desc. Num. Order
DC	54.77%	DC	61.10%	HI	2.78	HI	$599	AZ	15.3%	1
NY	43.93%	NY	47.82%	CA	2.74	CA	$561	OK	14.7%	2
HI	42.16%	HI	46.13%	UT	2.67	NJ	$521	WY	14.4%	3
CA	41.20%	RI	45.32%	MS	2.65	CT	$510	TX	13.0%	4
NV	40.65%	NV	45.23%	AK	2.58	MA	$506	LA	12.5%	5
MA	37.03%	CA	44.38%	LA	2.57	AK	$503	FL	12.4%	6
RI	36.95%	AK	43.90%	TX	2.55	NH	$479	GA	12.2%	7
AK	35.65%	MA	40.75%	NM	2.52	MD	$473	NH	11.8%	8
MD	34.97%	TX	39.13%	ID	2.51	NV	$445	SC	11.5%	9
WA	34.48%	MD	37.83%	GA	2.49	DC	$441	CO	11.4%	10
OR	34.13%	CO	37.76%	AR	2.48	NY	$428	NM	11.4%	11
TX	33.90%	WA	37.43%	AZ	2.46	DE	$425	KS	11.1%	12
IL	33.35%	OR	36.92%	MD	2.45	RI	$416	MO	10.7%	13
CO	32.78%	AZ	35.82%	AL	2.44	VA	$411	AR	10.4%	14
CT	32.02%	IL	35.77%	VA	2.43	FL	$402	WV	10.1%	15
NJ	31.91%	NJ	35.11%	OK	2.41	WA	$383	MT	9.6%	16
GA	31.45%	GA	35.07%	NJ	2.40	VT	$374	TN	9.6%	17
VA	30.94%	ND	34.43%	FL	2.39	AZ	$370	MS	9.5%	18
NE	30.57%	CT	34.38%	KY	2.39	IL	$369	AL	9.3%	19
OH	30.41%	LA	34.10%	NC	2.39	CO	$362	NC	9.2%	20
SD	30.05%	SD	33.92%	WY	2.39	ME	$358	NV	9.1%	21
ND	30.01%	VA	33.70%	DE	2.38	MN	$348	ND	9.0%	22
LA	29.79%	NE	33.53%	NY	2.38	GA	$344	UT	8.6%	23
AZ	29.55%	WI	33.30%	IL	2.37	OR	$344	AK	8.5%	24
WI	29.52%	FL	32.77%	NV	2.35	MI	$343	ME	8.4%	25
TN	29.25%	MT	32.75%	TN	2.35	WI	$331	IN	8.3%	26
KS	29.02%	NM	32.57%	SD	2.34	TX	$328	KY	8.2%	27
UT	28.63%	OH	32.52%	OR	2.33	PA	$322	VA	8.1%	28
NC	28.57%	WY	32.16%	WV	2.33	NM	$312	IL	8.0%	29
NM	27.96%	KS	32.07%	KS	2.31	UT	$300	DC	7.9%	30
IA	27.89%	NC	31.99%	MI	2.31	OH	$296	MN	7.9%	31
MO	27.85%	TN	31.97%	CT	2.30	IN	$291	RI	7.9%	32
KY	27.83%	OK	31.92%	IN	2.30	KS	$285	DE	7.8%	33
MT	27.76%	UT	31.88%	WA	2.30	NC	$284	NE	7.7%	34
FL	27.58%	NH	31.81%	MT	2.28	MO	$282	OH	7.5%	35
OK	27.37%	MO	31.23%	NE	2.27	NE	$282	VT	7.5%	36
IN	27.36%	VT	30.99%	OH	2.27	SC	$276	NJ	7.4%	37
AR	27.11%	AR	30.44%	WI	2.26	TN	$273	ID	7.3%	38
PA	26.73%	KY	30.39%	CO	2.25	WY	$270	SD	7.3%	39
WY	26.69%	SC	30.15%	IA	2.25	ND	$266	MI	7.2%	40
SC	26.64%	IA	29.97%	SC	2.25	ID	$261	PA	7.2%	41
AL	26.63%	ID	29.94%	MA	2.24	LA	$260	CT	6.9%	42
ID	26.13%	DE	29.77%	MO	2.24	OK	$259	MA	6.9%	43
NH	25.96%	IN	29.75%	NH	2.24	MT	$251	MD	6.8%	44
MI	25.77%	AL	29.53%	RI	2.23	KY	$250	IA	6.4%	45
MS	25.71%	ME	29.53%	VT	2.22	SD	$242	CA	5.9%	46
DE	25.42%	PA	29.36%	ME	2.20	AR	$230	WA	5.8%	47
MN	25.11%	MI	29.00%	PA	2.19	AL	$229	HI	5.4%	48
VT	24.07%	MS	28.50%	ND	2.18	WV	$221	OR	5.3%	49
ME	23.41%	MN	28.17%	DC	2.12	IA	$216	NY	4.9%	50
WV	22.85%	WV	25.92%	MN	2.08	MS	$215	WI	4.7%	51

Source: Bureau of the Census, U.S. Dept. of Commerce

OWNER-OCCUPIED HOUSING UNITS

As % of Housing Units		As % of Occup. Units		Persons per Unit		Median Value		Desc. Num. Order
WV	65.28%	WV	74.08%	UT	3.38	HI	$245,300	1
IA	65.17%	MN	71.83%	HI	3.19	CA	$195,500	2
IN	64.60%	MS	71.50%	AK	2.97	CT	$177,800	3
MS	64.49%	MI	71.00%	NJ	2.87	MA	$162,800	4
PA	64.32%	PA	70.64%	NY	2.86	NJ	$162,300	5
MN	64.04%	AL	70.47%	NM	2.85	RI	$133,500	6
KY	63.74%	ME	70.47%	TX	2.85	NY	$131,600	7
AL	63.57%	IN	70.25%	CA	2.84	NH	$129,400	8
MI	63.09%	DE	70.23%	LA	2.83	DC	$123,900	9
OH	63.09%	ID	70.06%	ID	2.82	MD	$116,500	10
TN	62.24%	IA	70.03%	MA	2.82	DE	$100,100	11
AR	61.95%	SC	69.85%	IL	2.81	NV	$95,700	12
SC	61.70%	KY	69.61%	MI	2.80	VT	$95,500	13
KS	61.46%	AR	69.56%	NH	2.80	AK	$94,400	14
MO	61.33%	VT	69.01%	MD	2.79	WA	$93,400	15
UT	61.16%	MO	68.77%	WI	2.79	VA	$91,000	16
ID	61.15%	NH	68.19%	MN	2.78	ME	$87,400	17
CT	61.13%	UT	68.12%	MS	2.78	CO	$82,700	18
VA	60.87%	OK	68.08%	RI	2.78	IL	$80,900	19
NC	60.74%	TN	68.03%	GA	2.76	AZ	$80,100	20
NE	60.61%	NC	68.01%	SC	2.75	FL	$77,100	21
MD	60.11%	KS	67.93%	CT	2.74	MN	$74,000	22
DE	59.95%	WY	67.84%	ND	2.74	GA	$71,300	23
IL	59.90%	OH	67.48%	OH	2.74	NM	$70,100	24
WI	59.12%	NM	67.43%	WY	2.74	PA	$69,700	25
NJ	58.97%	MT	67.25%	IN	2.73	UT	$68,900	26
SD	58.53%	FL	67.23%	VT	2.73	OR	$67,100	27
OK	58.39%	WI	66.70%	PA	2.72	NC	$65,800	28
OR	58.31%	RI	66.51%	AZ	2.71	OH	$63,500	29
GA	58.25%	NE	66.47%	DE	2.71	WI	$62,500	30
NM	57.90%	VA	66.30%	ME	2.71	WY	$61,600	31
WA	57.65%	SD	66.08%	SD	2.71	SC	$61,100	32
LA	57.56%	LA	65.89%	AL	2.70	MI	$60,600	33
ND	57.16%	CT	65.62%	VA	2.70	MO	$59,800	34
MT	57.01%	ND	65.57%	KY	2.69	TX	$59,600	35
FL	56.59%	MD	65.03%	NE	2.68	LA	$58,500	36
WY	56.31%	GA	64.93%	WA	2.68	TN	$58,400	37
ME	55.85%	NJ	64.89%	MO	2.67	ID	$58,200	38
NH	55.64%	IL	64.23%	NV	2.67	MT	$56,600	39
RI	54.22%	AZ	64.18%	CO	2.66	IN	$53,900	40
CO	54.03%	OR	63.08%	TN	2.66	AL	$53,700	41
MA	53.85%	WA	62.57%	MT	2.65	KS	$52,200	42
VT	53.59%	CO	62.24%	KS	2.64	ND	$50,800	43
AZ	52.94%	TX	60.87%	IA	2.63	KY	$50,500	44
TX	52.72%	MA	59.25%	WV	2.63	NE	$50,400	45
CA	51.63%	AK	56.10%	NC	2.62	OK	$48,100	46
HI	49.23%	CA	55.62%	OR	2.62	WV	$47,900	47
NV	49.22%	NV	54.77%	AR	2.61	AR	$46,300	48
NY	47.94%	HI	53.87%	OK	2.59	MS	$45,600	49
AK	45.57%	NY	52.18%	DC	2.50	SD	$45,200	50
DC	34.87%	DC	38.90%	FL	2.49	IA	$15,900	51

Source: Bureau of the Census, U.S. Dept. of Commerce

CRIME

CRIME RATE PER 100,000 POPULATION (1993)

Total		Violent Crime		Murder		Aggrav. Assault		Robbery		Rape	
DC	11,761.1	DC	2,921.8	DC	78.5	DC	1,557.6	DC	1,229.6	AK	83.8
FL	8,351.0	FL	1,206.0	LA	20.3	FL	785.7	NY	561.2	DE	77.0
AZ	7,431.7	CA	1,077.8	MS	13.5	SC	773.4	MD	434.7	MI	71.1
LA	6,846.6	NY	1,073.5	NY	13.3	NM	731.1	CA	405.1	WA	64.4
CA	6,456.9	LA	1,061.7	CA	13.1	LA	715.0	IL	381.2	NV	60.9
TX	6,439.1	SC	1,023.4	MD	12.7	CA	621.8	FL	357.6	DC	56.1
HI	6,277.0	MD	997.8	TX	11.9	MA	592.0	NV	340.1	TX	55.0
NM	6,266.1	IL	959.7	AL	11.6	AL	574.3	NJ	296.0	FL	53.8
GA	6,193.0	NM	929.7	GA	11.4	AK	545.6	LA	283.6	SC	52.3
NV	6,180.1	NV	875.2	IL	11.4	IL	532.6	GA	248.0	NM	52.1
MD	6,106.5	MA	804.9	MO	11.3	MD	506.4	MO	241.8	OR	51.3
WA	5,952.3	MI	791.5	NC	11.3	AZ	505.7	MI	238.5	TN	49.9
SC	5,903.4	AL	780.4	NV	10.4	TN	485.5	TX	224.4	OK	49.3
OR	5,765.6	TN	765.8	SC	10.3	MI	472.1	TN	220.1	OH	49.1
NC	5,652.3	TX	762.1	AR	10.2	NY	471.0	CT	196.7	CO	45.8
IL	5,617.9	AK	760.8	TN	10.2	TX	470.0	OH	192.7	UT	44.6
AK	5,567.9	MO	744.4	MI	9.8	NV	463.9	NC	192.4	SD	44.5
NY	5,551.3	GA	723.1	AK	9.0	MO	455.2	SC	187.3	NH	44.4
CO	5,526.8	AZ	715.0	FL	8.9	OK	455.0	DE	186.7	MD	44.0
MI	5,452.5	DE	685.9	AZ	8.6	NC	441.3	PA	179.0	MS	42.6
OK	5,294.3	NC	679.3	OK	8.4	GA	428.3	MA	175.7	AR	42.4
TN	5,239.5	OK	634.8	VA	8.3	DE	417.1	AZ	162.9	LA	42.3
UT	5,237.4	NJ	626.9	NM	8.0	AR	415.0	AL	159.5	VT	39.8
MO	5,095.4	AR	593.3	IN	7.5	CO	399.0	VA	142.0	IN	39.1
KS	4,975.3	CO	567.3	WV	6.9	KY	331.0	MS	139.3	AZ	37.8
MA	4,893.9	WA	514.6	PA	6.8	KS	326.3	NM	138.4	CA	37.7
AL	4,878.8	OH	504.1	KY	6.6	IN	322.6	WA	137.1	MO	36.2
DE	4,872.1	OR	503.1	KS	6.4	OR	317.6	OR	129.6	GA	35.4
AR	4,810.7	KS	496.4	CT	6.3	WA	307.9	AR	124.9	ID	35.3
NJ	4,800.8	IN	489.1	OH	6.0	NJ	297.0	KS	123.6	MN	35.2
MT	4,790.0	KY	462.7	CO	5.8	RI	268.1	AK	122.4	AL	35.1
CT	4,650.4	CT	456.2	NJ	5.3	OH	256.3	OK	121.8	IL	34.6
RI	4,499.0	MS	433.9	WA	5.2	NE	252.0	IN	119.8	KS	34.3
OH	4,485.3	PA	417.5	DE	5.0	IA	244.8	CO	116.7	KY	34.3
IN	4,465.1	RI	401.7	OR	4.6	MS	238.0	WI	113.4	NC	34.3
MS	4,418.3	VA	372.2	WI	4.4	WY	231.3	MN	112.7	WY	34.3
MN	4,386.2	NE	339.1	MA	3.9	CT	228.7	HI	103.6	HI	33.6
WY	4,163.0	MN	327.2	NE	3.9	ID	226.7	RI	101.1	MA	33.4
NE	4,117.1	IA	325.5	RI	3.9	PA	205.0	KY	90.4	VA	32.1
VA	4,115.5	UT	301.0	HI	3.8	UT	194.7	UT	58.6	RI	28.6
WI	4,054.1	WY	286.2	VT	3.6	VA	189.8	NE	55.4	NJ	28.1
VT	3,972.4	ID	281.8	MN	3.4	MN	175.8	IA	53.9	MT	27.9
IA	3,846.4	WI	264.4	SD	3.4	SD	145.0	WV	43.0	NE	27.8
ID	3,845.1	HI	261.2	WY	3.4	WV	138.5	MT	32.4	NY	27.5
PA	3,271.4	SD	208.4	UT	3.1	WI	121.4	NH	27.3	ME	26.6
KY	3,259.7	WV	208.4	MT	3.0	HI	120.1	ME	21.3	PA	26.5
ME	3,153.9	MT	177.5	ID	2.9	MT	114.2	WY	17.2	WI	25.2
SD	2,958.2	NH	137.8	IA	2.3	ME	76.3	ID	16.9	CT	24.4
NH	2,905.0	ME	125.7	NH	2.0	NH	64.1	SD	15.0	IA	24.4
ND	2,820.3	VT	114.2	ND	1.7	VT	61.8	VT	9.0	ND	23.5
WV	2,532.6	ND	82.2	ME	1.6	ND	48.7	ND	8.3	WV	20.1

Source: FBI, *Uniform Crime Reports*

CRIME RATE PER 100,000 POPULATION (1993) (CONTINUED)

Property Crime		Burglary		Larceny-Theft		Motor Vehicle Theft		Desc. Num. Order
DC	8,839.3	DC	1,995.5	DC	5,449.0	DC	1,394.8	1
FL	7,145.0	FL	1,835.4	HI	4,429.4	CA	1,023.0	2
AZ	6,716.7	NC	1,515.8	FL	4,413.9	FL	895.7	3
HI	6,015.8	AZ	1,465.5	AZ	4,387.4	AZ	863.8	4
LA	5,784.9	NM	1,421.2	WA	3,914.4	NY	835.0	5
TX	5,677.0	LA	1,368.3	UT	3,903.4	MA	816.1	6
GA	5,469.8	CA	1,327.0	LA	3,802.9	NV	738.3	7
WA	5,437.7	SC	1,309.2	TX	3,687.3	NJ	714.0	8
CA	5,379.1	GA	1,307.3	OR	3,656.9	TX	692.3	9
NM	5,336.4	TX	1,297.3	MT	3,652.1	MD	683.4	10
NV	5,304.9	MS	1,285.8	GA	3,568.7	RI	646.3	11
OR	5,262.5	NV	1,245.0	AK	3,539.4	MI	615.0	12
MD	5,108.7	OK	1,235.0	NM	3,510.1	LA	613.7	13
NC	4,973.0	TN	1,182.6	CO	3,499.4	CT	595.5	14
CO	4,959.5	HI	1,135.7	NV	3,321.6	GA	593.8	15
UT	4,936.3	MD	1,132.8	MD	3,292.5	TN	591.0	16
SC	4,880.0	KS	1,132.2	SC	3,226.8	OR	580.7	17
AK	4,807.2	AR	1,099.3	NC	3,168.8	IL	558.7	18
MI	4,661.0	AL	1,088.6	IL	3,084.0	MO	547.7	19
OK	4,659.4	WA	1,067.2	WY	3,078.7	OK	480.7	20
IL	4,658.2	RI	1,040.9	MI	3,063.2	WA	456.1	21
MT	4,612.5	MO	1,025.5	CA	3,029.1	AK	450.9	22
KS	4,478.8	OR	1,024.8	KS	3,024.0	HI	450.8	23
NY	4,477.8	IL	1,015.5	DE	2,979.0	CO	450.3	24
TN	4,473.8	CO	1,009.8	OK	2,943.7	PA	440.0	25
MO	4,351.0	MA	1,001.7	NE	2,912.9	OH	435.3	26
AR	4,217.5	NY	998.6	MN	2,872.0	IN	428.1	27
CT	4,194.2	MI	982.7	VT	2,851.2	NM	405.1	28
DE	4,186.3	CT	978.1	AR	2,795.7	WI	364.7	29
NJ	4,174.0	NJ	974.0	VA	2,790.1	SC	344.0	30
AL	4,098.4	DE	892.0	MO	2,777.8	MN	342.6	31
RI	4,097.3	OH	878.1	WI	2,762.0	AL	337.8	32
MA	4,089.0	VT	874.3	ID	2,711.1	MS	335.1	33
MN	4,059.0	IN	852.0	TN	2,700.2	KS	322.7	34
MS	3,984.4	MN	844.5	IN	2,695.9	AR	322.5	35
OH	3,981.2	AK	816.9	AL	2,672.0	DE	315.3	36
IN	3,976.0	UT	790.8	OH	2,667.7	NC	288.5	37
WY	3,876.8	KY	740.1	NY	2,644.2	VA	258.5	38
VT	3,858.2	IA	730.7	CT	2,620.6	MT	246.2	39
WI	3,789.7	ME	719.0	IA	2,599.4	UT	242.2	40
NE	3,778.0	MT	714.2	NJ	2,486.1	KY	216.2	41
VA	3,743.3	ID	668.8	RI	2,410.1	NE	201.6	42
ID	3,563.3	VA	667.7	MS	2,363.5	NH	194.0	43
IA	3,521.0	NE	663.5	MA	2,271.3	IA	190.8	44
ME	3,028.2	WI	663.0	ND	2,216.2	ID	183.4	45
PA	2,853.9	WY	643.2	ME	2,174.7	WV	161.5	46
KY	2,797.0	WV	599.1	SD	2,086.0	WY	154.9	47
NH	2,767.2	PA	582.0	NH	2,058.0	ND	148.7	48
SD	2,749.8	SD	549.2	KY	1,840.7	ME	134.4	49
ND	2,738.1	NH	515.1	PA	1,831.7	VT	132.0	50
WV	2,324.2	ND	373.2	WV	1,563.5	SD	114.5	51

TEACHING AND LEARNING

ENROLLMENTS, PUBLIC SCHOOLS

	Pop. 3 & Over in School		% of Pop. 3+ in School		Public Schools, 1992-93		Public Schools per 100,000 Pop.	Desc. Num. Order
CA	8,300,046	UT	37.7%	CA	7,665	MT	109.20	1
TX	4,805,895	WY	31.1%	TX	6,184	SD	103.30	2
NY	4,656,218	ID	30.8%	IL	4,185	ND	101.10	3
IL	3,031,673	AK	30.2%	NY	4,032	NE	90.65	4
FL	2,926,662	NM	30.2%	OH	3,821	WY	88.36	5
PA	2,829,553	TX	29.7%	MI	3,340	AK	84.16	6
OH	2,798,226	MS	29.6%	PA	3,197	VT	69.88	7
MI	2,581,042	LA	29.5%	FL	2,594	ME	59.98	8
NJ	1,867,402	CA	29.3%	NJ	2,292	KS	58.90	9
GA	1,643,859	MI	29.1%	MO	2,188	OK	57.05	10
NC	1,624,913	ND	29.1%	WI	2,030	ID	56.75	11
VA	1,546,257	NE	28.7%	WA	2,017	IA	55.56	12
MA	1,530,134	CO	28.5%	NC	1,948	WV	52.52	13
IN	1,436,188	AZ	28.4%	IN	1,902	AR	45.51	14
WI	1,302,230	KS	28.2%	OK	1,829	NM	44.28	15
MO	1,292,623	MT	28.2%	VA	1,816	MO	42.13	16
WA	1,252,312	MN	28.1%	MA	1,772	OR	40.91	17
MD	1,212,333	SD	27.9%	GA	1,724	WI	40.62	18
LA	1,185,759	IL	27.8%	MN	1622	CO	40.40	19
MN	1,175,027	OK	27.8%	IA	1,560	NH	40.39	20
TN	1,171,640	WI	27.8%	KS	1,483	UT	39.43	21
AL	1,056,402	IA	27.7%	NE	1,454	WA	39.20	22
AZ	991,122	HI	27.4%	LA	1,453	MS	37.43	23
KY	918,315	SC	27.4%	CO	1,399	KY	37.17	24
SC	913,010	AL	27.3%	KY	1,395	MN	36.25	25
CO	896,144	IN	27.1%	AL	1,294	IL	36.05	26
OK	838,811	VT	27.1%	MD	1,263	MI	35.45	27
CT	805,486	NY	27.0%	OR	1,217	TX	35.00	28
IA	737,729	OH	27.0%	AZ	1,118	OH	34.72	29
MS	727,486	DE	26.9%	SC	1,104	LA	34.00	30
OR	724,233	WA	26.9%	TN	1,094	IN	33.65	31
KS	668,365	GA	26.6%	AR	1,090	AL	31.32	32
UT	610,696	MD	26.6%	CT	993	RI	31.24	33
AR	582,405	OR	26.6%	MS	978	DC	30.89	34
WV	436,513	MA	26.5%	WV	949	SC	30.71	35
NM	435,989	RI	26.5%	MT	899	CT	30.28	36
NE	433,409	MO	26.4%	ME	742	MA	29.54	37
ME	304,868	NH	26.1%	SD	733	NJ	29.34	38
ID	295,638	VA	26.1%	UT	714	AZ	29.15	39
HI	290,578	KY	26.0%	NM	700	NV	28.78	40
NV	280,411	DC	25.9%	ND	642	NC	28.49	41
NH	276,765	ME	25.9%	ID	605	VA	28.42	42
RI	254,635	AR	25.8%	AK	494	PA	26.66	43
MT	215,759	CT	25.6%	NH	450	MD	25.70	44
SD	185,246	NC	25.6%	WY	410	DE	25.51	45
ND	177,543	NJ	25.2%	VT	399	GA	25.48	46
DE	171,219	WV	25.2%	NV	383	CA	24.80	47
AK	156,357	TN	25.0%	RI	313	NY	22.28	48
DC	151,248	PA	24.8%	HI	238	TN	21.79	49
VT	145,988	NV	24.4%	DC	181	HI	20.64	50
WY	134,739	FL	23.5%	DE	176	FL	19.20	51

Source: Bureau of the Census, U.S. Dept of Commerce; National Center for Education Statistics, U.S. Dept. of Education

PUBLIC SCHOOLS: SALARIES AND EXPENDITURES

	Teachers' Avg. Salary, 1992-93		Expend. per Capita, 1990-91		Expend. per Pupil, 1991-92	Desc. Num. Order
CT	$51,233	AK	$9,776.41	DC	$9,549	1
NY	$47,089	DC	$6,935.39	NJ	$9,317	2
AK	$46,984	NY	$5,457.12	NY	$8,527	3
MA	$46,206	WY	$5,063.84	AK	$8,450	4
NJ	$46,024	HI	$4,597.48	CT	$8,017	5
MI	$44,956	CT	$4,443.02	VT	$6,944	6
PA	$43,220	MN	$4,250.02	MD	$6,679	7
CA	$42,975	MA	$4,104.51	PA	$6,613	8
MD	$41,071	NJ	$4,093.46	RI	$6,546	9
DC	$40,967	DE	$4,092.90	MA	$6,408	10
IL	$40,935	CA	$3,978.45	MI	$6,268	11
RI	$39,641	RI	$3,867.15	WI	$6,139	12
AZ	$39,211	VT	$3,864.55	DE	$6,093	13
DE	$38,667	WA	$3,810.26	OR	$5,913	14
HI	$38,560	NV	$3,740.07	WY	$5,812	15
WA	$38,371	MD	$3,716.45	NH	$5,790	16
OR	$38,164	WI	$3,672.24	OH	$5,694	17
WI	$37,618	OR	$3,631.26	IL	$5,670	18
NH	$37,400	ME	$3,628.44	ME	$5,652	19
MN	$37,160	MI	$3,603.62	MT	$5,423	20
IN	$37,042	ND	$3,541.28	HI	$5,420	21
NV	$36,690	MT	$3,503.02	MN	$5,409	22
OH	$36,563	AZ	$3,421.61	WA	$5,271	23
CO	$35,514	CO	$3,418.99	NE	$5,263	24
KS	$35,157	IA	$3,416.89	FL	$5,243	25
VT	$34,076	FL	$3,412.17	CO	$5,172	26
VA	$33,945	NM	$3,358.76	WV	$5,109	27
FL	$33,315	LA	$3,350.68	IA	$5,096	28
KY	$33,187	VA	$3,318.70	IN	$5,074	29
ME	$32,650	IL	$3,293.58	KS	$5,007	30
GA	$32,535	NE	$3,266.98	NV	$4,926	31
WV	$32,242	GA	$3,213.36	VA	$4,880	32
IA	$31,991	KS	$3,199.99	MO	$4,830	33
WY	$31,820	OH	$3,194.63	CA	$4,746	34
SC	$31,392	PA	$3,192.89	KY	$4,719	35
MO	$31,391	SC	$3,138.01	TX	$4,632	36
NC	$31,305	NH	$3,057.74	NC	$4,555	37
NE	$31,298	NC	$3,035.26	ND	$4,441	38
TX	$31,241	UT	$3,015.33	SC	$4,436	39
TN	$30,842	IN	$2,993.85	AZ	$4,381	40
LA	$29,914	SD	$2,949.43	GA	$4,375	41
MT	$29,590	KY	$2,946.69	LA	$4,354	42
AR	$29,232	AL	$2,942.29	SD	$4,173	43
UT	$28,953	OK	$2,908.26	OK	$4,078	44
AL	$28,913	TX	$2,895.44	AR	$4,031	45
ID	$28,898	WV	$2,865.60	NM	$3,765	46
NM	$28,090	ID	$2,852.09	TN	$3,692	47
OK	$27,568	TN	$2,757.08	AL	$3,616	48
ND	$26,733	MS	$2,695.57	ID	$3,556	49
MS	$25,876	MO	$2,663.88	MS	$3,245	50
SD	$24,918	AR	$2,439.92	UT	$3,040	51

Source: National Education Association, (copyright); National Center for Education Statistics, U.S. Dept. of Education

SAT AND ACT TESTS

% of Grads. Taking SAT, 1993		Mean Verbal Scores		Mean Math Scores		% of Grads. Taking ACT, 1995		Mean ACT Scores		Desc. Num. Order
CT	88%	IA	520	IA	583	LA	75%	OR	22.6	1
MA	81%	ND	518	ND	583	NE	75%	NH	22.3	2
NH	78%	SD	502	SD	558	ND	75%	WA	22.2	3
DC	76%	UT	500	MN	556	MS	73%	WI	22.0	4
NJ	76%	KS	494	WI	551	KS	72%	MN	21.9	5
NY	74%	MN	489	UT	549	SD	68%	HI	21.8	6
RI	71%	TN	486	KS	548	TN	68%	IA	21.8	7
PA	70%	WI	485	NE	544	IL	67%	MT	21.8	8
ME	69%	OK	482	IL	541	UT	67%	NY	21.7	9
DE	68%	LA	481	MO	532	WY	66%	VT	21.7	10
VT	68%	MS	481	TN	531	OK	65%	DE	21.6	11
MD	66%	MO	481	OK	530	IA	64%	ME	21.5	12
GA	65%	AL	480	MI	528	MI	64%	CO	21.4	13
VA	63%	NE	479	LA	527	MO	64%	CT	21.4	14
IN	61%	AR	478	AL	526	WI	64%	NE	21.4	15
SC	61%	NM	478	NM	525	AR	63%	UT	21.4	16
NC	60%	KY	476	KY	522	CO	63%	MO	21.3	17
HI	56%	IL	475	MS	521	KY	63%	NV	21.3	18
OR	56%	MI	469	AR	519	ID	61%	WY	21.3	19
FL	52%	ID	465	MT	516	AL	60%	ID	21.2	20
WA	52%	WY	463	CO	509	MN	59%	IN	21.2	21
CA	47%	MT	459	ID	507	NM	59%	KS	21.2	22
TX	45%	CO	454	WY	507	OH	59%	ND	21.2	23
AK	42%	OH	454	OH	505	MT	56%	OH	21.2	24
AZ	28%	AZ	444	AZ	497	WV	56%	SD	21.2	25
CO	28%	NH	442	OR	492	NV	42%	IL	21.1	26
NV	28%	OR	441	NV	488	AK	40%	MI	21.1	27
MT	24%	WV	439	NH	487	FL	34%	AK	21.0	28
OH	22%	AK	438	WA	486	TX	33%	AZ	21.0	29
ID	18%	WA	435	WV	485	AZ	29%	CA	20.9	30
WV	17%	NV	432	CA	484	IN	22%	MA	20.9	31
IL	15%	MD	431	HI	478	GA	18%	FL	20.7	32
TN	13%	CT	430	MD	478	NY	18%	MD	20.6	33
WY	13%	DE	429	AK	477	WA	17%	PA	20.6	34
KY	11%	MA	427	MA	476	HI	14%	RI	20.6	35
MI	11%	VT	426	CT	474	OR	14%	VA	20.6	36
MO	11%	VA	425	NJ	473	SC	14%	NJ	20.4	37
NM	11%	ME	422	TX	472	CA	12%	OK	20.3	38
MN	10%	NJ	419	NY	471	MD	12%	TN	20.3	39
NE	10%	RI	419	VA	469	NC	12%	AR	20.2	40
WI	10%	PA	418	VT	467	PA	7%	GA	20.2	41
AL	9%	FL	416	FL	466	VA	6%	KY	20.1	42
KS	9%	NY	416	DE	465	DC	5%	NM	20.1	43
LA	9%	CA	415	RI	464	DE	4%	TX	20.1	44
OK	9%	TX	413	ME	463	MA	4%	AL	20.0	45
AR	6%	IN	409	IN	460	VT	4%	WV	20.0	46
ND	6%	NC	406	PA	460	CT	3%	NC	19.6	47
SD	6%	DC	405	NC	453	NJ	3%	LA	19.4	48
IA	5%	HI	401	GA	445	ME	2%	SC	19.1	49
MS	4%	GA	399	SC	442	NH	2%	DC	18.9	50
UT	4%	SC	396	DC	441	RI	2%	MS	18.8	51

Source: SAT: National Center for Education Statistics, U.S. Dept. of Education; ACT: American College Testing Program

PERCENT OF POPULATION OVER 25 COMPLETING CERTAIN LEVELS

Less Than 9th Grade		High School		College Degree		Desc. Num. Order
KY	19.0%	AK	86.6%	DC	33.3%	1
WV	16.8%	UT	85.1%	CT	27.2%	2
TN	16.0%	CO	84.4%	MA	27.2%	3
MS	15.6%	WA	83.8%	CO	27.0%	4
AR	15.2%	WY	83.0%	MD	26.5%	5
ND	15.0%	MN	82.4%	NJ	24.9%	6
LA	14.7%	NH	82.2%	VA	24.5%	7
AL	13.7%	NE	81.8%	NH	24.4%	8
SC	13.6%	OR	81.5%	VT	24.3%	9
TX	13.5%	KS	81.3%	CA	23.4%	10
SD	13.4%	MT	81.0%	NY	23.1%	11
NC	12.7%	VT	80.8%	AK	23.0%	12
GA	12.0%	HI	80.1%	HI	22.9%	13
MO	11.6%	IA	80.1%	WA	22.9%	14
NM	11.4%	MA	80.0%	UT	22.3%	15
CA	11.2%	ID	79.7%	MN	21.8%	16
VA	11.2%	CT	79.2%	DE	21.4%	17
RI	11.1%	ME	78.8%	RI	21.3%	18
IL	10.3%	NV	78.8%	KS	21.1%	19
NY	10.2%	AZ	78.7%	IL	21.0%	20
HI	10.1%	WI	78.6%	OR	20.6%	21
OK	9.8%	MD	78.4%	NM	20.4%	22
DC	9.6%	DE	77.5%	AZ	20.3%	23
FL	9.5%	SD	77.1%	TX	20.3%	24
WI	9.5%	MI	76.8%	MT	19.8%	25
NJ	9.4%	NJ	76.7%	GA	19.3%	26
PA	9.4%	ND	76.7%	NE	18.9%	27
IA	9.2%	CA	76.2%	ME	18.8%	28
AZ	9.0%	IL	76.2%	WY	18.8%	29
ME	8.8%	OH	75.7%	FL	18.3%	30
VT	8.7%	IN	75.6%	ND	18.1%	31
MN	8.6%	VA	75.2%	PA	17.9%	32
IN	8.5%	NM	75.1%	MO	17.8%	33
CT	8.4%	NY	74.8%	OK	17.8%	34
MT	8.1%	PA	74.7%	ID	17.7%	35
MA	8.0%	OK	74.6%	WI	17.7%	36
NE	8.0%	FL	74.4%	MI	17.4%	37
MD	7.9%	MO	73.9%	NC	17.4%	38
OH	7.9%	DC	73.1%	SD	17.2%	39
MI	7.8%	TX	72.1%	OH	17.0%	40
KS	7.7%	RI	72.0%	IA	16.9%	41
ID	7.4%	GA	70.9%	SC	16.6%	42
DE	7.2%	NC	70.0%	LA	16.1%	43
NH	6.7%	LA	68.3%	TN	16.0%	44
OR	6.2%	SC	68.3%	AL	15.7%	45
NV	6.0%	TN	67.1%	IN	15.6%	46
WY	5.7%	AL	66.9%	NV	15.3%	47
CO	5.6%	AR	66.3%	MS	14.7%	48
WA	5.5%	WV	66.0%	KY	13.6%	49
AK	5.1%	KY	64.6%	AR	13.3%	50
UT	3.4%	MS	64.3%	WV	12.3%	51

Source: Bureau of the Census, U.S. Dept. of Commerce

HIGHER EDUCATION INSTITUTIONS (1993-94)

	Higher Education Instit.			Per 100,000 Pop.	Desc. Num. Order
CA	328		VT	3.84	1
NY	314		ND	3.14	2
PA	219		DC	3.12	3
TX	178		SD	2.78	4
IL	169		NH	2.68	5
OH	156		ME	2.51	6
NC	122		MT	2.39	7
MA	117		IA	2.16	8
GA	116		MN	2.16	9
FL	108		NE	2.04	10
MI	106		KS	2.00	11
MN	98		NM	1.98	12
MO	98		MA	1.95	13
VA	87		AL	1.91	14
AL	80		WY	1.90	15
TN	78		MO	1.88	16
IN	77		PA	1.82	17
WI	64		MS	1.79	18
KY	62		NC	1.76	19
WA	62		NY	1.73	20
IA	61		GA	1.69	21
NJ	61		CO	1.66	22
CO	59		KY	1.64	23
SC	59		SC	1.62	24
MD	57		WV	1.54	25
KS	51		TN	1.53	26
MS	47		AR	1.45	27
OK	46		OR	1.45	28
OR	44		IL	1.44	29
AZ	42		OK	1.42	30
CT	42		OH	1.41	31
AR	35		RI	1.39	32
LA	33		HI	1.36	33
NE	33		IN	1.35	34
NM	32		VA	1.35	35
ME	31		AK	1.33	36
NH	30		DE	1.29	37
WV	28		CT	1.28	38
VT	22		WI	1.27	39
MT	20		WA	1.18	40
ND	20		MD	1.15	41
SD	20		MI	1.12	42
DC	18		AZ	1.07	43
HI	16		CA	1.04	44
UT	16		ID	1.00	45
RI	14		TX	0.99	46
ID	11		UT	0.86	47
DE	9		FL	0.79	48
NV	9		NJ	0.78	49
WY	9		LA	0.77	50
AK	8		NV	0.65	51

Source: National Center for Education Statistics, U.S. Dept. of Education

ENROLLMENT IN INSTITUTIONS OF HIGHER EDUCATION

	Total Enroll., 1992		% of Total Pop.	Desc. Num. Order
CA	1,977,249	DC	13.98%	1
NY	1,069,772	RI	7.90%	2
TX	938,526	NE	7.64%	3
IL	748,033	UT	7.35%	4
PA	629,832	AZ	7.19%	5
FL	618,285	MA	7.05%	6
OH	573,183	CO	6.94%	7
MI	559,729	WY	6.80%	8
MA	422,976	KS	6.73%	9
NC	383,453	VT	6.55%	10
VA	354,172	IL	6.44%	11
NJ	342,446	CA	6.40%	12
WI	307,902	ND	6.37%	13
IN	296,912	IA	6.33%	14
MO	296,617	NM	6.28%	15
GA	293,162	DE	6.20%	16
WA	276,484	WI	6.16%	17
AZ	275,599	MN	6.10%	18
MN	272,920	MI	5.94%	19
MD	268,399	NY	5.91%	20
TN	242,970	NH	5.74%	21
CO	240,163	MO	5.71%	22
AL	230,537	OK	5.68%	23
LA	204,379	OR	5.63%	24
KY	188,320	NC	5.61%	25
OK	182,105	AL	5.58%	26
IA	177,813	VA	5.54%	27
SC	171,443	MD	5.46%	28
KS	169,419	ID	5.42%	29
OR	167,415	WA	5.37%	30
CT	165,874	TX	5.31%	31
UT	133,083	HI	5.30%	32
MS	123,754	SD	5.30%	33
NE	122,603	AK	5.26%	34
NM	99,276	IN	5.25%	35
AR	97,435	PA	5.25%	36
WV	90,252	OH	5.21%	37
DC	81,909	CT	5.06%	38
RI	79,165	KY	5.02%	39
NH	63,924	WV	4.99%	40
NV	63,877	TN	4.84%	41
HI	61,162	MT	4.82%	42
ME	57,977	NV	4.80%	43
ID	57,798	LA	4.78%	44
DE	42,763	SC	4.77%	45
ND	40,470	MS	4.74%	46
MT	39,644	ME	4.69%	47
SD	37,596	FL	4.58%	48
VT	37,377	NJ	4.38%	49
WY	31,548	GA	4.33%	50
AK	30,902	AR	4.07%	51

Source: National Center for Education Statistics, U.S. Dept. of Education

PUBLIC LIBRARIES

Volumes Per Capita		State & Local Govt. Expend. Per Capita		State Govt. Expend. Per Capita		Local Govt. Expend. Per Capita		Desc. Num. Order
ME	4.88	AK	$36.18	HI	$19.44	DC	$32.16	1
MA	4.32	DC	$32.16	AK	$10.10	AK	$26.07	2
WY	4.28	CT	$28.10	GA	$6.68	CT	$23.38	3
VT	4.14	WA	$25.46	RI	$5.72	WA	$22.91	4
SD	4.13	NV	$23.99	MD	$5.60	NV	$21.41	5
KS	4.04	MD	$23.84	IL	$5.48	IN	$21.28	6
NH	3.98	MA	$23.71	NY	$5.01	MA	$20.16	7
IA	3.82	NY	$23.53	WV	$5.01	WI	$19.56	8
NE	3.75	WY	$23.32	CT	$4.72	WY	$19.55	9
NY	3.70	IN	$22.43	VT	$4.69	AZ	$19.47	10
NJ	3.56	IL	$22.15	SD	$4.26	NY	$18.52	11
CT	3.42	WI	$21.53	WY	$3.76	MD	$18.24	12
IN	3.39	AZ	$21.20	MA	$3.55	NJ	$17.76	13
MO	3.38	VA	$21.06	VA	$3.41	VA	$17.65	14
ID	3.37	NJ	$21.01	NJ	$3.25	CO	$17.54	15
OH	3.37	HI	$19.81	KY	$3.12	CA	$17.07	16
AK	3.13	CO	$18.87	MI	$2.99	MN	$17.04	17
IL	3.13	CA	$18.75	MT	$2.97	IL	$16.66	18
WI	3.11	IA	$18.55	DE	$2.93	IA	$16.30	19
MT	3.01	MN	$18.42	ME	$2.92	OR	$15.47	20
DC	2.77	OR	$17.01	ND	$2.80	OH	$15.32	21
ND	2.76	NH	$16.47	NC	$2.71	NH	$14.22	22
RI	2.74	OH	$16.01	PA	$2.67	UT	$13.64	23
CO	2.62	UT	$15.86	NV	$2.58	LA	$12.03	24
MN	2.58	RI	$15.64	WA	$2.55	FL	$11.82	25
WA	2.56	SD	$14.81	TN	$2.53	MO	$11.50	26
UT	2.47	NC	$14.11	AR	$2.51	NC	$11.40	27
MI	2.43	MI	$14.03	ID	$2.45	MI	$11.05	28
NM	2.41	FL	$13.88	SC	$2.30	NM	$10.73	29
MD	2.34	NM	$12.89	IA	$2.25	KS	$10.70	30
VA	2.33	NE	$12.59	MS	$2.25	SD	$10.56	31
OR	2.32	MO	$12.58	NH	$2.24	NE	$10.40	32
TX	2.22	LA	$12.56	UT	$2.22	RI	$9.93	33
HI	2.15	KS	$12.42	NE	$2.19	ID	$9.89	34
WV	2.15	ID	$12.33	NM	$2.16	ME	$9.28	35
PA	2.08	ME	$12.20	AL	$2.11	MT	$8.74	36
LA	2.03	VT	$12.06	FL	$2.06	TX	$7.94	37
OK	2.01	MT	$11.71	WI	$1.97	SC	$7.83	38
AR	1.97	SC	$10.14	OK	$1.87	OK	$7.68	39
CA	1.95	DE	$10.02	AZ	$1.73	VT	$7.37	40
MS	1.88	ND	$9.98	KS	$1.71	ND	$7.18	41
KY	1.87	KY	$9.69	CA	$1.69	DE	$7.09	42
AZ	1.86	OK	$9.56	OR	$1.54	KY	$6.57	43
AL	1.81	TX	$9.11	MN	$1.39	AL	$6.12	44
NC	1.74	PA	$8.39	CO	$1.33	PA	$5.72	45
GA	1.70	AL	$8.24	TX	$1.17	TN	$5.47	46
DE	1.68	GA	$8.13	IN	$1.15	AR	$4.74	47
TN	1.56	TN	$8.01	MO	$1.09	MS	$3.48	48
FL	1.54	WV	$7.26	OH	$0.68	WV	$2.25	49
NV	1.51	AR	$7.25	LA	$0.53	GA	$1.45	50
SC	1.49	MS	$5.73	DC	$0.00	HI	$0.38	51

Sources: U.S. Dept. of Education; Bureau of the Census, U.S. Dept. of Commerce

LAW ENFORCEMENT, COURTS, AND PRISONS

EXPENDITURES, POLICE, PRISONERS

	Total Expend., 1992		Expend. Per Capita, 1992		Police per 10,000 Pop., 1993		Prisoners per 100,000 Pop., 1993		Under Sentence of Death, 1993	Desc. Num. Order
CA	$14,032,000,000	DC	$1,229	DC	75.95	DC	18,730.57	CA	363	1
NY	$9,000,000,000	AK	$623	NJ	35.74	DE	6,031.52	TX	357	2
FL	$5,153,000,000	NY	$497	NY	31.66	LA	5,237.30	FL	324	3
TX	$4,596,000,000	CA	$454	LA	31.47	SC	5,152.62	PA	169	4
IL	$3,255,000,000	NV	$454	DE	29.65	OK	5,075.47	IL	152	5
MI	$2,985,000,000	FL	$382	GA	28.12	AK	4,520.07	OH	129	6
PA	$2,944,000,000	DE	$375	MD	26.27	AZ	4,514.83	OK	122	7
NJ	$2,887,000,000	NJ	$369	CT	25.72	AL	4,454.44	AL	120	8
OH	$2,883,000,000	AZ	$366	IL	25.70	NV	4,441.39	AZ	112	9
GA	$1,806,000,000	HI	$352	MA	24.60	CT	4,176.63	NC	99	10
MA	$1,781,000,000	MD	$348	FL	24.32	MI	4,156.24	TN	98	11
MD	$1,709,000,000	CT	$333	NV	24.04	MD	4,087.13	GA	96	12
VA	$1,698,000,000	WA	$327	KS	23.86	GA	4,025.35	MO	80	13
WA	$1,679,000,000	WY	$319	PA	23.80	TX	3,891.19	MS	50	14
NC	$1,609,000,000	MI	$316	WY	23.65	FL	3,864.78	VA	48	15
WI	$1,467,000,000	CO	$303	CO	23.29	CA	3,842.49	IN	47	16
AZ	$1,404,000,000	RI	$302	HI	23.06	MS	3,752.65	SC	47	17
TN	$1,135,000,000	MA	$297	NC	22.74	OH	3,674.26	LA	45	18
LA	$1,096,000,000	WI	$294	WI	22.57	NY	3,556.93	NV	42	19
CT	$1,091,000,000	NM	$293	RI	22.43	AR	3,555.23	AR	33	20
MN	$1,078,000,000	OR	$286	TX	21.59	VA	3,530.05	KY	30	21
CO	$1,051,000,000	IL	$280	NM	21.28	NC	3,149.02	ID	22	22
IN	$1,026,000,000	GA	$267	CA	21.02	MO	3,090.35	DE	15	23
MO	$1,020,000,000	VA	$266	VA	20.89	NJ	3,032.32	MD	15	24
SC	$869,000,000	OH	$262	SC	20.55	IL	2,951.82	OR	12	25
OR	$851,000,000	TX	$260	AL	20.53	RI	2,783.00	NE	11	26
AL	$825,000,000	LA	$256	TN	20.50	KY	2,751.71	UT	9	27
KY	$722,000,000	PA	$245	NH	20.46	HI	2,683.53	NJ	7	28
DC	$719,000,000	MN	$241	AZ	20.06	CO	2,654.88	MT	6	29
OK	$623,000,000	NH	$241	MI	19.79	IN	2,535.93	CT	5	30
NV	$607,000,000	SC	$241	MO	19.65	TN	2,517.47	CO	3	31
KS	$604,000,000	KS	$240	OK	19.09	WY	2,402.13	SD	2	32
NM	$463,000,000	NC	$235	UT	18.58	ID	2,369.09	NM	1	33
IA	$452,000,000	TN	$226	ID	18.36	KS	2,259.17			34
HI	$407,000,000	ID	$220	KY	18.31	PA	2,165.42			35
UT	$396,000,000	UT	$219	NE	18.07	NM	2,163.37			36
AK	$366,000,000	MT	$210	OH	17.92	OR	2,160.46			37
AR	$366,000,000	VT	$207	MS	17.68	SD	2,153.95			38
MS	$356,000,000	ME	$201	AK	17.41	VT	2,123.26			39
NE	$310,000,000	AL	$199	WV	17.07	WA	1,981.18			40
RI	$303,000,000	MO	$197	ME	16.15	MT	1,832.34			41
NH	$269,000,000	NE	$194	MN	15.94	WI	1,740.88			42
DE	$259,000,000	OK	$194	MT	15.94	IA	1,736.26			43
ME	$248,000,000	KY	$192	IA	15.92	MA	1,667.33			44
ID	$234,000,000	IN	$181	WA	15.92	NH	1,579.18			45
WV	$212,000,000	SD	$170	IN	15.90	NE	1,561.07			46
MT	$173,000,000	IA	$161	OR	15.73	UT	1,552.69			47
WY	$148,000,000	ND	$155	ND	15.69	ME	1,184.68			48
SD	$121,000,000	AR	$153	VT	14.50	WV	992.85			49
VT	$118,000,000	MS	$136	AR	13.94	MN	928.38			50
ND	$98,000,000	WV	$117	SD	13.23	ND	781.79			51

Sources: FBI, *Uniform Crime Reports*; Bureau of Justice Statistics, U.S. Dept. of Justice

RELIGION

Population 18 and over, By Religious Preferences

Christian		Jewish		Muslim		Hindu		Buddhist	
LA	94.70%	NY	6.90%	NY	0.80%	NY	0.60%	CA	0.70%
ND	94.50%	NJ	4.30%	CA	0.60%	NJ	0.30%	NH	0.50%
MS	94.20%	FL	3.60%	DC	0.60%	CO	0.20%	OR	0.50%
SD	94.00%	MA	3.50%	NJ	0.60%	GA	0.20%	WA	0.50%
AL	93.30%	MD	2.80%	IL	0.40%	IL	0.20%	MA	0.40%
SC	93.00%	CT	2.40%	MA	0.40%	MD	0.20%	NV	0.40%
GA	91.10%	CA	2.30%	OH	0.40%	MI	0.20%	VA	0.40%
NC	90.60%	DC	2.30%	RI	0.40%	NE	0.20%	DC	0.30%
TN	90.60%	CO	1.80%	GA	0.30%	WY	0.20%	KS	0.30%
WI	90.20%	PA	1.70%	MI	0.30%	AL	0.10%	WI	0.30%
TX	90.00%	AZ	1.60%	PA	0.30%	CA	0.10%	AR	0.20%
KS	89.90%	RI	1.60%	SD	0.30%	CT	0.10%	CT	0.20%
KY	89.80%	IL	1.50%	AL	0.20%	FL	0.10%	ID	0.20%
AR	89.60%	DE	1.40%	AZ	0.20%	IA	0.10%	NY	0.20%
IA	89.30%	VT	1.10%	MD	0.20%	KS	0.10%	OK	0.20%
MN	89.30%	VA	1.10%	NH	0.20%	ME	0.10%	TX	0.20%
MO	88.70%	NH	1.00%	NC	0.20%	MA	0.10%	AZ	0.10%
NE	88.40%	NV	0.90%	SC	0.20%	MN	0.10%	CO	0.10%
PA	87.90%	MI	0.80%	TX	0.20%	OH	0.10%	FL	0.10%
UT	87.60%	MN	0.80%	VA	0.20%	OK	0.10%	GA	0.10%
IN	87.50%	NM	0.70%	WI	0.20%	PA	0.10%	IL	0.10%
RI	87.50%	OH	0.70%	CT	0.10%	VA	0.10%	IN	0.10%
VA	87.40%	TX	0.70%	FL	0.10%	WA	0.10%	KY	0.10%
WV	86.50%	UT	0.70%	IN	0.10%	WV	0.10%	LA	0.10%
OK	86.20%	MS	0.60%	KS	0.10%	AK	NA	ME	0.10%
OH	86.10%	MO	0.60%	LA	0.10%	AZ	NA	MD	0.10%
IL	85.60%	GA	0.50%	MN	0.10%	AR	NA	MI	0.10%
NV	85.50%	NE	0.50%	OR	0.10%	DE	NA	MN	0.10%
CT	85.40%	NC	0.50%	TN	0.10%	DC	NA	MO	0.10%
DE	85.40%	ME	0.40%	WV	0.10%	HI	NA	NE	0.10%
DC	85.30%	ND	0.40%	AK	NA	ID	NA	NJ	0.10%
NM	85.20%	OR	0.40%	AR	NA	IN	NA	NM	0.10%
MT	85.00%	WA	0.40%	CO	NA	KY	NA	NC	0.10%
NJ	85.00%	WI	0.40%	DE	NA	LA	NA	OH	0.10%
ME	84.90%	IN	0.30%	HI	NA	MS	NA	PA	0.10%
MD	84.80%	KS	0.30%	ID	NA	MO	NA	SC	0.10%
MI	84.70%	SC	0.30%	IA	NA	MT	NA	TN	0.10%
FL	84.20%	TN	0.30%	KY	NA	NV	NA	UT	0.10%
VT	83.60%	KY	0.20%	ME	NA	NH	NA	WV	0.10%
MA	82.30%	LA	0.20%	MS	NA	NM	NA	AL	NA
ID	81.90%	OK	0.20%	MO	NA	NC	NA	AK	NA
WY	81.90%	SD	0.20%	MT	NA	ND	NA	DE	NA
CO	79.90%	AL	0.10%	NE	NA	OR	NA	HI	NA
NY	79.80%	AR	0.10%	NV	NA	RI	NA	IA	NA
AZ	79.50%	WV	0.10%	NM	NA	SC	NA	MS	NA
NH	78.30%	AK	NA	ND	NA	SD	NA	MT	NA
WA	77.10%	HI	NA	OK	NA	TN	NA	ND	NA
CA	77.00%	ID	NA	UT	NA	TX	NA	RI	NA
OR	76.10%	IA	NA	VT	NA	UT	NA	SD	NA
AK	NA	MT	NA	WA	NA	VT	NA	VT	NA
HI	NA	WY	NA	WY	NA	WI	NA	WY	NA

Source: *Religious Composition of State Population, 1990*, a report by The National Survey of Religious Identification

POPULATION 18 AND OVER, BY RELIGIOUS PREFERENCES (CONTINUED)

	Unitarian		Agnostic		Other		None		Refused to Respond	Desc. Num. Order
VT	1.10%	WA	1.40%	WV	2.90%	OR	17.20%	DE	5.70%	1
NV	0.90%	CA	1.20%	NH	2.70%	WA	14.00%	OK	4.20%	2
MA	0.80%	NH	1.20%	WA	2.70%	WY	13.50%	CT	3.90%	3
CO	0.70%	OR	1.20%	DC	2.50%	NH	13.40%	WA	3.30%	4
ME	0.60%	VT	1.20%	OH	2.40%	CA	13.00%	WY	3.30%	5
NE	0.50%	AZ	1.10%	AZ	2.30%	AZ	12.20%	AR	3.20%	6
WA	0.50%	CO	1.10%	MI	2.30%	ID	11.90%	ID	3.10%	7
CA	0.40%	ID	1.10%	PA	2.30%	CO	11.40%	MA	3.10%	8
ID	0.40%	IA	1.10%	OK	2.10%	VT	11.40%	NY	2.90%	9
IL	0.40%	FL	1.00%	CO	2.00%	MT	10.20%	RI	2.90%	10
KS	0.40%	MA	1.00%	IA	2.00%	ME	10.00%	UT	2.90%	11
MN	0.40%	NM	1.00%	CA	1.90%	NM	10.00%	AZ	2.80%	12
OR	0.40%	SD	1.00%	IN	1.90%	MI	8.70%	CA	2.80%	13
RI	0.40%	ME	0.90%	NC	1.70%	NV	8.10%	CO	2.80%	14
CT	0.30%	NV	0.90%	OR	1.70%	WV	8.00%	IL	2.80%	15
FL	0.30%	UT	0.90%	VA	1.70%	UT	7.80%	MT	2.70%	16
MD	0.30%	MD	0.70%	TX	1.60%	IN	7.40%	NJ	2.70%	17
MI	0.30%	PA	0.70%	NE	1.50%	OH	7.40%	NH	2.50%	18
MT	0.30%	IL	0.60%	NY	1.50%	MA	7.30%	ND	2.50%	19
NM	0.30%	KS	0.60%	GA	1.40%	DE	7.20%	OR	2.40%	20
NY	0.30%	MN	0.60%	ID	1.40%	FL	7.20%	IN	2.30%	21
SD	0.30%	MT	0.60%	IL	1.40%	MD	7.20%	MD	2.30%	22
AZ	0.20%	NJ	0.60%	MD	1.40%	IL	7.00%	DC	2.20%	23
AR	0.20%	NY	0.60%	CT	1.30%	NE	7.00%	ME	2.20%	24
KY	0.20%	TX	0.60%	FL	1.30%	KY	6.50%	MN	2.20%	25
MO	0.20%	VA	0.60%	MS	1.30%	MO	6.50%	MO	2.20%	26
NH	0.20%	CT	0.50%	MO	1.30%	OK	6.50%	OH	2.20%	27
TX	0.20%	DC	0.50%	NV	1.30%	NY	6.40%	FL	2.10%	28
VA	0.20%	MI	0.50%	KY	1.20%	VA	6.40%	MI	2.10%	29
WI	0.20%	MS	0.50%	MT	1.20%	DC	6.30%	NV	2.00%	30
AL	0.10%	OH	0.50%	SC	1.20%	WI	6.10%	PA	1.90%	31
GA	0.10%	RI	0.50%	MA	1.10%	RI	6.00%	VA	1.90%	32
IN	0.10%	WY	0.50%	NM	1.10%	TN	6.00%	WV	1.90%	33
IA	0.10%	MO	0.40%	TN	1.00%	IA	5.90%	SC	1.80%	34
NJ	0.10%	ND	0.40%	KS	0.90%	AR	5.80%	KS	1.70%	35
NC	0.10%	OK	0.40%	VT	0.90%	CT	5.80%	KY	1.70%	36
OH	0.10%	GA	0.30%	AL	0.80%	KS	5.70%	NE	1.70%	37
OK	0.10%	IN	0.30%	LA	0.80%	MN	5.60%	NC	1.70%	38
PA	0.10%	KY	0.30%	ME	0.80%	NJ	5.50%	NM	1.60%	39
TN	0.10%	NC	0.30%	MN	0.80%	PA	4.90%	TN	1.60%	40
UT	0.10%	WI	0.30%	NJ	0.80%	TX	4.90%	TX	1.60%	41
WV	0.10%	AL	0.20%	WI	0.80%	NC	4.80%	IA	1.50%	42
AK	NA	AR	0.20%	AR	0.70%	GA	4.60%	WI	1.50%	43
DE	NA	SC	0.20%	RI	0.70%	AL	3.90%	GA	1.40%	44
DC	NA	TN	0.20%	SD	0.70%	SC	3.20%	AL	1.30%	45
HI	NA	WV	0.20%	ND	0.60%	LA	2.90%	LA	1.20%	46
LA	NA	NE	0.10%	WY	0.60%	MS	2.80%	SD	1.00%	47
MS	NA	AK	NA	DE	0.30%	SD	2.50%	VT	0.70%	48
ND	NA	DE	NA	AK	NA	ND	1.60%	MS	0.60%	49
SC	NA	HI	NA	HI	NA	AK	NA	AK	NA	50
WY	NA	LA	NA	UT	NA	HI	NA	HI	NA	51

MAKING A LIVING

INCOME, POVERTY STATUS, EXPENDITURE FOR ENERGY

Personal Income Per Capita, 1994		Disposable Income Per Capita, 1994		Median Income, Hshlds., 1993		Pop. Below Poverty Level, 1993		Pop. 65+ Below Poverty Level		Energy Expend., 1992	Desc. Num. Order
DC	$31,136	DC	$25,832	AK	$42,931	DC	26.4%	MS	29.4%	WY	$3,334	1
CT	$29,402	CT	$24,732	HI	$42,662	LA	26.4%	LA	24.1%	AK	$3,175	2
NJ	$28,038	NJ	$23,929	NJ	$40,500	MS	24.7%	AL	24.0%	LA	$2,893	3
NY	$25,999	NY	$22,047	MD	$39,939	WV	22.2%	AR	22.9%	ND	$2,471	4
MA	$25,616	MA	$21,649	CT	$39,516	KY	20.4%	TN	20.9%	TX	$2,454	5
MD	$24,933	MD	$21,293	NH	$37,964	AR	20.0%	KY	20.6%	KS	$2,103	6
HI	$24,057	AK	$21,175	MA	$37,064	OK	19.9%	SC	20.5%	MT	$2,091	7
NV	$24,023	NV	$20,815	VA	$36,433	TN	19.6%	GA	20.4%	WV	$2,079	8
AK	$23,788	NH	$20,780	DE	$36,064	SC	18.7%	NC	19.5%	ME	$2,077	9
IL	$23,784	HI	$20,587	NV	$35,814	CA	18.2%	TX	18.4%	NJ	$2,066	10
NH	$23,434	IL	$20,587	UT	$35,786	FL	17.8%	OK	17.9%	IN	$2,051	11
DE	$22,828	WA	$19,886	WA	$35,655	AL	17.4%	DC	17.2%	AL	$2,019	12
WA	$22,610	CA	$19,593	CO	$34,488	NM	17.4%	WV	16.7%	VT	$2,005	13
VA	$22,594	RI	$19,544	CA	$34,073	TX	17.4%	NM	16.5%	CT	$1,980	14
CA	$22,493	MI	$19,517	MN	$33,682	NY	16.4%	SD	15.5%	DE	$1,970	15
MN	$22,453	VA	$19,501	RI	$33,509	MO	16.1%	MO	14.8%	AR	$1,959	16
CO	$22,333	PA	$19,418	OR	$33,138	AZ	15.4%	ND	14.6%	DC	$1,954	17
MI	$22,333	DE	$19,381	IL	$32,875	ME	15.4%	VA	14.1%	KY	$1,935	18
PA	$22,324	FL	$19,076	MI	$32,662	MI	15.4%	ME	14.0%	OH	$1,920	19
RI	$22,251	CO	$19,022	WI	$31,766	MT	14.9%	MT	12.5%	NC	$1,913	20
FL	$21,677	MN	$18,919	NY	$31,697	NC	14.4%	VT	12.4%	NM	$1,899	21
WI	$21,019	WY	$18,271	GA	$31,663	SD	14.2%	NE	12.2%	TN	$1,896	22
OH	$20,928	MO	$18,226	OH	$31,285	IL	13.6%	MN	12.1%	NV	$1,894	23
KS	$20,869	OH	$18,195	VT	$31,065	GA	13.5%	KS	12.0%	IA	$1,889	24
MO	$20,717	WI	$18,151	ID	$31,010	WY	13.3%	NY	11.9%	NE	$1,889	25
NE	$20,488	KS	$18,140	NE	$31,008	PA	13.2%	RI	11.6%	OK	$1,887	26
WY	$20,436	NE	$18,089	PA	$30,995	ID	13.1%	ID	11.5%	MS	$1,883	27
OR	$20,419	IN	$17,801	AZ	$30,510	KS	13.1%	IA	11.2%	PA	$1,875	28
IN	$20,378	VT	$17,763	KS	$29,770	OH	13.0%	CO	11.0%	SC	$1,869	29
IA	$20,265	SD	$17,751	IN	$29,475	WI	12.6%	AZ	10.8%	RI	$1,865	30
GA	$20,251	GA	$17,677	WY	$29,442	IN	12.2%	FL	10.8%	GA	$1,861	31
VT	$20,224	TX	$17,668	NC	$28,820	WA	12.1%	IN	10.8%	IL	$1,832	32
TX	$19,857	ME	$17,559	TX	$28,727	OR	11.8%	MI	10.8%	SD	$1,818	33
NC	$19,669	IA	$17,529	MO	$28,682	MN	11.6%	IL	10.7%	ID	$1,811	34
ME	$19,663	OR	$17,419	IA	$28,663	ND	11.2%	OH	10.7%	MA	$1,810	35
SD	$19,577	TN	$17,387	FL	$28,550	RI	11.2%	WY	10.7%	AZ	$1,797	36
TN	$19,482	NC	$17,116	ND	$28,118	NJ	10.9%	PA	10.6%	NH	$1,796	37
AZ	$19,001	AZ	$16,748	SD	$27,737	MA	10.7%	MD	10.5%	MO	$1,779	38
ND	$18,546	ND	$16,664	ME	$27,438	UT	10.7%	NH	10.2%	MI	$1,775	39
ID	$18,231	ID	$16,293	DC	$27,304	IA	10.3%	DE	10.1%	VA	$1,761	40
AL	$18,010	AL	$16,022	NM	$26,758	NE	10.3%	OR	10.1%	WA	$1,728	41
MT	$17,865	LA	$15,754	MT	$26,470	DE	10.2%	NV	9.6%	MN	$1,721	42
KY	$17,807	SC	$15,709	LA	$26,312	VT	10.0%	MA	9.4%	OR	$1,716	43
OK	$17,744	MT	$15,615	OK	$26,260	CO	9.9%	WA	9.1%	HI	$1,702	44
SC	$17,695	OK	$15,575	SC	$26,053	NH	9.9%	WI	9.1%	MD	$1,670	45
LA	$17,651	KY	$15,446	TN	$25,102	NV	9.8%	UT	8.8%	WI	$1,630	46
WV	$17,208	WV	$15,445	AL	$25,082	MD	9.7%	NJ	8.5%	CA	$1,600	47
NM	$17,106	NM	$15,308	KY	$24,376	VA	9.7%	HI	8.0%	NY	$1,588	48
UT	$17,043	AR	$14,995	AR	$23,039	AK	9.1%	AK	7.6%	UT	$1,580	49
AR	$16,898	UT	$14,938	WV	$22,421	CT	8.5%	CA	7.6%	CO	$1,571	50
MS	$15,838	MS	$14,362	MS	$22,191	HI	8.0%	CT	7.2%	FL	$1,510	51

Source: Bureau of Economic Analysis, U.S. Dept. of Commerce; Energy Information Administration, U.S. Dept. of Energy

ECONOMY

CIVILIAN LABOR FORCE

	Civ. Labor Force, 1994		% of Pop. in Labor Force		Females in Labor Force		Job Growth, 1980-90	Desc. Num. Order
CA	15,471,000	MN	56.16%	DC	48.73%	AL	18.99%	1
TX	9,385,000	VT	55.34%	HI	48.71%	NV	53.41%	2
NY	8,571,000	IA	55.32%	RI	48.32%	FL	50.14%	3
FL	6,824,000	NH	55.23%	VT	48.29%	AZ	48.44%	4
IL	6,000,000	DC	55.09%	MD	48.01%	AK	40.53%	5
PA	5,829,000	WI	55.00%	SC	47.76%	GA	36.84%	6
OH	5,537,000	CO	54.60%	NC	47.71%	NH	36.67%	7
MI	4,753,000	DE	54.39%	IN	47.61%	DE	35.15%	8
NJ	3,991,000	NE	53.97%	TN	47.56%	VA	34.17%	9
NC	3,609,000	MD	53.76%	NE	47.49%	WA	33.51%	10
GA	3,566,000	NV	53.47%	VA	47.40%	CA	32.26%	11
VA	3,422,000	OR	53.24%	CT	47.39%	MD	31.22%	12
MA	3,179,000	IN	53.13%	ME	47.31%	UT	30.88%	13
IN	3,056,000	ND	52.98%	MN	47.25%	VT	30.60%	14
WI	2,795,000	CT	52.70%	GA	47.00%	ME	29.08%	15
WA	2,708,000	MA	52.62%	MT	46.91%	NC	28.18%	16
MO	2,695,000	WY	52.31%	KS	46.88%	SC	27.41%	17
MD	2,691,000	VA	52.23%	SD	46.79%	NM	25.65%	18
TN	2,664,000	ID	52.16%	ND	46.75%	HI	25.55%	19
MN	2,565,000	KS	52.11%	KY	46.74%	CO	24.50%	20
AL	2,031,000	SD	51.87%	MA	46.62%	TN	23.09%	21
CO	1,996,000	TN	51.48%	WI	46.48%	NJ	21.77%	22
AZ	1,988,000	UT	51.10%	FL	46.37%	TX	21.07%	23
LA	1,939,000	TX	51.07%	OH	46.27%	OR	20.40%	24
SC	1,828,000	IL	51.06%	LA	46.26%	MN	19.26%	25
KY	1,825,000	MO	51.06%	NY	46.26%	MO	19.25%	26
CT	1,726,000	MT	51.05%	IL	46.25%	KY	18.85%	27
OR	1,643,000	NC	51.05%	AL	46.18%	CT	18.58%	28
IA	1,565,000	WA	50.68%	MO	46.16%	MI	18.31%	29
OK	1,540,000	RI	50.65%	MS	46.09%	AR	18.13%	30
KS	1,331,000	GA	50.55%	IA	46.07%	MA	17.77%	31
MS	1,254,000	NJ	50.49%	AK	45.90%	IN	17.67%	32
AR	1,207,000	AK	50.33%	AR	45.90%	ID	16.89%	33
UT	975,000	MI	50.05%	MI	45.89%	WI	16.82%	34
NE	876,000	SC	49.89%	CO	45.84%	NY	15.42%	35
WV	788,000	OH	49.87%	WY	45.78%	SD	15.30%	36
NV	779,000	HI	49.45%	NH	45.70%	RI	15.26%	37
NM	770,000	ME	49.44%	NJ	45.38%	KS	14.47%	38
NH	628,000	CA	49.22%	WA	45.38%	OH	13.71%	39
ME	613,000	AR	49.21%	AZ	45.27%	IL	13.49%	40
ID	591,000	FL	48.91%	PA	45.27%	NE	12.30%	41
HI	583,000	AZ	48.79%	DE	45.05%	PA	11.23%	42
RI	505,000	PA	48.37%	OK	45.00%	DC	11.01%	43
MT	437,000	AL	48.14%	OR	44.98%	MT	9.42%	44
DE	384,000	KY	47.69%	ID	44.84%	MS	8.85%	45
SD	374,000	OK	47.27%	WV	44.80%	ND	7.07%	46
ND	338,000	NY	47.17%	UT	44.62%	IA	7.04%	47
VT	321,000	MS	46.98%	NM	44.42%	OK	6.51%	48
DC	314,000	NM	46.55%	TX	44.39%	LA	2.46%	49
AK	305,000	LA	44.94%	NV	44.29%	WV	-1.13%	50
WY	249,000	WV	43.25%	CA	44.08%	WY	-4.34%	51

Source: Bureau of Economic Analysis, U.S. Dept. of Commerce; Bureau of Labor Statistics, U.S. Dept. of Labor

PERCENTAGE OF STATES' WORKERS IN SELECTED INDUSTRIES (1994)

Manufactur.		Transport., Commun., Public Util.		Trade		Finance, Insur., Real Estate		Service		Govt.		Desc. Num. Order
NC	25.3%	AK	8.1%	ND	22.1%	CT	9.9%	DC	34.4%	DC	31.2%	1
IN	24.3%	KS	8.1%	FL	21.6%	DE	9.5%	NV	33.8%	AK	27.7%	2
SC	23.7%	NJ	7.4%	WV	20.7%	NY	8.2%	MA	29.2%	MD	23.7%	3
MI	23.3%	TX	6.7%	ME	20.6%	NJ	8.0%	RI	25.9%	NM	21.9%	4
TN	22.8%	WY	6.7%	NE	20.5%	HI	7.4%	FL	25.6%	WY	21.7%	5
WI	22.6%	HI	6.6%	MO	20.4%	IL	7.2%	HI	25.4%	MT	20.5%	6
AR	22.4%	CO	6.5%	MI	20.2%	MA	7.2%	NY	25.3%	HI	20.4%	7
OH	22.3%	WV	6.4%	PA	20.1%	FL	7.0%	MD	25.2%	UT	20.2%	8
NH	21.9%	GA	6.2%	TX	20.0%	WA	6.6%	PA	24.8%	ND	19.2%	9
AL	21.6%	MS	6.1%	LA	19.8%	AZ	6.4%	NJ	24.6%	LA	18.9%	10
RI	21.5%	LA	6.0%	IL	19.7%	CA	6.2%	VT	24.5%	VA	18.9%	11
MS	20.8%	MO	6.0%	WA	19.7%	MD	6.2%	CO	24.1%	WV	18.8%	12
CT	20.3%	FL	5.9%	IA	19.6%	PA	6.1%	VA	23.7%	WA	18.6%	13
DE	19.1%	KY	5.9%	HI	19.4%	KS	6.0%	CT	23.4%	OK	18.5%	14
PA	17.8%	AL	5.8%	MN	19.4%	CO	5.9%	NH	23.4%	NY	18.4%	15
IL	17.5%	AZ	5.8%	SC	19.4%	OR	5.9%	DE	23.1%	SD	17.4%	16
ME	17.5%	AR	5.8%	SD	19.4%	RI	5.7%	IL	23.1%	KS	17.2%	17
MO	17.5%	IL	5.8%	NH	19.3%	MN	5.6%	MN	23.0%	MS	16.9%	18
IA	17.0%	VA	5.8%	OH	19.3%	NE	5.6%	AZ	22.6%	OR	16.9%	19
KY	16.3%	MD	5.6%	MT	19.2%	DC	5.5%	MO	22.5%	AZ	16.7%	20
GA	16.2%	MT	5.6%	NM	19.2%	IN	5.5%	ME	21.9%	GA	16.6%	21
MA	16.2%	NV	5.6%	UT	19.2%	IA	5.5%	OH	21.9%	TX	16.4%	22
KS	15.7%	PA	5.6%	NV	19.1%	GA	5.4%	GA	21.3%	ID	16.3%	23
VT	15.7%	UT	5.5%	NJ	19.1%	NV	5.3%	CA	21.2%	NE	15.6%	24
MN	15.3%	NE	5.3%	RI	19.1%	VA	5.3%	MI	21.0%	MN	15.4%	25
ID	15.2%	OK	5.3%	KY.	19.0%	ME	5.2%	WI	21.0%	SC	15.3%	26
NJ	15.2%	TN	5.3%	OR	19.0%	OH	5.2%	OR	20.8%	IA	15.2%	27
WV	14.8%	NY	5.2%	WY	19.0%	UT	5.2%	WA	20.6%	CO	15.1%	28
CA	14.5%	WA	5.2%	AZ	18.9%	WI	5.2%	TX	20.6%	AL	14.9%	29
UT	14.4%	CA	5.1%	MD	18.9%	NH	5.0%	NM	20.5%	CA	14.8%	30
OK	14.3%	IN	5.1%	CO	18.8%	TX	5.0%	UT	20.5%	FL	14.8%	31
OR	13.5%	ID	5.0%	ID	18.8%	KY	4.9%	LA	20.2%	KY	14.7%	32
NY	13.0%	NC	4.9%	MA	18.8%	LA	4.9%	NE	20.1%	NJ	14.7%	33
VA	13.0%	OH	4.9%	TN	18.6%	MO	4.8%	IN	19.7%	NC	14.7%	34
NE	12.8%	NM	4.8%	AR	18.5%	SC	4.8%	ND	19.6%	AR	14.5%	35
TX	12.7%	MN	4.6%	CA	18.4%	MI	4.7%	OK	19.6%	MI	14.3%	36
CO	12.5%	MA	4.5%	NC	18.3%	AL	4.5%	TN	19.6%	OH	14.1%	37
WA	12.0%	CT	4.4%	VA	18.3%	NM	4.4%	AK	19.1%	WI	13.9%	38
SD	11.4%	DE	4.4%	KS	18.1%	OK	4.4%	KS	19.1%	TN	13.7%	39
AZ	10.7%	MI	4.4%	AL	18.0%	SD	4.4%	WV	19.1%	VT	13.4%	40
LA	10.5%	OR	4.4%	CT	18.0%	AR	4.3%	KY	19.0%	IL	13.3%	41
FL	9.0%	NH	4.3%	IN	17.9%	AK	4.2%	SD	18.5%	ME	13.3%	42
MD	7.3%	ND	4.3%	DE	17.8%	VT	4.2%	AL	18.4%	NV	13.1%	43
NM	6.1%	SC	4.3%	VT	17.7%	WY	4.2%	IA	18.2%	MO	12.8%	44
MT	5.9%	IA	4.1%	WI	17.6%	NC	4.1%	MT	18.2%	MA	12.7%	45
ND	5.9%	ME	4.1%	AK	17.2%	TN	4.1%	ID	17.6%	RI	12.7%	46
NV	5.3%	WI	4.0%	MS	17.1%	WV	4.0%	NC	17.5%	IN	12.6%	47
WY	4.3%	VT	3.9%	OK	17.0%	ND	3.9%	SC	17.1%	DE	12.5%	48
DC	3.8%	DC	3.8%	NY	16.8%	ID	3.8%	MS	16.5%	PA	12.2%	49
AK	3.7%	SD	3.7%	GA	16.3%	MS	3.6%	AR	16.4%	CT	11.7%	50
HI	3.5%	RI	3.3%	DC	10.5%	MT	3.4%	WY	15.4%	NH	11.2%	51

Source: Bureau of Labor Statistics, U.S. Dept of Labor

FOREIGN EXPORTS, GROSS STATE PRODUCT, AND PATENTS

	Exports Value, 1994		Exports per Person, 1993		State Product per Person, 1993		Patents per 100,000 Pop., 1993	Desc. Num. Order
CA	$66,292,000,000	WA	$4,422.42	DC	$63,973.06	DE	74.64	1
TX	$51,818,000,000	AK	$4,052.81	AK	$45,694.20	CT	53.26	2
NY	$25,912,000,000	LA	$3,371.73	DE	$30,882.35	MA	41.61	3
MI	$25,830,000,000	TX	$2,819.57	CT	$29,170.46	NJ	41.07	4
WA	$23,629,000,000	MI	$2,720.09	WY	$28,384.28	MN	39.06	5
IL	$19,097,000,000	VT	$2,363.79	NJ	$27,423.72	NH	35.94	6
OH	$19,007,000,000	DE	$2,121.81	HI	$27,336.86	MI	32.90	7
FL	$16,287,000,000	CA	$2,109.13	NY	$26,384.35	ID	32.36	8
LA	$14,549,000,000	OR	$1,977.64	MA	$25,991.34	CA	30.65	9
NC	$11,863,000,000	MA	$1,853.83	NV	$25,680.93	CO	29.57	10
PA	$11,650,000,000	CT	$1,729.47	CA	$25,118.36	NY	29.50	11
MA	$11,199,000,000	OH	$1,712.03	IL	$24,208.24	IL	28.34	12
NJ	$10,519,000,000	NC	$1,677.93	WA	$23,714.63	RI	27.50	13
VA	$9,573,000,000	IL	$1,625.00	MN	$23,255.81	OR	26.99	14
IN	$8,256,000,000	AZ	$1,586.99	VA	$23,063.46	OH	26.91	15
GA	$8,237,000,000	WI	$1,519.48	MD	$23,050.01	VT	26.74	16
WI	$7,722,000,000	VA	$1,461.08	CO	$22,848.66	WI	26.49	17
TN	$6,749,000,000	MN	$1,449.75	TX	$22,832.10	UT	25.32	18
MN	$6,621,000,000	IN	$1,435.33	LA	$22,400.38	PA	24.88	19
AZ	$6,467,000,000	SC	$1,429.04	NE	$21,984.92	AZ	23.52	20
OR	$6,103,000,000	NY	$1,426.17	NC	$21,919.43	MD	21.60	21
CT	$5,664,000,000	NJ	$1,330.85	GA	$21,739.13	OK	21.06	22
SC	$5,236,000,000	TN	$1,304.15	NH	$21,660.65	TX	20.67	23
MD	$4,874,000,000	ID	$1,293.91	PA	$21,344.27	WA	20.44	24
KY	$4,803,000,000	KY	$1,255.03	KS	$21,268.06	IN	19.40	25
AL	$3,895,000,000	UT	$1,234.28	RI	$20,916.33	NM	16.03	26
CO	$3,802,000,000	KS	$1,185.59	OH	$20,856.20	FL	15.40	27
MO	$3,541,000,000	GA	$1,167.54	WI	$20,812.29	IA	15.38	28
IA	$3,214,000,000	FL	$1,167.28	MO	$20,550.60	NC	15.36	29
KS	$3,028,000,000	IA	$1,136.09	TN	$20,404.04	VA	15.19	30
AK	$2,456,000,000	CO	$1,039.93	IN	$20,346.24	MO	14.27	31
UT	$2,355,000,000	MD	$973.63	OR	$20,205.48	SC	13.80	32
OK	$2,110,000,000	NE	$969.19	MI	$20,170.76	NV	13.17	33
MS	$1,846,000,000	PA	$966.64	IA	$20,057.31	MT	12.84	34
AR	$1,672,000,000	DC	$957.89	SD	$19,943.02	TN	12.50	35
WV	$1,586,000,000	RI	$925.78	NM	$19,392.37	GA	12.47	36
NE	$1,573,000,000	AL	$923.20	VT	$19,366.20	KS	12.47	37
DE	$1,498,000,000	NH	$879.51	FL	$19,190.25	NE	11.84	38
ID	$1,466,000,000	ME	$879.03	ND	$18,927.44	ME	11.45	39
VT	$1,371,000,000	WV	$870.47	KY	$18,842.53	LA	11.19	40
ME	$1,090,000,000	WY	$756.30	AZ	$18,681.61	AK	10.70	41
NH	$1,000,000,000	ND	$717.87	UT	$18,675.72	DC	10.36	42
RI	$923,000,000	MS	$691.64	ME	$18,593.37	ND	10.36	43
NV	$621,000,000	AR	$681.61	SC	$18,554.96	WV	9.90	44
DC	$546,000,000	MO	$670.90	OK	$18,308.08	WY	9.15	45
NM	$526,000,000	OK	$647.64	ID	$18,286.81	HI	9.09	46
ND	$458,000,000	NV	$426.22	AL	$18,106.19	KY	8.51	47
WY	$360,000,000	SD	$409.15	MT	$17,326.73	AL	7.75	48
MT	$328,000,000	MT	$383.18	AR	$17,292.28	AR	6.35	49
HI	$297,000,000	NM	$318.02	WV	$16,120.07	SD	6.10	50
SD	$295,000,000	HI	$251.91	MS	$15,805.71	MS	5.30	51

Source: Bureau of Economic Analysis, U.S. Dept. of Labor; Bureau of the Census, U.S. Dept. of Commerce; *U.S. Merchandise Trade*; U.S. Patent and Trademark Office

BUSINESSES

	Total Bus., 1991		New Bus. Incorp., 1990		New Bus. Incorp., 1991		As % of Total Bus., 1991
CA	1,097,465	FL	82,172	FL	81,083	DE	138.74%
TX	844,821	NY	65,569	NY	63,808	NV	28.58%
NY	605,384	CA	39,111	CA	36,561	FL	19.49%
IL	441,411	TX	35,523	TX	34,571	HI	12.16%
FL	415,975	DE	29,861	DE	29,887	MD	11.09%
PA	367,348	IL	29,279	IL	29,068	NJ	10.64%
OH	341,253	NJ	28,281	NJ	27,994	NY	10.54%
MI	320,693	MI	22,204	MI	20,099	GA	9.45%
NJ	263,070	PA	19,431	GA	18,098	VA	8.71%
NC	209,770	GA	18,891	OH	17,895	CO	8.66%
MA	201,385	OH	18,094	PA	17,340	UT	8.55%
VA	193,800	VA	17,376	VA	16,883	DC	7.88%
GA	191,583	MD	16,674	MD	16,463	RI	7.50%
WA	183,769	MA	12,468	CO	13,583	LA	7.06%
MN	176,738	NC	12,376	NC	11,944	AR	6.72%
WI	175,870	CO	12,257	MA	11,706	AZ	6.70%
MO	172,165	NV	12,031	WA	11,521	IL	6.59%
IA	168,153	WA	11,948	NV	11,030	OR	6.59%
IN	160,619	IN	10,608	IN	10,205	AK	6.49%
CO	156,891	AZ	10,129	AZ	9,832	IN	6.35%
TN	151,392	MO	9,761	MN	9,564	WA	6.27%
MD	148,454	MN	9,678	MO	9,521	MI	6.27%
AZ	146,672	CT	9,138	LA	8,973	CT	6.10%
CT	139,462	LA	8,974	CT	8,501	KY	6.07%
OR	127,176	OR	8,525	OR	8,375	OK	5.94%
LA	127,163	TN	8,290	TN	8,306	MA	5.81%
OK	119,162	WI	7,334	OK	7,073	NC	5.69%
AL	114,123	SC	7,158	WI	6,994	VT	5.64%
KY	111,784	OK	7,152	KY	6,782	MO	5.53%
KS	107,489	KY	6,669	AL	6,116	NH	5.51%
SC	103,796	AR	6,111	SC	5,700	SC	5.49%
MS	79,509	AL	6,092	AR	5,326	TN	5.49%
AR	79,276	IA	4,381	UT	4,973	MN	5.41%
NE	71,814	KS	4,249	IA	4,531	AL	5.36%
UT	58,156	UT	4,147	KS	3,930	WY	5.25%
NM	55,334	HI	3,794	HI	3,792	OH	5.24%
WV	51,655	MS	3,405	MS	3,602	ME	5.10%
ID	46,787	RI	3,000	NE	3,093	NM	4.90%
ME	45,619	NE	2,934	NM	2,713	PA	4.72%
MT	43,961	NM	2,854	RI	2,458	MS	4.53%
NH	43,357	NH	2,679	NH	2,387	NE	4.31%
SD	39,038	WV	2,542	ME	2,326	WV	4.30%
NV	38,593	ME	2,428	DC	2,256	ID	4.16%
RI	32,764	DC	2,256	WV	2,219	TX	4.09%
ND	32,361	ID	1,909	ID	1,944	WI	3.98%
HI	31,188	VT	1,650	MT	1,572	KS	3.66%
DC	28,638	MT	1,519	VT	1,486	MT	3.58%
WY	26,383	AK	1,345	WY	1,386	CA	3.33%
VT	26,339	WY	1,171	AK	1,250	IA	2.69%
DE	21,542	SD	1,078	SD	1,040	SD	2.66%
AK	19,262	ND	860	ND	820	ND	2.53%

Source: Dun & Bradstreet; Bureau of Economic Analysis, U.S. Dept. of Commerce

BUSINESSES (CONTINUED)

% Change New Bus., 1990-91		Bus. Failures, 1990		Bus. Failures, 1991		Failures as % of Tot. Bus., 1991		Change in Bus. Failures, 1990-91		Desc. Num. Order
UT	19.92%	CA	14,466	CA	8,968	OK	1.34%	IA	+92.0%	1
WY	18.36%	TX	6,976	TX	6,742	CO	1.33%	HI	+51.8%	2
CO	10.82%	NY	5,563	FL	3,665	GA	1.01%	MT	+20.1%	3
MS	5.79%	FL	5,180	NY	3,284	TN	0.97%	WY	+10.6%	4
NE	5.42%	PA	3,622	OH	2,262	KY	0.95%	CO	+7.6%	5
MT	3.49%	GA	3,367	PA	2,228	MA	0.95%	LA	+4.6%	6
IA	3.42%	IL	3,027	IL	2,149	LA	0.91%	ND	+2.9%	7
ID	1.83%	MA	2,806	MI	2,109	FL	0.88%	IN	-0.3%	8
KY	1.69%	OH	2,751	CO	2,091	CA	0.82%	TX	-3.4%	9
AL	0.39%	NJ	2,715	GA	1,944	VA	0.82%	MI	-7.2%	10
TN	0.19%	VA	2,283	MA	1,913	TX	0.80%	OK	-12.6%	11
DE	0.09%	MI	2,273	OK	1,597	AZ	0.74%	KY	-12.9%	12
DC	0.00%	AZ	2,210	VA	1,597	IN	0.73%	MS	-12.9%	13
LA	-0.01%	TN	1,992	TN	1,475	KS	0.71%	AK	-13.3%	14
HI	-0.05%	CO	1,944	NJ	1,265	MO	0.71%	SD	-13.4%	15
IL	-0.72%	OK	1,827	MO	1,221	SD	0.69%	OH	-17.8%	16
NJ	-1.01%	IN	1,723	IN	1,171	ID	0.67%	NM	-21.0%	17
OH	-1.10%	MO	1,575	LA	1,152	WY	0.67%	MO	-22.4%	18
OK	-1.10%	MN	1,566	AZ	1,090	MI	0.66%	KS	-23.3%	19
MN	-1.18%	WA	1,418	KY	1,063	NV	0.66%	NC	-24.0%	20
MD	-1.27%	NC	1,350	NC	1,026	OH	0.66%	ID	-25.0%	21
FL	-1.33%	MD	1,314	WA	860	AK	0.64%	TN	-26.0%	22
OR	-1.76%	OR	1,304	KS	763	NH	0.64%	WI	-26.0%	23
MO	-2.46%	KY	1,221	MD	693	UT	0.64%	UT	-27.5%	24
TX	-2.68%	LA	1,101	AL	678	PA	0.61%	IL	-29.0%	25
NY	-2.69%	AL	1,022	WI	666	AL	0.59%	FL	-29.2%	26
VA	-2.84%	KS	995	OR	591	NM	0.58%	VA	-30.0%	27
AZ	-2.93%	WI	900	IA	553	MS	0.57%	SC	-30.6%	28
NC	-3.49%	CT	898	MN	529	RI	0.56%	MA	-31.8%	29
SD	-3.53%	NH	853	MS	453	NY	0.54%	NE	-33.1%	30
WA	-3.57%	SC	598	CT	435	NE	0.50%	AL	-33.7%	31
IN	-3.80%	NV	545	SC	415	IL	0.49%	CA	-38.0%	32
GA	-4.20%	NE	535	UT	372	NC	0.49%	PA	-38.5%	33
ME	-4.20%	MS	520	NE	358	HI	0.48%	WV	-39.2%	34
WI	-4.64%	UT	513	NM	319	NJ	0.48%	WA	-39.4%	35
ND	-4.65%	AR	477	ID	312	MD	0.47%	NY	-41.0%	36
NM	-4.94%	RI	454	NH	279	WA	0.47%	GA	-42.3%	37
MA	-6.11%	WV	395	SD	271	OR	0.46%	AR	-44.2%	38
CA	-6.52%	ME	392	AR	266	WV	0.46%	MD	-47.3%	39
CT	-6.97%	ID	390	NV	255	ME	0.44%	ME	-49.2%	40
AK	-7.06%	NM	386	WV	240	ND	0.44%	DC	-49.5%	41
KS	-7.51%	SD	313	ME	199	MT	0.43%	AZ	-50.7%	42
NV	-8.32%	IA	288	MT	191	SC	0.40%	CT	-51.6%	43
MI	-9.48%	DC	198	RI	183	WI	0.38%	NV	-53.2%	44
VT	-9.94%	VT	187	WY	178	DE	0.37%	OR	-54.7%	45
PA	-10.76%	WY	161	HI	149	DC	0.37%	VT	-58.3%	46
NH	-10.90%	MT	159	ND	144	AR	0.34%	RI	-59.7%	47
WV	-12.71%	DE	158	AK	124	IA	0.33%	MN	-66.2%	48
AR	-12.85%	AK	143	DC	100	CT	0.31%	NH	-67.3%	49
RI	-18.07%	ND	140	DE	80	MN	0.30%	DE	-97.5%	50
SC	-20.37%	HI	72	VT	78	VT	0.30%	NJ	-114.6%	51

AGRICULTURE

	Farm Income Mktg., 1993		Farm Income Avg. per Farm		Farm Income Avg. per Acre		Avg. Value of Prop. per Acre, 1994
CA	$19,850,000,000.00	CA	$261,184.21	CT	$1,264.56	RI	$5,334
TX	$12,617,000,000.00	AZ	$240,250.00	DE	$942.42	NJ	$4,840
IA	$10,001,000,000.00	DE	$207,333.33	RI	$877.78	CT	$4,686
NE	$8,909,000,000.00	NE	$161,981.82	NJ	$848.56	MA	$3,992
IL	$8,082,000,000.00	CO	$157,038.46	MA	$724.49	MD	$2,866
KS	$7,363,000,000.00	FL	$147,435.90	CA	$667.99	DE	$2,641
MN	$6,574,000,000.00	NV	$144,500.00	MD	$619.50	NH	$2,374
FL	$5,750,000,000.00	ID	$135,571.43	NC	$581.71	FL	$2,205
NC	$5,457,000,000.00	CT	$130,250.00	FL	$558.47	PA	$1,910
WI	$5,250,000,000.00	WA	$127,055.56	PA	$469.58	CA	$1,722
IN	$5,118,000,000.00	HI	$123,000.00	GA	$347.87	IL	$1,645
WA	$4,574,000,000.00	NM	$115,785.71	NY	$343.20	IN	$1,473
OH	$4,393,000,000.00	KS	$113,276.92	IN	$319.84	OH	$1,386
AR	$4,382,000,000.00	IL	$101,025.00	HI	$316.20	NC	$1,349
GA	$4,211,000,000.00	IA	$100,010.00	VT	$315.72	VA	$1,338
CO	$4,083,000,000.00	AR	$95,260.87	MI	$314.32	IA	$1,316
MO	$4,053,000,000.00	SD	$94,857.14	NH	$312.26	VT	$1,262
OK	$3,869,000,000.00	GA	$93,577.78	WI	$307.67	NY	$1,251
PA	$3,712,000,000.00	NC	$92,491.53	ME	$305.00	MI	$1,212
KY	$3,376,000,000.00	MD	$91,066.67	IA	$300.33	KY	$1,144
MI	$3,367,000,000.00	WY	$90,777.78	AL	$290.68	ME	$1,081
SD	$3,320,000,000.00	ND	$88,878.79	OH	$289.01	TN	$1,054
ND	$2,933,000,000.00	NJ	$88,250.00	WA	$286.16	GA	$983
AL	$2,910,000,000.00	IN	$81,238.10	IL	$285.38	WI	$975
ID	$2,847,000,000.00	RI	$79,000.00	AR	$284.36	LA	$973
NY	$2,817,000,000.00	MN	$75,563.22	VA	$240.47	AL	$964
MS	$2,605,000,000.00	NY	$74,131.58	SC	$239.98	SC	$923
OR	$2,476,000,000.00	PA	$72,784.31	KY	$239.35	MN	$900
VA	$2,068,000,000.00	MT	$71,240.00	MN	$221.59	WA	$898
TN	$2,039,000,000.00	MA	$71,000.00	ID	$205.72	MS	$814
AZ	$1,922,000,000.00	VT	$69,142.86	LA	$203.99	AR	$800
MT	$1,781,000,000.00	TX	$68,200.00	MS	$200.59	ID	$784
LA	$1,757,000,000.00	OR	$66,918.92	NE	$189.23	MO	$762
NM	$1,621,000,000.00	MS	$66,794.87	TN	$164.65	OR	$740
MD	$1,366,000,000.00	WI	$66,455.70	KS	$154.12	WV	$713
SC	$1,221,000,000.00	MI	$64,750.00	OR	$141.48	NE	$635
WY	$817,000,000.00	AL	$61,914.89	MO	$134.16	KS	$537
UT	$804,000,000.00	UT	$61,846.15	CO	$122.11	OK	$534
NJ	$706,000,000.00	ME	$61,000.00	OK	$113.76	UT	$508
DE	$622,000,000.00	LA	$60,586.21	WV	$109.46	TX	$493
CT	$521,000,000.00	OH	$57,802.63	TX	$97.01	CO	$430
MA	$497,000,000.00	OK	$54,492.96	SD	$74.05	ND	$409
HI	$492,000,000.00	NH	$54,333.33	ND	$72.61	SD	$388
VT	$484,000,000.00	SC	$50,875.00	UT	$71.75	AZ	$314
ME	$427,000,000.00	VA	$48,093.02	AZ	$52.72	MT	$302
WV	$405,000,000.00	MO	$38,235.85	NV	$38.97	NM	$240
NV	$289,000,000.00	KY	$37,098.90	NM	$35.37	NV	$229
NH	$163,000,000.00	AK	$27,000.00	MT	$29.14	WY	$169
RI	$79,000,000.00	TN	$23,709.30	WY	$24.26	AK	NA
AK	$27,000,000.00	WV	$20,250.00	AK	$15.35	DC	NA
DC	NA	DC	NA	DC	NA	HI	NA

Source: Economic Research Service, U.S. Dept. of Agriculture

AGRICULTURE (CONTINUED)

% Increase, 1990-94		Govt. Payments, 1993		Govt. Payments Avg. per Farm		Govt. Pay. Avg. per Acre		Desc. Num. Order
UT	30.59%	TX	$1,421,000,000	ND	$17,121.21	AR	$45.75	1
OR	29.60%	IA	$1,230,000,000	AR	$15,326.09	LA	$42.61	2
NY	28.44%	IL	$851,000,000	NE	$14,654.55	IA	$36.94	3
MT	26.89%	MN	$823,000,000	AZ	$14,250.00	IL	$30.05	4
NM	22.45%	NE	$806,000,000	MT	$13,520.00	MS	$29.57	5
WI	21.42%	KS	$784,000,000	LA	$12,655.17	MN	$27.74	6
MI	20.60%	AR	$705,000,000	SD	$12,342.86	IN	$23.68	7
ND	20.29%	ND	$565,000,000	IA	$12,300.00	MI	$22.50	8
CO	20.11%	CA	$522,000,000	KS	$12,061.54	SC	$20.24	9
IA	19.42%	MO	$455,000,000	IL	$10,637.50	GA	$18.67	10
AZ	19.39%	SD	$432,000,000	MS	$9,846.15	WI	$18.17	11
ID	18.61%	MS	$384,000,000	CO	$9,615.38	CA	$17.57	12
IL	18.43%	IN	$379,000,000	MN	$9,459.77	OH	$17.43	13
MD	18.43%	LA	$367,000,000	TX	$7,681.08	NE	$17.12	14
IN	18.41%	MT	$338,000,000	ID	$7,571.43	KS	$16.41	15
SD	18.29%	OK	$324,000,000	CA	$6,868.42	MO	$15.06	16
NV	18.04%	WI	$310,000,000	IN	$6,015.87	ME	$14.29	17
DE	16.91%	OH	$265,000,000	WA	$5,750.00	NC	$14.07	18
KY	16.62%	CO	$250,000,000	NM	$5,428.57	ND	$13.99	19
WV	16.31%	MI	$241,000,000	GA	$5,022.22	AL	$13.68	20
KS	16.23%	GA	$226,000,000	WY	$4,777.78	TN	$13.00	21
NE	15.45%	WA	$207,000,000	MI	$4,634.62	WA	$12.95	22
WA	15.28%	TN	$161,000,000	OK	$4,563.38	MD	$11.79	23
OH	15.12%	ID	$159,000,000	MO	$4,292.45	ID	$11.49	24
AL	14.90%	AL	$137,000,000	SC	$4,291.67	TX	$10.93	25
WY	13.42%	NC	$132,000,000	WI	$3,924.05	FL	$10.78	26
MO	12.22%	AZ	$114,000,000	NV	$3,500.00	SD	$9.64	27
MS	11.81%	FL	$111,000,000	OH	$3,486.84	OK	$9.53	28
MN	11.80%	SC	$103,000,000	AL	$2,914.89	DE	$9.09	29
OK	7.44%	KY	$97,000,000	ME	$2,857.14	NY	$8.77	30
NC	6.81%	OR	$93,000,000	FL	$2,846.15	NJ	$8.41	31
AR	6.67%	NM	$76,000,000	UT	$2,846.15	CO	$7.48	32
LA	6.34%	NY	$72,000,000	OR	$2,513.51	CT	$7.28	33
NH	6.12%	VA	$46,000,000	NC	$2,237.29	KY	$6.88	34
CT	6.09%	PA	$45,000,000	AK	$2,000.00	MA	$5.83	35
MA	6.09%	WY	$43,000,000	DE	$2,000.00	PA	$5.69	36
RI	6.09%	UT	$37,000,000	NY	$1,894.74	MT	$5.53	37
ME	6.08%	MD	$26,000,000	TN	$1,872.09	VA	$5.35	38
VT	6.05%	ME	$20,000,000	MD	$1,733.33	OR	$5.31	39
TN	5.82%	NV	$7,000,000	VA	$1,069.77	NH	$3.83	40
FL	5.76%	NJ	$7,000,000	KY	$1,065.93	UT	$3.30	41
PA	5.70%	DE	$6,000,000	PA	$882.35	AZ	$3.13	42
NJ	4.45%	WV	$6,000,000	NJ	$875.00	VT	$1.96	43
SC	1.54%	MA	$4,000,000	CT	$750.00	HI	$1.93	44
CA	1.06%	CT	$3,000,000	HI	$750.00	NM	$1.66	45
TX	-0.40%	HI	$3,000,000	NH	$666.67	WV	$1.62	46
GA	-2.87%	VT	$3,000,000	MA	$571.43	WY	$1.28	47
VA	-11.74%	AK	$2,000,000	VT	$428.57	AK	$1.14	48
AK	NA	NH	$2,000,000	WV	$300.00	NV	$0.94	49
DC	NA	RI	under $500,000	DC	NA	DC	NA	50
HI	NA	DC	NA	RI	NA	RI	NA	51

TRAVEL AND TRANSPORTATION

VEHICLE REGISTRATIONS (1993)

	Motor Vehicle Reg.		Reg. per 1,000 Pop.		Motor- cycle Reg.		Reg. per 1,000 Pop.	Desc. Num. Order
CA	22,824,000	WY	1,187.23	CA	587,000	IA	52.82	1
TX	13,118,000	SD	1,120.67	OH	233,000	WI	39.06	2
FL	10,170,000	MT	1,116.53	IL	201,000	SD	36.06	3
NY	10,163,000	ND	1,039.25	WI	197,000	NH	32.03	4
OH	9,279,000	TN	974.48	NY	195,000	VT	29.51	5
PA	8,282,000	IA	970.58	FL	189,000	ID	29.09	6
IL	8,070,000	ID	930.00	PA	172,000	ND	28.26	7
MI	7,399,000	NE	892.13	IA	149,000	MN	27.85	8
NJ	5,641,000	NM	879.33	TX	144,000	MT	26.16	9
GA	5,632,000	OR	864.58	MI	137,000	WY	25.53	10
VA	5,408,000	OK	857.10	MN	126,000	ME	25.00	11
NC	5,365,000	NH	853.20	WA	109,000	CO	24.69	12
TN	4,964,000	CO	850.73	IN	96,000	OH	21.07	13
IN	4,670,000	WA	839.13	NJ	89,000	KS	20.91	14
WA	4,413,000	OH	838.89	CO	88,000	WA	20.73	15
MO	4,066,000	VT	838.54	TN	84,000	HI	20.58	16
MA	3,837,000	VA	835.47	AZ	73,000	OR	20.10	17
WI	3,815,000	ME	829.03	MA	68,000	AK	20.07	18
MN	3,716,000	MN	821.40	NC	64,000	RI	20.00	19
MD	3,560,000	IN	818.44	VA	62,000	NM	19.18	20
AL	3,390,000	AK	817.73	OR	61,000	CA	18.80	21
LA	3,166,000	GA	816.00	MO	57,000	AZ	18.50	22
CO	3,032,000	AL	810.81	OK	56,000	OK	17.32	23
AZ	2,892,000	DE	795.13	GA	55,000	IL	17.20	24
OK	2,771,000	CT	791.34	KS	53,000	IN	16.82	25
IA	2,738,000	MI	782.14	MD	41,000	TN	16.49	26
SC	2,684,000	MO	776.70	AL	40,000	MI	14.48	27
KY	2,629,000	NC	771.72	CT	37,000	NV	14.47	28
OR	2,624,000	KS	758.19	NH	36,000	DE	14.33	29
CT	2,594,000	MS	757.58	LA	35,000	PA	14.30	30
MS	2,000,000	WI	756.34	SC	34,000	FL	13.77	31
KS	1,922,000	FL	740.93	ID	32,000	UT	12.37	32
AR	1,528,000	WV	739.82	KY	32,000	NE	11.78	33
NE	1,439,000	SC	739.39	ME	31,000	NJ	11.32	34
NM	1,421,000	LA	738.00	NM	31,000	MA	11.30	35
WV	1,345,000	AZ	733.08	MS	28,000	CT	11.29	36
UT	1,335,000	CA	731.14	SD	26,000	MO	10.89	37
ME	1,028,000	TX	727.89	HI	24,000	NY	10.74	38
ID	1,023,000	MD	718.03	UT	23,000	MS	10.61	39
NH	959,000	NJ	717.78	MT	22,000	WV	10.45	40
MT	939,000	UT	717.74	NV	20,000	VA	9.58	41
NV	937,000	RI	695.00	RI	20,000	AL	9.57	42
SD	808,000	KY	692.94	NE	19,000	SC	9.37	43
HI	763,000	IL	690.57	WV	19,000	NC	9.21	44
RI	695,000	PA	688.45	ND	18,000	KY	8.43	45
ND	662,000	NV	678.00	VT	17,000	MD	8.27	46
WY	558,000	HI	654.37	AR	14,000	LA	8.16	47
DE	555,000	MA	637.59	AK	12,000	TX	7.99	48
AK	489,000	AR	629.84	WY	12,000	GA	7.97	49
VT	483,000	NY	559.85	DE	10,000	AR	5.77	50
DC	264,000	DC	455.96	DC	2,000	DC	3.45	51

Source: Federal Highway Administration, U.S. Dept. of Transportation

TRENDS AMONG DRIVERS; MOTOR VEHICLE DEATHS (1993)

	Licenses per 1,000 Pop.		Deaths per 100,000 Pop.		Annual Vehicle-Miles per Person		Avg. Trip for Workers	Desc. Num. Order
FL	784.06	MS	30.80	WY	14,468	NY	28.6 min.	1
OR	781.88	NM	26.79	NM	11,696	DC	27.1 min.	2
NH	773.13	WY	25.53	GA	11,359	MD	27.0 min.	3
VT	748.26	AL	24.30	AL	11,313	NJ	25.3 min.	4
WY	744.68	AR	24.03	OK	10,981	IL	25.1 min.	5
AK	732.44	WV	23.60	IN	10,603	CA	24.6 min.	6
ME	730.65	SC	23.28	MO	10,468	VA	24.0 min.	7
CO	726.99	KY	23.09	ID	10,455	HI	23.8 min.	8
DE	724.93	MT	23.07	KY	10,438	GA	22.7 min.	9
OK	722.55	TN	23.07	VT	10,417	MA	22.7 min.	10
AR	721.76	ID	21.18	MT	10,345	LA	22.3 min.	11
AL	719.68	OK	20.79	SD	10,264	TX	22.2 min.	12
WV	716.17	LA	20.54	TN	10,228	WA	22.0 min.	13
NM	710.40	GA	20.37	MS	10,189	NH	21.9 min.	14
VA	707.55	AZ	20.35	NC	9,997	FL	21.8 min.	15
NE	707.38	NC	19.91	SC	9,945	AZ	21.6 min.	16
NV	706.22	FL	19.62	AZ	9,937	MO	21.6 min.	17
WA	703.37	AK	19.57	VA	9,918	PA	21.6 min.	18
SD	703.19	VT	19.44	AR	9,893	TN	21.5 min.	19
ID	700.00	SD	19.42	DE	9,885	AL	21.2 min.	20
KS	699.80	NV	19.03	ME	9,839	MI	21.2 min.	21
TN	695.52	MO	18.13	WI	9,754	CT	21.1 min.	22
NJ	694.62	OR	17.20	ND	9,733	WV	21.0 min.	23
WI	694.29	KS	16.88	KS	9,507	CO	20.7 min.	24
MA	691.43	TX	16.85	OR	9,357	KY	20.7 min.	25
OH	690.26	UT	16.29	MN	9,328	OH	20.7 min.	26
MI	689.96	DE	16.19	TX	9,300	MS	20.6 min.	27
ND	687.60	NE	15.75	WV	9,241	SC	20.5 min.	28
NC	679.66	CO	15.74	UT	9,194	IN	20.4 min.	29
RI	675.00	IN	15.62	CO	9,175	DE	20.0 min.	30
IA	673.17	IA	15.49	NE	9,175	NV	19.8 min.	31
SC	669.70	ME	15.00	NH	9,164	NC	19.8 min.	32
PA	669.58	MI	14.89	MI	9,059	OR	19.6 min.	33
GA	668.36	ND	13.97	IA	8,898	OK	19.3 min.	34
AZ	665.15	WI	13.94	FL	8,779	RI	19.2 min.	35
CT	665.04	MD	13.55	OH	8,770	MN	19.1 min.	36
IN	664.39	VA	13.52	WA	8,766	NM	19.1 min.	37
MO	663.23	OH	13.42	MD	8,733	AR	19.0 min.	38
MD	660.35	PA	12.71	CA	8,534	ME	19.0 min.	39
TX	658.97	WA	12.59	LA	8,485	UT	18.9 min.	40
KY	650.76	CA	12.50	NV	8,394	WI	18.3 min.	41
CA	644.62	IL	11.91	CT	8,237	VT	18.0 min.	42
UT	639.78	MN	11.89	MA	7,760	ID	17.3 min.	43
IL	638.54	HI	11.49	IL	7,676	KS	17.2 min.	44
MT	631.39	NH	10.85	NJ	7,596	AK	16.7 min.	45
HI	629.50	CT	10.43	PA	7,539	IA	16.2 min.	46
DC	623.49	NJ	10.01	RI	7,200	NE	15.8 min.	47
MS	621.21	NY	9.67	HI	6,947	WY	15.4 min.	48
LA	600.70	MA	7.88	AK	6,522	MT	14.8 min.	49
MN	582.89	RI	7.40	NY	6,181	SD	13.8 min.	50
NY	568.89	DC	(NA)	DC	6,045	ND	13.0 min.	51

Source: Federal Highway Administration, U.S. Dept. of Transportation

ROADWAY MILEAGE (1993)

Public Roads & Streets, Total Mileage		Total Mileage per 1,000 Pop.		Rural Mileage		Rural Mileage per 1,000 Pop.	
TX	294,142	ND	136.15	TX	215,010	ND	133.30
CA	169,201	SD	115.54	KS	123,676	SD	112.96
IL	136,965	MT	82.96	MN	115,073	MT	80.13
KS	133,256	WY	80.09	MO	105,637	WY	75.01
MN	129,959	NE	57.47	IA	103,490	NE	54.34
MO	121,787	ID	53.49	IL	101,784	ID	50.38
MI	117,659	KS	52.57	OK	99,673	KS	48.79
PA	117,038	IA	39.95	WI	95,387	IA	36.69
OH	113,823	NM	37.63	MI	89,485	NM	34.01
FL	112,808	OK	34.79	CA	88,140	OK	30.83
IA	112,708	NV	33.12	NE	87,648	NV	29.80
OK	112,467	AR	31.82	OR	86,008	AR	28.69
NY	111,882	OR	31.64	ND	84,909	OR	28.34
WI	110,978	MN	28.73	GA	84,605	MN	25.44
GA	110,879	MS	27.59	PA	84,422	MS	24.59
OR	96,036	VT	24.59	OH	82,255	VT	22.30
NC	96,028	MO	23.26	SD	81,445	AK	20.25
NE	92,702	AK	23.16	NC	74,305	MO	20.18
IN	92,374	CO	22.09	IN	73,112	WI	18.91
AL	92,209	AL	22.05	AL	72,828	UT	18.50
ND	86,727	WI	22.00	NY	72,589	CO	18.47
TN	85,037	UT	21.78	AR	69,597	WV	17.55
SD	83,305	WV	19.28	TN	68,516	AL	17.42
WA	79,428	KY	19.14	MT	67,388	KY	16.47
CO	78,721	ME	18.15	CO	65,818	ME	16.07
AR	77,192	SC	17.67	MS	64,930	SC	14.78
MS	72,834	TN	16.69	FL	63,630	TN	13.45
KY	72,632	TX	16.32	KY	62,493	IN	12.81
MT	69,768	IN	16.19	WA	62,210	GA	12.26
VA	68,429	GA	16.06	ID	55,419	TX	11.93
SC	64,158	WA	15.10	NM	54,961	WA	11.83
NM	60,812	AZ	14.14	SC	53,637	NH	10.74
LA	59,599	LA	13.89	VA	52,848	NC	10.69
ID	58,835	NC	13.81	LA	45,833	LA	10.68
AZ	55,763	NH	13.29	NV	41,181	AZ	9.99
NV	45,778	MI	12.44	AZ	39,423	MI	9.46
UT	40,508	IL	11.72	WY	35,256	IL	8.71
WY	37,642	VA	10.57	UT	34,402	VA	8.16
NJ	35,097	OH	10.29	WV	31,908	OH	7.44
WV	35,045	PA	9.73	ME	19,927	PA	7.02
MA	30,563	FL	8.22	MD	15,642	DE	5.27
MD	29,313	DE	7.94	VT	12,842	FL	4.64
ME	22,510	CT	6.21	AK	12,107	NY	4.00
CT	20,357	NY	6.16	NH	12,069	MD	3.15
NH	14,938	RI	6.06	NJ	11,068	CA	2.82
VT	14,166	MD	5.91	MA	10,927	CT	2.69
AK	13,849	CA	5.42	CT	8,814	HI	1.98
RI	6,057	MA	5.08	DE	3,675	MA	1.82
DE	5,544	NJ	4.47	HI	2,307	NJ	1.41
HI	4,106	HI	3.52	RI	1,334	RI	1.33
DC	1,107	DC	1.91	DC	NA	DC	NA

Source: Federal Highway Administration, U.S. Dept. of Transportation

ROADWAY MILEAGE (1993) (CONTINUED)

	Urban Mileage		Urban Mileage per 1,000 Pop.		Interstate Mileage		Interstate Mileage per 1,000 Pop.		Desc. Num. Order
AL	19,381	WY	5.08	TX	3,234	WY	1.94	1
CA	81,061	RI	4.72	CA	2,423	AK	1.82	2
TX	79,132	AL	4.64	IL	2,051	MT	1.41	3
FL	49,178	TX	4.39	PA	1,588	SD	0.94	4
NY	39,293	AZ	4.14	OH	1,573	ND	0.90	5
IL	35,181	OK	3.96	NY	1,500	NM	0.62	6
PA	32,616	GA	3.81	FL	1,443	ID	0.56	7
OH	31,568	KS	3.78	GA	1,243	VT	0.56	8
MI	28,174	CO	3.62	MI	1,240	UT	0.50	9
GA	26,274	NM	3.62	MT	1,190	NV	0.39	10
NJ	24,029	FL	3.58	AZ	1,189	KS	0.34	11
NC	21,723	CT	3.52	MO	1,178	AZ	0.30	12
MA	19,636	IN	3.38	IN	1,138	ME	0.30	13
IN	19,262	NV	3.33	VA	1,106	NE	0.30	14
WA	17,218	OR	3.30	AK	1,087	WV	0.30	15
TN	16,521	MN	3.29	TN	1,062	OK	0.29	16
AZ	16,340	UT	3.28	NM	998	IA	0.28	17
MO	16,150	IA	3.27	NC	970	CO	0.27	18
WI	15,591	WA	3.27	CO	954	MS	0.26	19
VA	15,581	MA	3.26	UT	937	OR	0.24	20
MN	14,886	TN	3.24	OK	929	MO	0.23	21
LA	13,766	LA	3.21	MN	914	AL	0.22	22
MD	13,671	AR	3.13	WY	914	AR	0.22	23
CO	12,903	NE	3.13	AL	899	SC	0.22	24
OK	12,794	NC	3.12	KS	871	TN	0.21	25
CT	11,543	ID	3.11	LA	871	IN	0.20	26
SC	10,521	MO	3.09	SC	810	KY	0.20	27
KY	10,139	WI	3.09	IA	783	LA	0.20	28
OR	10,028	NJ	3.06	WA	763	MN	0.20	29
KS	9,580	IL	3.01	KY	761	NH	0.20	30
IA	9,218	MS	2.99	OR	727	GA	0.18	31
MS	7,904	MI	2.98	MS	685	IL	0.18	32
AR	7,595	AK	2.91	SD	678	TX	0.18	33
UT	6,106	SC	2.90	WI	638	VA	0.17	34
NM	5,851	ND	2.85	ID	611	WA	0.15	35
NE	5,054	OH	2.85	ND	571	NC	0.14	36
RI	4,723	MT	2.83	MA	565	OH	0.14	37
NV	4,597	MD	2.76	WV	550	MI	0.13	38
ID	3,416	PA	2.71	NV	545	PA	0.13	39
WV	3,137	DE	2.68	AR	543	WI	0.13	40
NH	2,869	KY	2.67	MD	482	FL	0.11	41
ME	2,583	CA	2.60	NE	481	CT	0.10	42
WY	2,386	SD	2.58	NJ	413	MD	0.10	43
MT	2,380	NH	2.55	ME	366	MA	0.09	44
DE	1,869	VA	2.41	CT	343	CA	0.08	45
SD	1,860	VT	2.30	VT	320	NY	0.08	46
ND	1,818	NY	2.16	NH	224	RI	0.07	47
HI	1,799	ME	2.08	RI	70	DE	0.06	48
AK	1,742	DC	1.91	HI	44	NJ	0.05	49
VT	1,324	WV	1.73	DE	41	HI	0.04	50
DC	1,107	HI	1.54	DC	14	DC	0.02	51

GOVERNMENT

REVENUES (1993)

	Total Revenue		Total Revenue Per Capita		Gaming Revenue Per Capita[1]	Desc. Num. Order
CA	$108,222,000,000	AK	$12,304.35	MA	$318.21	1
NY	$78,209,000,000	HI	$4,753.86	NV	$282.92	2
TX	$42,019,000,000	WY	$4,640.43	NJ	$198.12	3
OH	$38,341,000,000	NY	$4,308.32	CT	$187.31	4
PA	$37,779,000,000	DE	$4,120.34	OR	$176.94	5
FL	$33,216,000,000	NM	$3,900.37	MD	$170.23	6
IL	$30,351,000,000	CT	$3,887.74	OH	$164.27	7
NJ	$29,614,000,000	WA	$3,789.69	FL	$154.74	8
MI	$28,760,000,000	NJ	$3,768.16	IL	$132.12	9
MA	$21,493,000,000	RI	$3,765.00	VA	$127.14	10
WA	$19,930,000,000	WI	$3,702.82	RI	$127.00	11
NC	$19,377,000,000	MT	$3,594.53	NY	$123.07	12
WI	$18,677,000,000	ND	$3,591.84	MI	$122.83	13
GA	$16,565,000,000	MN	$3,590.85	DE	$121.78	14
VA	$16,307,000,000	MA	$3,571.45	KY	$121.24	15
MN	$16,245,000,000	OR	$3,567.05	PA	$111.89	16
MD	$14,842,000,000	CA	$3,466.76	LA	$108.86	17
IN	$14,653,000,000	OH	$3,466.32	SD	$108.18	18
LA	$13,348,000,000	VT	$3,390.63	NH	$96.09	19
CT	$12,744,000,000	WV	$3,326.18	ME	$95.97	20
MO	$12,559,000,000	NV	$3,256.15	WI	$95.16	21
TN	$11,864,000,000	ME	$3,166.13	TX	$94.38	22
AL	$11,389,000,000	PA	$3,140.40	IN	$81.84	23
KY	$11,011,000,000	LA	$3,111.42	VT	$81.60	24
AZ	$10,843,000,000	ID	$3,098.18	MN	$81.56	25
OR	$10,826,000,000	MI	$3,040.17	CO	$72.11	26
SC	$10,637,000,000	MD	$2,993.55	IA	$70.54	27
CO	$10,028,000,000	SC	$2,930.30	WA	$70.36	28
OK	$8,679,000,000	IA	$2,915.28	AZ	$63.88	29
IA	$8,224,000,000	KY	$2,902.21	WV	$60.51	30
AK	$7,358,000,000	UT	$2,875.27	CA	$56.41	31
MS	$7,205,000,000	CO	$2,813.69	ID	$52.73	32
KS	$6,730,000,000	NC	$2,787.26	MO	$46.04	33
AR	$6,446,000,000	AZ	$2,748.54	KS	$43.39	34
NM	$6,303,000,000	MS	$2,729.17	MT	$41.62	35
WV	$6,047,000,000	AL	$2,723.99	ND	$10.99	36
HI	$5,543,000,000	SD	$2,693.48	AR	$7.01	37
UT	$5,348,000,000	OK	$2,684.50	NE	$6.82	38
NV	$4,500,000,000	NH	$2,678.83	SC	$6.61	39
ME	$3,926,000,000	AR	$2,657.05	OK	$3.09	40
NE	$3,890,000,000	KS	$2,654.83	AK	$1.67	41
RI	$3,765,000,000	IL	$2,597.21	AL	$1.44	42
ID	$3,408,000,000	IN	$2,568.00	DC	NA	43
MT	$3,023,000,000	VA	$2,519.23	GA	$0.00	44
NH	$3,011,000,000	FL	$2,419.93	HI	$0.00	45
DE	$2,876,000,000	NE	$2,411.66	MS	$0.00	46
ND	$2,288,000,000	GA	$2,400.03	NM	$0.00	47
WY	$2,181,000,000	MO	$2,399.04	NC	$0.00	48
VT	$1,953,000,000	TX	$2,331.54	TN	$0.00	49
SD	$1,942,000,000	TN	$2,329.01	UT	$0.00	50
DC	NA	DC	NA	WY	$0.00	51

[1] Revenues from parimutuel and amusement taxes and lotteries
Source: Bureau of the Census, U.S. Dept. of Commerce

EXPENDITURES AND DEBT (1993)

	Total Expend.		Expend. Per Capita		Debt Outstanding		Debt Outstanding Per Capita	Desc. Num. Order
CA	$104,567,000,000	AK	$9,068.56	NY	$59,219,000,000	AK	$7,403.01	1
NY	$74,280,000,000	HI	$4,807.89	CA	$41,295,000,000	RI	$5,147.00	2
TX	$39,091,000,000	RI	$4,176.00	MA	$25,415,000,000	DE	$5,000.00	3
PA	$34,359,000,000	NY	$4,091.89	NJ	$21,779,000,000	NM	$4,701.11	4
OH	$31,665,000,000	WY	$4,014.89	IL	$19,893,000,000	NH	$4,663.70	5
FL	$30,103,000,000	CT	$3,815.44	FL	$13,635,000,000	HI	$4,307.89	6
NJ	$28,923,000,000	NJ	$3,680.24	PA	$12,989,000,000	MA	$4,223.16	7
IL	$28,133,000,000	DE	$3,663.32	CT	$12,848,000,000	CT	$3,919.46	8
MI	$27,051,000,000	MA	$3,582.09	OH	$12,486,000,000	NY	$3,262.22	9
MA	$21,557,000,000	NM	$3,464.73	LA	$9,585,000,000	NJ	$2,771.22	10
WA	$18,003,000,000	WA	$3,423.27	MI	$8,849,000,000	SD	$2,521.50	11
NC	$16,916,000,000	CA	$3,349.68	MD	$8,731,000,000	VT	$2,463.54	12
GA	$15,308,000,000	ND	$3,342.23	TX	$8,684,000,000	ME	$2,418.55	13
VA	$14,721,000,000	WV	$3,268.98	WA	$7,848,000,000	LA	$2,234.27	14
WI	$14,621,000,000	VT	$3,210.07	WI	$7,674,000,000	MT	$2,079.67	15
MN	$14,295,000,000	MT	$3,166.47	NM	$7,597,000,000	OR	$1,917.96	16
IN	$14,136,000,000	MN	$3,159.81	VA	$7,438,000,000	KY	$1,797.58	17
MD	$13,537,000,000	ME	$3,136.29	KY	$6,820,000,000	MD	$1,760.99	18
LA	$12,893,000,000	LA	$3,005.36	MO	$6,516,000,000	IL	$1,702.29	19
CT	$12,507,000,000	OR	$2,969.69	OR	$5,821,000,000	WY	$1,661.70	20
TN	$11,028,000,000	NV	$2,931.26	IN	$5,458,000,000	WI	$1,521.41	21
MO	$10,809,000,000	WI	$2,898.69	NH	$5,242,000,000	WA	$1,492.30	22
KY	$10,543,000,000	OH	$2,862.76	RI	$5,147,000,000	WV	$1,476.35	23
SC	$10,388,000,000	SC	$2,861.71	HI	$5,023,000,000	SC	$1,350.14	24
AL	$10,242,000,000	MI	$2,859.51	SC	$4,901,000,000	CA	$1,322.84	25
AZ	$9,783,000,000	PA	$2,856.11	GA	$4,519,000,000	ND	$1,302.98	26
OR	$9,013,000,000	KY	$2,778.86	AK	$4,427,000,000	MO	$1,244.70	27
CO	$8,673,000,000	IA	$2,752.92	AL	$4,163,000,000	NV	$1,196.09	28
OK	$8,272,000,000	MD	$2,730.33	MN	$4,145,000,000	UT	$1,179.03	29
IA	$7,766,000,000	NH	$2,642.35	NC	$4,002,000,000	ID	$1,172.73	30
MS	$6,235,000,000	UT	$2,598.92	DE	$3,490,000,000	VA	$1,149.08	31
WV	$5,943,000,000	OK	$2,558.61	OK	$3,191,000,000	OH	$1,128.83	32
AR	$5,915,000,000	ID	$2,523.64	CO	$3,117,000,000	PA	$1,079.72	33
KS	$5,742,000,000	AZ	$2,479.85	AZ	$3,053,000,000	AL	$995.69	34
HI	$5,606,000,000	IN	$2,477.39	ME	$2,999,000,000	FL	$993.37	35
NM	$5,599,000,000	AL	$2,449.65	WV	$2,684,000,000	OK	$987.01	36
AK	$5,423,000,000	AR	$2,438.17	TN	$2,632,000,000	NE	$983.88	37
UT	$4,834,000,000	CO	$2,433.50	UT	$2,193,000,000	IN	$956.54	38
RI	$4,176,000,000	NC	$2,433.26	AR	$1,884,000,000	MI	$935.41	39
NV	$4,051,000,000	IL	$2,407.41	IA	$1,837,000,000	MN	$916.22	40
ME	$3,889,000,000	NE	$2,370.12	SD	$1,818,000,000	CO	$874.58	41
NE	$3,823,000,000	MS	$2,361.74	MT	$1,749,000,000	AR	$776.59	42
NH	$2,970,000,000	SD	$2,338.42	MS	$1,659,000,000	AZ	$773.89	43
ID	$2,776,000,000	VA	$2,274.22	NV	$1,653,000,000	GA	$654.74	44
MT	$2,663,000,000	KS	$2,265.09	NE	$1,587,000,000	IA	$651.19	45
DE	$2,557,000,000	GA	$2,217.91	VT	$1,419,000,000	MS	$628.41	46
ND	$2,129,000,000	FL	$2,193.14	ID	$1,290,000,000	NC	$575.66	47
WY	$1,887,000,000	TX	$2,169.07	KS	$935,000,000	TN	$516.69	48
VT	$1,849,000,000	TN	$2,164.90	ND	$830,000,000	TX	$481.86	49
SD	$1,686,000,000	MO	$2,064.76	WY	$781,000,000	KS	$368.84	50
DC	NA	DC	NA	DC	NA	DC	NA	51

Source: Bureau of the Census, U.S. Dept. of Commerce

INDEXES

Below you will find three separate indexes to *The World Almanac of the U.S.A.*

The INDEX TO PEOPLE lists not only individuals but also groups of people such as the Creek Indians or the Amish. The INDEX TO PLACES includes each of the fifty states, islands under U.S. jurisdiction, cities (followed by state abbreviation), and geographical features such as mountain ranges and lakes. Page ranges in **boldface** indicate the main article on each state, in Part II: Portraits of the States. THE INDEX TO TOPICS covers Parts I and III of the text. Information on most topics listed within that index can also be found in each state article in Part II.

INDEX TO PLACES

INDEX TO TOPICS